P9-DED-517

GEORGE MEREDITH

THE EGOIST

AN ANNOTATED TEXT
BACKGROUNDS
CRITICISM

Edited by

ROBERT M. ADAMS

UNIVERSITY OF CALIFORNIA AT LOS ANGELES

W · W · NORTON & COMPANY
New York   *London*

Gillian Beer: Selection from "The Two Masks and the Idea of Comedy," in *Meredith: A Change of Masks* (London: Athlone Press, 1970), pp. 114–39. Reprinted by permission of the publisher and the author.

Jenni Calder: "Insurrection," in *Women and Marriage in Victorian Fiction* (New York: Oxford University Press, 1976), pp. 181–88. Reprinted by permission of the publisher.

John Goode: *"The Egoist:* Anatomy or Striptease?" in *Meredith Now*, edited by Ian Fletcher (London: Routledge & Kegan Paul, 1971), pp. 205–21. Reprinted by permission of the publisher.

Charles J. Hill: "Theme and Image in *The Egoist*," from *The University of Kansas City Review*, vol. 20, no. 4, Summer 1954, pp. 281–85. Reprinted by permission of the author and the publisher.

Richard B. Hudson: "The Meaning of Egoism in George Meredith's *'The Egoist,'*" from *The Trollopian* (Nineteenth Century Fiction), III (1948–49), pp. 163–76. Reprinted by permission of the publisher.

John Lucas: "Meredith's Reputation," from *Meredith Now*, edited by Ian Fletcher (London: Routledge & Kegan Paul, 1971), pp. 1–13. Reprinted by permission of the publisher.

Robert D. Mayo: "The Egoist and the Willow Pattern," from *English Literary History*, IX, 1942, pp. 71–78. Copyright © The Johns Hopkins University Press. Reprinted by permission of The Johns Hopkins University Press.

Michael Sundell: "The Function of Flitch in *The Egoist*," from *Nineteenth Century Fiction*, vol. 24, no. 2 (September 1969), pp. 227–35. Reprinted by permission of the publisher.

Virginia Woolf: "The Novels of George Meredith," from *The Second Common Reader* by Virginia Woolf, copyright 1932 by Harcourt Brace Jovanovich, Inc.; renewed 1960 by Leonard Woolf. Selection reprinted by permission of the publishers. English source is *The Common Reader, Second Series*; selection reprinted by permission of the author's literary estate and The Hogarth Press.

Published simultaneously in Canada by George J. McLeod Limited, Toronto.

FIRST EDITION

Library of Congress Cataloging in Publication Data
Meredith, George, 1828–1909.
The egoist.
(A Norton critical edition)
1. Meredith, George, 1828–1909. The egoist.
I. Adams, Robert Martin, 1915–   II. Title.
PZ3.M54Eg   1978   [PR5006]   823'.8   77–25313
ISBN 0–393–04431–9
ISBN 0–393–09171–6 pbk.

Printed in the United States of America.
1 2 3 4 5 6 7 8 9 10

Contents

Preface

When George Meredith set about writing *The Egoist* in the late 1870s, the movement for the improvement of women's social position and for the assertion of women's legal rights was just gaining momentum. For a long time the voices of isolated precursors had been heard in the land. Mary Astell was one of the first to speak out when in 1697 she published *A Serious Proposal to the Ladies, wherein a Method is Offered for the Improvement of their Minds*; but it was almost a hundred years later when Mary Wollstonecraft wrote her trenchant *Vindication of the Rights of Women* (1792). Other and less powerful voices were raised both before and after these authors, but essentially the cries of protest were isolated and intermittent; not surprisingly, they accomplished very little. But, starting about the middle of the nineteenth century, the individual, occasional voices started to blend into a chorus, and the message they delivered started to echo down the corridors of power.

In 1847 the first stirrings of agitation began, aimed at gaining for women the right to vote; in 1848, Queens College, the first dedicated to providing higher education for women, opened in London. A decade later, *The Englishwoman's Journal* began to offer women an independent voice. In 1861, John Stuart Mill, with the encouragement of his wife, wrote *The Subjection of Women* (though he did not publish it until eight years later); and in 1865, when he was elected to Parliament, he made votes for women part not only of his election platform but of his legislative program. Between 1870 and 1880 petitions calling for women's suffrage were forwarded to Parliament every year, and they had on the average 200,000 signatures attached to them. Women began to be accepted in the universities (Newnham and Girton colleges opened, at Cambridge, during the 1870s) and in the professions. Finally, starting in 1870, Parliament passed a series of important acts under the common title of Married Women's Property Acts; their general tendency was to give women increased control over the money and the children of a marriage at a level that we can start to recognize as distinctively modern.

The rising arc of the movement for women's rights intersected in 1879 with the line of George Meredith's career as a writer of fiction, and gave us, not precisely the character, but the fearful situation of Clara Middleton. She appeals to us not on the basis of legal or ethical technicalities, but as a human being caught in an inhuman system of commodity relationships. By her father, by Willoughby, by "right-thinking society" as a whole, she is valued for her purity, her docility, her serviceability to men. Meredith's intuition of the suffocating web that can be woven about a young woman by playing on these "virtues" of hers is a tremendous imaginative achievement. What makes her struggle so exasperating is that breaking the net would be so easy for her, if only she would forfeit her fragile reputation. How she guides herself surely, instinctively, without calculation or crudity, through a labyrinth of blinding dilemmas to safety is the heart of Meredith's book.

He had written, before *The Egoist*, about a dozen books, among them several volumes of poetry, an oriental fantasy, and eight novels. His reviews were often good and his sales invariably small. He was understood to be a clever, difficult author, and these were qualities that readers appreciated even less a hundred years ago than they do today. To gain a living, Meredith therefore turned his pen to periodical journalism, as Vernon Whitford in the novel plans to do; in addition, he worked on a retainer basis as literary adviser for the publishing house of Chapman & Hall. When he began to write *The Egoist*, he was fifty years old, and had not yet enjoyed any popular success at all. But none of his earlier work had struck quite so resonant a theme as the story of Sir Willoughby Patterne and "his" Clara. *The Egoist* did not gain instant, bestseller popularity for Meredith—that came with an even later book, *Diana of the Crossways*, in consequence of its supposed closeness to a political scandal of the day. But *The Egoist*, as it approaches its century mark, is by all odds the novel of Meredith's that has best stood the test of time. It is likely to prove a permanent part of the heritage, for in Sir Willoughby Patterne Meredith uncovered a figure of comic fatuity whose roots go deeper than any particular set of legal or social arrangements.

We have all known Sir Willoughby. He flourishes, only slightly transformed, in the guise of a college president, a professor of English, or a conoisseur of art; he is one of the "oldest inhabitants" of a small town; he is chairman of the board; there is a streak of him in any politician you care to name. Wherever men act like peacocks, preening and swelling and strutting for the admiration of women and the envy of other men, there Sir Willoughby is found, and there the comic imps foregather. Willoughby himself as Meredith drew him is a rare and (to us) exotic flower; but the process from which he grew is common as dirt. And, as with dirt, there's no good professing to be above it; the stuff is not only common, it's common to us all. One of the chief qualities that gives Meredith's novel its enduring interest is his awareness of the primitive inside the civilized. [Human life, as we can't help being aware nowadays, is built around a core of instincts, the original uses of which are largely anachronistic, but which must somehow be adapted to civilized ends] The comic spirit as wielded primarily by women does some of this civilizing work on the interior barbarians who are universal among us. The comic spirit is the cutting edge of culture; we need its keen and flashing blade. But without the primal instincts that culture is constantly alert to lop, men would be tame and hollow creatures indeed. Culture and instinct are permanently and inconclusively at war; civilization is unthinkable without its discontents.

Thus I think it is a superficial view of *The Egoist* which complains that adequate poetic justice isn't in the end visited on Willoughby. He should be stripped and whipped, some think, as the moral monster he is; he and the social order that bred him should be arraigned, denounced, rejected. Of course that isn't the method of comedy, but it doesn't answer, either, to the deeper vision of the case—which is simply that the Willoughby in us is immortal, universal, and consequently not subject to moral approval or disapproval. You might as well denounce the law of gravity, Meredith seems to be saying, as expect to eradicate egoism from the character of men—or, for that matter, of women either, though certainly under Victorian circumstances they got less chance to display the quality. Comedy, in any case, is not the cure for this or any other social condition; it is a state of mind particularly open to cool, inconclusive, distanced observation. Of this stance *The Egoist* is the supreme example in English.

ROBERT M. ADAMS

The Text of

The Egoist

CONTENTS OF *THE EGOIST*

PRELUDE

A CHAPTER OF WHICH THE LAST PAGE ONLY IS OF ANY
IMPORTANCE

COMEDY is a game played to throw reflections upon
social life, and it deals with human nature in the drawing-
room of civilized men and women, where we have no dust [Satire]
of the struggling outer world, no mire, no violent crashes,
to make the correctness of the representation convincing.
Credulity is not wooed through the impressionable senses;
nor have we recourse to the small circular glow of the
watchmaker's eye to raise in bright relief minutest grains
of evidence for the routing of incredulity.[1] The Comic
Spirit conceives a definite situation for a number of characters, and rejects all accessories in the exclusive pursuit
of them and their speech. For, being a spirit, he hunts
the spirit in men; vision and ardour constitute his merit:
he has not a thought of persuading you to believe in
him. Follow and you will see. But there is a question
of the value of a run at his heels. [as hounds]

Now the world is possessed of a certain big book, the
biggest book on earth; that might indeed be called the
Book of Earth; whose title is the Book of Egoism, and it
is a book full of the world's wisdom. So full of it, and
of such dimensions is this book, in which the generations
have written ever since they took to writing, that to be
profitable to us the Book needs a powerful compression.

Who, says the notable humourist, in allusion to this
Book, who can studiously travel through sheets of leaves
now capable of a stretch from the Lizard to the last few
poor pulmonary snips and shreds of leagues dancing on
their toes for cold, explorers tell us, and catching breath
by good luck, like dogs at bones about a table, on the edge
of the Pole?[2] Inordinate unvaried length, sheer longin-
quity, staggers the heart, ages the very heart of us at a
view. And how if we manage finally to print one of
our pages on the crow-scalp of that solitary majestic out-

1. "watchmaker's eye": hidden behind
its magnifying glass (*loupe*) for close
vision.
2. "Lizard": a headland at the south-
west tip of Cornwall, the southernmost
point of England. The Book of Egoism,
laid out leaf to leaf, would cover the
British Isles.

sider ?[3] We may with effort get even him into the Book;
yet the knowledge we want will not be more present with
us than it was when the chapters hung their end over the
cliff you ken of at Dover, where sits our great lord and
master contemplating the seas without upon the reflex of
that within![4]

In other words, as I venture to translate him (humour-
ists are difficult: it is a piece of their humour to puzzle
our wits), the inward mirror, the embracing and condensing spirit, is required to give us those interminable mile-
post piles of matter (extending well-nigh to the very Pole)
in essence, in chosen samples, digestibly. I conceive
him to indicate that the realistic method of a conscientious transcription of all the visible, and a repetition of all
the audible, is mainly accountable for our present branfulness, and for that prolongation of the vasty and the
noisy, out of which, as from an undrained fen, steams
the malady of sameness, our modern malady.[5] We have
the malady, whatever may be the cure or the cause. We
drove in a body to Science the other day for an antidote;
which was as if tired pedestrians should mount the engine-
box of headlong trains; and Science introduced us to our
o'er-hoary ancestry — them in the Oriental posture: whereupon we set up a primeval chattering to rival the Amazon
forest nigh nightfall, cured, we fancied.[6] And before daybreak our disease was hanging on to us again, with the
extension of a tail. We had it fore and aft. We were
the same, and animals into the bargain. That is all we
got from Science.

Art is the specific.[7] We have little to learn of apes, and
they may be left. The chief consideration for us is, what
particular practice of Art in letters is the best for the
perusal of the Book of our common wisdom; so that with
clearer minds and livelier manners we may escape, as it
were, into daylight and song from a land of fog-horns.
Shall we read it by the watchmaker's eye in luminous
rings eruptive of the infinitesimal, or pointed with examples and types under the broad Alpine survey of the spirit
born of our united social intelligence, which is the Comic
Spirit? Wise men say the latter. They tell us that
there is a constant tendency in the Book to accumulate
excess of substance, and such repleteness, obscuring the
glass it holds to mankind, renders us inexact in the recognition of our individual countenances: a perilous thing for
civilization. And these wise men are strong in their

3. "crow-scalp": the top leaf, one supposes, on the mountain of leaves making
up the book.
4. "Dover": the cliff in *King Lear*, Act
IV. Meredith fancies Shakespeare atop
it, comparing the immeasurable oceans
outside and inside himself.
5. "branfulness": an excess of bran
(chaff) and a deficiency of grain.
6. "ancestry": the anthropoids, whose
possible relation to man had been disturbing Victorian England since Darwin's
Origin of Species (1859). Monkeys "hun-
ker down" on their heels, and Meredith
refers to it as an "Oriental posture."
7. The precise cure, the right solution.

opinion that we should encourage the Comic Spirit, who is, after all, our own offspring, to relieve the Book. Comedy, they say, is the true diversion, as it is likewise the key of the great Book, the music of the Book. They tell us how it condenses whole sections of the Book in a sentence, volumes in a character; so that a fair part of a book outstripping thousands of leagues when unrolled, may be compassed in one comic sitting.

For verily, say they, we must read what we can of it, at least the page before us, if we would be men. One, with an index on the Book, cries out, in a style pardonable to his fervency:[8] The remedy of your frightful affliction is here, through the stillatory of Comedy, and not in Science, nor yet in Speed, whose name is but another for voracity. Why, to be alive, to be quick in the soul, there should be diversity in the companion throbs of your pulses. Interrogate them. They lump along like the old lob-legs of Dobbin the horse; or do their business like cudgels of carpet-thwackers expelling dust, or the cottage-clock pendulum teaching the infant hour over midnight simple arithmetic. This too in spite of Bacchus.[9] And let them gallop; let them gallop with the God bestriding them, gallop to Hymen, gallop to Hades, they strike the same note.[1] Monstrous monotonousness has enfolded us as with the arms of Amphitrite![2] We hear a shout of war for a diversion. — Comedy he pronounces to be our means of reading swiftly and comprehensively.[3] She it is who proposes the correcting of pretentiousness, of inflation, of dulness, and of the vestiges of rawness and grossness to be found among us. She is the ultimate civilizer, the polisher, a sweet cook. If, he says, she watches over sentimentalism with a birch-rod, she is not opposed to romance. You may love, and warmly love, so long as you are honest. Do not offend reason. A lover pretending too much by one foot's length of pretence, will have that foot caught in her trap. In Comedy is the singular scene of charity issuing of disdain under the stroke of honourable laughter: an Ariel released by Prospero's wand from the fetters of the damned witch Sycorax.[4] And this laughter of reason refreshed is floriferous, like the magical great gale of the shifty Spring deciding for Summer.[5] You hear it giving the delicate spirit his liberty. Listen, for comparison, to an unleavened society: a low as of the udderful cow past milking hour![6] O for a titled ecclesiastic to curse to excommuni-

8. "index": index finger; "stillatory": distillery.
9. Drink, liquor—from the Roman god of wine, Bacchus.
1. "Hymen . . . Hades": whatever our human destination (marriage or hell or both), our pulses keep the same monotonous time.
2. Amph-i-trí-te is a sea-nymph, wife of the sea-god Poseidon; into her bower drowned men are gathered.

3. "he": still the man with an index on the book, above.
4. Shakespeare, *The Tempest*, Act I; Prospero, when he came to the island, freed Ariel from the hag Sycorax.
5. "floriferous": flower-bearing.
6. The delicate ironies of the free comic spirit are contrasted with bovine society, content with its gross satisfactions, sensitive only to gross discontents.

cation that unholy thing!—So far an enthusiast perhaps; but he should have a hearing.

Concerning pathos, no ship can now set sail without pathos; and we are not totally deficient of pathos; which is, I do not accurately know what, if not the ballast, reducible to moisture by patent process, on board our modern vessel; for it can hardly be the cargo, and the general water-supply has other uses; and ships well charged with it seem to sail the stiffest:—there is a touch of pathos.[7] The Egoist surely inspires pity. He who would desire to clothe himself at everybody's expense, and is of that desire condemned to strip himself stark naked, he, if pathos ever had a form, might be taken for the actual person. Only he is not allowed to rush at you, roll you over and squeeze your body for the briny drops. There is the innovation.

You may as well know him out of hand, as a gentleman of our time and country, of wealth and station; a not flexile figure, do what we may with him; the humour of whom scarcely dimples the surface and is distinguishable but by very penetrative, very wicked imps, whose fits of roaring below at some generally imperceptible stroke of his quality, have first made the mild literary angels aware of something comic in him, when they were one and all about to describe the gentleman on the heading of the records baldly (where brevity is most complimentary) as a gentleman of family and property, an idol of a decorous island that admires the concrete. Imps have their freakish wickedness in them to kindle detective vision: malignly do they love to uncover ridiculousness in imposing figures. Wherever they catch sight of Egoism they pitch their camps, they circle and squat, and forthwith they trim their lanterns, confident of the ludicrous to come. So confident that their grip of an English gentleman, in whom they have spied their game, never relaxes until he begins insensibly to frolic and antic, unknown to himself, and comes out in the native steam which is their scent of the chase. Instantly off they scour, Egoist and imps. They will, it is known of them, dog a great House for centuries, and be at the birth of all the new heirs in succession, diligently taking confirmatory notes, to join hands and chime their chorus in one of their merry rings round the tottering pillar of the House, when his turn arrives; as if they had (possibly they had) smelt of old date a doomed colossus of Egoism in that unborn, unconceived inheritor of the stuff of the family. They dare not be chuckling while Egoism is valiant, while sober, while socially valuable, nationally serviceable. They wait.

Aforetime a grand old Egoism built the House. It would appear that ever finer essences of it are demanded to sus-

7. "moisture": tears; so also "briny drops," below.

tain the structure: but especially would it appear that a reversion to the gross original, beneath a mask and in a vein of fineness, is an earthquake at the foundations of the House.\ Better that it should not have consented to motion, and have held stubbornly to all ancestral ways, than have bred that anachronic spectre.[8] The sight, however, is one to make our squatting imps in circle grow restless on their haunches, as they bend eyes instantly, ears at full cock, for the commencement of the comic drama of the suicide. If this line of verse be not yet in our literature,

Through very love of self himself he slew,

let it be admitted for his epitaph.

CHAPTER 1

A MINOR INCIDENT SHOWING AN HEREDITARY APTITUDE IN THE USE OF THE KNIFE

THERE was an ominously anxious watch of eyes visible and invisible[1] over the infancy of Willoughby, fifth in descent from Simon Patterne, of Patterne Hall, premier of this family, a lawyer, a man of solid acquirements and stout ambition, who well understood the foundation-work of a House, and was endowed with the power of saying No to those first agents of destruction, besieging relatives. He said it with the resonant emphasis of death to younger sons.[2] For if the oak is to become a stately tree, we must provide against the crowding of timber. Also the tree beset with parasites prospers not. A great House in its beginning lives, we may truly say, by the knife. Soil is easily got, and so are bricks, and a wife, and children come of wishing for them, but the vigorous use of the knife is a natural gift and points to growth. Pauper Patternes were numerous when the fifth head of the race was the hope of his county. A Patterne was in the Marines.[3]

The country and the chief of this family were simultaneously informed of the existence of one Lieutenant Crossjay Patterne, of the corps of the famous hard fighters, through an act of heroism of the unpretending cool sort which kindles British blood, on the part of the modest

8. Sir Willoughby Patterne, in whom the greedy instincts of his ancestors survive under a veneer of social graces.
1. Parents and imps; "premier": the first-born, the eldest son.
2. Primogeniture is the law of England; the oldest son inherits the title and the estate, the younger sons whatever the father wants to give them, generally nothing.
3. As distinguished from county regiments, rich in tradition and social prestige (the Hampshire Rifles, Seaforth Highlanders, etc.), the Marines were plebian fighters.

young officer, in the storming of some eastern riverain
stronghold, somewhere about the coast of China.[4] The
officer's youth was assumed on the strength of his rank,
perhaps likewise from the tale of his modesty: "he had
only done his duty." Our Willoughby was then at College, emulous of the generous enthusiasm of his years, and
strangely impressed by the report, and the printing of his
name in the newspapers. He thought over it for several
months, when, coming to his title and heritage, he sent
Lieutenant Crossjay Patterne a cheque for a sum of money
amounting to the gallant fellow's pay per annum, at the
same time showing his acquaintance with the first, or
chemical, principles of generosity, in the remark to friends
at home, that "blood is thicker than water." The man is
a Marine, but he is a Patterne. How any Patterne should
have drifted into the Marines, is of the order of questions
which are senselessly asked of the great dispensary.[5] In
the complimentary letter accompanying his cheque, the
lieutenant was invited to present himself at the ancestral
Hall, when convenient to him, and he was assured that he
had given his relative and friend a taste for a soldier's
life. Young Sir Willoughby was fond of talking of his
"military namesake and distant cousin, young Patterne —
the Marine." It was funny; and not less laughable was
the description of his namesake's deed of valour: with the
rescued British sailor inebriate, and the hauling off to
captivity of the three braves of the black dragon on a yellow ground, and the tying of them together back to back by
their pigtails, and driving of them into our lines upon a
newly devised dying-top style of march that inclined to
the oblique, like the astonished six eyes of the celestial
prisoners, for straight they could not go.[6] The humour of
gentlemen at home is always highly excited by such cool
feats. We are a small island, but you see what we do.
The ladies at the Hall, Sir Willoughby's mother, and his
aunts Eleanor and Isabel, were more affected than he by
the circumstance of their having a Patterne in the
Marines. But how then! We English have ducal blood
in business: we have, genealogists tell us, royal blood in
common trades. For all our pride we are a queer people;
and you may be ordering butcher's meat of a Tudor, sitting on the cane-bottom chairs of a Plantagenet. By and
by you may . . . but cherish your reverence.[7] Young
Willoughby made a kind of shock-head or football hero of
his gallant distant cousin, and wondered occasionally that
the fellow had been content to despatch a letter of effusive

---

4. During the mid-nineteenth century the
British entered China by force to export
religion, manufactured goods, and opium.
Merchants worked hand in glove with the
military to force open Chinese ports and
rivers—hence "riverain," on the analogy
of "sovereign."

5. He who dispenses (Fate), with the
overtone of a free clinic.

6. "dying-top": a top which is losing
momentum and so wobbling.

7. Presumably, you may meet in trade
some members of the royal family.

thanks without availing himself of the invitation to partake of the hospitalities of Patterne.[8]

He was one afternoon parading between showers on the stately garden terrace of the Hall, in company with his affianced, the beautiful and dashing Constantia Durham, followed by knots of ladies and gentlemen vowed to fresh air before dinner, while it was to be had. Chancing with his usual happy fortune (we call these things dealt to us out of the great hidden dispensary, chance) to glance up the avenue of limes, as he was in the act of turning on his heel at the end of the terrace, and it should be added, discoursing with passion's privilege of the passion of love to Miss Durham, Sir Willoughby, who was anything but obtuse, experienced a presentiment upon espying a thick-set stumpy man crossing the gravel space from the avenue to the front steps of the Hall, decidedly *not* bearing the stamp of the gentleman "on his hat, his coat, his feet, or anything that was his," Willoughby subsequently observed to the ladies of his family in the Scriptural style of gentlemen who do bear the stamp. His brief sketch of the creature was repulsive. The visitor carried a bag, and his coat-collar was up, his hat was melancholy; he had the appearance of a bankrupt tradesman absconding; no gloves, no umbrella.

As to the incident we have to note, it was very slight. The card of Lieutenant Patterne was handed to Sir Willoughby, who laid it on the salver, saying to the footman, "Not at home."

He had been disappointed in the age, grossly deceived in the appearance of the man claiming to be his relative in this unseasonable fashion; and his acute instinct advised him swiftly of the absurdity of introducing to his friends a heavy unpresentable senior as the celebrated gallant Lieutenant of Marines, and the same as a member of his family! He had talked of the man too much, too enthusiastically, to be able to do so. A young subaltern, even if passably vulgar in figure, can be shuffled through by the aid of the heroical story humourously exaggerated in apology for his aspect. Nothing can be done with a mature and stumpy Marine of that rank. Considerateness dismisses him on the spot, without parley. It was performed by a gentleman supremely advanced at a very early age in the art of cutting.

Young Sir Willoughby spoke a word of the rejected visitor to Miss Durham, in response to her startled look: "I shall drop him a cheque," he said, for she seemed personally wounded, and had a face of crimson.

The young lady did not reply.

Dating from the humble departure of Lieutenant Crossjay Patterne up the limes-avenue under a gathering rain-

cloud, the ring of imps in attendance on Sir Willoughby
maintained their station with strict observation of his
movements at all hours; and were comparisons in quest,
the sympathetic eagerness of the eyes of caged monkeys
for the hand about to feed them, would supply one.[9] They
perceived in him a fresh development and very subtle
manifestation of the very old thing from which he had
sprung.

CHAPTER 2

THE YOUNG SIR WILLOUGHBY

THESE little scoundrel imps, who have attained to some
respectability as the dogs and pets of the Comic Spirit,
had been curiously attentive three years earlier, long before the public announcement of his engagement to the
beautiful Miss Durham, on the day of Sir Willoughby's
majority, when Mrs. Mountstuart Jenkinson said her word
of him. Mrs. Mountstuart was a lady certain to say the
remembered, if not the right, thing. Again and again was
it confirmed on days of high celebration, days of birth or
bridal, how sure she was to hit the mark that rang the bell;
and away her word went over the county: and had she been
an uncharitable woman she could have ruled the county
with an iron rod of caricature, so sharp was her touch.[1] A
grain of malice would have sent county faces and characters
awry into the currency.[2] She was wealthy and kindly, and
resembled our mother Nature in her reasonable antipa-
thies to one or two things which none can defend, and her
decided preference of persons that shone in the sun.[3] Her
word sprang out of her. She looked at you, and forth it
came: and it stuck to you, as nothing laboured or literary
could have adhered. Her saying of Lætitia Dale: "Here
she comes, with a romantic tale on her eyelashes," was a
portrait of Lætitia. And that of Vernon Whitford: "He is
a Phœbus Apollo turned fasting friar," painted the sunken
brilliancy of the lean long-walker and scholar at a stroke.

Of the young Sir Willoughby, her word was brief; and
there was the merit of it on a day when he was hearing
from sunrise to the setting of the moon salutes in his
honour, songs of praise and Ciceronian eulogy. Rich,
handsome, courteous, generous, lord of the Hall, the feast,
and the dance, he excited his guests of both sexes to a
holiday of flattery. And, says Mrs. Mountstuart, while

9. "limes-avenue": avenue of linden
trees; "in quest": called for.
1. "the county": County society in England is the local gentry (and aristocracy, if any)—quite separate, most of
the year, from the world of the court and
the metropolis.
2. "would have sent": would have made
distorted and ugly pictures of her neigh-
bors pass for true ones.
3. I.e., the favored and successful.

grand phrases were mouthing round about him: " *You see he has a leg.*"

That you saw, of course. But after she had spoken you saw much more. Mrs. Mountstuart said it just as others utter empty nothings, with never a hint of a stress. Her word was taken up, and very soon, from the extreme end of the long drawing-room, the circulation of something of Mrs. Mountstuart's was distinctly perceptible. Lady Patterne sent a little Hebe down, skirting the dancers, for an accurate report of it; and even the inappreciative lips of a very young lady transmitting the word could not damp the impression of its weighty truthfulness.[4] It was perfect! Adulation of the young Sir Willoughby's beauty and wit, and aristocratic bearing and mien, and of his moral virtues, was common: welcome if you like, as a form of homage; but common, almost vulgar, beside Mrs. Mountstuart's quiet little touch of nature. In seeming to say infinitely less than others, as Miss Isabel Patterne pointed out to Lady Busshe, Mrs. Mountstuart comprised all that the others had said, by showing the needlessness of allusions to the saliently evident. She was the aristocrat reproving the provincial. "He is everything you have had the goodness to remark, ladies and dear sirs, he talks charmingly, dances divinely, rides with the air of a commander-in-chief, has the most natural grand pose possible without ceasing for a moment to be the young English gentleman he is. Alcibiades, fresh from a Louis XIV. perruquier, could not surpass him: whatever you please; I could outdo you in sublime comparisons, were I minded to pelt him.[5] Have you noticed that he has a leg?"

So might it be amplified. A simple-seeming word of this import is the triumph of the spiritual, and where it passes for coin of value, the society has reached a high refinement: Arcadian by the æsthetic route.[6] Observation of Willoughby was not, as Miss Eleanor Patterne pointed out to Lady Culmer, drawn down to the leg, but directed to estimate him from the leg upward. That, however, is prosaic. Dwell a short space on Mrs. Mountstuart's word; and whither, into what fair region, and with how decorously voluptuous a sensation, do not we fly, who have, through mournful veneration of the Martyr Charles, a coy attachment to the Court of his Merrie Son, where the leg was ribanded with love-knots and reigned.[7] Oh! it was a

4. "Hebe": handmaiden, cupbearer (from Greek mythology).
5. "Alcibiades": the great rake and tricky diplomat of Periclean Athens, improved (rather grotesquely) by a full wig from the court of Louis XIV, the Grand Monarque of the late seventeenth and early eighteenth centuries.
6. Mythologically, Arcadia is a simple, natural, but crude society; England, having passed through the pastoral poets, is now a refined and elegant Arcadia.
7. Charles Stuart, Charles the First, "martyred," i.e., executed, by the Puri-

tans in 1649. His "Merrie Son" was bawdy Charles II of Restoration fame. Sir Willoughby is a Cavalier; a humble, practical fellow like Crossjay Patterne (of the Marines) is identified with the "Roundheads," the Puritans, whose descendants now populate America. This conflict between two Englands, one of the ruling class, one of the working class, both dating back to the Civil Wars of 1640–60, is important to Meredith's novel, and can be found as well in another novel, that of Benjamin Disraeli, *Sybil: or the Two Nations* (1845).

naughty Court. Yet have we dreamed of it as the period
when an English cavalier was grace incarnate; far from
the boor now hustling us in another sphere; beautifully
mannered, every gesture dulcet. And if the ladies were
. . . we will hope they have been traduced. But if they
were, if they were too tender, ah! gentlemen were gentlemen then — worth perishing for! There is this dream in
the English country; and it must be an aspiration after
some form of melodious gentlemanliness which is imagined
to have inhabited the island at one time; as among our
poets the dream of the period of a circle of chivalry here
is encouraged for the pleasure of the imagination.

Mrs. Mountstuart touched a thrilling chord. "In spite
of men's hateful modern costume, you see he has a leg."

That is, the leg of the born cavalier is before you: and
obscure it as you will, dress degenerately, there it is for
ladies who have eyes. You *see* it: or, you see *he* has it.
Miss Isabel and Miss Eleanor disputed the incidence of
the emphasis, but surely, though a slight difference of
meaning may be heard, either will do: many, with a good
show of reason, throw the accent upon *leg*. And the
ladies knew for a fact that Willoughby's leg was exquisite;
he had a cavalier court-suit in his wardrobe. Mrs.
Mountstuart signified that the leg was to be seen because
it was a burning leg. There it is, and it *will* shine
through! He has the leg of Rochester, Buckingham,
Dorset, Suckling;[8] the leg that smiles, that winks, is
obsequious to you, yet perforce of beauty self-satisfied;
that twinkles to a tender midway between imperiousness
and seductiveness, audacity and discretion; between "you
shall worship me," and "I am devoted to you;" is your
lord, your slave, alternately and in one. It is a leg of
ebb and flow and high-tide ripples. Such a leg, when it
has done with pretending to retire, will walk straight into
the hearts of women. Nothing so fatal to them.

Self-satisfied it must be. Humbleness does not win
multitudes or the sex. It must be vain to have a sheen.
Captivating melodies (to prove to you the unavoidableness
of self-satisfaction when you know that you have hit perfection), listen to them closely, have an inner pipe of that
conceit almost ludicrous when you detect the chirp.

And you need not be reminded that he has the leg without the naughtiness. You see eminent in him what we
would fain have brought about in a nation that has lost
its leg in gaining a possibly cleaner morality. And that
is often contested; but there is no doubt of the loss of the
leg.

Well, footmen and courtiers and Scottish highlanders,
and the corps de ballet, draymen too, have legs, and staring legs, shapely enough.[9] But what are they? not the

---

8. Famous courtiers of the Stuart era,
great court gentlemen.

9. footmen . . . draymen: heavy-handed,
thick-limbed porters.

modulated instrument we mean — simply legs for leg-work, dumb as the brutes. Our cavalier's is the poetic leg, a portent, a valiance.[1] He has it as Cicero had a tongue. It is a lute to scatter songs to his mistress; a rapier, is she obdurate. In sooth a leg with brains in it, soul.

And its shadows are an ambush, its lights a surprise. It blushes, it pales, can whisper, exclaim. It is a peep, a part revelation, just sufferable, of the Olympian god — Jove playing carpet-knight.[2]

For the young Sir Willoughby's family and his thoughtful admirers, it is not too much to say that Mrs. Mountstuart's little word fetched an epoch of our history to colour the evening of his arrival at man's estate.[3] He was all that Merrie Charles's Court should have been, subtracting not a sparkle from what it was. Under this light he danced, and you may consider the effect of it on his company.

He had received the domestic education of a prince. Little princes abound in a land of heaped riches. Where they have not to yield military service to an Imperial master, they are necessarily here and there dainty during youth, sometimes unmanageable, and as they are bound in no personal duty to the State, each is for himself, with full present, and what is more, luxurious prospective leisure for the practice of that allegiance. They are sometimes enervated by it: that must be in continental countries. Happily our climate and our brave blood precipitate the greater number upon the hunting-field, to do the public service of heading the chase of the fox, with benefit to their constitutions.[4] Hence a manly as well as useful race of little princes, and Willoughby was as manly as any. He cultivated himself, he would not be outdone in popular accomplishments. Had the standard of the public taste been set in philosophy, and the national enthusiasm centred in philosophers, he would at least have worked at books. He did work at science, and had a laboratory. His admirable passion to excel, however, was chiefly directed in his youth upon sport; and so great was the passion in him, that it was commonly the presence of rivals which led him to the declaration of love.[5]

He knew himself nevertheless to be the most constant of men in his attachment to the sex. He had never discouraged Lætitia Dale's devotion to him, and even when he followed in the sweeping tide of the beautiful Constantia Durham (whom Mrs. Mountstuart called "The Racing Cutter"), he thought of Lætitia, and looked at

---

1. "valiance": a heroic deed or statement. Cicero, as the greatest of orators, had a tongue indeed.
2. Pagan divinities are suggested; a "carpet-knight" is, however, only a parlor hero.
3. The age of twenty-one. He is therefore twenty-four "now" when first engaged to Miss Durham.
4. "the public service": spoken with bitter irony.
5. For an analysis of the strength of jealousy in structuring the "love" of fictional characters, see **René Girard**, *Mensonge romantique et vérité romanesque* (Paris: Grasset, 1961).

her. She was a shy violet.

Willoughby's comportment while the showers of adulation drenched him might be likened to the composure of Indian Gods undergoing worship, but unlike them he reposed upon no seat of amplitude to preserve him from a betrayal of intoxication; he had to continue tripping, dancing, exactly balancing himself, head to right, head to left, addressing his idolaters in phrases of perfect choiceness.[6] This is only to say, that it is easier to be a wooden idol than one in the flesh; yet Willoughby was equal to his task. The little prince's education teaches him that he is other than you, and by virtue of the instruction he receives, and also something, we know not what, within, he is enabled to maintain his posture where you would be tottering. Urchins upon whose curly pates grey seniors lay their hands with conventional encomium and speculation look older than they are immediately, and Willoughby looked older than his years, not for want of freshness, but because he felt that he had to stand eminently and correctly poised.

Hearing of Mrs. Mountstuart's word on him, he smiled and said: "It is at her service."

The speech was communicated to her, and she proposed to attach a dedicatory strip of silk. And then they came together, and there was wit and repartee suitable to the electrical atmosphere of the dancing-room, on the march to a magical hall of supper. Willoughby conducted Mrs. Mountstuart to the supper-table.

"Were I," said she, "twenty years younger, I think I would marry you, to cure my infatuation."

"Then let me tell you in advance, madam," said he, "that I will do everything to obtain a new lease of it, except divorce you."

They were infinitely wittier, but so much was heard and may be reported.

"It makes the business of choosing a wife for him superhumanly difficult!" Mrs. Mountstuart observed, after listening to the praises she had set going again when the ladies were weeded of us, in Lady Patterne's Indian room, and could converse unhampered upon their own ethereal themes.[7]

"Willoughby will choose a wife for himself," said his mother.

6. "Indian Gods": Buddhas.
7. After dinner it was customary for the ladies to retire and talk scandal, while the gentlemen indulged in port, cigars ("the weed"), and scandal by themselves.

CHAPTER 3

not constant to him

CONSTANTIA DURHAM

THE great question for the county was debated in many households, daughter-thronged and daughterless, long subsequent to the memorable day of Willoughby's coming of age. Lady Busshe was for Constantia Durham. She laughed at Mrs. Mountstuart Jenkinson's notion of Lætitia Dale. She was a little older than Mrs. Mountstuart, and had known Willoughby's father, whose marriage into the wealthiest branch of the Whitford family had been strictly sagacious. "Patternes marry money: they are not romantic people," she said. Miss Durham had money, and she had health and beauty: three mighty qualifications for a Patterne bride. Her father, Sir John Durham, was a large landowner in the western division of the county; a pompous gentleman, the picture of a father-in-law for Willoughby. The father of Miss Dale was a battered army surgeon from India, tenant of one of Sir Willoughby's cottages bordering Patterne Park. His girl was portionless and a poetess. Her writing of the song in celebration of the young baronet's birthday was thought a clever venture, bold as only your timid creatures can be bold. She let the cat out of her bag of verse before the multitude; she almost proposed to her hero in her rhymes. She was pretty; her eyelashes were long and dark, her eyes dark blue, and her soul was ready to shoot like a rocket out of them at a look from Willoughby. And he looked, he certainly looked, though he did not dance with her once that night, and danced repeatedly with Miss Durham. He gave Lætitia to Vernon Whitford for the final dance of the night, and he may have looked at her so much in pity of an elegant girl allied to such a partner. The "Phœbus Apollo turned fasting friar" had entirely forgotten his musical gifts in motion. He crossed himself and crossed his bewildered lady, and crossed everybody in the figure, extorting shouts of cordial laughter from his cousin Willoughby. Be it said that the hour was four in the morning, when dancers must laugh at somebody, if only to refresh their feet, and the wit of the hour administers to the wildest laughter. Vernon was likened to Theseus in the maze, entirely dependent upon his Ariadne; to a fly released from a jam-pot; to a "salvage," or green, man caught in a web of nymphs and made to go the paces.[1] Willoughby was inexhaustible in

---

1. Theseus ventured into the maze built by Daedalus, but after killing the Minotaur he was able to get out only because Ariadne held one end of a string that he had unwound behind him as he went in. The "salvage" or wild man is a figure in Spenser's *Faerie Queene*; Vernon, more "natural" than his overcivilized counterparts, is also a "green" man.

the happy similes he poured out to Miss Durham across the lines of Sir Roger de Coverley, and they were not forgotten, they procured him a reputation as a convivial sparkler.[2] Rumour went the round that he intended to give Lætitia to Vernon for good, when he could decide to take Miss Durham to himself; his generosity was famous; but that decision, though the rope was in the form of a knot, seemed reluctant for the conclusive close haul; it preferred the state of slackness; and if he courted Lætitia on behalf of his cousin, his cousinly love must have been greater than his passion, one had to suppose. He was generous enough for it, or for marrying the portionless girl himself.

There was a story of a brilliant young widow of our aristocracy who had very nearly snared him. Why should he object to marry into our aristocracy? Mrs. Mountstuart asked him, and he replied, that the girls of that class have no money, and he doubted the quality of their blood. He had his eyes awake. His duty to his House was a foremost thought with him, and for such a reason he may have been more anxious to give the slim and not robust Lætitia to Vernon than accede to his personal inclination. The mention of the widow singularly offended him, notwithstanding the high rank of the lady named. "A widow?" he said. "I!" He spoke to a widow; an oldish one truly; but his wrath at the suggestion of his union with a widow, led him to be for the moment oblivious of the minor shades of good taste.[3] He desired Mrs. Mountstuart to contradict the story in positive terms. He repeated his desire; he was urgent to have it contradicted, and said again, "A widow!" straightening his whole figure to the erectness of the letter I. She was a widow unmarried a second time, and it has been known of the stedfast women who retain the name of their first husband, or do not hamper his title with a little new squire at their skirts, that they can partially approve the objections indicated by Sir Willoughby. They are thinking of themselves when they do so, and they will rarely say, "I might have married;" rarely within them will they avow that, with their permission, it might have been. They can catch an idea of a gentleman's view of the widow's cap. But a niceness that could feel sharply wounded by the simple rumour of his alliance with the young relict of an earl, was mystifying. Sir Willoughby unbent. His military letter I took a careless glance at itself lounging idly and proudly at ease in the glass of his mind, decked with a wanton wreath, as he dropped a hint, generously vague, just to show the origin of the rumour, and the excellent basis it had for not being credited. He was chidden.

2. "Sir Roger de Coverley" is the title of an air and of a dance performed to it—giving rise through its old-fashioned merriment to the name of a character in Addison's *Spectator*.
3. He is of course grossly rude.

Mrs. Mountstuart read him a lecture. She was however able to contradict the tale of the young countess. "There is no fear of his marrying her, my dears."

Meanwhile there was a fear that he would lose his chance of marrying the beautiful Miss Durham.

The dilemmas of little princes are often grave. They should be dwelt on now and then for an example to poor, struggling commoners of the slings and arrows assailing fortune's most favoured men, that we may preach contentment to the wretch who cannot muster wherewithal to marry a wife, or has done it and trots the streets, pack-laden, to maintain the dame and troops of children painfully reared to fill subordinate stations. According to our reading, a moral is always welcome in a moral country, and especially so when silly envy is to be chastised by it, the restless craving for change rebuked.[4] Young Sir Willoughby, then, stood in this dilemma: — a lady was at either hand of him; the only two that had ever, apart from metropolitan conquests, not to be recited, touched his emotions.[5] Susceptible to beauty, he had never seen so beautiful a girl as Constantia Durham. Equally susceptible to admiration of himself, he considered Lætitia Dale a paragon of cleverness. He stood between the queenly rose and the modest violet. One he bowed to; the other bowed to him. He could not have both; it is the law governing princes and pedestrians alike. But which could he forfeit? His growing acquaintance with the world taught him to put an increasing price on the sentiments of Miss Dale. Still Constantia's beauty was of a kind to send away beholders aching. She had the glory of the racing cutter full sail on a winning breeze; and she did not court to win him, she flew. In his more reflective hour the attractiveness of that lady which held the mirror to his features was paramount. But he had passionate snatches when the magnetism of the flyer drew him in her wake. Further to add to the complexity, he loved his liberty; he was princelier free; he had more subjects, more slaves; he ruled arrogantly in the world of women; he was more himself. His metropolitan experiences did not answer to his liking the particular question, Do **we** bind the woman down to us idolatrously by making a wife of her?

In the midst of his deliberations, a report of the hot pursuit of Miss Durham, casually mentioned to him by Lady Busshe, drew an immediate proposal from Sir Willoughby. She accepted him, and they were engaged. She

---

4. "moral . . . in a moral country": ironic, once again, to the point of sarcasm.
5. "metropolitan conquests": London girls, with latent overtones of easy pickings. The novel repeatedly suggests that Sir Willoughby has had all the casual connections he wants. These were thought perfectly condonable, even admirable, in a gentleman, though unthinkable in a lady. But see below for the suggestion that the London girls judged Willoughby too sharply for his own complete comfort.

had been nibbled at, all but eaten up, while he hung dubitative; and though that was the cause of his winning her, it offended his niceness. She had not come to him out of cloistral purity, out of perfect radiancy. Spiritually, likewise, was he a little prince, a despotic prince. He wished for her to have come to him out of an egg-shell, somewhat more astonished at things than a chicken, but as completely enclosed before he tapped the shell, and seeing him with her sex's eyes first of all men. She talked frankly of her cousins and friends, young males. She could have replied to his bitter wish: "Had you asked me on the night of your twenty-first birthday, Willoughby!" Since then she had been in the dust of the world, and he conceived his peculiar antipathy, destined to be so fatal to him, from the earlier hours of his engagement. He was quaintly incapable of a jealousy of individuals. A young Captain Oxford had been foremost in the swarm pursuing Constantia.[6] Willoughby thought as little of Captain Oxford as he did of Vernon Whitford. His enemy was the world, the mass, which confounds us in a lump, which has breathed on her whom we have selected, whom we cannot, can never, rub quite clear of her contact with the abominated crowd. The pleasure of the world is to bowl down our soldierly letter I; to encroach on our identity, soil our niceness. To begin to think is the beginning of disgust of the world.

As soon as the engagement was published, all the county said that there had not been a chance for Lætitia, and Mrs. Mountstuart Jenkinson humbly remarked, in an attitude of penitence, "I'm not a witch." Lady Busshe could claim to be one; she had foretold the event. Lætitia was of the same opinion as the county. She had looked up, but not hopefully. She had only looked up to the brightest, and, as he was the highest, how could she have hoped? She was the solitary companion of a sick father, whose inveterate prognostic of her, that she would live to rule at Patterne Hall, tortured the poor girl in proportion as he seemed to derive comfort from it. The noise of the engagement merely silenced him; recluse invalids cling obstinately to their ideas. He had observed Sir Willoughby in the society of his daughter, when the young baronet revived to a sprightly boyishness immediately. Indeed, as big boy and little girl, they had played together of old. Willoughby had been a handsome fair boy. The portrait of him at the Hall, in a hat, leaning on his pony, with crossed legs and long flaxen curls over his shoulders, was the image of her soul's most present angel; and, as a man, he had — she did not suppose intentionally — subjected her nature to bow to him; so submissive was she, that it

6. Captain Oxford is named after the university and a street in central London, both societies where Willoughby's peculiar predominance is subject to challenge.

was fuller happiness for her to think him right in all his actions than to imagine the circumstances different. This may appear to resemble the ecstacy of the devotee of Juggernaut.[7] It is a form of the passion inspired by little princes, and we need not marvel that a conservative sex should assist to keep them in their lofty places. What were there otherwise to look up to? We should have no dazzling beacon-lights if they were levelled and treated as clod earth; and it is worth while for here and there a woman to be burnt, so long as women's general adoration of an ideal young man shall be preserved.[8] Purity is our demand of them. They may justly cry for attraction. They cannot have it brighter than in the universal bearing of the eyes of their sisters upon a little prince, one who has the ostensible virtues in his pay, and can practise them without injuring himself to make himself unsightly. Let the races of men be by-and-by astonished at their Gods, if they please. Meantime they had better continue to worship.

Lætitia did continue. She saw Miss Durham at Patterne on several occasions. She admired the pair. She had a wish to witness the bridal ceremony. She was looking forward to the day with that mixture of eagerness and withholding which we have as we draw nigh the disenchanting termination of an enchanting romance, when Sir Willoughby met her on a Sunday morning, as she crossed his park solitarily to church. They were within ten days of the appointed ceremony. He should have been away at Miss Durham's end of the county. He had, Lætitia knew, ridden over to her the day before; but here he was; and very unwontedly, quite surprisingly, he presented his arm to conduct Lætitia to the church-door, and talked and laughed in a way that reminded her of a hunting gentleman she had seen once rising to his feet, staggering from an ugly fall across hedge and fence into one of the lanes of her short winter walks: "All's well, all sound, never better, only a scratch!" the gentleman had said, as he reeled and pressed a bleeding head. Sir Willoughby chattered of his felicity in meeting her. "I am really wonderfully lucky," he said, and he said that and other things over and over, incessantly talking, and telling an anecdote of county occurrences, and laughing at it with a mouth that would not widen. He went on talking in the church porch, and murmuring softly some steps up the aisle, passing the pews of Mrs. Mountstuart Jenkinson and Lady Busshe. Of course he was entertaining, but what a strangeness it was to Lætitia! His face would have been half under an antique bonnet. It came very

7. Worshippers of the Indian god Jagannath (he is an aspect of Vishnu) were popularly but erroneously supposed to fling themselves under the wheels of the wagon bearing the god's image, to be crushed on the festive day.

8. Meredith touches sharply yet swiftly and only intermittently on the theme of barbaric cruelties surviving in the midst of "civilization."

close to hers, and the scrutiny he bent on her was most solicitous.

After the service, he avoided the great ladies by sauntering up to within a yard or two of where she sat; he craved her hand on his arm to lead her forth by the park entrance to the church, all the while bending to her, discoursing rapidly, appearing radiantly interested in her quiet replies, with fits of intentness that stared itself out into dim abstraction. She hazarded the briefest replies for fear of not having understood him.

One question she asked: "Miss Durham is well, I trust?"

And he answered, "Durham?" and said, "There is no Miss Durham to my knowledge."

The impression he left with her was, that he might yesterday during his ride have had an accident and fallen on his head.

She would have asked that, if she had not known him for so thorough an Englishman, in his dislike to have it thought that accidents could hurt even when they happened to him.

He called the next day to claim her for a walk. He assured her she had promised it, and he appealed to her father, who could not testify to a promise he had not heard, but begged her to leave him to have her walk. So once more she was in the park with Sir Willoughby, listening to his raptures over old days. A word of assent from her sufficed him. "I am now myself," was one of the remarks he repeated this day. She dilated on the beauty of the Park and the Hall to gratify him.

He did not speak of Miss Durham, and Lætitia became afraid to mention her name.

At their parting, Willoughby promised Lætitia that he would call on the morrow. He did not come; and she could well excuse him, after her hearing of the tale.

It was a lamentable tale. He had ridden to Sir John Durham's mansion, a distance of thirty miles, to hear, on his arrival, that Constantia had quitted her father's house two days previously on a visit to an aunt in London, and had just sent word that she was the <u>wife of Captain Oxford</u>, hussar, and messmate of one of her brothers. A letter from the bride awaited Willoughby at the Hall. He had ridden back at night, not caring how he used his horse in order to get swiftly home, so forgetful of himself was he under the terrible blow. That was the night of Saturday. On the day following, being Sunday, he met Lætitia in his park, led her to church, led her out of it, and the day after that, previous to his <u>disappearance</u> for some weeks, was walking with her in full view of the carriages along the road.

He had indeed, you see, been very fortunately, if not considerately, liberated by Miss Durham. He, as a man

of honour, could not have taken the initiative, but the
frenzy of a jealous girl might urge her to such a course;
and how little he suffered from it had been shown to the
world. Miss Durham, the story went, was his mother's
choice for him, against his heart's inclinations; which had
finally subdued Lady Patterne. Consequently, there was
no longer an obstacle between Sir Willoughby and Miss
Dale. It was a pleasant and romantic story, and it put
most people in good humour with the county's favourite,
as his choice of a portionless girl of no position would
not have done without the shock of astonishment at the
conduct of Miss Durham, and the desire to feel that so
prevailing a gentleman was not in any degree pitiable.
Constantia was called "that mad thing." Lætitia broke
forth in novel and abundant merits; and one of the chief
points of requisition in relation to Patterne — a Lady Willoughby who would entertain well and animate the dead-
ness of the Hall, became a certainty when her gentleness
and liveliness and exceeding cleverness were considered.
She was often a visitor at the Hall by Lady Patterne's
express invitation, and sometimes on these occasions Willoughby was there too, superintending the fitting up of
his laboratory, though he was not at home to the county;
it was not expected that he should be yet. He had taken
heartily to the pursuit of science, and spoke of little else.
Science, he said, was in our days the sole object worth a
devoted pursuit. But the sweeping remark could hardly
apply to Lætitia, of whom he was the courteous quiet
wooer you behold when a man has broken loose from an
unhappy tangle to return to the lady of his first and
strongest affections.

Some months of homely courtship ensued, and then, the
decent interval prescribed by the situation having elapsed,
Sir Willoughby Patterne left his native land on a tour of
the globe.

CHAPTER 4

LÆTITIA DALE

THAT was another surprise to the county.

Let us not inquire into the feelings of patiently starving women: they must obtain some sustenance of their
own, since, as you perceive, they live; evidently they
are not in need of a great amount of nourishment; and
we may set them down for creatures with a rushlight of
animal fire to warm them.[1] They cannot have much vitality
who are so little exclamatory. A corresponding sentiment
of patient compassion, akin to scorn, is provoked by per-

1. "rushlight": a weak, flickering candle.

sons having the opportunity for pathos and declining to use it. The public bosom was open to Lætitia for several weeks, and had she run to it to bewail herself, she would have been cherished in thankfulness for a country drama. There would have been a party against her, cold people, critical of her pretensions to rise from an unrecognized sphere to be mistress of Patterne Hall; but there would also have been a party against Sir Willoughby, composed of the two or three revolutionists, tired of the yoke, which are to be found in England when there is a stir; a larger number of born sympathetics, ever ready to yield the tear for the tear; and here and there a Samaritan soul prompt to succour poor humanity in distress. The opportunity passed undramatized. Lætitia presented herself at church with a face mildly devout, according to her custom, and she accepted invitations to the Hall, she assisted at the reading of Willoughby's letters to his family, and fed on dry husks of him wherein her name was not mentioned; never one note of the summoning call for pathos did this young lady blow.

So, very soon the public bosom closed. She had, under the fresh interpretation of affairs, too small a spirit to be Lady Willoughby of Patterne; she could not have entertained becomingly; he must have seen that the girl was not the match for him in station, and off he went to conquer the remainder of a troublesome first attachment, no longer extremely disturbing, to judge from the tenor of his letters: really incomparable letters! Lady Busshe and Mrs. Mountstuart Jenkinson enjoyed a perusal of them. Sir Willoughby appeared as a splendid young representative island lord in these letters to his family, despatched from the principal cities of the United States of America. He would give them a sketch of "our democratic cousins," he said. Such cousins! They might all have been in the Marines. He carried his English standard over that Continent, and by simply jotting down facts, he left an idea of the results of the measurement to his family and friends at home. He was an adept in the irony of incongruously grouping. The nature of the Equality under the stars and stripes was presented in this manner. Equality! Reflections came occasionally: "These cousins of ours are highly amusing. I am among the descendants of the Roundheads.[2] Now and then an allusion to old domestic differences, in perfect good temper. We go on in our way; they theirs, in the apparent belief that Republicanism operates remarkable changes in human nature. Vernon tries hard to think it does. The upper ten of our cousins are the Infernal of Paris.[3] The rest of them is Radical England, as far as I am acquainted with that

2. Cromwell's Puritans.
3. The "Infernal of Paris" was the ruling clique of the French Revolution. Travel-ing to America in the 1870's, Willoughby would have met in the presidency Ulysses S. Grant, hardly a flaming radical.

section of my country." — Where we compared, they were
absurd; where we contrasted, they were monstrous. The
contrast of Vernon's letters with Willoughby's was just as
extreme. You could hardly have taken them for relatives
travelling together, or Vernon Whitford for a born and
bred Englishman. The same scenes furnished by these
two pens might have been sketched in different hemispheres. Vernon had no irony. He had nothing of Willoughby's epistolary creative power, which, causing his
family and friends to exclaim, "How like him that is!"
conjured them across the broad Atlantic to behold and
clap hands at his lordliness.

They saw him distinctly, as with the naked eye: a
word, a turn of the pen, or a word unsaid, offered the picture of him in America, Japan, China, Australia, nay, the
Continent of Europe, holding an English review of his
Maker's grotesques. Vernon seemed a sheepish fellow,
without stature abroad, glad of a compliment, grateful for
a dinner, endeavouring sadly to digest all he saw and
heard. But one was a Patterne; the other a Whitford.
One had genius; the other pottered after him with the title
of student. One was the English gentleman wherever he
went; the other was a new kind of thing, nondescript,
produced in England of late, and not likely to come to
much good himself, or do much good to the country.

Vernon's dancing in America was capitally described by
Willoughby. "Adieu to our cousins!" the latter wrote on
his voyage to Japan. "I may possibly have had some
vogue in their ball-rooms, and in showing them an English
seat on horseback: I must resign myself if I have not been
popular among them. I could not sing their national song
— if a congery of States be a nation — and I must confess I
listened with frigid politeness to their singing of it.[4] A great
people, no doubt. Adieu to them. I have had to tear old
Vernon away. He had serious thoughts of settling, means
to correspond with some of them." On the whole, forgetting two or more "traits of insolence" on the part of his
hosts, which he cited, Willoughby escaped pretty comfortably. The President had been, consciously or not, uncivil,
but one knew his origin! Upon these interjections, placable flicks of the lionly tail addressed to Britannia the
Ruler, who expected him in some mildish way to lash
terga cauda in retiring, Sir Willoughby Patterne passed
from a land of alien manners; and ever after he spoke of
America respectfully and pensively, with a tail tucked in,
as it were.[5] His travels were profitable to himself. The
fact is, that there are cousins who come to greatness and
must be pacified, or they will prove annoying. Heaven
forefend a collision between cousins![6]

4. "congery": muddled combination.
5. The whole sentence is built on the old
metaphor for Americans teasing Britons,
"twisting the lion's tail." "Terga cauda"
is a kind of pig-Latin for "tail on back."
6. The cousins are Britain and America,
on the overt plane; Vernon and Willoughby, covertly.

Willoughby returned to his England after an absence of three years.7 On a fair April morning, the last of the month, he drove along his park palings, and by the luck of things, Lætitia was the first of his friends whom he met. She was crossing from field to field with a band of school-children, gathering wild flowers for the morrow May-day. He sprang to the ground and seized her hand. "Lætitia Dale!" he said. He panted. "Your name is sweet English music! And you are well?" The anxious question permitted him to read deeply in her eyes. He found the man he sought there, squeezed him passionately, and let her go, saying, "I could not have prayed for a lovelier home-scene to welcome me than you and these children flower-gathering. I don't believe in chance. It was decreed that we should meet. Do not you think so?"

Lætitia breathed faintly of her gladness.

He begged her to distribute a gold coin among the little ones; asked for the names of some of them, and repeated, "Mary, Susan, Charlotte—only the Christian names, pray!8 Well, my dears, you will bring your garlands to the Hall to-morrow morning; and mind, early! no slugabeds to-morrow; I suppose I am browned, Lætitia?"9 He smiled in apology for the foreign sun, and murmured with rapture: "The green of this English country is unsurpassed. It is wonderful. Leave England and be baked, if you would appreciate it. You can't, unless you taste exile as I have done — for how many years? How many?"

"Three," said Lætitia.

"Thirty!" said he. "It seems to me that length. At least, I am immensely older. But looking at you, I could think it less than three. You have not changed. You are absolutely unchanged. I am bound to hope so. I shall see you soon. I have much to talk of, much to tell you. I shall hasten to call on your father. I have specially to speak with him. I — what happiness this is, Lætitia! But I must not forget I have a mother. Adieu; for some hours — not for many!"

He pressed her hand again. He was gone.

She dismissed the children to their homes. Plucking primroses was hard labour now — a dusty business. She could have wished that her planet had not descended to earth, his presence agitated her so; but his enthusiastic patriotism was like a shower that in the Spring season of the year sweeps against the hard-binding East and melts the air, and brings out new colours, makes life flow; and her thoughts recurred in wonderment to the behaviour of Constantia Durham. That was Lætitia's manner of taking

---

7. He is now, therefore, twenty-seven.
8. He really does not want to know who they are.
9. The garlands are for May Day. "No slugabeds tomorrow" is a recall of the Cavalier poet Robert Herrick in "Corinna's Going a-Maying": "Get up, sweet slug-a-bed, and see / The dew bespangling herb and tree."

up her weakness once more. She could almost have reviled the woman who had given this beneficent magician, this pathetic exile, of the aristocratic sunburnt visage and deeply-scrutinizing eyes, cause for grief. How deeply his eyes could read! The starveling of patience awoke to the idea of a feast. The sense of hunger came with it, and hope came, and patience fled. She would have rejected hope to keep patience nigh her; but surely it cannot always be Winter! said her reasoning blood, and we must excuse her as best we can if she was assured by her restored warmth that Willoughby came in the order of the revolving seasons, marking a long Winter past. He had specially to speak with her father, he had said. What could that mean? What but—! She dared not phrase it or view it.

At their next meeting she was "Miss Dale."

A week later he was closeted with her father.

Mr. Dale, in the evening of that pregnant day, eulogized Sir Willoughby as a landlord. A new lease of the cottage was to be granted him on the old terms, he said. Except that Sir Willoughby had congratulated him in the possession of an excellent daughter, their interview was one of landlord and tenant, it appeared; and Lætitia said, "So we shall not have to leave the cottage?" in a tone of satisfaction, while she quietly gave a wrench to the neck of the young hope in her breast. At night her diary received the line: "This day I was a fool. To-morrow?"

To-morrow and many days after there were dashes instead of words.

Patience travelled back to her sullenly. As we must have some kind of food, and she had nothing else, she took to that and found it dryer than of yore. It is a composing but a lean dietary. The dead are patient, and we get a certain likeness to them in feeding on it unintermittingly over-long. Her hollowed cheeks with the fallen leaf in them pleaded against herself to justify her idol for not looking down on one like her. She saw him when he was at the Hall. He did not notice any change. He was exceedingly gentle and courteous. More than once she discovered his eyes dwelling on her, and then he looked hurriedly at his mother, and Lætitia had to shut her mind from thinking, lest thinking should be a sin and hope a guilty spectre. But had his mother objected to her? She could not avoid asking herself. His tour of the globe had been undertaken at his mother's desire; she was an ambitious lady, in failing health; and she wished to have him living with her at Patterne, yet seemed to agree that he did wisely to reside in London.

One day Sir Willoughby, in the quiet manner which was his humour, informed her that he had become a country gentleman; he had abandoned London, he loathed it as the burial-place of the individual man. He intended to sit

down on his estates and have his cousin Vernon Whitford
to assist him in managing them, he said; and very amusing
was his description of his cousin's shifts to live by literature, and add enough to a beggarly income to get his usual
two months of the year in the Alps. Previous to his great
tour, Willoughby had spoken of Vernon's judgement with
derision; nor was it entirely unknown that Vernon had
offended his family pride by some extravagant act. But
after their return he acknowledged Vernon's talents, and
seemed unable to do without him.

The new arrangement gave Lætitia a companion for her
walks. Pedestrianism was a sour business to Willoughby,
whose exclamation of the word indicated a willingness for
any amount of exercise on horseback; but she had no horse,
and so, while he hunted, Lætitia and Vernon walked, and
the neighbourhood speculated on the circumstances, until
the ladies Eleanor and Isabel Patterne engaged her more
frequently for carriage exercise, and Sir Willoughby was
observed riding beside them.

A real and sunny pleasure befell Lætitia, in the establishment of young Crossjay Patterne under her roof; the
son of the lieutenant, now captain, of Marines; a boy of
twelve, with the sprights of twelve boys in him, for whose
board and lodgement Vernon provided by arrangement
with her father.[1] Vernon was one of your men that have
no occupation for their money, no bills to pay for repair of
their property, and are insane to spend. He had heard of
Captain Patterne's large family, and proposed to have his
eldest boy at the Hall, to teach him; but Willoughby declined to house the son of such a father, predicting that the
boy's hair would be red, his skin eruptive, and his prac-
tices detestable. So Vernon, having obtained Mr. Dale's
consent to accommodate this youth, stalked off to Devonport, and brought back a rosy-cheeked, round-bodied rogue
of a boy, who fell upon meats and puddings, and defeated
them, with a captivating simplicity in his confession that
he had never had enough to eat in his life. He had gone
through a training for a plentiful table. At first, after a
number of helps, young Crossjay would sit and sigh
heavily, in contemplation of the unfinished dish. Subsequently he told his host and hostess that he had two sisters
above his own age, and three brothers and two sisters
younger than he: "All hungry!" said the boy.

His pathos was most comical. It was a good month before he could see pudding taken away from table without
a sigh of regret that he could not finish it as deputy for
the Devonport household.[2] The pranks of the little fellow,
and his revel in a country life, and muddy wildness in it,
amused Lætitia from morning to night. She, when she

1. The point is quietly made that Vernon,
poor and dependent, is paying for the
support of wealthy Willoughby's kinsman.

2. The royal dockyards near Plymouth,
by Willoughby's standards a sad and
grubby environment.

had caught him, taught him in the morning; Vernon,
favoured by the chase, in the afternoon. Young Crossjay
would have enlivened any household. He was not only
indolent, he was opposed to the acquisition of knowledge
through the medium of books, and would say: "But I
don't want to!" in a tone to make a logician thoughtful.
Nature was very strong in him. He had, on each return
of the hour for instruction, to be plucked out of the earth,
rank of the soil, like a root, for the exercise of his big
round headpiece on those tyrannous puzzles. But the
habits of birds, and the place for their eggs, and the management of rabbits, and the tickling of fish, and poaching
joys with combative boys of the district, and how to
wheedle a cook for a luncheon for a whole day in the rain,
he soon knew of his great nature.[3] His passion for our
naval service was a means of screwing his attention to
lessons after he had begun to understand that the desert
had to be traversed to attain midshipman's rank. He
boasted ardently of his fighting father, and, chancing to
be near the Hall as he was talking to Vernon and Lætitia
of his father, he propounded a question close to his heart;
and he put it in these words, following: "My father's the
one to lead an army!" when he paused: "I say, Mr.
Whitford, Sir Willoughby's kind to me, and gives me
crown-pieces, why wouldn't he see my father, and my
father came here ten miles in the rain to see him, and had
to walk ten miles back, and sleep at an inn?"

The only answer to be given was, that Sir Willoughby
could not have been at home. "Oh! my father saw him,
and Sir Willoughby said he was not at home," the boy
replied, producing an odd ring in the ear by his repetition
of "not at home" in the same voice as the apology, plainly
innocent of malice. Vernon told Lætitia, however, that
the boy never asked an explanation of Sir Willoughby.

Unlike the horse of the adage, it was easier to compel
young Crossjay to drink of the waters of instruction than
to get him to the brink. His heart was not so antagonistic
as his nature, and by degrees, owing to a proper mixture
of discipline and cajolery, he imbibed. He was whistling
at the cook's windows after a day of wicked truancy, on
an April night, and reported adventures over the supper
supplied to him. Lætitia entered the kitchen with a reproving forefinger. He jumped to kiss her, and went on
chattering of a place fifteen miles distant, where he had
seen Sir Willoughby riding with a young lady. The
impossibility that the boy should have got so far on foot
made Lætitia doubtful of his veracity, until she heard that
a gentleman had taken him up on the road in a gig, and
had driven him to a farm to show him strings of birds'

3. In tickling fish one stalks the wary
creatures so stealthily that one can touch
them in the water.

eggs and stuffed birds of every English kind, kingfishers, yaffles, black woodpeckers, goat-sucker owls, more mouth than head, with dusty, dark-spotted wings, like moths; all very circumstantial. Still, in spite of his tea at the farm, and ride back by rail at the gentleman's expense, the tale seemed fictitious to Lætitia until Crossjay related how that he had stood to salute on the road to the railway, and taken off his cap to Sir Willoughby, and Sir Willoughby had passed him, not noticing him, though the young lady did, and looked back and nodded. The hue of truth was in that picture.

Strange eclipse, when the hue of truth comes shadowing over our bright ideal planet. It will not seem the planet's fault, but truth's. Reality is the offender; delusion our treasure that we are robbed of. Then begins with us the term of wilful delusion, and its necessary accompaniment of the disgust of reality; exhausting the heart much more than patient endurance of starvation.

Hints were dropping about the neighbourhood; the hedgeways twittered, the tree-tops cawed. Mrs. Mountstuart Jenkinson was loud on the subject: "Patterne is to have a mistress at last, you say? But there never was a doubt of his marrying — he must marry; and, so long as he does not marry a foreign woman, we have no cause to complain. He met her at Cherriton. Both were struck at the same moment. Her father is, I hear, some sort of learned man; money; no land. No house either, I believe. People who spend half their time on the Continent. They are now for a year at Upton Park. The very girl to settle down and entertain when she does think of settling. Eighteen, perfect manners; you need not ask if a beauty. Sir Willoughby will have his dues. We must teach her to make amends to him — but don't listen to Lady Busshe! He was too young at twenty-three or twenty-four. No young man is ever jilted; he is allowed to escape. A young man married is a fire-eater bound over to keep the peace; if he keeps it he worries it. At thirty-one or thirty-two he is ripe for his command, because he knows how to bend. And Sir Willoughby is a splendid creature, only wanting a wife to complete him. For a man like that to go on running about would never do. Soberly — no! It would soon be getting ridiculous. He has been no worse than other men, probably better — infinitely more excusable; but now we have him, and it was time we should. I shall see her and study her, sharply, you may be sure; though I fancy I can rely on his judgement."

In confirmation of the swelling buzz, the Rev. Dr. Middleton and his daughter paid a flying visit to the Hall, where they were seen only by the members of the Patterne family. Young Crossjay had a short conversation with Miss Middleton, and ran to the cottage full of her — she loved the navy and had a merry face. She had a smile of very pleasant humour, according to Vernon. The young lady was outlined to Lætitia as tall, elegant, lively; and painted as carrying youth like a flag. With her smile of "very pleasant humour," she could not but be winning.

Vernon spoke more of her father, a scholar of high repute; happily, a scholar of an independent fortune. His maturer recollection of Miss Middleton grew poetic, or he described her in an image to suit a poetic ear: "She gives you an idea of the Mountain Echo.[4] Dr. Middleton has one of the grandest heads in England."

"What is her Christian name?" said Lætitia.

He thought her Christian name was Clara.

Lætitia went to bed and walked through the day conceiving the Mountain Echo, the swift wild spirit, Clara by name, sent fleeting on a far half-circle by the voice it is roused to subserve; sweeter than beautiful, high above drawing-room beauties as the colours of the sky; and if, at the same time, elegant and of loveable smiling, could a man resist her? To inspire the title of Mountain Echo in any mind, a young lady must be singularly spiritualized. Her father doated on her, Vernon said. Who would not? It seemed an additional cruelty that the grace of a poetical attractiveness should be round her, for this was robbing Lætitia of some of her own little fortune, mystical though that might be. But a man like Sir Willoughby had claims on poetry, possessing as he did every manly grace; and to think that Miss Middleton had won him by virtue of something native to her likewise, though mystically, touched Lætitia with a faint sense of relationship to the chosen girl. "What is in me, he sees on her." It decked her pride to think so, as a wreath on the grave stone. She encouraged her imagination to brood over Clara, and invested her designedly with romantic charms, in spite of pain: the ascetic zealot hugs his share of heaven — most bitter, most blessed — in his hair shirt and scourge, and Lætitia's happiness was to glorify Clara. Through that chosen rival, through her comprehension of the spirit of Sir Willoughby's choice of one such as Clara, she was linked to him yet.

Her mood of ecstatic fidelity was a dangerous exaltation: one that in a desert will distort the brain, and in the world where the idol dwells will put him, should he come nigh, to its own furnace-test, and get a clear brain out of a burnt heart. She was frequently at the Hall, helping to nurse Lady Patterne. Sir Willoughby had hitherto treated her as a dear insignificant friend, to whom it was unnecessary that he should mention the object of his rides to Upton Park.

He had, however, in the contemplation of what he was

4. Especially in the Alps, mountains often make echoes; Meredith may have some particular one in mind. But the phrase by itself suggests loftiness, purity, mystery.

gaining, fallen into anxiety about what he might be losing. She belonged to his brilliant youth; her devotion was the bride of his youth; he was a man who lived backwards almost as intensely as in the present; and, notwithstanding Lætitia's praiseworthy zeal in attending on his mother, he suspected some unfaithfulness: hardly without cause: she had not looked paler of late, her eyes had not reproached him; the secret of the old days between them had been as little concealed as it was exposed. She might have buried it, after the way of women, whose bosoms can be tombs, if we and the world allow them to be; absolutely sepulchres, where you lie dead, ghastly. Even if not dead and horrible to think of, you may be lying cold, somewhere in a corner. Even if embalmed, you may not be much visited. And how is the world to know you are embalmed? You are no better than a rotting wretch to the world that does not have peeps of you in the woman's breast, and see lights burning and an occasional exhibition of the services of worship. There are women — tell us not of her of Ephesus! — that have embalmed you, and have quitted the world to keep the tapers alight, and a stranger comes, and they, who have your image before them, will suddenly blow out the vestal flames and treat you as dust to fatten the garden of their bosoms for a fresh flower of love.[5] Sir Willoughby knew it; he had experience of it in the form of the stranger; and he knew the stranger's feelings toward his predecessor and the lady.

He waylaid Lætitia to talk of himself and his plans: the project of a run to Italy. Enviable? Yes, but in England you live the higher moral life. Italy boasts of sensual beauty; the spiritual is yours. "I know Italy well; I have often wished to act as cicerone to you there.[6] As it is, I suppose I shall be with those who know the land as well as I do, and will not be particularly enthusiastic: . . . if you are what you were?" He was guilty of this perplexing twist from one person to another in a sentence more than once. While he talked exclusively of himself, it seemed to her a condescension. In time he talked principally of her, beginning with her admirable care of his mother; and he wished to introduce "a Miss Middleton" to her; he wanted her opinion of Miss Middleton; he relied on her intuition of character, had never known it err.

"If I supposed it could err, Miss Dale, I should not be so certain of myself. I am bound up in my good opinion of you, you see; and you must continue the same, or where shall I be?" Thus he was led to dwell upon friendship, and the charm of the friendship of men and women, "Pla-

5. A flighty allusion to Diana of Ephesus, late representative of a cult originally dedicated to an Amazon. Such warlike virgins would not mourn over a slight.

6. "cicerone": guide, from the oratorical habits of Italian tour-guides: in allusion to the Roman rhetorician, Cicero.

tonism," as it was called. "I have laughed at it in the
world, but not in the depth of my heart. The world's
platonic attachments are laughable enough. You have
taught me that the ideal of friendship *is* possible — when
we find two who are capable of a disinterested esteem.
The rest of life is duty; duty to parents, duty to country.
But friendship is the holiday of those who can be friends.
Wives are plentiful, friends are rare. I know *how* rare!"

Lætitia swallowed her thoughts as they sprang up.
Why was he torturing her? — to give himself a holiday?
She could bear to lose him — she was used to it — and bear
his indifference, but not that he should disfigure himself;
it made her poor. It was as if he required an oath of her
when he said: "Italy! But I shall never see a day in
Italy to compare with the day of my return to England,
or know a pleasure so exquisite as your welcome of me!
Will you be true to that? May I look forward to just
another such meeting?"

He pressed her for an answer. She gave the best she
could. He was dissatisfied, and to her hearing it was
hardly in the tone of manliness that he entreated her to
reassure him; he womanized his language. She had to say:
"I am afraid I cannot undertake to make it an appointment, Sir Willoughby," before he recovered his alertness,
which he did, for he was anything but obtuse, with the
reply, "You would keep it if you promised, and freeze at
your post. So, as accidents happen, we must leave it to
fate. The will's the thing. You know my detestation of
changes. At least I have you for my tenant, and wherever I am, I see your light at the end of my park."

"Neither my father nor I would willingly quit Ivy
Cottage," said Lætitia.

"So far, then," he murmured. "You will give me a
long notice, and it must be with my consent if you think
of quitting?"

"I could almost engage to do that," she said.

"You love the place?"

"Yes; I am the most contented of cottagers."

"I believe, Miss Dale, it would be well for my happiness were I a cottager."

"That is the dream of the palace. But to be one, and
not to wish to be other, is quiet sleep in comparison."

"You paint a cottage in colours that tempt one to run
from big houses and households."

"You would run back to them faster, Sir Willoughby."

"You may know me," said he, bowing and passing on
contentedly. He stopped: "But I am not ambitious."

"Perhaps you are too proud for ambition, Sir Willoughby."

"You hit me to the life!"

He passed on regretfully. Clara Middleton did not study
and know him like Lætitia Dale.

Lætitia was left to think it pleased him to play at cat and mouse. She had not "hit him to the life," or she would have marvelled in acknowledging how sincere he was.

At her next sitting by the bedside of Lady Patterne, she received a certain measure of insight that might have helped her to fathom him, if only she could have kept her feelings down. The old lady was affectionately confidential in talking of her one subject, her son. "And here is another dashing girl, my dear; she has money and health and beauty; and so has he; and it appears a fortunate union; I hope and pray it may be; but we begin to read the world when our eyes grow dim, because we read the plain lines, and I ask myself whether money and health and beauty on both sides, have not been the mutual attraction. We tried it before; and that girl Durham was honest, whatever we may call her. I should have desired an appreciative, thoughtful partner for him, a woman of mind, with another sort of wealth and beauty. She was honest, she ran away in time; there was a worse thing possible than that. And now we have the same chapter, and the same kind of person, who may not be quite as honest; and I shall not see the end of it. Promise me you will always be good to him; be my son's friend; his Egeria, he names you.[7] Be what you were to him when that girl broke his heart, and no one, not even his mother, was allowed to see that he suffered anything. Comfort him in his sensitiveness. Willoughby has the most entire faith in you. Were that destroyed — I shudder! You are, he says, and he has often said, his image of the constant woman. . . ."

Lætitia's hearing took in no more. She repeated to herself for days: "His image of the constant woman!" Now, when he was a second time forsaking her, his praise of her constancy wore the painful ludicrousness of the look of a whimper on the face.

CHAPTER 5

CLARA MIDDLETON

THE great meeting of Sir Willoughby Patterne and Miss Middleton had taken place at Cherriton Grange, the seat of a county grandee, where this young lady of eighteen was first seen rising above the horizon. She had money and health and beauty, the triune of perfect starriness, which makes all men astronomers. He looked on her,

---

7. Egeria was the nymph who inspired Numa with his conception of the Roman religion, fled to the woods after his death, and there remained faithful to him: Ovid, *Metamorphoses*, XV.

expecting her to look at him. But as soon as he looked he found that he must be in motion to win a look in return. He was one of a pack; many were ahead of him, the whole of them were eager. He had to debate within himself how best to communicate to her that he was Willoughby Patterne, before her gloves were too much soiled to flatter his niceness, for here and there, all around, she was yielding her hand to partners — obscurant males whose touch leaves a stain. Far too generally gracious was Her Starriness to please him. The effect of it, nevertheless, was to hurry him with all his might into the heat of the chase, while yet he knew no more of her than that he was competing for a prize and Willoughby Patterne only one of dozens to the young lady.

A deeper student of Science than his rivals, he appreciated Nature's compliment in the fair one's choice of you. We now scientifically know that in this department of the universal struggle, success is awarded to the bettermost.[1] You spread a handsomer tail than your fellows, you dress a finer top-knot, you pipe a newer note, have a longer stride; she reviews you in competition, and selects you. The superlative is magnetic to her. She may be looking elsewhere, and you will see — the superlative will simply have to beckon, away she glides. She cannot help herself; it is her nature, and her nature is the guarantee for the noblest race of men to come of her. In complimenting you, she is a promise of superior offspring. Science thus — or it is better to say, an acquaintance with science facilitates the cultivation of aristocracy. Consequently a successful pursuit and a wresting of her from a body of competitors, tells you that you are the best man. What is more, it tells the world so.

Willoughby aired his amiable superlatives in the eye of Miss Middleton; he had a leg. He was the heir of successful competitors. He had a style, a tone, an artist tailor, an authority of manner: he had in the hopeful ardour of the chase among a multitude a freshness that gave him advantage; and together with his undeviating energy when there was a prize to be won and possessed, these were scarcely resistible. He spared no pains, for he was adust and athirst for the winning-post. He courted her father, aware that men likewise, and parents pre-eminently, have their preference for the larger offer, the deeper pocket, the broader lands, the respectfuller consideration. Men, after their fashion, as well as women, distinguish the bettermost, and aid him to succeed, as Dr. Middleton certainly did in the crisis of the memorable question proposed to his daughter within a month of Willoughby's reception at Upton Park. The young lady was

---

1. "scientifically know": i.e., from the book of Mr. Darwin, *The Origin of Species*.

astonished at his whirlwind wooing of her, and bent to it
like a sapling. She begged for time; Willoughby could
barely wait. She unhesitatingly owned that she liked no
one better, and he consented. A calm examination of his
position told him that it was unfair so long as he stood
engaged and she did not. She pleaded a desire to see a
little of the world before she plighted herself. She
alarmed him; he assumed the amazing God of Love under
the subtlest guise of the divinity. Willingly would he
obey her behests, resignedly languish, were it not for his
mother's desire to see the future lady of Patterne established there before she died. Love shone cunningly
through the mask of filial duty, but the plea of urgency
was reasonable. Dr. Middleton thought it reasonable,
supposing his daughter to have an inclination. She had
no disinclination, though she had a maidenly desire to see
a little of the world — grace for one year, she said. Willoughby reduced the year to six months, and granted that
term, for which, in gratitude, she submitted to stand engaged; and that was no light whispering of a word. She
was implored to enter the state of captivity by the pronunciation of vows — a private but a binding ceremonial.
She had health and beauty, and money to gild these gifts:
not that he stipulated for money with his bride, but it
adds a lustre to dazzle the world; and, moreover, the pack
of rival pursuers hung close behind, yelping and raising
their dolorous throats to the moon. Captive she must be.

He made her engagement no light whispering matter.
It was a solemn plighting of a troth. Why not? Having
said, I am yours, she could say, I am wholly yours, I am
yours for ever, I swear it, I will never swerve from it, I
am your wife in heart, yours utterly; our engagement is
written above. To this she considerately appended, "as
far as I am concerned;" a piece of somewhat chilling
generosity, and he forced her to pass him through love's
catechism in turn, and came out with fervent answers that
bound him to her too indissolubly to let her doubt of her
being loved. And I am loved! she exclaimed to her
heart's echoes, in simple faith and wonderment. Hardly
had she begun to think of love ere the apparition arose in
her path. She had not thought of love with any warmth,
and here it was. She had only dreamed of love as one of
the distant blessings of the mighty world, lying somewhere in the world's forests, across wild seas, veiled,
encompassed with beautiful perils, a throbbing secresy,
but too remote to quicken her bosom's throbs. Her chief
idea of it was, the enrichment of the world by love.

Thus did Miss Middleton acquiesce in the principle of
selection.

And then did the best man of a host blow his triumphant
horn, and loudly.

He looked the fittest; he justified the dictum of Science. The survival of the Patternes was assured. "I would," he said to his admirer, Mrs. Mountstuart Jenkinson, "have bargained for health above everything, but she has everything besides — lineage, beauty, breeding: is what they call an heiress, and is the most accomplished of her sex." With a delicate art he conveyed to the lady's understanding that Miss Middleton had been snatched from a crowd, without a breath of the crowd having offended his niceness. He did it through sarcasm at your modern young women, who run about the world nibbling and nibbled at, until they know one sex as well as the other, and are not a whit less cognizant of the market than men; pure, possibly; it is not so easy to say innocent; decidedly not our feminine ideal. Miss Middleton was different: she was the true ideal, fresh-gathered morning fruit in a basket, warranted by her bloom.

Women do not defend their younger sisters for doing what they perhaps have done — lifting a veil to be seen, and peeping at a world where innocence is as poor a guarantee as a babe's caul against shipwreck.[2] Women of the world never think of attacking the sensual stipulation for perfect bloom, silver purity, which is redolent of the Oriental origin of the love-passion of their lords. Mrs. Mountstuart congratulated Sir Willoughby on the prize he had won in the fair western-eastern.[3]

"Let me see her," she said; and Miss Middleton was introduced and critically observed.

She had the mouth that smiles in repose. The lips met full on the centre of the bow and thinned along to a lifting dimple; the eyelids also lifted slightly at the outer corners and seemed, like the lip into the limpid cheek, quickening up the temples, as with a run of light, or the ascension indicated off a shoot of colour. Her features were playfellows of one another, none of them pretending to rigid correctness, nor the nose to the ordinary dignity of governess among merry girls, despite which the nose was of a fair design, not acutely interrogative or inviting to gambols. Aspens imaged in water, waiting for the breeze, would offer a susceptible lover some suggestion of her face: a pure smooth-white face, tenderly flushed in the cheeks, where the gentle dints were faintly intermelting even during quietness. Her eyes were brown, set well between mild lids, often shadowed, not unwakeful. Her hair of lighter brown, swelling above her temples on the sweep to the knot, imposed the triangle of the fabulous wild woodland visage from brow to mouth and chin, evidently in agreement with her taste; and the triangle suited

2. "caul": the thin membrane protecting a baby's tender skull during childbirth.
3. Willoughby is to be an Oriental Sultan, Clara the shrouded, guarded, submissive beauty of his harem.

her; but her face was not significant of a tameless wildness or of weakness; her equable shut mouth threw its
long curve to guard the small round chin from that effect;
her eyes wavered only in humour, they were steady when
thoughtfulness was awakened; and at such seasons the
build of her winter-beechwood hair lost the touch of
nymph-like and whimsical, and strangely, by mere outline, added to her appearance of studious concentration.
Observe the hawk on stretched wings over the prey he
spies, for an idea of this change in the look of a young
lady whom Vernon Whitford could liken to the Mountain
Echo, and Mrs. Mountstuart Jenkinson pronounced to be
"a dainty rogue in porcelain."[4]

Vernon's fancy of her must have sprung from her
prompt and most musical responsiveness. He preferred
the society of her learned father to that of a girl under
twenty engaged to his cousin, but the charm of her ready
tongue and her voice was to his intelligent understanding
wit, natural wit, crystal wit, as opposed to the paste-
sparkle of the wit of the town.[5] In his encomiums he did
not quote Miss Middleton's wit; nevertheless he ventured
to speak of it to Mrs. Mountstuart, causing that lady to
say: "Ah, well, I have not noticed the wit. You may
have the art of drawing it out."

No one had noticed the wit. The corrupted hearing of
people required a collision of sounds, Vernon supposed.
For his part, to prove their excellence, he recollected a
great many of Miss Middleton's remarks; they came flying to him; and as long as he forbore to speak them aloud,
they had a curious wealth of meaning. It could not be all
her manner, however much his own manner might spoil
them. It might be, to a certain degree, her quickness at
catching the hue and shade of evanescent conversation.
Possibly by remembering the whole of a conversation
wherein she had her place, the wit was to be tested; only
how could any one retain the heavy portion? As there
was no use in being argumentative on a subject affording
him personally, and apparently solitarily, refreshment and
enjoyment, Vernon resolved to keep it to himself. The
eulogies of her beauty, a possession in which he did not
consider her so very conspicuous, irritated him in consequence. To flatter Sir Willoughby, it was the fashion to
exalt her as one of the types of beauty: the one providen-
tially selected to set off his masculine type. She was
compared to those delicate flowers, the ladies of the Court
of China, on rice-paper.[6] A little French dressing would
make her at home on the sward by the fountain among the
lutes and whisperers of the bewitching silken shepherd-

4. "rogue": In addition to its common
meaning of "playful rascal"—a meaning
that stretches sometimes as far as "out-
law"—the word has the meaning among
ceramists of "crack" or "flaw."

5. "paste-sparkle": Of artificial brilliants:
costume jewelry.
6. Delicate Chinese drawings are made
on rice paper. But French dressing won't
improve it.

esses, who live though they never were. Lady Busshe was reminded of the favourite lineaments of the women of Leonardo, the angels of Luini.[7] Lady Culmer had seen crayon sketches of demoiselles of the French aristocracy resembling her. Some one mentioned an antique statue of a figure breathing into a flute: and the mouth at the flute-stop might have a distant semblance of the bend of her mouth, but this comparison was repelled as grotesque.

For once Mrs. Mountstuart Jenkinson was unsuccessful. Her "dainty rogue in porcelain" displeased Sir Willoughby. "Why rogue?" he said. The lady's fame for hitting the mark fretted him, and the grace of his bride's fine bearing stood to support him in his objection. Clara was young, healthy, handsome; she was therefore fitted to be his wife, the mother of his children, his companion picture. Certainly they looked well side by side. In walking with her, in drooping to her, the whole man was made conscious of the female image of himself by her exquisite unlikeness. She completed him, added the softer lines wanting to his portrait before the world. He had wooed her rageingly; he courted her becomingly; with the manly self-possession enlivened by watchful tact which is pleasing to girls. He never seemed to undervalue himself in valuing her: a secret priceless in the courtship of young women that have heads; the lover doubles their sense of personal worth through not forfeiting his own. Those were proud and happy days when he rode Black Norman over to Upton Park, and his lady looked forth for him and knew him coming by the faster beating of her heart.

Her mind, too, was receptive. She took impressions of his characteristics, and supplied him a feast. She remembered his chance phrases; noted his ways, his peculiarities, as no one of her sex had done. He thanked his cousin Vernon for saying she had wit. She had it, and of so high a flavour that the more he thought of the epigram launched at her, the more he grew displeased. With the wit to understand him, and the heart to worship, she had a dignity rarely seen in young ladies.

"Why rogue?" he insisted with Mrs. Mountstuart.

"I said — in porcelain," she replied.

"Rogue perplexes me."

"Porcelain explains it."

"She has the keenest sense of honour."

"I am sure she is a paragon of rectitude."

"She has a beautiful bearing."

"The carriage of a young princess!"

"I find her perfect."

"And still she may be a dainty rogue in porcelain."

"Are you judging by the mind or the person, ma'am?"

"Both."

7. Leonardo da Vinci and Bernardo Luini, Italian artists famous for the *sfumato*, the heavy-lidded, shadowy features of their Lombard models.

"And which is which?"

"There's no distinction."

"Rogue and mistress of Patterne do not go together."

"Why not? She will be a novelty to our neighbourhood and an animation of the Hall."

"To be frank, rogue does not rightly match with *me*."

"Take her for a supplement."

"You like her?"

"In love with her! I can imagine life-long amusement in her company. Attend to my advice: prize the porcelain and play with the rogue."

Sir Willoughby nodded unilluminated. There was nothing of rogue in himself, so there could be nothing of it in his bride. Elfishness, tricksiness, freakishness, were antipathetic to his nature; and he argued that it was impossible he should have chosen for his complement a person deserving the title. It would not have been sanctioned by his guardian genius. His closer acquaintance with Miss Middleton squared with his first impressions; you know that this is convincing; the common jury justifies the presentation of the case to them by the grand jury; and his original conclusion, that she was essentially feminine, in other words, a parasite and a chalice, Clara's conduct confirmed from day to day.[8] He began to instruct her in the knowledge of himself without reserve, and she, as she grew less timid with him, became more reflective.

"I judge by character," he said to Mrs. Mountstuart.

"If you have caught the character of a girl," said she.

"I think I am not far off it."

"So it was thought by the man who dived for the moon in a well."

"How women despise their sex!"

"Not a bit. She has no character yet. You are forming it, and pray be advised and be merry; the solid is your safest guide; physiognomy and manners will give you more of a girl's character than all the divings you can do. She is a charming young woman, only she is one of that sort."

"Of what sort?" Sir Willoughby asked impatiently.

"Rogues in porcelain."

"I am persuaded I shall never comprehend it!"

"I cannot help you one bit further."

"The word rogue!"

"It was dainty rogue."

"Brittle, would you say?"

"I am quite unable to say."

"An innocent naughtiness?"

"Prettily moulded in a delicate substance."

"You are thinking of some piece of Dresden you suppose her to resemble."

"I dare say."

8. "a parasite and a chalice": The phrase catches with stunning concision two classic definitions of female function as formulated by male chauvinists.

"Artificial?"

"You would not have her natural?"

"I am heartily satisfied with her from head to foot, my dear Mrs. Mountstuart."

"Nothing could be better. And sometimes she will lead, and generally you will lead, and everything will go well, my dear Sir Willoughby."

Like all rapid phrasers, Mrs. Mountstuart detested the analysis of her sentence. It had an outline in vagueness, and was flung out to be apprehended, not dissected. Her directions for the reading of Miss Middleton's character were the same that she practised in reading Sir Willoughby's, whose physiognomy and manners bespoke him what she presumed him to be, a splendidly proud gentleman, with good reason.

Mrs. Mountstuart's advice was wiser than her procédure, for she stopped short where he declined to begin. He dived below the surface without studying that index-page. He had won Miss Middleton's hand; he believed he had captured her heart; but he was not so certain of his possession of her soul, and he went after it. Our enamoured gentleman had therefore no tally of Nature's writing above to set beside his discoveries in the deeps. Now it is a dangerous accompaniment of this habit of diving, that where we do not light on the discoveries we anticipate, we fall to work sowing and planting; which becomes a disturbance of the gentle bosom. Miss Middleton's features were legible as to the mainspring of her character. He could have seen that she had a spirit with a natural love of liberty, and required the next thing to liberty, spaciousness, if she was to own allegiance. Those features, unhappily, instead of serving for an introduction to the within, were treated as the mirror of himself. They were indeed of an amiable sweetness to tempt an accepted lover to angle for the first person in the second.[9] But he had made the discovery that their minds differed on one or two points, and a difference of view in his bride was obnoxious to his repose. He struck at it recurringly to show her error under various aspects. He desired to shape her character to the feminine of his own, and betrayed the surprise of a slight disappointment at her advocacy of her ideas. She said immediately: "It is not too late, Willoughby," and wounded him, for he wanted her simply to be material in his hands for him to mould her; he had no other thought. He lectured her on the theme of the infinity of love. How was it not too late? They were plighted; they were one eternally; they could not be parted. She listened gravely, conceiving the infinity as a narrow dwelling where a voice droned and ceased not. However, she listened. She became an attentive listener.

9. i.e., to angle for allegiance within a grant of freedom, also to angle for me in you.

CHAPTER 6

HIS COURTSHIP

THE world was the principal topic of dissension between
these lovers. His opinion of the world affected her like
a creature threatened with a deprivation of air. He explained to his darling that lovers of necessity do loathe the
world. They live in the world, they accept its benefits,
and assist it as well as they can. In their hearts they
must despise it, shut it out, that their love for one another
may pour in a clear channel, and with all the force they
have. They cannot enjoy the sense of security for their
love unless they fence away the world. It is, you will
allow, gross; it is a beast.[1] Formally we thank it for the
good we get of it; only we two have an inner temple
where the worship we conduct is actually, if you would
but see it, an excommunication of the world. We abhor
that beast to adore that divinity. This gives us our oneness, our isolation, our happiness. This is to love with
the soul. Do you see, darling?

She shook her head; she could not see it. She would
admit none of the notorious errors of the world; its back-
biting, selfishness, coarseness, intrusiveness, infectious-
ness. She was young. She might, Willoughby thought,
have let herself be led: she was not docile. She must be
up in arms as a champion of the world: and one saw she
was hugging her dream of a romantic world, nothing else.
She spoilt the secret bower-song he delighted to tell over
to her. And how, Powers of Love! is love-making to be
pursued if we may not kick the world out of our bower
and wash our hands of it? Love that does not spurn the
world when lovers curtain themselves is a love — is it not
so? — that seems to the unwhipped scoffing world to go
slinking into basiation's obscurity,[2] instead of on a glorious
march behind the screen. Our hero had a strong sentiment as to the policy of scorning the world for the sake of
defending his personal pride and (to his honour, be it said)
his lady's delicacy.

The act of scorning put them both above the world, said,
retro Sathanas![3] So much, as a piece of tactics: he was
highly civilized: in the second instance, he knew it to be
the world which must furnish the dry sticks for the bon-
fire of a woman's worship. He knew, too, that he was
prescribing poetry to his betrothed, practicable poetry.
She had a liking for poetry, and sometimes quoted the
stuff in defiance of his pursed mouth and pained murmur:

1. "Your people," said Alexander Ham-
ilton, "is a great beast."
2. "basiation's obscurity": kissing in
dark corners.
3. "Get thee behind me, Satan."

"I am no poet;" but his poetry of the enclosed and fortified bower, without nonsensical rhymes to catch the ears
of women, appeared incomprehensible to her, if not adverse.
She would not burn the world for him; she would not,
though a purer poetry is little imaginable, reduce herself
to ashes, or incense, or essence, in honour of him, and so,
by love's transmutation, literally be the man she was to
marry. She preferred to be herself, with the egoism of
women! She said it: she said: "I must be myself to be
of any value to you, Willoughby." He was indefatigable
in his lectures on the æsthetics of love. Frequently, for
an indemnification to her (he had no desire that she should
be a loser by ceasing to admire the world), he dwelt on
his own youthful ideas; and his original fancies about the
world were presented to her as a substitute for the theme.

Miss Middleton bore it well, for she was sure that he
meant well. Bearing so well what was distasteful to her,
she became less well able to bear what she had merely noted
in observation before: his view of scholarship; his manner
toward Mr. Vernon Whitford, of whom her father spoke
warmly; the rumour concerning his treatment of a Miss
Dale. And the country tale of Constantia Durham sang
itself to her in a new key. He had no contempt for the
world's praises. Mr. Whitford wrote the letters to the
county paper which gained him applause at various great
houses, and he accepted it, and betrayed a tingling fright
lest he should be the victim of a sneer of the world he
contemned. Recollecting his remarks, her mind was
afflicted by the "something illogical" in him that we readily discover when our natures are no longer running free.
and then at once we yearn for a disputation. She resolved
that she would one day, one distant day, provoke it —
upon what? The special point eluded her. The world is
too huge a client, and too pervious, too spotty, for a girl
to defend against a man.[4] That "something illogical" had
stirred her feelings more than her intellect to revolt. She
could not constitute herself the advocate of Mr. Whitford.
Still she marked the disputation for an event to come.

Meditating on it, she fell to picturing Sir Willoughby's
face at the first accents of his bride's decided disagreement
with him. The picture once conjured up would not be
laid. He was handsome; so correctly handsome, that a
slight unfriendly touch precipitated him into caricature.
His habitual air of happy pride, of indignant contentment
rather, could easily be overdone. Surprise, when he threw
emphasis on it, stretched him with the tall eyebrows of a
mask — limitless under the spell of caricature; and in time,
whenever she was not pleased by her thoughts, she had
that, and not his likeness, for the vision of him. And it
was unjust, contrary to her deeper feelings; she rebuked
herself, and as much as her naughty spirit permitted, she

4. "pervious": vulnerable.

tried to look on him as the world did; an effort inducing
reflections upon the blessings of ignorance. She seemed
to herself beset by a circle of imps, hardly responsible for
her thoughts.

He outshone Mr. Whitford in his behaviour to young
Crossjay. She had seen him with the boy, and he was
amused, indulgent, almost frolicsome, in contradistinction
to Mr. Whitford's tutorly sharpness. He had the English
father's tone of a liberal allowance for boy's tastes and
pranks, and he ministered to the partiality of the genus for
pocket-money. He did not play the schoolmaster, like
bookworms who get poor little lads in their grasp.

Mr. Whitford avoided her very much. He came to
Upton Park on a visit to her father, and she was not
particularly sorry that she saw him only at table. He
treated her by fits to a level scrutiny of deep-set eyes unpleasantly penetrating. She had liked his eyes. They
became unbearable; they dwelt in the memory as if they
had left a phosphorescent line. She had been taken by
playmate boys in her infancy to peep into hedge-leaves,
where the mother-bird brooded on the nest; and the eyes of
the bird in that marvellous dark thickset home, had sent
her away with worlds of fancy. Mr. Whitford's gaze
revived her susceptibility, but not the old happy wondering.
She was glad of his absence, after a certain hour that she
passed with Willoughby, a wretched hour to remember.
Mr. Whitford had left, and Willoughby came, bringing bad
news of his mother's health. Lady Patterne was fast failing. Her son spoke of the loss she would be to him; he
spoke of the dreadfulness of death. He alluded to his own
death to come, carelessly, with a philosophical air.

"All of us must go! our time is short."

"Very," she assented.

It sounded like want of feeling.

"If you lose me, Clara!"

"But you are strong, Willoughby."

"I may be cut off to-morrow."

"Do not talk in such a manner."

"It is as well that it should be faced."

"I cannot see what purpose it serves."

"Should you lose me, my love!"

"Willoughby!"

"Oh, the bitter pang of leaving you!"

"Dear Willoughby, you are distressed; your mother may
recover; let us hope she will; I will help to nurse her; I
have offered, you know; I am ready, most anxious. I
believe I am a good nurse."

"It is this belief — that one does not die with death!"

"That is our comfort."

"When we love?"

"Does it not promise that we meet again?"

" To walk the world and see you perhaps . . . with another ! "

" See me ? — Where ? Here ? "

" Wedded . . . to another. You! my bride ; whom I call mine ; and you are ! You would be still — in that hor-ror ! But all things are possible ; women are women ; they swim in infidelity, from wave to wave ! I know them."

" Willoughby, do not torment yourself and me, I beg you."

He meditated profoundly, and asked her : " Could you be such a saint among women ? "

" I think I am a more than usually childish girl."

" Not to forget me ? "

" Oh ! no."

" Still to be mine ? "

" I am yours."

" To plight yourself ? "

" It is done."

" Be mine beyond death ? "

" Married is married, I think."

" Clara ! to dedicate your life to our love ! Never one touch ! not one whisper ! not a thought, not a dream ! Could you ? — it agonizes me to imagine . . . be inviolate ? mine above ? — mine before all men, though I am gone : — true to my dust ? Tell me. Give me that assurance. True to my name ! — Oh ! I hear them. ' His relict.' [5] Buzzings about Lady Patterne. ' The widow.' If you knew their talk of widows ! Shut your ears, my angel ! But if she holds them off and keeps her path, they are forced to respect her. The dead husband is not the dishonoured wretch they fancied him, because he was out of their way. He lives in the heart of his wife. Clara ! my Clara ! as I live in yours, whether here or away ; whether you are a wife or widow, there is no distinction for love — I am your husband — say it — eter-nally. I must have peace ; I cannot endure the pain. Depressed, yes ; I have cause to be. But it has haunted me ever since we joined hands. To have you — to lose you ! "

" Is it not possible that I may be the first to die ? " said Miss Middleton.

" And lose you, with the thought that you, lovely as you are, and the dogs of the world barking round you, might . . . Is it any wonder that I have my feeling for the world ? This hand ! — the thought is horrible. You would be sur-rounded ; men are brutes ; the scent of unfaithfulness ex-cites them, overjoys them. And I helpless ! The thought is maddening. I see a ring of monkeys grinning. There is your beauty, and man's delight in desecrating. You would be worried night and day to quit my name, to . . . I feel the blow now. You would have no rest for them, nothing to cling to without your oath."

5. The legal term for a widow.

"An oath!" said Miss Middleton.

"It is no delusion, my love, when I tell you that with this thought upon me I see a ring of monkey-faces grinning at me: they haunt me. But you do swear it! Once, and I will never trouble you on the subject again. My weakness! if you like. You will learn that it is love, a man's love, stronger than death."

"An oath?" she said, and moved her lips to recall what she might have said and forgotten. "To what? what oath?"

"That you will be true to me dead as well as living! Whisper it."

"Willoughby, I shall be true to my vows at the altar."

"To me! me!"

"It will be to you."

"To my soul. No heaven can be for me — I see none, only torture, unless I have your word, Clara. I trust it. I will trust it implicitly. My confidence in you is absolute."

"Then you need not be troubled."

"It is for *you*, my love; that you may be armed and strong when I am not by to protect you."

"Our views of the world are opposed, Willoughby."

"Consent; gratify me; swear it. Say, 'Beyond death.' Whisper it. I ask for nothing more. Women think the husband's grave breaks the bond, cuts the tie, sets them loose. They wed the flesh — pah! What I call on you for is nobility: the transcendant nobility of faithfulness beyond death. '*His* widow!' let them say; a saint in widowhood."

"My vows at the altar must suffice."

"You will not? Clara!"

"I am plighted to you."

"Not a word? — a simple promise? But you love me?"

"I have given you the best proof of it that I can."

"Consider how utterly I place confidence in you."

"I hope it is well placed."

"I could kneel to you, to worship you, if you would, Clara!"

"Kneel to heaven, not to me, Willoughby. I am . . . I wish I were able to tell what I am. I may be inconstant: I do not know myself. Think; question yourself whether I am really the person you should marry. Your wife should have great qualities of mind and soul. I will consent to hear that I do not possess them, and abide by the verdict."

"You do; you do possess them!" Willoughby cried. "When you know better what the world is, you will understand my anxiety. Alive, I am strong to shield you from it; dead, helpless — that is all. You would be clad in mail, steel-proof, inviolable, if you would . . . But try to enter into my mind; think with me, feel with me. When you have once comprehended the intensity of the love of a man like me, you will not require asking. It is the difference of

the elect and the vulgar; of the ideal of love from the
coupling of the herds. We will let it drop. At least, I
have your hand. As long as I live I have your hand. Ought
I not to be satisfied? I am; only, I see farther than most
men, and feel more deeply. And now I must ride to my
mother's bedside. She dies Lady Patterne! It might have
been that she . . . but she is a woman of women! With
a father-in-law! Just heaven! Could I have stood by her
then with the same feelings of reverence? A very little,
my love, and everything gained for us by civilization crum-
bles; we fall back to the first mortar-bowl we were bruised
and stirred in. My thoughts, when I take my stand to
watch by her, come to this conclusion, that, especially in
women, distinction is the thing to be aimed at. Otherwise
we are a weltering human mass. Women must teach us to
venerate them, or we may as well be bleating and barking
and bellowing. So, now enough. You have but to think a
little. I must be off. It may have happened during
my absence. I will write. I shall hear from you? Come
and see me mount Black Norman. My respects to your
father. I have no time to pay them in person. One!"

He took the one — love's mystical number — from which
commonly spring multitudes; but, on the present occasion,
it was a single one, and cold. She watched him riding away
on his gallant horse as handsome a cavalier as the world
could show, and the contrast of his recent language and his
fine figure was a riddle that froze her blood. Speech so
foreign to her ears, unnatural in tone, unmanlike even for a
lover (who is allowed a softer dialect), set her vainly sounding for the source and drift of it. She was glad of not
having to encounter eyes like Mr. Vernon Whitford's.

On behalf of Sir Willoughby, it is to be said that his
mother, without infringing on the degree of respect for his
decisions and sentiments exacted by him, had talked to him
of Miss Middleton, suggesting a volatility of temperament
in the young lady, that struck him as consentaneous with
Mrs. Mountstuart's "rogue in porcelain," and alarmed him
as the independent observations of two world-wise women.
Nor was it incumbent upon him personally to credit the
volatility in order, as far as he could, to effect the soul-
insurance of his bride, that he might hold the security of
the policy. The desire for it was in him; his mother had
merely tolled a warning bell that he had put in motion before.
Clara was not a Constantia. But she was a woman, and he
had been deceived by women, as a man fostering his high
ideal of them will surely be. The strain he adopted was
quite natural to his passion and his theme. The language
of the primitive sentiments of men is of the same expression
at all times, minus the primitive colours when a modern
gentleman addresses his lady.

Lady Patterne died in the Winter season of the new year.
In April Dr. Middleton had to quit Upton Park, and he had

not found a place of residence, nor did he quite know what
to do with himself in the prospect of his daughter's marriage
and desertion of him. Sir Willoughby proposed to find him
a house within a circuit of the neighbourhood of Patterne.
Moreover, he invited the Rev. Doctor and his daughter to
come to Patterne from Upton for a month, and make acquaintance with his aunts, the ladies Eleanor and Isabel
Patterne, so that it might not be so strange to Clara to have
them as her housemates after her marriage. Dr. Middleton
omitted to consult his daughter before accepting the invitation, and it appeared, when he did speak to her, that it
should have been done. But she said mildly, " Very well,
papa."

Sir Willoughby had to visit the metropolis and an estate
in another county, whence he wrote to his betrothed daily.
He returned to Patterne in time to arrange for the welcome
of his guests ; too late, however, to ride over to them ; and,
meanwhile, during his absence, Miss Middleton had bethought herself that she ought to have given her last days of
freedom to her friends. After the weeks to be passed at
Patterne, very few weeks were left to her, and she had a wish
to run to Switzerland or Tyrol and see the Alps ; a quaint
idea, her father thought. She repeated it seriously, and Dr.
Middleton perceived a feminine shuttle of indecision at
work in her head, frightful to him, considering that they
signified hesitation between the excellent library and capital
wine-cellar of Patterne Hall, together with the society of
that promising young scholar Mr. Vernon Whitford, on the
one side, and a career of hotels — equivalent to being rammed
into monster artillery with a crowd every night, and shot off
on a day's journey through space every morning — on the
other.

" You will have your travelling and your Alps after the
ceremony," he said.

" I think I would rather stay at home," said she.

Dr. Middleton rejoined : "*I* would."

" But I am not married yet, papa."

" As good, my dear."

" A little change of scene, I thought . . ."

" We have accepted Willoughby's invitation. And he
helps me to a house near you."

" You wish to be near me, papa ? "

" Proximate — at a remove : communicable."

" Why should we separate ? "

" For the reason, my dear, that you exchange a father for
a husband."

" If I do not want to exchange ? "

" To purchase, you must pay, my child. Husbands are
not given for nothing."

" No. But I should have you, papa ! "

" Should ? "

" They have not yet parted us, dear papa."

"What does that mean?" he asked fussily. He was in a gentle stew already, apprehensive of a disturbance of the serenity precious to scholars by postponements of the ceremony, and a prolongation of a father's worries.

"Oh, the common meaning, papa," she said, seeing how it was with him.

"Ah," said he, nodding and blinking gradually back to a state of composure, glad to be appeased on any terms; for mutability is but another name for the sex, and it is the enemy of the scholar.

She suggested that two weeks at Patterne would offer plenty of time to inspect the empty houses of the district, and should be sufficient, considering the claims of friends, and the necessity for going the round of London shops.

"Two or three weeks," he agreed hurriedly, by way of compromise with that fearful prospect.

CHAPTER 7

THE BETROTHED

DURING the drive from Upton to Patterne, Miss Middleton hoped, she partly believed, that there was to be a change in Sir Willoughby's manner of courtship. He had been so different a wooer. She remembered with some half-conscious desperation of fervour what she had thought of him at his first approaches, and in accepting him. Had she seen him with the eyes of the world, thinking they were her own? That look of his, the look of "indignant contentment," had then been a most noble conquering look, splendid as a general's plume at the gallop. It could not have altered. Was it that her eyes had altered?

The spirit of those days rose up within her to reproach her and whisper of their renewal: she remembered her rosy dreams and the image she had of him, her throbbing pride in him, her choking richness of happiness: and also her vain attempting to be very humble, usually ending in a carol, quaint to think of, not without charm, but quaint, puzzling.

Now men whose incomes have been restricted to the extent that they must live on their capital, soon grow relieved of the forethoughtful anguish wasting them by the hilarious comforts of the lap upon which they have sunk back, insomuch that they are apt to solace themselves for their intolerable anticipations of famine in the household by giving loose to one fit or more of reckless lavishness. Lovers in like manner live on their capital from failure of income: they, too, for the sake of stifling apprehension and piping

to the present hour, are lavish of their stock, so as rapidly
to attenuate it: they have their fits of intoxication in view
of coming famine: they force memory into play, love retro-
spectively, enter the old house of the past and ravage the
larder, and would gladly, even resolutely, continue in illusion
if it were possible for the broadest honey-store of reminiscences to hold out for a length of time against a mortal
appetite: which in good sooth stands on the alternative of a
consumption of the hive or of the creature it is for nourishing. Here do lovers show that they are perishable. More
than the poor clay world they need fresh supplies, right
wholesome juices; as it were, life in the burst of the bud,
fruits yet on the tree, rather than potted provender. The
latter is excellent for by-and-by, when there will be a vast
deal more to remember, and appetite shall have but one
tooth remaining. Should their minds perchance have been
saturated by their first impressions and have retained them,
loving by the accountable light of reason, they may have
fair harvests, as in the early time; but that case is rare.
In other words, love is an affair of two, and is only for two
that can be as quick, as constant in intercommunication as
are sun and earth, through the cloud or face to face. They
take their breath of life from one another in signs of affection, proofs of faithfulness, incentives to admiration. Thus
it is with men and women in love's good season. But a
solitary soul dragging a log, must make the log a God to
rejoice in the burden. That is not love.

Clara was the least fitted of all women to drag a log.
Few girls would be so rapid in exhausting capital. She
was feminine indeed, but she wanted comradeship, a living
and frank exchange of the best in both, with the deeper
feelings untroubled. To be fixed at the mouth of a mine,
and to have to descend it daily, and not to discover great
opulence below; on the contrary, to be chilled in subterranean sunlessness, without any substantial quality that she
could grasp, only the mystery of inefficient tallow-light in
those caverns of the complacent talking man: this appeared
to her too extreme a probation for two or three weeks.
How of a lifetime of it!

She was compelled by her nature to hope, expect, and
believe that Sir Willoughby would again be the man she
had known when she accepted him. Very singularly,
to show her simple spirit at the time, she was unaware of
any physical coldness to him; she knew of nothing but her
mind at work, objecting to this and that, desiring changes.
She did not dream of being on the giddy ridge of the passive or negative sentiment of love, where one step to the
wrong side precipitates us into the state of repulsion.

Her eyes were lively at their meeting — so were his.
She liked to see him on the steps, with young Crossjay
under his arm. Sir Willoughby told her in his pleasantest
humour of the boy's having got into the laboratory that

morning to escape his taskmaster, and blown out the windows. She administered a chiding to the delinquent in the same spirit, while Sir Willoughby led her on his arm across the threshold, whispering, "Soon for good!" In reply to the whisper, she begged for more of the story of young Crossjay. "Come into the laboratory," said he, a little less laughingly than softly; and Clara begged her father to come and see young Crossjay's latest pranks. Sir Willoughby whispered to her of the length of their separation, and his joy to welcome her to the house where she would reign as mistress *very* soon. He numbered the weeks. He whispered, "Come." In the hurry of the moment she did not examine a lightning terror that shot through her. It passed, and was no more than the shadow which bends the summer grasses, leaving a ruffle of her ideas, in wonder of her having feared herself for something. Her father was with them. She and Willoughby were not yet alone.

Young Crossjay had not accomplished so fine a piece of destruction as Sir Willoughby's humour proclaimed of him. He had connected a battery with a train of gunpowder, shattering a window-frame and unsettling some bricks. Dr. Middleton asked if the youth was excluded from the library, and rejoiced to hear that it was a sealed door to him. Thither they went. Vernon Whitford was away on one of his long walks.

"There, papa, you see he is not so very faithful to you," said Clara.

Dr. Middleton stood frowning over MS notes on the table, in Vernon's handwriting. He flung up the hair from his forehead and dropped into a seat to inspect them closely. He was now immoveable. Clara was obliged to leave him there. She was led to think that Willoughby had drawn them to the library with the design to be rid of her protector, and she began to fear him. She proposed to pay her respects to the ladies Eleanor and Isabel. They were not seen, and a footman reported in the drawing-room that they were out driving. She grasped young Crossjay's hand. Sir Willoughby despatched him to Mrs. Montague, the housekeeper, for a tea of cakes and jam.

"Off!" he said, and the boy had to run.

Clara saw herself without a shield.

"And the garden!" she cried. "I love the garden; I must go and see what flowers are up with you. In Spring I care most for wild-flowers, and if you will show me daffodils, and crocuses, and anemones . . ."

"My dearest Clara! my bride!" said he.

"Because they are vulgar flowers?" she asked him artlessly, to account for his detaining her.

Why would he not wait to deserve her! — no, not deserve — to reconcile her with her real position; not reconcile, but to repair the image of him in her mind, before he claimed his apparent right!

He did not wait. He pressed her to his bosom.

"You are mine, my Clara — utterly mine; every thought, every feeling. We are one: the world may do its worst. I have been longing for you, looking forward. You save me from a thousand vexations. One is perpetually crossed. That is all outside us. We two! With you I am secure! Soon! I could not tell you whether the world's alive or dead. My dearest!"

She came out of it with the sensations of the frightened child that has had its dip in sea-water, sharpened to think that after all it was not so severe a trial. Such was her idea; and she said to herself immediately: What am I that I should complain? Two minutes earlier she would not have thought it; but humiliated pride falls lower than humbleness.

She did not blame him; she fell in her own esteem; less because she was the betrothed Clara Middleton, which was now palpable as a shot in the breast of a bird, than that she was a captured woman, of whom it is absolutely expected that she must submit, and when she would rather be gazing at flowers. Clara had shame of her sex. They cannot take a step without becoming bondwomen; into what a slavery! For herself, her trial was over, she thought. As for herself, she merely complained of a prematureness and crudity best unanalyzed. In truth, she could hardly be said to complain. She did but criticize him and wonder that a man was unable to perceive, or was not arrested by perceiving, unwillingness, discordance, dull compliance; the bondwoman's due instead of the bride's consent. Oh, sharp distinction, as between two spheres!

She meted him justice; she admitted that he had spoken in a lover-like tone. Had it not been for the iteration of "the world," she would not have objected critically to his words, though they were words of downright appropriation. He had the right to use them, since she was to be married to him. But if he had only waited before playing the privileged lover!

Sir Willoughby was enraptured with her. Even so purely, coldly, statue-like, Dian-like, would he have prescribed his bride's reception of his caress.[1] The suffusion of crimson coming over her subsequently, showing her divinely feminine in reflective bashfulness, agreed with his highest definitions of female character.

"Let me conduct you to the garden, my love," he said.

She replied, "I think I would rather go to my room."

"I will send you a wild-flower posy."

"Flowers, no; I do not like them to be gathered."

"I will wait for you on the lawn."

1. "Dian-like": like the chaste and virginal goddess Diana.

"My head is rather heavy."

His deep concern and tenderness brought him close.

She assured him sparklingly that she was well: she was ready to accompany him to the garden and stroll over the park.

"Head*ache* it is not," she said.

But she had to pay the fee for inviting a solicitous accepted gentleman's proximity.

This time she blamed herself and him, and the world he abused, and destiny into the bargain. And she cared less about the probation; but she craved for liberty. With a frigidity that astonished her, she marvelled at the act of kissing, and at the obligation it forced upon an inanimate person to be an accomplice. Why was she not free? By what strange right was it that she was treated as a possession?

"I will try to walk off the heaviness," she said.

"My own girl must not fatigue herself."

"Oh, no; I shall not."

"Sit with me. Your Willoughby is your devoted attendant."

"I have a desire for the air."

"Then we will walk out."

She was horrified to think how far she had drawn away from him, and now placed her hand on his arm to appease her self-accusations and propitiate duty. He spoke as she had wished; his manner was what she had wished; she was his bride, almost his wife; her conduct was a kind of madness; she could not understand it.

Good sense and duty counselled her to control her wayward spirit.

He fondled her hand, and to that she grew accustomed; her hand was at a distance. And what is a hand? Leaving it where it was, she treated it as a link between herself and dutiful goodness. Two months hence she was a bondwoman for life! She regretted that she had not gone to her room to strengthen herself with a review of her situation, and meet him thoroughly resigned to her fate. She fancied she would have come down to him amicably. It was his present respectfulness and easy conversation that tricked her burning nerves with the fancy. Five weeks of perfect liberty in the mountains, she thought, would have prepared her for the day of bells. All that she required was a separation offering new scenes, where she might reflect undisturbed, feel clear again.

He led her about the flower-beds; too much as if he were giving a convalescent an airing. She chafed at it, and pricked herself with remorse. In contrition she expatiated on the beauty of the garden.

"All is yours, my Clara."

An oppressive load it seemed to her! She passively yielded to the man in his form of attentive courtier; his mansion, estates, and wealth overwhelmed her. They suggested the price to be paid. Yet she recollected that on her last departure through the park she had been proud of the rolling green and spreading trees. Poison of some sort must be operating in her. / She had not come to him to-day with this feeling of sullen antagonism; she had caught it here.

"You have been well, my Clara?"

"Quite."

"Not a hint of illness?"

"None."

"My bride must have her health if all the doctors in the kingdom die for it! My darling!"

"And tell me: the dogs?"

"Dogs and horses are in very good condition."

"I am glad. Do you know, I love those ancient French châteaux and farms in one, where salon windows look on poultry-yard and stalls. I like that homeliness with beasts and peasants."

He bowed indulgently.

"I am afraid we can't do it for you in England, my 'lara."

"No."

"And I like the farm," said he. "But I think our drawing-rooms have a better atmosphere off the garden. As to our peasantry, we cannot, I apprehend, modify our class demarcations without risk of disintegrating the social structure."

"Perhaps. I proposed nothing."

"My love, I would entreat you to propose, if I were convinced that I could obey."

"You are very good."

"I find my merit nowhere but in your satisfaction."

Although she was not thirsting for dulcet sayings, the peacefulness of other than invitations to the exposition of his mysteries and of their isolation in oneness, inspired her with such calm that she beat about in her brain, as if it were in the brain, for the specific injury he had committed. Sweeping from sensation to sensation, the young, whom sensations impel and distract, can rarely date their disturbance from a particular one; unless it be some great villain injury that has been done: and Clara had not felt an individual shame in his caress; the shame of her sex was but a passing protest that left no stamp. So she conceived she had been behaving cruelly, and said, "Willoughby;" because she was aware of the omission of his name in her previous remarks.

His whole attention was given to her.

She had to invent the sequel: "I was going to beg you, Willoughby, do not seek to spoil me. You compliment me. Compliments are not suited to me. You think too highly of me. It is nearly as bad as to be slighted. I am

. . . I am a . . ." But she could not follow his example: even as far as she had gone, her prim little sketch
of herself, set beside her real, ugly, earnest feelings, rang
of a mincing simplicity, and was a step in falseness. How
could she display what she was?

"Do I not know you?" he said.

The melodious bass notes, expressive of conviction on
that point, signified, as well as the words, that no answer
was the right answer. She could not dissent without
turning his music to discord, his complacency to amazement. She held her tongue, knowing that he did not
know her, and speculating on the division made bare by
their degrees of the knowledge; a deep cleft.

He alluded to friends in her neighbourhood and his own.
The bridesmaids were mentioned.

"Miss Dale, you will hear from my Aunt Eleanor, declines, on the plea of indifferent health. She is rather a
morbid person, with all her really estimable qualities. It
will do no harm to have none but young ladies of your own
age; a bouquet of young buds: though one blowing flower
among them . . . However, she has decided. My principal annoyance has been Vernon's refusal to act as my
best man."

"Mr. Whitford refuses?"

"He half refuses. I do not take no from him. His
pretext is a dislike to the ceremony."

"I share it with him."

"I sympathize with you. If we might say the words
and pass from sight! There is a way of cutting off the
world: I have it at times completely: I lose it again, as
if it were a cabalistic phrase one had to utter. But with
you! You give it me for good. It will be for ever, eternally, my Clara. Nothing can harm, nothing touch us;
we are one another's. Let the world fight it out: we
have nothing to do with it."

"If Mr. Whitford should persist in refusing?"

"So entirely one, that there never can be question of
external influences. I am, we will say, riding home from
the hunt: I see you awaiting me: I read your heart as
though you were beside me. And I know that I am coming to the one who reads mine! You have me, you have me
like an open book, you, and only you!"

"I am to be always at home?" Clara said, unheeded,
and relieved by his not hearing.

"Have you realized it? — that we are invulnerable!
The world cannot hurt us: it cannot touch us. Felicity is
ours, and we are impervious in the enjoyment of it.
Something divine! surely something divine on earth?
Clara! — being to one another that between which the
world can never interpose! What I do is right: what
you do is right. Perfect to one another! Each new day
we rise to study and delight in new secrets. Away with

the crowd! We have not even to say it; we are in an atmosphere where the world cannot breathe."

"O the world!" Clara partly carolled on a sigh that sank deep.

Hearing him talk as one exulting on the mountain top, when she knew him to be in the abyss, was very strange, provocative of scorn.

"My letters?" he said incitingly.

"I read them."

"Circumstances have imposed a long courtship on us, my Clara: and I, perhaps lamenting the laws of decorum — I have done so! — still felt the benefit of the gradual initiation. It is not good for women to be surprised by a sudden revelation of man's character. We also have things to learn: — there is matter for learning everywhere. Some day you will tell me the difference of what you think of me now, from what you thought when we first . . . ?"

An impulse of double-minded acquiescence caused Clara to stammer as on a sob, —

"I — I daresay I shall."

She added: "If it is necessary."

Then she cried out. "Why do you attack the world? You always make me pity it."

He smiled at her youthfulness. "I have passed through that stage. It leads to my sentiment. Pity it, by all means."

"No," said she, "but pity it, side with it, not consider it so bad. The world has faults; glaciers have crevasses, mountains have chasms; but is not the effect of the whole sublime? not to admire the mountain and the glacier because they can be cruel, seems to me . . . And the world is beautiful."

"The world of nature, yes. The world of men?"

"Yes."

"My love, I suspect you to be thinking of the world of ball-rooms."

"I am thinking of the world that contains real and great generosity, true heroism. We see it round us."

"We read of it. The world of the romance-writer!"

"No: the living world. I am sure it is our duty to love it. I am sure we weaken ourselves if we do not. If I did not, I should be looking on mist, hearing a perpetual boom instead of music. I remember hearing Mr. Whitford say that cynicism is intellectual dandyism without the coxcomb's feathers; and it seems to me that cynics are only happy in making the world as barren to others as they have made it for themselves."

"Old Vernon!" ejaculated Sir Willoughby, with a countenance rather uneasy, as if it had been flicked with a glove. "He strings his phrases by the dozen."

"Papa contradicts that, and says he is very clever and very simple."

"As to cynics, my dear Clara, oh! certainly, certainly: you are right. They are laughable, contemptible. But understand me, I mean, we cannot feel, or if we feel we cannot so intensely feel, our oneness, except by dividing ourselves from the world."

"Is it an art?"

"If you like. It is our poetry! But does not love shun the world? Two that love must have their substance in isolation."

"No: they will be eating themselves up."

"The purer the beauty, the more it will be out of the world."

"But not opposed."

"Put it in this way," Willoughby condescended. "Has experience the same opinion of the world as ignorance?"

"It should have more charity."

"Does virtue feel at home in the world?"

"Where it should be an example, to my idea."

"Is the world agreeable to holiness?"

"Then, are you in favour of monasteries?"

He poured a little runlet of half-laughter over her head, of the sound assumed by genial compassion.

It is irritating to hear that when we imagine we have spoken to the point.

"Now in my letters, Clara . . ."

"I have no memory, Willoughby!"

"You will however have observed that I am not completely myself in my letters . . ."

"In your letters to men, you may be."

The remark threw a pause across his thoughts. He was of a sensitiveness terribly tender. A single stroke on it reverberated swellingly within the man, and most, and infuriately searching, at the spots where he had been wounded, especially where he feared the world might have guessed the wound. Did she imply that he had no hand for love-letters? Was it her meaning that women would not have much taste for his epistolary correspondence? She had spoken in the plural, with an accent on "men." Had she heard of Constantia? Had she formed her own judgement about the creature? The supernatural sensitiveness of Sir Willoughby shrieked a peal of affirmatives. He had often meditated on the moral obligation of his unfolding to Clara the whole truth of his conduct to Constantia; for whom, as for other suicides, there were excuses. He at least was bound to supply them. She had behaved badly; but had he not given her some cause? If so, manliness was bound to confess it.

Supposing Clara heard the world's version first! Men whose pride is their backbone suffer convulsions where

other men are barely aware **of** a shock, and Sir Willoughby
was taken with galvanic jumpings of the spirit within him,
at the idea of the world whispering to Clara that he had
been jilted.

"My letters to men, you say, my love?"

"Your letters of business."

"Completely myself in my letters of business?" He
stared indeed.

She relaxed the tension of his figure by remarking:
"You are able to express yourself to men as your meaning
dictates. In writing to . . . to us it is, I suppose, more
difficult."

"True, my love. I will not exactly say difficult. I
can acknowledge no difficulty. Language, I should say,
is not fitted to express emotion. Passion rejects it."

"For dumb-show and pantomime?"

"No: but the writing of it coldly."

"Ah, coldly!"

"My letters disappoint you?"

"I have not implied that they do."

"My feelings, dearest, are too strong for transcription.
I feel, pen in hand, like the mythological Titan at war
with Jove, strong enough to hurl mountains, and finding
nothing but pebbles. The simile is a good one. You must
not judge of me by my letters."

"I do not; I like them," said Clara.[2]

She blushed, eyed him hurriedly, and seeing him complacent, resumed: "I prefer the pebble to the mountain;
but if you read poetry you would not think human speech
incapable of . . ."

"My love, I detest artifice. Poetry is a profession."

"Our poets would prove to you . . ."

"As I have often observed, Clara, I am no poet."

"I have not accused you, Willoughby."

"No poet, and with no wish to be a poet. Were I one,
my life would supply material, I can assure you, my love.
My conscience is not entirely at rest. Perhaps the heaviest matter troubling it is that in which I was least wilfully guilty. You have heard of a Miss Durham?"

"I have heard — yes — of her."

"She may be happy. I trust she is. If she is not, I
cannot escape some blame. An instance of the difference
between myself and the world, now. The world charges
it upon her. I have interceded to exonerate her."

"That was generous, Willoughby."

"Stay. I fear I was the primary offender. But I, Clara,
I, under a sense of honour, acting under a sense of honour,
would have carried my engagement through."

"What had you done?"

"The story is long, dating from an early day, in the

---

2. Clara has said it all in words of one syllable.

' downy antiquity of my youth,' as Vernon says."

"Mr. Whitford says that ?"

"One of old Vernon's odd sayings. It 's a story of an early fascination."

"Papa tells me Mr. Whitford speaks at times with wise humour."

"Family considerations — the lady's health among other things; her position in the calculations of relatives — intervened. Still there was the fascination. I have to own it. Grounds for feminine jealousy."

"Is it at an end ?"

"Now ? with you ? my darling Clara! indeed at an end, or could I have opened my inmost heart to you! Could I have spoken of myself so unreservedly that in part you know me as I know myself! Oh! but would it have been possible to enclose you with myself in that intimate union ? so secret, unassailable!"

"You did not speak to her as you speak to me ?"

"In no degree."

"What *could* have! . . ." Clara checked the murmured exclamation.

Sir Willoughby's expoundings on his latest of texts would have poured forth, had not a footman stepped across the lawn to inform him that his builder was in the laboratory and requested permission to consult with him.

Clara's plea of a horror of a talk of bricks and joists excused her from accompanying him. He had hardly been satisfied by her manner, he knew not why. He left her, convinced that he must do and say more to reach down to her female intelligence.

She saw young Crossjay, springing with pots of jam in him, join his patron at a bound, and taking a lift of arms, fly aloft, clapping heels. Her reflections were confused. Sir Willoughby was admirable with the lad. "Is he two men ?" she thought: and the thought ensued: "Am I unjust ?" She headed a run with young Crossjay to divert her mind.

CHAPTER 8

A RUN WITH THE TRUANT: A WALK WITH THE MASTER.

THE sight of Miss Middleton running inflamed young Crossjay with the passion of the game of hare and hounds. He shouted a view-halloo, and flung up his legs. She was fleet; she ran as though a hundred little feet were bearing her onward smooth as water over the lawn and the sweeps of grass of the park, so swiftly did the hidden pair multiply one another to speed her. So sweet was she in her flowing pace, that the boy, as became his age, translated admiration into a dogged frenzy of pursuit, and continued pounding along, when far outstripped, determined to run her down or die. Suddenly her flight wound to an end in a dozen twittering steps, and she sank. Young Crossjay attained her, with just breath enough to say, " You are a runner! "

" I forgot you had been having your tea, my poor boy," said she.

" And you don't pant a bit! " was his encomium.

"Dear me, no; not more than a bird. You might as well try to catch a bird."

Young Crossjay gave a knowing nod. "Wait till I get my second wind."

"Now you must confess that girls run faster than boys."

" They may at the start."

" They do everything better."

" They 're flash-in-the-pans."

" They learn their lessons."

" You can't make soldiers or sailors of them, though."

"And that is untrue. Have you never read of Mary Ambree? and Mistress Hannah Snell of Pondicherry? And there was the bride of the celebrated William Taylor. And what do you say to Joan of Arc? What do you say to Boadicea?[1] I suppose you have never heard of the Amazons."

" They were n't English."

"Then, it is your own countrywomen you decry, sir! "

Young Crossjay betrayed anxiety about his false position, and begged for the stories of Mary Ambree and the others who were English.

"See, you will not read for yourself, you hide and play truant with Mr. Whitford, and the consequence is you are ignorant of your country's history! "

Miss Middleton rebuked him, enjoying his wriggle between a perception of her fun and an acknowledgement of his peccancy. She commanded him to tell her which was the glorious Valentine's day of our naval annals; the name of the hero of the day, and the name of his ship.[2] To these questions his answers were as ready as the guns of the good ship *Captain* for the Spanish four-decker.

"And that you owe to Mr. Whitford," said Miss Middleton.

"He bought me the books," young Crossjay growled, and plucked at grass-blades and bit them, foreseeing dimly but certainly the termination of all this.

1. Crossjay is not to be blamed for ignorance of Mary Ambree; she is the heroine of a ballad, published in 1680, describing her bravery at the battle of "Gaunt." Hannah Snell is more historical; she fought in India during the eighteenth century. The wife of the celebrated William Taylor is not to be found, nor is he. Boadicea was the warlike queen of an ancient British tribe; Romans finally defeated her.
2. "Valentine's day": February 14, 1797, when Sir John Jervis, ably supported by Nelson in the *Captain*, won the battle of Saint Vincent.

Miss Middleton lay back on the grass, and said: "Are you going to be fond of me, Crossjay?"

The boy sat blinking. His desire was to prove to her that he was immoderately fond of her already; and he might have flown at her neck had she been sitting up, but her recumbency and eyelids half closed excited wonder in him and awe. His young heart beat fast.

"Because, my dear boy," she said, leaning on her elbow, "you are a very nice boy, but an ungrateful boy, and there is no telling whether you will not punish anyone who cares for you. Come along with me; pluck me some of these cowslips, and the speedwells near them; I think we both love wild-flowers." She rose and took his arm. "You shall row me on the lake while I talk to you seriously."

It was she, however, who took the sculls at the boat-house, for she had been a playfellow with boys, and knew that one of them engaged in a manly exercise is not likely to listen to a woman.

"Now, Crossjay," she said. Dense gloom overcame him like a cowl. She bent across her hands to laugh. "As if I were going to lecture you, you silly boy!" He began to brighten dubiously. "I used to be as fond of birdsnesting as you are. I like brave boys, and I like you for wanting to enter the Royal Navy. Only, how can you if you do not learn? You must get the captains to pass you, you know. Somebody spoils you: Miss Dale or Mr. Whitford."

"Do they!" sang out young Crossjay.

"Sir Willoughby does?"

"I don't know about spoil. I can come round him."

"I am sure he is very kind to you. I daresay you think Mr. Whitford rather severe. You should remember he has to teach you, so that you may pass for the navy. You must not dislike him because he makes you work. Supposing you had blown yourself up to-day! You would have thought it better to have been working with Mr. Whitford."

"Sir Willoughby says, when he's married, you won't let me hide."

"Ah! It is wrong to pet a big boy like you. Does not he what you call tip you, Crossjay?"

"Generally half-crown pieces. I've had a crown-piece. I've had sovereigns."

"And for that you do as he bids you? and he indulges you because you . . . Well, but though Mr. Whitford does not give you money, he gives you his time, he tries to get you into the navy."

"He pays for me."

"What do you say?"

"My keep. And, as for liking him, if he were at the bottom of the water here, I'd go down after him. I mean to learn. We 're both of us here at six o'clock in the morning, when it 's light, and have a swim. He taught me. Only, I never cared for school-books."

" Are you quite certain that Mr. Whitford pays for you ? "

"My father told me he did, and I must obey him. He heard my father was poor, with a family. He went down to see my father. My father came here once, and Sir Willoughby would n't see him. I know Mr. Whitford does. And Miss Dale told me he did. My mother says she thinks he does it to make up to us for my father's long walk in the rain, and the cold he caught coming here to Patterne."

"So you see you should not vex him, Crossjay. He is a good friend to your father and to you. You ought to love him."

" I like him, and I like his face."

" Why his face ? "

" It 's not like those faces! Miss Dale and I talk about him. She thinks that Sir Willoughby is the best-looking man ever born."

" Were you not speaking of Mr. Whitford ? "

" Yes; old Vernon. That 's what Sir Willoughby calls him," young Crossjay excused himself to her look of surprise. " Do you know what he makes me think of ? — his eyes, I mean. He makes me think of Robinson Crusoe's old goat in the cavern.[3] I like him because he 's always the same, and you 're not positive about some people. Miss Middleton, if you look on at cricket, in comes a safe man for ten runs. He may get more, and he never gets less; and you should hear the old farmers talk of him in the booth. That 's just my feeling."

Miss Middleton understood that some illustration from the cricketing-field was intended to throw light on the boy's feeling for Mr. Whitford. Young Crossjay was evidently warming to speak from his heart. But the sun was low, she had to dress for the dinner-table, and she landed him with regret, as at a holiday over. Before they parted, he offered to swim across the lake in his clothes, or dive to the bed for anything she pleased to throw, declaring solemnly that it should not be lost.

She walked back at a slow pace, and sang to herself above her darker-flowing thoughts, like the reed-warbler on the branch beside the night-stream; a simple song of a light-hearted sound, independent of the shifting black and grey of the flood underneath.

A step was at her heels.

" I see you have been petting my scapegrace."

"Mr. Whitford! Yes; not petting, I hope. I tried to give him a lecture. He 's a dear lad, but, I fancy, trying."

She was in fine sunset colour, unable to arrest the

3. Just after Robinson Crusoe finds a first footprint on the beach, he is scared by a goat in a cave.

mounting tide. She had been rowing, she said; and, as he directed his eyes, according to his wont, <u>penetratingly</u>, she defended herself by fixing her mind on Robinson Crusoe's old goat in the recess of the cavern.

"I must have him away from here very soon," said Vernon. "Here he's quite spoilt. Speak of him to Willoughby. I can't guess at his ideas of the boy's future, but the chance of passing for the navy won't bear trifling with; and if ever there was a lad made for the navy, it's Crossjay."

The incident of the explosion in the laboratory was new to Vernon.

"And Willoughby laughed?" he said. "There are seaport crammers who stuff young fellows for examination, and we shall have to pack off the boy at once to the best one of the lot we can find. I would rather have had him under me up to the last three months, and have made sure of some roots to what is knocked into his head. But he's ruined here. And I am going. So I shall not trouble him for many weeks longer. Dr. Middleton is well?"

"My father is well, yes. He pounced like a falcon on your notes in the library."

Vernon came out with a chuckle.

"They were left to attract him. I am in for a controversy."

"Papa will not spare you, to judge from his look."

"I know the look."

"Have you walked far to-day?"

"Nine and a half hours. My Flibbertigibbet is too much for me at times, and I had to walk off my temper."[4]

She cast her eyes on him, thinking of the pleasure of dealing with a temper honestly coltish, and manfully open to a specific.[5]

"All those hours were required?"

"Not quite so long."

"You are training for your Alpine tour."

"It's doubtful whether I shall get to the Alps this year. I leave the Hall, and shall probably be in London with a pen to sell."

"Willoughby knows that you leave him?"

"As much as Mont Blanc knows that he is going to be = *Willoughby* climbed by a party below. He sees a speck or two in the valley."

"He has not spoken of it."

"He would attribute it to changes . . ." *in his marital status?* Vernon did not conclude the sentence.

She became breathless, without emotion, but checked by the barrier confronting an impulse to ask, What changes? She stooped to pluck a cowslip.

"I saw daffodils lower down the park," she said. "One

4. "Flibbertigibbet": the foul fiend, as in *King Lear*, used euphemistically here for ill humor.
5. Cure.

or two; they're nearly over."

"We are well-off for wild-flowers here," he answered.

"Do not leave him, Mr. Whitford."

"He will not want me."

"You are devoted to him."

"I can't pretend that."

"Then it is the changes you imagine you foresee . . . ? If any occur, why should they drive you away?"

"Well, I'm two and thirty, and have never been in the fray: a kind of nondescript, half-scholar, and by nature half billman or bowman or musketeer; if I'm worth anything, London's the field for me.[6] But that's what I have to try."

"Papa will not like your serving with your pen in London: he will say you are worth too much for that."

"Good men are at it; I should not care to be ranked above them."

"They are wasted, he says."

"Error! If they have their private ambition, they may suppose they are wasted. But the value to the world of a private ambition I do not clearly understand."

"You have not an evil opinion of the world?" said Miss Middleton, sick at heart as she spoke, with the sensation of having invited herself to take a drop of poison.

He replied: "One might as well have an evil opinion of a river: here it's muddy, there it's clear; one day troubled, another at rest. We have to treat it with common sense."

"Love it?"

"In the sense of serving it."

"Not think it beautiful?"

"Part of it is, part of it the reverse."

"Papa would quote the 'mulier formosa.'"[7]

"Except that 'fish' is too good for the black extremity. 'Woman' is excellent for the upper."

"How do you say that? — not cynically, I believe. Your view commends itself to my reason."

She was grateful to him for not stating it in ideal contrast with Sir Willoughby's view. If he had, so intensely did her youthful blood desire to be enamoured of the world, that she felt he would have lifted her off her feet. For a moment a gulf beneath had been threatening. When she said, "Love it?" a little enthusiasm would have wafted her into space fierily as wine; but the sober, "In the sense of serving it," entered her brain, and was matter for reflection upon it and him.

She could think of him in pleasant liberty, uncorrected by her woman's instinct of peril. He had neither arts nor graces; nothing of his cousin's easy social front-face. She had once witnessed the military precision of his danc-

6. "billman": footsoldier with a pike.
7. Horace in his *Art of Poetry* deplores the lack of order that results in a gro-

tesque figure, a beautiful woman ("mulier formosa") on top, a fish-tail below.

ing, and had to learn to like him before she ceased to pray that she might never be the victim of it as his partner. He walked heroically, his pedestrian vigour being famous, but that means one who walks away from the sex, not excelling in the recreations where men and women join hands. He was not much of a horseman either. Sir Willoughby enjoyed seeing him on horseback. And he could scarcely be said to shine in a drawing-room, unless when seated beside a person ready for real talk. Even more than his merits, his demerits pointed him out as a man to be a friend to a young woman who wanted one. His way of life pictured to her troubled spirit an enviable smoothness: and his having achieved that smooth way she considered a sign of strength; and she wished to lean in idea upon some friendly strength. His reputation for indifference to the frivolous charms of girls clothed him with a noble coldness, and gave him the distinction of a far-seen solitary iceberg in Southern waters. The popular notion of hereditary titled aristocracy resembles her sentiment for a man that would not flatter and could not be flattered by her sex: he appeared superior almost to awfulness.[8] She was young, but she had received much flattery in her ears, and by it she had been snared; and he, disdaining to practise the fowler's arts or to cast a thought on small fowls, appeared to her to have a pride founded on natural loftiness.

They had not spoken for a while, when Vernon said abruptly: "The boy's future rather depends on you, Miss Middleton. I mean to leave as soon as possible, and I do not like his being here without me, though you will look after him, I have no doubt. But you may not at first see where the spoiling hurts him. He should be packed off at once to the crammer, before you are Lady Patterne. Use your influence. Willoughby will support the lad at your request. The cost cannot be great. There are strong grounds against my having him in London, even if I could manage it. May I count on you?"

"I will mention it: I will do my best," said Miss Middleton, strangely dejected. *because he is leaving*

They were now on the lawn, where Sir Willoughby was walking with the ladies Eleanor and Isabel, his maiden aunts.

"You seem to have coursed the hare and captured the hart," he said to his bride.

"Started the truant and run down the pedagogue," said Vernon.

"Ay, you won't listen to me about the management of that boy," Sir Willoughby retorted.

The ladies embraced Miss Middleton. One offered up an ejaculation in eulogy of her looks, the other of her

---

8. To the point of awing her.

healthfulness: then both remarked that with indulgence young Crossjay could be induced to do anything. Clara wondered whether inclination or Sir Willoughby had disciplined their individuality out of them and made them his shadows, his echoes. She gazed from them to him, and feared him. But as yet she had not experienced the power in him which could threaten and wrestle to subject the members of his household to the state of satellites. Though she had in fact been giving battle to it for several months, she had held her own too well to perceive definitely the character of the spirit opposing her.

She said to the ladies: "Ah, no! Mr. Whitford has chosen the only method for teaching a boy like Crossjay."

"I propose to make a man of him," said Sir Willoughby.

"What is to become of him if he learns nothing?"

"If he pleases me, he will be provided for. I have never abandoned a dependant."

Clara let her eyes rest on his, and without turning or dropping, shut them.

The effect was discomforting to him. He was very sensitive to the intentions of eyes and tones; which was one secret of his rigid grasp of the dwellers in his household. They were taught that they had to render agreement under sharp scrutiny. Studious eyes, devoid of warmth, devoid of the shyness of sex, that suddenly closed on their look, signified a want of comprehension of some kind, it might be hostility of understanding. Was it possible he did not possess her utterly? He frowned up.

Clara saw the lift of his brows, and thought: "My mind is my own, married or not."

It was the point in dispute.

CHAPTER 9

CLARA AND LÆTITIA MEET: THEY ARE COMPARED

An hour before the time for lessons next morning young Crossjay was on the lawn with a big bunch of wild-flowers. He left them at the Hall-door for Miss Middleton, and vanished into bushes.

These vulgar weeds were about to be dismissed to the dust-heap by the great officials of the household; but as it happened that Miss Middleton had seen them from the window in Crossjay's hands, the discovery was made that they were indeed his presentation-bouquet, and a footman received orders to place them before her. She was very pleased. The arrangement of the flowers bore witness to fairer fingers than the boy's own in the disposition of the rings of colour, red campion and anemone, cowslip and

speedwell, primroses and wood-hyacinths; and rising out
of the blue was a branch bearing thick white blossom, so
thick, and of so pure a whiteness, that Miss Middleton,
while praising Crossjay for soliciting the aid of Miss Dale,
was at a loss to name the tree.

"It is a gardener's improvement on the Vestal of the
forest, the wild cherry," said Dr. Middleton, "and in this
case we may admit the gardener's claim to be valid,
though I believe that, with his gift of double-blossom, he
has improved away the fruit.[1] Call this the Vestal of civilization, then; he has at least done something to vindicate the
beauty of the office as well as the justness of the title."

"It is Vernon's Holy Tree the young rascal has been
despoiling," said Sir Willoughby merrily.

Miss Middleton was informed that this double-blossom
wild cherry-tree was worshipped by Mr. Whitford.

Sir Willoughby promised he would conduct her to it.
"You," he said to her, "can bear the trial; few complexions can; it is to most ladies a crueller test than snow.
Miss Dale, for example, becomes old lace within a dozen
yards of it. I should like to place her under the tree
beside you."

"Dear me, though; but that is investing the hamadryad with novel and terrible functions," exclaimed Dr.
Middleton.[2]

Clara said, "Miss Dale could drag me into a superior
Court to show me fading beside her in gifts more valuable
than a complexion."

"She has a fine ability," said Vernon.

All the world knew, so Clara knew of Miss Dale's
romantic admiration of Sir Willoughby; she was curious to
see Miss Dale and study the nature of a devotion that might
be, within reason, imitable — for a man who could speak
with such steely coldness of the poor lady he had fascinated?
Well, perhaps it was good for the hearts of women to be
beneath a frost; to be schooled, restrained, turned inward
on their dreams. Yes, then, his coldness was desireable; it
encouraged an ideal of him. It suggested and seemed to
propose to Clara's mind the divineness of separation instead
of the deadly accuracy of an intimate perusal. She tried to
look on him as Miss Dale might look, and while partly despising her for the dupery she envied, and more than criticizing him for the inhuman numbness of sentiment which
offered up his worshipper to point a complimentary comparison, she was able to imagine a distance whence it would
be possible to observe him uncritically, kindly, admiringly;
as the moon a handsome mortal, for example.

In the midst of her thoughts, she surprised herself by
saying: "I certainly was difficult to instruct. I might see
things clearer if I had a fine ability, I never remember to

1. "Vestal": The Vestal Virgins were
priestesses of ancient Rome, clad always
in white.
2. "hamadryad": wood nymph.

have been perfectly pleased with my immediate lesson . . ."[3]

She stopped, wondering whither her tongue was leading her; then added, to save herself, " And that may be why I feel for poor Crossjay."

Mr. Whitford apparently did not think it remarkable that she should have been set off gabbling of " a fine ability," though the eulogistic phrase had been pronounced by him with an impressiveness to make his ear aware of an echo.

Sir Willoughby dispersed her vapourish confusion. "Exactly," he said. " I have insisted with Vernon, I don't know how often, that you must have the lad by his affections. He won't bear driving. It had no effect on me. Boys of spirit kick at it. I think I know boys, Clara."

He found himself addressing eyes that regarded him as though he were a small speck, a pin's head, in the circle of their remote contemplation. They were wide; they closed. She opened them to gaze elsewhere.

He was very sensitive.

Even then, when knowingly wounding him, or because of it, she was trying to climb back to that altitude of the thin division of neutral ground, from which we see a lover's faults and are above them, pure surveyors. She climbed unsuccessfully, it is true; soon despairing and using the effort as a pretext to fall back lower.[4]

Dr. Middleton withdrew Sir Willoughby's attention from the imperceptible annoyance, —

"No, sir, no: the birch! the birch![5] Boys of spirit commonly turn into solid men, and the solider the men the more surely do they vote for Busby. For me, I pray he may be immortal in Great Britain. Sea-air nor mountain-air is half so bracing. I venture to say that the power to take a licking is better worth having than the power to administer one. Horse him and birch him if Crossjay runs from his books."

" It is your opinion, sir ? " his host bowed to him affably, shocked on behalf of the ladies.

" So positively so, sir, that I will undertake without knowledge of their antecedents, to lay my finger on the men in public life who have not had early Busby. They are ill-balanced men. Their seat of reason is not a concrete. They won't take rough and smooth as they come. They make bad blood, can't forgive, sniff right and left for approbation, and are excited to anger if an East wind does not flatter them. Why, sir, when they have grown to be seniors, you find these men mixed up with the nonsense of their youth; you see they are unthreshed. We English beat the world because we take a licking well. I hold it for a surety of a proper sweetness of blood."

3. "immediate lesson": her subconscious means Willoughby.
4. Vernon's metaphor of Mont Blanc (p. 61) dominates the metaphors used to describe Clara's thoughts.
5. Flogging with birch rods was accepted practice at English public schools. Doctor Busby was a famous practitioner of corporal punishment in the seventeenth century. "Horsing" is laying one boy on another's back, or over a chair, to flog him.

The smile of Sir Willoughby waxed ever softer as the shakes of his head increased in contradictoriness. " And yet," said he, with the air of conceding a little after having answered the Rev. Doctor and convicted him of error, " Jack requires it to keep him in order. On board ship your argument may apply. Not, I suspect, among gentlemen. No."

" Good night to your gentlemen ! " said Dr. Middleton.

Clara heard Miss Eleanor and Miss Isabel interchange remarks, —

" Willoughby would not have suffered it ! "

" It would entirely have altered him ! "

She sighed and put a tooth on her underlip. The gift of humourous fancy is in women fenced round with forbidding placards; they have to choke it; if they perceive a piece of humour, for instance, the young Willoughby grasped by his master, and his horrified relatives rigid at the sight of preparations for the deed of sacrilege, they have to blindfold the mind's eye. They are society's hard-drilled soldiery, Prussians that must both march and think in step. It is for the advantage of the civilized world, if you like, since men have decreed it, or matrons have so read the decree; but here and there a younger woman, haply an uncorrected insurgent of the sex matured here and there, feels that her lot was cast with her head in a narrower pit than her limbs.

Clara speculated as to whether Miss Dale might be perchance a person of a certain liberty of mind. She asked for some little, only some little, free play of mind in a house that seemed to wear, as it were, a cap of iron. Sir Willoughby not merely ruled, he throned, he inspired: and how? She had noticed an irascible sensitiveness in him alert against a shadow of disagreement; and as he was kind when perfectly appeased, the sop was offered by him for submission. She noticed that even Mr. Whitford forbore to alarm the sentiment of authority in his cousin. If he did not breathe Sir Willoughby, like the ladies Eleanor and Isabel, he would either acquiesce in a syllable, or be silent. He never strongly dissented. The habit of the house, with its iron cap, was on him; as it was on the servants, and would be, oh, shudders of the shipwrecked that see their end in drowning! on the wife.

"When do I meet Miss Dale ? " she inquired.

"This very evening, at dinner," replied Sir Willoughby. Then, thought she, there is that to look forward to!

She indulged her morbid fit, and shut up her senses that she might live in the anticipation of meeting Miss Dale; and, long before the approach of the hour, her hope of encountering any other than another dull adherent of Sir Willoughby had fled. So she was languid for two of the three minutes when she sat alone with Lætitia in the drawing-room before the ladies had assembled.

" It is Miss Middleton ? " Lætitia said, advancing to her.

·" My jealousy tells me; for you have won my boy Crossjay's

heart, and done more to bring him to obedience in a few minutes than we have been able to do in months."

"His wild-flowers were so welcome to me," said Clara.

"He was very modest over them. And I mention it because boys of his age usually thrust their gifts in our faces fresh as they pluck them, and you were to be treated quite differently."

"We saw his good fairy's hand."

"She resigns her office; but I pray you not to love him too well in return; for he ought to be away reading with one of those men who get boys through their examinations. He is, we all think, a born sailor, and his place is in the navy."

"But, Miss Dale, I love him so well that I shall consult his interests and not my own selfishness. And, if I have influence, he will not be a week with you longer. It should have been spoken of to-day; I must have been in some dream; I thought of it, I know. I will not forget to do what may be in my power."

Clara's heart sank at the renewed engagement and plighting of herself involved in her asking a favour, urging any sort of petition. The cause was good. Besides, she was plighted already.

"Sir Willoughby is really fond of the boy," she said.

"He is fond of exciting fondness in the boy," said Miss Dale. "He has not dealt much with children. I am sure he likes Crossjay; he could not otherwise be so forbearing; it is wonderful what he endures and laughs at."

Sir Willoughby entered. The presence of Miss Dale illuminated him as the burning taper lights up consecrated plate.[6] Deeply respecting her for her constancy, esteeming her for a model of taste, he was never in her society without that happy consciousness of shining which calls forth the treasures of the man; and these it is no exaggeration to term unbounded, when all that comes from him is taken for gold.

The effect of the evening on Clara was to render her distrustful of her later antagonism. She had unknowingly passed into the spirit of Miss Dale, Sir Willoughby aiding; for she could sympathize with the view of his constant admirer on seeing him so cordially and smoothly gay; as one may say, domestically witty, the most agreeable form of wit. Mrs. Mountstuart Jenkinson discerned that he had a leg of physical perfection; Miss Dale distinguished it in him in the vital essence; and before either of these ladies he was not simply a radiant, he was a productive creature, so true it is that praise is our fructifying sun. He had even a touch of the romantic air which Clara remembered as her first impression of the favourite of the county: and strange she found it to observe this resuscitated idea confronting her

---

6. Heavy silver vessels often used on the altar in religious ceremonies.

experience. What if she had been captious, inconsiderate ?
O blissful revival of the sense of peace! The happiness of
pain departing was all that she looked for, and her conception of liberty was to learn to love her chains, provided that
he would spare her the caress. In this mood she sternly
condemned Constantia. "We must try to do good; we must
not be thinking of ourselves ; we must make the best of our
path in life." She revolved these infantile precepts with
humble earnestness; and not to be tardy in her striving to
do good, with a remote but pleasurable glimpse of Mr.
Whitford hearing of it, she took the opportunity to speak
to Sir Willoughby on the subject of young Crossjay, at a
moment when, alighting from horseback, he had shown himself to advantage among a gallant cantering company. He
showed to great advantage on horseback among men, being
invariably the best mounted, and he had a cavalierly style,
possibly cultivated, but effective. On foot his raised head
and half-dropped eyelids too palpably assumed superiority.
"Willoughby, I want to speak," she said, and shrank as
she spoke, lest he should immediately grant everything in
the mood of courtship, and invade her respite; "I want
to speak of that dear boy Crossjay. You are fond of him.
He is rather an idle boy here, and wasting time . . ."

"Now you are here, and when you are here for good, my
love, for good . . . " he fluted away in loverliness, forgetful
of Crossjay, whom he presently took up. "The boy recognizes his most sovereign lady, and will do your bidding,
though you should order him to learn his lessons ! Who
would not obey ? Your beauty alone commands. But what
is there beyond ? — a grace, a hue divine, that sets you not
so much above as apart, severed from the world."

Clara produced an active smile in duty, and pursued : "If
Crossjay were sent at once to some house where men prepare
boys to pass for the navy, he would have his chance, and
the navy is distinctly his profession. His father is a brave
man, and he inherits bravery, and he has a passion for a
sailor's life; only he must be able to pass his examination,
and he has not much time."

Sir Willoughby gave a slight laugh in sad amusement.

"My dear Clara, you adore the world; and I suppose you
have to learn that there is not a question in this wrangling
world about which we have not disputes and contests ad
nauseam.[7] I have my notions concerning Crossjay, Vernon
has his. I should wish to make a gentleman of him.
Vernon marks him for a sailor. But Vernon is the lad's
protector, I am not. Vernon took him from his father to
instruct him, and he has a right to say what shall be done
with him. I do not interfere. Only I can't prevent the lad
from liking me. Old Vernon seems to feel it. I assure you
I hold entirely aloof. If I am asked, in spite of my dis-

7. To the point of disgust.

approval of Vernon's plans for the boy, to subscribe to his
departure, I can but shrug, because, as you see, I have never
opposed. Old Vernon pays for him, he is the master, he
decides, and if Crossjay is blown from the mast-head in a
gale, the blame does not fall on me. These, my dear, are
matters of reason."

"I would not venture to intrude on them," said Clara,
"if I had not suspected that money . . . "

"Yes," cried Willoughby; "and it is a part. And let
old Vernon surrender the boy to me, I will immediately
relieve him of the burden on his purse. Can I do that, my
dear, for the furtherance of a scheme I condemn? The
point is this: latterly I have invited Captain Patterne to
visit me: just previous to his departure for the African
Coast, where Government despatches Marines when there is
no other way of killing them, I sent him a special invitation. He thanked me and curtly declined. The man, I
may almost say, is my pensioner. Well, he calls himself
a Patterne, he is undoubtedly a man of courage, he has
elements of our blood, and the name. I think I am to be
approved for desiring to make a better gentleman of the son
than I behold in the father: and seeing that life from an
early age on board ship has anything but made a gentleman
of the father, I hold that I am right in shaping another
course for the son."

"Naval officers . . . " Clara suggested.

"Some," said Willoughby. "But they must be men of
birth, coming out of homes of good breeding. Strip them of
the halo of the title of naval officers, and I fear you would
not often say gentlemen when they step into a drawing-
room. I went so far as to fancy I had some claim to make
young Crossjay something different. It can be done: the
Patterne comes out in his behaviour to you, my love: it can
be done. But if I take him, I claim undisputed sway over
him. I cannot make a gentleman of the fellow if I am to
compete with this person and that. In fine, he must look
up to me, he must have one model."

"Would you, then, provide for him subsequently?"

"According to his behaviour."

"Would not that be precarious for him?"

"More so than the profession you appear inclined to
choose for him?"

"But there he would be under clear regulations."

"With me he would have to respond to affection."

"Would you secure to him a settled income? For an idle
gentleman is bad enough; a penniless gentleman! . . ."

"He has only to please me, my dear, and he will be
launched and protected."

"But if he does not succeed in pleasing you!"

"Is it so difficult?"

"Oh!" Clara fretted.

"You see, my love, I answer you," said Sir Willoughby.

He resumed: "But let old Vernon have his trial with the lad. He has his own ideas. Let him carry them out. I shall watch the experiment."

Clara was for abandoning her task in sheer faintness.

"Is not the question one of money?" she said shyly, knowing Mr. Whitford to be poor.

"Old Vernon chooses to spend his money that way," replied Sir Willoughby. "If it saves him from breaking his shins and risking his neck on his Alps, we may consider it well employed."

"Yes," Clara's voice occupied a pause.

She seized her languor as it were a curling snake and cast it off. "But I understand that Mr. Whitford wants your assistance. Is he not — not rich? When he leaves the Hall to try his fortune in literature in London, he may not be so well able to support Crossjay and obtain the instruction necessary for the boy: and it would be generous to help him."

"Leaves the Hall!" exclaimed Willoughby. "I have not heard a word of it. He made a bad start at the beginning, and I should have thought that would have tamed him: had to throw over his Fellowship; ahem. Then he received a small legacy some time back, and wanted to be off to push his luck in Literature: rank gambling, as I told him. Londonizing can do him no good. I thought that nonsense of his was over years ago. What is it he has from me? — about a hundred and fifty a year: and it might be doubled for the asking: and all the books he requires: and these writers and scholars no sooner think of a book than they must have it. And do not suppose me to complain. I am a man who will not have a single shilling expended by those who serve immediately about my person. I confess to exacting that kind of dependancy. Feudalism is not an objectionable thing if you can be sure of the lord. You know, Clara, and you should know me in my weakness too, I do not claim servitude, I stipulate for affection. I claim to be surrounded by persons loving me. And with one? ... dearest! So that we two can shut out the world: we live what is the dream of others. Nothing imaginable can be sweeter. It is a veritable heaven on earth. To be the possessor of the whole of you! Your thoughts, hopes, all."

Sir Willoughby intensified his imagination to conceive more: he could not, or could not express it, and pursued: "But what is this talk of Vernon's leaving me? He cannot leave. He has barely a hundred a year of his own. You see, I consider him. I do not speak of the ingratitude of the wish to leave. You know, my dear, I have a deadly abhorrence of partings and such like. As far as I can, I surround myself with healthy people specially to guard myself from having my feelings wrung; and excepting Miss Dale, whom you like — my darling does like her?" — the answer satisfied him; "with that one exception, I am not aware of a case that threatens to torment me. And here is a man, under no compulsion, talking of leaving the Hall! In the name of goodness, why? But why? Am I to imagine that the sight of perfect felicity distresses him? We are told that the world is 'desperately wicked.' I do not like to think it of my friends; yet otherwise their conduct is often hard to account for."

"If it were true, you would not punish Crossjay?" Clara feebly interposed.

"I should certainly take Crossjay and make a man of him after my own model, my dear. But who spoke to you of this?"

"Mr. Whitford himself. And let me give you my opinion, Willoughby, that he will take Crossjay with him rather than leave him, if there is a fear of the boy's missing his chance of the navy."

"Marines appear to be in the ascendant," said Sir Willoughby, astonished at the locution and pleading in the interests of a son of one. "Then Crossjay he must take. I cannot accept half the boy. I am," he laughed, "the legitimate claimant in the application for judgement before the wise King. Besides, the boy has a dose of my blood in him; he has none of Vernon's, not one drop."

"Ah!"

"You see, my love."

"Oh! I do see; yes."

"I put forth no pretensions to perfection," Sir Willoughby continued. "I can bear a considerable amount of provocation; still I can be offended, and I am unforgiving when I have been offended. Speak to Vernon, if a natural occasion should spring up. I shall, of course, have to speak to him. You may, Clara, have observed a man who passed me on the road as we were cantering home, without a hint of a touch to his hat. That man is a tenant of mine, farming six hundred acres, Hoppner by name: a man bound to remember that I have, independently of my position, obliged him frequently. His lease of my ground has five years to run.[8] I must say I detest the churlishness of our country population, and where it comes across me I chastise it. Vernon is a different matter: he will only require to be spoken to. One would fancy the old fellow laboured now and then under a magnetic attraction to beggary. My love," he bent to her and checked their pacing up and down, "you are tired?"

"I am very tired to-day," said Clara.

His arm was offered. She laid two fingers on it, and they dropped when he attempted to press them to his rib.

8. Willoughby implies that the lease will not be renewed. Total social subservience of tenant to landlord, a feudal remnant, was fading from the countryside. This is very backward behavior.

He did not insist. To walk beside her was to share in the stateliness of her walking.

He placed himself at a corner of the doorway for her to pass him into the house, and doated on her cheek, her ear, and the softly dusky nape of her neck, where this way and that the little lighter-coloured irreclaimable curls running truant from the comb and the knot — curls, half-curls, root-curls, vine-ringlets, wedding-rings, fledgeling feathers, tufts of down, blown wisps — waved or fell, waved over or up or involutedly, or strayed, loose and downward, in the form of small silken paws, hardly any of them much thicker than a crayon shading, cunninger than long round locks of gold to trick the heart.

Lætitia had nothing to show resembling such beauty.

[margin note: physical]

CHAPTER 10

IN WHICH SIR WILLOUGHBY CHANCES TO SUPPLY THE TITLE FOR HIMSELF

Now Vernon was useful to his cousin; he was the accomplished secretary of a man who governed his estates shrewdly and diligently, but had been once or twice unlucky in his judgements pronounced from the magisterial bench as a Justice of the Peace, on which occasions a half-column of trenchant English supported by an apposite classical quotation impressed Sir Willoughby with the value of such a secretary in a controversy. He had no fear of that fiery dragon of scorching breath — the newspaper Press — while Vernon was his right-hand man; and as he intended to enter Parliament, he foresaw the greater need of him. Furthermore, he liked his cousin to date his own controversial writings, on classical subjects, from Patterne Hall. It caused his house to shine in a foreign field; proved the service of scholarship by giving it a flavour of a bookish aristocracy that, though not so well worth having, and indeed in itself contemptible, is above the material and titular; one cannot quite say how. There, however, is the flavour. Dainty sauces are the life, the nobility, of famous dishes; taken alone, the former would be nauseating, the latter plebeian. It is thus, or somewhat so, when you have a poet, still better a scholar, attached to your household. Sir Willoughby deserved to have him, for he was above his county friends in his apprehension of the flavour bestowed by the man; and having him, he had made them conscious of their deficiency. His cook, M. Dehors, pupil of the great Godefroy, was not the only French cook in the county; but his cousin and secretary, the rising scholar, the elegant

[margin note: Willoughby needs Vernon]

essayist, was an unparalleled decoration; of his kind, of
course. Personally, we laugh at him; you had better not,
unless you are fain to show that the higher world of polite
literature is unknown to you. Sir Willoughby could create
an abject silence at a county dinner-table, by an allusion
to Vernon "at work at home upon his Etruscans or his
Dorians;" and he paused a moment to let the allusion sink,
laughed audibly to himself over his eccentric cousin, and
let him rest.

In addition, Sir Willoughby abhorred the loss of a familiar face in his domestic circle. He thought ill of servants
who could accept their dismissal without petitioning to stay
with him. A servant that gave warning partook of a certain fiendishness. Vernon's project of leaving the Hall
offended and alarmed the sensitive gentleman. "I shall
have to hand Letty Dale to him at last!" he thought, yielding in bitter generosity to the conditions imposed on him
by the ungenerousness of another. For, since his engagement to Miss Middleton, his electrically forethoughtful
mind had seen in Miss Dale, if she stayed in the neighbourhood, and remained unmarried, the governess of his infant
children, often consulting with him. But here was a prospect dashed out. The two, then, may marry, and live in a
cottage on the borders of his park; and Vernon can retain
his post, and Lætitia her devotion. The risk of her casting
it off had to be faced. Marriage has been known to have
such an effect on the most faithful of women, that a great
passion fades to naught in their volatile bosoms when they
have taken a husband. We see in women especially the
triumph of the animal over the spiritual. Nevertheless,
risks must be run for a purpose in view.

Having no taste for a discussion with Vernon, whom it
was his habit to confound by breaking away from him
abruptly when he had delivered his opinion, he left it to
both the persons interesting themselves in young Crossjay
to imagine that he was meditating on the question of the
lad, and to imagine that it would be wise to leave him to
meditate; for he could be preternaturally acute in reading
any of his fellow-creatures if they crossed the current of
his feelings. And, meanwhile, he instructed the ladies
Eleanor and Isabel to bring Lætitia Dale on a visit to the
Hall, where dinner-parties were soon to be given and a
pleasing talker would be wanted; where also a woman of
intellect, steeped in a splendid sentiment, hitherto a miracle
of female constancy, might stir a younger woman to some
emulation. Definitely to resolve to bestow Lætitia upon
Vernon, was more than he could do; enough that he held
the card.

Regarding Clara, his genius for perusing the heart which
was not in perfect harmony with him through the series of
responsive movements to his own, informed him of a something in her character that might have suggested to Mrs.

Mountstuart Jenkinson her indefensible, absurd "rogue in porcelain." Idea there was none in that phrase; yet, if you looked on Clara as a delicately inimitable porcelain beauty, the suspicion of a delicately inimitable ripple over her features touched a thought of innocent roguery, wild-wood roguery; the likeness to the costly and lovely substance appeared to admit a fitness in the dubious epithet. He detested but was haunted by the phrase.

She certainly had at times the look of the nymph that has gazed too long on the faun, and has unwittingly copied his lurking lip and long sliding eye. Her play with young Crossjay resembled a return of the lady to the cat; she flung herself into it as if her real vitality had been in suspense till she saw the boy. Sir Willoughby by no means disapproved of a physical liveliness that promised him health in his mate; but he began to feel in their conversations that she did not sufficiently think of making herself a nest for him. Steely points were opposed to him when he, figuratively, bared his bosom to be taken to the softest and fairest. She reasoned: in other words, armed her ignorance. She reasoned against him publicly, and lured Vernon to support her. Influence is to be counted for power, and her influence over Vernon was displayed in her persuading him to dance one evening at Lady Culmer's, after his melancholy exhibitions of himself in the art; and not only did she persuade him to stand up fronting her, she manœuvred him through the dance like a clever boy cajoling a top to come to him without reeling, both to Vernon's contentment and to Sir Willoughby's; for he was the last man to object to a manifestation of power in his bride. Considering her influence with Vernon, he renewed the discourse upon young Crossjay; and, as he was addicted to system, he took her into his confidence, that she might be taught to look to him and act for him.

"Old Vernon has not spoken to you again of that lad?" he said.

"Yes, Mr. Whitford has asked me."

"He does not ask me, my dear!"

"He may fancy me of greater aid than I am."

"You see, my love, if he puts Crossjay on me, he will be off. He has this craze for 'enlisting' his pen in London, as he calls it; and I am accustomed to him; I don't like to think of him as a hack scribe, writing nonsense from dictation to earn a pitiful subsistence; I want him here; and, supposing he goes, he offends me; he loses a friend; and it will not be the first time that a friend has tried me too far; but, if he offends me, he is extinct."

"Is what?" cried Clara, with a look of fright.

"He becomes to me at once as if he had never been. He is extinct."

"In spite of your affection?"

"On account of it, I might say. Our nature is mysterious, and mine as much so as any. Whatever my regrets, he goes out. This is not a language I talk to the world. I do the man no harm; I am not to be named unchristian. But! . . ."

Sir Willoughby mildly shrugged, and indicated a spreading out of the arms.

"But do, do talk to me as you talk to the world, Willoughby; give me some relief!"

"My own Clara, we are one. You should know me, at my worst, we will say, if you like, as well as at my best."

"Should I speak too?"

"What could you have to confess?"

She hung silent: the wave of an insane resolution swelled in her bosom and subsided before she said, "Cowardice, incapacity to speak."

"Women!" said he.

We do not expect so much of women; the heroic virtues as little as the vices. They have not to unfold the scroll of character.

He resumed, and by his tone she understood that she was now in the inner temple of him: "I tell you these things; I quite acknowledge they do not elevate me. They help to constitute my character. I tell you most humbly that I have in me much too much of the fallen archangel's pride."

Clara bowed her head over a sustained indrawn breath.

"It must be pride," he said, in a revery superinduced by her thoughtfulness over the revelation, and glorying in the black flames demoniacal wherewith he crowned himself.

"Can you not correct it?" said she.

He replied, profoundly vexed by disappointment: "I am what I am. It might be demonstrated to you mathematically that it is corrected by equivalents or substitutions in my character. If it be a failing — assuming that."

"It seems one to me: so cruelly to punish Mr. Whitford for seeking to improve his fortunes."

"He reflects on my share in his fortunes. He has had but to apply to me, for his honorarium to be doubled."

"He wishes for independence."

"Independence of *me!*"

"Liberty!"

"At my expense!"

"Oh, Willoughby."

"Ay, but this is the world, and I know it, my love; and beautiful as your incredulity may be, you will find it more comforting to confide in my knowledge of the selfishness of the world. My sweetest, you will? — you do! For a breath of difference between us is intolerable. Do you not feel how it breaks our magic ring? One small fissure, and we have the world with its muddy deluge! — But my subject was old Vernon. Yes, I pay for Crossjay, if Vernon consents to stay. I waive my own scheme for the lad, though I think it the better one. Now, then, to induce Vernon to stay. He has his ideas about staying under a mistress of the household; and therefore, not to contest it — he is a man of no argument; a sort of lunatic determination takes the place of it with old Vernon! — let him settle close by me, in one of my cottages; very well, and to settle him we must marry him."

" Who is there?" said Clara, beating for the lady in her mind.

" Women," said Willoughby, "are born match-makers, and the most persuasive is a young bride. With a man — and a man like old Vernon! — she is irresistible. It is my wish, and that arms you. It is your wish, that subjugates him. If he goes, he goes for good. If he stays, he is my friend. I deal simply with him, as with every one. It is the secret of authority. Now Miss Dale will soon lose her father. He exists on a pension; she has the prospect of having to leave the neighbourhood of the Hall, unless she is established near us. Her whole heart is in this region; it is the poor soul's passion. Count on her agreeing. But she will require a little wooing: and old Vernon wooing! Picture the scene to yourself, my love. His notion of wooing, I suspect, will be to treat the lady like a lexicon, and turn over the leaves for the word, and fly through the leaves for another word, and so get a sentence. Don't frown at the poor old fellow, my Clara; some have the language on their tongues, and some have not. Some are very dry sticks; manly men, honest fellows, but so cut away, so polished away from the sex, that they are in absolute want of outsiders to supply the silken filaments to attach them. Actually!" Sir Willoughby laughed in Clara's face to relax the dreamy stoniness of her look. " But I can assure you, my dearest, I have seen it. Vernon does not know how to speak — as *we* speak. He has, or he had, what is called a sneaking affection for Miss Dale. It was the most amusing thing possible : his courtship! — the air of a dog with an uneasy conscience, trying to reconcile himself with his master! We were all in fits of laughter. Of course it came to nothing."

" Will Mr. Whitford," said Clara, " offend you to extinction if he declines?"

Willoughby breathed an affectionate "Tush," to her silliness.

" We bring them together, as we best can. You see, Clara, I desire, and I will make some sacrifices to detain him."

" But what do you sacrifice? — a cottage?" said Clara, combative at all points.

" An ideal, perhaps. I lay no stress on sacrifice. I strongly object to separations. And therefore, you will say, I prepare the ground for unions? Put your influence to good service, my love. I believe you could persuade him to give us the Highland fling on the drawing-room table."

" There is nothing to say to him of Crossjay?"

"We hold Crossjay in reserve."

"It is urgent."

"Trust me. I have my ideas. I am not idle. That boy bids fair for a capital horseman. Eventualities might . . ." Sir Willoughby murmured to himself, and addressing his bride: "The cavalry? If we put him into the cavalry, we might make a gentleman of him — not be ashamed of him. Or, under certain eventualities, the Guards. Think it over, my love. De Craye, who will, I assume, act best man for me, supposing old Vernon to pull at the collar, is a Lieutenant-Colonel in the Guards, a thorough gentleman — of the brainless class, if you like, but an elegant fellow; an Irishman; you will see him, and I should like to set a naval lieutenant beside him in a drawing-room, for you to compare them and consider the model you would choose for a boy you are interested in.[1] Horace is grace and gallantry incarnate; fatuous, probably: I have always been too friendly with him to examine closely. He made himself one of my dogs, though my elder, and seemed to like to be at my heels. One of the few men's faces I can call admirably handsome; — with nothing behind it, perhaps. As Vernon says, 'a nothing picked by the vultures and bleached by the desert.' Not a bad talker, if you are satisfied with keeping up the ball. He will amuse you. Old Horace does not know how amusing he is!"

"Did Mr. Whitford say that of Colonel De Craye?"

"I forget the person of whom he said it. So you have noticed old Vernon's foible? Quote him one of his epigrams, and he is in motion head and heels! It is an infallible receipt for tuning him. If I want to have him in good temper, I have only to remark, 'as you said.' I straighten his back instantly."

"I," said Clara, "have noticed chiefly his anxiety concerning the boy; for which I admire him."

"Creditable, if not particularly far-sighted and sagacious. Well then, my dear, attack him at once: lead him to the subject of our fair neighbour. She is to be our guest for a week or so, and the whole affair might be concluded far enough to fix him before she leaves. She is at present awaiting the arrival of a cousin to attend on her father. A little gentle pushing will precipitate old Vernon on his knees as far as he ever can unbend them; but when a lady is made ready to expect a declaration, you know, why, she does not — does she? — demand the entire formula? — though some beautiful fortresses . . ."

He enfolded her. Clara was growing hardened to it. To this she was fated; and not seeing any way of escape, she invoked a friendly frost to strike her blood, and passed through the minute unfeelingly. Having passed it, she reproached herself for making so much of it, thinking it a

1. "pull at the collar": decline obstinately.

lesser endurance than to listen to him. What could she do? — she was caged; by her word of honour, as she at one time thought; by her cowardice, at another; and dimly sensible that the latter was a stronger lock than the former, she mused on the abstract question whether a woman's cowardice can be so absolute as to cast her into the jaws of her aversion. Is it to be conceived? Is there not a moment when it stands at bay? But haggard-visaged Honour then starts up claiming to be dealt with in turn; for having courage restored to her, she must have the courage to break with honour, she must dare to be faithless, and not merely say, I will be brave, but be brave enough to be dishonourable. The cage of a plighted woman hungering for her disengagement has two keepers, a noble and a vile; where on earth is creature so dreadfully enclosed? It lies with her to overcome what degrades her, that she may win to liberty by overcoming what exalts.

Contemplating her situation, this idea (or vapour of youth taking the godlike semblance of an idea) sprang, born of her present sickness, in Clara's mind; that it must be an ill-constructed tumbling world where the hour of ignorance is made the creator of our destiny by being forced to the decisive elections upon which life's main issues hang. Her teacher had brought her to contemplate his view of the world.

She thought likewise: how must a man despise women, who can expose himself as he does to me!

Miss Middleton owed it to Sir Willoughby Patterne that she ceased to think like a girl. When had the great change begun? Glancing back, she could imagine that it was near the period we call, in love, the first — almost from the first. And she was led to imagine it through having become barred from imagining her own emotions of that season. They were so dead as not to arise even under the forms of shadows in fancy. Without imputing blame to him, for she was reasonable so far, she deemed herself a person entrapped. In a dream somehow she had committed herself to a life-long imprisonment; and, oh terror! not in a quiet dungeon; the barren walls closed round her, talked, called for ardour, expected admiration.

She was unable to say why she could not give it; why she retreated more and more inwardly; why she invoked the frost to kill her tenderest feelings. She was in revolt, until a whisper of the day of bells reduced her to blank submission; out of which a breath of peace drew her to revolt again in gradual rapid stages, and once more the aspect of that singular day of merry blackness felled her to earth. It was alive, it advanced, it had a mouth, it had a song. She received letters of bridesmaids writing of it, and felt them as waves that hurl a log of wreck to shore. Following which afflicting sense of antagonism to the whole circle sweeping on with her, she considered the possibility of her being in a commencement of madness. Otherwise might she not be accused of a capriciousness quite as deplorable to consider? She had written to certain of those young ladies not very long since of this gentleman — how? — in what tone? And was it her madness then? — her recovery now? It seemed to her that to have written of him enthusiastically resembled madness more than to shudder away from the union; but standing alone, opposing all she has consented to set in motion, is too strange to a girl for perfect justification to be found in reason when she seeks it.

Sir Willoughby was destined himself to supply her with that key of special insight which revealed and stamped him in a title to fortify her spirit of revolt, consecrate it almost.

The popular physician of the county and famous anecdotal wit, Dr. Corney, had been a guest at dinner overnight, and the next day there was talk of him, and of the resources of his art displayed by Armand Dehors on his hearing that he was to minister to the tastes of a gathering of hommes d'esprit.[2] Sir Willoughby glanced at Dehors with his customary benevolent irony in speaking of the persons, great in their way, who served him. "Why he cannot give us daily so good a dinner, one must, I suppose, go to French nature to learn. The French are in the habit of making up for all their deficiencies with enthusiasm. They have no reverence; if I had said to him, 'I want something particularly excellent, Dehors,' I should have had a commonplace dinner. But they have enthusiasm on draught, and that is what we must pull at. Know one Frenchman and you know France. I have had Dehors under my eye two years, and I can mount his enthusiasm at a word. He took hommes d'esprit to denote men of letters. Frenchmen have destroyed their nobility, so, for the sake of excitement, they put up the literary man — not to worship him; that they can't do; it's to put themselves in a state of effervescence. They will not have real greatness above them, so they have sham. That they may justly call it equality, perhaps! Ay, for all your shake of the head, my good Vernon! You see, human nature comes round again, try as we may to upset it, and the French only differ from us in wading through blood to discover that they are at their old trick once more: 'I am your equal, sir, your born equal. Oh! you are a man of letters? Allow me to be in a bubble about you.' Yes, Vernon, and I believe the fellow looks up to you as the head of the establishment. I am not jealous. Provided he attends to his functions! There's a French philosopher who's for naming the days of the year after the birthdays of French men of letters, Voltaire-day, Rousseau-day, Racine-day, so on.[3] Perhaps

---

2. "Armand Dehors": The cook's name means Armand Outside, perhaps because his concern is the inner man. "Hommes d'esprit": men of wit.

3. "French philosopher": This is Auguste Comte, who planned not only calendars but cities to celebrate the great culture-heroes. Meredith admired him.

Vernon will inform us who takes April 1st."

"A few trifling errors are of no consequence when you are in the vein of satire," said Vernon. "Be satisfied with knowing a nation in the person of a cook."

"They may be reading us English off in a jockey!" said Dr. Middleton. "I believe that jockeys are the exchange we make for cooks; and our neighbours do not get the best of the bargain."

"No, but, my dear good Vernon, it's nonsensical," said Sir Willoughby; "why be bawling every day the name of men of letters?"

"Philosophers."

"Well, philosophers."

"Of all countries and times. And they are the bene-factors of humanity."

"Bene . . . !" Sir Willoughby's derisive laugh broke the word. "There's a pretension in all that, irreconcilable with English sound sense. Surely you see it?"

"We might," said Vernon, "if you like, give alternative titles to the days, or have alternating days, devoted to our great families that performed meritorious deeds upon such a day."

The rebel Clara, delighting in his banter, was heard "Can we furnish sufficient?"

"A poet or two could help us."

"Perhaps a statesman," she suggested.

"A pugilist, if wanted."

"For blowy days," observed Dr. Middleton, and hastily in penitence picked up the conversation he had unintention-ally prostrated, with a general remark on new-fangled notions, and a word aside to Vernon; which created the blissful suspicion in Clara, that her father was indisposed to second Sir Willoughby's opinions even when sharing them.

Sir Willoughby had led the conversation. Displeased that the lead should be withdrawn from him, he turned to Clara and related one of the after-dinner anecdotes of Dr. Corney; and another, with a vast deal of human nature in it, concerning a valetudinarian gentleman, whose wife chanced to be desperately ill, and he went to the physicians assembled in consultation outside the sick-room, imploring them by all he valued, and in tears, to save the poor patient for him, saying: "She is everything to me, everything, and if she dies I am compelled to run the risks of marrying again; I must marry again; for she has accustomed me so to the little attentions of a wife, that in truth I can't, I can't lose her! She must be saved!" And the loving husband of any devoted wife wrung his hands.

"Now, there, Clara, there you have the Egoist," added Sir Willoughby. "That is the perfect Egoist. You see what he comes to — and his wife! The man was utterly unconscious of giving vent to the grossest selfishness."

"An Egoist!" said Clara.

"Beware of marrying an Egoist, my dear!" He bowed gallantly; and so blindly fatuous did he appear to her, that she could hardly believe him guilty of uttering the words she had heard from him, and kept her eyes on him vacantly till she came to a sudden full stop in the thoughts directing her gaze. She looked at Vernon, she looked at her father, and at the ladies Eleanor and Isabel. None of them saw the man in the word, none noticed the word; yet this word was her medical herb, her illuminating lamp, the key of him (and, alas, but she thought it by feeling her need of one), the advocate pleading in apology for her. Egoist! She beheld him — unfortunate, self-designated man that he was! — in his good qualities as well as bad under the implacable lamp, and his good were drenched in his first person singular. His generosity roared of *I* louder than the rest. Conceive him at the age of Dr. Corney's hero : "Pray, save my wife for me. I shall positively have to get another if I lose her, and one who may not love me half so well, or understand the peculiarities of my character and appreciate my attitudes." He was in his thirty-second year, therefore a young man, strong and healthy, yet his garrulous return to his principal theme, his emphasis on I and me, lent him the seeming of an old man spotted with decaying youth.

"Beware of marrying an Egoist."

Would he help her to escape? The idea of the scene ensuing upon her petition for release, and the being dragged round the walls of his egoism, and having her head knocked against the corners, alarmed her with sensations of sickness.

There was the example of Constantia. But that desperate young lady had been assisted by a gallant, loving gentleman; she had met a Captain Oxford.

Clara brooded on those two until they seemed heroic. She questioned herself: Could she . . . ? were one to come? She shut her eyes in languor, leaning the wrong way of her wishes, yet unable to say No.

Sir Willoughby had positively said beware! Marrying him would be a deed committed in spite of his express warning. She went so far as to conceive him subsequently saying, "I warned you." She conceived the state of marriage with him as that of a woman tied not to a man of heart, but to an obelisk lettered all over with hieroglyphics, and everlastingly hearing him expound them, relishingly renewing his lectures on them.

Full surely this immovable stone-man would not release her. This petrifaction of egoism would from amazedly to austerely refuse the petition. His pride would debar him from understanding her desire to be released. And if she resolved on it, without doing it straightway in Constantia's manner, the miserable bewilderment of her father, for whom such a complication would be a tragic dilemma, had to be thought of. Her father, with all his tenderness for his child, would make a stand on a point of honour; though certain to yield to her, he would be distressed, in a tempest of worry; and Dr. Middleton thus afflicted threw up his arms, he shunned books, shunned speech, and resembled a castaway on the ocean, with nothing between himself and his calamity. As for the world it would be barking at her heels. She might call the man she wrenched her hand from, Egoist; jilt, the world would call her. She dwelt bitterly on her agreement with Sir Willoughby regarding the world, laying it to his charge that her garden had become a place of nettles, her horizon an unlighted fourth side of a square.

Clara passed from person to person visiting the Hall. There was universal, and as she was compelled to see, honest admiration of the host. Not a soul had a suspicion of his cloaked nature. Her agony of hypocrisy in accepting their compliments as the bride of Sir Willoughby Patterne was poorly moderated by contempt of them for their infatuation. She tried to cheat herself with the thought that they were right and that she was the foolish and wicked inconstant. In her anxiety to strangle the rebelliousness which had been communicated from her mind to her blood, and was present with her whether her mind was in action or not, she encouraged the ladies Eleanor and Isabel to magnify the fictitious man of their idolatry, hoping that she might enter into them imaginatively, that she might to some degree subdue herself to the necessity of her position. If she partly succeeded in stupefying her antagonism, five minutes of him undid the work.

He requested her to wear the Patterne Pearls for a dinner-party of grand ladies, telling her that he would commission Miss Isabel to take them to her. Clara begged leave to decline them, on the plea of having no right to wear them. He laughed at her modish modesty. "But really it might almost be classed with affectation," said he. "I give you the right. Virtually you are my wife."

"No."

"Before heaven?"

"No. We are not married."

"As my betrothed, will you wear them, to please me?"

"I would rather not. I cannot wear borrowed jewels. These I cannot wear. Forgive me, I cannot. And, Willoughby," she said, scorning herself for want of fortitude in not keeping to the simply blunt provocative refusal, "does one not look like a victim decked for the sacrifice —the garlanded heifer you see on Greek vases, in that array of jewelry?"

"My dear Clara!" exclaimed the astonished lover, "how can you term them borrowed, when they are the Patterne jewels, our family heirloom pearls, unmatched, I venture to affirm, decidedly in my county and many others, and passing to the use of the mistress of the house in the natural course of things?"

"They are yours, they are not mine."

"Prospectively they are yours."

"It would be to anticipate the fact to wear them."

"With my consent, my approval? at my request?"

"I am not yet . . . I never may be . . ."

"My wife?" He laughed triumphantly, and silenced her by manly smothering.

Her scruple was perhaps an honourable one, he said. Perhaps the jewels were safer in their iron box. He had merely intended a surprise and gratification to her.

Courage was coming to enable her to speak more plainly, when his discontinuing to insist on her wearing the jewels, under an appearance of deference to her wishes, disarmed her by touching her sympathies.

She said, however, "I fear we do not often agree, Willoughby."

"When you are a little older!" was the irritating answer.

"It would then be too late to make the discovery."

"The discovery, I apprehend, is not imperative, my love."

"It seems to me that our minds are opposed."

"I should," said he, "have been awake to it at a single indication, be sure."

"But I know," she pursued, "I have learnt, that the ideal of conduct for women is to subject their minds to the part of an accompaniment."

"For women, my love? my wife will be in natural harmony with me."

"Ah!" She compressed her lips. The yawn would come. "I am sleepier here than anywhere."

"Ours, my Clara, is the finest air of the kingdom. It has the effect of sea-air."

"But if I am always asleep here?"

"We shall have to make a public exhibition of the Beauty."

This dash of his liveliness defeated her.

She left him, feeling the contempt of the brain feverishly quickened and fine-pointed, for the brain chewing the cud in the happy pastures of unawakenedness. So violent was the fever, so keen her introspection, that she spared few, and Vernon was not among them. Young Crossjay, whom she considered the least able of all to act as an ally, was the only one she courted with a real desire to please him; he was the one she affectionately envied; he was the youngest, the freest, he had the world before him, and he did not know how horrible the world was, or could be made to look. She loved the boy from expecting nothing of him. Others, Vernon Whitford, for instance, could help, and moved no hand. He read her case. A

scrutiny so penetrating under its air of abstract thoughtfulness, though his eyes did but rest on her a second or
two, signified that he read her line by line, and to the end
— excepting what she thought of him for probing her with
that sharp steel of insight without a purpose.

She knew her mind's injustice. It was her case, her
lamentable case — the impatient panic-stricken nerves of a
captured wild creature, which cried for help. She exaggerated her sufferings to get strength to throw them off,
and lost it in the recognition that they were exaggerated:
and out of the conflict issued recklessness, with a cry as
wild as any coming of madness; for she did not blush in
saying to herself, "If some one loved me!" Before hearing of Constantia, she had mused upon liberty as a virgin
Goddess, — men were out of her thoughts; even the figure
of a rescuer, if one dawned in her mind, was more angel
than hero. That fair childish maidenliness had ceased.
With her body straining in her dragon's grasp, with the
savour of loathing, unable to contend, unable to speak
aloud, she began to speak to herself, and all the health
of her nature made her outcry womanly, — "If I were
loved!" — not for the sake of love, but for free breathing;
and her utterance of it was to ensure life and enduringness
to the wish, as the yearning of a mother on a drowning
ship is to get her infant to shore. "If some noble gentleman could see me as I am and not disdain to aid me! Oh!
to be caught up out of this prison of thorns and brambles.
I cannot tear my own way out. I am a coward. My cry
for help confesses that. A beckoning of a finger would
change me, I believe. I could fly bleeding and through
hootings to a comrade. Oh! a comrade. I do not want
a lover. I should find another Egoist, not so bad, but
enough to make me take a breath like death. I could
follow a soldier, like poor Sally or Molly. He stakes his
life for his country, and a woman may be proud of the
worst of men who do that. Constantia met a soldier.
Perhaps she prayed and her prayer was altered. She did
ill. But, oh, how I love her for it! His name was Harry
Oxford. Papa would call him her Perseus.[4] She must
have felt that there was no explaining what she suffered.
She had only to act, to plunge. First she fixed her mind
on Harry Oxford. To be able to speak his name and see
him awaiting her, must have been relief, a reprieve. She
did not waver, she cut the links, she signed herself over.
O brave girl! what do you think of me? But I have
no Harry Whitford, I am alone.[5] Let anything be said
against women; we must be very bad to have such bad
things written of us: only, say this, that to ask them to

4. In classical mythology, Perseus rescued
the enchained Andromeda from a fearful
sea-beast.
5. "Harry Whitford": Clara has made,

as we would say now, a Freudian slip.
Meredith knew about it without benefit
of Freud.

sign themselves over by oath, and ceremony, because of an ignorant promise, to the man they have been mistaken in, is . . . it is —" the sudden consciousness that she had put another name for Oxford, struck her a buffet, drowning her in crimson.

CHAPTER 11

THE DOUBLE-BLOSSOM WILD CHERRY-TREE

Sir Willoughby chose a moment when Clara was with him and he had a good retreat through folding-windows to the lawn, in case of cogency on the enemy's part, to attack his cousin regarding the preposterous plot to upset the family by a scamper to London: "By the way, Vernon, what is this you 've been mumbling to everybody save me, about leaving us to pitch yourself into the stew-pot and be made broth of ? — London is no better, and you are fit for considerably better. Don't, I beg you, continue to annoy me. Take a run abroad, if you are restless. Take two or three months, and join us as we are travelling home; and then think of settling, pray. Follow my example, if you like. You can have one of my cottages, or a place built for you. Anything to keep a man from destroying the sense of stability about one. In London, my dear old fellow, you lose your identity. What are you there? I ask you, what? One has the feeling of the house crumbling when a man is perpetually for shifting and cannot fix himself. Here you are known, you can study at your ease; up in London you are nobody; I tell you honestly, I feel it myself; a week of London literally drives me home to discover the individual where I left him. Be advised. You don't mean to go."

"I have the intention," said Vernon.

"Why ?"

"I 've mentioned it to you."

"To my face ?"

"Over your shoulder, is generally the only chance you give me."

"You have not mentioned it to me, to my knowledge. As to the reason, I might hear a dozen of your reasons, and I should not understand one. It 's against your interests and against my wishes. Come, friend, I am not the only one you distress. Why, Vernon, you yourself have said that the English would be very perfect Jews if they could manage to live on the patriarchal system. You said it, yes, you said it! — but I recollect it clearly. Oh! as for your double-meanings, you said the thing, and you jeered at the incapacity of English families to live together, on account of bad temper; and now you are the first to break up our union! I decidedly do not profess to be perfect Jew, but I do . . ."

Sir Willoughby caught signs of a probably smiling commerce between his bride and his cousin. He raised his face, appeared to be consulting his eyelids, and resolved to laugh: "Well, I own it, I do like the idea of living patriarchally." He turned to Clara. "The Rev. Doctor one of us!"

"My father?" she said.

"Why not?"

"Papa's habits are those of a scholar."

"That you might not be separated from him, my dear."

Clara thanked Sir Willoughby for the kindness of thinking of her father, mentally analyzing the kindness, in which at least she found no unkindness, scarcely egoism, though she knew it to be there.

"We might propose it," said he.

"As a compliment?"

"If he would condescend to accept it as a compliment. These great scholars! . . . And if Vernon goes, our inducement for Dr. Middleton to stay . . . But it is too absurd for discussion. Oh, Vernon, about Master Crossjay; I will see to it."

He was about to give Vernon his shoulder and step into the garden, when Clara said, "You will have Crossjay trained for the navy, Willoughby? There is not a day to lose."

"Yes, yes; I will see to it. Depend on me for holding the young rascal in view."

He presented his hand to her to lead her over the step to the gravel, surprised to behold how flushed she was

She responded to the invitation by putting her hand forth from a bent elbow, with hesitating fingers. "It should not be postponed, Willoughby."

Her attitude suggested a <u>stipulation</u> before she touched him.

"It's an affair of money, as you know, Willoughby," said Vernon. "If I'm in London, I can't well provide for the boy for some time to come, or it's not certain that I can."

"Why on earth should you go!"

"That's another matter. I want you to take my place with him."

"In which case the circumstances are changed. I am responsible for him, and I have a right to bring him up according to my own prescription."

"We are likely to have one idle lout the more."

"I guarantee to make a gentleman of him."

"We have too many of your gentlemen already."

"You can't have enough, my good Vernon."

"They're the national apology for indolence. Training a penniless boy to be one of them is nearly as bad as an

education in a thieves' den; he will be just as much at war
with society, if not game for the police."

"Vernon, have you seen Crossjay's father, the now Captain of Marines? I think you have."

"He's a good man and a very gallant officer."

"And in spite of his qualities he's a cub, and an old
cub. He is a captain now, but he takes that rank very
late, you will own. There you have what you call a good
man, undoubtedly a gallant officer, neutralized by the
fact that he is not a gentleman. Holding intercourse
with him is out of the question. No wonder Government
declines to advance him rapidly. Young Crossjay does
not bear your name. He bears mine, and on that point
alone I should have a voice in the settlement of his career.
And I say emphatically that a drawing-room approval
of a young man is the best certificate for his general
chances in life. I know of a City of London merchant of
some sort, and I know a firm of lawyers, who will have
none but University men in their office; at least, they
have the preference."

"Crossjay has a bullet head, fit neither for the University nor the drawing-room," said Vernon; "equal to fighting and dying for you, and that's all."

Sir Willoughby contented himself with replying, "The
lad is a favourite of mine."

His anxiety to escape a rejoinder caused him to step
into the garden, leaving Clara behind him. "My love!"
said he, in apology as he turned to her. She could not
look stern, but she had a look without a dimple to soften
it, and her eyes shone. For she had wagered in her heart
that the dialogue she provoked upon Crossjay would expose
the Egoist. And there were other motives, wrapped up
and intertwisted, unrecognizable, sufficient to strike her
with worse than the flush of her self-knowledge of wickedness when she detained him to speak of Crossjay before
Vernon.

At last it had been seen that she was conscious of
suffering in her association with this Egoist! Vernon
stood for the world taken into her confidence. The world,
then, would not think so ill of her, she thought hopefully,
at the same time that she thought most evilly of herself.
But self-accusations were for the day of reckoning; she
would and must have the world with her, or the belief
that it was coming to her, in the terrible struggle she foresaw within her horizon of self, now her utter boundary.
She needed it for the inevitable conflict. Little sacrifices
of her honesty might be made. Considering how weak she
was, how solitary, how dismally entangled, daily disgraced
beyond the power of any veiling to conceal from her fiery
sensations, a little hypocrisy was a poor girl's natural
weapon. She crushed her conscientious mind with the
assurance that it was magnifying trifles: not entirely

unaware that she was magnifying trifles: not entirely
unaware that she was thereby preparing it for a convenient
blindness in the presence of dread alternatives; but the
pride of laying such stress on small sins gave her purity
a blush of pleasure and overcame the inner warning. In
truth she dared not think evilly of herself for long, sailing into battle as she was. Nuns and anchorites may;
they have leisure. She regretted the forfeits she had to
pay for self-assistance and, if it might be won, the world's;
regretted, felt the peril of the loss, and took them up and
flung them.

"You see, old Vernon has no argument," Willoughby
said to her.

He drew her hand more securely on his arm, to make
her sensible that she leaned on a pillar of strength.

"Whenever the little brain is in doubt, perplexed,
undecided which course to adopt, she will come to me,
will she not? I shall always listen," he resumed soothingly. "My own! and I to you when the world vexes me.
So we round our completeness. You will know me; you
will know me in good time. I am not a mystery to those
to whom I unfold myself. I do not pretend to mystery:
yet, I will confess, your home — your heart's — Willoughby
is not exactly identical with the Willoughby before the
world. One must be armed against that rough beast."

Certain is the vengeance of the young upon monotony;
nothing more certain. They do not scheme it, but sameness
is a poison to their systems; and vengeance is their heartier
breathing, their stretch of the limbs, run in the fields;
nature avenges them.

"When does Colonel De Craye arrive?" said Clara.

"Horace? In two or three days. You wish him to be
on the spot to learn his part, my love?"

She had not flown forward to the thought of Colonel De
Craye's arrival; she knew not why she had mentioned
him; but now she flew back, shocked, first into shadowy
subterfuge, and then into the criminal's dock.

"I do not wish him to be here. I do not know that he
has a part to learn. I have no wish. Willoughby, did
you not say I should come to you and you would listen? —
will you listen? I am so commonplace that I shall not be
understood by you unless you take my words for the very
meaning of the words. I am unworthy. I am volatile.
I love my liberty. I want to be free . . ."

"Flitch!" he called.

It sounded necromantic.

"Pardon me, my love," he said. "The man you see
yonder violates my express injunction that he is not to
come on my grounds, and here I find him on the borders
of my garden!"

Sir Willoughby waved his hand to the abject figure of a
man standing to intercept him.

"Volatile, unworthy, liberty — my dearest!" he bent to her when the man had appeased him by departing, "you are at liberty within the law, like all good women; I shall control and direct your volatility; and your sense of worthiness must be re-established when we are more intimate; it is timidity. The sense of unworthiness is a guarantee of worthiness ensuing. I believe I am in the vein of a sermon! Whose the fault? The sight of that man was annoying.[1] Flitch was a stable-boy, groom, and coachman, like his father before him, at the Hall thirty years; his father died in our service. Mr. Flitch had not a single grievance here; only one day the demon seizes him with the notion of bettering himself, he wants his independence, and he presents himself to me with a story of a shop in our county town. — Flitch! remember, if you go you go for good. — Oh! he quite comprehended. — Very well; good-bye, Flitch; — The man was respectful: he looked the fool he was very soon to turn out to be. Since then, within a period of several years, I have had him, against my express injunctions, ten times on my grounds. It's curious to calculate. Of course the shop failed, and Flitch's independence consists in walking about with his hands in his empty pockets, and looking at the Hall from some elevation near."

"Is he married? Has he children?" said Clara.

"Nine; and a wife that cannot cook or sew or wash linen."

"You could not give him employment?"

"After his having dismissed himself?"

"It might be overlooked."

"Here he was happy. He decided to go elsewhere, to be free — of course, of my yoke. He quitted my service against my warning. Flitch, we will say, emigrated with his wife and nine children, and the ship foundered. He returns, but his place is filled; he is a ghost here, and I object to ghosts."

"Some work might be found for him."

"It will be the same with old Vernon, my dear. If he goes, he goes for good. It is the vital principle of my authority to insist on that. A dead leaf might as reasonably demand to return to the tree. Once off, off for all eternity! I am sorry, but such was your decision, my friend. I have, you see, Clara, elements in me —"

"Dreadful!"

"Exert your persuasive powers with Vernon. You can do well-nigh what you will with the old fellow. We have

---

1. "that man": Flitch, the banished coachman. His name means literally "a side of bacon, generally smoked," but he is also (unbeknownst to anyone) an emblem of domestic content. The Dunmow Flitch is awarded annually, in that Essex village, to the couple who will take an oath that they have lived through the year without strife. The custom, begun in the thirteenth century and long discontinued, had just been revived in 1855: Meredith specifically alludes to it in Chapter 18.

Miss Dale this evening for a week or two. Lead him to
some ideas of her. — Elements in me, I was remarking,
which will no more bear to be handled carelessly than
gunpowder. At the same time, there is no reason why
they should not be respected, managed with some degree
of regard for me and attention to consequences. Those
who have not done so have repented."

"You do not speak to others of the elements in you,"
said Clara.

"I certainly do not: I have but one bride," was his
handsome reply.

"Is it fair to me that you should show me the worst of
you?"

"All myself, my own?"

His ingratiating droop and familiar smile rendered
"All myself" so affectionately meaningful in its happy
reliance upon her excess of love, that at last she understood she was expected to worship him and uphold him for
whatsoever he might be, without any estimation of qualities: as indeed love does, or young love does: as she perhaps did once, before he chilled her senses. That was
before her "little brain" had become active and had turned
her senses to revolt.

It was on the full river of love that Sir Willoughby
supposed the whole floating bulk of his personality to be
securely sustained; and therefore it was that, believing
himself swimming at his ease, he discoursed of himself.

She went straight away from that idea with her mental
exclamation: "Why does he not paint himself in brighter
colours to me!" and the question: "Has he no ideal of
generosity and chivalry?"

But the unfortunate gentleman imagined himself to be
loved, on Love's very bosom. He fancied that everything
relating to himself excited maidenly curiosity, womanly
reverence, ardours to know more of him, which he was
ever willing to satisfy by repeating the same things. His
notion of women was the primitive black and white: there
are good women, bad women; and he possessed a good one.
His high opinion of himself fortified the belief that Providence, as a matter of justice and fitness, must necessarily
select a good one for him — or what are we to think of
Providence? And this female, shaped by that informing
hand, would naturally be in harmony with him, from the
centre of his profound identity to the raying circle of his
variations. Know the centre, you know the circle, and
you discover that the variations are simply characteristics,
but you must travel on the rays from the circle to get to
the centre. Consequently Sir Willoughby put Miss Middleton on one or other of these converging lines from time
to time. Us, too, he drags into the deeps, but when we
have harpooned a whale and are attached to the rope, down
we must go; the miracle is to see us rise again.

Women of mixed essences shading off the divine to the considerably lower, were outside his vision of woman. His mind could as little admit an angel in pottery as a rogue in porcelain. For him they were what they were when fashioned at the beginning; many cracked, many stained, here and there a perfect specimen designed for the elect of men. At a whisper of the world he shut the prude's door on them with a slam; himself would have branded them with the letters in the hue of fire. Privately he did so: and he was constituted by his extreme sensitiveness and taste for ultra-feminine refinement to be a severe critic of them during the carnival of egoism, the love-season. Constantia . . . can it be told? She had been, be it said, a fair and frank young merchant with him in that season; she was of a nature to be a mother of heroes; she met the salute, almost half-way, ingenuously unlike the coming mothers of the regiments of marionnettes, who retire in vapours, downcast, as by convention; ladies most flattering to the egoistical gentleman, for they proclaim him the "first." Constantia's offence had been no greater, but it was not that dramatic performance of purity which he desired of an affianced lady, and so the offence was great.

The love-season is the carnival of egoism, and it brings the touchstone to our natures. I speak of love, not the mask, and not of the flutings upon the theme of love, but of the passion; a flame having, like our mortality, death in it as well as life, that may or may not be lasting. Applied to Sir Willoughby, as to thousands of civilized males, the touchstone found him requiring to be dealt with by his betrothed as an original savage. She was required to play incessantly on the first reclaiming chord which led our ancestral satyr to the measures of the dance, the threading of the maze, and the setting conformably to his partner before it was accorded to him to spin her with both hands and a chirrup of his frisky heels. To keep him in awe and hold him enchained, there are things she must never do, dare never say, must not think. She must be cloistral. Now, strange and awful though it be to hear, women perceive this requirement of them in the spirit of the man; they perceive, too, and it may be gratefully, that they address their performances less to the taming of the green and prankish monsieur of the forest than to the pacification of a voracious æsthetic gluttony, craving them insatiably, through all the tenses, with shrieks of the lamentable letter "I" for their purity. Whether they see that it has its foundation in the sensual, and distinguish the ultra-refined but lineally great-grandson of the Hoof in this vast and dainty exacting appetite is uncertain.[2] They probably do not; the more the damage; for in the

---

2. Satyrs have goat-feet; modern gentlemen, though nicely shod, are satyrs at heart.

appeasement of the glutton they have to practise much
simulation; they are in their way losers like their ancient
mothers. It is the palpable and material of them still
which they are tempted to flourish wherewith to invite and
allay pursuit: a condition under which the spiritual,
wherein their hope lies, languishes. The capaciously
strong in soul among women will ultimately detect an
infinite grossness in the demand for purity infinite, spot-
less bloom. Earlier or later they see they have been victims of the singular Egoist, have worn a mask of ignorance
to be named innocent, have turned themselves into market
produce for his delight, and have really abandoned the
commodity in ministering to the lust for it, suffered
themselves to be dragged ages back in playing upon the
fleshly innocence of happy accident to gratify his jealous
greed of possession. when it should have been their task
to set the soul above the fairest fortune, and the gift of
strength in women beyond ornamental whiteness. Are
they not of a nature warriors, like men? — men's mates
to bear them heroes instead of puppets? But the devouring male Egoist prefers them as inanimate overwrought
polished pure-metal precious vessels, fresh from the hands
of the artificer, for him to walk away with hugging, call
all his own, drink of, and fill and drink of, and forget
that he stole them.

This running off on a by-road is no deviation from Sir
Willoughby Patterne and Miss Clara Middleton. He, a
fairly intelligent man, and very sensitive, was blinded to
what was going on within her visibly enough, by her pro-
duction of the article he demanded of her sex. He had to
leave the fair young lady to ride to his county-town, and
his design was to conduct her through the covert of a group
of laurels, there to revel in her soft confusion. She resisted; nay, resolutely returned to the lawn-sward. He
contrasted her with Constantia in the amorous time, and
rejoiced in his disappointment. He saw the Goddess
Modesty guarding Purity; and one would be bold to say
that he did not hear the Precepts, Purity's aged grannams
maternal and paternal, cawing approval of her over their
munching gums.[3] And if you ask whether a man, sensitive
and a lover, can be so blinded, you are condemned to re-
peruse the foregoing paragraph.

Miss Middleton was not sufficiently instructed in the
position of her sex to know that she had plunged herself
in the thick of the strife of one of their great battles.
Her personal position, however, was instilling knowledge
rapidly, as a disease in the frame teaches us what we are
and have to contend with. Could she marry this man?
He was evidently manageable. Could she condescend

admits his own philosophizing

---

3. "The Precepts" are the old and tired
forms of correct conduct for young girls.
Where Willoughby thinks her passionately chaste, she is only pretending conventionality as a mask for dislike.

to the use of arts in managing him to obtain a placable
life ? — a horror of swampy flatness! So vividly did the
sight of that dead heaven over an unvarying level earth,
swim on her fancy, that she shut her eyes in angry exclu-
sion of it as if it were outside, assailing her: and she
nearly stumbled upon young Crossjay.

"Oh! have I hurt you ?" he cried.

"No," said she, "it was my fault. Lead me somewhere,
away from everybody."

The boy took her hand, and she resumed her thoughts;
and, pressing his fingers and feeling warm to him both for
his presence and silence, so does the blood in youth lead
the mind, even cool and innocent blood, even with a touch,
that she said to herself: "And if I marry, and then . . .
Where will honour be then ? I marry him to be true to my
word of honour, and if then! . . ." An intolerable languor caused her to sigh profoundly. It is written as she
thought it; she thought in blanks, as girls do, and some
women. A shadow of the male Egoist is in the chamber
of their brains overawing them.

"Were I to marry, and to run!" There is the thought;
she is offered up to your mercy. We are dealing with
a girl feeling herself desperately situated, and not a
fool.

"I'm sure you're dead tired, though," said Crossjay.

"No, I am not; what makes you think so ?" said Clara.

"I do think so."

"But why do you think so ?"

"You're so hot."

"What makes you think that ?"

"You're so red."

"So are you, Crossjay."

"I'm only red in the middle of the cheeks, except when
I've been running. And then you talk to yourself, just
as boys do when they are blown."

"Do they ?"

"They say, ' I know I could have kept up longer,' or,
' my buckle broke,' all to themselves, when they break
down running."

"And you have noticed that ?"

"And, Miss Middleton, I don't wish you were a boy, but
I should like to live near you all my life and be a gentleman. I'm coming with Miss Dale this evening to stay at
the Hall and be looked after, instead of stopping with her
cousin who takes care of her father. Perhaps you and I'll
play chess at night."

"At night you will go to bed, Crossjay."

"Not if I have Sir Willoughby to catch hold of. He
says I'm an authority on birds' eggs. I can manage rabbits and poultry. Is n't a farmer a happy man? But he
does n't marry ladies. A cavalry officer has the best
chance."

"But you are going to be a naval officer."

"I don't know. It's not positive. I shall bring my two dormice, and make them perform gymnastics on the dinner-table. They're such dear little things. Naval officers are not like Sir Willoughby."

"No, they are not," said Clara; "they give their lives to their country."

"And then they're dead," said Crossjay.

Clara wished Sir Willoughby were confronting her: she could have spoken.

She asked the boy where Mr. Whitford was. Crossjay pointed very secretly in the direction of the double-blossom wild-cherry. Coming within gaze of the stem she beheld Vernon stretched at length, reading, she supposed; asleep, she discovered: his finger in the leaves of a book; and what book? She had a curiosity to know the title of the book he would read beneath these boughs, and grasping Crossjay's hand fast she craned her neck, as one timorous of a fall in peeping over chasms, for a glimpse of the page; but immediately, and still with a bent head, she turned her face to where the load of virginal blossom, whiter than summer-cloud on the sky, showered and drooped and clustered so thick as to claim colour and seem, like higher Alpine snows in noon-sunlight, a flush of white. From deep to deeper heavens of white, her eyes perched and soared. Wonder lived in her. Happiness in the beauty of the tree pressed to supplant it, and was more mortal and narrower. Reflection came, contracting her vision and weighing her to earth. Her reflection was: "He must be good who loves to lie and sleep beneath the branches of this tree!" She would rather have clung to her first impression: wonder so divine, so unbounded, was like soaring into homes of angel-crowded space, sweeping through folded and on to folded white fountain-bow of wings, in innumerable columns: but the thought of it was no recovery of it; she might as well have striven to be a child. The sensation of happiness promised to be less short-lived in memory, and would have been, had not her present disease of the longing for happiness ravaged every corner of it for the secret of its existence. The reflection took root. "He must be good! . . ." That reflection vowed to endure. Poor by comparison with what it displaced, it presented itself to her as conferring something on him, and she would not have had it absent though it robbed her.

She looked down. Vernon was dreamily looking up.

She plucked Crossjay hurriedly away, whispering that he had better not wake Mr. Whitford, and then she proposed to reverse their previous chase, and she be the hound and he the hare. Crossjay fetched a magnificent start. On his glancing behind he saw Miss Middleton walking listlessly, with a hand at her side.

"There's a regular girl!" said he, in some disgust; for his theory was, that girls always have something the matter with them to spoil a game.

CHAPTER 12

MISS MIDDLETON AND MR. VERNON WHITFORD

LOOKING upward, not quite awakened out of a transient doze, at a fair head circled in dazzling blossom, one may temporize awhile with common sense, and take it for a vision after the eyes have regained direction of the mind. Vernon did so until the plastic vision interwound with reality alarmingly. This is the embrace of a Melusine who will soon have the brain if she is encouraged.[1] Slight dalliance with her makes the very diminutive seem as big as life. He jumped to his feet, rattled his throat, planted firmness on his brows and mouth, and attacked the dream-giving earth with tremendous long strides, that his blood might be lively at the throne of understanding. Miss Middleton and young Crossjay were within hail: it was her face he had seen, and still the idea of a vision, chased from his reasonable wits, knocked hard and again for readmission. There was little for a man of humble mind toward the sex to think of in the fact of a young lady's bending rather low to peep at him asleep, except that the poise of her slender figure, between an air of spying and of listening, vividly recalled his likening of her to the Mountain Echo. Man or maid sleeping in the open air provokes your tip-toe curiosity. Men, it is known, have in that state cruelly been kissed; and no rights are bestowed on them, they are teased by a vapourish rapture; what has happened to them the poor fellows barely divine: they have a crazy step from that day. But a vision is not so distracting; it is our own, we can put it aside and return to it, play at rich and poor with it, and are not to be summoned before your laws and rules for secreting it in our treasury. Besides, it is the golden key of all the possible: new worlds expand beneath the dawn it brings us. Just outside reality, it illumines, enriches, and softens real things; — and to desire it in preference to the simple fact, is a damning proof of enervation.

Such was Vernon's winding up of his brief drama of fantasy. He was aware of the fantastical element in him and soon had it under. Which of us who is of any worth is without it? He had not much vanity to trouble him, and passion was quiet, so his task was not gigantic. Especially be it remarked, that he was a man of quick

---

1. Melusine is the water-sprite of French legend, like Undine among the Germans.

pace, the sovereign remedy for the dispersing of the mental fen-mist. He had tried it and knew that nonsense is to be walked off.

Near the end of the park young Crossjay overtook him, and after acting the pumped one a trifle more than needful, cried: "I say, Mr. Whitford, there's Miss Middleton with her handkerchief out."

"What for, my lad?" said Vernon.

"I'm sure I don't know. All of a sudden she bumped down. And, look what fellows girls are!—here she comes as if nothing had happened, and I saw her feel at her side."

Clara was shaking her head to express a denial. "I am not at all unwell," she said when she came near. "I guessed Crossjay's business in running up to you; he's a good-for-nothing, officious boy. I was tired, and rested for a moment."

Crossjay peered at her eyelids. Vernon looked away and said: "Are you too tired for a stroll?"

"Not now."

"Shall it be brisk?"

"You have the lead."

He led at a swing of the legs that accelerated young Crossjay's to the double, but she with her short swift equal steps glided along easily on a line by his shoulder, and he groaned to think that of all the girls of earth this one should have been chosen for the position of fine lady.

"You won't tire me," said she, in answer to his look.

"You remind me of the little Piedmontese Bersaglieri on the march."[2]

"I have seen them trotting into Como from Milan."

"They cover a quantity of ground in a day, if the ground's flat. You want another sort of step for the mountains."

"I should not attempt to dance up."

"They soon tame romantic notions of them."

"The mountains tame luxurious dreams, you mean. I see how they are conquered. I can plod. Anything to be high up!"

"Well, there you have the secret of good work: to plod on and still keep the passion fresh."

"Yes, when we have an aim in view."

"We always have one."

"Captives have?"

"More than the rest of us."

Ignorant man! What of wives miserably wedded? What aim in view have these most woeful captives? Horror shrouds it, and shame reddens through the folds to tell of innermost horror.

"Take me back to the mountains, if you please, Mr. Whitford," Miss Middleton said, fallen out of sympathy

2. "Piedmontese Bersaglieri": picked infantrymen of Northern Italy.

with him. "Captives have death in view, but that is not
an aim."

"Why may not captives expect a release?"

"Hardly from a tyrant."

"If you are thinking of tyrants, it may be so. Say the
tyrant dies?"

"The prison-gates are unlocked and out comes a skeleton. But why will you talk of skeletons! The very
name of mountain seems life in comparison with any other
subject."

"I assure you," said Vernon, with the fervour of a man
lighting on an actual truth in his conversation with a
young lady, "it's not the first time I have thought you
would be at home in the Alps. You would walk and
climb as well as you dance."

She liked to hear Clara Middleton talked of, and of her
having been thought of: and giving him friendly eyes,
barely noticing that he was in a glow, she said, "If you
speak so encouragingly I shall fancy we are near an
ascent."

"I wish we were," said he.

"We can realize it by dwelling on it, don't you think?"

"We can begin climbing."

"Oh!" she squeezed herself shadowily.

"Which mountain shall it be?" said Vernon in the
right real earnest tone.

Miss Middleton suggested a lady's mountain first, for
a trial. "And then, if you think well enough of me — if
I have not stumbled more than twice, or asked more than
ten times how far it is from the top, I should like to be
promoted to scale a giant."

They went up some of the lesser heights of Switzerland
and Styria, and settled in South Tyrol, the young lady
preferring this district for the strenuous exercise of her
climbing powers because she loved Italian colour; and it
seemed an exceedingly good reason to the genial imagination she had awakened in Mr. Whitford: "Though," said
he abruptly, "you are not so much Italian as French."[3]

She hoped she was English, she remarked.

"Of course you are English; . . . yes." He moderated
his assent with the halting affirmative.

She inquired wonderingly why he spoke in apparent
hesitation.

"Well, you have French feet, for example: French wits;
French impatience," he lowered his voice, "and charm."

"And love of compliments."

"Possibly. I was not conscious of paying them."

"And a disposition to rebel?"

"To challenge authority, at least."

"That is a dreadful character."

"At all events it is a character."

3. "Styria": a province of Austria.

"Fit for an Alpine comrade?"

"For the best of comrades anywhere."

"It is not a piece of drawing-room sculpture: that is the most one can say for it!" she dropped a dramatic sigh.

Had he been willing she would have continued the theme, for the pleasure a poor creature long gnawing her sensations finds in seeing herself from the outside. It fell away. After a silence, she could not renew it: and he was evidently indifferent, having to his own satisfaction dissected and stamped her a foreigner. With it passed her holiday. She had forgotten Sir Willoughby: she remembered him and said, "You knew Miss Durham, Mr. Whitford."

He answered briefly, "I did."

"Was she . . .?" some hot-faced inquiry peered forth and withdrew.

"Very handsome," said Vernon.

"English?"

"Yes: the dashing style of English."

"Very courageous."

"I daresay she had a kind of courage."

"She did very wrong."

"I won't say no. She discovered a man more of a match with herself; luckily not too late. We're at the mercy . . ."

"Was she not unpardonable?"

"I should be sorry to think that of any one."

"But you agree that she did wrong."

"I suppose I do. She made a mistake and she corrected it. If she had not, she would have made a greater mistake."

"The manner . . ."

"That was bad — as far as we know. The world has not much right to judge. A false start must now and then be made. It's better not to take notice of it, I think."

"What is it we are at the mercy of?"

"Currents of feeling, our natures. I am the last man to preach on the subject: young ladies are enigmas to me; I fancy they must have a natural perception of the husband suitable to them, and the reverse; and if they have a certain degree of courage, it follows that they please themselves."

"They are not to reflect on the harm they do?" said Miss Middleton.

"By all means let them reflect; they hurt nobody by doing that."

"But a breach of faith!"

"If the faith can be kept through life, all's well."

"And then there is the cruelty, the injury!"

"I really think that if a young lady came to me to inform me she must break our engagement — I have never been put to the proof, but to suppose it: — I should not think her cruel."

"Then she would not be much of a loss."

"And I should not think so for this reason, that it is impossible for a girl to come to such a resolution without previously showing signs of it to her . . . the man she is engaged to. I think it unfair to engage a girl for longer than a week or two, just time enough for her preparations and publications."

"If he is always intent on himself, signs are likely to be unheeded by him," said Miss Middleton.

He did not answer, and she said quickly, —

"It must always be a cruelty. The world will think so. It is an act of inconstancy."

"If they knew one another well before they were engaged."

"Are you not singularly tolerant?" said she.

To which Vernon replied with airy cordiality, —

"In some cases it is right to judge by results; we 'll leave severity to the historian, who is bound to be a professional moralist and put pleas of human nature out of the scales. The lady in question may have been to blame, but no hearts were broken, and here we have four happy instead of two miserable."

His persecuting geniality of countenance appealed to her to confirm this judgement by results, and she nodded and said, "Four," as the awe-stricken speak.

From that moment until young Crossjay fell into the green-rutted lane from a tree, and was got on his legs half-stunned, with a hanging lip and a face like the inside of a flayed eel-skin, she might have been walking in the desert, and alone, for the pleasure she had in society.

They led the fated lad home between them, singularly drawn together by their joint ministrations to him, in which her delicacy had to stand fire, and sweet good nature made naught of any trial. They were hand in hand with the little fellow as physician and professional nurse.

CHAPTER 13

THE FIRST EFFORT AFTER FREEDOM

Crossjay's accident was only another proof, as Vernon told Miss Dale, that the boy was but half monkey.

"Something fresh?" she exclaimed on seeing him brought into the Hall, where she had just arrived.

"Simply a continuation," said Vernon. "He is not so prehensile as he should be. He probably in extremity relies on the tail that has been docked. Are you a man, Crossjay ?"

"I should think I was!" Crossjay replied with an old man's voice, and a ghastly twitch for a smile overwhelmed the compassionate ladies.

Miss Dale took possession of him. "You err in the other direction," she remarked to Vernon.

"But a little bracing roughness is better than spoiling him," said Miss Middleton.

She did not receive an answer, and she thought, "Whatever Willoughby does is right, to this lady !"

Clara's impression was renewed when Sir Willoughby sat beside Miss Dale in the evening; and certainly she had never seen him shine so picturesquely as in his bearing with Miss Dale. The sprightly sallies of the two, their rallyings, their laughter, and her fine eyes, and his handsome gestures, won attention like a fencing match of a couple keen with the foils to display the mutual skill. And it was his design that she should admire the display; he was anything but obtuse; enjoying the match as he did and necessarily did to act so excellent a part in it, he meant the observer to see the man he was with a lady not of raw understanding. So it went on from day to day for three days.

She fancied once that she detected the agreeable stirring of the brood of jealousy, and found it neither in her heart nor in her mind, but in the book of wishes, well known to the young, where they write matter which may sometimes be independent of both those volcanic albums. Jealousy would have been a relief to her, a dear devil's aid. She studied the complexion of jealousy to delude herself with the sense of the spirit being in her, and all the while she laughed, as at a vile theatre whereof the imperfection of the stage machinery rather than the performance is the wretched source of amusement.

Vernon had deeply depressed her. She was hunted by the figure 4. *Four happy instead of two miserable.* He had said it, involving her among the four; and so it must be, she considered, and she must be as happy as she could; for not only was he incapable of perceiving her state, he was unable to imagine other circumstances to surround her. How, to be just to him, were they imaginable by him or any one ?

Her horrible isolation of secresy in a world amiable in unsuspectingness, frightened her. To fling away her secret, to conform, to be unrebellious, uncritical, submissive, became an impatient desire; and the task did not appear so difficult since Miss Dale's arrival. Endearments had been rarer, more formal; living bodily untroubled and unashamed, and, as she phrased it, having no one to care for her, she turned insensibly in the direction where she was due; she slightly imitated Miss Dale's colloquial

responsiveness. To tell truth, she felt vivacious in a
moderate way with Willoughby after seeing him with
Miss Dale. Liberty wore the aspect of a towering prison-
wall; the desperate undertaking of climbing one side and
dropping to the other was more than she, unaided, could
resolve on; consequently, as no one cared for her, a
worthless creature might as well cease dreaming and stipulating for the fulfilment of her dreams; she might as well
yield to her fate: nay, make the best of it.

Sir Willoughby was flattered and satisfied. Clara's
adopted vivacity proved his thorough knowledge of feminine nature; nor did her feebleness in sustaining it dis-
please him. A steady look of hers had of late perplexed
the man, and he was comforted by signs of her inefficiency
where he excelled. The effort and the failure were both
of good omen.

But she could not continue the effort. He had over-
weighted her too much for the mimicry of a sentiment to
harden and have an apparently natural place among her
impulses; and now an idea came to her that he might, it
might be hoped, possibly see in Miss Dale, by present
contrast, the mate he sought; by contrast with an unan-
swering creature like herself, he might perhaps realize
in Miss Dale's greater accomplishments and her devotion
to him the merit of suitability; he might be induced to do
her justice. Dim as the loophole was, Clara fixed her
mind on it till it gathered light. And as a prelude to
action, she plunged herself into a state of such profound
humility, that to accuse it of being simulated would be
venturesome, though it was not positive. The tempers of
the young are liquid fires in isles of quicksand; the precious metals not yet cooled in a solid earth. Her compassion for Lætitia was less forced; but really she was almost
as earnest in her self-abasement, for she had not latterly
been brilliant, not even adequate to the ordinary require-
ments of conversation. She had no courage, no wit, no
diligence, nothing that she could distinguish save discontentment like a corroding acid, and she went so far in
sincerity as with a curious shift of feeling to pity the man
plighted to her. If it suited her purpose to pity Sir Willoughby, she was not moved by policy, be assured; her
needs were her nature, her moods her mind; she had the
capacity to make anything serve her by passing into it
with the glance which discerned its usefulness; and this
is how it is that the young, when they are in trouble,
without approaching the elevation of scientific hypocrites,
can teach that able class lessons in hypocrisy.

"Why should not Willoughby be happy?" she said; and
the explanation was pushed forth by the second thought:
"Then I shall be free!" Still that thought came second.

The desire for the happiness of Willoughby was fervent
on his behalf, and wafted her far from friends and letters
to a narrow Tyrolean valley, where a shallow river ran,

with the indentations of a remotely-seen army of winding ranks in column, topaz over the pebbles, to hollows of ravishing emerald. There sat Liberty, after her fearful leap over the prison-wall, at peace to watch the water and the falls of sunshine on the mountain above, between descending pine-stem shadows. Clara's wish for his happiness, as soon as she had housed herself in the imagination of her freedom, was of a purity that made it seem exceedingly easy for her to speak to him.

The opportunity was offered by Sir Willoughby. Every morning after breakfast, Miss Dale walked across the park to see her father, and on this occasion Sir Willoughby and Miss Middleton went with her as far as the lake, all three discoursing of the beauty of various trees, birches, aspens, poplars, beeches, then in their new green. Miss Dale loved the aspen, Miss Middleton the beech, Sir Willoughby the birch, and pretty things were said by each in praise of the favoured object, particularly by Miss Dale. So much so that when she had gone on he recalled one of her remarks, and said: "I believe, if the whole place were swept away to-morrow, Lætitia Dale could reconstruct it, and put those aspens on the north of the lake in number and situation correctly where you have them now. I would guarantee her description of it in absence correct."

"Why should she be absent?" said Clara, palpitating.

"Well, why!" returned Sir Willoughby. "As you say, there is no reason why. The art of life, and mine will be principally a country life — town is not life, but a tornado whirling atoms — the art is to associate a group of sympathetic friends in our neighbourhood; and it is a fact worth noting that if ever I feel tired of the place, a short talk with Lætitia Dale refreshes it more than a month or two on the Continent. She has the well of enthusiasm. And there is a great advantage in having a cultivated person at command, with whom one can chat of any topic under the sun. I repeat, you have no need of town if you have friends like Lætitia Dale within call. My mother esteemed her highly."

"Willoughby, she is not obliged to go."

"I hope not. And, my love, I rejoice that you have taken to her. Her father's health is poor. She would be a young spinster to live alone in a country cottage."

"What of your scheme?"

"Old Vernon is a very foolish fellow."

"He has declined?"

"Not a word on the subject! I have only to propose it to be snubbed, I know."

"You may not be aware how you throw him into the shade with her."

"Nothing seems to teach him the art of dialogue with ladies."

"Are not gentlemen shy when they see themselves outshone ? "

" He has n't it, my love : Vernon is deficient in the lady's
tongue."

" I respect him for that."

" Outshone, you say ? I do not know of any shining —
save to one, who lights me, path and person ! "

The identity of the one was conveyed to her in a bow and
a soft pressure.

" Not only has he not the lady's tongue, which I hold to
be a man's proper accomplishment," continued Sir Willoughby, " he cannot turn his advantages to account. Here
has Miss Dale been with him now four days in the house.
They are exactly on the same footing as when she entered it.
You ask ? I will tell you. It is this : it is want of warmth.
Old Vernon is a scholar — and a fish. Well, perhaps he has
cause to be shy of matrimony : but he is a fish."

" You are reconciled to his leaving you ? "

" False alarm ! The resolution to do anything unaccustomed is quite beyond old Vernon."

" But if Mr. Oxford — Whitford . . . your swans coming
sailing up the lake, how beautiful they look when they are
indignant ! I was going to ask you, surely men witnessing
a marked admiration for some one else will naturally be
discouraged ? "

Sir Willoughby stiffened with sudden enlightenment.
Though the word jealousy had not been spoken, the drift of
her observations was clear. · Smiling inwardly, he said, and
the sentences were not enigmas to her : " Surely, too, young
ladies . . . a little ? — Too far ? But an old friendship !
About the same as the fitting of an old glove to a hand.
Hand and glove have only to meet. Where there is natural
harmony you would not have discord. Ay, but you have it
if you check the harmony. My dear girl ! You child ! "

He had actually, in this parabolic and commendable
obscureness, for which she thanked him in her soul, struck
the very point she had not named and did not wish to hear
named, but wished him to strike. His exultation, of the
compressed sort, was extreme, on hearing her cry out, —

" Young ladies may be. Oh ! not I, not I. I can convince you. Not that. Believe me, Willoughby. I do not
know what it is to feel that, or anything like it. I cannot
conceive a claim on any one's life — as a claim : or the continuation of an engagement not founded on perfect, *perfect*
sympathy. How should I feel it, then ? It is, as you say
of Mr. Ox — Whitford, beyond me."

Sir Willoughby caught up the Ox — Whitford.

Bursting with laughter in his joyful pride, he called it a
portrait of old Vernon in society. For she thought a trifle
too highly of Vernon, as here and there a raw young lady
does think of the friends of her plighted man : which is
waste of substance properly belonging to him : as it were,
in the loftier sense, an expenditure in genuflexions to way-

side idols of the reverence she should bring intact to the
temple. Derision instructs her.

Of the other subject — her jealousy — he had no desire to
hear more. She had winced : the woman had been touched
to smarting in the girl : enough. She attempted the subject
once, but faintly, and his careless parrying threw her out.
Clara could have bitten her tongue for that reiterated stupid
slip on the name of Whitford ; and because she was innocent
at heart she persisted in asking herself how she could be
guilty of it.

" You both know the botanic titles of these wild-flowers,"
she said.

"Who ?" he inquired.

"You and Miss Dale."

Sir Willoughby shrugged. He was amused. *non sequitur*

"No woman on earth will grace a barouche so exquisitely
as my Clara!"[1]

"Where ?" said she.

"During our annual two months in London. I drive a
barouche there, and venture to prophecy that my equipage
will create the greatest excitement of any in London. I see
old Horace De Craye gazing!"

She sighed. She could not drag him to the word, or a
hint of it necessary to her subject.

But there it was ; she saw it. She had nearly let it go,
and blushed at being obliged to name it.

" Jealousy, do you mean, Willoughby ? the people in
London would be jealous ? — Colonel De Craye ? How
strange ! That is a sentiment I cannot understand."

Sir Willoughby gesticulated the " Of course not " of an
established assurance to the contrary.

" Indeed, Willoughby, I do not."

"Certainly not."

He was now in her trap. And he was imagining himself
to be anatomizing her feminine nature.

" Can I give you a proof, Willoughby ? I am so utterly
incapable of it that — listen to me — were you to come to me
to tell me, as you might, how much better suited to you
Miss Dale has appeared than I am — and I fear I am not ; it
should be spoken plainly ; unsuited altogether, perhaps — I
would, I beseech you to believe — you must believe me — give
you . . . give you your freedom instantly ; most truly ; and
engage to speak of you as I should think of you. Willoughby, you would have no one to praise you in public
and in private as I should, for you would be to me the most
honest, truthful, chivalrous gentleman alive. And in that
case I would undertake to declare that she would not admire
you more than I : Miss Dale would not ; she would not
admire you more than I ; not even Miss Dale ! "

This, her first direct leap for liberty, set Clara panting,

1. "grace a barouche": look so well in an open carriage.

and so much had she to say that the nervous and the intellectual halves of her clashed like cymbals, dazing and stunning her with the appositeness of things to be said, and dividing her in indecision as to the cunningest to move him, of the many pressing.

The condition of feminine jealousy stood revealed.

He had driven her farther than he intended.

"Come, let me allay these . . ." he soothed her with hand and voice while seeking for his phrase; "these magnified pin-points. Now, my Clara! on my honour! and when I put it forward in attestation, my honour has the most serious meaning speech can have; ordinarily my word has to suffice for bonds, promises or asseverations: on my honour! not merely is there, my poor child! no ground of suspicion, I assure you, I declare to you, the fact of the case is the very reverse. Now, mark me; of her sentiments I cannot pretend to speak; I did not, to my knowledge, originate, I am not responsible for them, and I am, before the law, as we will say, ignorant of them: that is, I have never heard a declaration of them, and I am, therefore, under pain of the stigma of excessive fatuity, bound to be noncognizant. But as to myself, I can speak for myself, and, on my honour! Clara — to be as direct as possible, even to baldness, and you know I loathe it — I could not, I repeat, *I could not marry Lœtitia Dale!* Let me impress it on you. No flatteries — we are all susceptible more or less — no conceivable condition could bring it about; no amount of admiration. She and I are excellent friends; we cannot be more. When you see us together, the natural concord of our minds is of course misleading. She is a woman of genius. I do not conceal, I profess my admiration of her. There are times when, I confess, I require a Lœtitia Dale to bring me out, give and take. I am indebted to her for the enjoyment of the duet few know, few can accord with, fewer still are allowed the privilege of playing with a human being. I am indebted, I own, and I feel deep gratitude; I own to a lively friendship for Miss Dale, but if she is displeasing in the sight of my bride by . . . by the breadth of an eyelash, then . . ."

Sir Willoughby's arm waved Miss Dale off away into outer darkness in the wilderness.

Clara shut her eyes and rolled her eyeballs in a frenzy of unuttered revolt.

But she was not engaged in the colloquy to be an advocate of Miss Dale or of common humanity.

"Ah!" she said, simply determining that the subject should not drop.

"And, ah!" he mocked her tenderly. "True, though! And who knows better than my Clara that I require youth, health, beauty, and the other undefinable attributes fitting with mine and beseeming the station of the lady called to preside over my household and represent me? What says my other self? my fairer? But you are! my love, you are! Understand my nature rightly, and you . . ."

"I do! I do!" interposed Clara: "if I did not by this time I should be idiotic. Let me assure you, I understand it. Oh! listen to me: one moment. Miss Dale regards me as the happiest woman on earth. Willoughby, if I possessed her good qualities, her heart and mind, no doubt I should be. It is my wish — you must hear me, hear me out — my wish, my earnest wish, my burning prayer, my wish to make way for her. She appreciates you: I do not — to my shame, I do not. She worships you: I do not, I cannot. You are the rising sun to her. It has been so for years. No one can account for love: I daresay not for the impossibility of loving . . . loving where we should; all love bewilders me. I was not created to understand it. But she loves you, she has pined. I believe it has destroyed the health you demand as one item in your list. But you, Willoughby, can restore that. Travelling, and . . . and your society, the pleasure of your society would certainly restore it. You look so handsome together! She has unbounded devotion: as for me I cannot idolize. I see faults; I see them daily. They astonish and wound me. Your pride would not bear to hear them spoken of, least of all by your wife. You warned me to beware — that is, you said, you said something."

Her busy brain missed the subterfuge to cover her slip of the tongue.

Sir Willoughby struck in: "And when I say that the entire concatenation is based on an erroneous observation of facts, and an erroneous deduction from that erroneous observation! — ? No, no. Have confidence in me. I propose it to you in this instance, purely to save you from deception. You are cold, my love? you shivered."

"I am not cold," said Clara. "Some one, I suppose, was walking over my grave."

The gulf of a caress hove in view like an enormous billow hollowing under the curled ridge.

She stooped to a buttercup; the monster swept by.

"Your grave!" he exclaimed over her head; "my own girl!"

"Is not the orchis naturally a stranger in ground so far away from the chalk, Willoughby?"

"I am incompetent to pronounce an opinion on such important matters. My mother had a passion for every description of flower. I fancy I have some recollection of her scattering the flower you mention over the park."

"If she were living now!"

"We should be happy in the blessing of the most estimable of women, my Clara."

"She would have listened to me. She would have realized what I mean."

"Indeed, Clara — poor soul!" he murmured to himself

aloud : " indeed you are absolutely in error. If I have
seemed — but I repeat, you are deceived. The idea of
' fitness ' is a total hallucination. Supposing you — I do it
even in play painfully — entirely out of the way, unthought
of . . . "

" Extinct," Clara said low.

" Non-existent for me," he selected a preferable term.
" Suppose it ; I should still, in spite of an admiration I have
never thought it incumbent on me to conceal, still be — I
speak emphatically — *utterly incapable of the offer of my
hand to Miss Dale.* It may be that she is embedded in my
mind as a friend, and nothing but a friend. I received the
stamp in early youth. People have noticed it — we do, it
seems, bring one another out, reflecting, counter-reflecting "

She glanced up at him with a shrewd satisfaction to see
that her wicked shaft had stuck.

" You do : it is a common remark," she said. " The
instantaneous difference when she comes near, any one
might notice."

" My love," he opened the iron gate into the garden,
" you encourage the naughty little suspicion."

" But it is a beautiful sight, Willoughby. I like to see
you together. I like it as I like to see colours match."

" Very well. There is no harm, then. We shall often be
together. I like my fair friend. But the instant ! — you
have only to express a sentiment of disapprobation."

" And you dismiss her."

" I dismiss her. That is, as to the word, I constitute
myself your echo, to clear any vestige of suspicion. She
goes."

" That is a case of a person doomed to extinction without
offending."

" Not without : for whoever offends my bride, my wife,
my sovereign lady, offends me : very deeply offends me."

" Then the caprices of your wife . . . " Clara stamped
her foot imperceptibly on the lawn-sward, which was irre-
sponsibly soft to her fretfulness. She broke from the
inconsequent meaningless mild tone of irony, and said :
' Willoughby, women have their honour to swear by equally
with men : — girls have : they have to swear an oath at the
altar : may I to you now? Take it for uttered when I tell
you that nothing would make me happier than your union
with Miss Dale. I have spoken as much as I can. Tell
me you release me."

With the well-known screw-smile of duty upholding
weariness worn to inanition, he rejoined : " Allow me once
more to reiterate, that it is repulsive, inconceivable, that I
should *ever, under any mortal conditions, bring myself to the
point of taking Miss Dale for my wife.* You reduce me
to this perfectly childish protestation — pitiably childish !
But, my love, have I to remind you that you and I are
plighted, and that I am an honourable man ? "

" I know it, I feel it, <u>release</u> me ! " cried Clara.

Sir Willoughby severely reprehended his shortsighted-
ness for seeing but the one proximate object in the particular attention he had bestowed on Miss Dale. He could
not disavow that they had been marked, and with an object,
and he was distressed by the unwonted want of wisdom
through which he had been drawn to overshoot his object.
His design to excite a touch of the insane emotion in Clara's
bosom was too successful, and, " I was not thinking of her,"
he said to himself in his candour, contrite.

She cried again: " Will you not, Willoughby ? — release
me ? "

He begged her to take his arm.

To consent to touch him while petitioning for a detachment, appeared discordant to Clara, but, if she expected
him to accede, it was right that she should do as much as
she could, and she surrendered her hand at arm's length,
disdaining the imprisoned fingers. He pressed them and
said: " Dr. Middleton is in the library. I see Vernon is
at work with Crossjay in the West-room — the boy has had
sufficient for the day. Now, is it not like old Vernon to
drive his books at a cracked head before it's half-mended ? "

He signalled to young Crossjay, who was up and out
through the folding windows in a twinkling.

" And you will go in, and talk to Vernon of the lady in
question," Sir Willoughby whispered to Clara. " Use your
best persuasions in our joint names. You have my warrant
for saying that money is no consideration ; house and income
are assured. You can hardly have taken me seriously when
I requested you to undertake Vernon before. I was quite
in earnest then as now. I prepare Miss Dale. I will not
have a wedding on *our* wedding-day : but either before or
after it, I gladly speed their alliance. I think now I give
you the best proof possible ; and though I know that with
women a delusion may be seen to be groundless and still be
cherished, I rely on your good sense."

Vernon was at the window and stood aside for her to
enter. Sir Willoughby used a gentle insistence with her.
She bent her head <u>as if she were stepping into a cave. So</u>
<u>frigid was she, that a ridiculous dread of calling Mr. Whit-</u>
<u>ford Mr. Oxford was her only present anxiety when Sir</u>
<u>Willoughby had closed the window on them.</u>

CHAPTER 14

SIR WILLOUGHBY AND LÆTITIA

"I PREPARE Miss Dale."

Sir Willoughby thought of his promise to Clara. He trifled awhile with young Crossjay, and then sent the boy flying, and wrapped himself in meditation. So shall you see standing many a statue of statesmen who have died in harness for their country.

In the hundred and fourth chapter of the thirteenth volume of the BOOK of EGOISM, it is written: *Possession without obligation to the object possessed approaches felicity.*

It is the rarest condition of ownership. For example: the possession of land is not without obligation both to the soil and the tax-collector; the possession of fine clothing is oppressed by obligation: gold, jewelry, works of art, enviable household furniture, are positive fetters: the possession of a wife we find surcharged with obligation. In all these cases, possession is a gentle term for enslavement, bestowing the sort of felicity attained to by the helot drunk.[1] You can have the joy, the pride, the intoxication of possession: you can have no free soul.

But there is one instance of possession, and that the most perfect, which leaves us free, under not a shadow of obligation, receiving ever, never giving, or if giving, giving only of our waste; as it were (sauf votre respect), by form of perspiration, radiation, if you like; unconscious poral bountifulness; and it is a beneficial process for the system.[2] Our possession of an adoring female's worship is this instance.

The soft cherishable Parsee is hardly at any season other than prostrate.[3] She craves nothing save that you continue in being — her sun: which is your firm constitutional endeavour: and thus you have a most exact alliance; she supplying spirit to your matter, while at the same time presenting matter to your spirit, verily a comfortable apposition. The Gods do bless it.

That they do so indeed is evident in the men they select for such a felicitous crown and aureole. Weak men would be rendered nervous by the flattery of a woman's worship; or they would be for returning it, at least partially, as though it could be bandied to and fro without emulgence of the poetry; or they would be pitiful, and quite spoil the thing.[4] Some would be for transforming the beautiful soli-

---

1. Spartan masters used to get their slaves ("helots") drunk as a lesson for the young against intoxication.
2. "sauf votre respect": "I beg your pardon."

3. "Parsee": here, an Indian devotee; literally, a Zoroastrian of Persian descent living in India.
4. "emulgence": the act of milking out.

tary vestal flame by the first effort of the multiplication-
table into your hearth-fire of slippered affection.[5] So these
men are not they whom the Gods have ever selected, but
rather men of a pattern with themselves, very high and very
solid men, who maintain the crown by holding divinely independent of the great emotion they have sown.

Even for them a pass of danger is ahead, as we shall see
in our sample of one among the highest of them.

A clear approach to felicity had long been the portion of
Sir Willoughby Patterne in his relations with Lætitia Dale.
She belonged to him; he was quite unshackled by her. She
was everything that is good in a parasite, nothing that is
bad. His dedicated critic she was, reviewing him with a
favour equal to perfect efficiency in her office; and whatever
the world might say of him, to her the happy gentleman
could constantly turn for his refreshing balsamic bath.[6] She
flew to the soul in him, pleasingly arousing sensations of
that inhabitant; and he allowed her the right to fly, in the
manner of kings, as we have heard, consenting to the privileges acted on by cats. These may not address their
Majesties, but they may stare; nor will it be contested that
the attentive circular eyes of the humble domestic creatures
are an embellishment to Royal pomp and grandeur, such
truly as should one day gain for them an inweaving and
figurement — in the place of bees, ermine tufts, and their
various present decorations — upon the august great robes
back-flowing and foaming over the gaspy page-boys.

Further to quote from the same volume of THE BOOK :
*There is pain in the surrendering of that we are fain to
relinquish.*

The idea is too exquisitely attenuate, as are those of the
whole body-guard of the heart of Egoism, and will slip
through you unless you shall have made a study of the
gross of volumes of the first and second sections of THE
BOOK, and that will take you up to senility ; or you must
make a personal entry into the pages, perchance; or an
escape out of them. There was once a venerable gentleman
for whom a white hair grew on the cop of his nose, laughing
at removals.[7] He resigned himself to it in the end, and
lastingly contemplated the apparition. It does not concern
us what effect was produced on his countenance and his
mind; enough that he saw a fine thing, but not so fine as
the idea cited above ; which has been between the two eyes
of humanity ever since women were sought in marriage.
With yonder old gentleman it may have been a ghostly hair
or a disease of the optic nerves; but for us it is a real
growth, and humanity might profitably imitate him in his
patient speculation upon it.

5. "multiplication-table": One times one
is an emblem of marriage; one man times
one woman equals one flesh.

6. Balsam or balm is the universal medi-
cation.

7. "cop": tip.

Sir Willoughby Patterne, though ready in the pursuit of duty and policy (an oft-united couple) to cast Miss Dale away, had to consider that he was not simply, so to speak, casting her over a hedge, he was casting her for a man to catch her; and this was a much greater trial than it had been on the previous occasion, when she went over bump to the ground. In the arms of a husband, there was no knowing how soon she might forget her soul's fidelity. It had not hurt him to sketch the project of the conjunction; benevolence assisted him; but he winced and smarted on seeing it take shape. It sullied his idea of Lætitia.

Still, if, in spite of so great a change in her fortune, her spirit could be guaranteed changeless, he, for the sake of pacifying his bride, and to keep two serviceable persons near him at command, might resolve to join them. The vision of his resolution brought with it a certain pallid contempt of the physically faithless woman; no wonder he betook himself to THE BOOK, and opened it on the scorching chapters treating of the sex, and the execrable wiles of that foremost creature of the chase, who runs for life. She is not spared in the Biggest of Books. But close it.

The writing in it having been done chiefly by men, men naturally receive their fortification from its wisdom, and half a dozen of the popular sentences for the confusion of women (cut in brass worn to a polish like sombre gold), refreshed Sir Willoughby for his undertaking.

An examination of Lætitia's faded complexion braced him very cordially.

His Clara jealous of this poor leaf!

He could have desired the transfusion of a quality or two from Lætitia to his bride; but you cannot, as in cookery, obtain a mixture of the essences of these creatures; and if, as it is possible to do, and as he had been doing recently with the pair of them at the Hall, you stew them in one pot, you are far likelier to intensify their little birth-marks of individuality. Had they a tendency to excellence, it might be otherwise; they might then make the exchanges we wish for; or scientifically concocted in a harem for a sufficient length of time by a sultan anything but obtuse, they might. It is however fruitless to dwell on what was only a glimpse of a wild regret, like the crossing of two express trains along the rails in Sir Willoughby's head.

The ladies Eleanor and Isabel were sitting with Miss Dale, all three at work on embroideries. He had merely to look at Miss Eleanor. She rose. She looked at Miss Isabel, and rattled her châtelaine to account for her departure.[8] After a decent interval Miss Isabel glided out. Such was the perfect discipline of the household.

Sir Willoughby played an air on the knee of his crossed leg.

8. "châtelaine": a chain on which women used to carry purse, keys, etc.

Lætitia grew conscious of a meaning in the silence. She said, " You have not been vexed by affairs to-day ? "

" Affairs," he replied, " must be peculiarly vexatious to trouble me. Concerning the country or my personal affairs ? "

" I fancy I was alluding to the country."

" I trust I am as good a patriot as any man living," said he ; " but I am used to the follies of my countrymen, and we are on board a stout ship. At the worst, it 's no worse than a rise in rates and taxes ; soup at the Hall-gates, perhaps ; licence to fell timber in one of the outer copses, or some dozen loads of coal. You hit my feudalism."

" The knight in armour has gone," said Lætitia, " and the castle with the drawbridge. Immunity for our island has gone too since we took to commerce."

" We bartered independence for commerce. You hit our old controversy. Ay, but we do not want this overgrown population ! However, we will put politics and sociology and the pack of their modern barbarous words aside. You read me intuitively. I have been, I will not say annoyed, but ruffled. I have much to do, and going into Parliament would make me almost helpless if I lose Vernon. You know of some absurd notion he has ? — literary fame, and bachelor's chambers, and a chop-house, and the rest of it."

She knew ; and thinking differently in the matter of literary fame, she flushed, and ashamed of the flush, frowned.

He bent over to her with the perusing earnestness of a gentleman about to trifle.

" You cannot intend that frown ? "

" Did I frown ? "

" You do."

" Now ? "

" Fiercely."

" Oh ! "

" Will you smile to reassure me ? "

" Willingly, as well as I can."

A gloom overcame him. With no woman on earth did he shine so as to recall to himself seigneur and dame of the old French Court, as he did with Lætitia Dale. He did not wish the period revived, but reserved it as a garden to stray into when he was in the mood for displaying elegance and brightness in the society of a lady ; and in speech Lætitia helped him to the nice delusion. She was not devoid of grace of bearing, either.

Would she preserve her beautiful responsiveness to his ascendancy ? Hitherto she had, and for years, and quite fresh. But how of her as a married woman ? Our souls are hideously subject to the conditions of our animal nature ! A wife, possibly mother, it was within sober calculation that there would be great changes in her. And the hint of any

change appeared a total change to one of the lofty order
who, when they are called on to relinquish possession
instead of aspiring to it, say, All or nothing!

Well, but if there was danger of the marriage-tie affecting
the slightest alteration of her character or habit of mind,
wherefore press it upon a tolerably hardened spinster!

Besides, though he did once put her hand in Vernon's for
the dance, he remembered acutely that the injury then done
by his generosity to his tender sensitiveness had sickened
and tarnished the effulgence of two or three successive
anniversaries of his coming of age. Nor had he altogether
yet got over the passion of greed for the whole group of the
well-favoured of the fair sex, which in his early youth had
made it bitter for him to submit to the fickleness, not to say
immodest fickleness, of any handsome one of them in yielding her hand to a man, and suffering herself to be led away.
Ladies whom he had only heard of as ladies of some beauty,
incurred his wrath for having lovers or taking husbands.
He was of a vast embrace; and do not exclaim, in covetous-
ness — for well he knew that even under Moslem law he
could not have them all; — but as the enamoured custodian
of the sex's purity, that blushes at such big spots as lovers
and husbands; and it was unbearable to see it sacrificed for
others. Without their purity what are they! — what are
fruiterer's plums? — unsaleable. O for the bloom on them!

"As I said, I lose my right hand in Vernon," he resumed,
"and I am, it seems, inevitably to lose him, unless we contrive to fasten him down here. I think, my dear Miss Dale,
you have my character. At least, I should recommend my
future biographer to you — with a caution, of course. You
would have to write selfishness with a dash under it. I cannot endure to lose a member of my household — not under
any circumstances; and a change of feeling to me on the part
of any of my friends because of marriage, I think hard. I
would ask you, how can it be for Vernon's good to quit an
easy pleasant home for the wretched profession of Literature? — wretchedly paying, I mean," he bowed to the
authoress. "Let him leave the house, if he imagines he
will not harmonize with its young mistress. He is queer,
though a good fellow. But he ought, in that event, to
have an establishment. And my scheme for Vernon — men,
Miss Dale, do not change to their old friends when they
marry — my scheme, which would cause the alteration in
his system of life to be barely perceptible, is to build him
a poetical little cottage, large enough for a couple, on the
borders of my park. I have the spot in my eye. The
point is, can he live alone there? Men, I say, do not change.
How is it that we cannot say the same of women?

Lætitia remarked: "The generic woman appears to have
an extraordinary faculty for swallowing the individual."

"As to the individual, as to a particular person, I may be

wrong. Precisely because it is her case I think of, my
strong friendship inspires the fear: unworthy of both, no
doubt, but trace it to the source. Even pure friendship,
such is the taint in us, knows a kind of jealousy; though I
would gladly see her established, and near me, happy and
contributing to my happiness with her incomparable social
charm. Her I do not estimate generically, be sure."

"If you do me the honour to allude to me, Sir Willoughby," said Lætitia. "I am my father's housemate."

"What wooer would take that for a refusal? He would
beg to be a third in the house and a sharer of your affectionate burden. Honestly, why not? And I may be arguing against my own happiness: it may be the end of me!"

"The end?"

"Old friends are captious, exacting. No, not the end.
Yet if my friend is not the same to me, it is the end to that
form of friendship: not to the degree possibly. But when
one is used to the form! And do you, in its application to
friendship, scorn the word 'use'? We are creatures of
custom. I am, I confess, a poltroon in my affections; I
dread changes. The shadow of the tenth of an inch in the
customary elevation of an eyelid!— to give you an idea of
my susceptibility. And, my dear Miss Dale, I throw myself
on your charity, with all my weakness bare, let me add, as I
could do to none but you. Consider, then, if I lose you!
The fear is due to my pusillanimity entirely. High-souled
women may be wives, mothers, and still reserve that home
for their friend. They can and will conquer the viler conditions of human life. Our states, I have always contended,
our various phases have to be passed through, and there
is no disgrace in it so long as they do not levy toll on the
quintessential, the spiritual element. You understand me?
I am no adept in these abstract elucidations."

"You explain yourself clearly," said Lætitia.

"I have never pretended that psychology was my forte,"
said he, feeling overshadowed by her cold commendation:
he was not less acutely sensitive to the fractional divisions
of tones than of eyelids, being, as it were, a melody with
which everything was out of tune that did not modestly or
mutely accord; and to bear about a melody in your person
is incomparably more searching than the best of touchstones
and talismans ever invented. "Your father's health has
improved latterly?"

"He did not complain of his health when I saw him this
morning. My cousin Amelia is with him, and she is an
excellent nurse."

"He has a liking for Vernon."

"He has a great respect for Mr. Whitford."

"You have?"

"Oh! yes; I have it equally."

"For a foundation, that is the surest. I would have the

friends dearest to me begin on that. The headlong match is ! — how can we describe it? By its finale, I am afraid. Vernon's abilities are really to be respected. His shyness is his malady. I suppose he reflected that he was not a capitalist. He might, one would think, have addressed himself to me; my purse is not locked."

"No, Sir Willoughby!" Lætitia said warmly, for his donations in charity were famous.

Her eyes gave him the food he enjoyed, and basking in them, he continued, —

"Vernon's income would at once have been regulated commensurately with a new position requiring an increase. This money, money, money! But the world will have it so. Happily I have inherited habits of business and personal economy. Vernon is a man who would do fifty times more with a companion appreciating his abilities and making light of his little deficiencies. They are palpable, small enough. He has always been aware of my wishes : — when perhaps the fulfilment might have sent me off on another tour of the world, home-bird though I am! When was it that our friendship commenced ? In my boyhood, I know. Very many years back."

"I am in my thirtieth year," said Lætitia.

Surprised and pained by a baldness resembling the deeds of ladies (they have been known, either through absence of mind, or mania, to displace a wig) in the deadly intimacy which slaughters poetic admiration, Sir Willoughby punished her by deliberately reckoning that she did not look less.

"Genius," he observed, "is unacquainted with wrinkles : " hardly one of his prettiest speeches ; but he had been wounded, and he never could recover immediately. Coming on him in a mood of sentiment, the wound was sharp. He could very well have calculated the lady's age. It was the jarring clash of her brazen declaration of it upon his low rich flute-notes that shocked him.

He glanced at the gold cathedral-clock on the mantel-piece, and proposed a stroll on the lawn before dinner. Lætitia gathered up her embroidery work.

" As a rule," he said, " authoresses are not needlewomen."

" I shall resign the needle or the pen if it stamps me an exception," she replied.

He attempted a compliment on her truly exceptional character. As when the player's finger rests in distraction on the organ, it was without measure and disgusted his own hearing. Nevertheless she had been so good as to diminish his apprehension that the marriage of a lady in her thirtieth year with his cousin Vernon would be so much of a loss to him ; hence, while parading the lawn, now and then casting an eye at the window of the room where his Clara and Vernon were in council, the schemes he indulged for his prospective comfort and his feelings of the moment were in such striving harmony as that to which we hear orchestral musicians bringing their instruments under the process called tuning. It is not perfect, but it promises to be so soon. We are not angels, which have their dulcimers ever on the choral pitch. We are mortals, attaining the celestial accord with effort, through a stage of pain. Some degree of pain was necessary to Sir Willoughby, otherwise he would not have seen his generosity confronting him. He grew, therefore, tenderly inclined to Lætitia once more, so far as to say within himself, " For conversation she would be a valuable wife." And this valuable wife he was presenting to his cousin.

Apparently, considering the duration of the conference of his Clara and Vernon, his cousin required strong persuasion to accept the present.

CHAPTER 15

THE PETITION FOR A RELEASE

NEITHER Clara nor Vernon appeared at the mid-day table. Dr. Middleton talked with Miss Dale on classical matters, like a good-natured giant giving a child the jump from stone to stone across a brawling mountain ford, so that an unedified audience might really suppose, upon seeing her over the difficulty, she had done something for herself. Sir Willoughby was proud of her, and therefore anxious to settle her business while he was in the humour to lose her. He hoped to finish it by shooting a word or two at Vernon before dinner. Clara's petition to be set free, released from *him*, had vaguely frightened even more than it offended his pride.

Miss Isabel quitted the room.

She came back, saying, "They decline to lunch."

"Then we may rise," remarked Sir Willoughby.

"She was weeping," Miss Isabel murmured to him.

"Girlish enough," he said.

The two elderly ladies went away together. Miss Dale, pursuing her theme with the Rev. Doctor, was invited by him to a course in the library. Sir Willoughby walked up and down the lawn, taking a glance at the West-room as he swung round on the turn of his leg. Growing impatient, he looked in at the window and found the room vacant.

Nothing was to be seen of Clara and Vernon during the afternoon. Near the dinner-hour the ladies were informed by Miss Middleton's maid that her mistress was lying down on her bed, too unwell with headache to be present. Young Crossjay brought a message from Vernon (delayed by birds' eggs in the delivery), to say that he was off over the hills, and thought of dining with Dr. Corney.

Sir Willoughby despatched condolences to his bride. He was not well able to employ his mind on its customary topic, being, like the dome of a bell, a man of so pervading a ring within himself concerning himself, that the recollection of a doubtful speech or unpleasant circumstance touching him closely, deranged his inward peace; and as dubious and unpleasant things will often occur, he had great need of a worshipper, and was often compelled to appeal to her for signs of antidotal idolatry. In this instance, when the need of a worshipper was sharply felt, he obtained no signs at all. The Rev. Doctor had fascinated Miss Dale; so that, both within and without, Sir Willoughby was uncomforted. His themes in public were those of an English gentleman; horses, dogs, game, sport, intrigue, scandal, politics, wines, the manly themes; with a condescension to ladies' tattle, and approbation of a racy anecdote. What interest could he possibly take in the Athenian Theatre and the girl whose flute-playing behind the scenes, imitating the nightingale, enraptured a Greek audience! He would have suspected a motive in Miss Dale's eager attentiveness, if the motive could have been conceived. Besides, the ancients were not decorous; they did not, as we make our moderns do, write for ladies. He ventured at the dinner-table to interrupt Dr. Middleton once, —

"Miss Dale will do wisely, I think, sir, by confining herself to your present edition of the classics."

"That," replied Dr. Middleton, "is the observation of a student of the dictionary of classical mythology in the English tongue."[1]

"The Theatre is a matter of climate, sir. You will grant me that."

"If quick wits come of climate, it is as you say, sir."

"With us it seems a matter of painful fostering, or the need of it," said Miss Dale, with a question to Dr. Middleton, excluding Sir Willoughby, as though he had been a temporary disturbance of the flow of their dialogue.

The ladies Eleanor and Isabel, previously excellent listeners to the learned talk, saw the necessity of coming to his rescue; but you cannot converse with your aunts, inmates of your house, on general subjects at table; the attempt increased his discomposure; he considered that he had ill-chosen his father-in-law; that scholars are an impolite race; that young or youngish women are devotees of power in any form, and will be absorbed by a scholar for a variation of a man; concluding that he must have a round of dinner-parties to friends, especially ladies, appreciating him, during the Doctor's visit. Clara's headache above, and Dr. Middleton's unmannerliness below, affected his instincts in a way to make him apprehend that a stroke of misfortune was impending; thunder was in the air. Still he learnt

---

1. I.e., a complete ignoramus, indirectly described.

something, by which he was to profit subsequently. The
topic of Wine withdrew the Doctor from his classics ; it was
magical on him. A strong fraternity of taste was discovered
in the sentiments of host and guest upon particular wines
and vintages; they kindled one another by naming great
years of the grape, and if Sir Willoughby had to sacrifice
the ladies to the topic, he much regretted a condition of
things that compelled him to sin against his habit, for the
sake of being in the conversation and probing an elderly
gentleman's foible.

Late at night he heard the house-bell, and meeting Vernon
in the hall, invited him to enter the laboratory and tell him
Dr. Corney's last. Vernon was brief; Corney had not let
fly a single anecdote, he said, and lighted his candle.

"By the way, Vernon, you had a talk with Miss
Middleton ? "

" She will speak to you to-morrow at twelve."

"To-morrow at twelve ? "

"It gives her four and twenty hours."

Sir Willoughby determined that his perplexity should be
seen ; but Vernon said good night to him, and was shooting
up the stairs before the dramatic exhibition of surprise had
yielded to speech.

Thunder was in the air and a blow coming. Sir Willoughby's instincts were awake to the many signs, nor,
though silenced, were they hushed by his harping on the
frantic excesses to which women are driven by the passion of
jealousy. He believed in Clara's jealousy because he really
had intended to rouse it; under the form of emulation, feebly.
He could not suppose she had spoken of it to Vernon. But
as for the seriousness of her desire to be released from her
engagement, that was little credible. Still the fixing of an
hour for her to speak to him after an interval of four and
twenty hours, left an opening for the incredible to add its
weight to the suspicious mass : and who would have fancied
Clara Middleton so wild a victim of the intemperate passion !
He muttered to himself several assuageing observations to
excuse a young lady half-demented, and rejected them in a
lump for their nonsensical inapplicability to Clara. In order
to obtain some sleep, he consented to blame himself slightly,
in the style of the enamoured historian of erring Beauties
alluding to their peccadilloes. He had done it to edify her.
Sleep, however, failed him. That an inordinate jealousy
argued an overpowering love, solved his problem until he
tried to fit the proposition to Clara's character. He had
discerned nothing southern in her. Latterly, with the
blushing Day in prospect, she had contracted and frozen.
There was no reading either of her or the mystery.

In the morning, at the breakfast-table, a confession of
sleeplessness was general. Excepting Miss Dale and Dr.
Middleton, none had slept a wink. "I, sir," the Doctor
replied to Sir Willoughby, "slept like a lexicon in your

library when Mr. Whitford and I are out of it."

Vernon incidentally mentioned that he had been writing through the night.

"You fellows kill yourselves," Sir Willoughby reproved him. "For my part, I make it a principle to get through my work without self-slaughter."

Clara watched her father for a symptom of ridicule. He gazed mildly on the systematic worker. She was unable to guess whether she would have in him an ally or a judge. The latter, she feared. Now that she had embraced the strife, she saw the division of the line where she stood from that one where the world places girls who are affianced wives : her father could hardly be with her ; it had gone too far. He loved her, but he would certainly take her to be moved by a maddish whim ; he would not try to understand her case. The scholar's detestation of a disarrangement of human affairs that had been by miracle contrived to run smoothly, would of itself rank him against her ; and with the world to back his view of her, he might behave like a despotic father. How could she defend herself before him ? At one thought of Sir Willoughby, her tongue made ready, and feminine craft was alert to prompt it ; but to her father she could imagine herself opposing only dumbness and obstinacy.

"It is not exactly the same kind of work," she said.

Dr. Middleton rewarded her with a bushy eyebrow's beam of his revolving humour at the baronet's notion of work.

So little was needed to quicken her that she sunned herself in the beam, coaxing her father's eyes to stay with hers as long as she could, and beginning to hope he might be won to her side, if she confessed she had been more in the wrong than she felt ; owned to him, that is, her error in not earlier disturbing his peace.

"I do not say it is the same," observed Sir Willoughby, bowing to their alliance of opinion. "My poor work is for the day, and Vernon's, no doubt, for the day to come. I contend, nevertheless, for the preservation of health, as the chief implement of work."

"Of continued work : there I agree with you," said Dr. Middleton cordially.

Clara's heart sank ; so little was needed to deaden her.

Accuse her of an overweening antagonism to her betrothed ; yet remember that though the words had not been uttered to give her good reason for it, nature reads nature : captives may be stript of everything save that power to read their tyrant ; remember also that she was not, as she well knew, blameless ; her rage at him was partly against herself.

The rising from table left her to Sir Willoughby. She swam away after Miss Dale, exclaiming : "The laboratory ! Will you have me for a companion on your walk to see your father ? One breathes earth and heaven to-day out of doors.

Isn't it Summer with a Spring-breeze? I will wander about your garden and not hurry your visit, I promise."

"I shall be very happy indeed. But I am going immediately," said Lætitia, seeing Sir Willoughby hovering to snap up his bride.

"Yes; and a garden-hat and I am on the march."

"I will wait for you on the terrace."

"You will not have to wait."

"Five minutes at the most," Sir Willoughby said to Lætitia, and she passed out, leaving them alone together.

"Well, and my love!" he addressed his bride almost huggingly; "and what is the story? and how did you succeed with old Vernon yesterday? He will and he won't? He's a very woman in these affairs. I can't forgive him for giving you a headache. You were found weeping."'

"Yes, I cried," said Clara.

"And now tell me about it. You know, my dear girl, whether he does or does n't, our keeping him somewhere in the neighbourhood — perhaps not in the house — that is the material point. It can hardly be necessary in these days to urge marriages on. I'm sure the country is over . . . Most marriages ought to be celebrated with the funeral knell!"

"I think so," said Clara.

"It will come to this, that marriages of consequence, and none but those, will be hailed with joyful peals."

"Do not say such things in public, Willoughby."

"Only to you, to you! Don't think me likely to expose myself to the world. Well, and I sounded Miss Dale, and there will be no violent obstacle. And now about Vernon?"

"I will speak to you, Willoughby, when I return from my walk with Miss Dale, soon after twelve."

"Twelve!" said he.

"I name an hour. It seems childish. I can explain it. But it is named, I cannot deny, because I am a rather childish person perhaps, and have it prescribed to me to delay my speaking for a certain length of time. I may tell you at once that Mr. Whitford is not to be persuaded by me, and the breaking of our engagement would not induce him to remain."

"Vernon used those words?"

"It was I."

"'The breaking of our engagement'! Come into the laboratory, my love."

"I shall not have time."

"Time shall stop rather than interfere with our conversation! 'The breaking . . .'! but it's a sort of sacrilege to speak of it."

"That I feel; yet it has to be spoken of."

"Sometimes? Why? I can't conceive the occasion. You know, to me, Clara, plighted faith, the affiancing of

two lovers, is a piece of religion. I rank it as holy as
marriage; nay, to me it is holier; I really cannot tell you
how; I can only appeal to you in your bosom to understand
me. We read of divorces with comparative indifference.
They occur between couples who have rubbed off all
romance."

She could have asked him in her fit of ironic iciness, on
hearing him thus blindly challenge her to speak out, whether
the romance might be his piece of religion.

He propitiated the more unwarlike sentiments in her by
ejaculating: "Poor souls! let them go their several ways.
Married people no longer lovers are in the category of the
unnameable. But the hint of the breaking of an engagement — our engagement! — between *us?* Oh!"

"Oh!" Clara came out with a swan's note swelling over
mechanical imitation of him to dolorousness illimitable.
"Oh!" she breathed short, "let it be now. Do not speak,
till you have heard me. My head may not be clear by-and-
by. And two scenes — twice will be beyond my endurance.
I am penitent for the wrong I have done you. I grieve for
you. All the blame is mine. Willoughby, you must release
me. Do not let me hear a word of that word; jealousy is
unknown to me . . . Happy if I could call you friend and
see you with a worthier than I, who might by-and-by call
me friend! You have my plighted troth . . . given in
ignorance of my feelings. Reprobate a weak and foolish
girl's ignorance. I have thought of it, and I cannot see
wickedness, though the blame is great, shameful. You have
none. You are without any blame. You will not suffer as
I do. You will be generous to me? I have no respect for
myself when I beg you to be generous and release me."

"But this was the . . . " Willoughby preserved his
calmness, "this, then, the subject of your interview with
Vernon?"

"I have spoken to him. I did my commission, and I
spoke to him."

"Of me?"

"Of myself. I see how I hurt you; I could not avoid it.
Yes, of you, as far as we are related. I said I believed you
would release me. I said I could be true to my plighted
word, but that you would not insist. Could a gentleman
insist? But not a step beyond; not love; I have none.
And, Willoughby, treat me as one perfectly worthless; I
am. I should have known it a year back. I was deceived
in myself. There should be love."

"Should be!" Willoughby's tone was a pungent comment on her.

"Love, then, I find I have not. I think I am antagonistic to it. What people say of it I have not experienced. I
find I was mistaken. It is lightly said, but very painful.
You understand me, that my prayer is for liberty, that I
may not be tied. If you can release and pardon me, or

promise ultimately to pardon me, or say some kind word, I shall know it is because I am beneath you utterly that I have been unable to give you the love you should have with a wife. Only say to me, go! It is you who break the match, discovering my want of a heart. What people think of me matters little. My anxiety will be to save you annoyance."

She waited for him : he seemed on the verge of speaking.

He perceived her expectation ; he had nothing but clownish tumult within, and his dignity counselled him to disappoint her.

Swaying his head, like the oriental palm whose shade is a blessing to the perfervid wanderer below, smiling gravely, he was indirectly asking his dignity what he could say to maintain it and deal this mad young woman a bitterly compassionate rebuke. What to think, hung remoter. The thing to do struck him first.

He squeezed both her hands, threw the door wide open, and said, with countless blinkings : "In the laboratory we are uninterrupted. I was at a loss to guess where that most unpleasant effect on the senses came from. They are always 'guessing' through the nose. I mean, the remainder of breakfast here. Perhaps I satirized them too smartly — if you know the letters. When they are not 'calculating.' More offensive than débris of a midnight banquet! An American tour is instructive, though not so romantic. Not so romantic as Italy, I mean. Let us escape."

She held back from his arm. She had scattered his brains ; it was pitiable : but she was in the torrent and could not suffer a pause or a change of place.

"It must be here ; one minute more — I cannot go elsewhere to begin again. Speak to me here ; answer my request. Once ; one word. If you forgive me, it will be superhuman. But, release me."

"Seriously," he rejoined, "tea-cups and coffee-cups, bread-crumbs, egg-shells, caviare. butter, beef, bacon ! Can we ? The room reeks."

"Then I will go for my walk with Miss Dale. And you will speak to me when I return ? "

"At all seasons. You shall go with Miss Dale. But, my dear! my love! Seriously, where are we ? One hears of lover's quarrels. Now, I never quarrel. It is a characteristic of mine. And you speak of me to my cousin Vernon ! Seriously, plighted faith signifies plighted faith, as much as an iron-cable is iron to hold by. Some little twist of the mind ? To Vernon, of all men ! Tush ! she has been dreaming of a hero of perfection, and the comparison is unfavourable to her Willoughby. But, my Clara, when I say to you, that bride is bride, and you are mine, mine ! "

"Willoughby, you mentioned them, — those separations of two married. You said, if they do not love . . . Oh!

say, is it not better . . . instead of later ? "

He took advantage of her modesty in speaking to exclaim : " Where are we now ? Bride is bride, and wife is wife, and *affianced* is, in honour, *wedded*. You cannot be released. We are united. Recognize it : united. There is no possibility of releasing a wife ! "

" Not if she ran ? . . ."

This was too direct to be histrionically[2] misunderstood. He had driven her to the extremity of more distinctly imagining the circumstance she had cited, and with that cleared view the desperate creature gloried in launching such a bolt at the man's real or assumed insensibility as must, by shivering it, waken him.

But in a moment she stood in burning rose, with dimmed eyesight. She saw his horror, and seeing shared it ; shared just then only by seeing it; which led her to rejoice with the deepest of sighs that some shame was left in her.

"Ran ? ran ? ran ? " he said as rapidly as he blinked. "How ? where ? what idea ? . . ."

Close was he upon an explosion that would have sullied his conception of the purity of the younger members of the sex hauntingly.

That she, a young lady, maiden, of strictest education, should, and without his teaching, know that wives ran ! — know that by running they compelled their husbands to abandon pursuit, surrender possession ! — and that she should suggest it of herself as a wife ! — that she should speak of running ! —

His ideal, the common male Egoist ideal of a waxwork sex, would have been shocked to fragments had she spoken further to fill in the outlines of these awful interjections.

She was tempted : for during the last few minutes the fire of her situation had enlightened her understanding upon a subject far from her as the ice-fields of the North a short while before ; and the prospect offered to her courage if she would only outstare shame and seem at home in the doings of wickedness, was his loathing and dreading so vile a young woman. She restrained herself ; chiefly, after the first bridling of maidenly timidity, because she could not bear to lower the idea of her sex even in his esteem.

The door was open. She had thoughts of flying out to breathe in an interval of truce.

She reflected on her situation hurriedly askance,—

" If one must go through this, to be disentangled from an engagement, what must it be to poor women seeking to be free of a marriage ? "

Had she spoken it, Sir Willoughby might have learnt that she was not so iniquitously wise of the things of this world as her mere sex's instinct, roused to the intemperateness of a creature struggling with fetters, had made her appear in her dash to seize a weapon, indicated moreover by him.

2. "histrionically": like a play-actor.

Clara took up the old broken vow of women to vow it afresh: "Never to any man will I give my hand."

She replied to Sir Willoughby: "I have said all. I cannot explain what I have said."

She had heard a step in the passage. Vernon entered.

Perceiving them, he stated his mission in apology: "Dr. Middleton left a book in this room. I see it; it's a Heinsius."[3]

"Ha! by the way, a book; books would not be left here if they were not brought here, with my compliments to Dr. Middleton, who may do as he pleases, though seriously order is order," said Sir Willoughby. "Come away to the laboratory, Clara. It's a comment on human beings that wherever they have been there's a mess, and you admirers of them," he divided a sickly nod between Vernon and the stale breakfast-table, "must make what you can of it. Come, Clara."

Clara protested that she was engaged to walk with Miss Dale.

"Miss Dale is waiting in the hall," said Vernon.

"Miss Dale is waiting," said Clara.

"Walk with Miss Dale; walk with Miss Dale," Sir Willoughby remarked pressingly. "I will beg her to wait another two minutes. You shall find her in the hall when you come down."

He rang the bell and went out.

"Take Miss Dale into your confidence; she is quite trustworthy," Vernon said to Clara.

"I have not advanced one step," she replied.

"Recollect that you are in a position of your own choosing; and if, after thinking over it, you mean to escape you must make up your mind to pitched battles, and not be dejected if you are beaten in all of them; there is your only chance."

"Not my choosing; do not say choosing, Mr. Whitford. I did not choose. I was incapable of really choosing. I consented."

"It's the same in fact. But be sure of what you wish."

"Yes," she assented, taking it for her just punishment that she should be supposed not quite to know her wishes. "Your advice has helped me to-day."[4]

"Did I advise?"

"Do you regret advising?"

"I should certainly regret a word that intruded between you and him."

"But you will not leave the Hall yet? You will not leave me without a friend? If papa and I were to leave to-morrow, I foresee endless correspondence. I have to stay at least some days, and wear through it, and then, if I have

3. Daniel Heinsius, seventeenth-century Dutch editor of the classics.

4. We are left to guess what advice Clara got from Vernon in the great skipped scene between them; see the interval between Chapters 14 and 15.

to speak to my poor father you can imagine the effect on him."

Sir Willoughby came striding in, to correct the error of his going out.

"Miss Dale awaits you, my dear. You have bonnet, hat? — No? Have you forgotten your appointment to walk with her?"

"I am ready," said Clara, departing.

The two gentlemen behind her separated in the passage. They had not spoken.

She had read of the reproach upon women, that they divide the friendships of men. She reproached herself, but she was in action, driven by necessity, between sea and rock. Dreadful to think of! she was one of the creatures who are written about.

CHAPTER 16

CLARA AND LÆTITIA

In spite of his honourable caution, Vernon had said things to render Miss Middleton more angrily determined than she had been in the scene with Sir Willoughby. His counting on pitched battles and a defeat for her in all of them, made her previous feelings appear slack in comparison with the energy of combat now animating her. And she could vehemently declare that she had not chosen; she was too young, too ignorant to choose. He had wrongly used that word; it sounded malicious; and to call consenting the same in fact as choosing, was wilfully unjust. Mr. Whitford meant well; he was conscientious, very conscientious. But he was not the hero descending from heaven bright-sworded to smite a woman's fetters off her limbs and deliver her from the yawning mouth-abyss.[1]

His logical coolness of expostulation with her when she cast aside the silly mission entrusted to her by Sir Willough-by and wept for herself, was unheroic in proportion to its praiseworthiness. He had left it to her to do everything she wished done, stipulating simply that there should be a pause of four and twenty hours for her to consider of it before she proceeded in the attempt to extricate herself. Of consolation there had not been a word. Said he, "I am the last man to give advice in such a case." Yet she had by no means astonished him when her confession came out. It came out, she knew not how. It was led up to by his declining the idea of marriage, and her congratulating him on his exemption from the prospect of the yoke, but memory was too dull to revive the one or two fiery minutes of

1. The myth in Clara's mind is that of Perseus rescuing Andromeda.

broken language when she had been guilty of her dire misconduct.

This gentleman was no flatterer, scarcely a friend. He could look on her grief without soothing her. Supposing he had soothed her warmly ? All her sentiments collected in her bosom to dash in reprobation of him at the thought. She nevertheless condemned him for his excessive coolness; his transparent anxiety not to be compromised by a syllable; his air of saying, "I guessed as much, but why plead your case to me ?" And his recommendation to her to be quite sure she did know what she meant, was a little insulting. She exonerated him from the intention; he treated her as a girl. By what he said of Miss Dale, he proposed that lady for imitation.

"I must be myself or I shall be playing hypocrite to dig my own pitfall," she said to herself, while taking counsel with Lætitia as to the route for their walk, and admiring a becoming curve in her companion's hat.

Sir Willoughby, with many protestations of regret that letters of business debarred him from the pleasure of accompanying them, remarked upon the path proposed by Miss Dale: "In that case you must have a footman."

"Then we adopt the other," said Clara, and they set forth.

"Sir Willoughby," Miss Dale said to her, "is always in alarm about our unprotectedness."

Clara glanced up at the clouds and closed her parasol. She replied, "It inspires timidity."

There was that in the accent and character of the answer which warned Lætitia to expect the reverse of a quiet chatter with Miss Middleton.

"You are fond of walking ?" She chose a peaceful topic.

"Walking or riding; yes, of walking," said Clara. "The difficulty is to find companions."

"We shall lose Mr. Whitford next week."

"He goes ?"

"He will be a great loss to me, for I do not ride." Lætitia replied to the off-hand inquiry.

"Ah !"

Miss Middleton did not fan conversation when she simply breathed her voice.

Lætitia tried another neutral theme.

"The weather to-day suits our country," she said.

"England, or Patterne Park ? I am so devoted to mountains that I have no enthusiasm for flat land."

"Do you call our country flat, Miss Middleton ? We have undulations, hills, and we have sufficient diversity, meadows, rivers, copses, brooks, and good roads, and pretty by-paths."

"The prettiness is overwhelming. It is very pretty to see; but to live with, I think I prefer ugliness. I can imagine learning to love ugliness. It 's honest. However

young you are, you cannot be deceived by it. These parks
of rich people are a part of the prettiness. I would rather
have fields, commons."

"The parks give us delightful green walks, paths through
beautiful woods."

"If there is a right of way for the public."

"There should be," said Miss Dale, wondering; and Clara
cried: "I chafe at restraint; hedges and palings everywhere! I should have to travel ten years to sit down
contented among these fortifications. Of course I can read
of this rich kind of English country with pleasure in poetry.
But it seems to me to require poetry. What would you say
of human beings requiring it?"

"That they are not so companionable but that the haze of
distance improves the view."

"Then you do know that you are the wisest!"

Lætitia raised her dark eyelashes; she sought to understand. She could only fancy she did; and if she did, it
meant that Miss Middleton thought her wise in remaining
single.

Clara was full of a sombre preconception that her "jealousy" had been hinted to Miss Dale.

"You knew Miss Durham?" she said.

"Not intimately."

"As well as you know me?"

"Not so well."

"But you saw more of her?"

"She was more reserved with me."

"Oh! Miss Dale, I would not be reserved with you."

The thrill of the voice caused Lætitia to steal a look.
Clara's eyes were bright, and she had the readiness to run
to volubility of the fever-stricken; otherwise she did not
betray excitement.

"You will never allow any of these noble trees to be
felled, Miss Middleton."

"The axe is better than decay, do you not think?"

"I think your influence will be great and always used to
good purpose."

"My influence, Miss Dale? I have begged a favour this
morning and cannot obtain the grant."

It was lightly said, but Clara's face was more significant,
and "What?" leapt from Lætitia's lips.

Before she could excuse herself, Clara had answered,
"My liberty."

In another and higher tone Lætitia said: "What?"
and she looked round on her companion; she looked in
doubt that is open to conviction by a narrow aperture, and
slowly and painfully yields access. Clara saw the vacancy
of her expression gradually filling with woefulness.

"I have begged him to release me from my engagement,
Miss Dale."

"Sir Willoughby?"

"It is incredible to you. He refuses. You see I have no influence."

"Miss Middleton, it is terrible!"

"To be dragged to the marriage service against one's will? Yes."

"Oh! Miss Middleton."

"Do you not think so?"

"That cannot be your meaning."

"You do not suspect me of trifling? You know I would not. I am as much in earnest as a mouse in a trap."

"No, you will not misunderstand me! Miss Middleton, such a blow to Sir Willoughby would be shocking, most cruel! He is devoted to you."

"He was devoted to Miss Durham."

"Not so deeply : differently."

"Was he not very much courted at that time? He is now ; not so much : he is not so young. But my reason for speaking of Miss Durham was to exclaim at the strangeness of a girl winning her freedom to plunge into wedlock. Is it comprehensible to you? She flies from one dungeon into another. These are the acts which astonish men at our conduct, and cause them to ridicule and, I daresay, despise us."

"But, Miss Middleton, for Sir Willoughby to grant such a request, if it was made . . ."

"It was made, and by me, and will be made again. I throw it all on my unworthiness, Miss Dale. So the county will think of me, and quite justly. I would rather defend him than myself. He requires a different wife from anything I can be. That is my discovery ; unhappily a late one. The blame is all mine. The world cannot be too hard on me. But I must be free if I am to be kind in my judgements even of the gentleman I have injured."

"So noble a gentleman!" Lætitia sighed.

"I will subscribe to any eulogy of him," said Clara, with a penetrating thought as to the possibility of a lady experienced in him like Lætitia taking him for noble. "He has a noble air. I say it sincerely, that your appreciation of him proves his nobility." Her feeling of opposition to Sir Willoughby pushed her to this extravagance, gravely perplexing Lætitia. "And it is," added Clara, as if to support what she had said, "a withering rebuke to me ; I know him less, at least have not had so long an experience of him."

Lætitia pondered on an obscurity in these words which would have accused her thick intelligence but for a glimmer it threw on another most obscure communication. She feared it might be, strange though it seemed, jealousy, a shade of jealousy affecting Miss Middleton, as had been vaguely intimated by Sir Willoughby when they were waiting in the hall. "A little feminine ailment, a want of comprehension of a perfect friendship ; " those were his words to her : and he suggested vaguely that care must be taken in the eulogy of her friend.

She resolved to be explicit.

" I have not said that I think him beyond criticism, Miss Middleton."

" Noble ? "

" He has faults. When we have known a person for years the faults come out, but custom makes light of them ; and I suppose we feel flattered by seeing what it would be difficult to be blind to ! A very little flatters us ! — Now, do you not admire that view ? It is my favourite."

Clara gazed over rolling richness of foliage, wood and water, and church spire, a town and horizon hills. There sang a sky-lark.

" Not even the bird that does not fly away ! " she said ; meaning, she had no heart for the bird satisfied to rise and descend in this place.

Lætitia travelled to some notion, dim and immense, of Miss Middleton's fever of distaste. She shrank from it in a kind of dread lest it might be contagious and rob her of her one ever-fresh possession of the homely picturesque ; but Clara melted her by saying : " For your sake I could love it . . . in time ; or some dear old English scene. Since . . . since this . . . this change in me, I find I cannot separate landscape from associations. Now I learn how youth goes. I have grown years older in a week. — Miss Dale, if he were to give me my freedom ? if he were to cast me off ? if he stood alone ? "

" I should pity him."

" Him — not me ! Oh ! right. I hoped you would ; I knew you would."

Lætitia's attempt to shift Miss Middleton's shiftiness was vain ; for now she seemed really listening to the language of jealousy : — jealous of the ancient Letty Dale ! — and immediately before, the tone was quite void of it.

" Yes," she said, " but you make me feel myself in the dark, and when I do I have the habit of throwing myself for guidance upon such light as I have within. You shall know me, if you will, as well as I know myself. And do not think me far from the point when I say I have a feeble health. I am what the doctors call anæmic ; a rather bloodless creature. The blood is life, so I have not much life. Ten years back — eleven, if I must be precise, I thought of conquering the world with a pen ! The result is that I am glad of a fireside, and not sure of always having one ; and that is my achievement. My days are monotonous, but if I have a dread, it is that there will be an alteration in them. My father has very little money. We subsist on what private income he has, and his pension : he was an army doctor. I may by-and-by have to live in a town for pupils. I could be grateful to any one who would save me from that. I should be astonished at his choosing to have me burden his household as well. —

Have I now explained the nature of my pity? It would be the pity of common sympathy, pure lymph of pity, as nearly disembodied as can be. Last year's sheddings from the tree do not form an attractive garland. Their merit is, that they have not the ambition. I am like them. Now, Miss Middleton, I cannot make myself more bare to you. I hope you see my sincerity."

'I do see it," Clara said.

With the second heaving of her heart, she cried: "See it, and envy you that humility! proud if I could ape it! Oh! how proud if I could speak so truthfully true!— You would not have spoken so to me without some good feeling out of which friends are made. That I am sure of. To be very truthful to a person, one must have a liking. So I judge by myself. Do I presume too much?"

Kindness was on Lætitia's face.

"But now," said Clara, swimming on the wave in her bosom, "I tax you with the silliest suspicion ever entertained by one of your rank. Lady, you have deemed me capable of the meanest of our vices!— Hold this hand, Lætitia, my friend, will you? Something is going on in me."

Lætitia took her hand, and saw and felt that something was going on.

Clara said: "You are a woman."

It was her effort to account for the something.

She swam for a brilliant instant on tears, and yielded to the overflow.

When they had fallen, she remarked upon her first long breath quite coolly: "An encouraging picture of a rebel, is it not?"

Her companion murmured to soothe her.

"It's little, it's nothing," said Clara, pained to keep her lips in line.

They walked forward, holding hands, deep-hearted to one another.

"I like this country better now," the shaken girl resumed. "I could lie down in it and ask only for sleep. I should like to think of you here. How nobly self-respecting you must be, to speak as you did! Our dreams of heroes and heroines are cold glitter beside the reality. I have been lately thinking of myself as an outcast of my sex, and to have a good woman liking me a little . . . loving? Oh! Lætitia, my friend, I should have kissed you, and not made this exhibition of myself — and if you call it hysterics, woe to you! for I bit my tongue to keep it off when I had hardly strength to bring my teeth together — if that idea of jealousy had not been in your head. You had it from him."

"I have not alluded to it in any word that I can recollect."

"He can imagine no other cause for my wish to be released. I have noticed, it is his instinct to reckon on

women as constant by their nature. They are the needles,
and he the magnet. Jealousy of you, Miss Dale!
Lætitia, may I speak?"

"Say everything you please."

"I could wish:—Do you know my baptismal name?"

"Clara."

"At last! I could wish . . . that is, if it were your
wish. Yes, I could wish that. Next to independence, my
wish would be that. I risk offending you. Do not let
your delicacy take arms against me. I wish him happy in
the only way that he can be made happy. There is my
jealousy."

"Was it what you were going to say just now?"

"No."

"I thought not."

"I was going to say—and I believe the rack would not
make me truthful like you, Lætitia—well, has it ever
struck you: remember, I do see his merits; I speak to
his faithfullest friend, and I acknowledge he is attractive,
he has manly tastes and habits; but has it never struck
you . . . I have no right to ask; I know that men must
have faults, I do not expect them to be saints; I am not
one; I wish I were."

"Has it never struck me . . .?" Lætitia prompted
her.

"That very few women are able to be straightforwardly
sincere in their speech, however much they may desire to
be?"

"They are differently educated. Great misfortune
brings it to them."

"I am sure your answer is correct. Have you ever
known a woman who was entirely an Egoist?"

"Personally known one? We are not better than men."

"I do not pretend that we are. I have latterly become
an Egoist, thinking of no one but myself, scheming to
make use of every soul I meet. But then, women are in
the position of inferiors. They are hardly out of the
nursery when a lasso is round their necks; and if they
have beauty, no wonder they turn it to a weapon and make
as many captives as they can. I do not wonder! My
sense of shame at my natural weakness and the arrogance
of men would urge me to make hundreds captive, if that
is being a coquette. I should not have compassion for
those lofty birds, the hawks. To see them with their
wings clipped would amuse me. Is there any other way
of punishing them?"

"Consider what you lose in punishing them."

"I consider what they gain if we do not."

Lætitia supposed she was listening to discursive observations upon the inequality in the relations of the sexes.
A suspicion of a drift to a closer meaning had been lulled,
and the colour flooded her swiftly when Clara said: "Here

is the difference I see; I see it; I am certain of it: women who are called coquettes make their conquests not of the best of men; but men who are Egoists have *good* women for their victims; women on whose devoted constancy they feed; they drink it like blood. I am sure I am not taking the merely feminine view. They punish themselves too by passing over the one suitable to them, who could really give them what they crave to have, and they go where they . . ." Clara stopped. "I have not your power to express ideas," she said.

"Miss Middleton, you have a dreadful power," said Lætitia.

Clara smiled affectionately: "I am not aware of any. Whose cottage is this?"

"My father's. Will you not come in? into the garden?"

Clara took note of ivied windows and roses in the porch. She thanked Lætitia and said, "I will call for you in an hour."

"Are you walking on the road alone?" said Lætitia incredulously, with an eye to Sir Willoughby's dismay.

"I put my trust in the highroad," Clara replied, and turned away, but turned back to Lætitia and offered her face to be kissed.

The "dreadful power" of this young lady had fervently impressed Lætitia, and in kissing her she marvelled at her gentleness and girlishness.

Clara walked on, unconscious of her possession of power of any kind.

CHAPTER 17

THE PORCELAIN VASE

DURING the term of Clara's walk with Lætitia, Sir Willoughby's shrunken self-esteem, like a garment hung to the fire after exposure to tempestuous weather, recovered some of the sleekness of its velvet pile in the society of Mrs. Mountstuart Jenkinson, who represented to him the world he feared and tried to keep sunny for himself by all the arts he could exercise. She expected him to be the gay Sir Willoughby, and her look being as good as an incantation-summons, he produced the accustomed sprite, giving her sally for sally. Queens govern the polite. Popularity with men, serviceable as it is for winning favouritism with women, is of poor value to a sensitive gentleman, anxious even to prognostic apprehension on behalf of his pride, his comfort, and his prevalence. And men are grossly purchaseable; good wines have them, good cigars, a goodfellow air: they are never quite worth their

salt even then; you can make head against their ill looks.
But the looks of women will at one blow work on you the
downright difference which is between the cock of lordly
plume and the moulting. Happily they may be gained:
a clever tongue will gain them, a leg. They are with you
to a certainty if Nature is with you; if you are elegant
and discreet: if the sun is on you, and they see you shining in it; or if they have seen you well-stationed and
handsome in the sun. And once gained, they are your
mirrors for life, and far more constant than the glass.
That tale of their caprice is absurd. Hit their imaginations once, they are your slaves, only demanding common
courtier service of you. They will deny that you are age-
ing, they will cover you from scandal, they will refuse to
see you ridiculous. Sir Willoughby's instinct, or skin, or
outfloating feelers told him of these mysteries of the
influence of the sex; he had as little need to study them
as a lady breathed on.[1]

He had some need to know them, in fact; and with him
the need of a protection for himself called it forth; he
was intuitively a conjuror in self-defence, long-sighted,
wanting no directions to the herb he was to suck at when
fighting a serpent. His dulness of vision into the heart
of his enemy was compensated by the agile sensitiveness
obscuring but rendering him miraculously active, and without supposing his need immediate, he deemed it politic to
fascinate Mrs. Mountstuart and anticipate ghastly possibilities in the future by dropping a hint; not of Clara's
fickleness, you may be sure; of his own, rather; or more
justly, of an altered view of Clara's character. He
touched on the *rogue in porcelain*.

Set gently laughing by his relishing humour: "I get
nearer to it," he said.

"Remember, I'm in love with her," said Mrs. Mountstuart.

"That is our penalty."

"A pleasant one for you."

He assented. "Is the 'rogue' to be eliminated?"

"Ask, when she's a mother, my dear Sir Willoughby."

"This is how I read you: — "

"I shall accept any interpretation that is complimentary."

"Not one will satisfy me of being sufficiently so, and so
I leave it to the character to fill out the epigram."

"Do. What hurry is there? And don't be misled by
your objection to rogue; which would be reasonable if you
had not secured her."

The door of a hollow chamber of horrible reverberation
was opened within him by this remark.

He tried to say in jest, that it was not always a passion-

1. A lady touched by scandal.

ate admiration that held the rogue fast; but he muddled it in the thick of his conscious thunder, and Mrs. Mountstuart smiled to see him shot from the smooth-flowing dialogue into the cataracts by one simple reminder to the lover of his luck. Necessarily after a fall, the pitch of their conversation relaxed.

"Miss Dale is looking well," he said.

"Fairly: she ought to marry," said Mrs. Mountstuart.

He shook his head. "Persuade her."

She nodded: "Example may have some effect."

He looked extremely abstracted. "Yes, it is time. Where is the man you could recommend for her complement? She has now what was missing before, a ripe intelligence in addition to her happy disposition — romantic, you would say. I can't think women the worse for that."

"A dash of it."

"She calls it 'leafage.'"

"Very pretty. And have you relented about your horse Achmet?"

"I don't sell him under four hundred."

"Poor Johnny Busshe! You forget that his wife doles him out his money. You're a hard bargainer, Sir Willoughby."

"I mean the price to be prohibitive."

"Very well; and 'leafage' is good for hide and seek; especially when there is no rogue in ambush. And that's the worst I can say of Lætitia Dale. An exaggerated devotion is the scandal of our sex. They say you're the hardest man of business in the county too, and I can believe it; for at home and abroad your aim is to get the best of everybody. You see I've no leafage, I am perfectly matter-of-fact, bald."

"Nevertheless, my dear Mrs. Mountstuart, I can assure you that conversing with you has much the same exhilarating effect on me as conversing with Miss Dale."

"But, leafage! leafage! You hard bargainers have no compassion for devoted spinsters."

"I tell you my sentiments absolutely."

"And you have mine moderately expressed."

She recollected the purpose of her morning's visit, which was to engage Dr. Middleton to dine with her, and Sir Willoughby conducted her to the library door. "Insist," he said.

Awaiting her reappearance, the refreshment of the talk he had sustained, not without point, assisted him to distinguish in its complete abhorrent orb the offence committed against him by his bride.[2] And this he did through projecting it more and more away from him, so that in the outer distance it involved his personal emotions less, while observation was enabled to compass its vastness, and, as

---

2. "orb": sphere, as of a heavenly body.

it were, perceive the whole spherical mass of the wretched girl's guilt impudently turning on its axis.

Thus to detach an injury done to us, and plant it in space, for mathematical measurement of its weight and bulk, is an art; it may also be an instinct of self-preservation; otherwise, as when mountains crumble adjacent villages are crushed, men of feeling may at any moment be killed outright by the iniquitous and the callous. But, as an art, it should be known to those who are for practising an art so beneficent, that circumstances must lend their aid. Sir Willoughby's instinct even had sat dull and crushed before his conversation with Mrs. Mountstuart. She lifted him to one of his ideals of himself. Among gentlemen he was the English gentleman; with ladies his aim was the Gallican courtier of any period from Louis Treize to Louis Quinze.[3] He could doat on those who led him to talk in that character — backed by English solidity, you understand. Roast beef stood eminent behind the soufflé and champagne. An English squire excelling his fellows at hazardous leaps in public, he was additionally a polished whisperer, a lively dialoguer, one for witty bouts, with something in him — capacity for a drive and dig or two — beyond mere wit, as they soon learnt who called up his reserves, and had a bosom for pinking.[4] So much for his ideal of himself. Now, Clara not only never evoked, never responded to it, she repelled it; there was no flourishing of it near her. He considerately overlooked these facts in his ordinary calculations; he was a man of honour and she was a girl of beauty; but the accidental blossoming of his ideal, with Mrs. Mountstuart, on the very heels of Clara's offence, restored him to full command of his art of detachment, and he thrust her out, quite apart from himself, to contemplate her disgraceful revolutions.

Deeply read in the Book of Egoism that he was, he knew the wisdom of the sentence: *An injured pride that strikes not out will strike home.* What was he to strike with? Ten years younger, Lætitia might have been the instrument. To think of her now was preposterous. Beside Clara she had the hue of Winter under the springing bough. He tossed her away, vexed to the very soul by an ostentatious decay that shrank from comparison with the blooming creature he had to scourge in self-defence, by some agency or other.

Mrs. Mountstuart was on the step of her carriage when the silken parasols of the young ladies were descried on a slope of the park, where the yellow green of May-clothed beeches flowed over the brown ground of last year's leaves.

3. From 1610 to 1774—from the onset of the French ("Gallican") old régime up to a discreet period before the Revolution.

4. The code duello has a place in Willoughby's fantasy-life but not in his actual existence, which is more prudent.

"Who's the cavalier?" she inquired.

A gentleman escorted them.

"Vernon? No! he's pegging at Crossjay," quoth Willoughby.

Vernon and Crossjay came out for the boy's half-hour's run before his dinner. Crossjay spied Miss Middleton and was off to meet her at a bound. Vernon followed him leisurely.

"The rogue has no cousin, has she?" said Mrs. Mount-stuart.

"It's a family of one son or one daughter for generations," replied Willoughby.

"And Letty Dale?"

"Cousin!" he exclaimed, as if wealth had been imputed to Miss Dale; adding: "No male cousin."

A railway-station fly drove out of the avenue on the circle to the hall-entrance. Flitch was driver. He had no right to be there, he was doing wrong, but he was doing it under cover of an office, to support his wife and young ones, and his deprecating touches of the hat spoke of these apologies to his former master with dog-like pathos.

Sir Willoughby beckoned to him to approach.

"So you are here," he said. "You have luggage."

Flitch jumped from the box and read one of the labels aloud: "Lieut.-Colonel H. De Craye."

"And the colonel met the ladies? Overtook them?"

Here seemed to come dismal matter for Flitch to relate.

He began upon the abstract origin of it: he had lost his place in Sir Willoughby's establishment, and was obliged to look about for work where it was to be got, and though he knew he had no right to be where he was, he hoped to be forgiven because of the mouths he had to feed as a flyman attached to the railway station, where this gentleman, the colonel, hired him, and he believed Sir Willoughby would excuse him for driving a friend, which the colonel was, he recollected well, and the colonel recollected him, and he said, not noticing how he was rigged: "What! Flitch! back in your old place?—Am I expected?" and he told the colonel his unfortunate situation: "Not back, colonel; no such luck for me:" and Colonel De Craye was a very kind-hearted gentleman, as he always had been, and asked kindly after his family. And it might be that such poor work as he was doing now he might be deprived of, such is misfortune when it once harpoons a man; you may dive, and you may fly, but it sticks in you, once do a foolish thing. "May I humbly beg of you, if you'll be so good, Sir Willoughby," said Flitch, passing to evidence of the sad mishap. He opened the door of the fly, displaying fragments of broken porcelain.

"But, what, what! what's the story of this?" cried Sir Willoughby.

"What is it?" said Mrs. Mountstuart, pricking up her ears.

"It was a vaws," Flitch replied in elegy.

"A porcelain vase!" interpreted Sir Willoughby.

"China!" Mrs. Mountstuart faintly shrieked.

One of the pieces was handed to her inspection. She held it close, she held it distant. She sighed horribly. "The man had better have hanged himself," said she.

Flitch bestirred his misfortune-sodden features and members for a continuation of the doleful narrative.

"How did this occur?" Sir Willoughby peremptorily asked him.

Flitch appealed to his former master for testimony that he was a good and a careful driver.

Sir Willoughby thundered: "I tell you to tell me how this occurred."

"Not a drop, my lady! not since my supper last night, if there's any truth in me;" Flitch implored succour of Mrs. Mountstuart.

"Drive straight," she said, and braced him.

His narrative was then direct.

Near Piper's mill, where the Wicker brook crossed the Rebdon road, one of Hoppner's waggons, overloaded as uusal, was forcing the horses uphill, when Flitch drove down at an easy pace, and saw himself between Hoppner's cart come to a stand, and a young lady advancing: and just then the carter smacks his whip, the horses pull half mad. The young lady starts behind the cart, and up jumps the colonel, and to save the young lady, Flitch dashed ahead and did save her, he thanked heaven for it, and more when he came to see who the young lady was.

"She was alone?" said Sir Willoughby, in tragic amazement, staring at Flitch.

"Very well, you saved her, and you upset the fly," Mrs. Mountstuart jogged him on.

"Bartlett, our old head-keeper, was a witness, my lady; I had to drive half up the bank, and it's true — over the fly did go; and the vaws it shoots out against the twelfth milestone, just as though *there* was the chance for it! for nobody else was injured, and knocked against anything else, it never would have flown all to pieces, so that it took Bartlett and me ten minutes to collect every one, down to the smallest piece there was; and he said, and I can't help thinking myself, there was a Providence in it, for we all come together so as you might say we was made to do as we did."

"So then Horace adopted the prudent course of walking on with the ladies instead of trusting his limbs again to this capsizing fly," Sir Willoughby said to Mrs. Mountstuart; and she rejoined: "Lucky that no one was hurt."

Both of them eyed the nose of poor Flitch, and simultaneously they delivered a verdict of "Humph."

Mrs. Mountstuart handed the wretch a half-crown from her purse. Sir Willoughby directed the footman in attendance to unload the fly and gather up the fragments of porcelain carefully, bidding Flitch be quick in his departing.

"The colonel's wedding present! I shall call to-morrow," Mrs. Mountstuart waved her adieu.

"Come every day! — Yes, I suppose we may guess the destination of the vase." He bowed her off: and she cried, —

"Well, now the gift can be shared, if you 're either of you for a division." In the crash of the carriage-wheels he heard: "At any rate, there was a rogue in *that* porcelain."

These are the slaps we get from a heedless world.

As for the vase, it was Horace De Craye's loss. Wedding-present he would have to produce, and decidedly not in chips. It had the look of a costly vase, but that was no question for the moment: — What was meant by Clara being seen walking on the highroad alone? — What snare, traceable ad inferas, had ever induced Willoughby Patterne to make her the repository and fortress of his honour![5]

CHAPTER 18

COLONEL DE CRAYE

CLARA came along chatting and laughing with Colonel de Craye, young Crossjay's hand under one of her arms, and her parasol flashing; a dazzling offender; as if she wished to compel the spectator to recognize the dainty rogue in procelain; really insufferably fair: perfect in height and grace of movement; exquisitely-tressed; red-lipped, the colour striking out to a distance from her ivory skin: a sight to set the woodland dancing, and turn the heads of the town; though beautiful, a jury of art-critics might pronounce her not to be. Irregular features are condemned in beauty. Beautiful figure, they could say. A description of her figure and her walking would have won her any praises: and she wore a dress cunning to embrace the shape and flutter loose about it, in the spirit of a Summer's day. Calypso-clad, Dr. Middleton would have called her.[1] See the silver birch in a breeze: here it swells, there it scatters, and it is puffed to a round and it streams like a pennon, and now gives the glimpse and shine of the white stem's line within, now hurries over it, denying that it was visible, with a chatter along the sweeping folds, while still the white peeps through.

5. "ad inferas": to the infernal regions.
1. Like Calypso, the nymph who de-tained Odysseus so long on his wanderings.

She had the wonderful art of dressing to suit the season and the sky. To-day the art was ravishingly companionable with her sweet-lighted face: too sweet, too vividly-meaningful for pretty, if not of the strict severity for beautiful. Millinery would tell us that she wore a fichu of thin white muslin crossed in front on a dress of the same light stuff, trimmed with deep rose.[2] She carried a grey-silk parasol, traced at the borders with green creepers, and across the arm devoted to Crossjay, a length of trailing ivy, and in that hand a bunch of the first long grasses. These hues of red rose and green and pale green, ruffled and pouted in the billowy white of the dress ballooning and valleying softly, like a yacht before the sail bends low; but she walked not like one blown against; resembling rather the day of the south-west driving the clouds, gallantly firm in commotion; interfusing colour and varying in her features from laugh to smile and look of settled pleasure, like the heavens above the breeze.

Sir Willoughby, as he frequently had occasion to protest to Clara, was no poet: he was a more than commonly candid English gentleman in his avowed dislike of the poet's nonsense, verbiage, verse; not one of those latterly terrorized by the noise made about the fellow into silent contempt; a sentiment that may sleep, and has not to be defended. He loathed the fellow, fought the fellow. But he was one with the poet upon that prevailing theme of verse, the charms of women. He was, to his ill-luck, intensely susceptible, and where he led men after him to admire, his admiration became a fury. He could see at a glance that Horace De Craye admired Miss Middleton. Horace was a man of taste, could hardly, could not, do other than admire; but how curious that in the setting forth of Clara and Miss Dale, in his own contemplation and comparison of them, Sir Willoughby had given but a nodding approbation of his bride's appearance! He had not attached weight to it recently.

Her conduct, and foremost, if not chiefly, her having been discovered, positively met by his friend Horace, walking on the highroad without companion or attendant, increased a sense of pain so very unusual with him that he had cause to be indignant. Coming on this condition, his admiration of the girl who wounded him was as bitter a thing as a man could feel. Resentment, fed from the main springs of his nature, turned it to wormwood, and not a whit the less was it admiration when he resolved to chastise her with a formal indication of his disdain. Her present gaiety sounded to him like laughter heard in the shadow of the pulpit.

"You have escaped!" he said to her, while shaking the hand of his friend Horace and cordially welcoming him;

2. "fichu": a neckerchief or small triangular shawl fastened in front.

"My dear fellow! and by the way, you had a squeak for it, I hear from Flitch."

"I, Willoughby? not a bit," said the colonel; "we get into a fly to get out of it; and Flitch helped me out as well as in, good fellow; just dusting my coat as he did it. The only bit of bad management was that Miss Middleton had to step aside a trifle hurriedly."

"You knew Miss Middleton at once?"

"Flitch did me the favour to introduce me. He first precipitated me at Miss Middleton's feet, and then he introduced me, in old oriental fashion, to my sovereign."

Sir Willoughby's countenance was enough for his friend Horace. Quarter-wheeling to Clara, he said: "'T is the place I 'm to occupy for life, Miss Middleton, though one is not always fortunate to have a bright excuse for taking it at the commencement."

Clara said: "Happily you were not hurt, Colonel De Craye."

"I was in the hands of the Loves. Not the Graces, I 'm afraid; I 've an image of myself. Dear, no! My dear Willoughby, you never made such a headlong declaration as that. It would have looked like a magnificent impulse, if the posture had only been choicer. And Miss Middleton did n't laugh. At least I saw nothing but pity."

"You did not write," said Willoughby.

"Because it was a toss-up of a run to Ireland or here, and I came here not to go there; and by the way, fetched a jug with me to offer up to the Gods of ill-luck; and they accepted the propitiation."

"Was n't it packed in a box?"

"No, it was wrapped in paper, to show its elegant form. I caught sight of it in the shop yesterday and carried it off this morning, and presented it to Miss Middleton at noon, without any form at all."

Willoughby knew his friend Horace's mood when the Irish tongue in him threatened to wag.

"You see what may happen," he said to Clara.

"As far as I am in fault I regret it," she answered.

"Flitch says the accident occurred through his driving up the bank to save you from the wheels."

"Flitch may go and whisper that down the neck of his empty whisky flask," said Horace De Craye. "And then let him cork it."

"The consequence is that we have a porcelain vase broken. You should not walk on the road alone, Clara. You ought to have a companion, always. <u>It is the rule here</u>."

"I had left Miss Dale at the cottage."

"You ought to have had the dogs."

"Would they have been any protection to the vase?"

<u>Horace De Craye crowed cordially.</u> *appreciates her humor*

"I 'm afraid not, Miss Middleton. One must go to the

witches for protection to vases; and they 're all in the air now, having their own way with us, which accounts for the confusion in politics and society, and the rise in the price of broomsticks, to prove it true, as they tell us, that every nook and corner wants a mighty sweeping. Miss Dale looks beaming," said De Craye, wishing to divert Willoughby from his anger with sense as well as nonsense.

"You have not been visiting Ireland recently," said Sir Willoughby.

"No, nor making acquaintance with an actor in an Irish part in a drama cast in the green island. 'T is Flitch, my dear Willoughby, has been and stirred the native in me, and we 'll present him to you for the like good office when we hear after a number of years that you 've not wrinkled your forehead once at your liege lady. Take the poor old dog back home, will you? He 's crazed to be at the Hall. I say, Willoughby, it would be a good bit of work to take him back. Think of it; you 'll do the popular thing, I 'm sure. I 've a superstition that Flitch ought to drive you from the church-door. If I were in luck, I 'd have him drive me."

"The man 's a drunkard, Horace."

"He fuddles his poor nose. 'T is merely unction to the exile. Sober struggles below. He drinks to rock his heart, because he has one. Now let me intercede for poor Flitch."

"Not a word of him. He threw up his place."

"To try his fortune in the world, as the best of us do, though livery runs after us to tell us there 's no being an independent gentleman, and comes a cold day we haul on the metal-button coat again, with a good ha! of satisfac· tion. You 'll do the popular thing. Miss Middleton joins in the pleading."

"No pleading!"

"When I 've vowed upon my eloquence, Willoughby, I 'd bring you to pardon the poor dog?"

"Not a word of him!"

"Just one!"

Sir Willoughby battled with himself to repress a state of temper that put him to marked disadvantage beside his friend Horace in high spirits. Ordinarily he enjoyed these fits of Irish of him, which were Horace's fun and play, at times involuntary, and then they indicated a recklessness that might embrace mischief. De Craye, as Willoughby had often reminded him, was properly Norman. The blood of two or three Irish mothers in his line, however, was enough to dance him, and if his fine profile spoke of the stiffer race, his eyes and the quick run of the lip in the cheek, and a number of his qualities, were evidence of the maternal legacy.

"My word has been said about the man," Willoughby replied.

(handwritten: de Craye as foil which we perceive)

"But I've wagered on your heart against your word, and can't afford to lose; and there's a double reason for revoking for you!"

"I don't see either of them. Here are the ladies."

"You'll think of the poor beast, Willoughby."

"I hope for better occupation."

"If he drives a wheelbarrow at the Hall he'll be happier than on board a chariot at large. He's broken-hearted."

"He's too much in the way of breakages, my dear Horace."

"Oh! the vase! the bit of porcelain!" sang De Craye. "Well, we'll talk him over by-and-by."

"If it pleases you; but my rules are never amended."

"Inalterable, are they? — like those of an ancient people who might as well have worn a jacket of lead for the comfort they had of their boast. The beauty of laws for human creatures is their adaptability to new stitchings."

Colonel De Craye walked at the heels of his leader to make his bow to the ladies Eleanor and Isabel.

Sir Willoughby had guessed the person who inspired his friend Horace to plead so pertinaciously and inopportunely for the man Flitch; and it had not improved his temper or the pose of his rejoinders; he had winced under the contrast of his friend Horace's easy, laughing, sparkling, musical air and manner with his own stiffness; and he had seen Clara's face, too, scanning the contrast — he was fatally driven to exaggerate his discontentment, which did not restore him to serenity. He would have learnt more from what his abrupt swing round of the shoulder precluded his beholding. There was an interchange between Colonel De Craye and Miss Middleton; spontaneous on both sides. His was a look that said: "You were right;" hers: "I knew it." Her look was calmer, and after the first instant clouded as by wearifulness of sameness; his was brilliant, astonished, speculative, and admiring, pitiful: a look that poised over a revelation, called up the hosts of wonder to question strange fact.

It had passed unseen by Sir Willoughby. The observer was the one who could also supply the key of the secret. Miss Dale had found Colonel De Craye in company with Miss Middleton at her gateway. They were laughing and talking together like friends of old standing, De Craye as Irish as he could be: and the Irish tongue and gentlemanly manner are an irresistible challenge to the opening steps of familiarity when accident has broken the ice. Flitch was their theme; and: "Oh! but if we go up to Willoughby hand in hand, and bob a curtsey to 'm and beg his pardon for Mister Flitch, won't he melt to such a pair of suppliants? of course he will!" Miss Middleton said he would not. Colonel De Craye wagered he would; he knew Willoughby best. Miss Middleton looked simply grave; a way of asserting the contrary opin-

(handwritten bottom: De Craye — by many Irish blood English by nation)

ion that tells of rueful experience. "We'll see," said the colonel. They chatted like a couple unexpectedly discovering in one another a common dialect among strangers. Can there be an end to it when those two meet? They prattle, they fill the minutes, as though they were violently to be torn asunder at a coming signal, and must have it out while they can; it is a meeting of mountain brooks; not a colloquy but a chasing, impossible to say which flies, which follows, or what the topic, so interlinguistic are they and rapidly counterchanging. After their conversation of an hour before, Lætitia watched Miss Middleton in surprise at her lightness of mind. Clara bathed in mirth. A boy in a Summer stream shows not heartier refreshment of his whole being. Lætitia could now understand Vernon's idea of her wit. And it seemed that she also had Irish blood. Speaking of Ireland, Miss Middleton said she had cousins there, her only relatives.

"The laugh told me that," said Colonel De Craye.

Lætitia and Vernon paced up and down the lawn. Colonel De Craye was talking with English sedateness to the ladies Eleanor and Isabel. Clara and young Crossjay strayed.

"If I might advise, I would say, do not leave the Hall immediately, not yet," Lætitia said to Vernon.

"You know, then?"

"I cannot understand why it was that I was taken into her confidence."

"I counselled it."

"But it was done without an object that I can see."

"The speaking did her good."

"But how capricious! how changeful!"

"Better now than later."

"Surely she has only to ask to be released? — to ask earnestly: if it is her wish."

"You are mistaken."

"Why does she not make a confidant of her father?"

"That she will have to do. She wished to spare him."

"He cannot be spared if she is to break the engagement."

"She thought of sparing him the annoyance. Now there's to be a tussle he must share in it."

"Or she thought he might not side with her?"

"She has not a single instinct of cunning. You judge her harshly."

"She moved me on the walk out. Coming home I felt differently."

Vernon glanced at Colonel De Craye.

"She wants *good* guidance," continued Lætitia.

"She has not an idea of treachery."

"You think so? It may be true. But she seems one born devoid of patience, easily made reckless. There is a wildness . . . I judge by her way of speaking; that at least appeared sincere. She does not practise concealment. He will naturally find it almost incredible. The change in her, so sudden, so wayward, is unintelligible to me. To me it is the conduct of a creature untamed. He may hold her to her word and be justified."

"Let him look out if he does!"

"Is not that harsher than anything I have said of her?"

"I'm not appointed to praise her. I fancy I read the case; and it's a case of opposition of temperaments. We never can tell the person quite suited to us; it strikes us in a flash."

"That they are *not* suited to us? Oh, no; that comes by degrees."

"Yes, but the accumulation of evidence, or sentience, if you like, is combustible; we don't command the spark; it may be late in falling. And you argue in her favour. Consider her as a generous and impulsive girl, outwearied at last."

"By what?"

"By anything; by his loftiness, if you like. He flies too high for her, we will say."

"Sir Willoughby an eagle?"

"She may be tired of his eyrie."

The sound of the word in Vernon's mouth smote on a consciousness she had of his full grasp of Sir Willoughby, and her own timid knowledge, though he was not a man who played on words.

If he had eased his heart in stressing the first syllable, it was only temporary relief.[3] He was heavy-browed enough.

"But I cannot conceive what she expects me to do by confiding her sense of her position to me," said Lætitia.

"We none of us know what will be done. We hang on Willoughby, who hangs on whatever it is that supports him: and there we are in a swarm."

"You see the wisdom of staying, Mr. Whitford."

"It must be over in a day or two. Yes, I stay."

"She inclines to obey you."

"I should be sorry to stake my authority on her obedience. We must decide something about Crossjay, and get the money for his crammer, if it is to be got. If not, I may get a man to trust me. I mean to drag the boy away. Willoughby has been at him with the tune of gentleman, and has laid hold of him by one ear. When I say 'her obedience,' she is not in a situation, nor in a condition, to be led blindly by anybody. She must rely on herself, do everything herself. It's a knot that won't bear touching by any hand save hers."

"I fear . . ." said Lætitia.

"Have no such fear."

---

3. "in stressing the first syllable": maybe to make "eyrie" sound like "airy," maybe to make it sound like "I-ry."

"If it should come to his positively refusing."

"He faces the consequences."

"You do not think of her."

Vernon looked at his companion.

CHAPTER 19

COLONEL DE CRAYE AND CLARA MIDDLETON

Miss Middleton finished her stroll with Crossjay by winding her trailer of ivy in a wreath round his hat and sticking her bunch of grasses in the wreath. She then commanded him to sit on the ground beside a big rhododendron, there to await her return. Crossjay had informed her of a design he entertained to be off with a horde of boys nesting in high trees, and marking spots where wasps and hornets were to be attacked in Autumn: she thought it a dangerous business, and as the boy's dinner-bell had very little restraint over him when he was in the flush of a scheme of this description, she wished to make tolerably sure of him through the charm she not unreadily believed she could fling on lads of his age. "Promise me you will not move from here until I come back, and when I come I will give you a kiss." Crossjay promised. She left him and forgot him.

Seeing by her watch fifteen minutes to the ringing of the bell, a sudden resolve that she would speak to her father without another minute's delay, had prompted her like a superstitious impulse to abandon her aimless course and be direct. She knew what was good for her; she knew it now more clearly than in the morning. To be taken away instantly! was her cry. There could be no further doubt. Had there been any before? But she would not in the morning have suspected herself of a capacity for evil, and of a pressing need to be saved from herself. She was not pure of nature: it may be that we breed saintly souls which are: she was pure of will: fire rather than ice. And in beginning to see the elements she was made of, she did not shuffle them to a heap with her sweet looks to front her. She put to her account some strength, much weakness; she almost dared to gaze unblinking at a perilous evil tendency. The glimpse of it drove her to her father.

"He must take me away at once; to-morrow!"

She wished to spare her father. So unsparing of herself was she, that in her hesitation to speak to him of her change of feeling for Sir Willoughby, she would not suffer it to be attributed in her own mind to a daughter's anxious consideration about her father's loneliness; an idea she had indulged formerly. Acknowledging that it was imperative she should speak, she understood that she had refrained, even to the inflicting upon herself of such humiliation as to run dilating on her woes to others, because of the silliest of human desires to preserve her reputation for consistency. She had heard women abused for shallowness and flightiness: she had heard her father denounce them as veering weather-vanes, and his oft-repeated quid femina possit: for her sex's sake, and also to appear an exception to her sex, this reasoning creature desired to be thought consistent.[1]

Just on the instant of her addressing him, saying, "Father:" a note of seriousness in his ear: it struck her that the occasion for saying all had not yet arrived, and she quickly interposed, "Papa;" and helped him to look lighter. The petition to be taken away was uttered.

"To London?" said Dr. Middleton. "I don't know who'll take us in."

"To France, papa?"

"That means hotel-life."

"Only for two or three weeks."

"Weeks! I am under an engagement to dine with Mrs. Mountstuart Jenkinson five days hence: that is, on Thursday."

"Could we not find an excuse?"

"Break an engagement? No, my dear, not even to escape drinking a widow's wine."

"Does a word bind us?"

"Why, what else should?"

"I think I am not very well."

"We'll call in that man we met at dinner here: Corney: a capital doctor; an old-fashioned anecdotal doctor. How is it you are not well, my love? You look well. I cannot conceive your not being well."

"It is only that I want a change of air, papa."

"There we are — a change! semper eadem![2] Women will be wanting a change of air in Paradise; a change of angels too, I might surmise. A change from quarters like these to a French hotel, would be a descent! — 'this the seat, this mournful gloom for that celestial light.'[3] I am perfectly at home in the library here. That excellent fellow Whitford and I have real days: and I like him for showing fight to his elder and better."

"He is going to leave."

"I know nothing of it, and I shall append no credit to the tale until I do know. He is headstrong, but he answers to a rap."

Clara's bosom heaved. The speechless insurrection threatened her eyes.

A South-west shower lashed the window-panes and sug-

---

1. "quid femina possit": what a woman is capable of, i.e., anything.

2. "semper eadem": always the same.
3. Dr. Middleton quotes Milton's Satan.

gested to Dr. Middleton shuddering visions of the channel-passage on board a steamer.

"Corney shall see you: he is a sparkling draught in person; probably illiterate, if I may judge from one interruption of my discourse when he sat opposite me, but lettered enough to respect Learning and write out his prescription: I do not ask more of men or of physicians." Dr. Middleton said this rising, glancing at the clock and at the back of his hands. "'Quod autem secundum litteras difficillimum esse artificium?'⁴ But what after letters is the more difficult practice? 'Ego puto medicum.' The medicus next to the scholar: though I have not to my recollection required him next me, nor ever expected child of mine to be crying for that milk. Daughter she is — of the unexplained sex: we will send a messenger for Corney. Change, my dear, you will speedily have, to satisfy the most craving of women, if Willoughby, as I suppose, is in the neoteric fashion of spending a honey-moon on a railway: apt image, exposition and perpetuation of the state of mania conducting to the institution!⁵ In my time we lay by to brood on happiness; we had no thought of chasing it over a Continent, mistaking hurly-burly clothed in dust for the divinity we sought. A smaller generation sacrifices to excitement. Dust and hurly-burly must perforce be the issue. And that is your modern world. Now, my dear, let us go and wash our hands. Midday-bells expect immediate attention. They know of no ante-room of assembly."

Clara stood gathered up, despairing at opportunity lost. He had noticed her contracted shape and her eyes, and had talked magisterially to smother and overbear the something disagreeable prefigured in her appearance.

"You do not despise your girl, father?"

"I do not; I could not; I love her; I love my girl. But you need not sing to me like a gnat to propound that question, my dear."

"Then, father, tell Sir Willoughby to-day we have to leave to-morrow. You shall return in time for Mrs. Mountstuart's dinner. Friends will take us in, the Darletons, the Erpinghams. We can go to Oxford, where you are sure of welcome. A little will recover me. Do not mention doctors. But you see I am nervous. I am quite ashamed of it; I am well enough to laugh at it, only I cannot overcome it; and I feel that a day or two will restore me. Say you will. Say it in First-Lesson-Book language; anything above a primer splits my foolish head to-day."

Dr. Middleton shrugged, spreading out his arms.

"The office of ambassador from you to Willoughby, Clara? You decree me to the part of ball between two

---

4. Dr. Middleton translates each of his Latin sentences in the next.

5. "neoteric": newfangled; "the institution" is the madhouse.

bats. The Play being assured, the prologue is a bladder
of wind. I seem to be instructed in one of the mysteries
of erotic esotery, yet on my word I am no wiser. If Willoughby is to hear anything from you, he will hear it from
your lips."

"Yes, father, yes. We have differences. I am not fit
for contests at present; my head is giddy. I wish to
avoid an illness. He and I . . . I accuse myself."

"There is the bell!" ejaculated Dr. Middleton. "I 'll
debate on it with Willoughby."

"This afternoon?"

"Somewhen, before the dinner-bell. I cannot tie myself to the minute-hand of the clock, my dear child. And
let me direct you, for the next occasion when you shall
bring the vowels I and A, in verbally detached letters,
into collision, that you do not fill the hiatus with so pronounced a Y.[6] It is the vulgarization of our tongue of
which I y-accuse you. I do not like my girl to be guilty
of it."

He smiled to moderate the severity of the correction,
and kissed her forehead.

She declared her inability to sit and eat; she went to her
room, after begging him very earnestly to send her the
assurance that he had spoken. She had not shed a tear,
and she rejoiced in her self-control; it whispered to her
of true courage when she had given herself such evidence
of the reverse.

Shower and sunshine alternated through the half-hours
of the afternoon, like a procession of dark and fair holding
hands and passing. The shadow came, and she was chill;
the light yellow in moisture, and she buried her face not
to be caught up by cheerfulness. Believing that her head
ached, she afflicted herself with all the heavy symptoms
and oppressed her mind so thoroughly that its occupation
was to speculate on Lætitia Dale's modest enthusiasm for
rural pleasures, for this place especially, with its rich
foliage and peeps of scenic peace. The prospect of an
escape from it inspired thoughts of a loveable round of life
where the sun was not a naked ball of fire but a friend
clothed in woodland; where park and meadow swept to
well-known features East and West; and distantly circling
hills, and the hearts of poor cottagers too — sympathy with
whom assured her of goodness — were familiar, homely to
the dweller in the place, morning and night. And she
had the love of wild flowers, the watchful happiness in
the seasons; poets thrilled her, books absorbed. She
dwelt strongly on that sincerity of feeling; it gave root in
our earth; she needed it as she pressed a hand on her
eyeballs, conscious of acting the invalid, though the reasons she had for languishing under headache were so

6. The reference ("Y") is to her phrase Where she speaks her heart, he hears
just above, "I . . . I accuse myself." only phonemes.

convincing that her brain refused to disbelieve in it and
went some way to produce positive throbs. Otherwise she
had no excuse for shutting herself in her room. Vernon
Whitford would be sceptical. Headache or none, Colonel
De Craye must be thinking strangely of her; she had not
shown him any sign of illness. His laughter and his talk
sang about her and dispersed the fiction; he was the very
sea-wind for bracing unstrung nerves. Her ideas reverted
to Sir Willoughby, and at once they had no more cohesion
than the foam on a torrent-water.

But soon she was undergoing a variation of sentiment.
Her maid Barclay brought her this pencilled line from her
father, —

"Factum est; lætus est; amantium iræ, &c."[7]

That it was done, that Willoughby had put on an air of
glad acquiescence, and that her father assumed the existence of a lover's quarrel, was wonderful to her at first
sight, simple the succeeding minute. Willoughby indeed
must be tired of her, glad of her going. He would know
that it was not to return. She was grateful to him for
perhaps hinting at the amantium iræ, though she rejected
the folly of the verse. And she gazed over dear homely
country through her windows now. Happy the lady of
the place, if happy she can be in her choice! Clara Middleton envied her the double-blossom wild cherry-tree,
nothing else. One sprig of it, if it had not faded and
gone to dust-colour like crusty Alpine snow in the lower
hollows, and then she could depart, bearing away a memory of the best here! Her fiction of the headache pained
her no longer. She changed her muslin dress for silk;
she was contented with the first bonnet Barclay presented.
Amicable toward every one in the house, Willoughby
included, she threw up her window, breathed, blessed
mankind: and she thought: "If Willoughby would open
his heart to nature, he would be relieved of his wretched
opinion of the world." Nature was then sparkling refreshed in the last drops of a sweeping rain-curtain, favourably disposed for a background to her joyful optimism. A
little nibble of hunger within, real hunger, unknown to
her of late, added to this healthy view, without precipi-
tating her to appease it; she was more inclined to foster
it, for the sake of the sinewy activity of limb it gave her;
and in the style of young ladies very light of heart, she
went downstairs like a cascade; and like the meteor observed in its vanishing trace she alighted close to Colonel
De Craye and entered one of the rooms off the hall.

He cocked an eye at the half-shut door.

Now, you have only to be reminded that it is the habit
of the sportive gentleman of easy life, bewildered as he
would otherwise be by the tricks, twists, and windings of
the hunted sex, to parcel out fair women into classes; and

7. "It's been done; he is cheerful; lovers' quarrels (are soon over)."

some are flyers and some are runners; these birds are wild
on the wing, those expose their bosoms to the shot. For
him there is <u>no individual woman</u>. He grants her a characteristic only to enroll her in a class. <u>He is our immortal
dunce at learning to distinguish her as a personal variety,
of a separate growth.</u>

Colonel De Craye's cock of the eye at the door said that
he had seen a rageing coquette go behind it. He had his
excuse for forming the judgement. She had spoken strangely
of the fall of his wedding present, strangely of Willoughby;
or there was a sound of strangeness in an allusion to
her appointed husband; and she had treated Willoughby
strangely when they met. Above all, her word about Flitch
was curious. And then that look of hers! And subsequently she transferred her polite attentions to Willoughby's friend. After a charming colloquy, the sweetest
give and take rattle he had ever enjoyed with a girl, she
developed headache to avoid him; and next she developed
blindness, for the same purpose.

He was feeling hurt, but considered it preferable to feel
challenged.

Miss Middleton came out of another door. She had seen
him when she had passed him and when it was too late to
convey her recognition; and now she addressed him with
an air of having bowed as she went by.

"No one?" she said. "Am I alone in the house?"

"There is a figure naught," said he, "but it's as good as
annihilated, and no figure at all, if you put yourself on the
wrong side of it, and wish to be alone in the house."[8]

"Where is Willoughby?"

"Away on business."

"Riding?"

"Achmet is the horse, and pray don't let him be sold,
Miss Middleton. I am deputed to attend on you."

"I should like a stroll."

"Are you perfectly restored?"

"Perfectly."

"Strong?"

"I was never better."

"It was the answer of the ghost of the wicked old man's
wife when she came to persuade him he had one chance
remaining. Then, says he, I'll believe in heaven if ye'll
stop that bottle, and hurls it; and the bottle broke and he
committed suicide, not without suspicion of her laying a
trap for him. These showers curling away and leaving
sweet scents are divine, Miss Middleton. I have the privilege of the Christian name on the nuptial-day. This park
of Willoughby's is one of the best things in England.
There's a glimpse over the lake that smokes of a corner of
Killarney; tempts the eye to dream, I mean." De Craye
wound his finger spirally upward like a smoke-wreath.

---

8. "figure naught": i.e., himself.

" Are you for Irish scenery ? "

" Irish, English, Scottish."

" All 's one so long as it 's beautiful : yes, you speak for me. Cosmopolitanism of races is a different affair. I beg leave to doubt the true union of some; Irish and Saxon, for example, let Cupid be master of the ceremonies and the dwelling-place of the happy couple at the mouth of a Cornucopia. Yet I have seen a flower of Erin worn by a Saxon gentleman proudly; and the Hibernian courting a Rowena !⁹ So we 'll undo what I said, and consider it cancelled."

" Are you of the rebel party, Colonel De Craye ? "¹

" I am Protestant and Conservative, Miss Middleton."

" I have not a head for politics."

" The political heads I have seen would tempt me to that opinion."

" Did Willoughby say when he would be back ? "

" He named no particular time. Dr. Middleton and Mr. Whitford are in the library upon a battle of the books."

" Happy battle ! "

" You are accustomed to scholars. They are rather intolerant of us poor fellows."

" Of ignorance, perhaps; not of persons."

" Your father educated you himself, I presume."

" He gave me as much Latin as I could take. The fault is mine that it is little."

" Greek ? "

" A little Greek."

" Ah ! And you carry it like a feather."

" Because it is so light."

" Miss Middleton, I could sit down to be instructed, old as I am. When women beat us, I verily believe we are the most beaten dogs in existence. You like the theatre ? "

" Ours ? "

" Acting, then."

" Good acting, of course."

" May I venture to say you would act admirably ? "

" The venture is bold, for I have never tried."

" Let me see; there is Miss Dale and Mr. Whitford : you and I; sufficient for a two-act piece.² THE IRISHMAN IN SPAIN would do." He bent to touch the grass as she stepped on it. " The lawn is wet."

She signified that she had no dread of wet, and said. " English women afraid of the weather might as well be shut up."

De Craye proceeded : " Patrick O'Neill passes over from Hibernia to Iberia, a disinherited son of a father in the claws of the lawyers, with a letter of introduction to Don

9. Rowena is the fair Saxon lady in Scott's *Ivanhoe*.
1. I.e., "Are you for Irish independence?" The question was just coming to the fore of public attention, under pressure from radicals like Charles Stewart Parnell. Colonel De Craye is no such firebrand.
2. Note the omission of Willoughby, who has no instinct for play.

Beltran d'Arragon, a Grandee of the First Class, who has a daughter Doña Serafina (Miss Middleton), the proudest beauty of her day, in the custody of a dueña (Miss Dale), and plighted to Don Fernan, of the Guzman family (Mr. Whitford). There you have our dramatis personæ."

[handwritten margin note: gets her wish for Vernon]

"You are Patrick ? "

"Patrick himself. And I lose my letter, and I stand on the Prado of Madrid with the last portrait of Britannia in the palm of my hand, and crying in the purest brogue of my native land : ' It 's all through dropping a letter I 'm here in Iberia instead of Hibernia, worse luck to the spelling ! ' "[3]

"But Patrick will be sure to aspirate the initial letter of Hibernia."[4]

"That is clever criticism, upon my word, Miss Middleton ! So he would. And there we have two letters dropped. But he 'd do it in a groan, so that it would n't count for more than a ghost of one ; and everything goes on the stage, since it 's only the laugh we want on the brink of the action. Besides you are to suppose the performance before a London audience, who have a native opposition to the aspirate and would n't bear to hear him spoil a joke, as if he were a lord or a constable. It 's an instinct of the English democracy. So with my bit of coin turning over and over in an undecided way, whether it shall commit suicide to supply me a supper, I behold a pair of Spanish eyes like violet lightnings in the black heavens of that favoured clime. Won't you have violet ? "

"Violet forbids my impersonation."

"But the lustre on black is dark violet blue."

"You remind me that I have no pretention to black."

Colonel de Craye permitted himself to take a flitting gaze at Miss Middleton's eyes. "Chestnut," he said. "Well, and Spain is the land of chestnuts."

"Then it follows that I am a daughter of Spain."

"Clearly."

"Logically ! "

"By positive deduction."

"And how do I behold Patrick ? "

"As one looks upon a beast of burden."

"Oh ! "

Miss Middleton's exclamation was louder than the matter of the dialogue seemed to require. She caught her hands up.

In the line of the outer extremity of the rhododendron, screened from the house windows, young Crossjay lay at his length, with his head resting on a doubled arm, and his ivy-wreathed hat on his cheek, just where she had left him, commanding him to stay. Half-way toward him up the lawn, she saw the poor boy, and the spur of that pitiful sight set her gliding swiftly. Colonel De Craye followed,

3. "last portrait of Britannia": the figure on the British penny-piece. "The Prado" is the fashionable promenade of Madrid.

4. I.e., pronounce the "aitch," instead of making the word 'Ibernia, easy to confuse with Iberia.

pulling an end of his moustache.

Crossjay jumped to his feet.

"My dear, dear Crossjay!" she addressed him and reproached him. "And how hungry you must be! And you must be drenched! This is really too bad."

"You told me to wait here," said Crossjay, in shy self-defence.

"I did, and you should not have done it; foolish boy! I told him to wait for me here before luncheon, Colonel De Craye, and the foolish, foolish boy!—he has had nothing to eat and he must have been wet through two or three times. —because I did not come to him!"

"Quite right. And the lava might overflow him and take the mould of him, like the sentinel at Pompeii, if he's of the true stuff."[5]

"He may have caught cold, he may have a fever."

"He was under your orders to stay."

"I know, and I cannot forgive myself. Run in, Crossjay, and change your clothes. Oh! run, run to Mrs. Montague, and get her to give you a warm bath, and tell her from me to prepare some dinner for you. And change every garment you have. This is unpardonable of me. I said— 'not for politics'!—I begin to think I have not a head for anything. But could it be imagined that Crossjay would not move for the dinner-bell! through all that rain! I forgot you, Crossjay. I am so sorry; so sorry! You shall make me pay any forfeit you like. Remember I am deep deep in your debt. And now let me see you run fast. You shall come in to dessert this evening."[6]

Crossjay did not run. He touched her hand.

"You said something?"

"What did I say, Crossjay?"

"You promised."

"What did I promise?"

"Something."

"Name it, dear boy."

He mumbled " . . . kiss me."

Clara plumped down on him, enveloped him and kissed him.

The affectionately remorseful impulse was too quick for a conventional note of admonition to arrest her from paying that portion of her debt. When she had sped him off to Mrs. Montague, she was in a blush.

"Dear, dear Crossjay!" she said sighing:

"Yes, he's a good lad," remarked the colonel. "The fellow may well be a faithful soldier and stick to his post, if he receives promise of such a solde.[7] He is a great favourite with you."

---

5. The sentinel at Pompeii maintained his post when Vesuvius erupted, and was found there many centuries later.
6. Crossjay normally eats with the housekeeper, as children commonly did in great houses.
7. Reward.

"He is. You will do him a service by persuading Willoughby to send him to one of those men who get boys through their naval examination. And, Colonel de Craye, will you be kind enough to ask at the dinner-table that Crossjay may come in to dessert?"

"Certainly," said he, wondering.

"And will you look after him while you are here? See that no one spoils him. If you could get him away before you leave, it would be much to his advantage. He is born for the navy and should be preparing to enter it now." ~~Sets him working against Willoughby~~

"Certainly, certainly," said De Craye, wondering more.

"I thank you in advance."

"Shall I not be usurping? . ."

"No, we leave to-morrow."

"For a day?"

"For longer."

"Two?"

"It will be longer."

"A week? I shall not see you again?"

"I fear, not."

Colonel De Craye controlled his astonishment; he smothered a sensation of veritable pain, and amiably said "I feel a blow, but I am sure you would not willingly strike. We are all involved in the regrets."

Miss Middleton spoke of having to see Mrs. Montague, the housekeeper, with reference to the bath for Crossjay, and stepped off the grass. He bowed, watched her a moment, and for parallel reasons, running close enough to hit one mark, he commiserated his friend Willoughby. The winning or the losing of that young lady struck him as equally lamentable for Willoughby.

CHAPTER 20

AN AGED AND A GREAT WINE

THE leisurely promenade up and down the lawn with ladies and deferential gentlemen, in anticipation of the dinner-bell, was Dr. Middleton's evening pleasure. He walked as one who had formerly danced (in Apollo's time and the young God Cupid's), elastic on the muscles of the calf and foot, bearing his broad iron-grey head in grand elevation. The hard labour of the day approved the cooling exercise and the crowning refreshments of French cookery and wines of known vintages. He was happy at that hour in dispensing wisdom or nugae to his hearers, like the Western sun, whose habit it is, when he is fairly treated, to break out in quiet splendours, which by no means exhaust his treasury.[1] Blest indeed above his fellows, by the height of the bow-winged bird in a fair weather sunset sky above the pecking sparrow, is he that ever in the recurrent evening of his day sees the best of it ahead and soon to come. He has the rich reward of a youth and manhood of virtuous living.[2] Dr. Middleton misdoubted the future as well as the past of the man who did not, in becoming gravity, exult to dine. That man he deemed unfit for this world and the next.

An example of the good fruit of temperance, he had a comfortable pride in his digestion, and his political sentiments were attuned by his veneration of the Powers rewarding virtue. We must have a stable world where this is to be done.

The Rev. Doctor was a fine old picture; a specimen of art peculiarly English; combining in himself piety and epicurism, learning and gentlemanliness, with good room for each and a seat at one another's table : for the rest, a strong man, an athlete in his youth, a keen reader of facts and no reader of persons, genial, a giant at a task, a steady worker besides, but easily discomposed. He loved his daughter and he feared her. However much he liked her character, the dread of her sex and age was constantly present to warn him that he was not tied to perfect sanity while the damsel Clara remained unmarried. Her mother had been an amiable woman, of the poetical temperament nevertheless, too enthusiastic, imaginative, impulsive, for the repose of a sober scholar; an admirable woman, still, as you see, a woman, a firework. The girl resembled her. Why should she wish to run away from Patterne Hall for a single hour? Simply because she was of the sex born mutable and explosive. A husband was her proper custodian, justly relieving a father. With demagogues abroad and daughters at home, philosophy is needed for us to keep erect. Let the girl be Cicero's Tullia: well, she dies![3] The choicest of them will furnish us examples of a strange perversity.

Miss Dale was beside Dr. Middleton. Clara came to them and took the other side.

" I was telling Miss Dale that the signal for your subjection is my enfranchisement," he said to her, sighing and smiling. " We know the date. The date of an event to come certifies to it as a fact to be counted on."

"Are you anxious to lose me ?" Clara faltered.

" My dear, you have planted me on a field where I am to expect the trumpet, and when it blows I shall be quit of my nerves, no more."

Clara found nothing to seize on for a reply in these words. She thought upon the silence of Lætitia.

Sir Willoughby advanced, appearing in a cordial mood.

1. Aphorisms, adages.
2. "bow-winged bird": the swallow, loftier and swifter than the pecking sparrow.

3. She was the apple of the orator's eye, but died inconsiderately young.

" I need not ask you whether you are better," he said to Clara, sparkled to Lætitia, and raised a key to the level of Dr. Middleton's breast, remarking, " I am going down to my inner cellar."

" An inner cellar ! " exclaimed the doctor.

" Sacred from the butler. It is interdicted to Stoneman. Shall I offer myself as guide to you ? My cellars are worth a visit."

" Cellars are not catacombs. They are, if rightly constructed, rightly considered, cloisters, where the bottle meditates on joys to bestow, not on dust misused ! Have you anything great ? "

" A wine aged ninety."

" Is it associated with your pedigree, that you pronounce the age with such assurance ? "

" My grandfather inherited it."

" Your grandfather, Sir Willoughby, had meritorious off spring, not to speak of generous progenitors. What would have happened had it fallen into the female line ! I shall be glad to accompany you. Port ? Hermitage ? "[4]

" Port."

" Ah ! We are in England ! "

" There will just be time," said Sir Willoughby, inducing Dr. Middleton to step out.

A chirrup was in the Rev. Doctor's tone : " Hocks, too, have compassed age.[5] I have tasted senior Hocks. Their flavours are as a brook of many voices; they have depth also. Senatorial Port ! we say. We cannot say that of any other wine. Port is deep-sea deep. It is in its flavour deep; mark the difference. It is like a classic tragedy, organic in conception. An ancient Hermitage has the light of the antique; the merit that it can grow to an extreme old age; a merit. Neither of Hermitage nor of Hock can you say that it is the blood of those long years, retaining the strength of youth with the wisdom of age. To Port for that ! Port is our noblest legacy ! Observe, I do not compare the wines; I distinguish the qualities. Let them live together for our enrichment; they are not rivals like the Idæan Three.[6] Were they rivals, a fourth would challenge them. Burgundy has great genius. It does wonders within its period; it does all except to keep up in the race; it is short-lived. An aged Burgundy runs with a beardless Port. I cherish the fancy that Port speaks the sentences of wisdom, Burgundy sings the inspired Ode. Or put it, that Port is the Homeric hexameter, Burgundy the Pindaric dithyramb.[7] What do you say ? "

---

4. "Port," as its name implies, comes via the harbor of Oporto from Spain or Portugal; it is a rich, strong wine. "Hermitage" is a lighter, though still opulent French vintage, from the Rhone valley.

5. "Hocks": German white wines (from Hochheimer).

6. Hera, Athena, and Aphrodite, who disputed the prize of beauty before Paris on Mount Ida.

7. Classical verse forms, the first regular and majestic, the second nervous and exalted.

didn't follow

"The comparison is excellent, sir."

"The distinction, you would remark. Pindar astounds. But his elder brings us the more sustaining cup. One is a fountain of prodigious ascent. One is the unsounded purple sea of marching billows."

"A very fine distinction."

"I conceive you to be now commending the similes. They pertain to the time of the first critics of those poets. Touch the Greeks, and you can nothing new : all has been said : 'Graiis, . . . præter laudem, nullius avaris.'[8] Genius dedicated to Fame is immortal. We, sir, dedicate genius to the cloacaline floods. We do not address the unforgetting Gods, but the popular stomach."

Sir Willoughby was patient. He was about as accordantly coupled with Dr. Middleton in discourse as a drum duetting with a bass-viol; and when he struck in he received correction from the pedagogue-instrument. If he thumped affirmative or negative, he was wrong. However, he knew scholars to be an unmannered species ; and the Doctor's learnedness would be a subject to dilate on.

In the cellar, it was the turn for the drum. Dr. Middleton was tongue-tied there. Sir Willoughby gave the history of his wine in heads of chapters ; whence it came to the family originally, and how it had come down to him in the quantity to be seen. "Curiously, my grandfather, who inherited it, was a water-drinker. My father died early."

"Indeed ! Dear me !" the Doctor ejaculated in astonishment and condolence. The former glanced at the contrariety of man, the latter embraced his melancholy destiny.

He was impressed with respect for the family. This cool vaulted cellar, and the central square block, or enceinte, where the thick darkness was not penetrated by the intruding lamp, but rather took it as an eye, bore witness to forethoughtful practical solidity in the man who had built the house on such foundations.[9] A house having a great wine stored below, lives in our imaginations as a joyful house fast and splendidly rooted in the soil. And imagination has a place for the heir of the house. His grandfather a water-drinker, his father dying early, present circumstances to us arguing predestination to an illustrious heirship and career. Dr. Middleton's musings were coloured by the friendly vision of glasses of the great wine ; his mind was festive ; it pleased him, and he chose to indulge in his whimsical-robustious, grandiose-airy style of thinking : from which the festive mind will sometimes take a certain print that we cannot obliterate immediately. Expectation is grateful, you know ; in the mood of gratitude we are waxen. And he was a self-humouring gentleman.

He liked Sir Willoughby's tone in ordering the servant at

8. "To the Greeks, greedy for nothing except praise": Horace, *The Art of Poetry*; "cloacaline floods": a very round-about way of referring to the gastric juices.
9. "enceinte": enclosure.

his heels to take up "those two bottles : " it prescribed, without overdoing it, a proper amount of caution, and it named an agreeable number.

Watching the man's hand keenly, he said, —

"But here is the misfortune of a thing super-excellent: — not more than one in twenty will do it justice."

Sir Willoughby replied : "Very true, sir, and I think we may pass over the nineteen."

"Women, for example : and most men."

"This wine would be a sealed book to them."

"I believe it would.   It would be a grievous waste."

"Vernon is a claret-man : and so is Horace De Craye. They are both below the mark of this wine. They will join the ladies. Perhaps you and I, sir, might remain together."

"With the utmost good will on my part."

"I am anxious for your verdict, sir."

"You shall have it, sir, and not out of harmony with the chorus preceding me, I can predict. Cool, not frigid." Dr. Middleton summed the attributes of the cellar on quitting it: "North side and South. No musty damp. A pure air! Everything requisite. One might lie down oneself and keep sweet here."

Of all our venerable British of the two Isles professing a suckling attachment to an ancient port-wine, lawyer, doctor, squire, rosy admiral, city merchant, the classic scholar is he whose blood is most nuptial to the webbed bottle. The reason must be, that he is full of the old poets. He has their spirit to sing with, and the best that Time has done on earth to feed it. He may also perceive a resemblance in the wine to the studious mind, which is the obverse of our mortality, and throws off acids and crusty particles in the piling of the years, until it is fulgent by clarity. Port hymns to his conservatism. It is magical : at one sip he is off swimming in the purple flood of the ever-youthful antique.

By comparison, then, the enjoyment of others is brutish ; they have not the soul for it; but he is worthy of the wine, as are poets of Beauty.   In truth, these should be severally apportioned to them, scholar and poet, as his own good thing. Let it be so.

Meanwhile Dr. Middleton sipped.

After the departure of the ladies, Sir Willoughby had practised a studied curtness upon Vernon and Horace.

"You drink claret," he remarked to them, passing it round. "Port, I think, Dr. Middleton ? The wine before you may serve for a preface. We shall have *your* wine in five minutes."

The claret jug empty, Sir Willoughby offered to send for more. De Craye was languid over the question. Vernon rose from the table.

"We have a bottle of Dr. Middleton's Port coming in," Willoughby said to him.

"Mine, you call it?" cried the Rev. Doctor.

"It's a royal wine, that won't suffer sharing," said Vernon.

"We'll be with you, if you go into the billiard-room, Vernon."

"I shall hurry my drinking of good wine for no man." said the Rev. Doctor.

"Horace?"

"I'm beneath it, ephemeral, Willoughby. I am going to the ladies."

Vernon and De Craye retired upon the arrival of the wine; and Dr. Middleton sipped. He sipped and looked at the owner of it.

"Some thirty dozen?" he said.

"Fifty."

The Doctor nodded humbly.

"I shall remember, sir," his host addressed him, "whenever I have the honour of entertaining you, I am cellarer of that wine."

The Rev. Doctor set down his glass. "You have, sir, in some sense, an enviable post. It is a responsible one, if that be a blessing. On you it devolves to retard the day of the last dozen."

"Your opinion of the wine is favourable, sir?"

"I will say this:—shallow souls run to rhapsody:—I will say, that I am consoled for not having lived ninety years back, or at any period but the present, by this one glass of your ancestral wine."

"I am careful of it," Sir Willoughby said modestly; "still its natural destination is to those who can appreciate it. You do, sir."

"Still, my good friend, still! It is a charge: it is a possession, but part in trusteeship. Though we cannot declare it an entailed estate, our consciences are in some sort pledged that it shall be a succession not too considerably diminished."

"You will not object to drink it, sir, to the health of your grandchildren. And may you live to toast them in it on their marriage-day!"

"You colour the idea of a prolonged existence in seductive hues. Ha! It is a wine for Tithonus.[1] This wine would speed him to the rosy Morning—aha!"

"I will undertake to sit you through it up to morning," said Sir Willoughby, innocent of the Bacchic nuptiality of the allusion.

Dr. Middleton eyed the decanter. There is a grief in gladness, for a premonition of our mortal state. The amount of wine in the decanter did not promise to sustain

---

1. In mythology, aged and chilly Tithonus is married to rosy Aurora, who is normally glad to leave his cold, ungrateful bed every morning. But if he had drunk this wine, she might have stayed with him. Willoughby doesn't get the Doctor's weighty allusion.

w/Dr M — a communion ceremony sealing marriage

the starry roof of night and greet the dawn. "Old wine, my friend, denies us the full bottle !"

" Another bottle is to follow."

" No ! "

" It is ordered."

"I protest."

" It is uncorked."

" I entreat."

" It is decanted."

"I submit. But, mark, it must be honest partnership. You are my worthy host, sir, on that stipulation. Note the superiority of wine over Venus ! — I may say, the magnanimity of wine; our jealousy turns on him that will not share! But the corks, Willoughby. The corks excite my amazement."

"The corking is examined at regular intervals. I remember the occurrence in my father's time. I have seen to it once."

"It must be perilous as an operation for tracheotomy; which I should assume it to resemble in surgical skill and firmness of hand, not to mention the imminent gasp of the patient."

A fresh decanter was placed before the doctor.

He said : "I have but a girl to give !" He was melted.

Sir Willoughby replied : "I take her for the highest prize this world affords."

"I have beaten some small stock of Latin into her head, and a note of Greek. She contains a savour of the classics. I hoped once . . . but she is a girl. The nymph of the woods is in her. Still she will bring you her flower-cup of Hippocrene.[2] She has that aristocracy — the noblest. She is fair; a Beauty, some have said, who judge not by lines. Fair to me, Willoughby ! She is my sky. There were applicants. In Italy she was besought of me. She has no history. You are the first heading of the chapter. With you she will have her one tale, as it should be. 'Mulier tum bene olet,' you know.[3] Most fragrant she that smells of naught. She goes to you from me, from me alone, from her father to her husband. 'Ut flos in septis secretus nascitur hortis.' [4] . . . He murmured on the lines to, "'Sic virgo, dum. . . .' I shall feel the parting. She goes to one who will have my pride in her, and more. I will add, who will be envied. Mr. Whitford must write you a Carmen Nuptiale."

The heart of the unfortunate gentleman listening to Dr. Middleton set in for irregular leaps. His offended temper broke away from the image of Clara, revealing her as he

2. A classical fountain where the Muses live; its water is often used as a symbol of poetic inspiration.
3. "A women's best reputation is to have none": Cicero, *Letters to Atticus* II, 1, 1.
4. "As the hidden flower is born in fenced gardens"; the doctor is quoting an epithalamion or marriage poem by Catullus (LXII). The "Carmen Nuptiale" that he supposes Vernon will write is another such.

had seen her in the morning beside Horace De Craye, distressingly sweet; sweet with the breezy radiance of an English soft-breathing day; sweet with sharpness of young sap. Her eyes, her lips, her fluttering dress that played happy mother across her bosom, giving peeps of the veiled twins; and her laughter, her slim figure, peerless carriage, all her terrible sweetness touched his wound to the smarting quick.

Her wish to be free of him was his anguish. In his pain he thought sincerely. When the pain was easier he muffled himself in the idea of her jealousy of Lætitia Dale, and deemed the wish a fiction. But she had expressed it. That was the wound he sought to comfort; for the double reason, that he could love her better after punishing her, and that to meditate on doing so masked the fear of losing her — the dread abyss she had succeeded in forcing his nature to shudder at as a giddy edge possibly near, in spite of his arts of self-defence.

"What I shall do to-morrow evening!" he exclaimed. "I do not care to fling a bottle to Colonel De Craye and Vernon. I cannot open one for myself. To sit with the ladies will be sitting in the cold for me. When do you bring me back my bride, sir?"

"My dear Willoughby!" The Rev. Doctor puffed, composed himself, and sipped. "The expedition is an absurdity. I am unable to see the aim of it. She had a headache, vapours. They are over, and she will show a return of good sense. I have ever maintained that nonsense is not to be encouraged in girls. *I* can put my foot on it. My arrangements are for staying here a further ten days, in the terms of your hospitable invitation. And I stay."

"I applaud your resolution, sir. Will you prove firm?"

"I am never false to my engagement, Willoughby."

"Not under pressure."

"Under no pressure."

"Persuasion, I should have said."

"Certainly not. The weakness is in the yielding, either to persuasion or to pressure. The latter brings weight to bear on us; the former blows at our want of it."

"You gratify me, Dr. Middleton, and relieve me."

"I cordially dislike a breach in good habits, Willoughby. But I do remember — was I wrong? — informing Clara that you appeared light-hearted in regard to a departure, or gap in a visit, that was not, I must confess, to my liking."

"Simply, my dear Doctor, your pleasure was my pleasure; but make my pleasure yours, and you remain to crack many a bottle with your son-in-law."

"Excellently said. You have a courtly speech, Willoughby. I can imagine you to conduct a lover's quarrel with a politeness to read a lesson to well-bred damsels. Aha?"

"Spare me the futility of the quarrel."

" All 's well ? "

" Clara," replied Sir Willoughby, in dramatic epigram, " is perfection."

" I rejoice," the Rev. Doctor responded, taught thus to understand that the lover's quarrel between his daughter and his host was at an end.

He left the table a little after eleven o'clock. A short dialogue ensued upon the subject of the ladies. They must have gone to bed? Why yes; of course they must. It is good that they should go to bed early to preserve their complexions for us. Ladies are creation's glory, but they are anti-climax, following a wine of a century old. They are anti-climax, recoil, cross-current; morally, they are repentance, penance; imagerially, the frozen North on the young brown buds bursting to green. What know they of a critic in the palate, and a frame all revelry! And mark you, revelry in sobriety, containment in exultation: classic revelry. Can they, dear though they be to us, light up candelabras in the brain, to illuminate all history and solve the secret of the destiny of man? They cannot; they cannot sympathize with them that can. So therefore this division is between us; yet are we not turbaned Orientals, nor are they inmates of the harem. We are not Moslem. Be assured of it in the contemplation of the table's decanter.

Dr. Middleton said: " Then I go straight to bed."

" I will conduct you to your door, sir," said his host.

The piano was heard. Dr. Middleton laid his hand on the banisters, and remarked: " The ladies must have gone to bed? "

Vernon came out of the library and was hailed: " Fellow-student! "

He waved a good night to the Doctor and said to Willoughby: " The ladies are in the drawing-room."

" I am on my way upstairs," was the reply.

" Solitude and sleep, after such a wine as that; and fore-fend us human society! " the Doctor shouted. " But, Willoughby! "

" Sir."

" *One* to-morrow! "

" You dispose of the cellar, sir."

" I am fitter to drive the horses of the sun.[5] I would rigidly counsel, one, and no more. We have made a breach in the fiftieth dozen. Daily one, will preserve us from having to name the fortieth quite so unseasonably. The couple of bottles per diem prognosticates disintegration, with its accompanying recklessness. Constitutionally, let me add, I bear three. I speak for posterity."

During Dr. Middleton's allocution the ladies issued from the drawing-room, Clara foremost, for she had heard her father's voice, and desired to ask him this in reference

---

5. Foolish Phaethon tried to drive the sun's horses and almost incinerated the world.

to their departure: "Papa, will you tell me the hour to-morrow?"

She ran up the stairs to kiss him, saying again: "When will you be ready to-morrow morning?"

Dr. Middleton announced a stoutly deliberative mind in the bugle-notes of a repeated ahem. He bethought him of replying in his doctorial tongue. Clara's eager face admonished him to brevity: it began to look starved. Intruding on his vision of the houris crouched in the inner cellar to be the reward of valiant men, it annoyed him.[6] His brows joined. He said: "I shall not be ready to-morrow morning."

"In the afternoon?"

"Nor in the afternoon."

"When?"

"My dear, I am ready for bed at this moment, and know of no other readiness. Ladies," he bowed to the group in the hall below him, "may fair dreams pay court to you this night!"

Sir Willoughby had hastily descended and shaken the hands of the ladies, directed Horace De Craye to the laboratory for a smoking-room, and returned to Dr. Middleton. Vexed by the scene, uncertain of his temper if he stayed with Clara, for whom he had arranged that her disappointment should take place on the morrow, in his absence, he said, "Good night, good night," to her, with due fervour, bending over her flaccid finger-tips; then offered his arm to the Rev. Doctor.

"Ay, son Willoughby, in friendliness, if you will, though I am a man to bear my load," the father of the stupefied girl addressed him. "Candles, I believe, are on the first landing. Good night, my love. Clara!"

"Papa!"

"Good night."

"Oh!" she lifted her breast with the interjection, standing in shame of the curtained conspiracy and herself, "good night."

Her father wound up the stairs. She stepped down.

"There was an understanding that papa and I should go to London to-morrow early," she said unconcernedly to the ladies, and her voice was clear, but her face too legible. De Craye was heartily unhappy at the sight.

6. "houris": delectable female angels of the Mohammedan paradise.

CHAPTER 21

CLARA'S MEDITATIONS

Two were sleepless that night: Miss Middleton and Colonel De Craye.

She was in a fever, lying like stone, with her brain burning. Quick natures run out to calamity in any little shadow of it flung before. Terrors of apprehension drive them. They stop not short of the uttermost when they are on the wings of dread. A frown means tempest, a wind wreck; to see fire is to be seized by it. When it is the approach of their loathing that they fear, they are in the tragedy of the embrace at a breath; and then is the wrestle between themselves and horror; between themselves and evil, which promises aid; themselves and weakness, which calls on evil; themselves and the better part of them, which whispers no beguilement.

The false course she had taken through sophistical cowardice appalled the girl; she was lost. The advantage taken of it by Willoughby put on the form of strength, and made her feel abject, reptilious; she was lost, carried away on the flood of the cataract. He had won her father for an ally. Strangely, she knew not how, he had succeeded in swaying her father, who had previously not more than tolerated him. "Son Willoughby" on her father's lips meant something that scenes and scenes would have to struggle with, to the outwearying of her father and herself. She revolved the "Son Willoughby" through moods of stupefaction, contempt, revolt, subjection. It meant that she was vanquished. It meant that her father's esteem for her was forfeited. She saw him a gigantic image of discomposure.

Her recognition of her cowardly feebleness brought the brood of fatalism. What was the right of so miserable a creature as she to excite disturbance, let her fortunes be good or ill? It would be quieter to float, kinder to everybody. Thank heaven for the chances of a short life! Once in a net, desperation is graceless. We may be brutes in our earthly destinies; in our endurance of them we need not be brutish.

She was now in the luxury of passivity, when we throw our burden on the Powers above, and do not love them. The need to love them drew her out of it, that she might strive with the unbearable, and by sheer striving, even though she were graceless, come to love them humbly. It is here that the seed of good teaching supports a soul; for the condition might be mapped, and where kismet whispers us to shut eyes, and instruction bids us look up, is at a well-marked cross-road of the contest.[1]

1. "kismet": fate.

Quick of sensation, but not courageously resolved, she perceived how blunderingly she had acted. For a punishment, it seemed to her that she who had not known her mind must learn to conquer her nature, and submit. She had accepted Willoughby; therefore she accepted him. The fact became a matter of the past, past debating.

In the abstract, this contemplation of circumstances went well. A plain duty lay in her way. And then a disembodied thought flew round her, comparing her with Vernon to her discredit. He had for years borne much that was distasteful to him, for the purpose of studying, and with his poor income helping the poorer than himself. She dwelt on him in pity and envy; he had lived in this place, and so must she; and he had not been dishonoured by his modesty: he had not failed of self-control, because he had a life within. She was almost imagining she might imitate him, when the clash of a sharp physical thought: "The difference! the difference!" told her she was woman and never could submit. Can a woman have an inner life apart from him she is yoked to? She tried to nestle deep away in herself: in some corner where the abstract view had comforted her, to flee from thinking as her feminine blood directed. It was a vain effort. The difference, the cruel fate, the defencelessness of women, pursued her, strung her to wild horses' backs, tossed her on savage wastes. In her case duty was shame: hence, it could not be broadly duty. That intolerable difference proscribed the word.

But the fire of a brain burning high and kindling everything, lit up herself against herself: — Was one so volatile as she a person with a will? — Were they not a multitude of flitting wishes that she took for a will?— Was she, featherheaded that she was, a person to make a stand on physical pride? — If she could yield her hand without reflection (as she conceived she had done, from incapacity to conceive herself doing it reflectively), was she much better than purchaseable stuff that has nothing to say to the bargain?

Furthermore, said her incandescent reason, she had not suspected such art of cunning in Willoughby. Then might she not be deceived altogether — might she not have misread him? Stronger than she had fancied, might he not be likewise more estimable? The world was favourable to him: he was prized by his friends.

She reviewed him. It was all in one flash. It was not much less intentionally favourable than the world's review and that of his friends, but, beginning with the idea of them, she recollected — heard Willoughby's voice pronouncing his opinion of his friends and the world; of Vernon Whitford and Colonel De Craye, for example, and of men and women. An undefined agreement to have the same regard for him as his friends and the world had, provided that he kept at the same distance from her, was the termination of this phase, occupying about a minute in time, and reached through a

series of intensely vivid pictures : — his face, at her petition
to be released, lowering behind them for a background and a
comment.

"I cannot ! I cannot ! " she cried aloud ; and it struck her
that her repulsion was a holy warning. Better be graceless
than a loathing wife : better appear inconsistent. Why
should she not appear such as she was ?

Why ? We answer that question usually in angry reliance
on certain superb qualities, injured fine qualities of ours
undiscovered by the world, not much more than suspected
by ourselves, which are still our fortress, where pride sits at
home, solitary and impervious as an octogenarian conservative. But it is not possible to answer it so when the brain
is rageing like a pine-torch and the devouring illumination
leaves not a spot of our nature covert. The aspect of her
weakness was unrelieved, and frightened her back to her
loathing. From her loathing, as soon as her sensations had
quickened to realize it, she was hurled on her weakness.
She was graceless, she was inconsistent, she was volatile, she
was unprincipled, she was worse than a prey to wickedness
— capable of it ; she was only waiting to be misled. Nay,
the idea of being misled suffused her with languor ; for then
the battle would be over and she a happy weed of the
sea, no longer suffering those tugs at the roots, but leaving
it to the sea to heave and contend. She would be like Constantia then : like her in her fortunes : never so brave, she
feared.

Perhaps very like Constantia in her fortunes !

Poor troubled bodies waking up in the night to behold
visually the spectre cast forth from the perplexed machinery
inside them, stare at it for a space, till touching consciousness they dive down under the sheets with fish-like alacrity.
Clara looked at her thought, and suddenly headed downward in a crimson gulf.

She must have obtained absolution, or else it was oblivion,
below. Soon after the plunge, her first object of meditation
was Colonel De Craye. She thought of him calmly : he
seemed a refuge. He was very nice, he was a holiday character. His lithe figure, neat firm footing of the stag, swift
intelligent expression, and his ready frolicsomeness, pleasant
humour, cordial temper, and his Irishry, whereon he was at
liberty to play, as on the emblem harp of the Isle, were
soothing to think of. The suspicion that she tricked herself
with this calm observation of him was dismissed. Issuing
out of torture, her young nature eluded the irradiating brain,
in search of refreshment, and she luxuriated at a feast in
considering him — shower on a parched land that he was !
He spread new air abroad. She had no reason to suppose
he was not a good man : she could securely think of him.
Besides he was bound by his prospective office in support of
his friend Willoughby to be quite harmless. And besides
(you are not to expect logical sequences) the showery re-

freshment in thinking of him lay in the sort of assurance it
conveyed, that the more she thought, the less would he be
likely to figure as an obnoxious official : that is, as the man
to do by Willoughby at the altar what her father would,
under the supposition, be doing by her. Her mind reposed
on Colonel De Craye.

His name was Horace. Her father had worked with her
at Horace. She knew most of the Odes and some of the
Satires and Epistles of the poet. They reflected benevolent
beams on the gentleman of the poet's name. He too was
vivacious, had fun, common sense, elegance ; loved rusti-
city, he said, sighed for a country life, fancied retiring to
Canada to cultivate his own domain ; " modus agri non ita
magnus : " a delight.[2] And he, too, when in the country
sighed for town. There were strong features of resemblance. He had hinted in fun at not being rich. " Quæ
virtus et quanta sit vivere parvo."[3] But that quotation
applied to and belonged to Vernon Whitford. Even so little
disarranged her meditations.

She would have thought of Vernon, as her instinct of
safety prompted, had not his exactions been excessive, He
proposed to help her with advice only. She was to do
everything for herself, do and dare everything, decide upon
everything. He told her flatly that so would she learn to
know her own mind ; and flatly that it was her penance.
She had gained nothing by breaking down and pouring herself out to him. He would have her bring Willoughby and
her father face to face, and be witness of their interview —
herself the theme. What alternative was there ? — obedience to the word she had pledged. He talked of patience,
of self-examination and patience. But all of her — she was
all marked *urgent*. This house was a cage, and the world —
her brain was a cage, until she could obtain her prospect of
freedom.

As for the house, she might leave it ; yonder was the
dawn.

She went to her window to gaze at the first colour along
the grey. Small satisfaction came of gazing at that or at
herself. She shunned glass and sky. One and the other
stamped her as a slave in a frame. It seemed to her she
had been so long in this place that she was fixed here : it
was her world, and to imagine an Alp, was like seeking to
get back to childhood. Unless a miracle intervened, here
she would have to pass her days. Men are so little chivalrous now, that no miracle ever intervenes. Consequently
she was doomed.

She took a pen and began a letter to a dear friend, Lucy
Darleton, a promised bridesmaid, bidding her countermand
orders for her bridal dress, and purposing a tour in Switzer-

2. "modus agri non ita magnus": "a bit
of ground, not very much": Horace,
Satires, II, vi. But the Latin poet was
thinking of his Sabine farm, not of Canada.

3. "What virtue and how much of it is
involved in living poor." Horace, *Odes*,
II, xvi, says he "lives well on a little."

land. She wrote of the mountain country with real abandonment to imagination. It became a visioned loophole of escape. She rose and clasped a shawl over her night-dress to ward off chillness, and sitting to the table again, could not produce a word. The lines she had written were condemned : they were ludicrously inefficient. The letter was torn to pieces. She stood very clearly doomed.

After a fall of tears, upon looking at the scraps, she dressed herself, and sat by the window and watched the blackbird on the lawn as he hopped from shafts of dewy sunlight to the long-stretched dewy tree-shadows, considering in her mind that dark dews are more meaningful than bright, the beauty of the dews of woods more sweet than meadow-dews. It signified only that she was quieter. She had gone through her crisis in the anticipation of it. That is how quick natures will often be cold and hard, or not much moved, when the positive crisis arrives, and why it is that they are prepared for astonishing leaps over the gradations which should render their conduct comprehensible to us, if not excuseable. She watched the blackbird throw up his head stiff, and peck to right and left, dangling the worm each side his orange beak. Speckle-breasted thrushes were at work, and a wagtail that ran as with Clara's own little steps. Thrush and blackbird flew to the nest. They had wings. The lovely morning breathed of sweet earth into her open window and made it painful, in the dense twitter, chirp, cheep, and song of the air, to resist the innocent intoxication. O to love! was not said by her, but if she had sung, as her nature prompted, it would have been. Her war with Willoughby sprang of a desire to love repelled by distaste. Her cry for freedom was a cry to be free to love: she discovered it, half-shuddering: to love, oh! no — no shape of man, nor impalpable nature either: but to love unselfishness, and helpfulness, and planted strength in something. Then, loving and being loved a little, what strength would be hers! She could utter all the words needed to Willoughby and to her father, locked in her love : walking in this world, living in that.

Previously she had cried, despairing: If I were loved! Jealousy of Constantia's happiness, envy of her escape, ruled her then: and she remembered the cry, though not perfectly her plain-speaking to herself : she chose to think she had meant: If Willoughby were capable of truly loving! For now the fire of her brain had sunk, and refuges and subterfuges were round about it. The thought of personal love was encouraged, she chose to think, for the sake of the strength it lent her to carve her way to freedom. She had just before felt rather the reverse, but she could not exist with that feeling; and it was true that freedom was not so indistinct in her fancy as the idea of love.

Were men, when they were known, like him she knew too well ?

are there any men for her ?
are they all Willoughby's ?

The arch-tempter's question to her was there.

She put it away. Wherever she turned, it stood observ-ing her. She knew so much of one man, nothing of the rest: naturally she was curious. Vernon might be sworn to be unlike. But he was exceptional. What of the other in the house?

Maidens are commonly reduced to read the masters of their destinies by their instincts; and when these have been edged by over-activity, they must hoodwink their maidenli-ness to suffer themselves to read: and then they must dupe their minds, else men would soon see they were gifted to discern. Total ignorance being their pledge of purity to men, they have to expunge the writing of their perceptives on the tablets of the brain: they have to know not when they do know. The instinct of seeking to know, crossed by the task of blotting knowledge out, creates that conflict of the natural with the artificial creature to which their ulti-mately-revealed double-face, complained of by ever-dissatis-fied men, is owing. Wonder in no degree that they indulge a craving to be fools, or that many of them act the char-acter. Jeer at them as little for not showing growth. You have reared them to this pitch, and at this pitch they have partly civilized you. Supposing you to want it done wholly, you must yield just as many points in your requisitions as are needed to let the wits of young women reap their due harvest and be of good use to their souls. You will then have a fair battle, a braver, with better results.

Clara's inner eye traversed Colonel De Craye at a shot.

She had immediately to blot out the vision of the Captain Oxford in him, the revelation of his laughing contempt for Willoughby, the view of mercurial principles, the scribbled histories of light love-passages.

She blotted it out, kept it from her mind: so she knew him, knew him to be a sweeter and a variable Willoughby, a generous kind of Willoughby, a Willoughby-butterfly, without having the free mind to summarize him and picture him for a warning. Scattered features of him, such as the instincts call up, were not sufficiently impressive. Besides, the clouded mind was opposed to her receiving impressions.

Young Crossjay's voice in the still morning air came to her ears. The dear guileless chatter of the boy's voice! Why, assuredly it was young Crossjay who was the man she loved. And he loved her. And he was going to be an unselfish, sustaining, true, strong man, the man she longed for, for anchorage. Oh, the dear voice! woodpecker and thrush in one. He never ceased to chatter to Vernon Whit-ford walking beside him with a swinging stride off to the lake for their morning swim. Happy couple! The morning gave them both a freshness and innocence above human. They seemed to Clara made of morning air and clear lake-water. Crossjay's voice ran up and down a diatonic scale, with here and there a query in semitone, and a laugh on a ringing note. She wondered what he could have to talk of so incessantly and imagined all the dialogue. He prattled of his yesterday, to-day and to-morrow, which did not imply past and future, but his vivid present. She felt like one vainly trying to fly in hearing him; she felt old. The consolation she arrived at was to feel maternal. She wished to hug the boy.

Trot and stride, Crossjay and Vernon entered the park, careless about wet grass, not once looking at the house. Crossjay ranged ahead and picked flowers, bounding back to show them. Clara's heart beat at a fancy that her name was mentioned. If those flowers were for her she would prize them!

The two bathers dipped over an undulation.

Her loss of them rattled her chains.

Deeply dwelling on their troubles has the effect upon the young of helping to forgetfulness; for they cannot think without imagining, their imaginations are saturated with their pleasures, and the collision, though they are unable to exchange sad for sweet, distils an opiate.

"Am I solemnly engaged?" she asked herself. She seemed to be awakening.

She glanced at her bed, where she had passed the night of ineffectual moaning; and out on the high wave of grass, where Crossjay and his good friend had vanished.

Was the struggle all to be gone over again?

Little by little her intelligence of her actual position crept up to submerge her heart.

"I am in his house!" she said. It resembled a discovery, so strangely had her opiate and power of dreaming wrought through her tortures. She said it gasping. She was in his house, his guest, his betrothed, sworn to him. The fact stood out cut in steel on the pitiless daylight.

That consideration drove her to be an early wanderer in the wake of Crossjay.

Her station was among beeches on the flank of the boy's return; and while waiting there, the novelty of her waiting to waylay any one — she who had played the contrary part! — told her more than it pleased her to think. Yet she could admit that she did desire to speak with Vernon, as with a counsellor, harsh and curt, but wholesome.

The bathers reappeared on the grass-ridge, racing and flapping wet towels.

Some one hailed them. A sound of the galloping hoof drew her attention to the avenue. She saw Willoughby dash across the park-level, and dropping a word to Vernon, ride away. Then she allowed herself to be seen.

Crossjay shouted. Willoughby turned his head, but not his horse's head. The boy sprang up to Clara. He had swum across the lake and back; he had raced Mr. Whitford —and beaten him! How he wished Miss Middleton had been able to be one of them!

Clara listened to him enviously. Her thought was: We women are nailed to our sex!

She said: "And you have just been talking to Sir Willoughby."

Crossjay drew himself up to give an imitation of the baronet's hand-waving in adieu.

He would not have done that, had he not smelt sympathy with the performance.

She declined to smile. Crossjay repeated it, and laughed. He made a broader exhibition of it to Vernon approaching: "I say, Mr. Whitford, who's this?"

Vernon doubled to catch him. Crossjay fled and resumed his magnificent air in the distance.

"Good morning, Miss Middleton; you are out early," said Vernon, rather pale and stringy from his cold swim, and rather hard-eyed with the sharp exercise following it.

She had expected some of the kindness she wanted to reject, for he could speak very kindly, and she regarded him as her doctor of medicine, who would at least present the futile drug.

"Good morning," she replied.

"Willoughby will not be home till the evening."

"You could not have had a finer morning for your bath."

"No."

"I will walk as fast as you like."

"I'm perfectly warm."

"But you prefer fast walking."

"Out."

"Ah! yes, that I understand. The walk back! Why is Willoughby away to-day?"

"He has business."

After several steps, she said: "He makes very sure of papa."

"Not without reason, you will find," said Vernon.

"Can it be? I am bewildered. I had papa's promise."

"To leave the Hall for a day or two."

"It would have been . . ."

"Possibly. But other heads are at work as well as yours. If you had been in earnest about it, you would have taken your father into your confidence at once. That was the course I ventured to propose, on the supposition."

"In earnest! I cannot imagine that you doubt it. I wished to spare him."

"This is a case in which he can't be spared."

"If I had been bound to any other! I did not know then *who* held me a prisoner. I thought I had only to speak to him sincerely."

"Not many men would give up their prize for a word;

Willoughby the last of any."

"Prize" rang through her thrillingly from Vernon's mouth, and soothed her degradation.

She would have liked to protest that she was very little of a prize; a poor prize; not one at all in general estimation; only one to a man reckoning his property; no prize in the true sense.

The importunity of pain saved her.

"Does he think I can change again? Am I treated as something won in a lottery? To stay here is indeed, indeed, more than I can bear. And if he is calculating — Mr. Whitford, if he calculates on another change, his plotting to keep me here is inconsiderate, not very wise. Changes *may* occur in absence."

"Wise or not, he has the right to scheme his best to keep you."

She looked on Vernon with a shade of wondering reproach.

"Why? What right?"

"The right you admit when you ask him to release you. He has the right to think you deluded; and to think you may come to a better mood if you remain — a mood more agreeable to him, I mean. He has that right absolutely. You are bound to remember also that you stand in the wrong. You confess it when you appeal to his generosity. And every man has the right to retain a treasure in his hand if he can. Look straight at these facts."

"You expect me to be all reason!"

"Try to be. It's the way to learn whether you are really in earnest."

"I will try. It will drive me to worse!"

"Try honestly. What is wisest now is, in my opinion, for you to resolve to stay. I speak in the character of the person you sketched for yourself as requiring. Well, then, a friend repeats the same advice. You might have gone with your father: now you will only disturb him and annoy him. The chances are, he will refuse to go."

"Are women ever so changeable as men, then? Papa consented; he agreed; he had some of my feeling; I saw it. That was yesterday. And at night! He spoke to each of us at night in a different tone from usual. With me he was hardly affectionate. But when you advise me to stay, Mr. Whitford, you do not perhaps reflect that it would be at the sacrifice of all candour."

"Regard it as a probational term."

"It has gone too far with me."

"Take the matter into the head: try the case there."

"Are you not counselling me as if I were a woman of intellect?"

The crystal ring in her voice told him that tears were near to flowing.

He shuddered slightly. "You have intellect," he said,

nodded, and crossed the lawn, leaving her. He had to dress.

She was not permitted to feel lonely, for she was immediately joined by Colonel De Craye.

CHAPTER 22

THE RIDE

CROSSJAY darted up to her a nose ahead of the colonel.

"I say, Miss Middleton, we're to have the whole day to ourselves, after morning lessons. Will you come and fish with me and see me bird's-nest?"

"Not for the satisfaction of beholding another cracked crown, my son," the colonel interposed: and bowing to Clara: "Miss Middleton is handed over to my exclusive charge for the day — with her consent?"

"I scarcely know," said she, consulting a sensation of languor that seemed to contain some reminiscence. "If I am here. My father's plans are uncertain. I will speak to him. If I am here, perhaps Crossjay would like a ride in the afternoon."

"Oh! yes," cried the boy; "out over Bournden, through Mewsey up to Closham beacon, and down on Aspenwell, where there's a common for racing. And ford the stream!"

"An inducement for you," De Craye said to her.

She smiled and squeezed the boy's hand.

"We won't go without you, Crossjay."

"You don't carry a comb, my man, when you bathe?"

At this remark of the colonel's, young Crossjay conceived the appearance of his matted locks in the eyes of his adorable lady. He gave her one dear look through his redness, and fled.

"I like that boy," said De Craye.

"I love him," said Clara.

Crossjay's troubled eyelids in his honest young face became a picture for her.

"After all, Miss Middleton, Willoughby's notions about him are not so bad, if we consider that you will be in the place of a mother to him."

"I think them bad."

"You are disinclined to calculate the good fortune of the boy in having more of you on land than he would have in crown and anchor buttons!"

"You have talked of him with Willoughby."

"We had a talk last night."

Of how much? thought she.

"Willoughby returns?" she said.

"He dines here, I know; for he holds the key of the

inner cellar, and Dr. Middleton does him the honour to applaud his wine. Willoughby was good enough to tell me that he thought I might contribute to amuse you."

She was brooding in stupefaction on her father and the wine as she requested Colonel De Craye to persuade Willoughby to take the general view of Crossjay's future and act on it.

"He seems fond of the boy, too!" said De Craye musingly.

"You speak in doubt?"

"Not at all. But is he not — men are queer fish! — make allowance for us — a trifle tyrannical, pleasantly, with those he is fond of?"

"If they look right and left?"

It was meant for an interrogation: it was not with the sound of one that the words dropped. "My dear Crossjay!" she sighed. "I would willingly pay for him out of my own purse, and I will do so rather than have him miss his chance. I have not mustered resolution to propose it."

"I may be mistaken, Miss Middleton. He talked of the boy's fondness of him."

"He would."

"I suppose he is hardly peculiar in liking to play Pole-star."[1]

"He may not be."

"For the rest, your influence should be all powerful."

"It is not."

De Craye looked with a wandering eye at the heavens.

"We are having a spell of weather perfectly superb. And the odd thing is, that whenever we have splendid weather at home we 're all for rushing abroad. I 'm booked for a Mediterranean cruise — postponed to give place to your ceremony."

"That?" she could not control her accent.

"What worthier?"

She was guilty of a pause.

De Craye saved it from an awkward length. "I have written half an essay on Honeymoons, Miss Middleton."

"Is that the same as a half-written essay, Colonel De Craye?"

"Just the same, with the difference that it 's a whole essay written all on one side."

"On which side?"

"The bachelor's."

"Why does he trouble himself with such topics!"

"To warm himself for being left out in the cold."

"Does he feel envy?"

"He has to confess it."

"He has liberty."

"A commodity he can't tell the value of if there 's no one to buy."

1. The focus of attention, a guiding light.

" Why should he wish to sell ? "

" He 's bent on completing his essay."

" To make the reading dull."

" There we touch the key of the subject. For what is to rescue the pair from a monotony multiplied by two? And so a bachelor's recommendation, when each has discovered the right sort of person to be dull with, pushes them from the Church door on a round of adventures containing a spice of peril, if 't is to be had. Let them be in danger of their lives the first or second day. A bachelor's loneliness is a private affair of his own; he has n't to look into a face to be ashamed of feeling it and inflicting it at the same time; 't is his pillow; he can punch it an he pleases, and turn it over t' other side, if he 's for a mighty variation ; there 's a dream in it. But our poor couple are staring wide awake. All their dreaming 's done. They 've emptied their bottle of elixir, or broken it; and she has a thirst for the use of the tongue, and he to yawn with a crony; and they may converse, they 're not aware of it, more than the desert that has drunk a shower. So as soon as possible she 's away to the ladies, and he puts on his Club. That 's what your bachelor sees and would like to spare them; and if he did n't see something of the sort he 'd be off with a noose round his neck, on his knees in the dew to the morning milkmaid."

" The bachelor is happily warned and on his guard," said Clara, diverted, as he wished her to be. " Sketch me a few of the adventures you propose."

" I have a friend who rowed his bride from the Houses of Parliament up the Thames to the Severn on into North Wales. They shot some pretty weirs and rapids."

" That was nice."

" They had an infinity of adventures, and the best proof of the benefit they derived is, that they forgot everything about them except that the adventures occurred."

" Those two must have returned bright enough to please you."

" They returned, and shone like a wrecker's beacon to the mariner. You see, Miss Middleton, there was the landscape, and the exercise, and the occasional bit of danger. I think it 's to be recommended. The scene is always changing, and not too fast ; and 't is not too sublime, like big mountains, to tire them of their everlasting big Ohs. There 's the difference between going into a howling wind, and launching among zephyrs. They have fresh air and movement, and not in a railway carriage ; they can take in what they look on. And she has the steering ropes, and that 's a wise commencement. And my lord is all day making an exhibition of his manly strength, bowing before her some dozen to the minute ; and she, to help him, just inclines when she 's in the mood. And they 're face to face, in the nature of things, and are not under the obligation of looking the unutterable, because, you see, there's business in hand; and the boat's just the right sort of third party, who never interferes, but must be attended to. And they feel they're labouring together to get along, all in the proper proportion; and whether he has to labour in life or not, he proves his ability. What do you think of it, Miss Middleton?"

"I think you have only to propose it, Colonel De Craye."

"And if they capsize, why, 'tis a natural ducking!"

"You forgot the lady's dressing-bag."

"The stain on the metal for a constant reminder of his prowess in saving it! Well, and there's an alternative to that scheme and a finer : — This, then : they read dramatic pieces during courtship, to stop the saying of things over again till the drum of the ear becomes nothing but a drum to the poor head, and a little before they affix their signatures to the <u>fatal Registry-book</u> of the vestry, they enter into an engagement with a body of provincial actors to join the troop on the day of their nuptials, and away they go in their coach and four, and she is Lady Kitty Caper for a month, and he Sir Harry Highflyer. See the honeymoon spinning! The marvel to me is, that none of the young couples do it. They could enjoy the world, see life, amuse the company, and come back fresh to their own characters, instead of giving themselves a dose of Africa without a savage to diversify it: an impression they never get over, I'm told. Many a character of the happiest auspices has irreparable mischief done it by the ordinary honeymoon. For my part, I rather lean to the second plan of campaign."

Clara was expected to reply, and she said : "Probably because you are fond of acting. It would require capacity on both sides."

"Miss Middleton, *I* would undertake to breathe the enthusiasm for the stage and the adventure."

"You are recommending it generally."

"Let my gentleman only have a fund of enthusiasm. The lady will kindle. She always does at a spark."

"If he has not any?"

"Then I'm afraid they must be mortally dull."

She allowed her silence to speak; she knew that it did so too eloquently, and could not control the personal adumbration she gave to the one point of light revealed in, "if he has not any." Her figure seemed immediately to wear a cap and cloak of dulness.

She was full of revolt and anger, she was burning with her situation; if sensible of shame now at anything that she did, <u>it turned to wrath and threw the burden on the author of her desperate distress. The hour for blaming herself had gone by, to be renewed ultimately perhaps in a season of freedom.</u> She was bereft of her insight within at present, so blind to herself, that while conscious of an accurate reading of Willoughby's friend, she thanked him in her heart for seeking simply to amuse her and slightly succeeding. The afternoon's ride with him and Crossjay was an agreeable beguilement to her in prospect.

Lætitia came to divide her from Colonel De Craye. Dr. Middleton was not seen before his appearance at the break-fast-table, where a certain air of anxiety in his daughter's presence produced the semblance of a raised map at intervals on his forehead. Few sights on earth are more deserving of our sympathy than a good man who has a troubled con-science thrust on him.

The Rev. Doctor's perturbation was observed. The ladies Eleanor and Isabel, seeing his daughter to be the cause of it, blamed her and would have assisted him to escape, but Miss Dale, whom he courted with that object, was of the opposite faction. She made way for Clara to lead her father out. He called to Vernon, who merely nodded while leaving the room by the window with Crossjay.

Half an eye on Dr. Middleton's pathetic exit in captivity sufficed to tell Colonel De Craye that parties divided the house. At first he thought how deplorable it would be to lose Miss Middleton for two days or three : and it struck him that Vernon Whitford and Lætitia Dale were acting oddly in seconding her, their aim not being discernible. For he was of the order of gentlemen of the obscurely-clear in mind, who have a predetermined acuteness in their watch upon the human play, and mark men and women as pieces of a bad game of chess, each pursuing an interested course. His ex-perience of a section of the world had educated him — as gal-lant, frank, and manly a comrade as one could wish for — up to this point. But he soon abandoned speculations, which may be compared to a shaking of the anemometer, that will not let the troubled indicator take station. Reposing on his perceptions and his instincts, he fixed his attention on the chief persons, only glancing at the others to establish a pos-tulate, that where there are parties in a house, the most bewitching person present is the origin of them. It is ever Helen's achievement. Miss Middleton appeared to him be-witching beyond mortal ; sunny in her laughter, shadowy in her smiling ; a young lady shaped for perfect music with a lover.

She was that, and no less, to every man's eye on earth. High breeding did not freeze her lovely girlishness. — But Willoughby did. This reflection intervened to blot luxurious picturings of her, and made itself acceptable by leading him back to several instances of an evident want of harmony of the pair.

And now (for purely undirected impulse all within us is not, though we may be eye-bandaged agents under direction) it became necessary for an honourable gentleman to cast vehement rebukes at the fellow who did not comprehend the jewel he had won. How could Willoughby behave like so complete a donkey ! De Craye knew him to be in his interior stiff, strange, exacting : women had talked of him ; he had been too much for one woman — the dashing Constantia : he had worn one woman, sacrificing far more for him than Constantia, to death. Still, with such a prize as Clara Middleton, Willoughby's behaviour was past calculating in its contemptible absurdity. And during courtship ! And courtship of that girl ! It was the way of a man ten years after marriage.

The idea drew him to picture her doatingly in her young matronly bloom ten years after marriage : without a touch of age, matronly wise, womanly sweet : perhaps with a couple of little ones to love, never having known the love of a man.

To think of a girl like Clara Middleton never having, at nine and twenty, and with two fair children ! known the love of a man, or the loving of a man, possibly, became torture to the Colonel.

For a pacification, he had to reconsider that she was as yet only nineteen and unmarried.

But she was engaged and she was unloved. One might swear to it, that she was unloved. And she was not a girl to be satisfied with a big house and a high-nosed husband.

There was a rapid alteration of the sad history of Clara the unloved matron solaced by two little ones. A childless Clara tragically loving and beloved, flashed across the dark glass of the future.

Either way her fate was cruel.

Some astonishment moved De Craye in the contemplation of the distance he had stepped in this morass of fancy. He distinguished the choice open to him of forward or back, and he selected forward. But fancy was dead : the poetry hovering about her grew invisible to him : he stood in the morass ; that was all he knew ; and momently he plunged deeper ; and he was aware of an intense desire to see her face, that he might study her features again : he understood no more.

It was the clouding of the brain by the man's heart, which had come to the knowledge that it was caught.

A certain measure of astonishment moved him still. It had hitherto been his portion to do mischief to women and avoid the vengeance of the sex. What was there in Miss Middleton's face and air to ensnare a veteran handsome man of society numbering six and thirty years, nearly as many conquests ? "Each bullet has got its commission." He was hit at last. That accident effected by Mr. Flitch had fired the shot. Clean through the heart, does not tell us of our misfortune till the heart is asked to renew its natural beating. It fell into the condition of the porcelain vase over a thought of Miss Middleton standing above his prostrate form on the road, and walking beside him to the Hall. Her words ? What have they been ? She had not uttered words, she had shed meanings. He did not for an instant conceive that he had charmed her : the charm she had cast

on him was too thrilling for coxcombry to lift a head; still
she had enjoyed his prattle. In return for her touch upon
the Irish fountain in him, he had manifestly given her relief.
And could not one see that so sprightly a girl would soon
be deadened by a man like Willoughby? Deadened she
was: she had not responded to a compliment on her
approaching marriage. An allusion to it killed her smiling. The case of Mr. Flitch, with the half-wager about his
reinstation in the service of the Hall, was conclusive evidence of her opinion of Willoughby.

It became again necessary that he should abuse Willoughby for his folly. Why was the man worrying her?
In some way he was worrying her.

What if Willoughby as well as Miss Middleton wished
to be quit of the engagement? . . .

For just a second, the handsome woman-flattered officer
proved his man's heart more whole than he supposed it.
That great organ, instead of leaping at the thought, suffered a check.

Bear in mind, that his heart was not merely man's, it was
a conqueror's. He was of the race of amorous heroes who
glory in pursuing, overtaking, subduing: wresting the prize
from a rival, having her ripe from exquisitely feminine
inward conflicts, plucking her out of resistance in good old
primitive fashion. You win the creature in her delicious
flutterings. He liked her thus, in cooler blood, because of
society's admiration of the capturer, and somewhat because
of the strife, which always enhances the value of a prize,
and refreshes our vanity in recollection.

Moreover, he had been matched against Willoughby: the
circumstance had occurred two or three times. He could
name a lady he had won, a lady he had lost. Willoughby's
large fortune and grandeur of style had given him advantages at the start. But the start often means the race —
with women, and a bit of luck.

The gentle check upon the galloping heart of Colonel De
Craye endured no longer than a second — a simple side-
glance in a headlong pace. Clara's enchantingness for a
temperament like his, which is to say, for him specially, in
part through the testimony her conquest of himself presented as to her power of sway over the universal heart
known as man's, assured him she was worth winning even
from a hand that dropped her.

He had now a double reason for exclaiming at the folly
of Willoughby. Willoughby's treatment of her showed
either temper or weariness. Vanity and judgement led De
Craye to guess the former. Regarding her sentiments for
Willoughby, he had come to his own conclusion. The certainty of it caused him to assume that he possessed an
absolute knowledge of her character: she was an angel,
born supple; she was a heavenly soul, with half a dozen of
the tricks of earth. Skittish filly, was among his phrases;

but she had a bearing and a gaze that forbade the dip in
the common gutter for wherewithal to paint the creature
she was.

Now, then, to see whether he was wrong for the first
time in his life! If not wrong, he had a chance.

There could be nothing dishonourable in rescuing a girl
from an engagement she detested. An attempt to think it
a service to Willoughby failed midway. De Craye dismissed that chicanery. It would be a service to Willoughby in the end, without question. There was that to
soothe his manly honour. Meanwhile he had to face the
thought of Willoughby as an antagonist, and the world
looking heavy on his honour as a friend.

Such considerations drew him tenderly close to Miss
Middleton. It must, however be confessed that the mental
ardour of Colonel De Craye had been a little sobered by his
glance at the possibility of both of the couple being of one
mind on the subject of their betrothal. Desirable as it was
that they should be united in disagreeing, it reduced the
romance to platitude, and the third person in the drama to
the appearance of a stick. No man likes to play that part.
Memoirs of the favourites of Goddesses, if we had them,
would confirm it of men's tastes in this respect, though the
divinest be the prize. We behold what part they played.

De Craye happened to be crossing the hall from the laboratory to the stables when Clara shut the library-door behind
her. He said something whimsical, and did not stop, nor
did he look twice at the face he had been longing for.

What he had seen made him fear there would be no ride
out with her that day. Their next meeting reassured him;
she was dressed in her riding habit and wore a countenance
resolutely cheerful. He gave himself the word of command
to take his tone from her.

He was of a nature as quick as Clara's. Experience
pushed him farther than she could go in fancy; but experience laid a sobering finger on his practical steps, and bade
them hang upon her initiative. She talked little. Young
Crossjay cantering ahead was her favourite subject. She
was very much changed since the early morning: his liveliness, essayed by him at a hazard, was unsuccessful; grave
English pleased her best. The descent from that was
naturally to melancholy. She mentioned a regret she had
that the Veil was interdicted to women in Protestant countries.[2] De Craye was fortunately silent; he could think of
no other veil than the Moslem, and when her meaning
struck his witless head, he admitted to himself that devout
attendance on a young lady's mind stupefies man's intelligence. Half an hour later, he was as foolish in supposing
it a confidence. He was again saved by silence.

In Aspenwell village she drew a letter from her bosom
and called to Crossjay to post it. The boy sang out: "Miss

2. "the Veil": devotional celibacy; there are few Protestant nunneries.

Lucy Darleton!   What a nice name!"

Clara did not show that the name betrayed anything.

She said to De Craye: "It proves he should not be here thinking of nice names."

Her companion replied: " You may be right." He added, to avoid feeling too subservient: " Boys will."

" Not if they have stern masters to teach them their daily lessons, and some of the lessons of existence."

" Vernon Whitford is not stern enough ? "

" Mr. Whitford has to contend with other influences here."

" With Willoughby ? "

"Not with Willoughby."

He understood her.   She touched the delicate indication firmly.   The man's heart respected her for it; not many girls could be so thoughtful or dare to be so direct; he saw that she had become deeply serious, and he felt her love of the boy to be maternal, past maiden sentiment.

By this light of her seriousness, the posting of her letter in a distant village, not entrusting it to the Hall post-box, might have import; not that she would apprehend the violation of her private correspondence, but we like to see our letter of weighty meaning pass into the mouth of the public box.

Consequently this letter was important. It was to suppose a sequency in the conduct of a variable damsel. Coupled with her remark about the Veil, and with other things, not words, breathing from her (which were the breath of her condition), it was not unreasonably to be supposed.   She might even be a very consistent person.   If one only had the key of her!

She spoke once of an immediate visit to London, supposing that she could induce her father to go.   De Craye remembered the occurrence in the hall at night, and her aspect of distress.

They raced along Aspenwell Common to the ford; shallow, to the chagrin of young Crossjay, between whom and themselves they left a fitting space for his rapture in leading his pony to splash up and down, lord of the stream.

Swiftness of motion so strikes the blood on the brain that our thoughts are lightnings, the heart is master of them.

De Craye was heated by his gallop to venture on the angling question: " Am I to hear the names of the brides-maids ? "

The pace had nerved Clara to speak to it sharply : "There is no need."

" Have I no claim ? "

She was mute.

" Miss Lucy Darleton, for instance; whose name I am almost as much in love with as Crossjay."

" She will not be bridesmaid to me."

"She declines ?   Add my petition, I beg."

" To all ? or to her ? "

" Do all the bridesmaids decline ? "

" The scene is too ghastly."

" A marriage ? "

" Girls have grown sick of it."

" Of weddings ?   We 'll overcome the sickness."

" With some."

" Not with Miss Darleton ?   You tempt my eloquence."

" You wish it ? "

" To win her consent ?   Certainly."

" The scene ! "

" Do I wish that ? "

" Marriage ! " exclaimed Clara, dashing into the ford, fearful of her ungovernable wildness and of what it might have kindled. — You, father ! you have driven me to unmaidenliness ! — She forgot Willoughby in her father, who would not quit a comfortable house for her all but prostrate beseeching; would not bend his mind to her explanations, answered her with the horrid iteration of such deaf misunderstanding as may be associated with a tolling bell.

De Craye allowed her to catch Crossjay by herself. They entered a narrow lane, mysterious with possible birds' eggs in the May-green hedges. As there was not room for three abreast, the colonel made up the rearguard, and was consoled by having Miss Middleton's figure to contemplate ; but the readiness of her joining in Crossjay's pastime of the nest-hunt was not so pleasing to a man that she had wound to a pitch of excitement. Her scornful accent on " Marriage " rang through him. Apparently she was beginning to do with him just as she liked, herself entirely unconcerned.

She kept Crossjay beside her till she dismounted, and the colonel was left to the procession of elephantine ideas in his head, whose ponderousness he took for natural weight. We do not with impunity abandon the initiative. Men who have yielded it are like cavalry put on the defensive ; a very small force with an ictus will scatter them.[3]

Anxiety to recover lost ground reduced the dimensions of his ideas to a practical standard.

Two ideas were opposed like duellists bent on the slaughter of one another. Either she amazed him by confirming the suspicions he had gathered of her sentiments for Willoughby in the moments of his introduction to her; or she amazed him as a model for coquettes : — the married and the widowed might apply to her for lessons.

These combatants exchanged shots, but remained standing : the encounter was undecided. Whatever the result, no person so seductive as Clara Middleton had he ever met. Her cry of loathing, " Marriage ! " coming from a girl, rang faintly clear of an ancient virginal aspiration of the sex to escape from their coil, and bespoke a pure cold savage pride that transplanted his thirst for her to higher fields.

3. "ictus": impetus, determination.

CHAPTER 23

TREATS OF THE UNION OF TEMPER AND POLICY

Sir Willoughby meanwhile was on a line of conduct suiting his appreciation of his duty to himself. He had deluded himself with the simple notion that good fruit would come of the union of <u>temper and policy</u>.[1]

No delusion is older, none apparently so promising, both parties being eager for the alliance. Yet, the theorists upon human nature will say, they are obviously of adverse disposition. And this is true, inasmuch as neither of them will submit to the yoke of an established union ; as soon as they have done their mischief, they set to work tugging for a divorce. But they have attractions, the one for the other, which precipitate them to embrace whenever they meet in a breast ; each is earnest with the owner of it to get him to officiate forthwith as wedding-priest. And here is the reason : temper, to warrant its appearance, desires to be thought as deliberative as policy ; and policy, the sooner to prove its shrewdness, is impatient for the quick blood of temper.

It will be well for men to resolve at the first approaches of the amorous but fickle pair upon interdicting even an accidental temporary junction: for the astonishing sweetness of the couple when no more than the ghosts of them have come together in a projecting mind is an intoxication beyond fermented grapejuice or a witch's brewage; and under the guise of active wits they will lead us to the parental meditation of antics compared with which a Pagan Saturnalia were less impious in the sight of sanity.[2] <u>This is full-mouthed</u> language; but on our studious way through any human career we are subject to fits of moral elevation; the theme inspires it, and the sage residing in every civilized bosom approves it.

Decide at the outset, that temper is fatal to policy: hold them with both hands in division. One might add, be doubtful of your policy and repress your temper: it would be to suppose you wise. You can however, by incorporating two or three captains of the great army of truisms bequeathed to us by ancient wisdom, fix in your service those veteran old standfasts to check you. They will not be serviceless in their admonitions to your understanding, and they will so contrive to reconcile with it the natural caperings of the wayward young sprig Conduct, that the latter, who commonly learns to walk upright and straight from nothing softer than raps of a bludgeon on his crown, shall foot soberly, appearing at least wary of dangerous corners.

1. We would perhaps call these qualities severity and persuasion.
2. "Saturnalia": The festival of Saturn, toward the end of December, was a time of misrule and indulgence.

Now Willoughby had not to be taught that temper is fatal to policy; he was beginning to see in addition that the temper he encouraged was particularly obnoxious to the policy he adopted; and although his purpose in mounting horse after yesterday frowning on his bride was definite, and might be deemed sagacious, he bemoaned already the fatality pushing him ever farther from her in chase of a satisfaction impossible to grasp.

But the bare fact that her behaviour demanded a line of policy crossed the grain of his temper: it was very offensive.

Considering that she wounded him severely, her reversal of their proper parts, by taking the part belonging to him, and requiring his watchfulness, and the careful dealings he was accustomed to expect from others and had a right to exact of her, was injuriously unjust. The feelings of a man hereditarily sensitive to property accused her of a trespassing impudence, and knowing himself, by testimony of his household, his tenants and the neighbourhood, and the world as well, amiable when he received his dues, he contemplated her with an air of stiff-backed ill-treatment, not devoid of a certain sanctification of martyrdom.

His bitterest enemy would hardly declare that it was he who was in the wrong.

Clara herself had never been audacious enough to say that. Distaste of his person was inconceivable to the favourite of society. The capricious creature probably wanted a whipping to bring her to the understanding of the principle called mastery, which is in man.

But was he administering it? If he retained a hold on her, he could undoubtedly apply the scourge at leisure; any kind of scourge; he could shun her, look on her frigidly, unbend to her to find a warmer place for sarcasm, pityingly smile, ridicule, pay court elsewhere. He could do these things if he retained a hold on her; and he could do them well because of the faith he had in his renowned amiability; for in doing them, he could feel that he was other than he seemed, and his own cordial nature was there to comfort him while he bestowed punishment. Cordial indeed, the chills he endured were flung from the world. His heart was in that fiction: half the hearts now beating have a mild form of it to keep them merry: and the chastisement he desired to inflict was really no more than righteous vengeance for an offended goodness of heart. Clara figuratively, absolutely perhaps, on her knees, he would raise her and forgive her. He yearned for the situation. To let her understand how little she had known him! It would be worth the pain she had dealt, to pour forth the stream of re-established confidences, to paint himself to her as he was; as he was in the spirit, not as he was to the world: though the world had reason to do him honour.

First, however, she would have to be humbled.

Something whispered that his hold on her was lost.

In such a case, every blow he struck would set her flying farther, till the breach between them would be past bridging.

Determination not to let her go, was the best finish to this perpetually revolving round which went like the same old wheel-planks of a water-mill in his head at a review of the injury he sustained. He had come to it before, and he came to it again. There was his vengeance. It melted him, she was so sweet! She shone for him like the sunny breeze on water. Thinking of her caused a catch of his breath.

The dreadful young woman had a keener edge for the senses of men than sovereign beauty.

It would be madness to let her go.

She affected him like an outlook on the great Patterne estate after an absence, when his welcoming flag wept for pride above Patterne Hall.

It would be treason to let her go.

It would be cruelty to her.

He was bound to reflect that she was of tender age, and the foolishness of the wretch was excuseable to extreme youth.

We toss away a flower that we are tired of smelling and do not wish to carry. But the rose — young woman — is not cast off with impunity. A fiend in shape of man is always behind us to appropriate her. He that touches that rejected thing is larcenous. Willoughby had been sensible of it in the person of Lætitia: and by all the more that Clara's charms exceeded the faded creature's, he felt it now. Ten thousand Furies thickened about him at a thought of her lying by the roadside without his having crushed all bloom and odour out of her which might tempt even the curiosity of the fiend, man.

On the other hand, supposing her to lie there untouched, universally declined by the sniffing sagacious dog-fiend, a miserable spinster for years, he could conceive notions of his remorse. A soft remorse may be adopted as an agreeable sensation within view of the wasted penitent whom we have struck a trifle too hard. Seeing her penitent, he certainly would be willing to surround her with little offices of compromising kindness. It would depend on her age. Supposing her still youngish, there might be captivating passages between them; as thus, in a style not unfamiliar, —

"And was it my fault, my poor girl? Am I to blame, that you have passed a lonely unloved youth?"

"No, Willoughby; the irreparable error was mine, the blame is mine, mine only. I live to repent it. I do not seek, for I have not deserved, your pardon. Had I it, I should need my own self-esteem to presume to clasp it to a bosom ever unworthy of you."

"I may have been impatient, Clara: we are human!"

"Never be it mine to accuse one on whom I laid so heavy a weight of forbearance!"

"Still, my old love!—for I am merely quoting history in naming you so—I cannot have been perfectly blameless."

"To me you were, and are."

"Clara!"

"Willoughby!"

"Must I recognize the bitter truth that we two, once nearly one! so nearly one! are eternally separated?"

"I have envisaged it. My friend—I may call you friend: you have ever been my friend, my best friend! Oh, that eyes had been mine to know the friend I had!—Willoughby, in the darkness of night, and during days that were as night to my soul, I have seen the inexorable finger pointing my solitary way through the wilderness from a Paradise forfeited by my most wilful, my wanton, sin. We have met. It is more than I have merited. We part. In mercy let it be for ever. Oh, terrible word! Coined by the passions of our youth, it comes to us for our sole riches when we are bankrupt of earthly treasures, and is the passport given by Abnegation unto Woe that prays to quit this probationary sphere. Willoughby, we part. It is better so."

"Clara! one—one only—one last—one holy kiss!"

"If these poor lips, that once were sweet to you . . ."

The kiss, to continue the language of the imaginative composition of his time, favourite readings in which had inspired Sir Willoughby with a colloquy so pathetic, was imprinted.

Ay, she had the kiss, and no mean one. It was intended to swallow every vestige of dwindling attractiveness out of her, and there was a bit of scandal springing of it in the background that satisfactorily settled her business, and left her "enshrined in memory, a divine recollection, to him," as his popular romances would say, and have said for years.

Unhappily, the fancied salute of her lips encircled him with the breathing Clara. She rushed up from vacancy like a wind summoned to wreck a stately vessel.

His reverie had thrown him into severe commotion. The slave of a passion thinks in a ring, as hares run: he will cease where he began. Her sweetness had set him off, and he whirled back to her sweetness: and that being incalculable and he insatiable, you have the picture of his torments when you consider that her behaviour made her as a cloud to him.

Riding slack, horse and man, in the likeness of those two ajog homeward from the miry hunt, the horse pricked his ears, and Willoughby looked down from his road along the hills on the race headed by young Crossjay with a short start over Aspenwell Common to the ford. There was no mistaking who they were, though they were well-nigh a

mile distant below. He noticed that they did not over-
take the boy. They drew rein at the ford, talking not
simply face to face, but face in face. Willoughby's novel
feeling of he knew not what drew them up to him, enabling him to fancy them bathing in one another's eyes.
Then she sprang through the ford, De Craye following,
but not close after — and why not close? She had flicked
him with one of her peremptorily saucy speeches when
she was bold with the gallop. They were not unknown
to Willoughby. They signified intimacy.

Last night he had proposed to De Craye to take Miss
Middleton for a ride the next afternoon. It never came
to his mind then that he and his friend had formerly been
rivals. He wished Clara to be amused. Policy dictated
that every thread should be used to attach her to her
residence at the Hall until he could command his temper
to talk to her calmly and overwhelm her, as any man in
earnest, with command of temper and a point of vantage,
may be sure to whelm a young woman. Policy, adulter-
ated by temper, yet policy it was that had sent him on his
errand in the early morning to beat about for a house and
garden suitable to Dr. Middleton within a circuit of five,
six, or seven miles of Patterne Hall. If the Rev. Doctor
liked the house and took it (and Willoughby had seen the
place to suit him), the neighbourhood would be a chain
upon Clara: and if the house did not please a gentleman
rather hard to please (except in a venerable wine), an excuse would have been started for his visiting other houses,
and he had the response to his importunate daughter, that
he believed an excellent house was on view. Dr. Middleton had been prepared by numerous hints to meet Clara's
black misreading of a lover's quarrel, so that everything
looked full of promise as far as Willoughby's exercise of
policy went.

But the strange pang traversing him now convicted him
of a large adulteration of profitless temper with it. The
loyalty of De Craye to a friend, where a woman walked in
the drama, was notorious. It was there, and a most flexi-
ble thing it was: and it soon resembled reason manipulated
by the sophists.[3] Not to have reckoned on his peculiar
loyalty was proof of the blindness cast on us by temper.

And De Craye had an Irish tongue; and he had it under
control, so that he could talk good sense and airy nonsense
at discretion. The strongest overboiling of English Puritan contempt of a gabbler would not stop women from
liking it. Evidently Clara did like it, and Willoughby
thundered on her sex. Unto such brainless things as
these do we, under the irony of circumstances, confide our
honour!

3. Greek sophists were famous for their
ability to make reason serve any end
which at the moment they happened to
favor.

For he was no gabbler. He remembered having rattled
in earlier days; he had rattled with an object to gain,
desiring to be taken for an easy, careless, vivacious, charming fellow, as any young gentleman may be who gaily
wears the golden dish of Fifty thousand pounds per annum
nailed to the back of his very saintly young pate.[4] The
growth of the critical spirit in him, however, had informed
him that slang had been a principal component of his rattling; and as he justly supposed it a betraying art for his
race and for him, he passed through the prim and the
yawning phases of affected indifference, to the pure Puritanism of a leaden contempt of gabblers.

They snare women, you see — girls! How despicable
the host of girls! — at least, that girl below there!

Married women understood him: widows did. He
placed an exceedingly handsome and flattering young widow
of his acquaintance, Lady Mary Lewison, beside Clara for
a comparison, involuntarily; and at once, in a flash, in
despite of him (he would rather it had been otherwise),
and in despite of Lady Mary's high birth and connections
as well, the silver lustre of the maid sicklied the poor
widow.

The effect of the luckless comparison was to produce an
image of surpassingness in the features of Clara that gave
him the final, or mace-blow.[5] Jealousy invaded him.

He had hitherto been free of it, regarding jealousy as a
foreign devil, the accursed familiar of the vulgar. Luckless fellows might be victims of the disease; he was not;
and neither Captain Oxford, nor Vernon, nor De Craye,
nor any of his compeers, had given him one shrewd pinch:
the woman had, not the man; and she in quite a different
fashion from his present wallowing anguish: she had never
pulled him to earth's level, where jealousy gnaws the
grasses. He had boasted himself above the humiliating
visitation.

If that had been the case, we should not have needed to
trouble ourselves much about him. A run or two with the
pack of imps would have satisfied us. But he desired
Clara Middleton manfully enough at an intimation of
rivalry to be jealous; in a minute the foreign devil had
him, he was flame: flaming verdigris, one might almost
dare to say, for an exact illustration; such was actually
the colour; but accept it as unsaid.[6]

Remember the poets upon Jealousy. It is to be haunted
in the heaven of two by a Third; preceded or succeeded,
therefore surrounded, embraced, hugged by this infernal
Third: it is Love's bed of burning marl; to see and taste
the withering Third in the bosom of sweetness; to be

---

4. "golden dish": a nimbus, as of a painted saint.
5. With a studded club or mace.

6. "verdigris": green, traditional color of jealousy.

dragged through the past and find the fair Eden of it sulphurous; to be dragged to the gates of the future and glory to behold them blood: to adore the bitter creature trebly and with treble power to clutch her by the windpipe: it is to be cheated, derided, shamed, and abject and supplicating, and consciously demoniacal in treacherousness, and victoriously self-justified in revenge.

And still there is no change in what men feel, though in what they do the modern may be judicious.

You know the many paintings of man transformed to rageing beast by the curse: and this, the fieriest trial of our egoism, worked in the Egoist to produce division of himself from himself, a concentration of his thoughts upon another object, still himself, but in another breast, which had to be looked at and into for the discovery of him. By the gaping jaw-chasm of his greed we may gather comprehension of his insatiate force of jealousy. Let her go? Not though he were to become a mark of public scorn in strangling her with the yoke! His concentration was marvellous. Unused to the exercise of imaginative powers, he nevertheless conjured her before him visually till his eyeballs ached. He saw none but Clara, hated none, loved none, save the intolerable woman. What logic was in him deduced her to be individual and most distinctive from the circumstance that only she had ever wrought these pangs. She had made him ready for them, as we know. An idea of De Craye being no stranger to her when he arrived at the Hall, dashed him at De Craye for a second: it might be or might not be that they had a secret; — Clara was the spell. So prodigiously did he love and hate, that he had no permanent sense except for her. The soul of him writhed under her eyes at one moment, and the next it closed on her without mercy. She was his possession escaping; his own gliding away to the Third.

There would be pangs for him too, that Third! Standing at the altar to see her fast-bound, soul and body, to another, would be good roasting fire.

It would be good roasting fire for her too, should she be averse. To conceive her aversion was to burn her and devour her. She would then be his! — what say you? Burnt and devoured! Rivals would vanish then. Her reluctance to espouse the man she was plighted to, would cease to be uttered, cease to be felt.

At last he believed in her reluctance. All that had been wanted to bring him to the belief was the scene on the common; such a mere spark, or an imagined spark! But the presence of the Third was necessary; otherwise he would have had to suppose himself personally distasteful.

Women have us back to the conditions of primitive man, or they shoot us higher than the topmost star. But it is as we please. Let them tell us what we are to them: for us, they are our back and front of life: the poet's Lesbia,

the poet's Beatrice; ours is the choice.[7] And were it
proved that some of the bright things are in the pay of
Darkness, with the stamp of his coin on their palms, and
that some are the very angels we hear sung of, not the
less might we say that they find us out, they have us by
our leanings. They are to us what we hold of best or
worst within. By their state is our civilization judged:
and if it is hugely animal still, that is because primitive
men abound and will have their pasture. Since the lead
is ours, the leaders must bow their heads to the sentence.
Jealousy of a woman, is the primitive egoism seeking to
refine in a blood gone to savagery under apprehension of
an invasion of rights; it is in action the tiger threatened
by a rifle when his paw is rigid on quick flesh; he tears
the flesh for rage at the intruder. The Egoist, who is our
original male in giant form, had no bleeding victim beneath his paw, but there was the sex to mangle. Much as
he prefers the well-behaved among women, who can worship and fawn, and in whom terror can be inspired, in his
wrath he would make of Beatrice a Lesbia Quadrantaria.[8]

Let women tell us of their side of the battle. We are
not so much the test of the Egoist in them as they to us.
Movements of similarity shown in crowned and undiademed
ladies of intrepid independence, suggest their occasional
capacity to be like men when it is given to them to hunt.
At present they fly, and there is the difference. Our manner of the chase informs them of the creature we are.

Dimly as young women are informed, they have a youthful ardour of detestation that renders them less tolerant of
the Egoist than their perceptive elder sisters. What they
do perceive, however, they have a redoubtable grasp of,
and Clara's behaviour would be indefensible if her detective feminine vision might not sanction her acting on its
direction. Seeing him as she did, she turned from him
and shunned his house as the antre of an ogre.[9] She had
posted her letter to Lucy Darleton. Otherwise, if it had
been open to her to dismiss Colonel De Craye, she might,
with a warm kiss to Vernon's pupil, have seriously
thought of the next shrill steam-whistle across yonder
hills for a travelling companion on the way to her friend
Lucy; so abhorrent was to her the putting of her horse's
head toward the Hall. Oh, the breaking of bread there!
It had to be gone through for another day and more: that
is to say, forty hours, it might be six and forty hours!
and no prospect of sleep to speed any of them on wings!

Such were Clara's inward interjections while poor Willoughby burnt himself out with verdigris flame having the
savour of bad metal, till the hollow of his breast was not
unlike to a corroded old cuirass found, we will assume, by

7. "Lesbia . . . Beatrice": Rather different ladies (Lesbia voluptuous, Beatrice
sacred) admired by Catullus and Dante
respectively.

8. A very vulgar mistress indeed, a
streetcorner mistress.
9. "antre": cave.

criminal lantern-beams in a digging beside green-mantled pools of the sullen soil, lumped with a strange adhesive concrete. How else picture the sad man ? — the cavity felt empty to him, and heavy; sick of an ancient and mortal combat, and burning; deeply-dinted too:

> With the starry hole
> Whence fled the soul:

very sore; impotent for aught save sluggish agony; a specimen and the issue of strife.

Measurelessly to loathe was not sufficient to save him from pain: he tried it: nor to despise; he went to a depth there also. The fact that she was a healthy young woman, returned to the surface of his thoughts like the murdered body pitched into the river, which will not drown and calls upon the elements of dissolution to float it. His grand hereditary desire to transmit his estates, wealth and name to a solid posterity, while it prompted him in his loathing and contempt of a nature mean and ephemeral compared with his, attached him desperately to her splendid healthiness. The council of elders, whose descendant he was, pointed to this young woman for his mate. He had wooed her with the idea that they consented. O she was healthy! And he likewise; but, as if it had been a duel between two clearly designated by quality of blood to bid a House endure, she was the first who taught him what it was to have sensations of his mortality.

He could not forgive her. It seemed to him consequently politic to continue frigid and let her have a further taste of his shadow, when it was his burning wish to strain her in his arms to a flatness provoking his compassion.

"You have had your ride ?" he addressed her politely in the general assembly on the lawn.

"I have had my ride, yes," Clara replied.

"Agreeable, I trust?"

"Very agreeable."

So it appeared. Oh, blushless!

The next instant he was in conversation with Lætitia, questioning her upon a dejected droop of her eyelashes.

"I am, I think," said she, "constitutionally melancholy."

He murmured to her: "I believe in the existence of specifics, and not far to seek, for all our ailments except those we bear at the hands of others."

She did not dissent.

De Craye, whose humour for being convinced that Willoughby cared about as little for Miss Middleton as she for him was nourished by his immediate observation of them, dilated on the beauty of the ride and his fair companion's equestrian skill.

"You should start a travelling circus," Willoughby rejoined.

"But the idea's a worthy one! — There's another alternative to the expedition I proposed, Miss Middleton," said De Craye. "And I be clown? I haven't a scruple of objection. I must read up books of jokes."

"Don't," said Willoughby.

"I'd spoil my part! But a natural clown won't keep up an artificial performance for an entire month, you see; which is the length of time we propose. He'll exhaust his nature in a day and be bowled over by the dullest regular donkey-engine with paint on his cheeks and a nodding-topknot."

"What is this expedition ' we ' proposé ?"

De Craye was advised in his heart to spare Miss Middleton any allusion to honeymoons.

"Merely a game to cure dulness."

"Ah," Willoughby acquiesced. "A month, you said?"

"One'd like it to last for years !"

"Ah! You are driving one of Mr. Merriman's witticisms at me, Horace; I am dense."[1]

Willoughby bowed to Dr. Middleton and drew him from Vernon, filially taking his arm to talk with him closely.

De Craye saw Clara's look as her father and Willoughby went aside thus linked.

It lifted him over anxieties and casuistries concerning loyalty. Powder was in the look to make a warhorse breathe high and shiver for the signal.

CHAPTER 24

CONTAINS AN INSTANCE OF THE GENEROSITY OF WILLOUGHBY

OBSERVERS of a gathering complication and a character in action commonly resemble gleaners who are intent only on picking up the ears of grain and huddling their store. Disinterestedly or interestedly they wax over-eager for the little trifles, and make too much of them. Observers should begin upon the precept, that not all we see is worth hoarding, and that the things we see are to be weighed in the scale with what we know of the situation, before we commit ourselves to a measurement. And they may be accurate observers without being good judges. They do not think so, and their bent is to glean hurriedly and form conclusions as hasty, when their business should be to sift at each step, and question.

1. "Mr. Merriman": Willoughby's contemptuous phrase for a writer of joke books.

Miss Dale seconded Vernon Whitford in the occupation
of counting looks and tones, and noting scraps of dialogue.
She was quite disinterested; he quite believed that he
was; to this degree they were competent for their post;
and neither of them imagined they could be personally
involved in the dubious result of the scenes they witnessed.
They were but anxious observers, diligently collecting.
She fancied Clara susceptible to his advice: he had fancied it, and was considering it one of his vanities. Each
mentally compared Clara's abruptness in taking them into
her confidence with her abstention from any secret word
since the arrival of Colonel De Craye. Sir Willoughby
requested Lætitia to give Miss Middleton as much of her
company as she could; showing that he was on the alert.
Another Constantia Durham seemed beating her wings for
flight. The suddenness of the evident intimacy between
Clara and Colonel De Craye shocked Lætitia: their acquaintance could be computed by hours. Yet at their first
interview she had suspected the possibility of worse than
she now supposed to be; and she had begged Vernon not
immediately to quit the Hall, in consequence of that faint
suspicion. She had been led to it by meeting Clara and
De Craye at her cottage-gate, and finding them as fluent
and laughter-breathing in conversation as friends. Unable to realize the rapid advance to a familiarity, more
ostensible than actual, of two lively natures, after such
an introduction as they had undergone: and one of the two
pining in a drought of liveliness: Lætitia listened to their
wager of nothing at all — a *no* against a *yes* — in the case
of poor Flitch; and Clara's, "Willoughby will not forgive:" and De Craye's, "Oh! he's human:" and the
silence of Clara: and De Craye's hearty cry, "Flitch
shall be a gentleman's coachman in his old seat again, or
I haven't a tongue!" to which there was a negative of
Clara's head: — and it then struck Lætitia that this young
betrothed lady, whose alienated heart acknowledged no
lord an hour earlier, had met her match, and, as the
observer would have said, her destiny. She judged of the
alarming possibility by the recent revelation to herself of
Miss Middleton's character, and by Clara's having spoken
to a man as well (to Vernon), and previously. That a
young lady should speak on the subject of the inner holies
to a man, though he were Vernon Whitford, was incredible
to Lætitia; but it had to be accepted as one of the dread
facts of our inexplicable life, which drag our bodies at
their wheels and leave our minds exclaiming. Then, if
Clara could speak to Vernon, which Lætitia would not have
done for a mighty bribe, she could speak to De Craye,
Lætitia thought deductively: this being the logic of un-
trained heads opposed to the proceeding whereby their
condemnatory deduction hangs. — Clara must have spoken
to De Craye!

Lætitia remembered how winning and prevailing Miss Middleton could be in her confidences. A gentleman hearing her might forget his duty to his friend, she thought, for she had been strangely swayed by Clara: ideas of Sir Willoughby that she had never before imagined herself to entertain, had been sown in her, she thought; not asking herself whether the searchingness of the young lady had struck them and bidden them rise from where they lay embedded. Very gentle women take in that manner impressions of persons, especially of the worshipped person, wounding them; like the new fortifications with embankments of soft earth, where explosive missiles bury themselves harmlessly until they are plucked out; and it may be a reason why those injured ladies outlive a Clara Middleton similarly battered.

Vernon less than Lætitia took into account that Clara was in a state of fever, scarcely reasonable. Her confidences to him he had excused, as a piece of conduct, in sympathy with her position. He had not been greatly astonished by the circumstances confided; and, on the whole, as she was excited and unhappy, he excused her thoroughly; he could have extolled her: it was natural that she should come to him, brave in her to speak so frankly, a compliment that she should condescend to treat him as a friend. Her position excused her widely. But she was not excused for making a confidential friend of De Craye. There was a difference.] *double standard*

Well, the difference was, that De Craye had not the smarting sense of honour with women which our meditator had: an impartial judiciary, it will be seen: and he discriminated between himself and the other justly: but sensation surging to his brain at the same instant, he reproached Miss Middleton for not perceiving that difference as clearly, before she betrayed her position to De Craye, which Vernon assumed that she had done. Of course he did. She had been guilty of it once: why, then, in the mind of an offended friend, she would be guilty of it twice. There was evidence. Ladies, fatally predestined to appeal to that from which they have to be guarded, must expect severity when they run off their railed highroad: justice is out of the question: man's brains might, his blood cannot administer it to them. By chilling him to the bone, they may get what they cry for. But that is a method deadening to their point of appeal.

In the evening Miss Middleton and the colonel sang a duet. She had of late declined to sing. Her voice was noticeably firm. Sir Willoughby said to her, "You have recovered your richness of tone, Clara." She smiled and appeared happy in pleasing him. He named a French ballad. She went to the music-rack and gave the song unasked. He should have been satisfied, for she said to him at the finish: "Is that as you like it?" He broke from, a murmur to Miss Dale: "Admirable." Some one mentioned a Tuscan popular canzone. She waited for Willoughby's approval, and took his nod for a mandate.

Traitress! he could have bellowed.

He had read of this characteristic of caressing obedience of the women about to deceive. He had in his time profited by it.

"Is it intuitively or by their experience that our neighbours across Channel surpass us in the knowledge of your sex?" he said to Miss Dale and talked through Clara's apostrophe to the "Santissima Virgine Maria," still treating temper as a part of policy, without any effect on Clara; and that was matter for sickly green reflections. The lover who cannot wound has indeed lost anchorage; he is woefully adrift: he stabs air, which is to stab himself. Her complacent proof-armour bids him know himself supplanted.[1]

During the short conversational period before the ladies retired for the night, Miss Eleanor alluded to the wedding by chance. Miss Isabel replied to her, and addressed an interrogation to Clara. De Craye foiled it adroitly. Clara did not utter a syllable. Her bosom lifted to a wavering height and sank. Subsequently she looked at De Craye, vacantly, like a person awakened, but she looked. She was astonished by his readiness, and thankful for the succour. Her look was cold, wide, unfixed, with nothing of gratitude or of personal in it. The look however stood too long for Willoughby's endurance. Ejaculating, "Porcelain!" he uncrossed his legs: a signal for the ladies Eleanor and Isabel to retire. Vernon bowed to Clara as she was rising. He had not been once in her eyes, and he expected a partial recognition at the good-night. She said it, turning her head to Miss Isabel, who was condoling once more with Colonel De Craye over the ruins of his wedding-present, the porcelain vase, which she supposed to have been in Willoughby's mind when he displayed the signal. Vernon walked off to his room, dark as one smitten blind: bile tumet jecur: her stroke of neglect hit him there where a blow sends thick obscuration upon eyeballs and brain alike.[2]

Clara saw that she was paining him and regretted it when they were separated. That was her real friend! But he prescribed too hard a task. Besides she had done everything he demanded of her, except the consenting to stay where she was and wear out Willoughby, whose dexterity wearied her small stock of patience. She had vainly tried remonstrance and supplication with her father hoodwinked by his host, she refused to consider how: through wine? — the thought was repulsive.

1. "proof-armour": Armor of proof cannot be penetrated; the indifference of a mistress spells the doom of her lover.

2. "bile tumet jecor": The liver swells with bile, classical phrase for being in a rage, from Horace, *Odes*, I, 13.

Nevertheless she was drawn to the edge of it by the contemplation of her scheme of release. If Lucy Darleton was at home: if Lucy invited her to come: if she flew to Lucy: oh! then her father would have cause for anger. He would not remember that but for hateful wine ! . . .

What was there in this wine of great age which expelled reasonableness, fatherliness ? He was her dear father: she was his beloved child: yet something divided them; something closed her father's ears to her: and could it be that incomprehensible seduction of the wine ? Her dutifulness cried violently no. She bowed, stupefied, to his arguments for remaining awhile, and rose clear-headed and rebellious with the reminiscence of the many strong reasons she had urged against them.

The strangeness of men, young and old, the little things (she regarded a grand wine as a little thing) twisting and changing them, amazed her. And these are they by whom women are abused for variability! Only the most imperious reasons, never mean trifles, move women, thought she. Would women do an injury to one they loved for oceans of that — ah! pah! of men. They necessarily respect a father. "My dear, dear father!" Clara said in the solitude of her chamber, musing on all his goodness, and she endeavoured to reconcile the desperate sentiments of the position he forced her to sustain, with those of a venerating daughter. The blow which was to fall on him beat on her heavily in advance. "I have not one excuse!" she said, glancing at numbers and a mighty one. But the idea of her father suffering at her hands cast her down lower than self-justification. She sought to imagine herself sparing him. It was too fictitious.

The sanctuary of her chamber, the pure white room so homely to her maidenly feelings, whispered peace, only to follow the whisper with another that went through her swelling to a roar, and leaving her as a string of music unkindly smitten. If she stayed in this house her chamber would no longer be a sanctuary. Dolorous bondage! Insolent death is not worse. Death's worm we cannot keep away, but when he has us we are numb to dishonour, happily senseless.

Youth weighed her eyelids to sleep, though she was quivering, and quivering she awoke to the sound of her name beneath her window. "I can love still, for I love him," she said, as she luxuriated in young Crossjay's boy's voice, again envying him his bath in the lake waters, which seemed to her to have the power to wash away grief and chains. Then it was that she resolved to let Crossjay see the last of her in this place. He should be made gleeful by doing her a piece of service; he should escort her on her walk to the railway station next morning, thence be sent flying for a long day's truancy, with a little

note of apology on his behalf that she would write for him
to deliver to Vernon at night.

Crossjay came running to her after his breakfast with
Mrs. Montague, the housekeeper, to tell her he had called
her up.

"You won't to-morrow: I shall be up far ahead of you,"
said she; and musing on her father, while Crossjay vowed
to be up the first, she thought it her duty to plunge into
another expostulation.

Willoughby had need of Vernon on private affairs. Dr.
Middleton betook himself as usual to the library, after
answering, "I will ruin you yet," to Willoughby's liberal
offer to despatch an order to London for any books he
might want.

His fine unruffled air, as of a mountain in still morning
beams, made Clara not indisposed to a preliminary scene
with Willoughby that might save her from distressing
him, but she could not stop Willoughby; as little could
she look an invitation. He stood in the hall, holding
Vernon by the arm. She passed him; he did not speak,
and she entered the library.

"What now, my dear? what is it?" said Dr. Middleton,
seeing that the door was shut on them.

"Nothing, papa," she replied calmly.

"You've not locked the door, my child? You turned
something there: try the handle."

"I assure you, papa, the door is not locked."

"Mr. Whitford will be here instantly. We are engaged
on tough matter. Women have not, and opinion is universal that they never will have, a conception of the value
of time."

"We are vain and shallow, my dear papa."

"No, no, not you, Clara. But I suspect you to require
to learn by having work in progress how important is . . .
is a quiet commencement of the day's task. There is not
a scholar who will not tell you so. We must have a
retreat. These invasions! — So you intend to have another
ride to-day? They do you good. To-morrow we dine
with Mrs. Mountstuart Jenkinson, an estimable person
indeed, though I do not perfectly understand our accepting. — You have not to accuse me of sitting over wine
last night, my Clara! I never do it, unless I am appealed
to for my judgement upon a wine."

"I have come to entreat you to take me away, papa."

In the midst of the storm aroused by this renewal of
perplexity, Dr. Middleton replaced a book his elbow had
knocked over in his haste to dash the hair off his forehead,
crying: "Whither? To what spot? That reading of
Guide-books, and idle people's notes of Travel, and picturesque correspondence in the newspapers, unsettles man and
maid. My objection to the living in hotels is known. I
do not hesitate to say that I do cordially abhor it. I have

had penitentially to submit to it in your dear mother's time, καὶ τρισκακοδαίμων up to the full ten thousand times.[3] But will you not comprehend that to the older man his miseries are multiplied by his years! But is it utterly useless to solicit your sympathy with an old man, Clara?"

"General Darleton will take us in, papa."

"His table is detestable. I say nothing of that; but his wine is poison. Let that pass — I should rather say, let it not pass! — but our political views are not in accord. True, we are not under the obligation to propound them in presence, but we are destitute of an opinion in common. We have no discourse. Military men *have* produced, or diverged in, noteworthy epicures: they are often devout; they have blossomed in lettered men: they are gentlemen; the country rightly holds them in honour; but, in fine, I reject the proposal to go to General Darleton. — Tears?"

"No, papa."

"I do hope not. Here we have everything man can desire; without contest, an excellent host. You have your transitory tea-cup tempests, which you magnify to hurricanes, in the approved historic manner of the book of Cupid. And all the better; I repeat, it is the better that you should have them over in the infancy of the alliance. Come in!" Dr. Middleton shouted cheerily in response to a knock at the door.

He feared the door was locked: he had a fear that his daughter intended to keep it locked.

"Clara!" he cried.

She reluctantly turned the handle, and the ladies Eleanor and Isabel came in, apologizing with as much coherence as Dr. Middleton ever expected from their sex. They wished to speak to Clara, but they declined to take her away. In vain the Rev. Doctor assured them she was at their service; they protested that they had very few words to say and would not intrude one moment further than to speak them.

Like a shy deputation of young scholars before the master, these very words to come were preceded by none at all; a dismal and trying pause; refreshing however to Dr. Middleton, who joyfully anticipated that the ladies could be induced to take away Clara when they had finished.

"We may appear to you a little formal," Miss Isabel began, and turned to her sister.

"We have no intention to lay undue weight on our mission, if mission it can be called," said Miss Eleanor.

"Is it entrusted to you by Willoughby?" said Clara.

"Dear child, that you may know it all the more earnest with us, and our personal desire to contribute to your happiness: therefore does Willoughby entrust the speaking

---

3. "kai triskakodaimon": literally, "and three bad devils," meaning something like "with a vengeance."

of it to us."

Hereupon the sisters alternated in addressing Clara, and she gazed from one to the other, piecing fragments of empty signification to get the full meaning when she might.

"— And in saying your happiness, dear Clara, we have our Willoughby's in view, which is dependent on yours."

"— And we never could sanction that our own inclinations should stand in the way."

"— No. We love the old place: and if it were only our punishment for loving it too idolatrously, we should deem it ground enough for our departure."

"— Without, really, an idea of unkindness; none, not any."

"— Young wives naturally prefer to be undisputed queens of their own establishment."

"— Youth and age!"

"But I," said Clara, "have never mentioned, never had a thought . . ."

"— You have, dear child, a lover who in his solicitude for your happiness both sees what you desire and what is due to you."

"— And for us, Clara, to recognize what is due to you is to act on it."

"— Besides, dear, a sea-side cottage has always been one of our dreams."

"— We have not to learn that we are a couple of old maids, incongruous associates for a young wife in the government of a great house."

"— With our antiquated notions, questions of domestic management might arise, and with the best will in the world to be harmonious! . . ."

"— So, dear Clara, consider it settled."

"— From time to time gladly shall we be your guests."

"— Your guests, dear, not censorious critics."

"And you think me such an Egoist!— dear ladies! The suggestion of so cruel a piece of selfishness wounds me. I would not have had you leave the Hall. I like your society; I respect you. My complaint, if I had one, would be, that you do not sufficiently assert yourselves. I could have wished you to be here for an example to me. I would not have allowed you to go. What can he think me!— Did Willoughby speak of it this morning?"

It was hard to distinguish which was the completer dupe of these two echoes of one another in worship of a family idol.

"Willoughby," Miss Eleanor presented herself to be stamped with the title hanging ready for the first that should open her lips, "our Willoughby is observant — he is ever generous — and he is not less forethoughtful. His arrangement is for our good on all sides."

"An index is enough," said Miss Isabel, appearing in her turn the monster dupe.[4]

4. "index": mere indication.

"You will not have to leave, dear ladies. Were I mistress here I should oppose it."

"Willoughby blames himself for not reassuring you before."

"Indeed we blame ourselves for not undertaking to go."

"Did he speak of it first this morning?" said Clara; but she could draw no reply to that from them. They resumed the duet, and she resigned herself to have her ears boxed with nonsense.

"So, it is understood?" said Miss Eleanor.

"I see your kindness, ladies."

"And I am to be Aunt Eleanor again?"

"And I Aunt Isabel?"

Clara could have wrung her hands at the impediment which prohibited her delicacy from telling them why she could not name them so, as she had done in the earlier days of Willoughby's courtship. She kissed them warmly, ashamed of kissing, though the warmth was real.

They retired with a flow of excuses to Dr. Middleton for disturbing him. He stood at the door to bow them out, and holding the door for Clara to wind up the procession, discovered her at a far corner of the room.

He was debating upon the advisability of leaving her there, when Vernon Whitford crossed the hall from the laboratory door, a mirror of himself in his companion air of discomposure.

That was not important, so long as Vernon was a check on Clara; but the moment Clara, thus baffled, moved to quit the library, Dr. Middleton felt the horror of having an uncomfortable face opposite.

"No botheration, I hope? It's the worst thing possible to work on. Where have you been? I suspect your weak point is not to arm yourself in triple brass against bother and worry; and no good work can you do unless you do. You have come out of that laboratory."

"I have, sir. — Can I get you any book?" Vernon said to Clara.

She thanked him, promising to depart immediately.

"Now you are at the section of Italian literature, my love," said Dr. Middleton. "Well, Mr. Whitford, the laboratory — ah! — where the amount of labour done within the space of a year would not stretch an electric current between this Hall and the railway station : say, four miles, which I presume the distance to be. Well, sir, a dilettantism costly in time and machinery is as ornamental as foxes' tails and deers' horns to an independent gentleman whose fellows are contented with the latter decorations for their civic wreath. Willoughby, let me remark, has recently shown himself most considerate for my girl. As far as I could gather — I have been listening to a dialogue of ladies — he is as generous as he is discreet. There are certain combats in which to be the one to succumb is to claim the honours, — and that is what women will not learn. I doubt their seeing the glory of it."

"I have heard of it; I have been with Willoughby," Vernon said hastily, to shield Clara from her father's allusive attacks. He wished to convey to her that his interview with Willoughby had not been profitable in her interests, and that she had better at once, having him present to support her, pour out her whole heart to her father. But how was it to be conveyed? She would not meet his eyes, and he was too poor an intriguer to be ready on the instant to deal out the verbal obscurities which are transparencies to one.

"I shall regret it, if Willoughby has annoyed you, for he stands high in my favour," said Dr. Middleton.

Clara dropped a book. Her father started higher than the nervous impulse warranted in his chair. Vernon tried to win a glance, and she was conscious of his effort, but her angry and guilty feelings prompting her resolution to follow her own counsel, kept her eyelids on the defensive.

"I don't say he annoys me, sir. I am here to give him my advice, and if he does not accept it I have no right to be annoyed. Willoughby seems annoyed that Colonel De Craye should talk of going to-morrow or next day."

"He likes his friends about him. Upon my word, a man of a more genial heart you might march a day without finding. But you have it on the forehead, Mr. Whitford."

"Oh! no, sir."

"There," Dr. Middleton drew his finger along his brows.

Vernon felt along his own, and coined an excuse for their blackness; unaware that the direction of his mind toward Clara pushed him to a kind of clumsy double meaning, while he satisfied an inward and craving wrath, as he said: "By the way, I have been racking my head; I must apply to you, sir. I have a line, and I am uncertain of the run of the line. Will this pass, do you think?—

'In Asination's tongue he asinates:'

signifying, that he excels any man of us at donkey-dialect."

After a decent interval for the genius of criticism to seem to have been sitting under his frown, Dr. Middleton rejoined with sober jocularity: "No, sir, it will not pass, and your uncertainty in regard to the run of the line would only be extended were the line centipedal.[5] Our recommendation is, that you erase it before the arrival of the ferule.[6] This might do:—

'In Assignation's name he assignats:'

signifying, that he pre-eminently flourishes hypothetical promises to pay by appointment. That might pass. But

---

5. "centipedal": a hundred feet long.
6. "ferule": The ruler serves both to measure the scansion of a Latin line and to punish the careless schoolboy who wrote it.

you will forbear to cite me for your authority."

" The line would be acceptable if I could get it to apply," said Vernon.

" Or this . . . " Dr. Middleton was offering a second suggestion, but Clara fled, astonished at men as she never yet had been. Why, in a burning world they would be exercising their minds in absurdities ! And those two were scholars, learned men ! And both knew they were in the presence of a soul in a tragic fever !

A minute after she had closed the door they were deep in their work. Dr. Middleton forgot his alternative line.

" Nothing serious ? " he said in reproof of the want of honourable clearness on Vernon's brows.

" I trust not, sir : it 's a case for common sense."

" And you call that not serious ? "

" I take Hermann's praise of the versus dochmiachus to be not only serious but unexaggerated," said Vernon.[7]

Dr. Middleton assented and entered on the voiceful ground of Greek metres, shoving your dry dusty world from his elbows.

CHAPTER 25

THE FLIGHT IN WILD WEATHER

THE morning of Lucy Darleton's letter of reply to her friend Clara was fair before sunrise with luminous colours that are an omen to the husbandman. Clara had no weather-eye for the rich Eastern crimson, nor a quiet space within her for the beauty. She looked on it as her gate of promise, and it set her throbbing with a revived relief in radiant things which she once dreamed of to surround her life, but her accelerated pulses narrowed her thoughts upon the machinery of her project. She herself was metal, pointing all to her one aim when in motion. Nothing came amiss to it, everything was fuel ; fibs, evasions, the serene battalions of white lies parallel on the march with dainty rogue falsehoods. She had delivered herself of many yesterday in her engagements for to-day. Pressure was put on her to engage herself, and she did so liberally, throwing the burden of deceitfulness on the extraordinary pressure. " I want the early part of the morning ; the rest of the day I shall be at liberty." She said it to Willoughby, Miss Dale, Colonel De Craye, and only the third time was she aware of the delicious double meaning. Hence she associated it with the colonel.

Your loudest outcry against the wretch who breaks your rules, is in asking how a tolerably conscientious person could have done this and the other besides the main offence,

7. Gottfried Hermann (1772–1848) wrote a book on Greek meters, one of which is the dochmian verse.

which you vow you could overlook but for the minor objections pertaining to conscience, the incomprehensible and abominable lies, for example, or the brazen coolness of the lying. Yet you know that we live in an undisciplined world, where in our seasons of activity we are servants of our design, and that this comes of our passions, and those of our position. Our design shapes us for the work in hand, the passions man the ship, the position is their apology: and now should conscience be a passenger on board, a merely seeming swiftness of our vessel will keep him dumb as the unwilling guest of a pirate captain scudding from the cruiser half in cloven brine through rocks and shoals to save his black flag. Beware the false position.

That is easy to say : sometimes the tangle descends on us like a net of blight on a rose-bush. There is then an instant choice for us between courage to cut loose, and desperation if we do not. But not many men are trained to courage ; young women are trained to cowardice. For them to front an evil with plain speech is to be guilty of effrontery and forfeit the waxen polish of purity, and therewith their commanding place in the market. They are trained to please man's taste, for which purpose they soon learn to live out of themselves, and look on themselves as he looks, almost as little disturbed as he by the undiscovered. Without courage, conscience is a sorry guest ; and if all goes well with the pirate captain, conscience will be made to walk the plank for being of no service to either party.

Clara's fibs and evasions disturbed her not in the least that morning. She had chosen desperation, and she thought herself very brave because she was just brave enough to fly from her abhorrence. She was light-hearted, or more truly, drunken-hearted. Her quick nature realized the way out of prison as vividly and suddenly as it had sunk suddenly and leadenly under the sense of imprisonment. Vernon crossed her mind : that was a friend ! Yes, and there was a guide ; but he would disapprove, and even he thwarting her way to sacred liberty must be thrust aside.

What would he think? They might never meet, for her to know. Or one day in the Alps they might meet, a middle-aged couple, he famous, she regretful only to have fallen below his lofty standard. "For, Mr. Whitford," says she, very earnestly, "I did wish at that time, believe me or not, to merit your approbation." The brows of the phantom Vernon whom she conjured up were stern, as she had seen them yesterday in the library.

She gave herself a chiding for thinking of him when her mind should be intent on that which he was opposed to.

It was a livelier relaxation to think of young Crossjay's shamefaced confession presently, that he had been a laggard in bed while she swept the dews. She laughed at him, and immediately Crossjay popped out on her from behind a tree, causing her to clap hand to heart and stand fast. A conspirator is not of the stuff to bear surprises. He feared he had hurt her and was manly in his efforts to soothe : he had been up "hours," he said, and had watched her coming along the avenue, and did not mean to startle her : it was the kind of fun he played with fellows, and if he had hurt her, she might do anything to him she liked, and she would see if he could not stand to be punished. He was urgent with her to inflict corporal punishment on him.

" I shall leave it to the boatswain to do that when you 're in the navy," said Clara.

" The boatswain dare n't strike an officer ! so now you see what you know of the navy," said Crossjay.

"But you could not have been out before me, you naughty boy, for I found all the locks and bolts when I went to the door."

" But you did n't go to the back-door, and Sir Willoughby's private door : you came out by the hall-door ; and I know what you want, Miss Middleton, you want not to pay what you 've lost."

" What have I lost, Crossjay ? "

" Your wager."

" What was that ? "

" You know."

" Speak."

" A kiss."

" Nothing of the sort. But, dear boy, I don't love you less for not kissing you. All that is nonsense : you have to think only of learning, and to be truthful. Never tell a story : suffer anything rather than be dishonest." She was particularly impressive upon the silliness and wickedness of falsehood, and added : " Do you hear ? "

" Yes : but you kissed me when I had been out in the rain that day."

" Because I promised."

" And, Miss Middleton, you betted a kiss yesterday."

" I am sure, Crossjay — no, I will not say I am sure : but can you say you are sure you were out first this morning ? Well, will you say you are sure that when you left the house you did not see me in the avenue ? You can't : ah ! "

" Miss Middleton, I do really believe I was dressed first."

" Always be truthful, my dear boy, and then you may feel that Clara Middleton will always love you."

" But, Miss Middleton, when you 're married you won't be Clara Middleton."

" I certainly shall, Crossjay."

" No, you won't, because I 'm so fond of your name ! "

She considered and said : " You have warned me, Crossjay, and I shall not marry. I shall wait," she was going to say, " for you," but turned the hesitation to a period. " Is the village where I posted my letter the day before yesterday too far for you ? "

Crossjay howled in contempt. "Next to Clara my favourite's Lucy," he said.

"I thought Clara came next to Nelson," said she; "and a long way off too, if you're not going to be a landlubber."

"I'm not going to be a landlubber, Miss Middleton, you may be absolutely positive on your solemn word."

"You're getting to talk like one a little now and then, Crossjay."

"Then I won't talk at all."

He stuck to his resolution for one whole minute.

Clara hoped that on this morning of a doubtful though imperative venture she had done some good.

They walked fast to cover the distance to the village post-office and back before the breakfast hour: and they had plenty of time, arriving too early for the opening of the door, so that Crossjay began to dance with an appetite, and was despatched to besiege a bakery. Clara felt lonely without him, apprehensively timid in the shuttered unmoving village street. She was glad of his return. When at last her letter was handed to her, on the testimony of the postman that she was the lawful applicant, Crossjay and she put on a sharp trot to be back at the Hall in good time. She took a swallowing glance of the first page of Lucy's writing, —

"Telegraph, and I will meet you. I will supply you with everything you can want for the two nights, if you cannot stop longer."

That was the gist of the letter. A second, less voracious glance at it along the road brought sweetness: — Lucy wrote, —

"Do I love you as I did? my best friend, you must fall into unhappiness to have the answer to that."

Clara broke a silence.

"Yes, dear Crossjay, and if you like you shall have another walk with me after breakfast. But remember, you must not say where you have gone with me. I shall give you twenty shillings to go and buy those bird's eggs and the butterflies you want for your collection; and mind, promise me, to-day is your last day of truancy. Tell Mr. Whitford how ungrateful you know you have been, that he may have some hope of you. You know the way across the fields to the railway station?"

"You save a mile; you drop on the road by Combline's mill, and then there's another five-minutes' cut, and the rest's road."

"Then, Crossjay, immediately after breakfast run round behind the pheasantry, and there I'll find you. And if any one comes to you before I come, say you are admiring the plumage of the Himalaya — the beautiful Indian bird; and if we're found together, we run a race, and of course you can catch me, but you mustn't until we're out of sight. Tell Mr. Vernon at night — tell Mr. Whitford at night you

had the money from me as part of my allowance to you for
pocket-money. I used to like to have pocket-money, Crossjay. And you may tell him I gave you the holiday, and I
may write to him for his excuse, if he is not too harsh to
grant it. He can be very harsh."

"You look right into his eyes next time, Miss Middleton.
I used to think him awful, till he made me look at him.
He says men ought to look straight at one another, just as
we do when he gives me my boxing-lesson, and then we won't
have quarrelling half so much. I can't recollect everything
he says."

"You are not bound to, Crossjay."

"No, but you like to hear."

"Really, dear boy, I can't accuse myself of having told
you that."

"No, but, Miss Middleton, you do. And he's fond of
your singing and playing on the piano, and watches
you."

"We shall be late if we don't mind," said Clara, starting
to a pace close on a run.

They were in time for a circuit in the park to the wild
double cherry-blossom, no longer all white. Clara gazed
up from under it, where she had imagined a fairer visible
heavenliness than any other sight of earth had ever given
her. That was when Vernon lay beneath. But she had
certainly looked above, not at him. The tree seemed sorrowful in its withering flowers of the colour of trodden
snow.

Crossjay resumed the conversation.

"He says ladies don't like him much."

"Who says that?"

"Mr. Whitford."

"Were those his words?"

"I forget the words: but he said they wouldn't be taught
by him, like me ever since you came; and since you came
I've liked him ten times more."

"The more you like him the more I shall like you,
Crossjay."

The boy raised a shout and scampered away to Sir
Willoughby, at the appearance of whom Clara felt herself
nipped and curling inward. Crossjay ran up to him with
every sign of pleasure. Yet he had not mentioned him
during the walk; and Clara took it for a sign that the boy
understood the entire satisfaction Willoughby had in mere
shows of affection, and acted up to it. Hardly blaming
Crossjay, she was a critic of the scene, for the reason that
youthful creatures who have ceased to love a person, hunger
for evidence against him to confirm their hard animus, which
will seem to them sometimes, when he is not immediately
irritating them, brutish, because they cannot analyze it and
reduce it to the multitude of just antagonisms whereof it
came. It has passed by large accumulation into a sombre

and speechless load upon the senses, and fresh evidence, the smallest item, is a champion to speak for it. Being about to do wrong, she grasped at this eagerly, and brooded on the little of vital and truthful that there was in the man, and how he corrupted the boy. Nevertheless she instinctively imitated Crossjay in an almost sparkling salute to him.

"Good morning, Willoughby; it was not a morning to lose : have you been out long ? "

He retained her hand. "My dear Clara ! and you, have you not over-fatigued yourself ? Where have you been ? "

"Round — everywhere ! And I am certainly not tired."

"Only you and Crossjay ? You should have loosened the dogs."

"Their barking would have annoyed the house."

"Less than I am annoyed to think of you without protection."

He kissed her fingers : it was a loving speech.

"The household . . ." said Clara, but would not insist to convict him of what he could not have perceived.

"If you outstrip me another morning, Clara, promise me to take the dogs; will you ? "

"Yes."

"To-day I am altogether yours."

"Are you ? "

"From the first to the last hour of it ! — So you fall in with Horace's humour pleasantly ? "

"He is very amusing."

"As good as though one had hired him."

"Here comes Colonel De Craye."

"He must think we *have* hired him ! "

She noticed the bitterness of Willoughby's tone. He sang out a good morning to De Craye, and remarked that he must go to the stables.

"Darleton ? Darleton, Miss Middleton ? " said the colonel, rising from his bow to her : "a daughter of General Darleton ? If so, I have had the honour to dance with her. And have not you ? — practised with her, I mean ; or gone off in a triumph to dance it out as young ladies do ? So you know what a delightful partner she is."

"She is ! " cried Clara, enthusiastic for her succouring friend, whose letter was the treasure in her bosom.

"Oddly, the name did not strike me yesterday, Miss Middleton. In the middle of the night it rang a little silver bell in my ear, and I remembered the lady I was half in love with, if only for her dancing. She is dark, of your height, as light on her feet; a sister in another colour. Now that I know her to be your friend ! . . ."

"Why, you may meet her, Colonel De Craye."

"It 'll be to offer her a castaway. And one only meets a charming girl to hear that she 's engaged ! 'T is not a line of a ballad, Miss Middleton, but out of the heart."

"Lucy Darleton . . . You were leading me to talk

seriously to you, Colonel De Craye."

"Will you one day?—and not think me a perpetual tumbler! You have heard of <u>melancholy clowns</u>. You would find the face not so laughable behind my paint. When I was thirteen years younger I was loved, and my dearest sank to the grave. Since then I have not been quite at home in life; probably because of finding no one so charitable as she. 'T is easy to win smiles and hands, but not so easy to win a woman whose faith you would trust as your own heart before the enemy. I was poor then. She said: 'The day after my twenty-first birthday;' and that day I went for her, and I wondered they did not refuse me at the door. I was shown upstairs, and I saw her, and saw death. She wished to marry me, to leave me her fortune!"

"Then never marry," said Clara in an underbreath.

She glanced behind.

Sir Willoughby was close, walking on turf.

"I must be cunning to escape him after breakfast," she thought.

He had discarded his foolishness of the previous days, and the thought in him could have replied: "I am a dolt if I let you out of my sight."

Vernon appeared, formal as usual of late. Clara begged his excuse for withdrawing Crossjay from his morning swim. He nodded.

De Craye called to Willoughby for a book of the trains.

"There's a card in the smoking-room; eleven, one, and four are the hours, if you must go," said Willoughby.

"You leave the Hall, Colonel De Craye?"

"In two or three days, Miss Middleton."

She did not request him to stay: his announcement produced no effect on her. Consequently, thought he—well, what? nothing: well, then, that she might not be minded to stay herself. Otherwise she would have regretted the loss of an amusing companion: that is the modest way of putting it. There is a modest and a vain for the same sentiment; and both may be simultaneously in the same breast; and each one as honest as the other; so shy is man's vanity in the presence of here and there a lady. She liked him: she did not care a pin for him—how could she? yet she liked him: O to be able to do her some kindling bit of service! These were his consecutive fancies, resolving naturally to the exclamation, and built on the conviction that she did not love Willoughby, and waited for a spirited lift from circumstances. His call for a book of the trains had been a sheer piece of impromptu, in the mind as well as on the mouth. It sprang, unknown to him, of conjectures he had indulged yesterday and the day before. This morning she would have an answer to her letter to her friend, Miss Lucy Darleton, the pretty dark girl, whom De Craye was astonished not to have noticed more when he danced with her. She, pretty as she was, had come to his recollection through the name and rank of her father, a famous general of cavalry, and tactician in that arm. The colonel despised himself for not having been devoted to Clara Middleton's friend.

The morning's letters were on the bronze plate in the hall. Clara passed on her way to her room without inspecting them. De Craye opened an envelope and went upstairs to scribble a line. Sir Willoughby observed their absence at the solemn reading to the domestic servants in advance of breakfast.[1] Three chairs were unoccupied. Vernon had his own notions of a mechanical service — and a precious profit he derived from them! but the other two seats returned the stare Willoughby cast at their backs with an impudence that reminded him of his friend Horace's calling for a book of the trains, when a minute afterward he admitted he was going to stay at the Hall another two days, or three. The man possessed by jealousy is never in need of matter for it: he magnifies; grass is jungle, hillocks are mountains. Willoughby's legs crossing and uncrossing audibly, and his tight-folded arms and clearing of the throat, were faint indications of his condition.

"Are you in fair health this morning, Willoughby?" Dr. Middleton said to him after he had closed his volumes.

"The thing is not much questioned by those who know me intimately," he replied.

"Willoughby unwell!" and "He is health incarnate!" exclaimed the ladies Eleanor and Isabel.

Lætitia grieved for him. Sunrays on a pest-stricken city, she thought, were like the smile of his face. She believed that he deeply loved Clara and had learnt more of her alienation.

He went into the hall to look up the well for the pair of malefactors; on fire with what he could not reveal to a soul.

De Craye was in the housekeeper's room, talking to young Crossjay and Mrs. Montague just come up to breakfast. He had heard the boy chattering, and as the door was ajar, he peeped in, and was invited to enter. Mrs. Montague was very fond of hearing him talk; he paid her the familiar respect which a lady of fallen fortunes, at a certain period after the fall, enjoys as a befittingly sad souvenir, and the respectfulness of the lord of the house was more chilling.

She bewailed the boy's trying his constitution with long walks before he had anything in him to walk on.

"And where did you go this morning, my lad?" said De Craye.

"Ah, you know the ground, colonel," said Crossjay. "I am hungry! I shall eat three eggs and some bacon, and

---

1. Prayers for the entire household, especially the staff, were customary in Victorian stately homes. "Mechanical service" is Vernon's severe judgment. Dr. Middleton, being in orders, presides.

buttered cakes, and jam, then begin again, on my second cup of coffee."

"It's not braggadocio," remarked Mrs. Montague. "He waits empty from five in the morning till nine, and then he comes famished to my table, and eats too much."

"Oh! Mrs. Montague, that is what the country people call roemancing. For, Colonel De Craye, I had a bun at seven o'clock. Miss Middleton forced me to go and buy it."

"A stale bun, my boy?"

"Yesterday's: there wasn't much of a stopper to you in it, like a new bun."

"And where did you leave Miss Middleton when you went to buy the bun? You should never leave a lady; and the street of a country town is lonely at that early hour. Crossjay, you surprise me."

"She forced me to go, colonel. Indeed she did. What do I care for a bun! And she was quite safe. We could hear the people stirring in the post-office, and I met our postman going for his letter-bag. I didn't want to go: bother the bun! — but you can't disobey Miss Middleton. I never want to, and wouldn't."

"There we're of the same mind," said the colonel, and Crossjay shouted, for the lady whom they exalted was at the door.

"You will be too tired for a ride this morning," De Craye said to her, descending the stairs.

She swung a bonnet by the ribands: "I don't think of riding to-day."

"Why did you not depute your mission to me?"

"I like to bear my own burdens, as far as I can."

"Miss Darleton is well?"

"I presume so."

"Will you try her recollection of me?"

"It will probably be quite as lively as yours was."

"Shall you see her soon?"

"I hope so."

Sir Willoughby met her at the foot of the stairs, but refrained from giving her a hand that shook

"We shall have the day together," he said.

Clara bowed.

At the breakfast-table she faced a clock.

De Craye took out his watch. "You are five and a half minutes too slow by that clock, Willoughby."

"The man omitted to come from Rendon to set it last week, Horace. He will find the hour too late here for him when he does come."

One of the ladies compared the time of her watch with De Craye's, and Clara looked at hers and gratefully noted that she was four minutes in arrear.

She left the breakfast-room at a quarter to ten, after kissing her father. Willoughby was behind her. He had been

soothed by thinking of his personal advantages over De
Craye, and he felt assured that if he could be solitary with
his eccentric bride and fold her in himself, he would, cutting
temper adrift, be the man he had been to her not so many
days back. Considering how few days back, his temper was
roused, but he controlled it.

They were slightly dissenting, as De Craye stepped into
the hall.

"A present worth examining," Willoughby said to her :
"and I do not dwell on the costliness. Come presently, then.
I am at your disposal all day. I will drive you in the afternoon to call on Lady Busshe to offer your thanks : but you
must see it first. It is laid out in the laboratory."

"There is time before the afternoon," said Clara.

"Wedding presents ? " interposed De Craye.

"A porcelain service from Lady Busshe, Horace."

"Not in fragments ? Let me have a look at it. I 'm
haunted by an idea that porcelain always goes to pieces.
I 'll have a look and take a hint. We 're in the laboratory,
Miss Middleton."

He put his arm under Willoughby's. The resistance to
him was momentary : Willoughby had the satisfaction of the
thought that De Craye being with him was not with Clara ;
and seeing her giving orders to her maid Barclay, he deferred
his claim on her company for some short period.

De Craye detained him in the laboratory, first over the
China cups and saucers, and then with the latest of London
— tales of youngest Cupid upon subterranean adventures,
having high titles to light him. Willoughby liked the tale
thus illuminated, for without the title there was no special
savour in such affairs, and it pulled down his betters in rank.
He was of a morality to reprobate the erring dame while he
enjoyed the incidents. He could not help interrupting De
Craye to point at Vernon through the window, striding this
way and that, evidently on the hunt for young Crossjay.
"No one here knows how to manage the boy except myself.
But go on, Horace," he said, checking his contemptuous
laugh ; and Vernon did look ridiculous, out there half-
drenched already in a white rain, again shuffled off by the
little rascal. It seemed that he was determined to have
his runaway : he struck up the avenue at full pedestrian
racing pace.

"A man looks a fool cutting after a cricket-ball ; but
putting on steam in a storm of rain to catch a young villain
out of sight, beats anything I 've witnessed," Willoughby
resumed, in his amusement.

"Aiha ! " said De Craye, waving a hand to accompany
the melodious accent, "there are things to beat that for
fun."

He had smoked in the laboratory, so Willoughby directed
a servant to transfer the porcelain service to one of the
sitting-rooms for Clara's inspection of it.

"You're a bold man," De Craye remarked. "The luck may be with you, though. I would n't handle the fragile treasure for a trifle."

"I believe in my luck," said Willoughby.

Clara was now sought for. The lord of the house desired her presence impatiently, and had to wait. She was in none of the lower rooms. Barclay, her maid, upon interrogation, declared she was in none of the upper. Willoughby turned sharp on De Craye: he was there.

The ladies Eleanor and Isabel, and Miss Dale, were consulted. They had nothing to say about Clara's movements, more than that they could not understand her exceeding restlessness. The idea of her being out of doors grew serious; heaven was black, hard thunder rolled, and lightning flushed the battering rain. Men bearing umbrellas, shawls, and cloaks were despatched on a circuit of the park. De Craye said: "I 'll be one."

"No," cried Willoughby, starting to intercept him, "I can't allow it."

"I've the scent of a hound, Willoughby; I 'll soon be on the track."

"My dear Horace, I won't let you go."

"Adieu, dear boy! and if the lady's discoverable, I 'm the one to find her."

He stepped to the umbrella-stand. There was then a general question whether Clara had taken her umbrella. Barclay said she had. The fact indicated a wider stroll than round inside the park: Crossjay was likewise absent. De Craye nodded to himself.

Willoughby struck a rattling blow on the barometer.

"Where 's Pollington?" he called, and sent word for his man Pollington to bring big fishing-boots and waterproof wrappers.

An urgent debate within him was in progress.

Should he go forth alone on his chance of discovering Clara and forgiving her under his umbrella and cloak? or should he prevent De Craye from going forth alone on the chance he vaunted so impudently?

"You will offend me, Horace, if you insist," he said.

"Regard me as an instrument of destiny, Willoughby," replied De Craye.

"Then we go in company."

"But that 's an addition of one that cancels the other by conjunction, and 's worse than simple division: for I can't trust my wits unless I rely on them alone, you see."

"Upon my word, you talk at times most unintelligible stuff, to be frank with you, Horace. Give it in English."

"'T is not suited perhaps to the genius of the language, for I thought I talked English."

"Oh! there 's English gibberish as well as Irish, we know!"

"And a deal foolisher when they do go at it; for it won't

bear squeezing, we think, like Irish."

"Where!" exclaimed the ladies, "where can she be! The storm is terrible."

Lætitia suggested the boathouse.

"For Crossjay had n't a swim this morning!" said De Craye.

No one reflected on the absurdity that Clara should think of taking Crossjay for a swim in the lake, and immediately after his breakfast: it was accepted as a suggestion at least that she and Crossjay had gone to the lake for a row.

In the hopefulness of the idea, Willoughby suffered De Craye to go on his chance unaccompanied. He was near chuckling. He projected a plan for dismissing Crossjay and remaining in the boathouse with Clara, luxuriating in the prestige which would attach to him for seeking and finding her. Deadly sentiments intervened. Still he might expect to be alone with her where she could not slip from him.

The throwing open of the hall-doors for the gentlemen presented a framed picture of a deluge. All the young-leaved trees were steely black, without a gradation of green, drooping and pouring, and the song of rain had become an inveterate hiss.

The ladies beholding it exclaimed against Clara, even apostrophized her, so dark are trivial errors when circumstances frown. She must be mad to tempt such weather: she was very giddy; she was never at rest. Clara! Clara! how could you be so wild! Ought we not to tell Dr. Middleton?

Lætitia induced them to spare him.

"Which way do you take?" said Willoughby, rather fearful that his companion was not to be got rid of now.

"Any way," said De Craye. "I chuck up my head like a halfpenny and go by the toss."

This enraging nonsense drove off Willoughby. De Craye saw him cast a furtive eye at his heels to make sure he was not followed, and thought: "Jove! he may be fond of her. But he's not on the track. She's a determined girl, if I'm correct. She's a girl of a hundred thousand. Girls like that make the right sort of wives for the right men. They're the girls to make men think of marrying. To-morrow! only give me the chance. They stick to you fast when they do stick."

Then a thought of her flower-like drapery and face caused him fervently to hope she had escaped the storm.

Calling at the West park-lodge he heard that Miss Middleton had been seen passing through the gate with Master Crossjay; but she had not been seen coming back. Mr. Vernon Whitford had passed through half an hour later.

"After his young man!" said the colonel.

The lodge-keeper's wife and daughter knew of Master

Crossjay's pranks; Mr. Whitford, they said, had made inquiries about him, and must have caught him and sent him
home to change his dripping things; for Master Crossjay
had come back, and had declined shelter in the lodge; he
seemed to be crying; he went away soaking over the wet
grass, hanging his head. The opinion at the lodge was,
that Master Crossjay was unhappy.

"He very properly received a wigging from Mr. Whitford, I have no doubt," said Colonel De Craye.[2]

Mother and daughter supposed it to be the case, and
considered Crossjay very wilful for not going straight home
to the Hall to change his wet clothes; he was drenched.

De Craye drew out his watch. The time was ten minutes
past eleven. If the surmise he had distantly spied was
correct, Miss Middleton would have been caught in the
storm midway to her destination. By his guess at her
character (knowledge of it, he would have said), he judged
that no storm would daunt her on a predetermined expedition. He deduced in consequence that she was at the
present moment flying to her friend the charming brunette
Lucy Darleton.

Still, as there was a possibility of the rain having been
too much for her, and as he had no other speculation concerning the route she had taken, he decided upon keeping
along the road to Rendon, with a keen eye at cottage and
farmhouse windows.

CHAPTER 26

VERNON IN PURSUIT

THE lodge-keeper had a son, who was a chum of Master
Crossjay's, and errant-fellow with him upon many adventures; for this boy's passion was to become a gamekeeper,
and accompanied by one of the head-gamekeeper's young-
sters, he and Crossjay, were in the habit of rangeing over the
country, preparing for a profession delightful to the tastes
of all three. Crossjay's prospective connection with the
mysterious ocean bestowed the title of captain on him by
common consent; he led them, and when missing for lessons
he was generally in the society of Jacob Croom or Jonathan
Fernaway. Vernon made sure of Crossjay when he perceived Jacob Croom sitting on a stool in the little lodge-
parlour. Jacob's appearance of a diligent perusal of a book
he had presented to the lad, he took for a decent piece of
trickery. It was with amazement that he heard from the
mother and daughter, as well as Jacob, of Miss Middleton's
going through the gate before ten o'clock with Crossjay

2. "wigging": scolding.

beside her, the latter too hurried to spare a nod to Jacob. That she, of all on earth, should be encouraging Crossjay to truancy was incredible. Vernon had to fall back upon Greek and Latin aphoristic shots at the sex to believe it.

Rain was universal; a thick robe of it swept from hill to hill; thunder rumbled remote, and between the ruffled roars the downpour pressed on the land with a great noise of eager gobbling, much like that of the swine's trough fresh filled, as though a vast assembly of the hungered had seated themselves clamorously and fallen to on meats and drinks in a silence, save of the chaps. A rapid walker poetically and humourously minded gathers multitudes of images on his way. And rain, the heaviest you can meet, is a lively companion when the resolute pacer scorns discomfort of wet clothes and squealing boots. South-western rain-clouds, too, are never long sullen: they enfold and will have the earth in a good strong glut of the kissing overflow; then, as a hawk with feathers on his beak of the bird in his claw lifts head, they rise and take veiled feature in long climbing watery lines: at any moment they may break the veil and show soft upper cloud, show sun on it, show sky, green near the verge they spring from, of the green of grass in early dew; or, along a travelling sweep that rolls asunder overhead, heaven's laughter of purest blue among titanic white shoulders: it may mean fair smiling for awhile, or be the lightest interlude; but the watery lines, and the drifting, the chasing, the upsoaring, all in a shadowy fingering of form, and the animation of the leaves of the trees pointing them on, the bending of the tree-tops, the snapping of branches, and the hurrahings of the stubborn hedge at wrestle with the flaws, yielding but a leaf at most, and that on a fling, make a glory of contest and wildness without aid of colour to inflame the man who is at home in them from old association on road, heath and mountain. Let him be drenched, his heart will sing. And thou, trim cockney, that jeerest, consider thyself, to whom it may occur to be out in such a scene, and with what steps of a nervous dancing master it would be thine to play the hunted rat of the elements, for the preservation of the one imagined dry spot about thee, somewhere on thy luckless person! The taking of rain and sun alike befits men of our climate, and he who would have the secret of a strengthening intoxication must court the clouds of the South-west with a lover's blood.

Vernon's happy recklessness was dashed by fears for Miss Middleton. Apart from those fears, he had the pleasure of a gull wheeling among foam-streaks of the wave. He supposed the Swiss and Tyrol Alps to have hidden their heads from him for many a day to come, and the springing and chiming South-west was the next best thing. A milder rain descended; the country expanded darkly defined underneath the moving curtain; the clouds were as he liked to see them, scaling; but their skirts dragged. Torrents were in store, for they coursed streamingly still and had not the higher lift, or eagle ascent, which he knew for one of the signs of fairness, nor had the hills any belt of mist-like vapour.

On a step of the stile leading to the short-cut to Rendon young Crossjay was espied. A man-tramp sat on the top bar.

"There you are; what are you doing there? Where's Miss Middleton?" said Vernon. "Now, take care before you open your mouth."

Crossjay shut the mouth he had opened.

"The lady has gone away over to a station, sir," said the tramp.

"You fool!" roared Crossjay, ready to fly at him.

"But ain't it, now, young gentleman? Can you say it ain't?"

"I gave you a' shilling, you ass!"

"You give me that sum, young gentleman, to stop here and take care of you, and here I stopped."

"Mr. Whitford!" Crossjay appealed to his master, and broke off in disgust. "Take care of me! As if anybody who knows me would think I wanted taking care of! Why, what a beast you must be, you fellow!"

"Just as you like, young gentleman. I chaunted you all I know, to keep up your downcast spirits. You did want comforting. You wanted it rarely. You cried like an infant."

"I let you 'chaunt' as you call it, to keep you from swearing."

"And why did I swear, young gentleman? because I've got an itchy coat in the wet, and no shirt for a lining. And no breakfast to give me a stomach for this kind of weather. That's what I've come to in this world! I'm a walking moral. No wonder I swears, when I don't strike up a chaunt."

"But why are you sitting here, wet through, Crossjay? Be off home at once, and change, and get ready for me."

"Mr. Whitford, I promised, and I tossed this fellow a shilling not to go bothering Miss Middleton."

"The lady wouldn't have none o' the young gentleman, sir, and I offered to go pioneer for her to the station, behind her, at a respectful distance."

"As if! — you treacherous cur!" Crossjay ground his teeth at the betrayer. "Well, Mr. Whitford, and I didn't trust him, and I stuck to him, or he'd have been after her whining about his coat and stomach, and talking of his being a moral. He repeats that to everybody."

"She has gone to the station?" said Vernon.

Not a word on that subject was to be won from Crossjay.

"How long since?" Vernon partly addressed Mr. Tramp.

The latter became seized with shivers as he supplied the information that it might be a quarter of an hour or twenty

minutes. "But what's time to me, sir! If I had reg'lar
meals, I should carry a clock in my inside. I got the rheu-
matics instead."

"Way there!" Vernon cried, and took the stile at a vault.

"That's what gentlemen can do, who sleeps in their beds
warm," moaned the tramp. "They've no joints."

Vernon handed him a half-crown piece, for he had been
of use for once.

"Mr. Whitford, let me come. If you tell me to come I
may. Do let me come," Crossjay begged with great entreaty. "I sha'n't see her for . . . "

"Be off, quick!" Vernon cut him short and pushed on.

The tramp and Crossjay were audible to him; Crossjay
spurning the consolations of the professional sad man.

Vernon sprang across the fields, timing himself by his
watch to reach Rendon station ten minutes before eleven,
though without clearly questioning the nature of the resolution which precipitated him. Dropping to the road, he had
better foothold than on the slippery field-path, and he ran.
His principal hope was that Clara would have missed her
way. Another pelting of rain agitated him on her behalf.
Might she not as well be suffered to go? — and sit three
hours and more in a railway-carriage with wet feet!

He clasped the visionary little feet to warm them on his
breast. — But Willoughby's obstinate fatuity deserved the
blow! — But neither she nor her father deserved the scandal. But she was desperate. Could reasoning touch her?
If not, what would? He knew of nothing. Yesterday he
had spoken strongly to Willoughby, to plead with him to
favour her departure and give her leisure to sound her
mind, and he had left his cousin, convinced that Clara's
best measure was flight: a man so cunning in a pretended
obtuseness backed by senseless pride, and in petty tricks
that sprang of a grovelling tyranny, could only be taught
by facts.

Her recent treatment of him, however, was very strange;
so strange that he might have known himself better if he
had reflected on the bound with which it shot him to a
hard suspicion. De Craye had prepared the world to hear
that he was leaving the Hall. Were they in concert? The
idea struck at his heart colder than if her damp little feet
had been there.

Vernon's full exoneration of her for making a confidant
of himself, did not extend its leniency to the young lady's
character when there was question of her doing the same
with a second gentleman. He could suspect much: he
could even expect to find De Craye at the station.

That idea drew him up in his run, to meditate on the
part he should play; and by drove little Dr. Corney on the
way to Rendon, and hailed him, and gave his cheerless
figure the nearest approach to an Irish hug in the form
of a dry seat under an umbrella and waterproof covering.

"Though it is the worst I can do for you, if you decline to supplement it with a dose of hot brandy and water at the Dolphin," said he: "and I 'll see you take it, if you please. I 'm bound to ease a Rendon patient out of the world. Medicine 's one of their superstitions, which they cling to the harder the more useless it gets. Pill and priest launch him happy between them. — 'And what 's on your conscience, Pat ? — It 's whether your blessing, your Riverence, would disagree with another drop. — Then, put the horse before the cart, my son, and you shall have the two in harmony, and God speed ye !' — Rendon station, did you say, Vernon ? You shall have my prescription at the Railway Arms, if you 're hurried. You have the look. What is it ? Can I help ?"

"No. And don't ask."

"You 're like the Irish Grenadier who had a bullet in a humiliating situation. Here 's Rendon, and through it we go with a spanking clatter. Here 's Dr. Corney's dog-cart posthaste again. For there 's no dying without him now, and Repentance is on the death-bed for not calling him in before ! Half a charge of humbug hurts no son of a gun, friend Vernon, if he 'd have his firing take effect. Be tender to 't in man or woman, particularly woman. So, by goes the meteoric doctor, and I 'll bring noses to windowpanes, you 'll see, which reminds me of the sweetest young lady *I* ever saw, and the luckiest man. When is she off for her bridal trousseau ? And when are they spliced ? I 'll not call her perfection, for that 's a post, afraid to move. But she 's a dancing sprig of the tree next it. Poetry 's wanted to speak of her. I 'm Irish and inflammable, I suppose, but I never looked on a girl to make a man comprehend the entire holy meaning of the word rapturous, like that one. And away she goes ! We 'll not say another word. But you 're a Grecian, friend Vernon. Now, could n't you think her just a whiff of an idea of a daughter of a peccadillo-Goddess ?"[1]

"Deuce take you, Corney, drop me here ; I shall be late for the train," said Vernon, laying hand on the doctor's arm to check him on the way to the station in view.

Dr. Corney had a Celtic intelligence for a meaning behind an illogical tongue. He drew up, observing : "Two minutes run won't hurt you."

He slightly fancied he might have given offence, though he was well acquainted with Vernon and had a cordial grasp at the parting.

The truth must be told, that Vernon could not at the moment bear any more talk from an Irishman. Dr. Corney had succeeded in persuading him not to wonder at Clara Middleton's liking for Colonel De Craye.

---

1. A nymph or wood sprite given to agreeable minor sins (peccadillos).

CHAPTER 27

AT THE RAILWAY STATION

CLARA stood in the waiting-room contemplating the white rails of the rain-swept line. Her lips parted at the sight of Vernon.

"You have your ticket?" said he.

She nodded, and breathed more freely; the matter of fact question was reassuring.

"You are wet," he resumed; and it could not be denied.

"A little. I do not feel it."

"I must beg you to come to the inn hard by : half a dozen steps. We shall see your train signalled. Come."

She thought him startlingly authoritative, but he had good sense to back him; and depressed as she was by the dampness, she was disposed to yield to reason if he continued to respect her independence. So she submitted outwardly, resisted inwardly, on the watch to stop him from taking any decisive lead.

"Shall we be sure to see the signal, Mr. Whitford?"

"I 'll provide for that."

He spoke to the station-clerk, and conducted her across the road.

"You are quite alone, Miss Middleton?"

"I am : I have not brought my maid."

"You must take off boots and stockings at once, and have them dried. I 'll put you in the hands of the landlady."

"But my train!"

"You have full fifteen minutes, besides fair chances of delay."

He seemed reasonable, the reverse of hostile, in spite of his commanding air, and that was not unpleasant in one friendly to her adventure. She controlled her alert mistrustfulness and passed from him to the landlady, for her feet were wet and cold, the skirts of her dress were soiled; generally inspecting herself, she was an object to be shuddered at, and she was grateful to Vernon for his inattention to her appearance.

Vernon ordered Dr. Corney's dose, and was ushered upstairs to a room of portraits, where the publican's ancestors and family sat against the walls, flat on their canvas as weeds of the botanist's portfolio, although corpulency was pretty generally insisted on, and there were formidable battalions of bust among the females. All of them had the aspect of the national energy which has vanquished obstacles to subside on its ideal. They all gazed straight at the guest. "Drink, and come to this!" they might have been labelled to say to him. He was in the private Walhalla of a large class of his countrymen.[1] The existing host had taken forethought to be of the party in his prime, and in the central place, looking fresh-flattened there, and sanguine from the performance. By-and-by a son would shove him aside; meanwhile he shelved his parent, according to the manners of energy.

One should not be a critic of our works of Art in uncomfortable garments. Vernon turned from the portraits to a stuffed pike in a glass-case, and plunged into sympathy with the fish for a refuge.

Clara soon rejoined him, saying: " But you, you must be very wet. You are without an umbrella. You must be wet through, Mr. Whitford."

" We 're all wet through to-day," said Vernon. " Crossjay 's wet through, and a tramp he met."

" The horrid man! But Crossjay should have turned back when I told him. Cannot the landlord assist you ? You are not tied to time. I begged Crossjay to turn back when it began to rain: when it became heavy I compelled him. So you met my poor Crossjay ? "

" You have not to blame him for betraying you. The tramp did that. I was thrown on your track quite by accident. Now pardon me for using authority: and don't be alarmed, Miss Middleton; you are perfectly free for me; but you must not run a risk to your health. I met Dr. Corney coming along, and he prescribed hot brandy and water for a wet skin; especially for sitting in it. There 's the stuff on the table; I see you have been aware of a singular odour; you must consent to sip some, as medicine; merely to give you warmth."

" Impossible, Mr. Whitford : I could not taste it. But pray obey Dr. Corney, if he ordered it for you."

" I can't unless you do."

" I will, then : I will try."

She held the glass, attempted, and was baffled by the reek of it.

" Try: you can do anything," said Vernon.

" Now that you find me here, Mr. Whitford ! Anything for myself, it would seem, and nothing to save a friend. But I will really try."

" It must be a good mouthful."

" I will try. And you will finish the glass ? "

" With your permission, if you do not leave too much."

They were to drink out of the same glass; and she was to drink some of this infamous mixture: and she was in a kind of hotel alone with him : and he was drenched in running after her : — all this came of breaking loose for an hour !

" Oh ! what a misfortune that it should be such a day, Mr. Whitford."

1. "private Walhalla": the parlor of the pub, the hall of Norse gods, very strange to a Grecian like Vernon. The "manners of energy" are rude and direct.

" Did you not choose the day ? "

" Not the weather."

" And the worst of it is, that Willoughby will come upon Crossjay wet to the bone, and pump him and get nothing but shufflings, blank lies, and then find him out and chase him from the house."

Clara drank immediately, and more than she intended. She held the glass as an enemy to be delivered from, gasping, uncertain of her breath.

" Never let me be asked to endure such a thing again ! "

" You are unlikely to be running away from father and friends again."

She panted still with the fiery liquid she had gulped : and she wondered that it should belie its reputation in not fortifying her, but rendering her painfully susceptible to his remarks.

" Mr. Whitford, I need not seek to know what you think of me."

" What I think ? I don't think at all; I wish to serve you, if I can."

" Am I right in supposing you a little afraid of me ? You should not be. I have deceived no one. I have opened my heart to you, and am not ashamed of having done so."

" It is an excellent habit, they say."

" It is not a habit with me."

He was touched, and for that reason, in his dissatisfaction with himself, not unwilling to hurt. " We take our turn, Miss Middleton. I 'm no hero, and a bad conspirator, so I am not of much avail."

" You have been reserved — but I am going, and I leave my character behind. You condemned me to the poison-bowl; you have not touched it yourself."

" In vino veritas : if I do I shall be speaking my mind."[2]

" Then do, for the sake of mind and body."

" It won't be complimentary."

" You can be harsh. Only say everything."

" Have we time ? "

They looked at their watches.

" Six minutes," Clara said.

Vernon's had stopped, penetrated by his total drenching.

She reproached herself. He laughed to quiet her. " My dies solemnes are sure to give me duckings; I 'm used to them.[3] As for the watch, it will remind me that it stopped when you went."

She raised the glass to him. She was happier and hoped for some little harshness and kindness mixed that she might carry away to travel with and think over.

He turned the glass as she had given it, turned it round

<hr />

2. "In vino veritas": "in wine is truth," a proverb ancient and dubious.
3. "dies solemnes": literally, "my sol-emn days," but also the opposite, "holidays."

in putting it to his lips: a scarce perceptible manœuvre, but
that she had given it expressly on one side.

It may be hoped that it was not done by design. Done
even accidentally, without a taint of contrivance, it was an
affliction to see, and coiled through her, causing her to
shrink and redden.

Fugitives are subject to strange incidents; they are not
vessels lying safe in harbour. She shut her lips tight, as
if they had been stung. The realizing sensitiveness of her
quick nature accused them of a loss of bloom. And the
man who made her smart like this was formal as a railway-
official on a platform!

"Now we are both pledged in the poison-bowl," said he.
"And it has the taste of rank poison, I confess. But the
doctor prescribed it, and at sea we must be sailors. Now,
Miss Middleton, time presses: will you return with me?"

"No! no!"

"Where do you propose to go?"

"To London; to a friend — Miss Darleton."

"What message is there for your father?"

"Say, I have left a letter for him in a letter to be
delivered to you."

"To me. And what message for Willoughby?"

"My maid Barclay will hand him a letter at noon."

"You have sealed Crossjay's fate."

"How?"

"He is probably at this instant undergoing an interrogation. You may guess at his replies. The letter will expose
him, and Willoughby does not pardon."

"I regret it. I cannot avoid it. Poor boy! My dear
Crossjay! I did not think of how Willoughby might punish
him. I was very thoughtless. Mr. Whitford, my pin-money
shall go for his education. Later, when I am a little older,
I shall be able to support him."

"That's an encumbrance; you should not tie yourself to
drag it about. You are inalterable, of course, but circumstances are not, and as it happens, women are more subject
to them than we are."

"But I will not be!"

"Your command of them is shown at the present
moment."

"Because I determine to be free?"

"No: because you do the contrary; you don't determine;
you run away from the difficulty, and leave it to your father
and friends to bear. As for Crossjay, you see you destroy
one of his chances. I should have carried him off before
this, if I had not thought it prudent to keep him on terms
with Willoughby. We'll let Crossjay stand aside. He'll
behave like a man of honour, imitating others who have had
to do the same for ladies."

"Have spoken falsely to shelter cowards, you mean, Mr.
Whitford. Oh! I know. — I have but two minutes. The

die is cast. I cannot go back. I must get ready. Will you
see me to the station? I would rather you should hurry
home."

"I will see the last of you. I will wait for you here. An
express runs ahead of your train, and I have arranged with
the clerk for a signal; I have an eye on the window."

"You are still my best friend, Mr. Whitford."

"Though — ?"

"Well, though you do not perfectly understand **what**
torments have driven me to this."

"Carried on tides and blown by winds?"

"Ah! you do not understand."

"Mysteries?"

"Sufferings are not mysteries, they are very simple
facts."

"Well, then, I don't understand. But decide at once. I
wish you to have your free will."

She left the room.

Dry stockings and boots are better for travelling in than
wet ones, but in spite of her direct resolve, she felt when
drawing them on like one that has been tripped. The goal
was desirable, the ardour was damped. Vernon's wish
that she should have her free will, compelled her to sound
it: and it was of course to go, to be liberated, to cast off
incubus:— and hurt her father? injure Crossjay? distress
her friends? No, and ten times no!

She returned to Vernon in haste, to shun the reflex of
her mind.

He was looking at a closed carriage drawn up at the
station-door.

"Shall we run over now, Mr. Whitford?"

"There's no signal. Here it's not so chilly."

"I ventured to enclose my letter to papa in yours, trusting you would attend to my request to you to break the
news to him gently and plead for me."

"We will all do the utmost we can."

"I am doomed to vex those who care for me. I tried to
follow your counsel."

"First you spoke to me, and then you spoke to Miss
Dale; and at least you have a clear conscience."

"No."

"What burdens it?"

"I have done nothing to burden it."

"Then it's a clear conscience?"

"No."

Vernon's shoulders jerked. Our patience with an innocent duplicity in women is measured by the place it assigns
to us and another. If he had liked he could have thought:
"You have not done but meditated something to trouble conscience." That was evident, and her speaking of it was
proof too of the willingness to be clear. He would not help
her. Man's blood, which is the link with women and re-

sponsive to them on the instant for or against, obscured
him. He shrugged anew when she said: "My character
would have been degraded utterly by my staying there.
Could you advise it?"

"Certainly not the degradation of your character," he
said, black on the subject of De Craye, and not lightened by
feelings which made him sharply sensible of the beggarly
dependent that he was, or poor adventuring scribbler that
he was to become.

"Why did you pursue me and wish to stop me, Mr.
Whitford?" said Clara, on the spur of a wound from his
tone.

He replied: "I suppose I'm a busybody: I was never
aware of it till now."

"You are my friend. Only you speak in irony so much.
That was irony, about my clear conscience. I spoke to
you and to Miss Dale: and then I rested and drifted. Can
you not feel for me, that to mention it is like a scorching
furnace? Willoughby has entangled papa. He schemes
incessantly to keep me entangled. I fly from his cunning
as much as from anything. I dread it. I have told you that
I am more to blame than he, but I must accuse him.
And wedding-presents! and congratulations! And to be
his guest!"

"All that makes up a plea in mitigation," said Vernon.

"It is not sufficient for you?" she asked him timidly.

"You have a masculine good sense that tells you you
won't be respected if you run. Three more days there
might cover a retreat with your father."

"He will not listen to me! He confuses me; Willoughby
has bewitched him."

"Commission me: I will see that he listens."

"And go back? Oh! no. To London! Besides there is
the dining with Mrs. Mountstuart this evening; and I like
her very well, but I must avoid her. She has a kind of
idolatry . . . And what answers can I give? I supplicate
her with looks. She observes them, my efforts to divert
them from being painful produce a comic expression to her,
and I am a charming 'rogue,' and I am entertained on the
topic she assumes to be principally interesting me. I must
avoid her. The thought of her leaves me no choice. She
is clever. She could tattoo me with epigrams."

"Stay: there you can hold your own."

"She has told me you give me credit for a spice of wit.
I have not discovered my possession. We have spoken of
it; we call it your delusion. She grants me some beauty;
that must be hers."

"There's no delusion in one case or the other, Miss Middleton. You have beauty and wit: public opinion will
say, wildness: indifference to your reputation, will be
charged on you, and your friends will have to admit it.
But you will be out of *this* difficulty."

"Ah!—to weave a second?"

"Impossible to judge until we see how you escape the first. — And I have no more to say. I love your father. His humour of sententiousness and doctorial stilts is a mask he delights in, but you ought to know him and not be frightened by it. If you sat with him an hour at a Latin task, and if you took his hand and told him you could not leave him, and no tears!— he would answer you at once. It would involve a day or two further: disagreeable to you, no doubt: preferable to the present mode of escape, as I think. But I have no power whatever to persuade. I have not the 'lady's tongue.' My appeal is always to reason."

"It is a compliment. I loathe the 'lady's tongue.'"

"It.'s a distinctly good gift, and I wish I had it. I might have succeeded instead of failing, and appearing to pay a compliment."

"Surely the express train is very late, Mr. Whitford?"

"The express has gone by."

"Then we will cross over."

"You would rather not be seen by Mrs. Mountstuart. That is her carriage drawn up at the station, and she is in it."

Clara looked, and with the sinking of her heart said: "I must brave her!"

"In that case, I will take my leave of you here, Miss Middleton."

She gave him her hand. "Why is Mrs. Mountstuart at the station to-day?"

"I suppose she has driven to meet one of the guests for her dinner-party. Professor Crooklyn was promised to your father, and he may be coming by the down-train."

"Go back to the Hall!" exclaimed Clara. "How can I? I have no more endurance left in me. If I had some support!— if it were the sense of secretly doing wrong, it might help me through. I am in a web. I cannot do right. whatever I do. There is only the thought of saving Crossjay. Yes, and sparing papa. — Good-bye, Mr. Whitford. I shall remember your kindness gratefully. I cannot go back."

"You will not?" said he, tempting her to hesitate.

"No."

"But if you are seen by Mrs. Mountstuart, you must go back. I'll do my best to take her away. Should she see you, you must patch up a story and apply to her for a lift. That, I think, is imperative."

"Not to my mind," said Clara.

He bowed hurriedly and withdrew. After her confession, peculiar to her, of possibly finding sustainment in secretly doing wrong, her flying or remaining seemed to him a choice of evils: and whilst she stood in bewildered speculation on his reason for pursuing her — which was not evident — he remembered the special fear inciting him, and so far did her justice as to have at himself on that subject. [He had done something perhaps to save her from a cold: such was his only consolatory thought.] He had also behaved like a man of honour, taking no personal advantage of her situation; but to reflect on it recalled his astonishing dryness. The strict man of honour plays a part that he should not reflect on till about the fall of the curtain, otherwise he will be likely sometimes to feel the shiver of foolishness at his good conduct.

CHAPTER 28

THE RETURN

POSTED in observation at a corner of the window, Clara saw Vernon cross the road to Mrs. Mountstuart Jenkinson's carriage, transformed to the leanest pattern of himself by narrowed shoulders and raised coat-collar. He had such an air of saying, "Tom's a-cold," that her skin crept in sympathy.

Presently he left the carriage and went into the station: a bell had rung. Was it her train? He approved her going, for he was employed in assisting her to go: a proceeding at variance with many things he had said, but he was as full of contradiction to-day as women are accused of being. The train came up. She trembled: no signal had appeared, and Vernon must have deceived her.

He returned; he entered the carriage, and the wheels were soon in motion. Immediately thereupon, Flitch's fly drove past, containing Colonel De Craye.

Vernon could not but have perceived him!

But what was it that had brought the colonel to this place? The pressure of Vernon's mind was on her and foiled her efforts to assert her perfect innocence, though she knew she had done nothing to allure the colonel hither. Excepting Willoughby, Colonel De Craye was the last person she would have wished to encounter.

She had now a dread of hearing the bell which would tell her that Vernon had not deceived her, and that she was out of his hands, in the hands of some one else.

She bit at her glove; she glanced at the concentrated eyes of the publican's family portraits, all looking as one; she noticed the empty tumbler, and went round to it and touched it, and the silly spoon in it.

A little yielding to desperation shoots us to strange distances!

Vernon had asked her whether she was alone. Connecting that inquiry, singular in itself, and singular in his manner of putting it, with the glass of burning liquid, she repeated: "He must have seen Colonel De Craye!" and she stared at the empty glass, as at something that witnessed to something: for Vernon was not your supple cavalier assiduously on the smirk to pin a gallantry to commonplaces. But all the doors are not open in a young lady's consciousness, quick of nature though she may be: some are locked and keyless, some will not open to the key, some are defended by ghosts inside. She could not have said what the something witnessed to. If we by chance know more, we have still no right to make it more prominent than it was with her. And the smell of the glass was odious; it disgraced her. She had an impulse to pocket the spoon for a memento, to show it to grandchildren for a warning. Even the prelude to the morality to be uttered on the occasion sprang to her lips: "Here, my dears, is a spoon you would be ashamed to use in your teacups, yet it was of more value to me at one period of my life than silver and gold in pointing out, &c. :" the conclusion was hazy, like the conception; she had her idea.

And in this mood she ran downstairs and met Colonel De Craye on the station steps.

The bright illumination of his face was that of the confident man confirmed in a risky guess in the crisis of doubt and dispute.

"Miss Middleton!" his joyful surprise predominated: the pride of an accurate forecast, adding: "I am not too late to be of service?"

She thanked him for the offer.

"Have you dismissed the fly, Colonel De Craye?"

"I have just been getting change to pay Mr. Flitch. He passed me on the road. He is interwound with our fates, to a certainty. I had only to jump in; I knew it, and rolled along like a magician commanding a genie."

"Have I been . . .?"

"Not seriously, nobody doubts your being under shelter. You will allow me to protect you? My time is yours."

"I was thinking of a running visit to my friend Miss Darleton."

"May I venture? I had the fancy that you wished to see Miss Darleton to-day. You cannot make the journey unescorted."

"Please retain the fly. Where is Willoughby?"

"He is in jack-boots. But may I not, Miss Middleton? I shall never be forgiven, if you refuse me."

"There has been searching for me?"

"Some hallooing. But why am I rejected? Besides I don't require the fly; I shall walk if I am banished. Flitch is a wonderful conjuror, but the virtue is out of him for the next four and twenty hours. And it will be an opportunity to me to make my bow to Miss Darleton!"

"She is rigorous on the conventionalities, Colonel De Craye."

"I'll appear before her as an ignoramus or a rebel, whichever she likes best to take in leading strings. I remember her. I was greatly struck by her."

"Upon recollection!"

"Memory did n't happen to be handy at the first mention of the lady's name. As the general said of his ammunition and transport, there 's the army! — but it was leagues in the rear. Like the footman who went to sleep after smelling fire in the house, I was thinking of other things. It will serve me right to be forgotten — if I am. I 've a curiosity to know: a remainder of my coxcombry. Not that exactly: a wish to see the impression I made on your friend. — None at all? But any pebble casts a ripple."

"That is hardly an impression," said Clara, pacifying her irresoluteness with this light talk.

"The utmost to be hoped for by men like me! I have your permission? — one minute — I will get my ticket."

"Do not," said Clara.

"Your man-servant entreats you!"

She signified a decided negative with the head, but her eyes were dreamy. She breathed deep: this thing done would cut the cord.[1] Her sensation of languor swept over her.

De Craye took a stride. He was accosted by one of the railway-porters. Flitch's fly was in request for a gentleman. A portly old gentleman bothered about luggage appeared on the landing.

"The gentleman can have it," said De Craye, handing Flitch his money.

"Open the door," Clara said to Flitch.

He tugged at the handle with enthusiasm. The door was open: she stepped in.

"Then, mount the box and I 'll jump up beside you," De Craye called out, after the passion of regretful astonishment had melted from his features.

Clara directed him to the seat fronting her; he protested indifference to the wet; she kept the door unshut. His temper would have preferred to buffet the angry weather. The invitation was too sweet.

She heard now the bell of her own train. Driving beside the railway embankment she met the train: it was eighteen minutes late, by her watch. And why, when it flung up its whale-spouts of steam, she was not journeying in it she could not tell. She had acted of her free will: that she could say. Vernon had not induced her to remain; assuredly her present companion had not; and her whole heart was for flight: yet she was driving back to the Hall, not devoid of calmness. She speculated on the circumstance enough to think herself incomprehensible, and there left it,

1. "this thing": allowing De Craye to accompany her to London. Her intuitive decision not to do this, partly provoked by his eagerness to do it, lies too deep for description, but is communicated in her contradictory command, "Open the door," below.

intent on the scene to come with Willoughby.

"I must choose a better day for London," she remarked.

De Craye bowed, but did not remove his eyes from her.

"Miss Middleton, you do not trust me."

She answered: "Say in what way. It seems to me that I do."

"I may speak?"

"If it depends on my authority."

"Fully?"

"Whatever you have to say. Let me stipulate, be not very grave. I want cheering in wet weather."

"Miss Middleton, Flitch is charioteer once more. Think of it. [There's a tide that carries him perpetually to the place whence he was cast forth, and a thread that ties us to him in continuity.] I have not the honour to be a friend of long standing: one ventures on one's devotion: it dates from the first moment of my seeing you. Flitch is to blame, if any one. Perhaps the spell would be broken, were he reinstated in his ancient office."

"Perhaps it would," said Clara, not with her best of smiles. Willoughby's pride of relentlessness appeared to her to be receiving a blow by rebound, and that seemed high justice.

"I am afraid you were right; the poor fellow has no chance," De Craye pursued. He paused, as for decorum in the presence of misfortune, and laughed sparklingly: "Unless I engage him, or pretend to! I verily believe that Flitch's melancholy person on the skirts of the Hall completes the picture of the Eden within. — Why will you not put some trust in me, Miss Middleton?"

"But why should you not pretend to engage him, then, Colonel De Craye?"

"We'll plot it, if you like. Can you trust me for that?"

"For any act of disinterested kindness, I am sure."

"You mean it?"

"Without reserve. You could talk publicly of taking him to London."

"Miss Middleton, just now you were going. My arrival changed your mind. You distrust me: and ought I to wonder? The wonder would be all the other way. You have not had the sort of report of me which would persuade you to confide, even in a case of extremity. I guessed you were going. Do you ask me, how? I cannot say. Through what they call sympathy, and that's inexplicable. There's natural sympathy, natural antipathy. People have to live together to discover how deep it is!"

Clara breathed her dumb admission of this truth.

The fly jolted and threatened to lurch.

"Flitch! my dear man!" the colonel gave a murmuring

remonstrance; "for," said he to Clara, whom his apostrophe to Flitch had set smiling, "we 're not safe with him, however we make believe, and he 'll be jerking the heart out of me before he has done. — But if two of us have not the misfortune to be united when they come to the discovery, there 's hope. That is, if one has courage, and the other has wisdom. Otherwise they may go to the yoke in spite of themselves. The great enemy is Pride, who has them both in a coach and drives them to the fatal door, and the only thing to do is to knock him off his box while there 's a minute to spare. And as there 's no pride like the pride of possession, the deadliest wound to him is to make that doubtful. Pride won't be taught wisdom in any other fashion. But one must have the courage to do it!"

De Craye trifled with the window-sash, to give his words time to sink in solution.

Who but Willoughby stood for Pride? And who, swayed by languor, had dreamed of a method that would be surest and swiftest to teach him the wisdom of surrendering her?

"You know, Miss Middleton, I study character," said the colonel.

"I see that you do," she answered.

"You intend to return?"

"Oh! decidedly."

"The day is unfavourable for travelling, I must say."

"It is."

"You may count on my discretion in the fullest degree. I throw myself on your generosity when I assure you that it was not my design to surprise a secret. I guessed the station, and went there, to put myself at your disposal."

"Did you," said Clara, reddening slightly, "chance to see Mrs. Mountstuart Jenkinson's carriage pass you when you drove up to the station?"

De Craye had passed a carriage. "I did not see the lady. She was in it?"

"Yes. And therefore it is better to put discretion on one side: we may be certain she saw you."

"But not you, Miss Middleton?"

"I prefer to think that I am seen. I have a description of courage, Colonel De Craye, when it is forced on me."

"I have not suspected the reverse. Courage wants training, as well as other fine capacities. Mine is often rusty and rheumatic."

"I cannot hear of concealment or plotting."

"Except, pray, to advance the cause of poor Flitch!"

"He shall be excepted."

The colonel screwed his head round for a glance at his coachman's back.

"Perfectly guaranteed to-day!" he said of Flitch's look of solidity. "The convulsion of the elements appears to sober our friend; he is only dangerous in calms. Five minutes will bring us to the park-gates."

Clara leaned forward to gaze at the hedgeways in the neighbourhood of the Hall, strangely renewing their familiarity with her. Both in thought and sensation she was like a flower beaten to earth, and she thanked her feminine mask for not showing how nerveless and languid she was. She could have accused Vernon of a treacherous cunning for imposing it on her free will to decide her fate.

Involuntarily she sighed.

"There is a train at three," said De Craye, with splendid promptitude.

"Yes, and one at five. We dine with Mrs. Mountstuart to-night. And I have a passion for solitude! I think I was never intended for obligations. The moment I am bound I begin to brood on freedom."

"Ladies who say that, Miss Middleton! . . ."

"What of them?"

"They 're feeling too much alone."

She could not combat the remark: by her self-assurance that she had the principle of faithfulness, she acknowledged to herself the truth of it:—there is no freedom for the weak! Vernon had said that once. She tried to resist the weight of it, and her sheer inability precipitated her into a sense of pitiful dependence.

Half an hour earlier it would have been a perilous condition to be traversing in the society of a closely-scanning reader of fair faces. Circumstances had changed. They were at the gates of the park.

"Shall I leave you?" said De Craye.

"Why should you?" she replied.

He bent to her gracefully.

The mild subservience flattered Clara's languor. He had not compelled her to be watchful on her guard, and she was unaware that he passed it when she acquiesced to his observation: "An anticipatory story is a trap to the teller."

"It is," she said. She had been thinking as much.

He threw up his head to consult the brain comically with a dozen little blinks.

"No, you are right, Miss Middleton, inventing beforehand never prospers; 't is a way to trip our own cleverness. Truth and mother-wit are the best counsellors: and as you are the former, I 'll try to act up to the character you assign me."

Some tangle, more prospective than present, seemed to be about her as she reflected. But her intention being to speak to Willoughby without subterfuge, she was grateful to her companion for not tempting her to swerve. No one could doubt his talent for elegant fibbing, and she was in the humour both to admire and adopt the art, so she was glad to be rescued from herself. How mother-wit was to second truth, she did not inquire, and as she did not happen to be thinking of Crossjay, she was not troubled by having to consider how truth and his tale of the morning would be likely to harmonize.

Driving down the park she had full occupation in questioning whether her return would be pleasing to Vernon, who was the virtual cause of it, though he had done so little to promote it: so little that she really doubted his pleasure in seeing her return.

CHAPTER 29

IN WHICH THE SENSITIVENESS OF SIR WILLOUGHBY IS EXPLAINED: AND HE RECEIVES MUCH INSTRUCTION

THE Hall-clock over the stables was then striking twelve. It was the hour for her flight to be made known, and Clara sat in a turmoil of dim apprehension that prepared her nervous frame for a painful blush on her being asked by Colonel De Craye whether she had set her watch correctly. He must, she understood, have seen through her at the breakfast-table: and was she not cruelly indebted to him for her evasion of Willoughby? Such perspicacity of vision distressed and frightened her; at the same time she was obliged to acknowledge that he had not presumed on it. Her dignity was in no way the worse for him. But it had been at a man's mercy, and there was the affliction.

She jumped from the fly as if she were leaving danger behind. She could at the moment have greeted Willoughby with a conventionally friendly smile. The doors were thrown open and young Crossjay flew out to her. He hung and danced on her hand, pressed the hand to his mouth, hardly believing that he saw and touched her, and in a lingo of dashes and asterisks related how Sir Willoughby had found him under the boathouse eaves and pumped him, and had been sent off to Hoppner's farm, where there was a sick child, and on along the road to a labourer's cottage: "For I said you're so kind to poor people, Miss Middleton; that's true, now that *is* true. And I said you would n't have me with you for fear of contagion!" This was what she had feared.

"Every crack and bang in a boy's vocabulary," remarked the colonel, listening to him after he had paid Flitch.

The latter touched his hat till he had drawn attention to himself, when he exclaimed with rosy melancholy: "Ah!

my lady, ah! colonel, if ever I lives to drink some of the old port wine in the old Hall at Christmastide!" Their healths would on that occasion be drunk, it was implied. He threw up his eyes at the windows, humped his body and drove away.

"Then Mr. Whitford has not come back?" said Clara to Crossjay.

"No, Miss Middleton. Sir Willoughby has, and he's upstairs in his room dressing."

"Have you seen Barclay?"

"She has just gone into the laboratory. I told her Sir Willoughby was n't there."

"Tell me, Crossjay, had she a letter?"

"She had something."

"Run: say I am here; I want the letter, it is mine."

Crossjay sprang away and plunged into the arms of Sir Willoughby.

"One has to catch the fellow like a football," exclaimed the injured gentleman, doubled across the boy and holding him fast, that he might have an object to trifle with, to give himself countenance: he needed it. "Clara, you have not been exposed to the weather?"

"Hardly at all."

"I rejoice. You found shelter?"

"Yes."

"In one of the cottages?"

"Not in a cottage; but I was perfectly sheltered. Colonel De Craye passed a fly before he met me . . . "

"Flitch again!" ejaculated the colonel.

"Yes, you have luck, you have luck," Willoughby addressed him, still clutching Crossjay and treating his tugs to get loose as an invitation to caresses. But the foil barely concealed his livid perturbation.

"Stay by me, sir," he said at last sharply to Crossjay, and Clara touched the boy's shoulder in admonishment of him.

She turned to the colonel as they stepped into the hall: "I have not thanked you, Colonel De Craye." She dropped her voice to its lowest: "A letter in my handwriting in the laboratory."

Crossjay cried aloud with pain.

"I have you!" Willoughby rallied him with a laugh not unlike the squeak of his victim.

"You squeeze awfully hard, sir!"

"Why, you milksop!"

"Am I! But I want to get a book."

"Where is the book?"

"In the laboratory."

Colonel De Craye, sauntering by the laboratory door, sung out: "I'll fetch you your book. What is it? EARLY NAVIGATORS? INFANT HYMNS? I think my cigar case is in here."

"Barclay speaks of a letter for me," Willoughby said to Clara, "marked to be delivered to me at noon!"

"In case of my not being back earlier: it was written to avert anxiety," she replied.

"You are very good."

"Oh! good! Call me anything but good. Here are the ladies. Dear ladies!" Clara swam to meet them as they issued from a morning-room into the hall, and interjections reigned for a couple of minutes.

Willoughby relinquished his grasp of Crossjay, who darted instantaneously at an angle to the laboratory. whither he followed, and he encountered De Craye coming out, but passed him in silence.

Crossjay was rangeing and peering all over the room. Willoughby went to his desk and the battery-table and the mantelpiece. He found no letter. Barclay had undoubtedly informed him that she had left a letter for him in the laboratory, by order of her mistress after breakfast. He hurried out and ran upstairs in time to see De Craye and Barclay breaking a conference.

He beckoned to her. The maid lengthened her upper lip and beat her dress down smooth: signs of the apprehension of a crisis and of the getting ready for action.

"My mistress's bell has just rung, Sir Willoughby."

"You had a letter for me."

"I said . . . "

"You said when I met you at the foot of the stairs that you had left a letter for me in the laboratory."

"It is lying on my mistress's toilet-table."

"Get it."

Barclay swept round with another of her demure grimaces. It was apparently necessary with her that she should talk to herself in this public manner.

Willoughby waited for her; but there was no reappearance of the maid.

Struck by the ridicule of his posture of expectation and of his whole behaviour, he went to his bedroom suite, shut himself in and paced the chambers, amazed at the creature he had become. Agitated like the commonest of wretches, destitute of self-control, not able to preserve a decent mask, he, accustomed to inflict these emotions and tremours upon others, was at once the puppet and dupe of an intriguing girl. His very stature seemed lessened. The glass did not say so, but the shrunken heart within him did, and wailfully too. Her compunction — "Call me anything but good" — coming after her return to the Hall beside De Craye, and after the visible passage of a secret between them in his presence, was a confession: it blew at him with the fury of a furnace-blast in his face. Egoist agony wrung the outcry from him that dupery is a more blest condition. He desired to be deceived.

He could desire such a thing only in a temporary transport; for above all he desired that no one should know of his being deceived: and were he a dupe the deceiver would know it, and her accomplice would know it, and the world would soon know of it: that world against whose tongue he stood defenceless. Within the shadow of his presence he compressed opinion, as a strong frost binds the springs of earth, but beyond it his shivering sensitiveness ran about in dread of a stripping in a wintry atmosphere. This was the ground of his hatred of the world: it was an appalling fear on behalf of his naked eidolon, the tender infant Self swaddled in his name before the world, for which he felt as the most highly civilized of men alone can feel, and which it was impossible for him to stretch out hands to protect.[1] There the poor little loveable creature ran for any mouth to blow on; and frost-nipped and bruised, it cried to him, and he was of no avail! Must we not detest a world that so treats us? We loathe it the more, by the measure of our contempt for them, when we have made the people within the shadow-circle of our person slavish.

And he had been once a young Prince in popularity: the world had been his possession. Clara's treatment of him was a robbery of land and subjects. His grander dream had been a marriage with a lady of so glowing a fame for beauty and attachment to her lord that the world perforce must take her for witness to merits which would silence detraction and almost, not quite (it was undesireable) extinguish envy. But for the nature of women his dream would have been realized. He could not bring himself to denounce Fortune. It had cost him a grievous pang to tell Horace De Craye he was lucky; he had been educated in the belief that Fortune specially prized and cherished little Willoughby: hence of necessity his maledictions fell upon women, or he would have forfeited the last blanket of a dream warm as poets revel in.

But if Clara deceived him, he inspired her with timidity. There was matter in that to make him wish to be deceived. She had not looked him much in the face: she had not crossed his eyes: she had looked deliberately downward, keeping her head up, to preserve an exterior pride. The attitude had its bewitchingness: the girl's physical pride of stature scorning to bend under a load of conscious guilt, had a certain black-angel beauty for which he felt a hugging hatred: and according to his policy when these fits of amorous meditation seized him, he burst from the present one in the mood of his more favourable conception of Clara, and sought her out.

The quality of the mood of hugging hatred is, that if you are disallowed the hug, you do not hate the fiercer.

Contrariwise the prescription of a decorous distance of two feet ten inches, which is by measurement the delimi-

1. "eidolon": image.

tation exacted of a rightly respectful deportment, has this miraculous effect on the great creature man, or often it has: that his peculiar hatred returns to the reluctant admiration begetting it, and his passion for the hug falls prostrate as one of the Faithful before the shrine: he is reduced to worship by fasting.

(For these mysteries, consult the sublime chapter in the GREAT BOOK, the Seventy-First on LOVE, wherein Nothing is written, but the Reader receives a Lanthorn, a Powder-cask and a Pick-axe, and therewith pursues his yellow-dusking path across the rubble of preceding excavators in the solitary quarry: a yet more instructive passage than the over-scrawled Seventieth, or French Section, whence the chapter opens, and where hitherto the polite world has halted.)[2]

The hurry of the hero is on us, we have no time to spare for mining-works: he hurried to catch her alone, to wreak his tortures on her in a bitter semblance of bodily worship, and satiated, then comfortably to spurn. He found her protected by Barclay on the stairs.

"That letter for me?" he said.

"I think I told you, Willoughby, there was a letter I left with Barclay to reassure you in case of my not return-ing early," said Clara. "It was unnecessary for her to deliver it."

"Indeed? But any letter, any writing, of yours, and from you to me! You have it still?"

"No, I have destroyed it."

"That was wrong."

"It could not have given you pleasure."

"My dear Clara, one line from you!"

"There were but three."

Barclay stood sucking her lips. A maid in the secrets of her mistress is a purchaseable maid, for if she will take a bribe with her right hand she will with her left; all that has to be calculated is the nature and amount of the bribe: such was the speculation indulged by Sir Willoughby, and he shrank from the thought and declined to know more than that he was on a volcanic hillside where a thin crust quaked over lava. This was a new condition with him, representing Clara's gain in their combat. Clara did not fear his questioning so much as he feared her candour.

Mutually timid, they were of course formally polite, and no plain-speaking could have told one another more dis-tinctly that each was defensive. Clara stood pledged to the fib; packed, sealed and posted; and he had only to ask to have it, supposing that he asked with a voice not exactly peremptory.

She said in her heart: "It is your fault: you are relent-less, and you would ruin Crossjay to punish him for devot-ing himself to me, like the poor thoughtless boy he is! and

2. "Lanthorn": lantern.

so I am bound in honour to do my utmost for him."

The reciprocal devotedness moreover served two purposes: it preserved her from brooding on the humiliation
of her lame flight and flutter back, and it quieted her mind
in regard to the precipitate intimacy of her relations with
Colonel De Craye. Willoughby's boast of his implacable
character was to blame. She was at war with him, and
she was compelled to put the case in that light. Crossjay
must be shielded from one who could not spare an offender,
so Colonel De Craye quite naturally was called on for his
help, and the colonel's dexterous aid appeared to her more
admirable than alarming.

Nevertheless she would not have answered a direct question falsely. She was for the fib, but not the lie; at a
word she could be disdainful of subterfuges. Her look said
that. Willoughby perceived it. She had written him a
letter of three lines: "There were but three:" and she had
destroyed the letter. Something perchance was repented
by her? Then she had done him an injury! Between
his wrath at the suspicion of an injury, and the prudence
enjoined by his abject coveting of her, he consented to be
fooled for the sake of vengeance, and something besides.

"Well! here you are, safe: I have you!" said he, with
courtly exultation: "and that is better than your handwriting. I have been all over the country after you."

"Why did you? We are not in a barbarous land," said
Clara.

"Crossjay talks of your visiting a sick child, my love:
—you have changed your dress?"

"You see."

"The boy declared you were going to that farm of Hoppner's and some cottage. I met at my gates a tramping
vagabond who swore to seeing you and the boy in a totally
contrary direction."

"Did you give him money?"

"I fancy so."

"Then he was paid for having seen me."

Willoughby tossed his head: it might be as she suggested; beggars are liars.

"But who sheltered you, my dear Clara? You had not
been heard of at Hoppner's."

"The people have been indemnified for their pains.
To pay them more would be to spoil them. You disperse
money too liberally. There was no fever in the place.
Who could have anticipated such a downpour! I want to
consult Miss Dale on the important theme of a dress I
think of wearing at Mrs. Mountstuart's to-night."

"Do. She is unerring."

"She has excellent taste."

"She dresses very simply herself."

"But it becomes her. She is one of the few women
whom I feel I could not improve with a touch."

"She has judgement."

He reflected and repeated his encomium.

The shadow of a dimple in Clara's cheek awakened him to the idea that she had struck him somewhere: and certainly he would never again be able to put up the fiction of her jealousy of Lætitia. What, then, could be this girl's motive for praying to be released? The interrogation humbled him: he fled from the answer.

Willoughby went in search of De Craye. That sprightly intriguer had no intention to let himself be caught solus.[3] He was undiscoverable until the assembly sounded, when Clara dropped a public word or two, and he spoke in perfect harmony with her. After that, he gave his company to Willoughby for an hour at billiards, and was well beaten.

The announcement of a visit of Mrs. Mountstuart Jenkinson took the gentlemen to the drawing-room, rather suspecting that something stood in the way of her dinnerparty. As it happened, she was lamenting only the loss of one of the jewels of the party: to wit, the great Professor Crooklyn, invited to meet Dr. Middleton at her table; and she related how she had driven to the station by appointment, the professor being notoriously a botherheaded traveller: as was shown by the fact that he had missed his train in town, for he had not arrived; nothing had been seen of him. She cited Vernon Whitford for her authority that the train had been inspected and the platform scoured to find the professor.

"And so," said she, "I drove home your Green Man to dry him; he was wet through and chattering; the man was exactly like a skeleton wrapped in a sponge, and if he escapes a cold he must be as invulnerable as he boasts himself.[4] These athletes are terrible boasters."

"They climb their Alps to crow," said Clara, excited by her apprehension that Mrs. Mountstuart would speak of having seen the colonel near the station.

There was a laugh, and Colonel De Craye laughed loudly as it flashed through him that a quick-witted impressionable girl like Miss Middleton must, before his arrival at the Hall, have speculated on such obdurate clay as Vernon Whitford was, with humourous despair at his uselessness to her. Glancing round, he saw Vernon standing fixed in a stare at the young lady.

"You heard that, Whitford?" he said, and Clara's face betokening an extremer contrition than he thought was demanded, the colonel rallied the Alpine climber for striving to be the tallest of them — Signor Excelsior! — and described these conquerors of mountains pancaked on the rocks in desperate embraces, bleached here, burnt there, barked all over, all to be able to say they had been up "so

---

3. "solus": alone.
4. "Green Man": Vernon, mockingly as before, a wild man of the woods.

high " — had conquered another mountain! He was extravagantly funny and self-satisfied: a conqueror of the sex having such different rewards of enterprise.

Vernon recovered in time to accept the absurdities heaped on him.

"Climbing peaks won't compare with hunting a wriggler," said he.

His allusion to the incessant pursuit of young Crossjay to pin him to lessons was appreciated.

Clara felt the thread of the look he cast from herself to Colonel De Craye. She was helpless, if he chose to misjudge her. Colonel De Craye did not!

Crossjay had the misfortune to enter the drawing-room while Mrs. Mountstuart was compassionating Vernon for his ducking in pursuit of the wriggler; which De Craye likened to "going through the river after his eel:" and immediately there was a cross-questioning of the boy between De Craye and Willoughby on the subject of his latest truancy, each gentleman trying to run him down in a palpable fib. They were succeeding brilliantly when Vernon put a stop to it by marching him off to hard labour. Mrs. Mountstuart was led away to inspect the beautiful porcelain service, the present of Lady Busshe. "Porcelain again!" she said to Willoughby, and would have signalled to the "dainty rogue" to come with them, had not Clara been leaning over to Lætitia, talking to her in an attitude too graceful to be disturbed. She called his attention to it, slightly wondering at his impatience. She departed to meet an afternoon train on the chance that it would land the professor. "But tell Dr. Middleton," said she, "I fear I shall have no one worthy of him! And," she added to Willoughby, as she walked out to her carriage, "I shall expect you to do the great-gunnery talk at table."

"Miss Dale keeps it up with him best," said Willoughby.

"She does everything best! But my dinner-table is involved, and I cannot count on a young woman to talk across it. I would hire a lion of a menagerie, if one were handy, rather than have a famous scholar at my table unsupported by another famous scholar. Dr. Middleton would ride down a duke when the wine is in him. He will terrify my poor flock. The truth is, we can't leaven him: I foresee undigested lumps of conversation, unless you devote yourself."

"I will devote myself," said Willoughby.

"I can calculate on Colonel De Craye and our porcelain beauty for any quantity of sparkles, if you promise that. They play well together. You are not to be one of the Gods to-night, but a kind of Jupiter's cupbearer; — Juno's, if you like: and Lady Busshe and Lady Culmer, and all your admirers shall know subsequently what you have done.[5] You see my alarm. I certainly did not rank Pro-

5. "Jupiter's cupbearer": Ganymede, an effeminate young person. Mrs. Mount-   stuart Jenkinson quickly corrects herself.

fessor Crooklyn among the possibly faithless, or I never would have ventured on Dr. Middleton at my table. My dinner-parties have hitherto been all successes. Naturally I feel the greater anxiety about this one. For a single failure is all the more conspicuous. The exception is everlastingly cited! It is not so much what people say, but my own sentiments. I hate to fail. However, if you are true we may do."

"Whenever the great gun goes off I will fall on my face, madam!"

"Something of that sort," said the dame smiling, and leaving him to reflect on the egoism of women. For the sake of her dinner-party he was to be a cipher in attendance on Dr. Middleton, and Clara and De Craye were to be encouraged in sparkling together! And it happened that he particularly wished to shine. The admiration of his county made him believe he had a flavour in general society that was not yet distinguished by his bride, and he was to relinquish his opportunity in order to please Mrs. Mountstuart! Had she been in the pay of his rival she could not have stipulated for more.

He remembered young Crossjay's instant quietude, after struggling in his grasp, when Clara laid her hand on the boy: and from that infinitesimal circumstance he deduced the boy's perception of a differing between himself and his bride, and a transfer of Crossjay's allegiance from him to her. She shone; she had the gift of female beauty; the boy was attracted to it. That boy must be made to feel his treason. But the point of the cogitation was, that similarly were Clara to see her affianced shining, as shine he could when lit up by admirers, there was the probability that the sensation of her littleness would animate her to take aim at him once more. And then was the time for her chastisement.

A visit to Dr. Middleton in the library satisfied him that she had not been renewing her entreaties to leave Patterne. No, the miserable coquette had now her pastime and was content to stay. Deceit was in the air: he heard the sound of the shuttle of deceit without seeing it; but on the whole, mindful of what he had dreaded during the hours of her absence, he was rather flattered, witheringly flattered.[6] What was it that he had dreaded? Nothing less than news of her running away. Indeed a silly fancy, a lover's fancy! yet it had led him so far as to suspect, after parting with De Craye in the rain, that his friend and his bride were in collusion, and that he should not see them again. He had actually shouted on the rainy road the theatric call "Fooled!" one of the stage-cries which are cries of nature! particularly the cry of nature with men who have driven other men to the cry.

Constantia Durham had taught him to believe women

6. "shuttle of deceit": The weaving of lies is done as with a shuttle on a loom.

capable of explosions of treason at half a minute's notice.
And strangely, to prove that women are all of a pack, she
had worn exactly the same placidity of countenance just
before she fled, as Clara yesterday and to-day; no nervousness, no flushes, no twitches of the brows, but smoothness,
ease of manner — an elegant sisterliness, one might almost
say: as if the creature had found a midway and border-
line to walk on between cruelty and kindness, and between
repulsion and attraction; so that up to the verge of her
breath she did forcefully attract, repelling at one foot's
length with her armour of chill serenity. Not with any
disdain, with no passion: such a line as she herself pursued she indicated to him on a neighbouring parallel.
The passion in her was like a place of waves evaporated to
a crust of salt. Clara's resemblance to Constantia in this
instance was ominous. For him whose tragic privilege it
had been to fold each of them in his arms, and weigh on
their eyelids, and see the dissolving mist-deeps in their
eyes, it was horrible. Once more the comparison overcame
him. Constantia he could condemn for revealing too much
to his manly sight: she had met him almost half way: well,
that was complimentary and sanguine: but her frankness
was a baldness often rendering it doubtful which of the
two, lady or gentleman, was the object of the chase — an
extreme perplexity to his manly soul. Now Clara's inner
spirit was shyer, shy as a doe down those rose-tinged
abysses; she allured both the lover and the hunter; forests
of heavenliness were in her flitting eyes. Here the difference of these fair women made his present fate an intolerable anguish. For if Constantia was like certain of the
ladies whom he had rendered unhappy, triumphed over,
as it is queerly called, Clara was not. Her individuality
as a woman was a thing he had to bow to. It was impossible to roll her up in the sex and bestow a kick on the
travelling bundle. Hence he loved her, though she hurt
him. Hence his wretchedness, and but for the hearty
sincerity of his faith in the Self he loved likewise and
more, he would have been hangdog abject.

As for De Craye, Willoughby recollected his own ex-
ploits too proudly to put his trust in a man. That fatal
conjunction of temper and policy had utterly thrown him
off his guard, or he would not have trusted the fellow
even in the first hour of his acquaintance with Clara. But
he had wished her to be amused while he wove his plans
to retain her at the Hall: — partly imagining that she
would weary of his neglect: vile delusion! In truth he
should have given festivities, he should have been the sun
of a circle, and have revealed himself to her in his more
dazzling form. He went near to calling himself foolish
after the tremendous reverberation of "Fooled!" had
ceased to shake him.

How behave? It slapped the poor gentleman's pride in

the face to ask. A private talk with her would rouse her to renew her supplications. He saw them flickering behind the girl's transparent calmness. That calmness really drew its dead ivory hue from the suppression of them: something as much he guessed; and he was not sure either of his temper or his policy if he should hear her repeat her profane request.

An impulse to address himself to Vernon and discourse with him jocularly on the childish whim of a young lady, moved perhaps by some whiff of jealousy, to shun the yoke, was checked. He had always taken so superior a pose with Vernon that he could not abandon it for a moment: on such a subject too! Besides Vernon was one of your men who entertain the ideas about women of fellows that have never conquered one: or only one, we will say in his case, knowing his secret history; and that one no flag to boast of. Densely ignorant of the sex, his nincompoopish idealizations, at other times preposterous, would now be annoying. He would probably presume on Clara's inconceivable lapse of dignity to read his master a lecture: he was quite equal to a philippic upon woman's rights.[7] This man had not been afraid to say that he talked common sense to women. He was an example of the consequence!

Another result was, that Vernon did not talk sense to men. Willoughby's wrath at Clara's exposure of him to his cousin dismissed the proposal of a colloquy so likely to sting his temper, and so certain to diminish his loftiness. Unwilling to speak to anybody, he was isolated, yet consciously begirt by the mysterious action going on all over the house, from Clara and De Craye to Lætitia and young Crossjay, down to Barclay the maid. His blind sensitiveness felt as we may suppose a spider to feel when plucked from his own web and set in the centre of another's. Lætitia looked her share in the mystery. A burden was on her eyelashes. How she could have come to any suspicion of the circumstances, he was unable to imagine. Her intense personal sympathy, it might be: he thought so with some gentle pity for her — of the paternal pat-back order of pity. She adored him, by decree of Venus; and the Goddess had not decreed that he should find consolation in adoring her. Nor could the temptings of prudent counsel in his head induce him to run the risk of such a total turnover as the incurring of Lætitia's pity of himself by confiding in her. He checked that impulse also, and more sovereignly. For him to be pitied by Lætitia seemed an upsetting of the scheme of Providence. Providence, otherwise the discriminating dispensation of the good things of life, had made him the beacon, her the bird: she was really the last person to whom he could unbosom. The idea of his being in a

---

7. "philippic": oration, like those of Demosthenes against Philip of Macedon.

position that suggested his doing so, thrilled him with fits of rage; and it appalled him. There appeared to be another Power. The same which had humiliated him once was menacing him anew. For it could not be Providence, whose favourite he had ever been. We must have a couple of Powers to account for discomfort when Egoism is the kernel of our religion. Benevolence had singled him for uncommon benefits: malignancy was at work to rob him of them. And you think well of the world, do you!

Of necessity he associated Clara with the darker Power pointing the knife at the quick of his pride. Still, he would have raised her weeping: he would have stanched her wounds bleeding: he had an infinite thirst for her misery, that he might ease his heart of its charitable love. Or let her commit herself, and be cast off! Only she must commit herself glaringly, and be cast off by the world as well. Contemplating her in the form of a discarded weed, he had a catch of the breath: she was fair. He implored his Power that Horace De Craye might not be the man! Why any man? An illness, fever, fire, runaway horses, personal disfigurement, a laming, were sufficient. And then a formal and noble offer on his part to keep to the engagement with the unhappy wreck: yes, and to lead the limping thing to the altar, if she insisted. His imagination conceived it, and the world's applause besides.

Nausea, together with a sense of duty to his line, extinguished that loathsome prospect of a mate, though without obscuring his chivalrous devotion to his gentleman's word of honour, which remained in his mind to compliment him permanently.

On the whole, he could reasonably hope to subdue her to admiration. He drank a glass of champagne at his dressing; an unaccustomed act, but, as he remarked casually to his man Pollington, for whom the rest of the bottle was left, he had taken no horse-exercise that day.

Having to speak to Vernon on business, he went to the schoolroom, where he discovered Clara, beautiful in full evening attire, with her arm on young Crossjay's shoulder, and heard that the hard taskmaker had abjured Mrs. Mountstuart's party, and had already excused himself, intending to keep Crossjay to the grindstone. Willoughby was for the boy, as usual, and more sparklingly than usual. Clara looked at him in some surprise. He rallied Vernon with great zest, quite silencing him when he said: "I bear witness that the fellow was here at his regular hour for lessons, and were you?" He laid his hand on Crossjay, touching Clara's hand.

"You will remember what I told you, Crossjay," said she, rising from the seat gracefully. "It is my command."

Crossjay frowned and puffed.

"But only if I'm questioned," he said.

"Certainly," she replied.

"Then I question the rascal," said Willoughby, causing a start. "What, sir, is your opinion of Miss Middleton in her robe of state this evening?"

"Now, the truth, Crossjay!" Clara held up a finger; and the boy could see she was playing at archness, but for Willoughby it was earnest. "The truth is not likely to offend you or me either," he murmured to her.

"I wish him never, never, on any excuse, to speak anything else."

"I always did think her a Beauty," Crossjay growled. He hated the having to say it.

"There!" exclaimed Sir Willoughby, and bent extending an arm to her. "You have not suffered from the truth, my Clara!"

Her answer was: "I was thinking how he might suffer if he were taught to tell the reverse."

"Oh! for a fair lady!"

"That is the worst of teaching, Willoughby."

"We'll leave it to the fellow's instinct; he has our blood in him. I could convince you, though, if I might cite circumstances. Yes! But yes! And yes again! The entire truth cannot invariably be told. I venture to say it should not."

"You would pardon it for the ' fair lady ' ?"

"Applaud, my love."

He squeezed the hand within his arm, contemplating her.

She was arrayed in a voluminous robe of pale blue silk vapourous with trimmings of light gauze of the same hue, gaze de Chambéry, matching her fair hair and clear skin for the complete overthrow of less inflammable men than Willoughby.[8]

"Clara!" sighed he.

"If so, it would really be generous," she said, "though the teaching is bad."

"I fancy I can be generous."

"Do we ever know?"

He turned his head to Vernon, issuing brief succinct instructions for letters to be written, and drew her into the hall, saying: "Know? There are people who do *not* know themselves, and as they are the majority they manufacture the axioms. And it is assumed that we have to swallow them. I may observe that I think I know. I decline to be engulfed in those majorities. ' Among them, but not of them.' I know this, that my aim in life is to be generous."

"Is it not an impulse or disposition rather than an aim?"

"So much I know," pursued Willoughby, refusing to be tripped. But she rang discordantly in his ear. His "fancy that he could be generous," and his "aim at being generous," had met with no response. "I have given

8. "gaze de Chambéry": light, translucent stuff, woven in southern France.

proofs," he said briefly, to drop a subject upon which he was not permitted to dilate; and he murmured: "People acquainted with me! . . ." She was asked if she expected him to boast of generous deeds. "From childhood!" she heard him mutter; and she said to herself: "Release me, and you shall be everything!"

The unhappy gentleman ached as he talked: for with men and with hosts of women to whom he was indifferent, never did he converse in this shambling, third-rate, sheepish manner, devoid of all highness of tone and the proper precision of an authority. He was unable to fathom the cause of it, but Clara imposed it on him, and only in anger could he throw it off. The temptation to an outburst that would flatter him with the sound of his authoritative voice had to be resisted on a night when he must be composed if he intended to shine, so he merely mentioned Lady Busshe's present, to gratify spleen by preparing the ground for dissension, and prudently acquiesced in her anticipated slipperiness. She would rather not look at it now, she said.

"Not now; very well," said he.

His immediate deference made her regretful. "There is hardly time, Willoughby."

"My dear, we shall have to express our thanks to her."

"I cannot."

His arm contracted sharply. He was obliged to be silent.

Dr. Middleton, Lætitia and the ladies Eleanor and Isabel joining them in the hall found two figures linked together in a shadowy indication of halves that have fallen apart and hang on the last thread of junction. Willoughby retained her hand on his arm; he held to it as the symbol of their alliance, and oppressed the girl's nerves by contact with a frame labouring for breath. De Craye looked on them from overhead. The carriages were at the door, and Willoughby said: "Where's Horace? I suppose he's taking a final shot at his Book of Anecdotes and neat collection of Irishisms."

"No," replied the colonel, descending. "That's a spring works of itself and has discovered the secret of continuous motion, more's the pity! — unless you'll be pleased to make it of use to Science."

He gave a laugh of good humour.

"Your laughter, Horace, is a capital comment on your wit."

Willoughby said it with the air of one who has flicked a whip.

"'Tis a genial advertisement of a vacancy," said De Craye.

"Precisely: three parts auctioneer to one for the property."

"Oh! if you have a musical quack, score it a point in his

favour, Willoughby, though you don't swallow his drug."

"If he means to be musical, let him keep time."

"Am I late?" said De Craye to the ladies, proving him-self an adept in the art of being gracefully vanquished and so winning tender hearts.

Willoughby had refreshed himself. At the back of his mind there was a suspicion that his adversary would not have yielded so flatly without an assurance of practically triumphing, secretly getting the better of him; and it filled him with venom for a further bout at the next oppor-tunity: but as he had been sarcastic and mordant, he had shown Clara what he could do in a way of speaking differ-ent from the lamentable cooing stuff, gasps and feeble protestations to which, he knew not how, she reduced him. Sharing the opinion of his race, that blunt personalities, or the pugilistic form, administered directly on the salient features, are exhibitions of mastery in such encounters, he felt strong and solid, eager for the successes of the evening. De Craye was in the first carriage as escort to the ladies Eleanor and Isabel. Willoughby, with Clara, Lætitia and Dr. Middleton followed, all silent, for the Rev. Doctor was ostensibly pondering; and Willoughby was damped a little when he unlocked his mouth to say:

"And yet I have not observed that Colonel De Craye is anything of a Celtiberian Egnatius meriting fustigation for an untimely display of well-whitened teeth, sir: ' quicquid est, ubicunque est, quodcunque agit, renidet: ' — ha? a morbus neither charming nor urbane to the gen-eral eye, however consolatory to the actor. [9] But this gen-tleman does not offend so, or I am so strangely prepos-sessed in his favour as to be an incompetent witness."

Dr. Middleton's persistent ha? eh? upon an honest frown of inquiry plucked an answer out of Willoughby that was meant to be humourously scornful and soon became apologetic under the Doctor's interrogatively grasping gaze.

"These Irishmen," Willoughby said, "will play the professional jester, as if it were an office they were born to. We must play critic now and then, otherwise we should have them deluging us with their Joe Millerisms."[1]

"With their *O'*Millerisms you would say, perhaps?"

Willoughby did his duty to the joke, but the Rev. Doctor, though he wore the paternal smile of a man that has begotten hilarity, was not perfectly propitiated, and pursued: "Nor to my apprehension is ' the man's laugh the comment on his wit' unchallengeably new: instances of

9. Doctor Middleton's entire speech is patched up from a poem by Catullus, in which he attacks Egnatius, a Celtiberian, for his silly grin. (Celtiberia was a dis-trict of ancient Spain.) The Latin means, "Whatever the matter, wherever he is or whatever he's doing, he gleams his teeth at you." "fustigation": whipping; "mor-bus": literally, illness, here, nothing more than a mannerism.

1. Comic sayings from Joe Miller's jest book, already antiquated and stale in Meredith's day.

cousinship germane to the phrase will recur to you. But it has to be noted that it was a phrase of assault; it was ostentatiously battery: and I would venture to remind you, friend, that among the elect, considering that it is as fatally facile to spring the laugh upon a man as to deprive him of his life, considering that we have only to condescend to the weapon, and that the more popular necessarily the more murderous that weapon is, — among the elect, to which it is your distinction to aspire to belong, the rule holds to abstain from any employment of the obvious, the percoct, and likewise, for your own sake, from the epitonic, the overstrained; for if the former, by readily assimilating with the understandings of your audience are empowered to commit assassination on your victim, the latter come under the charge of unseemliness, inasmuch as they are a description of public suicide.[2] Assuming, then, manslaughter to be your pastime, and hari-kari not to be your bent, the phrase, to escape criminality, must rise in you as you would have it to fall on him. ex improviso.[3] Am I right ? "

"I am in the habit of thinking it impossible, sir, that you can be in error," said Willoughby.

Dr. Middleton left it the more emphatic by saying nothing further.

Both his daughter and Miss Dale, who had disapproved the waspish snap at Colonel De Craye, were in wonderment of the art of speech which could so soothingly inform a gentleman that his behaviour had not been gentlemanly.

Willoughby was damped by what he comprehended of it for a few minutes. In proportion as he realized an evening with his ancient admirers he was restored, and he began to marvel greatly at his folly in not giving banquets and Balls, instead of making a solitude about himself and his bride. For solitude, thought he, is good for the man, the man being a creature consumed by passion; woman's love, on the contrary, will only be nourished by the reflex light she catches of you in the eyes of others, she having no passion of her own, but simply an instinct driving her to attach herself to whatsoever is most largely admired, most shining. So thinking, he determined to change his course of conduct, and he was happier. In the first gush of our wisdom drawn directly from experience, there is a mental intoxication that cancels the old world and establishes a new one, not allowing us to ask whether it is too late.

2. "epitonic": cooked through.   3. On the spur of the moment.

CHAPTER 30

TREATING OF THE DINNER-PARTY AT MRS. MOUNTSTUART
JENKINSON'S

VERNON and young Crossjay had tolerably steady work
together for a couple of hours, varied by the arrival of a
plate of meat on a tray for the master, and some interrogations put to him from time to time by the boy in reference to Miss Middleton. Crossjay made the discovery
that if he abstained from alluding to Miss Middleton's
beauty he might water his dusty path with her name
nearly as much as he liked. Mention of her beauty incurred a reprimand. On the first occasion his master was
wistful. "Is n't she glorious!" Crossjay fancied he had
started a sovereign receipt for blessed deviations. He
tried it again, but pedagogue-thunder broke over his
head.

"Yes, only I can't understand what she means, Mr.
Whitford," he excused himself. "First, I was not to tell;
I know I was n't, because she said so; she quite as good as
said so. Her last words were, 'Mind, Crossjay, you know
nothing about me,' when I stuck to that beast of a tramp,
who's a 'walking moral,' and gets money out of people by
snuffling it."

"Attend to your lesson, or you 'll be one," said Vernon.

"Yes, but, Mr. Whitford, now I *am* to tell. I 'm to
answer straight out to every question."

"Miss Middleton is anxious that you should be truthful."

"Yes, but in the morning she told me *not* to tell."

"She was in a hurry. She has it on her conscience that
you may have misunderstood her, and she wishes you never
to be guilty of an untruth, least of all on her account."

Crossjay committed an unspoken resolution to the air in
a violent sigh: "Ah!" and said: "If I were sure!"

"Do as she bids you, my boy."

"But I don't know what it is she wants."

"Hold to her last words to you."

"So I do. If she told me to run till I dropped, on
I'd go."

"She told you to study your lessons: do that."

Crossjay buckled to his book, invigorated by an imagination of his liege lady on the page.

After a studious interval, until the impression of his lady
had subsided, he resumed: "She's so funny! She's just
like a girl, and then she's a lady too. She's my idea of
a princess. And Colonel De Craye! Was n't he taught
dancing! When he says something funny he ducks, and
seems to be setting to his partner. I should like to be
as clever as her father. That is a clever man! I daresay

Colonel De Craye will dance with her to-night. I wish I was there."

"It's a dinner-party, not a dance," Vernon forced himself to say, to dispel that ugly vision.

"Isn't it, sir? I thought they danced after dinner parties. Mr. Whitford, have you ever seen her run?"

Vernon pointed him to his task.

They were silent for a lengthened period.

"But does Miss Middleton mean me to speak out if Sir Willoughby asks me?" said Crossjay.

"Certainly. You need n't make much of it. All's plain and simple."

"But I'm positive, Mr. Whitford, he was n't to hear of her going to the post-office with me before breakfast. And how did Colonel De Craye find her and bring her back, with that old Flitch? He's a man and can go where he pleases, and I'd have found her too, give me the chance. You know, I'm fond of Miss Dale, but she — I'm very fond of her — but you can't think she's a girl as well. And about Miss Dale, when she says a thing, there it is, clear. But Miss Middleton has a lot of meanings. Never mind; I go by what's inside, and I'm pretty sure to please her."

"Take your chin off your hand and your elbow off the book, and fix yourself," said Vernon, wrestling with the seduction of Crossjay's idolatry, for Miss Middleton's appearance had been preternaturally sweet on her departure, and the next pleasure to seeing her was hearing of her from the lips of this passionate young poet.

"Remember that you please her by speaking truth," Vernon added, and laid himself open to questions upon the truth, by which he learnt, with a perplexed sense of envy and sympathy, that the boy's idea of truth strongly approximated to his conception of what should be agreeable to Miss Middleton.

He was lonely, bereft of the bard, when he had tucked Crossjay up in his bed and left him. Books he could not read; thoughts were disturbing, A seat in the library and a stupid stare helped to pass the hours, and but for the spot of sadness moving meditation in spite of his effort to stun himself, he would have borne a happy resemblance to an idiot in the sun. He had verily no command of his reason. She was too beautiful! Whatever she did was best. That was the refrain of the fountain-song in him; the burden being her whims, variations, inconsistencies, wiles; her tremblings between good and naughty, that might be stamped to noble or to terrible; her sincereness, her duplicity, her courage, cowardice, possibilities for heroism and for treachery.[1] By dint of dwelling on the theme, he magnified the young lady to extraordinary stature. And he had sense enough to own that her character was yet liquid

---

1. "refrain": as it were, the chorus of a ballad; the burden is its underlying and   sometimes contrasting theme.

in the mould, and that she was a creature of only naturally youthful wildness provoked to freakishness by the ordeal of a situation shrewd as any that can happen to her sex in civilized life. But he was compelled to think of her extravagantly, and he leaned a little to the discrediting of her, because her actual image unmanned him and was unbearable: and to say at the end of it "She is too beautiful! whatever she does is best," smoothed away the wrong he did her. Had it been in his power he would have thought of her in the abstract — the stage contiguous to that which he adopted: but the attempt was luckless; the Stagyrite would have failed in it.[2] What philosopher could have set down that face of sun and breeze and nymph in shadow as a point in a problem?

The library-door was opened at midnight by Miss Dale. She closed it quietly. "You are not working, Mr. Whitford? I fancied you would wish to hear of the evening. Professor Crooklyn arrived after all! Mrs. Mountstuart is bewildered: she says she expected you, and that you did not excuse yourself to her, and she cannot comprehend, et cætera. That is to say, she chooses bewilderment to indulge in the exclamatory. She must be very much annoyed. The professor did come by the train she drove to meet!"

"I thought it probable," said Vernon.

"He had to remain a couple of hours at the Railway Inn: no conveyance was to be found for him. He thinks he has caught a cold, and cannot stifle his fretfulness about it. He may be as learned as Dr. Middleton; he has not the same happy constitution. Nothing more unfortunate could have occurred; he spoilt the party. Mrs. Mountstuart tried petting him, which drew attention to him and put us all in his key for several awkward minutes, more than once. She lost her head; she was unlike herself. I may be presumptuous in criticizing her, but should not the president of a dinner-table treat it like a battle-field, and let the guest that sinks descend, and not allow the voice of a discordant, however illustrious, to rule it? Of course, it is when I see failures that I fancy I could manage so well: comparison is prudently reserved in the other cases. I am a daring critic, no doubt because I know I shall never be tried by experiment. I have no ambition to be tried."

She did not notice a smile of Vernon's and continued: "Mrs. Mountstuart gave him the lead upon any subject he chose. I thought the Professor never would have ceased talking of a young lady who had been at the inn before him drinking hot brandy and water with a gentleman!"

"How did he hear of that?" cried Vernon, roused by the malignity of the Fates.

"From the landlady, trying to comfort him. And a story of her lending shoes and stockings while those of the young lady were drying. He has the dreadful snappish humourous

2. "Stagyrite": Aristotle, who was born in Stagira.

way of recounting which impresses it ; the table took up the
subject of this remarkable young lady, and whether she was
a lady of the neighbourhood, and who she could be that went
abroad on foot in heavy rain.   It was painful to me ; I knew
enough to be sure of who she was."

"Did she betray it ?"

"No."

"Did Willoughby look at her ?"

"Without suspicion then."

"Then ?"

"Colonel De Craye was diverting us, and he was very
amusing.   Mrs. Mountstuart told him afterwards that he
ought to be paid salvage for saving the wreck of her party.
Sir Willoughby was a little too cynical : he talked well ;
what he said was good, but it was not good-humoured : he
has not the reckless indifference of Colonel De Craye to
uttering nonsense that amusement may come of it.   And in
the drawing-room he lost such gaiety as he had.   I was close
to Mrs. Mountstuart when Professor Crooklyn approached
her and spoke in my hearing of *that* gentleman and *that*
young lady.   They were, you could see by his nods, Colonel
De Craye and Miss Middleton."

"And she at once mentioned it to Willoughby !"

"Colonel De Craye gave her no chance, if she sought it.
He courted her profusely.   Behind his rattle he must have
brains.   It ran in all directions to entertain her and her
circle."

"Willoughby knows nothing ?"

"I cannot judge.   He stood with Mrs. Mountstuart a
minute as we were taking leave.   She looked strange.   I
heard her say, 'The rogue.'   He laughed.   She lifted her
shoulders.   He scarcely opened his mouth on the way
home."

"The thing must run its course," Vernon said, with the
philosophical air which is desperation rendered decorous.
"Willoughby deserves it.   A man of full growth ought to
know that nothing on earth tempts Providence so much as
the binding of a young woman against her will.   Those two
are mutually attracted : they 're both . . . They meet and
the mischief's done : both are bright.   He can persuade
with a word.   Another might discourse like an angel and
it would be useless.   I said everything I could think of, to
no purpose.   And so it is : there are those attractions ! —
just as, with her, Willoughby is the reverse, he repels.
I 'm in about the same predicament — or should be if she
were plighted to me.   That is, for the length of five minutes ; about the space of time I should require for the
formality of handing her back her freedom.   How a sane
man can imagine a girl like that . . . ! But if she has
changed, she has changed !   You can't conciliate a withered
affection.   This detaining her, and tricking, and not listening, only increases her aversion ; she learns the art in turn.

Here she is, detained by fresh plots to keep Dr. Middleton at the Hall. That's true, is it not?" He saw that it was. "No, she's not to blame! She has told him her mind; he won't listen. The question then is, whether she keeps to her word, or breaks it. It's a dispute between a conventional idea of obligation and an injury to her nature. Which is the more dishonourable thing to do? Why, you and I see in a moment that her feelings guide her best. It's one of the few cases in which nature may be consulted like an oracle."

"Is she so sure of her nature?" said Miss Dale.

"You may doubt it; I do not. I am surprised at her coming back. De Craye is a man of the world, and advised it, I suppose. He — well, I never had the persuasive tongue, and my failing does n't count for much."

"But the suddenness of the intimacy!"

"The disaster is rather famous 'at first sight.'[3] He came in a fortunate hour . . . for him. A pigmy's a giant if he can manage to arrive in season. Did you not notice that there was danger, at their second or third glance? You counselled me to hang on here, where the amount of good I do in proportion to what I have to endure is microscopic."

"It was against your wishes, I know," said Lætitia, and when the words were out she feared that they were tentative. Her delicacy shrank from even seeming to sound him in relation to a situation so delicate as Miss Middleton's.

The same sentiment guarded him from betraying himself, and he said: "Partly against. We both foresaw the possible — because, like most prophets, we knew a little more of circumstances enabling us to see the fatal. A pigmy would have served, but De Craye is a handsome, intelligent, pleasant fellow."

"Sir Willoughby's friend!"

"Well, in these affairs! A great deal must be charged on the Goddess."

"That is really Pagan fatalism!"

"Our modern word for it is Nature. Science condescends to speak of natural selection. Look at these! They are both graceful and winning and witty, bright to mind and eye, made for one another, as country people say. I can't blame him. Besides we don't know that he's guilty. We're quite in the dark, except that we're certain how it must end. If the chance should occur to you of giving Willoughby a word of counsel — it may — you might, without irritating him as my knowledge of his plight does, hint at your eyes being open. His insane dread of a detective world makes him artificially blind. As soon as he fancies himself seen, he sets to work spinning a web, and he discerns nothing else. It's generally a clever kind of web; but if it's a tangle to others it's the same to him, and a veil as

---

3. "Who ever loved, that loved not at first sight?": Marlowe, *Hero and Leander.*

well. He is preparing the catastrophe, he forces the issue. Tell him of her extreme desire to depart. Treat her as mad, to soothe him. Otherwise one morning he will wake a second time . . . ! It is perfectly certain. And the second time it will be entirely his own fault. Inspire him with some philosophy."

" I have none."

"If I thought so, I would say you have better. There are two kinds of philosophy, mine and yours. Mine comes of coldness, yours of devotion."

" He is unlikely to choose me for his confidante."

Vernon meditated. " One can never quite guess what he will do, from never knowing the heat of the centre in him which precipitates his actions : he has a great art of concealment. As to me, as you perceive, my views are too philosophical to let me be of use to any of them. I blame only the one who holds to the bond. The sooner I am gone ! — in fact, I cannot stay on. So Dr. Middleton and the Professor did not strike fire together ? "

"Dr. Middleton was ready and pursued him, but Professor Crooklyn insisted on shivering. His line of blank verse : ' A Railway platform and a Railway inn !' became pathetic in repetition. He must have suffered."

"Somebody has to ! "

" Why the innocent ? "

" He arrives à propos.[4] But remember that Fridolin sometimes contrives to escape and have the guilty scorched. The Professor would not have suffered if he had missed his train, as he appears to be in the habit of doing. Thus his unaccustomed good fortune was the cause of his bad."

" You saw him on the platform ? "

" I am unacquainted with the Professor. I had to get Mrs. Mountstuart out of the way."

"She says she described him to you. ' Complexion of a sweetbread, consistency of a quenelle, grey, and like a Saint without his dish behind the head.' "[5]

" Her descriptions are strikingly accurate, but she forgot to sketch his back, and all that I saw was a narrow sloping back and a broad hat resting the brim on it. My report to her spoke of an old gentleman of dark complexion, as the only traveller on the platform. She has faith in the efficiency of her descriptive powers, and so she was willing to drive off immediately. — The intention was a start to London. Colonel De Craye came up and effected in five minutes what I could not compass in thirty."[6]

" But you saw Colonel De Craye pass you ? "

4. Opportunely. "Fridolin": the allusion is to a ballad by Schiller, "Der Gang nach dem Eisenhammer." Innocent Fridolin is sent on a fatal errand, but delays in order to worship in church and is saved when his wicked accuser is burnt alive in his stead.

5. "quenelle": meatball. Cookery controls at this point the mind of Mrs. Mountstart Jenkinson.

6. Vernon in his jealousy wholly misinterprets the reason for Clara's return. Nobody corrects him.

"My work was done; I should have been an intruder. Besides I was acting wet jacket with Mrs. Mountstuart to get her to drive off fast, or she might have jumped out in search of her Professor herself."[7]

"She says you were lean as a fork, with the wind whistling through the prongs."

"You see how easy it is to deceive one who is an artist in phrases. Avoid them, Miss Dale; they dazzle the penetration of the composer. That is why people of ability like Mrs. Mountstuart see so little; they are so bent on describing brilliantly. However, she is kind and charitable at heart. I have been considering to-night that, to cut this knot as it is now, Miss Middleton might do worse than speak straight out to Mrs. Mountstuart. No one else would have such influence with Willoughby. The simple fact of Mrs. Mountstuart's knowing of it would be almost enough. But courage would be required for that. Good night, Miss Dale."

"Good night, Mr. Whitford. You pardon me for disturbing you?"

Vernon pressed her hand reassuringly. He had but to look at her and review her history to think his cousin Willoughby punished by just retribution. Indeed for any maltreatment of the dear boy Love by man or by woman, coming under your cognizance, you, if you be of common soundness, shall behold the retributive blow struck in your time.

Miss Dale retired thinking how like she and Vernon were to one another in the toneless condition they had achieved through sorrow. He succeeded in masking himself from her, owing to her awe of the circumstances. She reproached herself for not having the same devotion to the cold idea of duty as he had; and though it provoked inquiry, she would not stop to ask why he had left Miss Middleton a prey to the sparkling colonel. It seemed a proof of the philosophy he preached.

As she was passing by young Crossjay's bedroom-door a face appeared. Sir Willoughby slowly emerged and presented himself in his full length, beseeching her to banish alarm.

He said it in a hushed voice, with a face qualified to create the sentiment.

"Are you tired? sleepy?" said he.

She protested that she was not; she intended to read for an hour.

He begged to have the hour dedicated to him. "I shall be relieved by conversing with a friend."

No subterfuge crossed her mind; she thought his midnight visit to the boy's bed-side a pretty feature in him; she was full of pity too; she yielded to the strange request, feeling that it did not become "an old woman" to attach importance even to the public discovery of midnight inter-

---

7. "acting wet jacket": pretending to be soaked through.

views involving herself as one, and feeling also that she
was being treated as an old friend in the form of a very old
woman. Her mind was bent on arresting any recurrence to
the project he had so frequently outlined in the tongue of
innuendo, of which, because of her repeated tremblings
under it, she thought him a master.[8]

He conducted her along the corridor to the private sitting-
room of the ladies Eleanor and Isabel.

"Deceit!" he said, while lighting the candles on the
mantelpiece.

She was earnestly compassionate, and a word that could
not relate to her personal destinies refreshed her by dis-
placing her apprehensive antagonism and giving pity free
play.

CHAPTER 31

SIR WILLOUGHBY ATTEMPTS AND ACHIEVES PATHOS

BOTH were seated. Apparently he would have preferred
to watch her dark downcast eyelashes in silence under sanction of his air of abstract meditation and the melancholy
superinducing it. Blood-colour was in her cheeks; the
party had inspirited her features. Might it be that lively
company, an absence of economical solicitudes and a flourishing home were all she required to make her bloom again?
The supposition was not hazardous in presence of her
heightened complexion.

She raised her eyes. He could not meet her look without
speaking.

"Can *you* forgive deceit?"

"It would be to boast of more charity than I know my
self to possess, were I to say that I can, Sir Willoughby. I
hope I am able to forgive. I cannot tell. I should like to
say yes."

"Could you live with the deceiver?"

"No."

"No. I could have given that answer for you. No semblance of union should be maintained between the deceiver
and ourselves. Lætitia!"

"Sir Willoughby?"

"Have I no right to your name?"

"If it please you to . . ."

"I speak as my thoughts run, and they did not know a
Miss Dale so well as a dear Lætitia: my truest friend! You
have talked with Clara Middleton?"

"We had a conversation."

8. The project is that of Chapter 14.   but sense demands "he."
Texts print "she had frequently outlined,"

Her brevity affrighted him. He flew off in a cloud.

" Reverting to that question of deceivers : is it not your opinion that to pardon, to condone, is to corrupt society by passing off as pure what is false ? Do we not," he wore the smile of haggard playfulness of a convalescent child the first day back to its toys, " Lætitia, do we not impose a counterfeit on the currency ? "

" Supposing it to be really deception."

" Apart from my loathing of deception, of falseness in any shape, upon any grounds, I hold it an imperious duty to expose, punish, off with it. I take it to be one of the forms of noxiousness which a good citizen is bound to extirpate. I am not myself good citizen enough, I confess, for much more than passive abhorrence. I do not forgive : I am at heart serious and I cannot forgive : — there is no possible reconciliation, there can be only an ostensible truce, between the two hostile powers dividing this world."

She glanced at him quickly.

" Good and evil ! " he said.

Her face expressed a surprise relapsing on the heart.

He spelt the puckers of her forehead to mean, that she feared he might be speaking unchristianly.

" You will find it so in all religions, my dear Lætitia : the Hindoo, the Persian, ours. It is universal; an experience of our humanity. Deceit and sincerity cannot live together. Truth must kill the lie, or the lie will kill truth. I do not forgive. All I say to the person is, go ! "

" But that is right ! that is generous ! " exclaimed Lætitia, glad to approve him for the sake of blinding her critical soul, and relieved by the idea of Clara's difficulty solved.

" *Capable* of generosity perhaps," he mused aloud.

She wounded him by not supplying the expected enthusiastic asseveration of her belief in his general tendency to magnanimity.

He said after a pause : " But the world is not likely to be impressed by anything not immediately gratifying it. People change, I find : as we increase in years we cease to be the heroes we were ! I myself am insensible to change : I do not admit the charge. Except in this, we will say : personal ambition. I have it no more. And what is it when we have it ? Decidedly a confession of inferiority ! That is, the desire to be distinguished is an acknowledgement of insufficiency. But I have still the craving for my dearest friends to think well of me. A weakness ? Call it so. Not a dishonourable weakness ! "

Lætitia racked her brain for the connection of his present speech with the preceding dialogue. She was baffled, from not knowing " the heat of the centre in him " as Vernon opaquely phrased it in charity to the object of her worship.

" Well," said he, unappeased, " and besides the passion to excel, I have changed somewhat in the heartiness of my thirst for the amusements incident to my station. I do not

care to keep a stud — I was once tempted : nor hounds. And
I can remember the day when I determined to have the
best kennels and the best breed of horses in the kingdom.
Puerile ! What is distinction of that sort, or of any acquisition and accomplishment ? We ask ! One's *self* is not the
greater. To seek it, owns to our smallness, in real fact ;
and when it is attained, what then ? My horses are good,
they are admired, I challenge the county to surpass them :
well ? These are but my horses ; the praise is of the
animals, not of me. I decline to share in it. Yet I know
men content to swallow the praise of their beasts and be
semi-equine. The littleness of one's fellows in the mob of
life is a very strange experience ! One may regret to have
lost the simplicity of one's forefathers, which could accept
those and other distinctions with a cordial pleasure, not to
say pride. As for instance, I am, as it is called, a dead shot.
'Give your acclamations, gentlemen, to my ancestors, from
whom I inherited a steady hand and quick sight.' They do
not touch *me*. Where I do not find myself — that *I* am
essentially I — no applause can move me. To speak to you
as I would speak to none, admiration — you know that in my
early youth I swam in flattery — I had to swim to avoid
drowning ! — admiration of my personal gifts has grown
tasteless. Changed, therefore, inasmuch as there has been
a growth of spirituality. We are all in submission to mortal
laws, and so far I have indeed changed. I may add that it
is unusual for country gentlemen to apply themselves to
scientific researches. These are, however, in the spirit of
the time. I apprehended that instinctively when at College.
I forsook the classics for science. And thereby escaped the
vice of domineering self-sufficiency peculiar to classical men,
of which you had an amusing example in the carriage, on
the way to Mrs. Mountstuart's this evening. Science is
modest ; slow, if you like : it deals with facts, and having
mastered them, it masters men ; of necessity, not with a
stupid loud-mouthed arrogance : words big and oddly-garbed
as the Pope's body-guard ![1] Of course, one bows to the
Infallible ; we must, when his giant-mercenaries level
bayonets ! "

Sir Willoughby offered Miss Dale half a minute that she
might in gentle feminine fashion acquiesce in the implied
reproof of Dr. Middleton's behaviour to him during the
drive to Mrs. Mountstuart's. She did not.

Her heart was accusing Clara of having done it a wrong
and a hurt. For while he talked he seemed to her to justify
Clara's feelings and her conduct : and her own reawakened
sensations of injury came to the surface a moment to look at
him, affirming that they pardoned him, and pitied, but
hardly wondered.

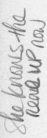

---

1. Swiss Guards at the Vatican used to
wear huge striped pantaloons ; Sir Willoughby is complaining of Dr. Middleton's speech at the end of Chapter 29.

The heat of the centre in him had administered the comfort he wanted, though the conclusive accordant notes he loved on woman's lips, that subservient harmony of another instrument desired of musicians when they have done their solo-playing, came not to wind up the performance : not a single bar. She did not speak. Probably his Lætitia was overcome, as he had long known her to be when they conversed ; nerve-subdued, unable to deploy her mental resources or her musical. Yet ordinarily she had command of the latter. — Was she too condoling ? Did a reason exist for it ? Had the impulsive and desperate girl spoken out to Lætitia to the fullest ? — shameless daughter of a domineering sire that she was ! Ghastlier inquiry (it struck the centre of him with a sounding ring), was Lætitia pitying him overmuch for worse than the pain of a little difference between lovers — for treason on the part of his bride ? Did she know of a rival ? know more than he ?

When the centre of him was violently struck he was a genius in penetration. He guessed that she did know : and by this was he presently helped to achieve pathos.

"So my election was for Science," he continued : "and if it makes me, as I fear, a rara avis among country gentlemen, it unites me, puts me in the main, I may say, in the only current of progress — a word sufficiently despicable in their political jargon. — You enjoyed your evening at Mrs. Mountstuart's ? "[2]

"Very greatly."

"She brings her Professor to dine here the day after to-morrow. Does it astonish you ? You started."

"I did not hear the invitation."

"It was arranged at the table : you and I were separated — cruelly, I told her : she declared that we see enough of one another, and that it was good for me that we should be separated ; neither of which is true. I may not have known what is the best for me : I do know what is good. If in my younger days I egregiously erred, that, taken of itself alone, is, assuming me to have sense and feeling, the surer proof of present wisdom. I can testify in person that wisdom is pain. If pain is to add to wisdom, let me suffer ! Do you approve of that, Lætitia ? "

"It is well said."

"It is felt. Those who themselves have suffered should know the benefit of the resolution."

"One may have suffered so much as to wish only for peace."

"True : but you ! have you ? "

"It would be for peace, if I prayed for an earthly gift."

Sir Willoughby dropped a smile on her. "I mentioned the Pope's parti-coloured body-guard just now. In my youth their singular attire impressed me. People tell me

2. "election": choice; "rara avis": rare bird.

they have been re-uniformed: I am sorry. They remain
one of my liveliest recollections of the Eternal City. They
affected my sense of humour, always alert in me, as you are
aware. We English have humour. It is the first thing
struck in us when we land on the Continent: our risible
faculties are generally active all through the tour. Humour,
or the clash of sense with novel examples of the absurd, is
our characteristic. I do not condescend to boisterous displays of it. I observe, and note the people's comicalities
for my correspondence. But you have read my letters —
most of them, if not all?"

"Many of them."

"I was with you then! — I was about to say — that
Swiss-guard reminded me — you have not been in Italy. I
have constantly regretted it. You are the very woman,
you have the soul for Italy. I know no other of whom I
could say it, with whom I should not feel that she was out
of place, discordant with me. Italy and Lætitia! often
have I joined you together. We shall see. I begin to
have hopes. Here you have literally stagnated. Why, a
dinner-party refreshes you! What would not travel do,
and that heavenly climate! You are a reader of history
and poetry. Well, poetry! I never yet saw the poetry
that expressed the tenth part of what I feel in the presence of beauty and magnificence, and when I really meditate — profoundly. Call me a positive mind. I feel: only
I feel too intensely for poetry. By the nature of it, poetry
cannot be sincere. I will have sincerity. Whatever
touches our emotions should be spontaneous, not a craft.
I know you are in favour of poetry. You would win me, if
any one could. But history! there I am with you. Walking over ruins: at night: the arches of the solemn black
amphitheatre pouring moonlight on us — the moonlight of
Italy!"

"You would not laugh there, Sir Willoughby?" said
Lætitia, rousing herself from a stupor of apprehensive
amazement, to utter something and realize actual circumstances.

"Besides, you, I think, or I am mistaken in you —" he
deviated from his projected speech — "you are not a victim
of the sense of association, and the ludicrous."

"I can understand the influence of it: I have at least a
conception of the humourous: but ridicule would not strike
me in the Coliseum of Rome. I could not bear it, no, Sir
Willoughby!"

She appeared to be taking him in very strong earnest,
by thus petitioning him not to laugh in the Coliseum, and
now he said: "Besides, you are one who could accommodate yourself to the society of the ladies, my aunts. Good
women, Lætitia! I cannot imagine them *de trop* in Italy,
or in a household.[3] I have of course reason to be partial in
my judgement."

3. *"de trop"*: in the way.

"They are excellent and most amiable ladies; I love them," said Lætitia fervently; the more strongly excited to fervour by her enlightenment as to his drift.

She read it, that he designed to take her to Italy with the ladies; — after giving Miss Middleton her liberty; that was necessarily implied. And that was truly generous. In his boyhood he had been famous for his bountifulness in scattering silver and gold. Might he not have caused himself to be misperused in later life?

Clara had spoken to her of the visit and mission of the ladies to the library: and Lætitia daringly conceived herself to be on the certain track of his meaning, she being able to enjoy their society as she supposed him to consider that Miss Middleton did not, and would not either abroad or at home.

Sir Willoughby asked her: "You could travel with them?"

"Indeed I could!"

"Honestly?"

"As affirmatively as one may protest. Delightedly."

"Agreed. It is an undertaking." He put his hand out. "Whether I be of the party or not! To Italy, Lætitia! It would give me pleasure to be with you, and it will, if I must be excluded, to think of you in Italy!"

His hand was out. She had to feign inattention or yield her own. She had not the effrontery to pretend not to see, and she yielded it. He pressed it, and whenever it shrank a quarter-inch to withdraw, he shook it up and down, as an instrument that had been lent him for due emphasis to his remarks. And very emphatic an amorous orator can make it upon a captive lady.

"I am unable to speak decisively on that or any subject. I am, I think you once quoted, 'tossed like a weed on the ocean.'[4] Of myself I can speak: I cannot speak for a second person. I am infinitely harassed. If I could cry, 'To Italy to-morrow!' Ah! . . . Do not set me down for complaining. I know the lot of man. But, Lætitia, deceit! deceit! It is a bad taste in the mouth. It sickens us of humanity. I compare it to an earthquake: we lose all our reliance on the solidity of the world. It is a betrayal not simply of the person; it is a betrayal of humankind. My friend! Constant friend! No, I will not despair. Yes, I have faults; I will remember them. Only, forgiveness is another question. Yes, the injury I *can* forgive: the falseness never. In the interests of humanity, no! So young, and such deceit!"

Lætitia's bosom rose: her hand was detained: a lady who has yielded it cannot wrestle to have it back: those outworks which protect her, treacherously shelter the enemy aiming at the citadel when he has taken them. In return for the silken armour bestowed on her by our civilization, it is exacted that she be soft and civil nigh up to perishing-point. She breathed tremulously high, saying on her top-

4. Willoughby seems to be mangling the poetry by muddling the images.

breath : "If it — it may not be so ; it can scarcely . . ." A deep sigh intervened. It saddened her that she knew so much.

"For when I love, I love," said Sir Willoughby ; "my friends and my servants know that. There can be no medium : not with me. I give all, I claim all. As I am absorbed, so must I absorb. We both cancel and create, we extinguish and we illumine one another. The error may be in the choice of an object : it is not in the passion. Perfect confidence, perfect abandonment. I repeat, I claim it because I give it. The selfishness of love may be denounced : it is a part of us ! My answer would be, it is an element only of the noblest of us ! Love, Lætitia ! I speak of love. But one who breaks faith to drag us through the mire, who betrays, betrays and hands us over to the world, whose prey we become identically because of virtues we were educated to think it a blessing to possess : tell me the name for that ! — Again : it has ever been a principle with me to respect the sex. But if we see women false, treacherous. . . . Why indulge in these abstract views, you would ask ! The world presses them on us, full as it is of the vilest specimens. They seek to pluck up every rooted principle : they sneer at our worship : they rob us of our religion. This bitter experience of the world drives us back to the antidote of what we knew before we plunged into it : of one . . . of something we esteemed and still esteem. Is that antidote strong enough to expel the poison ? I hope so ! I believe so ! To lose faith in womankind is terrible."

He studied her. She looked distressed : she was not moved.

She was thinking that, with the exception of a strain of haughtiness, he talked excellently to men, at least in the tone of the things he meant to say ; but that his manner of talking to women went to an excess in the artificial tongue — the tutored tongue of sentimental deference of the towering male : he fluted exceedingly ; and she wondered whether it was this which had wrecked him with Miss Middleton.

His intuitive sagacity counselled him to strive for pathos to move her. It was a task ; for while he perceived her to be not ignorant of his plight, he doubted her knowing the extent of it, and as his desire was merely to move her without an exposure of himself, he had to compass being pathetic as it were under the impediments of a mailed and gauntletted knight, who cannot easily heave the bosom, or show it heaving.

Moreover pathos is a tide : often it carries the awakener of it off his feet, and whirls him over and over, armour and all, in ignominious attitudes of helpless prostration, whereof he may well be ashamed in the retrospect. We cannot quite preserve our dignity when we stoop to the work of calling forth tears. Moses had probably to take a nimble jump away from the rock after that venerable Law-giver had knocked the water out of it.[5]

However, it was imperative in his mind that he should be sure he had the power to move her.

He began: clumsily at first, as yonder gauntletted knight attempting the briny handkerchief:

"What are we! We last but a very short time. Why not live to gratify our appetites? I might really ask myself why. All the means of satiating them are at my disposal. But no: I must aim at the highest: — at that which in my blindness I took for the highest. You know the sportsman's instinct, Lætitia; he is not tempted by the stationary object. Such are we in youth, toying with happiness, leaving it, to aim at the dazzling and attractive."

"We gain knowledge," said Lætitia.

"At what cost!"

The exclamation summoned self-pity to his aid, and pathos was handy.

"By paying half our lives for it and all our hopes! Yes, we gain knowledge, we are the wiser; very probably my value surpasses now what it was when I was happier. But the loss! That youthful bloom of the soul is like health to the body; once gone, it leaves cripples behind. Nay, my friend and precious friend, these four fingers I must retain. They seem to me the residue of a wreck: <u>you shall be released shortly</u>: absolutely, Lætitia, I have nothing else remaining. — We have spoken of deception: what of being undeceived? — when one whom we adored is laid bare, and the wretched consolation of a worthy object is denied to us. No misfortune can be like that. Were it death, we could worship still. Death would be preferable. But may you be spared to know a situation in which the comparison with your inferior is forced on you to your disadvantage and your loss because of your generously giving up your whole heart to the custody of some shallow, light-minded, self —!
. . . we will not deal in epithets. If I were to find as many bad names for the serpent as there are spots on his body, it would be serpent still, neither better nor worse.
. . . The loneliness! And the darkness! Our luminary is extinguished. Self-respect refuses to continue worshipping, but the affection will not be turned aside. We are literally in the dust, we grovel, we would fling away self-respect if we could; we would adopt for a model the creature preferred to us; we would humiliate, degrade ourselves; we cry for justice as if it were for pardon . . ."

"For pardon! when we are straining to grant it!" Lætitia murmured, and it was as much as she could do. She remembered how in her old misery her efforts after charity had twisted her round to feel herself the sinner, and beg forgiveness in prayer: a noble sentiment, that filled her

5. When Moses struck the rock in the wilderness and drew water from it, he must have got uncomfortably splashed; so with a modern tear-jerker like Willoughby.

with pity of the bosom in which it had sprung. There was no similarity between his idea and hers, but her idea had certainly been roused by his word "pardon," and he had the benefit of it in the moisture of her eyes. Her lips trembled, tears fell.

He had heard something; he had not caught the words, but they were manifestly favourable; her sign of emotion assured him of it and of the success he had sought. [There was one woman who bowed to him to all eternity! He had inspired one woman with the mysterious man-desired passion of self-abandonment, self-immolation!] The evidence was before him. At any instant he could, if he pleased, fly to her and command her enthusiasm.

He had, in fact, perhaps by sympathetic action, succeeded in striking the same springs of pathos in her which animated his lively endeavour to produce it in himself.

He kissed her hand; then released it, quitting his chair to bend above her soothingly.

"Do not weep, Lætitia, you see that I do not: I can smile. Help me to bear it; you must not unman me."

She tried to stop her crying; but self-pity threatened to rain all her long years of grief on her head, and she said: "I must go . . . I am unfit . . . good night, Sir Willoughby."

Fearing seriously that he had sunk his pride too low in her consideration, and had been carried farther than he intended on the tide of pathos, he remarked: "We will speak about Crossjay to-morrow. His deceitfulness has been gross.[6] As I said, I am grievously offended by deception. But you are tired. Good night, my dear friend."

"Good night, Sir Willoughby."

She was allowed to go forth.

Colonel De Craye coming up from the smoking-room, met her and noticed the state of her eyelids, as he wished her good-night. He saw Willoughby in the room she had quitted, but considerately passed without speaking, and without reflecting why he was considerate.

Our hero's review of the scene made him on the whole satisfied with his part in it. Of his power upon one woman he was now perfectly sure:—Clara had agonized him with a doubt of his personal mastery of any. One was a poor feast, but the pangs of his flesh during the last few days and the latest hours, caused him to snatch at it, hungrily if contemptuously. A poor feast, she was yet a fortress, a point of succour, both shield and lance; a cover and an impetus. He could now encounter Clara boldly. Should she resist and defy him, he would not be naked and alone; he foresaw that he might win honour in the world's eye from his position:—a matter to be thought of only in most urgent need. The effect on him of his recent exercise in

6. After pretending all through the scene that it is Clara he is talking about, Wil- loughby covers up by shifting to Crossjay.

pathos was to compose him to slumber. He was for the period well-satisfied.

His attendant imps were well-satisfied likewise, and danced a round about his bed after the vigilant gentleman had ceased to debate on the question of his unveiling of himself past forgiveness of her to Lætitia, and had surrendered unto benignant sleep the present direction of his affairs.

CHAPTER 32

LÆTITIA DALE DISCOVERS A SPIRITUAL CHANGE AND DR. MIDDLETON A PHYSICAL

CLARA tripped over the lawn in the early morning to Lætitia to greet her. She broke away from a colloquy with Colonel De Craye under Sir Willoughby's windows. The colonel had been one of the bathers, and he stood like a circus driver, flicking a wet towel at Crossjay capering.

"My dear, I am very unhappy!" said Clara.

"My dear, I bring you news," Lætitia replied.

"Tell me. But the poor boy is to be expelled! He burst into Crossjay's bed-room last night and dragged the sleeping boy out of bed to question him, and he had the truth.[1] That is one comfort: only Crossjay is to be driven from the Hall because he was untruthful previously — for me: to serve me; really, I feel it was at my command. Crossjay will be out of the way to-day and has promised to come back at night to try to be forgiven. You must help me, Lætitia."

"You are free, Clara! If you desire it, you have but to ask for your freedom."

"You mean . . . ?"

"He will release you."

"You are sure?"

"We had a long conversation last night."

"I owe it to you?"

"Nothing is owing to me. He volunteered it."

Clara made as if to lift her eyes in apostrophe. "Professor Crooklyn![2] Professor Crooklyn! I see. I did not guess that!"

"Give credit for some generosity, Clara; you are unjust."

"By-and-by: I will be more than just by-and-by. I will practise on the trumpet: I will lecture on the greatness of the souls of men when we know them thoroughly. At present we do but half know them, and we are unjust. You

---

1. We are to juxtapose this version of Willoughby's visit to Crossjay's room against Laetitia's gentle thoughts at the end of Chapter 30.
2. Clara assumes that Willoughby is re-

leasing her only because he has guessed, from Professor Crooklyn's conversation, that she was about to run away with De Craye, or actually did so.

are not deceived, Lætitia? There is to be no speaking to papa? no delusions? You have agitated me. I feel myself a very small person indeed. I feel I can understand those who admire him. He gives me back my word simply? clearly? without— Oh! that long wrangle in scenes and letters? And it will be arranged for papa and me to go not later than to-morrow? Never shall I be able to explain to any one how I fell into this! I am frightened at myself when I think of it. I take the whole blame: I have been scandalous. And, dear Lætitia! you came out so early in order to tell me?"

"I wished you to hear it."

"Take my heart."

"Present me with a part—but for good!"

"Fie! But you have a right to say it."

"I mean no unkindness; but is not the heart you allude to an alarmingly searching one?"

"Selfish it is, for I have been forgetting Crossjay. If we are going to be generous, is not Crossjay to be forgiven? If it were only that the boy's father is away fighting for his country, endangering his life day by day, and for a stipend not enough to support his family, we are bound to think of the boy! Poor dear silly lad! with his 'I say, Miss Middleton, why wouldn't (some one) see my father when he came here to call on him, and had to walk back ten miles in the rain?'—I could almost fancy that did me mischief . . . But we have a splendid morning after yesterday's rain. And we will be generous. Own, Lætitia, that it is possible to gild the most glorious day of creation."

"Doubtless the spirit may do it and make its hues permanent," said Lætitia.

"You to me, I to you, he to us. Well, then, if he does, it shall be one of my heavenly days. Which is for the probation of experience. We are not yet at sunset."

"Have you seen Mr. Whitford this morning?"

"He passed me."

"Do not imagine him ever ill-tempered."

"I had a governess, a learned lady, who taught me in person the picturesqueness of grumpiness. Her temper was ever perfect, because she was never in the wrong, but I being so, she was grumpy. She carried my iniquity under her brows, and looked out on me through it. I was a trying child."

Lætitia said, laughing: "I can believe it!"

"Yet I liked her and she liked me: we were a kind of foreground and background: she threw me into relief, and I was an apology for her existence."

"You picture her to me."

"She says of me now, that I am the only creature she has loved. Who knows that I may not come to say the same of her?"

"You would plague her and puzzle her still."

"Have I plagued and puzzled Mr. Whitford?"

"He reminds you of her?"

"You said you had her picture."

"Ah! do not laugh at him. He is a true friend."

"The man who can be a friend is the man who will presume to be a censor."

"A mild one."

"As to the sentence he pronounces, I am unable to speak, but his forehead is Rhadamanthine condemnation."[3]

"Dr. Middleton!"

Clara looked round. "Who? I? Did you hear an echo of papa? He would never have put Rhadamanthus over European souls; because it appears that Rhadamanthus judged only the Asiatic; so you are wrong, Miss Dale. My father is infatuated with Mr. Whitford. What can it be? We women cannot sound the depths of scholars, probably because their pearls have no value in our market; except when they deign to chasten an impertinent; and Mr. Whitford stands aloof from any notice of small fry. He is deep, studious, excellent; and does it not strike you that if he descended among us he would be like a Triton ashore?"[4]

Lætitia's habit of wholly subservient sweetness, which was her ideal of the feminine, not yet conciliated with her acuter character, owing to the absence of full pleasure from her life — the unhealed wound she had sustained and the cramp of a bondage of such old date as to seem iron — induced her to say, as if consenting: "You think he is not quite at home in society?" But she wished to defend him strenuously, and as a consequence she had to quit the self-imposed ideal of her daily acting, whereby — the case being unwonted, very novel to her — the lady's intelligence became confused through the process that quickened it; so sovereign a method of hoodwinking our bright selves is the acting of a part, however naturally it may come to us! and to this will each honest autobiographical member of the animated world bear witness.

She added: "You have not found him sympathetic? He is. You fancy him brooding, gloomy? He is the reverse, he is cheerful, he is indifferent to personal misfortune. Dr. Corney says there is no laugh like Vernon Whitford's, and no humour like his. Latterly he certainly . . . but it has not been your cruel word grumpiness. The truth is, he is anxious about Crossjay: and about other things; and he wants to leave. He is at a disadvantage beside very lively and careless gentlemen at present, but your 'Triton ashore' is unfair, it is ugly. He is, I can say, the truest man I know."

"I did not question his goodness, Lætitia."

3. Judge and ruler of the ancient underworld, Rhadamanthus assigned one to the particular torture one merited.

4. "Triton": a son and herald of Neptune in the shape of a sea-centaur—man, horse, and fish.

"You threw an accent on it."

"Did I? I must be like Crossjay, who declares he likes fun best."

"Crossjay ought to know him, if anybody should. Mr. Whitford has defended you against me, Clara, ever since I took to calling you Clara. Perhaps when you supposed him so like your ancient governess, he was meditating how he could aid you. Last night he gave me reasons for thinking you would do wisely to confide in Mrs. Mountstuart. It is no longer necessary. I merely mention it. He is a devoted friend."

"He is an untiring pedestrian."

"Oh!"

Colonel De Craye, after hovering near the ladies in the hope of seeing them divide, now adopted the method of making three that two may come of it.

As he joined them with his glittering chatter, Lætitia looked at Clara to consult her, and saw the face rosy as a bride's.

The suspicion she had nursed sprang out of her arms a muscular fact on the spot.

"Where is my dear boy?" Clara said.

"Out for a holiday," the colonel answered in her tone.

"Advise Mr. Whitford not to waste his time in searching for Crossjay, Lætitia. Crossjay is better out of the way to-day. At least, I thought so just now. Has he pocket-money, Colonel De Craye?"

"My lord can command his inn."

"How thoughtful you are!"

Lætitia's bosom swelled upon a mute exclamation, equivalent to: Woman! woman! snared ever by the sparkling and frivolous! undiscerning of the faithful, the modest and beneficent!

In the secret musings of moralists this dramatic rhetoric survives.

The comparison was all of her own making and she was indignant at the contrast, though to what end she was indignant she could not have said, for she had no idea of Vernon as a rival of De Craye in the favour of a plighted lady. But she was jealous on behalf of her sex: her sex's reputation seemed at stake, and the purity of it was menaced by Clara's idle preference of the shallower man. When the young lady spoke so carelessly of being like Crossjay, she did not perhaps know that a likeness, based on a similarity of their enthusiasms, loves, and appetites, has been established between women and boys. Lætitia had formerly chafed at it, rejecting it utterly, save when now and then in a season of bitterness she handed here and there a volatile young lady (none but the young) to be stamped with the degrading brand. Vernon might be as philosophical as he pleased. To her the gaiety of these two, Colonel De Craye and Clara Middleton, was distressingly musical: they harmonized painfully. The representative of her sex was hurt by it.

She had to stay beside them : Clara held her arm. The colonel's voice dropped at times to something very like a whisper. He was answered audibly and smoothly. The quick-witted gentleman accepted the correction: but in immediately paying assiduous attentions to Miss Dale, in the approved intriguer's fashion, he showed himself in need of another amounting to a reproof. Clara said : "We have been consulting, Lætitia, what is to be done to cure Professor Crooklyn of his cold." De Craye perceived that he had taken a wrong step, and he was mightily surprised that a lesson in intrigue should be read to him of all men. Miss Middleton's audacity was not so astonishing : he recognized grand capabilities in the young lady. Fearing lest she should proceed farther and cut away from him his vantage-ground of secrecy with her, he turned the subject and was adroitly submissive.

Clara's manner of meeting Sir Willoughby expressed a timid disposition to friendliness upon a veiled inquiry, understood by none save Lætitia, whose brain was racked to convey assurances to herself of her not having misinterpreted him. Could there be any doubt ? She resolved that there could not be ; and it was upon this basis of reason — that she fancied she had led him to it. Legitimate or not, the fancy sprang from a solid foundation. Yesterday morning she could not have conceived it. Now she was endowed to feel that she had power to influence him, because now, since the midnight, she felt some emancipation from the spell of his physical mastery. He did not appear to her as a different man, but she had grown sensible of being a stronger woman. He was no more the cloud over her, nor the magnet ; the cloud once heaven-suffused, the magnet fatally compelling her to sway round to him. She admired him still : his handsome air, his fine proportions, the courtesy of his bending to Clara and touching of her hand, excused a fanatical excess of admiration on the part of a woman in her youth, who is never the anatomist of the hero's lordly graces. But now she admired him piecemeal. When it came to the putting of him together, she did it coldly. To compassionate him was her utmost warmth. Without conceiving in him anything of the strange old monster of earth which had struck the awakened girl's mind of Miss Middleton, Lætitia classed him with other men : he was " one of them." And she did not bring her disenchantment as a charge against him. She accused herself, acknowledged the secret of the change to be, that her youthfulness was dead : — otherwise could she have given him compassion, and not herself have been carried on the flood of it ? The compassion was fervent, and pure too. She supposed he would supplicate ; she saw that Clara Middleton was pleasant with him only for what she expected of his generosity. She grieved. Sir Willoughby was fortified by her sorrowful gaze as he and Clara passed out together to the laboratory arm in arm.

Lætitia had to tell Vernon of the uselessness of his beating the house and grounds for Crossjay. Dr. Middleton held him fast in discussion upon an overnight's classical wrangle with Professor Crooklyn, which was to be renewed that day. The Professor had appointed to call expressly to renew it. "A fine scholar," said the Rev. Doctor, "but crotchetty, like all men who cannot stand their Port."

"I hear that he had a cold," Vernon remarked. "I hope the wine was good, sir."

As when the foreman of a sentimental jury is commissioned to inform an awful Bench exact in perspicuous English, of a verdict that must of necessity be pronounced in favour of the hanging of the culprit, yet would fain attenuate the crime of a palpable villain by a recommendation to mercy, such foreman, standing in the attentive eye of a master of grammatical construction, and feeling the weight of at least three sentences on his brain, together with a prospect of judicial interrogation for the discovery of his precise meaning, is oppressed, himself is put on trial in turn, and he hesitates, he recapitulates, the fear of involution leads him to be involved; as far as a man so posted may, he on his own behalf appeals for mercy; entreats that his indistinct statement of preposterous reasons may be taken for understood, and would gladly, were permission to do it credible, throw in an imploring word, that he may sink back among the crowd without for the one imperishable moment publicly swinging in his lordship's estimation: —much so, moved by chivalry toward a lady, courtesy to the recollection of a hostess, and particularly by the knowledge that his hearer would expect with a certain frigid rigour charity of him, Dr. Middleton paused, spoke and paused: he stammered. Ladies, he said, were famous poisoners in the Middle Ages. His opinion was, that we had a class of manufacturing wine-merchants on the watch for widows in this country. But he was bound to state the fact of his waking at his usual hour to the minute unassailed by headache. On the other hand, this was a condition of blessedness unanticipated when he went to bed. Mr. Whitford, however, was not to think that he entertained rancour toward the wine. It was no doubt dispensed with the honourable intention of cheering. [In point of flavour execrable, judging by results it was innocuous.]

"The test of it shall be the effect of it upon Professor Crooklyn, and his appearance in the forenoon according to promise," Dr. Middleton came to an end with his perturbed balancings. "If I hear more of the eight or twelve winds discharged at once upon a railway platform, and the young lady who dries herself of a drenching by drinking brandy and water with a gentleman at a railway inn, I shall solicit your sanction to my condemnation of the wine as anti-Bacchic and a counterfeit presentment. Do not misjudge me. Our hostess is not responsible. But widows should marry."

"You must contrive to stop the Professor, sir, if he should attack his hostess in that manner," said Vernon.

"Widows should marry!" Dr. Middleton repeated.

He murmured of objecting to be at the discretion of a butler: unless, he was careful to add, the aforesaid functionary could boast of an University education: and even then, said he, it requires a line of ancestry to train a man's taste.

The Rev. Doctor smothered a yawn. The repression of it caused a second one, a real monster, to come, big as our old friend of the sea advancing on the chained-up Beauty.[5]

Disconcerted by this damning evidence of indigestion, his countenance showed that he considered himself to have been too lenient to the wine of an unhusbanded hostess. He frowned terribly.

In the interval Lætitia told Vernon of Crossjay's flight for the day, hastily bidding the master to excuse him: she had no time to hint the grounds of excuse. Vernon mentally made a guess.

Dr. Middleton took his arm and discharged a volley at the crotchetty scholarship of Professor Crooklyn, whom to confute by book, he directed his march to the library. Having persuaded himself that he was dyspeptic, he had grown irascible. He denounced all dining out, eulogized Patterne Hall as if it were his home, and remembered he had dreamed in the night: — a most humiliating sign of physical disturbance. "But let me find a house in proximity to Patterne, as I am induced to suppose I shall," he said, "and here only am I to be met when I stir abroad."

Lætitia went to her room. She was complacently anxious, enough to prefer solitude and be willing to read. She was more seriously anxious about Crossjay than about any of the others. For Clara would be certain to speak very definitely, and how then could a gentleman oppose her? He would supplicate, and could she be brought to yield? It was not to be expected of a young lady who had turned from Sir Willoughby. His inferiors would have had a better chance. Whatever his faults, he had that element of greatness which excludes the intercession of pity. Supplication would be with him a form of condescension. It would be seen to be such. His was a monumental pride that could not stoop. She had preserved this image of the gentleman for a relic in the shipwreck of her idolatry. So she mused between the lines of her book, and finishing her

5. "friend of the sea": the monster from whom Andromeda was rescued by Perseus. In connection with the "strange old monster of earth," he surrounds Clara with mythological menaces and overtones.

reading and marking the page, she glanced down on the lawn. Dr. Middleton was there, and alone; his hands behind his back, his head bent. His meditative pace and unwonted perusal of the turf proclaimed that a non-sentimental jury within had delivered an unmitigated verdict upon the widow's wine. Lætitia hurried to find Vernon.

He was in the hall. As she drew near him, the laboratory door opened and shut.

"It is being decided," said Lætitia.

Vernon was paler than the hue of perfect calmness.

"I want to know whether I ought to take to my heels like Crossjay, and shun the Professor," he said.

They spoke in undertones, furtively watching the door.

"I wish what she wishes, I am sure, but it will go badly with the boy," said Lætitia.

"Oh, well, then I'll take him," said Vernon, "I would rather. I think I can manage it."

Again the laboratory door opened. This time it shut behind Miss Middleton. She was highly flushed. Seeing them, she shook the storm from her brows, with a dead smile: the best piece of serenity she could put on for public wear.

She took a breath before she moved.

Vernon strode out of the house.

Clara swept up to Lætitia.

"You were deceived!"

The hard sob of anger barred her voice.

Lætitia begged her to come to her room with her.

"I want air: I must be by myself," said Clara, catching at her garden-hat.

She walked swiftly to the portico-steps and turned to the right, to avoid the laboratory windows.

CHAPTER 33

IN WHICH THE COMIC MUSE HAS AN EYE ON TWO GOOD SOULS

Clara met Vernon on the bowling-green among the laurels. She asked him where her father was.

"Don't speak to him now," said Vernon.

"Mr. Whitford, will you?"

"It is not adviseable just now. Wait."

"Wait? Why not now?"

"He is not in the right humour."

She choked. There are times when there is no medicine for us in sages, we want slaves; we scorn to temporize, we must overbear. On she sped, as if she had made the mistake of exchanging words with a post.

The scene between herself and Willoughby was a thick mist in her head, except the burden and result of it, that he held to her fast, and would neither assist her to depart nor disengage her.

Oh, men! men! They astounded the girl; she could not define them to her understanding. Their motives, their tastes, their vanity, their tyranny, and the domino on their vanity, the baldness of their tyranny, clenched her in feminine antagonism to brute power.[1] She was not the less disposed to rebellion by a very present sense of the justice of what could be said to reprove her. She had but one answer: "Anything but marry him!" It threw her on her nature, our last and headlong advocate, who is quick as the flood to hurry us from the heights to our level, and lower, if there be accidental gaps in the channel. For say we have been guilty of misconduct: can we redeem it by violating that which we are and live by? The question sinks us back to the luxuriousness of a sunny relinquishment of effort in the direction against tide. Our nature becomes ingenious in devices, penetrative of the enemy, confidently citing its cause for being frankly elvish or worse. Clara saw a particular way of forcing herself to be surrendered.[2] She shut her eyes from it: the sight carried her too violently to her escape: but her heart caught it up and huzzaed. To press the points of her fingers at her bosom, looking up to the sky as she did, and cry, "I am not my own; I am his!" was instigation sufficient to make her heart leap up with all her body's blush to urge it to recklessness. A despairing creature then may say she has addressed the heavens and has had no answer to restrain her.

Happily for Miss Middleton she had walked some minutes in her chafing fit before the falcon eye of Colonel De Craye spied her away on one of the beech-knolls.

Vernon stood irresolute. It was decidedly not a moment for disturbing Dr. Middleton's composure. He meditated upon a conversation, as friendly as possible, with Willoughby. Round on the front-lawn he beheld Willoughby and Dr. Middleton together, the latter having halted to lend attentive ear to his excellent host. Unnoticed by them or disregarded, Vernon turned back to Lætitia, and sauntered talking with her of things current for as long as he could endure to listen to praise of his pure self-abnegation; proof of how well he had disguised himself, but it smacked unpleasantly to him. His humourous intimacy with men's minds likened the source of this distaste to the gallant all-or-nothing of the gambler, who hates the little when he cannot have the much, and would rather stalk

1. "domino": a cloak, draped over naked self-love.
2. "particular way": a man, any other man. Clara can always and easily escape via the door of scandal—for example, simply by riding in a railway car with Horace De Craye to London.

from the tables clean-picked than suffer ruin to be tickled
by driblets of the glorious fortune he has played for and
lost. If we are not to be beloved, spare us the small coin
of compliments on character: especially when they compliment only our acting. It is partly endurable to win eulogy
for our stately fortitude in losing, but Lætitia was unaware
that he flung away a stake; so she could not praise him
for his merits.

"Willoughby makes the pardoning of Crossjay condi-
tional," he said, "and the person pleading for him has
to grant the terms. How could you imagine Willoughby
would give her up! How could he! Who!... He should,
is easily said. I was no witness of the scene between them
just now, but I could have foretold the end of it; I could
almost recount the passages. The consequence is, that
everything depends upon the amount of courage she pos-
sesses. Dr. Middleton won't leave Patterne yet. And it
is of no use to speak to him to-day. And she is by nature
impatient, and is rendered desperate."

"Why is it of no use to speak to Dr. Middleton to-day?"
said Lætitia.

"He drank wine yesterday that did not agree with him;
he can't work. To-day he is looking forward to Patterne
Port. He is not likely to listen to any proposals to leave
to-day."

"Goodness!"

"I know the depth of that cry!"

"*You* are excluded, Mr. Whitford."

"Not a bit of it; I am in with the rest. Say that men
are to be exclaimed at. Men have a right to expect you to
know your own mind when you close on a bargain. You
don't know the world or yourselves very well, it's true;
still the original error is on your side, and upon that you
should fix your attention. She brought her father here,
and no sooner was he very comfortably established than she
wished to dislocate him."

"I cannot explain it; I cannot comprehend it," said
Lætitia.

"You are Constancy."

"No." She coloured. "I am 'in with the rest.' I do not
say I should have done the same. But I have the knowledge
that I must not sit in judgement on her. I can waver."

She coloured again. She was anxious that he should
know her to be not that stupid statue of Constancy in a
corner doting on the antic Deception. Reminiscences of
the interview over night made it oppressive to her to hear herself praised for always pointing like the needle. Her newly
enfranchised individuality pressed to assert its existence.
Vernon, however, not seeing this novelty, continued, to her
excessive discomfort, to baste her old abandoned image with
his praises. They checked hers; and moreover he had
suddenly conceived an envy of her life-long, uncomplain-

ing, almost unaspiring, constancy of sentiment. If you know lovers when they have not reason to be blissful, you will remember that in this mood of admiring envy they are given to fits of uncontrollable maundering. Praise of constancy, moreover, smote shadowily a certain inconstant, enough to seem to ruffle her smoothness and do no hurt. He found his consolation in it, and poor Lætitia writhed. Without designing to retort, she instinctively grasped at a weapon of defence in further exalting his devotedness; which reduced him to cast his head to the heavens and implore them to partially enlighten her. Nevertheless, maunder he must; and he recurred to it in a way so utterly unlike himself that Lætitia stared in his face. She wondered whether there could be anything secreted behind this everlasting theme of constancy. He took her awakened gaze for a summons to asseverations of sincerity, and out they came. She would have fled from him, but to think of flying was to think how little it was that urged her to fly, and yet the thought of remaining and listening to praises undeserved and no longer flattering, was a torture.

"Mr. Whitford, I bear no comparison with you."

"I do and must set you for my example, Miss Dale."

"Indeed you do wrongly; you do not know me."

"I could say that. For years! . . ."

"Pray, Mr. Whitford!"

"Well, I have admired it. You show us how self can be smothered."

"An echo would be a retort on you!"

"On me? I am never thinking of anything else."

"I could say that."

"You are necessarily conscious of not swerving."

"But I do; I waver dreadfully; I am not the same two days running."

"You are the same, with 'ravishing divisions' upon the same."[3]

"And you without the 'divisions.' I draw such support as I have from you."

"From some simulacrum of me, then. And that will show you how little you require support."

"I do not speak my own opinion only."

"Whose?"

"I am not alone."

"Again let me say, I wish I were like you!"

"Then let me add, I would willingly make the exchange!"

"You would be amazed at your bargain."

"Others would be!"

"Your exchange would give me the qualities I am in want of, Miss Dale."

"Negative, passive, at the best, Mr. Whitford. But *I* should have . . ."

---

3. "ravishing divisions": exquisite variations on a melody.

"Oh!—pardon me. But you inflict the sensations of a boy, with a dose of honesty in him, called up to receive a prize he has won by the dexterous use of a crib."

"And how do you suppose she feels, who has a crown of Queen o' the May forced on her head when she is verging on November?"

He rejected her analogy, and she his. They could neither of them bring to light the circumstances which made one another's admiration so unbearable. The more he exalted her for constancy, the more did her mind become bent upon critically examining the object of that imagined virtue; and the more she praised him for possessing the spirit of perfect friendliness, the fiercer grew the passion in him which disdained the imputation, hissing like a heated iron-bar that flings the water-drops to steam. He would none of it: would rather have stood exposed in his profound foolishness.

Amiable though they were, and mutually affectionate, they came to a stop in their walk, longing to separate, and not seeing how it was to be done, they had so knit themselves together with the pelting of their interlaudation.

"I think it is time for me to run home to my father for an hour," said Lætitia.

"I ought to be working," said Vernon.

Good progress was made to the disgarlanding of themselves thus far; yet, an acutely civilized pair, the abruptness of the transition from floweriness to commonplace affected them both, Lætitia chiefly, as she had broken the pause, and she remarked,—

"I am really Constancy in my opinions."

"Another title is customary where stiff opinions are concerned. Perhaps by-and-by you will learn your mistake, and then you will acknowledge the name for it."

"How?" said she. "What shall I learn?"

"If you learn that I am a grisly Egoist?"

"You? And it would not be egoism," added Lætitia, revealing to him at the same instant as to herself, that she swung suspended on a scarce credible guess.

"— Will nothing pierce your ears, Mr. Whitford?"

He heard the intruding voice, but he was bent on rubbing out the cloudy letters Lætitia had begun to spell, and he stammered in a tone of matter-of-fact: "Just that and no better;" then turned to Mrs. Mountstuart Jenkinson.

"— Or are you resolved you will never see Professor Crooklyn when you look on him?" said the great lady.

Vernon bowed to the Professor and apologized to him shufflingly and rapidly, incoherently, and with a red face; which induced Mrs. Mountstuart to scan Lætitia's.

After lecturing Vernon for his abandonment of her yes·terday evening, and flouting his protestations, she returned to the business of the day. "We walked from the lodge-gates to see the park and prepare ourselves for Dr. Middle-ton. We parted last night in the middle of a controversy and are rageing to resume it. Where is our redoubtable antagonist?"

Mrs. Mountstuart wheeled Professor Crooklyn round to accompany Vernon.

"We," she said, "are for modern English scholarship, opposed to the champion of German."

"The contrary," observed Professor Crooklyn.

"Oh. We," she corrected the error serenely, "are for German scholarship, opposed to English."

"Certain editions."

"We defend certain editions."

"Defend, is a term of imperfect application to my position, ma'am."

"My dear Professor, you have in Dr. Middleton a match for you in conscientious pugnacity, and you will not waste it upon me. There, there they are; there he is. Mr. Whitford will conduct you. I stand away from the first shock."

Mrs. Mountstuart fell back to Lætitia, saying: "He pores over a little inexactitude in phrases, and pecks at it like a domestic fowl."

Professor Crooklyn's attitude and air were so well described that Lætitia could have laughed.

"These mighty scholars have their flavour," the great lady hastened to add, lest her younger companion should be misled to suppose that they were not valuable to a governing hostess: "their shadow-fights are ridiculous, but they have their flavour at a table. Last night, no: I discard all mention of last night. We failed: as none else in this neighbourhood could fail, but we failed. If we have among us a cormorant devouring young lady who drinks up all the — ha! — brandy and water — of our inns and occupies all our flys, why, our condition is abnormal, and we must expect to fail: we are deprived of accommodation for accidental circumstances. How Mr. Whitford could have missed seeing Professor Crooklyn! And what was *he* doing at the station, Miss Dale?"

"Your portrait of Professor Crooklyn was too striking, Mrs. Mountstuart, and deceived him by its excellence. He appears to have seen only the blank side of the slate."

"Ah. He is a faithful friend of his cousin, do you not think?"

"He is the truest of friends."

"As for Dr. Middleton," Mrs. Mountstuart diverged from her inquiry, "he will swell the letters of my vocabulary to gigantic proportions if I see much of him: he is contagious."

"I believe it is a form of his humour."

"I caught it of him yesterday at my dinner-table in my distress, and must pass it off as a form of mine, while it lasts. I talked Dr. Middleton half the dreary night through to my pillow. Your candid opinion, my dear, come! As for me, I don't hesitate. We seemed to have sat down to a

solitary performance on the bass-viol. We were positively
an assembly of insects during thunder. My very soul
thanked Colonel De Craye for his diversions, but I heard
nothing but Dr. Middleton. It struck me that my table was
petrified, and every one sat listening to bowls played overhead."[4]

"I was amused."

"Really? You delight me. Who knows but that my
guests were sincere in their congratulations on a thoroughly
successful evening? I have fallen to this, you see! And I
know, wretched people! that as often as not it is their way
of condoling with one. I do it myself: but only where there
have been amiable efforts. But imagine *my* being congratulated for that!—Good morning, Sir Willoughby.—The
worst offender! and I am in no pleasant mood with him,"
Mrs. Mountstuart said aside to Lætitia, who drew back,
retiring.

Sir Willoughby came on a step or two. He stopped to
watch Lætitia's figure swimming to the house.

So, as, for instance, beside a stream, when a flower on the
surface extends its petals drowning to subside in the clear
still water, we exercise our privilege to be absent in the
charmed contemplation of a beautiful natural incident.

A smile of pleased abstraction melted on his features.

CHAPTER 34

MRS. MOUNTSTUART AND SIR WILLOUGHBY

"GOOD morning, my dear Mrs. Mountstuart," Sir Willoughby wakened himself to address the great lady. "Why
has she fled?"

"Has any one fled?"

"Lætitia Dale."

"Letty Dale? Oh! if you call that flying. Possibly to
renew a close conversation with Vernon Whitford, that I
cut short. You frightened me with your 'Shepherds-tell-
me' air and tone. Lead me to one of your garden-seats:
out of hearing to Dr. Middleton, I beg. He mesmerizes me,
he makes me talk Latin. I was curiously susceptible last
night. I know I shall everlastingly associate him with an
abortive entertainment and solos on big instruments. We
were flat."

"Horace was in good vein."[1]

"You were not."

"And Lætitia—Miss Dale talked well, I thought."

---

4. Dr. Middleton compared to rumbling
thunder compared to bowling balls rum-

bling down the alleys of the gods.
1. Fluent, amusing.

"She talked with you, and no doubt she talked well. We did not mix. The yeast was bad. You shot darts at Colonel De Craye : you tried to sting. You brought Dr. Middleton down on you. Dear me, that man is a reverberation in my head. Where is your lady and love ? "

"Who ? "

"Am I to name her ? "

"Clara ? I have not seen her for the last hour. Wandering, I suppose."

"A very pretty summer-bower," said Mrs. Mountstuart, seating herself. "Well, my dear Sir Willoughby, preferences, preferences are not to be accounted for, and one never knows whether to pity or congratulate, whatever may occur. I want to see Miss Middleton."

"Your ' dainty rogue in porcelain ' will be at your beck — you lunch with us ? — before you leave."

"So now you have taken to quoting me, have you ? "

"But ' a romantic tale on her eyelashes' is hardly descriptive any longer."

"Descriptive of whom ? Now you are upon Lætitia Dale ! "

"I quote you generally. She has now a graver look."

"And well may have ! "

"Not that the romance has entirely disappeared."

"No : it looks as if it were in print."

"You have hit it perfectly, as usual, ma'am."

Sir Willoughby mused.

Like one resuming his instrument to take up the melody in a concerted piece, he said . "I thought Lætitia Dale had a singularly animated air last night."

"Why ! —" Mrs. Mountstuart mildly gaped.

"I want a new description of her. You know, I collect your mottoes and sentences."

"It seems to me she is coming three parts out of her shell, and wearing it as a hood for convenience."

"Ready to issue forth at an invitation ? Admirable ! exact ! "

"Ay, my good Sir Willoughby, but are we so very admirable and exact ? Are we never to know our own minds ? "

He produced a polysyllabic sigh, like those many-jointed compounds of poets in happy languages, which are copious in a single expression : "Mine is known to me. It always has been. Cleverness in women is not uncommon. Intellect is the pearl. A woman of intellect is as good as a Greek statue ; she is divinely wrought, and she is divinely rare."

"Proceed," said the lady, confiding a cough to the air.

"The rarity of it : and it is not mere intellect, it is a sympathetic intellect ; or else it is an intellect in perfect accord with an intensely sympathetic disposition ; — the rarity of it makes it too precious to be parted with when once we have met it. I prize it the more the older I grow."

" Are we on the feminine or the neuter ? "

" I beg pardon ? "

" The universal or the individual ? "

He shrugged. " For the rest, psychological affinities may exist coincident with and entirely independent of material or moral prepossessions, relations, engagements, ties."

" Well, that is not the raving of passion, certainly," said Mrs. Mountstuart, "and it sounds as if it were a comfortable doctrine for men. On that plea, you might all of you be having Aspasia and a wife.[2] We saw your fair Middleton and Colonel De Craye at a distance as we entered the park. Professor Crooklyn is under some hallucination."

" What more likely ? "

The readiness and the double-bearing of the reply struck her comic sense with awe.

" The Professor must hear that. He insists on the fly, and the inn, and the wet boots, and the warming mixture, and the testimony of the landlady and the railway porter."

" I say, what more likely ? "

" Than that he should insist ? "

" If he is under the hallucination ! "

" He may convince others."

" I have only to repeat ! . . ."

"' What more likely ? ' It 's extremely philosophical. Coincident with a pursuit of the psychological affinities."

" Professor Crooklyn will hardly descend, I suppose, from his classical altitudes to lay his hallucinations before Dr. Middleton ? "

" Sir Willoughby, you are the pink of chivalry ! "

By harping on Lætitia, he had emboldened Mrs. Mountstuart to lift the curtain upon Clara. It was offensive to him, but the injury done to his pride had to be endured for the sake of his general plan of self-protection.

" Simply desirous to save my guests from annoyance of any kind," he said. " Dr. Middleton can look 'Olympus and thunder,' as Vernon calls it."

"Don't. I see him. That look ! It is Dictionary-bitten ! Angry, horned Dictionary ! — an apparition of Dictionary in the night — to a dunce ! "

" One would undergo a good deal to avoid the sight."

" What the man must be in a storm ! Speak as you please of yourself : you are a true and chivalrous knight to dread it for her. But now candidly, how is it you cannot condescend to a little management ? Listen to an old friend. You are too lordly. No lover can afford to be incomprehensible for half an hour. Stoop a little. Sermonizings are not to be thought of. You can govern unseen. You are to know that I am one who disbelieves in philosophy in love. I admire the look of it, I give no credit to the assumption. I rather like lovers to be out at times : it makes them

2. "Aspasia": a mistress—from the name of Pericles' extramarital friend.

picturesque, and it enlivens their monotony. I perceived she had a spot of wildness. It's proper that she should wear it off before marriage."

"Clara? The wildness of an infant!" said Willoughby, paternally musing over an inward shiver. "You saw her at a distance just now, or you might have heard her laughing. Horace diverts her excessively."

"I owe him my eternal gratitude for his behaviour last night. She was one of my bright faces. Her laughter was delicious; rain in the desert! It will tell you what the load on me was, when I assure you those two were merely a spectacle to me — points I scored in a lost game. And I know they were witty."

"They both have wit; a kind of wit," Willoughby assented.

"They struck together like a pair of cymbals."

"Not the highest description of instrument. However, they amuse me. I like to hear them when I am in the vein."

"That vein should be more at command with you, my friend. You can be perfect, if you like."

"Under your tuition."

Willoughby leaned to her, bowing languidly. He was easier in his pain for having hoodwinked the lady. She was the outer world to him; she could tune the world's voice; prescribe which of the two was to be pitied, himself or Clara; and he did not intend it to be himself, if it came to the worst.

They were far away from that at present, and he continued: "Probably a man's power of putting on a face is not equal to a girl's. I detest petty dissensions. Probably I show it when all is not quite smooth. Little fits of suspicion vex me. It is a weakness, not to play them off, I know. Men have to learn the arts which come to women by nature. I don't sympathize with suspicion, from having none myself."

His eyebrows shot up. That ill-omened man Flitch had sidled round by the bushes to within a few feet of him.

Flitch primarily defended himself against the accusation of drunkenness, which was hurled at him to account for his audacity in trespassing against the interdict: but he admitted that he had taken "something short" for a fortification in visiting scenes where he had once been happy — at Christmastide, when all the servants, and the butler at head, gray old Mr. Chessington, sat in rows, toasting the young heir of the old Hall in the old port wine! Happy had he been then, before ambition for a shop, to be his own master and an independent gentleman, had led him into his quagmire: — to look back envying a dog on the old estate, and sigh for the smell of Patterne stables, sweeter than Arabia, his drooping nose appeared to say.

He held up close against it something that imposed silence

on Sir Willoughby as effectually as a cunning exordium in oratory will enchain mobs to swallow what is not complimenting them: and this he displayed, secure in its being his license to drivel his abominable pathos. Sir Willoughby recognized Clara's purse. He understood at once how the man must have come by it: he was not so quick in devising a means of stopping the tale.[3] Flitch foiled him. "Intact," he replied to the question: "What have you there?" He repeated this grand word. And then he turned to Mrs. Mountstuart to speak of Paradise and Adam, in whom he saw the prototype of himself: also the Hebrew people in the bondage of Egypt, discoursed of by the clergymen, not without a likeness to him.

"Sorrows have done me one good, to send me attentive to church, my lady," said Flitch, "when I might have gone to London, the coachman's home, and been driving some honourable family with no great advantage to my morals, according to what I hear of. And a purse found under the seat of a fly in London would have a poor chance of returning *intact* to the young lady losing it."

"Put it down on that chair; inquiries will be made, and you will see Sir Willoughby," said Mrs. Mountstuart. "Intact, no doubt; it is not disputed."

With one motion of a finger she set the man rounding. Flitch halted: he was very regretful of the termination of his feast of pathos, and he wished to relate the finding of the purse, but he could not encounter Mrs. Mountstuart's look: he slouched away in very close resemblance to the ejected Adam of illustrated books.

"It's my belief that naturalness among the common people has died out of the kingdom," she said.

Willoughby charitably apologized for him. "He has been fuddling himself."

Her vigilant considerateness had dealt the sensitive gentleman a shock, plainly telling him she had her ideas of his actual posture. Nor was he unhurt by her superior acuteness and her display of authority on his grounds.

He said boldly, as he weighed the purse, half tossing it: "It's not unlike Clara's."

He feared that his lips and cheeks were twitching, and as he grew aware of a glassiness of aspect that would reflect any suspicion of a keen-eyed woman, he became bolder still: "Lætitia's, I know it is not. Hers is an ancient purse."

"A present from you!"

"How do you hit on that, my dear lady?"

"Deductively."

"Well, the purse looks as good as new in quality, like the owner."

"The poor dear has not much occasion for using it."

---

3. "come by it": She had been in the fly with De Craye.

" You are mistaken : she uses it daily."

" If it were better filled, Sir Willoughby, your old scheme might be arranged. The parties do not appear so unwilling. Professor Crooklyn and I came on them just now rather by surprise, and I assure you their heads were close, faces meeting, eyes musing."

" Impossible."

" Because when they approach the point, you won't allow it ! Selfish ! "

" Now," said Willoughby, very animatedly, " question Clara. Now, do, my dear Mrs. Mountstuart, do speak to Clara on that head ; she will convince you I have striven quite recently : — against myself, if you like. I have instructed her to aid me, given her the fullest instructions, carte blanche. *She* cannot possibly have a doubt. I may look to her to remove any you may entertain from your mind on the subject. I have proposed, seconded and chorussed it, and it will *not* be arranged. If you expect me to deplore that fact, I can only answer that my actions are under my control, my feelings are not. I will do everything consistent with the duties of a man of honour : perpetually running into fatal errors because he did not properly consult the dictates of those feelings at the right season. I can violate them : but I can no more command them than I can my destiny. They were crushed of old, and so let them be now. Sentiments, we won't discuss ; though you know that sentiments have a bearing on social life : are factors, as they say in their later jargon. I never speak of mine. To you I could. It is not necessary. If old Vernon, instead of flattening his chest at a desk had any manly ambition to take part in public affairs, she would be the woman for him. I have called her my Egeria. She would be his Cornelia.[4] One could swear of her that she would have noble offspring ! — But old Vernon has had his disappointment, and will moan over it up to the end. And she ? So it appears. I have tried ; yes, personally : without effect. In other matters I may have influence with her : not in that one. She declines. She will live and die Lætitia Dale. We are alone : I confess to you, I love the name. It 's an old song in my ears. Do not be too ready with a name for *me*. Believe me — I speak from my experience hitherto — there is a fatality in these things. I cannot conceal from my poor girl that this fatality exists . . ."

" Which is the poor girl at present ? " said Mrs. Mountstuart, cool in a mystification.

" And though she will tell you that I have authorized and — Clara Middleton — done as much as man can to institute the union you suggest, she will own that she is conscious of the presence of this — fatality, I call it for

4. Egeria, who was faithful to Numa (first king of ancient Rome) even after death ; Cornelia, mother of the Gracchi— of whom she said proudly, "These are my jewels."

want of a better title — between us. It drives her in one
direction, me in another — or would, if I submitted to the
pressure. She is not the first who has been conscious
of it."

"Are we laying hold of a third poor girl ? " said Mrs.
Mountstuart. "Ah! I remember. And I remember we
used to call it playing fast and loose in those days, not
fatality. It is very strange. It may be that you were
unblushingly courted in those days, and excuseable ; and we
all supposed . . . but away you went for your tour."

" My mother's medical receipt for me. Partially it succeeded. She was for grand marriages: not I. I could
make, I could not be, a sacrifice. And then I went in due
time to Dr. Cupid on my own account. She has the kind
of attraction . . . But one changes ! *On revient toujours.*[5]
First we begin with a liking : then we give ourselves up to
the passion for beauty : then comes the serious question of
suitableness of the mate to match us : and perhaps we
discover that we were wiser in early youth than somewhat
later. However, she has beauty. Now, Mrs. Mountstuart,
you do admire her. Chase the idea of the ' dainty rogue '
out of your view of her : you admire her : she is captivating ; she has a particular charm of her own, nay, she has
real beauty."

Mrs. Mountstuart fronted him to say: " Upon my word,
my dear Sir Willoughby, I think she has it to such a degree
that I don't know the man who could hold out against her
if she took the field. She is one of the women who are
dead shots with men. Whether it's in their tongues or
their eyes, or it's an effusion and an atmosphere — whatever
it is, it's a spell, another fatality for you ! "

"Animal ; not spiritual ! "

"Oh ! she hasn't the head of Letty Dale."

Sir Willoughby allowed Mrs. Mountstuart to pause and
follow her thoughts.

"Dear me ! " she exclaimed. "I noticed a change in
Letty Dale last night : and to-day. She looked fresher and
younger ; extremely well : which is not what I can say for
you, my friend. Fatalizing is not good for the complexion."

"Don't take away my health, pray ! " cried Willoughby,
with a snapping laugh.

"Be careful," said Mrs. Mountstuart. " You have got a
sentimental tone. You talk of 'feelings crushed of old.'
It is to a woman, not to a man that you speak, but that sort
of talk is a way of making the ground slippery. I listen in
vain for a natural tongue ; and when I don't hear it, I
suspect plotting in men. You show your under-teeth too at
times when you draw in a breath, like a condemned high-
caste Hindoo my husband took me to see in a jail in Calcutta, to give me some excitement when I was pining for
England. The creature did it regularly as he breathed ;

5. "One always comes back."

you did it last night, and you have been doing it to-day, as if the air cut you to the quick. You have been spoilt. You have been too much anointed. What I've just mentioned is a sign with me of a settled something on the brain of a man."

"The brain?" said Sir Willoughby, frowning.

"Yes, you laugh sourly, to look at," said she. "Mountstuart told me that the muscles of the mouth betray men sooner than the eyes, when they have cause to be uneasy in their minds."

"But, ma'am, I shall not break my word; I shall not, not; I intend, I have resolved to keep it. I do *not* fatalize, let my complexion be black or white. Despite my resemblance to a high-class malefactor of the Calcutta prisonwards . . ."

"Friend! friend! you know how I chatter."

He saluted her finger-ends. "Despite the extraordinary display of teeth, you will find me go to execution with perfect calmness; with a resignation as good as happiness."

"Like a Jacobite lord under the Georges."[6]

"You have told me that you wept to read of one: like him, then. My principles have not changed, if I have. When I was younger, I had an idea of a wife who would be with me in my thoughts as well as aims: a woman with a spirit of romance, and a brain of solid sense. I shall sooner or later dedicate myself to a public life; and shall, I suppose, want the counsellor or comforter who ought always to be found at home. It may be unfortunate that I have the ideal in my head. But I would never make rigorous demands for specific qualities. The cruellest thing in the world is to set up a living model before a wife, and compel her to copy it. In any case, here we are upon the road: the die is cast. I shall not reprieve myself. I cannot release her. Marriage represents facts, courtship fancies. She will be cured by-and-by of that coveting of everything that I do, feel, think, dream, imagine . . . ta-ta-ta-ta ad infinitum. Lætitia was invited here to show her the example of a fixed character — solid as any concrete substance you would choose to build on, and not a whit the less feminine."

"Ta-ta-ta-ta ad infinitum. You need not tell me you have a design in all that you do, Willoughby Patterne."

"You smell the autocrat? Yes, he can mould and govern the creatures about him. His toughest rebel is himself! If you see Clara . . . You wish to see her, I think you said?"

"Her behaviour to Lady Busshe last night was queer."

"If you will. She makes a mouth at porcelain. *Toujours la porcelaine!*[7] For me, her pettishness is one of her charms, I confess it. Ten years younger, I could not have compared them."

6. Four Scottish leaders of the Jacobite (pro-Stuart) rising of 1745 were executed by the House of Hanover which gave England four Georges in a row.
7. "Always this porcelain!"

"Whom ?"

"Lætitia and Clara."

"Sir Willoughby, in any case, to quote you, here we are all upon the road, and we must act as if events were going to happen; and I must ask her to help me on the subject of my wedding-present, for I don't want to have her making mouths at mine, however pretty — and she does it prettily."

"' Another dedicatory offering to the *rogue* in me!' she says of porcelain."

"Then porcelain it shall not be. I mean to consult her; I have come determined upon a chat with her. I think I understand. But she produces false impressions on those who don't know you both. 'I shall have that porcelain back,' says Lady Busshe to me, when we were shaking hands last night: 'I think,' says she, 'it should have been the Willow Pattern.' And she really said: 'he's in for being jilted a second time!'"

Sir Willoughby restrained a bound of his body that would have sent him up some feet into the air. He felt his skull thundered at within.

"Rather than that it should fall upon her!" ejaculated he, correcting his resemblance to the high-caste culprit as soon as it recurred to him.

"But you know Lady Busshe," said Mrs. Mountstuart, genuinely solicitous to ease the proud man of his pain. She could see through him to the depth of the skin, which his fencing sensitiveness vainly attempted to cover as it did the heart of him. "Lady Busshe is nothing without her flights, fads, and fancies. She has always insisted that you have an unfortunate nose. I remember her saying on the day of your majority, it was the nose of a monarch destined to lose a throne."

"Have I ever offended Lady Busshe ?"

"She trumpets you. She carries Lady Culmer with her too, and you may expect a visit of nods and hints and pots of alabaster. They worship you: you are the hope of England in their eyes, and no woman is worthy of you: but they are a pair of fatalists, and if you begin upon Letty Dale with them, you might as well forbid your banns. They will be all over the country exclaiming on predestination and marriages made in heaven."

"Clara and her father!" cried Sir Willoughby.

Dr. Middleton and his daughter appeared in the circle of shrubs and flowers.

"Bring her to me, and save me from the polyglot," said Mrs. Mountstuart, in affright at Dr. Middleton's manner of pouring forth into the ears of the downcast girl.

The leisure he loved that he might debate with his genius upon any next step was denied to Willoughby: he had to place his trust in the skill with which he had sown and prepared Mrs. Mountstuart's understanding to meet the girl — beautiful abhorred that she was! detested darling! thing to squeeze to death and throw to the dust, and mourn over!

He had to risk it; and at an hour when Lady Busshe's prognostic grievously impressed his intensely apprehensive nature.

As it happened that Dr. Middleton's notion of a disagreeable duty in colloquy was to deliver all that he contained, and escape the listening to a syllable of reply, Willoughby withdrew his daughter from him opportunely.

"Mrs. Mountstuart wants you, Clara."

"I shall be very happy," Clara replied, and put on a new face.

An imperceptible nervous shrinking was met by another force in her bosom, that pushed her to advance without a sign of reluctance. She seemed to glitter.

She was handed to Mrs. Mountstuart.

Dr. Middleton laid his hand over Willoughby's shoulder, retiring on a bow before the great lady of the district. He blew and said: "An opposition of female instincts to masculine intellect necessarily creates a corresponding antagonism of intellect to instinct."

"Her answer, sir? Her reasons? Has she named any?"

"The cat," said Dr. Middleton, taking breath for a sentence, "that humps her back in the figure of the letter H, or a Chinese bridge, has given the dog her answer and her reasons, we may presume: but he that undertakes to translate them into human speech might likewise venture to propose an addition to the alphabet and a continuation of Homer.[8] The one performance would be not more wonderful than the other. Daughters, Willoughby, daughters! Above most human peccancies, I do abhor a breach of faith. She will not be guilty of that. I demand a cheerful fulfilment of a pledge: and I sigh to think that I cannot count on it without administering a lecture."

"She will soon be my care, sir."

"She shall be. Why, she is as good as married. She is at the altar. She is in her house. She is — why, where is she not? She has entered the sanctuary. She is out of the market. This mænad shriek for freedom would happily entitle her to the Republican cap — the Phrygian — in a revolutionary Parisian procession.[9] To me it has no meaning: and but that I cannot credit child of mine with mania, I should be in trepidation of her wits."

Sir Willoughby's livelier fears were pacified by the information that Clara had simply emitted a cry. Clara had once or twice given him cause for starting and considering whether to think of her sex differently or condemningly of

---

8. "Chinese bridge": Dr. Middleton too has been staring at the willow pattern.
9. "mænad": Bacchanalian, as of a female worshipper of Dionysus. The Phryg-ian cap, looking rather like a loose nightcap, became during the French Revolution a symbol of revolutionary sentiments.

her, yet he could not deem her capable of fully unbosoming herself even to him, and under excitement. His idea of the cowardice of girls combined with his ideal of a waxwork sex to persuade him that though they are often (he had experienced it) wantonly desperate in their acts, their tongues are curbed by rosy pudency.[1] And this was in his favour. For if she proved speechless and stupid with Mrs. Mountstuart, the lady would turn her over, and beat her flat, beat her angular, in fine, turn her to any shape, despising her, and cordially believe him to be the model gentleman of Christendom. She would fill in the outlines he had sketched to her of a picture that he had small pride in by comparison with his early vision of a fortune-favoured, triumphing squire, whose career is like the sun's, intelligibly lordly to all comprehensions. Not like your model gentleman, that has to be expounded — a thing for abstract esteem! However, it was the choice left to him. And an alternative was enfolded in that. Mrs. Mountstuart's model gentleman could marry either one of two women, throwing the other overboard. He was bound to marry: he was bound to take to himself one of them: and whichever one he selected would cast a lustre on his reputation. At least she would rescue him from the claws of Lady Busshe, and her owl's hoot of "Willow Pattern," and her hag's shriek of "twice jilted." That flying infant Willoughby — his unprotected little incorporeal omnipresent Self (not thought of so much as passionately felt for) — would not be scoffed at as the luckless with women. A fall indeed from his original conception of his name of fame abroad! But Willoughby had the high consolation of knowing that others have fallen lower. There is the fate of the devils to comfort us, if we are driven hard. *For one of your pangs another bosom is racked by ten*, we read in the solacing Book.

With all these nice calculations at work, Willoughby stood above himself, contemplating his active machinery, which he could partly criticize but could not stop, in a singular wonderment at the aims and schemes and tremours of one who was handsome, manly, acceptable in the world's eyes: and had he not loved himself most heartily he would have been divided to the extent of repudiating that urgent and excited half of his being, whose motions appeared as those of a body of insects perpetually erecting and repairing a structure of extraordinary pettiness. He loved himself too seriously to dwell on the division for more than a minute or so. But having seen it, and for the first time, as he believed, his passion for the woman causing it became surcharged with bitterness, atrabiliar.[2]

A glance behind him, as he walked away with Dr. Middleton, showed Clara, cunning creature that she was, airily executing her malicious graces in the preliminary courtesies with Mrs. Mountstuart.

1. Modesty.   2. Troubled with black bile, bitter.

CHAPTER 35

MISS MIDDLETON AND MRS. MOUNTSTUART

"Sit beside me, fair Middleton," said the great lady.

"Gladly," said Clara, bowing to her title.

"I want to sound you, my dear."

Clara presented an open countenance with a dim interrogation on the forehead. "Yes?" she said submissively.

"You were one of my bright faces last night. I was in love with you. Delicate vessels ring sweetly to a fingernail, and if the wit is true, you answer to it; that I can see, and that is what I like. Most of the people one has at a table are drums. A rub-a-dub-dub on them is the only way to get a sound. When they can be persuaded to do it upon one another, they call it conversation."

"Colonel De Craye was very funny."

"Funny, and witty too."

"But never spiteful."

"These Irish or half-Irishmen are my taste. If they're not politicians, mind: I mean Irish gentlemen. I will never have another dinner-party without one. Our men's tempers are uncertain. You can't get them to forget themselves. And when the wine is in them the nature comes out, and they must be buffetting, and up start politics, and good-bye to harmony! My husband, I am sorry to say, was one of those who have a long account of ruined dinners against them. I have seen him and his friends red as the roast and white as the boiled with wrath on a popular topic they had excited themselves over, intrinsically not worth a snap of the fingers. In London!" exclaimed Mrs. Mountstuart, to aggravate the charge against her lord in the Shades.[1] "But town or country, the table should be sacred. I have heard women say it is a plot on the side of the men to teach us our littleness. I don't believe they have a plot. It would be to compliment them on a talent. I believe they fall upon one another blindly, simply because they are full: which is, we are told, the preparation for the fighting Englishman. They cannot eat and keep a truce. Did you notice that dreadful Mr. Capes?"

"The gentleman who frequently contradicted papa? But Colonel De Craye was good enough to relieve us."

"How, my dear?"

"You did not hear him? He took advantage of an interval when Mr. Capes was breathing after a pæan to his friend, the Governor—I think—of one of the Presidencies, to say to the lady beside him: 'He was a wonderful administrator and great logician; he married an Anglo-

---

1. "In the Shades" removes Mr. Mountstuart Jenkinson discreetly to the realm of the nonliving.

Indian widow, and soon after published a pamphlet in
favour of Suttee.'"[2]

"And what did the lady say?"

"She said, 'Oh.'"

"Hark at her! And was it heard?"

"Mr. Capes granted the widow, but declared he had never
seen the pamphlet in favour of Suttee, and disbelieved in
it. He insisted that it was to be named Satì. He was
vehement."

"Now I do remember: — which must have delighted the
colonel. And Mr. Capes retired from the front upon a
repetition of 'in toto, in toto.'[3] As if 'in toto' were the
language of a dinner-table! But what will ever teach
these men? Must we import Frenchmen to give them an
example in the art of conversation, as their grandfathers
brought over marquises to instruct them in salads? And
our young men too! Women have to take to the hunting-
field to be able to talk with them and be on a par with their
grooms. Now, there was Willoughby Patterne, a prince
among them formerly. Now, did you observe him last
night? did you notice how, instead of conversing, instead
of assisting me — as he was bound to do doubly, owing to
the defection of Vernon Whitford: a thing I don't yet comprehend — there he sat sharpening his lower lip for cutting
remarks. And at my best man! at Colonel De Craye! If
he had attacked Mr. Capes, with his Governor of Bomby, as
the man pronounces it, or Colonel Wildjohn and his Protestant Church in Danger, or Sir Wilson Pettifer harping on
his Monarchical Republic, or any other! No, he preferred
to be sarcastic upon friend Horace, and he had the worst of
it. Sarcasm is so silly! What is the gain if he has been
smart? People forget the epigram and remember the
other's good temper. On that field, my dear, you must
make up your mind to be beaten by 'friend Horace.' I
have my prejudices and I have my prepossessions, but I
love good temper, and I love wit, and when I see a man
possessed of both, I set my cap at him, and there's my flat
confession, and highly unfeminine it is."

"Not at all!" cried Clara.

"We are one, then."

Clara put up a mouth empty of words: she was quite one
with her. Mrs. Mountstuart pressed her hand. "When
one does get intimate with a dainty rogue!" she said.
"You forgive me all that, for I could vow that Willoughby
has betrayed me."

Clara looked soft, kind, bright, in turns, and clouded instantly when the lady resumed: "A friend of my own sex,
and young, and a close neighbour, is just what I would have
prayed for. And I'll excuse you, my dear, for not being so

2. The "Presidencies" were the major divisions of India under British rule. "Suttee": the practice, once frequent in India,
of a widow burning herself on her hus-

band's funeral pyre. See above, Chapter
6.

3. "in toto": completely, entirely.

anxious about the friendship of an old woman. But I shall be of use to you, you will find. In the first place, I never tap for secrets. In the second, I keep them. Thirdly, I have some power. And fourth, every young married woman has need of a friend like me. Yes, and Lady Patterne heading all the county will be the stronger for my backing. You don't look so mighty well pleased, my dear. Speak out."

"Dear Mrs. Mountstuart!"

"I tell you, I am very fond of Willoughby, but I saw the faults of the boy and see the man's. He has the pride of a king, and it's a pity if you offend it. He is prodigal in generosity, but he can't forgive. As to his own errors, you must be blind to them as a Saint. The secret of him is, that he is one of those excessively civilized creatures who aim at perfection : and I think he ought to be supported in his conceit of having attained it; for the more men of that class, the greater our influence. He excels in manly sports, because he won't be excelled in anything, but as men don't comprehend his fineness, he comes to us; and his wife must manage him by that key. You look down at the idea of manageing. It has to be done. One thing you may be assured of, he will be proud of you. His wife won't be very much enamoured of herself if she is not the happiest woman in the world. You will have the best horses, the best dresses, the finest jewels, in England; and an incomparable cook. The house will be changed the moment you enter it as Lady Patterne. And, my dear, just where he is, with all his graces, deficient of attraction, yours will tell. The sort of Othello he would make, or Leontes, I don't know, and none of us ever needs to know.[4] My impression is, that if even a shadow of a suspicion flitted across him, he is a sort of man to double-dye himself in guilt by way of vengeance in anticipation of an imagined offence. Not uncommon with men. I have heard strange stories of them : and so will you in your time to come, but not from me. No young woman shall ever be the sourer for having been my friend. One word of advice now we are on the topic : never play at counter-strokes with him. He will be certain to outstroke you, and you will be driven farther than you meant to go. They say we beat men at that game, and so we do, at the cost of beating ourselves. And if once we are started, it is a race-course ending on a precipice — over goes the winner. We must be moderately slavish to keep our place; which is given us in appearance; but appearances make up a remarkably large part of life, and far the most comfortable, so long as we are discreet at the right moment. He is a man whose pride, when hurt, would run his wife to perdition to solace it. If he married a troublesome widow, his pamphlet on Suttee would be out within the year. Vernon Whitford

---

4. Othello and Leontes are both Shakespearean victims of jealousy, the latter in   *A Winter's Tale*.

would receive instructions about it the first frosty moon. You like Miss Dale ? "

" I think I like her better than she likes me," said Clara.

" Have you never warmed together ? "

" I have tried it. She is not one bit to blame. I can see how it is that she misunderstands me : or justly condemns me, perhaps I should say."

" The hero of two women must die and be wept over in common before they can appreciate one another. You are not cold ? "

" No."

" You shuddered, my dear."

" Did I ? "

" I do sometimes. Feet will be walking over one's grave, wherever it lies. Be sure of this : Willoughby Patterne is a man of unimpeachable honour."

" I do not doubt it."

" He means to be devoted to you. He has been accustomed to have women hanging around him like votive offerings."[5]

" I . . . ! "

" You cannot : of course not : any one could see that at a glance. You are all the sweeter to me for not being tame. Marriage cures a multitude of indispositions."

" Oh ! Mrs. Mountstuart, will you listen to me ? "

" Presently. Don't threaten me with confidences. Eloquence is a terrible thing in woman. I suspect, my dear, that we both know as much as could be spoken."

" You hardly suspect the truth, I fear."

" Let me tell you one thing about jealous men — when they are not blackamoors married to disobedient daughters.[6] I speak of our civil creature of the drawing-rooms : and lovers, mind, not husbands : two distinct species, married or not : — they 're rarely given to jealousy unless they are flighty themselves. The jealousy fixes them. They have only to imagine that we are for some fun likewise and they grow as deferential as my footman, as harmless as the sportsman whose gun has burst. Ah ! my fair Middleton, am I pretending to teach you ? You have read him his lesson, and my table suffered for it last night, but I bear no rancour."

" You bewilder me, Mrs. Mountstuart."

" Not if I tell you that you have driven the poor man to try whether it would be possible for him to give you up."

" I have ? "

" Well, and you are successful."

" I am ? "

" Jump, my dear ! "

" He will ? "

" When men love stale instead of fresh, withered better than blooming, excellence in the abstract rather than the palpable. With their idle prate of feminine intellect, and a grotto nymph, and — and a mother of Gracchi![7] Why, he must think me dazed with admiration of him to talk to me! One listens, you know. And he is one of the men who cast a kind of physical spell on you while he has you by the ear, until you begin to think of it by talking to somebody else. I suppose there are clever people who do see deep into the breast while dialogue is in progress. One reads of them. No, my dear, you have very cleverly managed to show him that it is n't at all possible: he can't. And the real cause for alarm in my humble opinion is lest your amiable foil should have been a trifle, as he would say, deceived, too much in earnest, led too far. One may reprove him for not being wiser, but men won't learn without groaning, that they are simply weapons taken up to be put down when done with. Leave it to me to compose him. — Willoughby can't give you up. I 'm certain he has tried; his pride has been horribly wounded. You are shrewd, and he has had his lesson. If these little rufflings don't come before marriage they come after; so it 's not time lost; and it 's good to be able to look back on them. You are very white, my child."

"Can you, Mrs. Mountstuart, can you think I would be so heartlessly treacherous?"

"Be honest, fair Middleton, and answer me: Can you say you had not a corner of an idea of producing an effect on Willoughby?"

Clara checked the instinct of her tongue to defend her reddening cheeks, with a sense that she was disintegrating and crumbling; but she wanted this lady for a friend, and she had to submit to the conditions, and be red and silent.

Mrs. Mountstuart examined her leisurely.

"That will do. Conscience blushes. One knows it by the outer conflagration. Don't be hard on yourself: there you are in the other extreme. That blush of yours would count with me against any quantity of evidence — all the Crooklyns in the kingdom. You lost your purse."

"I discovered that it was lost this morning."

"Flitch has been here with it. Willoughby has it. You will ask him for it; he will demand payment: you will be a couple of yards' length or so of cramoisy:[8] and there ends the episode, nobody killed, only a poor man melancholy-wounded, and I must offer him my hand to mend him, vowing to prove to him that Suttee was properly abolished. Well, and now to business. I said I wanted to sound you. You have been overdone with porcelain. Poor Lady Busshe is in despair at your disappointment. Now, I mean my wedding-present to be to your taste."

"Madam!"

"Who is the madam you are imploring?"

"Dear Mrs. Mountstuart!"

"Well?"

7. Cf. Chapter 34, note 4.
8. "Cramoisy" is scarlet cloth; the phrase means she will blush.

"I shall fall in your esteem. Perhaps you will help me. No one else can. I am a prisoner: I am compelled to continue this imposture. Oh! I shun speaking much: you object to it and I dislike it: but I must endeavour to explain to you that I am unworthy of the position you think a proud one."

"Tut-tut; we are all unworthy, cross our arms, bow our heads; and accept the honours. Are you playing humble handmaid? What an old organ-tune that is! Well? Give me reasons."

"I do not wish to marry."

"He's the great match of the county!"

"I cannot marry him."

"Why, you are at the church-door with him! Cannot marry him?"

"It does not bind me."

"The church-door is as binding as the altar to an honourable girl. What have you been about? Since I am in for confidences, half ones won't do. We must have honourable young women as well as men of honour. You can't imagine he is to be thrown over now, at this hour? What have you against him? come!"

"I have found that I do not . . ."

"What?"

"Love him."

Mrs. Mountstuart grimaced transiently. "That is no answer. The cause!" she said. "What has he done?"

"Nothing."

"And when did you discover this nothing?"

"By degrees: unknown to myself; suddenly."

"Suddenly and by degrees? I suppose it's useless to ask for a head. But if all this is true, you ought not to be here."

"I wish to go; I am unable."

"Have you had a scene together?"

"I have expressed my wish."

"In roundabout? — girl's English?"

"Quite clearly. Oh! very clearly."

"Have you spoken to your father?"

"I have."

"And what does Dr. Middleton say?"

"It is incredible to him."

"To me too! I can understand little differences, little whims, caprices: we don't settle into harness for a tap on the shoulder, as a man becomes a knight: but to break and bounce away from an unhappy gentleman at the church-door is either madness or it's one of the things without a name. You think you are quite sure of yourself?"

"I am so sure, that I look back with regret on the time when I was not."

"But you were in love with him."

"I was mistaken."

" No love ? "

" I have none to give."

" Dear me ! — Yes, yes, but that tone of sorrowful conviction is often a trick, it 's not new : and I know that assumption of plain sense to pass off a monstrosity." Mrs. Mountstuart struck her lap : " Soh ! but I 've had to rack my brain for it : feminine disgust ? You have been hearing imputations on his past life ? moral character ? No ? Circumstances might make him behave unkindly, not unhandsomely : and we have no claim over a man 's past, or it 's too late to assert it. What is the case ? "

" We are quite divided."

" Nothing in the way of . . . nothing green-eyed ? "[9]

" Far from that ! "

" Then, name it."

" We disagree."

" Many a very good agreement is founded on disagreeing. It 's to be regretted that you are not portionless.[1] If you had been, you would have made very little of disagreeing. You are just as much bound in honour as if you had the ring on your finger."

" In honour ! But I appeal to his, I am no wife for him."

" But if he insists, you consent ? "

" I appeal to reason. Is it, madam . . ."

" But, I say, if he insists, you consent ! "

" He will insist upon his own misery as well as mine."

Mrs. Mountstuart rocked herself. " My poor Sir Willoughby ! What a fate ! — And I who took you for a clever girl ! Why, I have been admiring your management of him ! And here am I bound to take a lesson from Lady Busshe. My dear good Middleton, don 't let it be said that Lady Busshe saw deeper than I ! I put some little vanity in it, I own : I won't conceal it. She declares that when she sent her present — I don't believe her — she had a premonition that it would come back. Surely you won't justify the extravagances of a woman without common reverence : — for anatomize him as we please to ourselves, he is a splendid man (and I did it chiefly to encourage and come at you). We don't often behold such a lordly-looking man : so conversable too when he feels at home ; a picture of an English gentleman ! The very man we want married for our neighbourhood ! A woman who can openly talk of expecting him to be twice jilted ! You shrink. It is repulsive. It would be incomprehensible : except, of course, to Lady Busshe, who rushed to one of her violent conclusions and became a prophetess. Conceive a woman imagining it could happen twice to the same man ! I am not sure she did not send the identical present that arrived and returned once before : you know, the Durham engagement. She told me last night she had it back. I watched her listening very suspiciously to Professor Crooklyn. My dear, it is her passion to foretell

disasters — her passion! And when they are confirmed, she
triumphs, of course. We shall have her domineering over
us with sapient nods at every trifle occurring. The county
will be unendureable. Unsay it, my Middleton! And don't
answer like an oracle because I do all the talking. Pour out
to me. You'll soon come to a stop and find the want of
reason in the want of words. I assure you that's true.—
Let me have a good gaze at you. No," said Mrs. Mountstuart, after posturing herself to peruse Clara's features,
" brains you have : one can see it by the nose and the mouth.
I could vow you are the girl I thought you; you have your
wits on tiptoe. How of the heart ? "

" None," Clara sighed.

The sigh was partly voluntary, though unforced; as one
may with ready sincerity act a character that is our own
only through sympathy.

Mrs. Mountstuart felt the extra weight in the young lady's
falling breath. There was no necessity for a deep sigh over
an absence of heart or confession of it. If Clara did not
love the man to whom she was betrothed, sighing about it
signified — what ? some pretence : and a pretence is the
cloak of a secret. Girls do not sigh in that way with compassion for the man they have no heart for, unless at the
same time they should be oppressed by the knowledge or
dread of having a heart for some one else. As a rule, they
have no compassion to bestow on him : you might as reasonably expect a soldier to bewail the enemy he strikes in
action : they must be very disengaged to have it. And
supposing a show of the thing to be exhibited, when it has
not been worried out of them, there is a reserve in the
background : they are pitying themselves under a mask of
decent pity of their wretch.

So ran Mrs. Mountstuart's calculations, which were like
her suspicion, coarse and broad, not absolutely incorrect,
but not of an exact measure with the truth. That pin's
head of the truth is rarely hit by design. The search after
it of the professionally penetrative in the dark of a bosom
may bring it forth by the heavy knocking all about the
neighbourhood that we call good guessing, but it does not
come out clean; other matter adheres to it; and being
more it is less than truth. The unadulterate is to be had
only by faith in it or by waiting for it.

A lover! thought the sagacious dame. There was no
lover: some love there was : or rather, there was a preparation of the chamber, with no lamp yet lighted.

"Do you positively tell me you have no heart for the
position of first lady of the county?" said Mrs. Mountstuart.

Clara's reply was firm : " None whatever."

" My dear, I will believe you on one condition. — Look at
me. You have eyes. If you are for mischief, you are
armed for it. But how much better, when you have won a
prize, to settle down and wear it ! Lady Patterne will have

entire occupation for her flights and whimsies in leading the
county. And the man, surely the man — he behaved badly
last night : but a beauty like this," she pushed a finger at
Clara's cheek, and doated a half instant, "you have the very
beauty to break in an ogre's temper. And the man is as
governable as he is presentable. You have the beauty the
French call — no, it 's the beauty of a queen of elves : one
sees them lurking about you, one here, one there. Smile
— they dance : be doleful — they hang themselves. No,
there 's not a trace of satanic ; at least, not yet. And
come, come, my Middleton, the man is a man to be proud
of. You can send him into Parliament to wear off his
humours. To my thinking, he has a fine style : conscious ?
I never thought so before last night. I can't guess what
has happened to him recently. He was once a young
Grand Monarque.[2] He was really a superb young English
gentleman. Have you been wounding him ?"

"It is my misfortune to be obliged to wound him," said
Clara.

"Quite needlessly, my child, for marry him you must."

Clara's bosom rose : her shoulders rose too, narrowing,
and her head fell slightly back.

Mrs. Mountstuart exclaimed : "But the scandal ! You
would never, never think of following the example of that
Durham girl? — whether she was provoked to it by jealousy
or not. It seems to have gone so astonishingly far with you
in a very short time, that one is alarmed as to where you
will stop. Your look just now was downright revulsion."

"I fear it is. It is. I am past my own control. Dear
madam, you have my assurance that I will not behave
scandalously or dishonourably. What I would entreat of
you, is to help me. I know this of myself : I am not the
best of women. I am impatient, wickedly. I should be no
good wife. Feelings like mine teach me unhappy things of
myself."

"Rich, handsome, lordly, influential, brilliant health, fine
estates," Mrs. Mountstuart enumerated in petulant accents
as they started across her mind some of Sir Willoughby's
attributes for the attraction of the soul of woman. "I suppose you wish me to take you in earnest ?"

"I appeal to you for help."

"What help ?"

"Persuade him of the folly of pressing me to keep my
word."

"I will believe you, my dear Middleton, on one condition : — your talk of no heart is nonsense. A change like
this, if one is to believe in the change, occurs through the
heart, not because there is none. Don't you see that ?
But if you want me for a friend, you must not sham stupid.
It 's bad enough in itself : the imitation 's horrid. You
have to be honest with me, and answer me right out. You

2. Louis XIV.

came here on this visit intending to marry Willoughby
Patterne."

"Yes."

"And *gradually* you *suddenly* discovered, since you came
here, that you did not intend it, if you could find a means
of avoiding it."

"Oh! madam, yes, it is true."

"Now comes the test. And, my lovely Middleton, your
flaming cheeks won't suffice for me this time. The old serpent can blush like an innocent maid on occasion. You are
to speak, and you are to tell me in six words why that
was: and don't waste one on 'madam,' or 'Oh! Mrs.
Mountstuart.' Why did you change?"

"I came . . . when I came I was in some doubt. Indeed I speak the truth. I found I could not give him the
admiration he has, I daresay, a right to expect. I turned
— it surprised me: it surprises me now. But so completely! So that to think of marrying him is . . ."

"Defer the simile," Mrs. Mountstuart interposed. "If
you hit on a clever one, you will never get the better of it.
Now, by just as much as you have outstripped my limitation of words to you, you show me you are dishonest."

"I could make a vow."

"You would forswear yourself."

"Will you help me?"

"If you are perfectly ingenuous, I may try."

"Dear lady, what more can I say?"

"It may be difficult. You can reply to a catechism."

"I shall have your help?"

"Well, yes; though I don't like stipulations between
friends. There is no man living to whom you could willingly give your hand? That is my question. I cannot
possibly take a step unless I know. Reply briefly: there is
or there is not."

Clara sat back with bated breath, mentally taking the
leap into the abyss, realizing it, and the cold prudence of
abstention, and the delirium of the confession. Was there
such a man? It resembled freedom to think there was: to
avow it promised freedom.

"Oh! Mrs. Mountstuart."

"Well?"

"You will help me?"

"Upon my word, I shall begin to doubt your desire for
it."

"*Willingly* give my hand, madam?"

"For shame! And with wits like yours, can't you perceive where hesitation in answering such a question lands
you?"

"Dearest lady, will you give me your hand? may I
whisper?"

"You need not whisper: I won't look."

Clara's voice trembled on a tense chord.

" There is one . . . compared with him I feel my insignificance. If I could aid him."

" What necessity have you to tell me more than that there is one ? "

" Ah, madam, it is different: not as you imagine. You bid me be scrupulously truthful: I am : I wish you to know the different kind of feeling it is from what might be suspected from . . . a confession. To give my hand, is beyond any thought I have ever encouraged. If you had asked me whether there is one whom I admire — yes, I do. I cannot help admiring a beautiful and brave self-denying nature. It is one whom you must pity, and to pity casts you beneath him: for you pity him because it is his nobleness that has been the enemy of his fortunes. He lives for others."

Her voice was musically thrilling in that low muted tone of the very heart, impossible to deride or disbelieve.

Mrs. Mountstuart set her head nodding on springs.

" Is he clever ? "

" Very."

" He talks well ? "

" Yes."

" Handsome ? "

" He might be thought so."

" Witty ? "

" I think he is."

" Gay, cheerful? "

" In his manner."

" Why, the man would be a mountebank if he adopted any other. And poor ? "

" He is not wealthy."

Mrs. Mountstuart preserved a lengthened silence, but nipped Clara's fingers once or twice to reassure her without approving. " Of course he 's poor," she said at last ; "directly the reverse of what you *could* have, it *must* be. Well, my fair Middleton, I can't say you have been dishonest. I 'll help you as far as I 'm able. How, it is quite impossible to tell. We 're in the mire. The best way seems to me, to get this pitiable angel to cut some ridiculous capers and present you another view of him. I don't believe in his innocence. He knew you to be a plighted woman."

" He has not once by word or sign hinted a disloyalty."

" Then how do you know . . . ? "

" I do not know."

" He is not the cause of your wish to break your engagement ? "

" No."

" Then you have succeeded in just telling me nothing. What is ? "

" Ah! madam."

" You would break your engagement purely because the admirable creature is in existence ? "

Clara shook her head : she could not say : she was dizzy.

She had spoken out more than she had ever spoken to herself: and in doing so she had cast herself a step beyond the line she dared to contemplate.

"I won't detain you any longer," said Mrs. Mountstuart. "The more we learn, the more we are taught that we are not so wise as we thought we were. I have to go to school to Lady Busshe! I really took you for a very clever girl If you change again, you will notify the important circumstance to me, I trust."

"I will," said Clara, and no violent declaration of the impossibility of her changeing again would have had such an effect on her hearer.

Mrs. Mountstuart scanned her face for a new reading of it to match with her later impressions.

"I am to do as I please with the knowledge I have gained?"

"I am utterly in your hands, madam."

"I have not meant to be unkind."

"You have not been unkind; I could embrace you."

"I am rather too shattered, and kissing won't put me together. I laughed at Lady Busshe! No wonder you went off like a rocket with a disappointing bouquet when I told you you had been successful with poor Sir Willoughby and he could not give you up. I noticed that. A woman like Lady Busshe, always prying for the lamentable, would have required no further enlightenment. Has he a temper?"

Clara did not ask her to signalize the person thus abruptly obtruded.

"He has faults," she said.

"There's an end to Sir Willoughby, then! Though I don't say he will give you up even when he hears the worst, if he must hear it, as for his own sake he should. And I won't say he ought to give you up. He'll be the pitiable angel if he does. For you — but you don't deserve compliments; they would be immoral. You have behaved badly, badly, badly. I have never had such a right-about-face in my life. You will deserve the stigma: you will be notorious: you will be called Number Two. Think of that! Not even original! We will break the conference, or I shall twaddle to extinction. I think I heard the luncheon bell."

"It rang."

"You don't look fit for company, but you had better come."

"Oh! yes: every day it's the same."

"Whether you're in my hands or I'm in yours, we're a couple of arch-conspirators against the peace of the family whose table we're sitting at, and the more we rattle the viler we are, but we must do it to ease our minds."

Mrs. Mountstuart spread the skirts of her voluminous dress, remarking further: "At a certain age our teachers are young people: we learn by looking backward. It speaks highly for me that I have not called you mad. —Full of

faults, goodish-looking, not a bad talker, cheerful, poorish;
— and she prefers that to this!" the great lady exclaimed
in her reverie while emerging from the circle of shrubs upon
a view of the Hall.

Colonel De Craye advanced to her; certainly good-looking,
certainly cheerful, by no means a bad talker, nothing of a
Crœsus, and variegated with faults.[3]

His laughing smile attacked the irresolute hostility of her
mien, confident as the sparkle of sunlight in a breeze. The
effect of it on herself angered her on behalf of Sir Willoughby's bride.

"Good morning, Mrs. Mountstuart; I believe I am the
last to greet you."

"And how long do you remain here, Colonel De Craye?"

"I kissed earth when I arrived, like the Norman William,
and consequently I've an attachment to the soil, ma'am."[4]

"You are not going to take possession of it, I suppose?"

"A handful would satisfy me!"

"You play the Conqueror pretty much, I have heard.
But property is held more sacred than in the times of the
Norman William."

"And speaking of property, Miss Middleton, your purse
is found," he said.

"I know it is," she replied, as unaffectedly as Mrs. Mountstuart could have desired, though the ingenuous air of the
girl incensed her somewhat.

Clara passed on.

"You restore purses," observed Mrs. Mountstuart.

Her stress on the word, and her look, thrilled De Craye:
for there had been a long conversation between the young
lady and the dame.

"It was an article that dropped and was not stolen,"
said he.

"Barely sweet enough to keep, then!"

"I think I could have felt to it like poor Flitch, the
flyman, who was the finder."

"If you are conscious of these temptations to appropriate
what is not your own, you should quit the neighbourhood."

"And do it elsewhere? But that's not virtuous counsel."

"And I'm not counselling in the interests of your virtue,
Colonel De Craye."

"And I dared for a moment to hope that you were,
ma'am," he said, ruefully drooping.

They were close to the dining-room window, and Mrs.
Mountstuart preferred the terminating of a dialogue that
did not promise to leave her features the austerely iron cast
with which she had commenced it. She was under the spell
of gratitude for his behaviour yesterday evening at her
dinner-table; she could not be very severe.

---

3. "Crœsus": a fabulously wealthy Lyd-
ian king of antiquity.
4. William the Conqueror tripped when
first setting foot on English soil, but con-
verted the bad omen to a good one by
coming up with a handful of English
earth.

CHAPTER 36

ANIMATED CONVERSATION AT A LUNCHEON-TABLE

VERNON was crossing the hall to the dining-room as Mrs. Mountstuart stepped in. She called to him : " Are the champions reconciled ? "

He replied : " Hardly that, but they have consented to meet at an altar to offer up a victim to the Gods, in the shape of modern poetic imitations of the classical."

" That seems innocent enough. The Professor has not been anxious about his chest ? "

" He recollects his cough now and then."

" You must help him to forget it."

" Lady Busshe and Lady Culmer are here," said Vernon, not supposing it to be a grave announcement until the effect of it on Mrs. Mountstuart admonished him.

She dropped her voice : " Engage my fair friend for one of your walks the moment we rise from table. You may have to rescue her; but do. I mean it."

" She 's a capital walker," Vernon remarked in simpleton style.

" There 's no necessity for any of your pedestrian feats," Mrs. Mountstuart said, and let him go, turning to Colonel De Craye to pronounce an encomium on him : " The most open-minded man I know! Warranted to do perpetual service and no mischief. If you were all . . . instead of catching at every prize you covet! Yes, you would have your reward for unselfishness, I assure you. Yes, and where you seek it! That is what none of you men will believe."

" When you behold me in your own livery ! " cried the colonel.

" Do I ? " said she, dallying with a half-formed design to be confidential. " How is it one is always tempted to address you in the language of innuendo ? I can't guess."

" Except that as a dog does n't comprehend good English we naturally talk bad to him."

The great lady was tickled. Who could help being amused by this man ? And after all, if her fair Middleton chose to be a fool, there could be no gainsaying her, sorry though poor Sir Willoughby's friends must feel for him.

She tried not to smile.

" You are too absurd. Or a baby, you might have added."

" I had n't the daring."

" I 'll tell you what, Colonel De Craye, I shall end by falling in love with you; and without esteeming you, I fear."

" The second follows as surely as the flavour upon a draught of Bacchus, if you 'll but toss off the glass, ma'am."

" We women, sir, think it should be first."

" 'T is to transpose the seasons, and give October the blossom, and April the apple, and no sweet one! Esteem's a mellow thing that comes after bloom and fire, like an evening at home ; because if it went before it would have no father and could n't hope for progeny ; for there 'd be no nature in the business. So please, ma'am, keep to the original order, and you 'll be nature's child and I the most blest of mankind."

" Really, were I fifteen years younger. I am not so certain . . . I might try and make you harmless."

" Draw the teeth of the lamb so long as you pet him ! "

" I challenged you, colonel, and I won't complain of your pitch. But now lay your wit down beside your candour and descend to an every-day level with me for a minute."

" Is it innuendo? "

" No, though I daresay it would be easier for you to respond to, if it were."

" I 'm the straightforwardest of men at a word of command."

" This is a whisper. Be alert as you were last night. Shuffle the table well. A little liveliness will do it. I don't imagine malice, but there 's curiosity, which is often as bad, and not so lightly foiled. We have Lady Busshe and Lady Culmer here."

" To sweep the cobwebs out of the sky ! "

" Well, then, can you fence with broomsticks ? "

" I have had a bout with them in my time."

" They are terribly direct."

" They 'give point,' as Napoleon commanded his cavalry to do."

" You must help me to ward it."

" They will require variety in the conversation."

" Constant. You are an angel of intelligence, and if I have the judgeing of you, I 'm afraid you 'll be allowed to pass, in spite of the scandal above. Open the door; I don't unbonnet."

De Craye threw the door open.

Lady Busshe was at that moment saying : " And are we indeed to have you for a neighbour, Dr. Middleton ? "

The Rev. Doctor's reply was drowned by the new arrivals.

" I thought you had forsaken us," observed Sir Willoughby to Mrs. Mountstuart.

" And run away with Colonel De Craye ? I 'm too weighty, my dear friend. Besides, I have not looked at the wedding-presents yet."

" The very object of our call ! " exclaimed Lady Culmer.

" I have to confess I am in dire alarm about mine," Lady Busshe nodded across the table at Clara. " Oh! you may shake your head, but I would rather hear a rough truth than the most complimentary evasion."

" How would you define a rough truth, Dr. Middleton ? "

said Mrs. Mountstuart.

Like the trained warrior who is ready at all hours for the trumpet to arms, Dr. Middleton wakened up for judicial allocution in a trice.

"A rough truth, madam, I should define to be that description of truth which is not imparted to mankind without a powerful impregnation of the roughness of the teller."

"It is a rough truth, ma'am, that the world is composed of fools, and that the exceptions are knaves," Professor Crooklyn furnished the example avoided by the Rev. Doctor.

"Not to precipitate myself into the jaws of the first definition, which strikes me as being as happy as Jonah's whale, that could carry probably the most learned man of his time inside without the necessity of digesting him," said De Craye, "a rough truth is a rather strong charge of universal nature for the firing off of a modicum of personal fact."

"It is a rough truth that Plato is Moses atticizing," said Vernon to Dr. Middleton, to keep the diversion alive.[1]

"And that Aristotle had the globe under his cranium," rejoined the Rev. Doctor.

"And that the Moderns live on the Ancients."[2]

"And that not one in ten thousand can refer to the particular treasury he filches."

"The Art of our days is a revel of rough truth," remarked Professor Crooklyn.

"And the literature has laboriously mastered the adjective, wherever it may be in relation to the noun," Dr. Middleton added.

"Orson's first appearance at Court was in the figure of a rough truth, causing the Maids of Honour, accustomed to Tapestry Adams, astonishment and terror," said De Craye.[3]

That he might not be left out of the sprightly play, Sir Willoughby levelled a lance at the quintain, smiling on Lætitia: "In fine, caricature is rough truth."[4]

She said: "Is one end of it, and realistic directness is the other."

He bowed: "The palm is yours."[5]

Mrs. Mountstuart admired herself as each one trotted forth in turn characteristically, with one exception unaware of the aid which was being rendered to a distressed damsel wretchedly incapable of decent hypocrisy. Her intrepid lead had shown her hand to the colonel and drawn the enemy at a blow.

1. "Plato . . . atticizing": Plato is a Hebrew prophet and lawgiver in Greek clothing.
2. I.e., modern ideas have their roots in ancient ideas.
3. "court": an allusion to the Old French romance *Valentine and Orson.* Having been brought up by a bear, Orson at his first appearance in court was uncouth. "Tapestry Adams": the sort of Adam that might be represented in a tapestry— i.e., clipped, clean, and decently clothed.
4. "quintain": the five of them.
5. I.e., you win.

Sir Willoughby's "in fine," however, did not please her: still less did his lackadaisical Lothario-like bowing and smiling to Miss Dale: and he perceived it and was hurt. For how, carrying his tremendous load, was he to compete with these unhandicapped men in the game of nonsense she had such a fondness for starting at a table? He was further annoyed to hear Miss Eleanor and Miss Isabel Patterne agree together, that "caricature" was the final word of the definition. Relatives should know better than to deliver these awards to us in public.

"Well!" quoth Lady Busshe, expressive of stupefaction at the strange dust she had raised.

"Are they on view, Miss Middleton?" inquired Lady Culmer.

"There's a regiment of us on view and ready for inspection," Colonel De Craye bowed to her, but she would not be foiled. "Miss Middleton's admirers are always on view," said he.

"Are they to be seen?" said Lady Busshe.

Clara made her face a question, with a laudable smoothness.

"The wedding-presents," Lady Culmer explained.

"No."

"Otherwise, my dear, we are in danger of duplicating and triplicating and quadruplicating, not at all to the satisfaction of the bride."

"But there's a worse danger to encounter in the 'on view,' my lady," said De Craye; "and that's the magnetic attraction a display of wedding-presents is sure to have for the ineffable burglar, who must have a nuptial soul in him, for wherever there's that collection on view, he's never a league off. And 't is said he knows a lady's dressing-case presented to her on the occasion, fifteen years after the event."

"As many as fifteen?" said Mrs. Mountstuart.

"By computation of the police. And if the presents are on view, dogs are of no use, nor bolts, nor bars: — he's worse than Cupid. The only protection to be found, singular as it may be thought, is in a couple of bottles of the oldest Jamaica rum in the British Isles."

"Rum?" cried Lady Busshe.

"The liquor of the Royal Navy, my lady. And with your permission, I'll relate the tale in proof of it. I had a friend engaged to a young lady, niece of an old sea-captain of the old school, the Benbow school, the wooden leg and pigtail school; a perfectly salt old gentleman with a pickled tongue, and a dash of brine in every deed he committed.[6] He looked rolled over to you by the last wave on the shore, sparkling: he was Neptune's own for humour. And when his present to the bride was opened, sure enough there lay a couple of bottles of the oldest Jamaica rum in

6. Admiral Benbow, who died in 1702, was a type of the rough fighting sailor.

the British Isles, born before himself, and his father to
boot. 'T is a fabulous spirit I beg you to believe in, my
lady, the sole merit of the story being its portentous veracity. The bottles were tied to make them appear twins, as
they both had the same claim to seniority. And there was
a label on them, telling their great age, to maintain their
identity. They were in truth a pair of patriarchal bottles
rivalling many of the biggest houses in the kingdom for
antiquity. They would have made the donkey that stood
between the two bundles of hay look at them with obliquity: supposing him to have, for an animal, a rum taste,
and a turn for hilarity. Wonderful old bottles! So, on
the label, just over the date, was written large: UNCLE
BENJAMIN'S WEDDING-PRESENT TO HIS NIECE BESSY. Poor
Bessy shed tears of disappointment and indignation enough
to float the old gentleman on his native element, ship and
all. She vowed it was done curmudgeonly to vex her,
because her uncle hated wedding-presents and had grunted
at the exhibition of cups and saucers, and this and that
beautiful service, and épergnes and inkstands, mirrors,
knives and forks, dressing-cases, and the whole mighty
category.[7] She protested, she flung herself about, she
declared those two ugly bottles should not join the exhibition in the dining-room, where it was laid out for days, and
the family ate their meals where they could, on the walls,
like flies. But there was also Uncle Benjamin's legacy on
view, in the distance, so it was ruled against her that the
bottles should have their place. And one fine morning
down came the family after a fearful row of the domestics;
shouting, screaming, cries for the police, and murder top-
ping all. What did they see? They saw two prodigious
burglars extended along the floor, each with one of the
twin bottles in his hand, and a remainder of the horror of
the midnight hanging about his person like a blown fog,
sufficient to frighten them whilst they kicked the rascals
entirely intoxicated. Never was wilder disorder of wedding-
presents, and not one lost! — owing, you'll own, to Uncle
Benjy's two bottles of ancient Jamaica rum."

Colonel De Craye concluded with an asseveration of the
truth of the story.

"A most provident far-sighted old sea-captain!" exclaimed Mrs. Mountstuart, laughing at Lady Busshe and
Lady Culmer.

These ladies chimed in with her gingerly.

"And have you many more clever stories, Colonel De
Craye?" said Lady Busshe.

"Ah! my lady, when the tree begins to count its gold
't is nigh upon bankruptcy."

"Poetic!" ejaculated Lady Culmer, spying at Miss Mid-

---

7. "épergnes": silver table stands, capable of holding several different sorts of
thing—as, for example, candles and fruit.

dleton's rippled countenance, and noting that she and Sir
Willoughby had not interchanged word or look.

"But that in the case of your Patterne Port a bottle of
it would outvalue the catalogue of nuptial presents, Willoughby, I would recommend your stationing some such
constabulary to keep watch and ward," said Dr. Middleton
as he filled his glass, taking Bordeaux in the middle of the
day, under a consciousness of virtue and its reward to
come at half-past seven in the evening.[8]

"The dogs would require a dozen of that, sir," said De
Craye.

"Then it is not to be thought of. Indeed, one!" Dr.
Middleton negatived the idea.

"We are no further advanced than when we began,"
observed Lady Busshe.

"If we are marked to go by stages," Mrs. Mountstuart
assented.

"Why, then, we shall be called old coaches," remarked
the colonel.

"You," said Lady Culmer, "have the advantage of us in
a closer acquaintance with Miss Middleton. You know her
tastes, and how far they have been consulted in the little
souvenirs already grouped somewhere, although not yet for
inspection. I am at sea. And here is Lady Busshe in
deadly alarm. There is plenty of time to effect a change —
though we are drawing on rapidly to the fatal day, Miss
Middleton. We are, we are very near it. Oh! yes. I am
one who thinks that these little affairs should be spoken of
openly, without that ridiculous bourgeois affectation, so that
we may be sure of giving satisfaction. It is a transaction,
like everything else in life. I for my part wish to be remembered favourably. I put it as a test of breeding to
speak of these things as plain matter-of-fact. You marry;
I wish you to have something by you to remind you of me.
What shall it be? — useful or ornamental. For an ordinary
household the choice is not difficult. But where wealth
abounds we are in a dilemma."

"And with persons of decided tastes," added Lady Busshe.
"I am really very unhappy," she protested to Clara.

Sir Willoughby dropped Lætitia; Clara's look of a sedate
resolution to preserve silence on the topic of the nuptial
gifts, made a diversion imperative.

"Your porcelain was exquisitely chosen, and I profess to
be a connoisseur," he said. "I am poor in old Saxony, as
you know: I can match the county in Sèvres, and my in-
heritance of China will not easily be matched in the
country."[9]

"You may consider your Dragon vases a present from
young Crossjay," said De Craye.

---

8. Claret, as a lighter wine, is more suitable for lunchtime drinking than port,
which is reserved for after dinner.

9. "Saxony . . . Sèvres . . . China":
These are all varieties of collector's porcelain.

"How?"

"Has n't he abstained from breaking them? the capital boy! Porcelain and a boy in the house together is a case of prospective disaster fully equal to Flitch and a fly."

"You should understand that my friend Horace — whose wit is in this instance founded on another tale of a boy — brought us a magnificent piece of porcelain, destroyed by the capsizing of his conveyance from the station," said Sir Willoughby to Lady Busshe.

She and Lady Culmer gave out lamentable Ohs, while Miss Eleanor and Miss Isabel Patterne sketched the incident. Then the lady visitors fixed their eyes in united sympathy upon Clara: recovering from which, after a contemplation of marble, Lady Busshe emphasized: "No, you do not love porcelain, it is evident, Miss Middleton."

"I am glad to be assured of it," said Lady Culmer.

"Oh! I know that face: I know that look," Lady Busshe affected to remark rallyingly: "it is not the first time I have seen it."

Sir Willoughby smarted to his marrow. "We will rout these fancies of an over-scrupulous generosity, my dear Lady Busshe."

Her unwonted breach of delicacy in speaking publicly of her present, and the vulgar persistency of her sticking to the theme, very much perplexed him. And if he mistook her not, she had just alluded to the demoniacal Constantia Durham. It might be that he had mistaken her: he was on guard against his terrible sensitiveness. Nevertheless it was hard to account for this behaviour of a lady greatly his friend and admirer, a lady of birth. And Lady Culmer as well! — likewise a lady of birth. Were they in collusion? had they a suspicion? He turned to Lætitia's face for the antidote to his pain.

"Oh, but you are not one yet, and I shall require two voices to convince me," Lady Busshe rejoined after another stare at the marble.

"Lady Busshe, I beg you not to think me ungrateful," said Clara.

"Fiddle! — gratitude! it is to please your taste, to satisfy *you*. I care for gratitude as little as for flattery."

"But gratitude is flattering," said Vernon.

"Now, no metaphysics, Mr. Whitford."

"But do care a bit for flattery, my lady," said De Craye. "'T is the finest of the Arts; we might call it moral sculpture. Adepts in it can cut their friends to any shape they like by practising it with the requisite skill. I myself, poor hand as I am, have made a man act Solomon by constantly praising his wisdom. He took a sagacious turn at an early period of the dose. He weighed the smallest question of his daily occasions with a deliberation truly oriental. Had I pushed it, he 'd have hired a baby and a couple of mothers to squabble over the undivided morsel."[1]

"I shall hope for a day in London with you," said Lady Culmer to Clara.

"You did not forget the Queen of Sheba?" said Mrs. Mountstuart to De Craye.

"With her appearance, the game has to be resigned to her entirely," he rejoined.

"That is," Lady Culmer continued, "if you do not despise an old woman for your comrade on a shopping excursion"

"Despise whom we fleece!" exclaimed Dr. Middleton. "Oh, no, Lady Culmer, the sheep is sacred."

"I am not so sure," said Vernon.

"In what way, and to what extent, are you not so sure?" said Dr. Middleton.

"The natural tendency is to scorn the fleeced."

"I stand for the contrary. Pity, if you like: particularly when they bleat."

"This is to assume that makers of gifts are a fleeced people: I demur," said Mrs. Mountstuart.

"Madam, we are expected to give; we are incited to give; you have dubbed it the fashion to give; and the person refusing to give, or incapable of giving, may anticipate that he will be regarded as benignly as a sheep of a drooping and flaccid wool by the farmer, who is reminded by the poor beast's appearance of a strange dog that worried the flock. Even Captain Benjamin, as you have seen, was unable to withstand the demand on him. The hymenæal pair are licensed freebooters levying black mail on us; survivors of an uncivilized period. But in taking without mercy, I venture to trust that the manners of a happier era instruct them not to scorn us. I apprehend that Mr. Whitford has a lower order of latrons in his mind."[2]

"Permit me to say, sir, that you have not considered the ignoble aspect of the fleeced," said Vernon. "I appeal to the ladies: would they not, if they beheld an ostrich walking down a Queen's Drawing Room, clean-plucked, despise him though they were wearing his plumes?"

"An extreme supposition indeed," said Dr. Middleton, frowning over it: "scarcely legitimately to be suggested."

"I think it fair, sir, as an instance."

"Has the circumstance occurred, I would ask?"

"In life? a thousand times."

"I fear so," said Mrs. Mountstuart.

Lady Busshe showed symptoms of a desire to leave a profitless table.

Vernon started up, glancing at the window.

"Did you see Crossjay?" he said to Clara.

"No; I must, if he is there," said she.

---

1. Two women, disputing over a child, appealed to Solomon; he offered to split it in two, and declared the one who pro-

2. "latrons": thieves.

tested to be the true mother.

She made her way out, Vernon after her. They both had the excuse.

"Which way did the poor boy go?" she asked him.

"I have not the slightest idea," he replied. "But put on your bonnet, if you would escape that pair of inquisitors."

"Mr. Whitford, what humiliation!"

"I suspect you do not feel it the most, and the end of it can't be remote," said he.

Thus it happened that when Lady Busshe and Lady Culmer quitted the dining-room, Miss Middleton had spirited herself away from summoning voice and messenger.

Sir Willoughby apologized for her absence. "If I could be jealous, it would be of that boy Crossjay."

"You are an excellent man, and the best of cousins," was Lady Busshe's enigmatical answer.

The exceedingly lively conversation at his table was lauded by Lady Culmer.

"Though," said she, "what it all meant, and what was the drift of it, I couldn't tell to save my life. Is it every day the same with you here?"

"Very much."

"How you must enjoy a spell of dulness!"

"If you said, simplicity and not talking for effect! I generally cast anchor by Lætitia Dale."

"Ah!" Lady Busshe coughed. "But the fact is, Mrs. Mountstuart is mad for cleverness."

"I think, my lady, Lætitia Dale is to the full as clever as any of the stars Mrs. Mountstuart assembles, or I."

"Talkative cleverness, I mean."

"In conversation as well. Perhaps you have not yet given her a chance."

"Yes, yes, she is clever, of course, poor dear. She is looking better too."

"Handsome, I thought," said Lady Culmer.

"She varies," observed Sir Willoughby.

The ladies took seat in their carriage and fell at once into a close-bonnet colloquy. Not a single allusion had they made to the wedding-presents after leaving the luncheon-table. The cause of their visit was obvious.

CHAPTER 37

CONTAINS CLEVER FENCING AND INTIMATIONS OF THE NEED
FOR IT

THAT woman Lady Busshe had predicted, after the event, Constantia Durham's defection. She had also, subsequent to Willoughby's departure on his travels, uttered sceptical things concerning his rooted attachment to Lætitia Dale. In her bitter vulgarity, that beaten rival of Mrs. Mountstuart

Jenkinson for the leadership of the county had taken his nose
for a melancholy prognostic of his fortunes; she had recently
played on his name: she had spoken the hideous English of
his fate. Little as she knew, she was alive to the worst interpretation of appearances. No other eulogy occurred to
her now than to call him the best of cousins, because Vernon
Whitford was housed and clothed and fed by him. She had
nothing else to say for a man she thought luckless! She was
a woman barren of wit, stripped of style, but she was wealthy
and a gossip — a forge of showering sparks — and she carried
Lady Culmer with her. The two had driven from his house
to spread the malignant rumour abroad: already they blew
the biting world on his raw wound. Neither of them was
like Mrs. Mountstuart, a witty woman, who could be hoodwinked; they were dull women, who steadily kept on their
own scent of the fact, and the only way to confound such
inveterate forces was, to be ahead of them, and seize and
transform the expected fact, and astonish them, when they
came up to him, with a totally unanticipated fact.

"You see, you were in error, ladies."

"And so we were, Sir Willoughby, and we acknowledge
it. We never could have guessed *that!*"

Thus the phantom couple in the future delivered themselves, as well they might at the revelation. He could run
far ahead.

Ay, but to combat these dolts, facts had to be encountered,
deeds done in groaning earnest. These representatives of
the pig-sconces of the population judged by circumstances:
airy shows and seems had no effect on them.[1] Dexterity of
fence was thrown away.

A flying peep at the remorseless might of dulness in compelling us to a concrete performance counter to our inclinations, if we would deceive its terrible instinct, gave Willoughby for a moment the survey of a sage. His intensity
of personal feeling struck so vivid an illumination of mankind at intervals that he would have been individually wise,
had he not been moved by the source of his accurate perceptions to a personal feeling of opposition to his own sagacity.
He loathed and he despised the vision, so his mind had no
benefit of it, though he himself was whipped along. He
chose rather (and the choice is open to us all) to be flattered
by the distinction it revealed between himself and mankind.

But if he was not as others were, why was he discomfited,
solicitous, miserable? To think that it should be so, ran
dead against his conqueror's theories wherein he had been
trained, which, so long as he gained success awarded success
to native merit, grandeur to the grand in soul, as light kindles
light: nature presents the example. His early training, his
bright beginning of life, had taught him to look to earth's
principal fruits as his natural portion, and it was owing to
a girl that he stood a mark for tongues, naked, wincing at

1. "pig-sconces": grunting heads.

the possible malignity of a pair of harridans. Why not
whistle the girl away?

Why, then he would be free to enjoy, careless, younger
than his youth in the rebound to happiness!

And then would his nostrils begin to lift and sniff at the
creeping up of a thick pestiferous vapour. Then in that
volume of stench would he discern the sullen yellow eye of
malice. A malarious earth would hunt him all over it. The
breath of the world, the world's view of him, was partly his
vital breath, his view of himself. The ancestry of the tortured man had bequeathed him this condition of high civilization among their other bequests. Your withered contracted
Egoists of the hut and the grot reck not of public opinion;
they crave but for liberty and leisure to scratch themselves
and soothe an excessive scratch. Willoughby was expansive,
a blooming one, born to look down upon a tributary world,
and to exult in being looked to. Do we wonder at his con-
sternation in the prospect of that world's blowing foul on
him? Princes have their obligations to teach them they are
mortal, and the brilliant heir of a tributary world is equally
enchained by the homage it brings him; — more, inasmuch
as it is immaterial, elusive, not gathered by the tax, and he
cannot capitally punish the treasonable recusants. Still
must he be brilliant; he must court his people. He must
ever, both in his reputation and his person, aching though
he be, show them a face and a leg.

The wounded gentleman shut himself up in his laboratory,
where he could stride to and fro, and stretch out his arms
for physical relief, secure from observation of his fantastical
shapes, under the idea that he was meditating. There was
perhaps enough to make him fancy it in the heavy fire of
shots exchanged between his nerves and the situation; there
were notable flashes. He would not avow that he was in an
agony: it was merely a desire for exercise.

Quintessence of worldliness, Mrs. Mountstuart appeared
through his farthest window, swinging her skirts on a turn
at the end of the lawn, with Horace De Craye smirking
beside her. And the woman's vaunted penetration was unable to detect the histrionic Irishism of the fellow. Or she
liked him for his acting and nonsense; nor she only. The
voluble beast was created to snare women. Willoughby
became smitten with an adoration of steadfastness in women.
The incarnation of that divine quality crossed his eyes. She
was clad in beauty.

A horrible nondescript convulsion composed of yawn and
groan drove him to his instruments, to avert a renewal of
the shock; and while arranging and fixing them for their
unwonted task, he compared himself advantageously with
men like Vernon and De Craye, and others of the county,
his fellows in the hunting-field and on the Magistrate's
bench, who neither understood nor cared for solid work,
beneficial practical work, the work of Science.

He was obliged to relinquish it: his hand shook.

" Experiments will not advance much at this rate," he said, casting the noxious retardation on his enemies.

It was not to be contested that he must speak with Mrs. Mountstuart, however he might shrink from the trial of his facial muscles. Her not coming to him seemed ominous: nor was her behaviour at the luncheon-table quite obscure. She had evidently instigated the gentlemen to cross and counter-chatter Lady Busshe and Lady Culmer. For what purpose ?

Clara's features gave the answer.

They were implacable. And he could be the same.

In the solitude of his room he cried right out: " I swear it, I will never yield her to Horace De Craye ! She shall feel some of my torments, and try to get the better of them by knowing she deserves them." He had spoken it, and it was an oath upon the record.

Desire to do her intolerable hurt became an ecstasy in his veins, and produced another stretching fit, that terminated in a violent shake of the body and limbs ; during which he was a spectacle for Mrs. Mountstuart at one of the windows. He laughed as he went to her, saying : " No, no work to-day ; it won't be done, positively refuses."

" I am taking the Professor away," said she ; " he is fidgetty about the cold he caught."

Sir Willoughby stepped out to her. " I was trying at a bit of work for an hour, not to be idle all day."

" You work in that den of yours every day ? "

" Never less than an hour, if I can snatch it."

" It is a wonderful resource ! "

The remark set him throbbing and thinking that a prolongation of his crisis exposed him to the approaches of some organic malady, possibly heart-disease.

" A habit," he said. " In there I throw off the world."

" We shall see some results in due time."

" I promise none : I like to be abreast of the real knowledge of my day, that is all."

" And a pearl among country gentlemen ! "

" In your gracious consideration, my dear lady. Generally speaking, it would be more adviseable to become a chatterer and keep an anecdotal note-book. I could not do it, simply because I could not live with my own emptiness for the sake of making an occasional display of fireworks. I aim at solidity. It is a narrow aim, no doubt ; not much appreciated."

" Lætitia Dale appreciates it."

A smile of enforced ruefulness, like a leaf curling in heat, wrinkled his mouth.

Why did she not speak of her conversation with Clara ?

" Have they caught Crossjay ? " he said.

" Apparently they are giving chase to him."

The likelihood was, that Clara had been overcome by

timidity.

"Must you leave us?"

"I think it prudent to take Professor Crooklyn away."

"He still . . .?"

"The extraordinary resemblance!"

"A word aside to Dr. Middleton will dispel that."

"You are thoroughly good."

This hateful encomium of commiseration transfixed him. Then, she knew of his calamity!

"Philosophical," he said, "would be the proper term, I think."

"Colonel De Craye, by the way, promises me a visit when he leaves you."

"To-morrow?"

"The earlier the better. He is too captivating; he is delightful. He won me in five minutes. I don't accuse him. Nature gifted him to cast the spell. We are weak women, Sir Willoughby."

She knew!

"Like to like: the witty to the witty, ma'am."

"You won't compliment me with a little bit of jealousy?"

"I forbear from complimenting *him*."

"Be philosophical, of course, if you have the philosophy."

"I pretend to it. Probably I suppose myself to succeed because I have no great requirement of it; I cannot say. We are riddles to ourselves."

Mrs. Mountstuart pricked the turf with the point of her parasol. She looked down and she looked up.

"Well?" said he to her eyes.

"Well, and where is Lætitia Dale?"

He turned about to show his face elsewhere.

When he fronted her again she looked very fixedly, and set her head shaking.

"It will not do, my dear Sir Willoughby!"

"What?"

"It."

"I never could solve enigmas."

"Playing ta-ta-ta-ta ad infinitum, then.[2] Things have gone far. All parties would be happier for an excursion. Send her home."

"Lætitia? I can't part with her."

Mrs. Mountstuart put a tooth on her under lip as her head renewed its brushing negative.

"In what way can it be hurtful that she should be here, ma'am?" he ventured to persist.

"Think."

"She is proof."[3]

"Twice!"

The word was big artillery. He tried the affectation of a staring stupidity. She might have seen his heart thump, and he quitted the mask for an agreeable grimace.

2. "ad infinitum": forever.   3. Above suspicion.

" She is inaccessible. She is my friend. I guarantee
her, on my honour. Have no fear for her. I beg you to
have confidence in me. I would perish rather. No soul on
earth is to be compared with her."

Mrs. Mountstuart repeated, " Twice ! "

The low monosyllable, musically spoken in the same
tone of warning of a gentle ghost, rolled a thunder that
maddened him, but he dared not take it up to fight against
it on plain terms.

" Is it for my sake ? " he said.

" It will not do, Sir Willoughby ! "

She spurred him to a frenzy.

" My dear Mrs. Mountstuart, you have been listening to
tales. I am not a tyrant. I am one of the most easy-going
of men. Let us preserve the forms due to society: I say no
more. As for poor old Vernon, people call me a good sort
of cousin; I should like to see him comfortably married;
decently married this time. I have proposed to contribute
to his establishment. I mention it to show that the case
has been practically considered. He has had a tolerably
souring experience of the state; he might be inclined if,
say, you took him in hand for another venture. It's a
demoralizing lottery. However, Government sanctions it."

"But, Sir Willoughby, what is the use of my taking
him in hand, when, as you tell me, Lætitia Dale holds
back ? "

" She certainly does."

" Then we are talking to no purpose, unless you undertake to melt her."

He suffered a lurking smile to kindle to some strength of
meaning.

" You are not over-considerate in committing me to such
an office."

" You are afraid of the danger ? " she all but sneered.

Sharpened by her tone, he said, " I have such a love of
steadfastness of character, that I should be a poor advocate
in the endeavour to break it. And frankly, I know the
danger. I saved my honour when I made the attempt:
that is all I can say."

" Upon my word," Mrs. Mountstuart threw back her head
to let her eyes behold him summarily over their fine aqui-
line bridge, "you have the heart of mystification, my good
friend."

" Abandon the idea of Lætitia Dale."

" And marry your cousin Vernon to whom ? Where are
we ?"

" As I said, ma'am, I am an easy-going man. I really
have not a spice of the tyrant in me. An intemperate
creature held by the collar may have that notion of me,
while pulling to be released as promptly as it entered the
noose. But I do strictly and sternly object to the scandal of
violent separations, open breaches of solemn engagements, a

public rupture. Put it that I am the cause, I will not consent to a violation of decorum. Is that clear? It is just
possible for things to be arranged so that all parties may
be happy in their way without much hubbub. Mind, it is
not I who have willed it so. I am, and I am forced to be,
passive. But I will not be obstructive."

He paused, waving his hand to signify the vanity of the
more that might be said.

Some conception of him, dashed by incredulity, excited
the lady's intelligence.

"Well!" she exclaimed, "you have planted me in the
land of conjecture. As my husband used to say, I don't
see light, but I think I see the lynx that does. We won't
discuss it at present. I certainly must be a younger woman
than I supposed, for I am learning hard. — Here comes the
Professor, buttoned up to the ears, and Dr. Middleton flapping in the breeze. There will be a cough and a footnote
referring to the young lady at the station, if we stand
together, so please order my carriage."

"You found Clara complacent? roguish?"

"I will call to-morrow. You have simplified my task,
Sir Willoughby, very much; that is, assuming that I have
not entirely mistaken you. I am so far in the dark, that
I have to help myself by recollecting how Lady Busshe opposed my view of a certain matter formerly. Scepticism is
her forte. It will be the very oddest thing if after all . . . !
No, I shall own, romance has not departed. Are you fond of
dupes?"

"I detest the race."

"An excellent answer. I could pardon you for it." She
refrained from adding: "If you are making one of me."
Sir Willoughby went to ring for her carriage.

She knew. That was palpable: Clara had betrayed him.
"The earlier Colonel De Craye leaves Patterne Hall the
better:" she had said that: and, "all parties would be
happier for an excursion." She knew the position of things
and she guessed the remainder. But what she did not
know, and could not divine, was the man who fenced her.
He speculated further on the witty and the dull. These
latter are the redoubtable body. They will have facts to
convince them; they had, he confessed it to himself, precipitated him into the novel sphere of his dark hints to
Mrs. Mountstuart; from which the utter darkness might
allow him to escape, yet it embraced him singularly, and
even pleasantly, with the sense of a fact established.

It embraced him even very pleasantly. There was an end
to his tortures. He sailed on a tranquil sea, the husband
of a steadfast woman — no rogue. The exceeding beauty
of steadfastness in women clothed Lætitia in graces Clara
could not match. A tried, steadfast woman is the one
jewel of the sex. She points to her husband like the sun-
flower; her love illuminates him; she lives in him, for

him; she testifies to his worth; she drags the world to his feet; she leads the chorus of his praises; she justifies him in his own esteem. Surely there is not on earth such beauty!

If we have to pass through anguish to discover it and cherish the peace it gives, to clasp it, calling it ours, is a full reward.

Deep in his reverie, he said his adieux to Mrs. Mountstuart, and strolled up the avenue behind the carriage-wheels, unwilling to meet Lætitia till he had exhausted the fresh savour of the cud of fancy.

Supposing it done !—

It would be generous on his part. It would redound to his credit.

His home would be a fortress, impregnable to tongues. He would have divine security in his home.

One who read and knew and worshipped him would be sitting there starlike: sitting there, awaiting him, his fixed star.

It would be marriage with a mirror, with an echo; marriage with a shining mirror, a choric echo.

It would be marriage with an intellect, with a fine understanding; to make his home a fountain of repeatable wit: to make his dear old Patterne Hall the luminary of the county.

He revolved it as a chant: with anon and anon involuntarily a discordant animadversion on Lady Busshe. His attendant imps heard the angry inward cry.

Forthwith he set about painting Lætitia in delectable human colours, like a miniature of the past century, reserving her ideal figure for his private satisfaction. The world was to bow to her visible beauty, and he gave her enamel and glow, a taller stature, a swimming air, a transcendancy that exorcised the image of the old witch who had driven him to this.

The result in him was, that Lætitia became humanly and avowedly beautiful. Her dark eyelashes on the pallor of her cheeks lent their aid to the transformation, which was a necessity to him, so it was performed. He received the waxen impression.

His retinue of imps had a revel. We hear wonders of men, and we see a lifting up of hands in the world. The wonders would be explained, and never a hand need to interject, if the mystifying man were but accompanied and reported of by that monkey-eyed confraternity. They spy the heart and its twists.

The heart is the magical gentleman. None of them would follow where there was no heart. The twists of the heart are the comedy.

" *The secret of the heart is its pressing love of self*," says the Book.

By that secret the mystery of the organ is legible: and a

comparison of the heart to the mountain rillet is taken up to show us the unbaffled force of the little channel in seeking to swell its volume, strenuously, sinuously, ever in pursuit of self; the busiest as it is the most single-aiming of forces on our earth. And we are directed to the sinuosities for the posts of observation chiefly instructive.

Few maintain a stand there. People see, and they rush away to interchange liftings of hands at the sight, instead of patiently studying the phenomenon of energy.

Consequently a man in love with one woman, and in all but absolute consciousness, behind the thinnest of veils, preparing his mind to love another, will be barely credible. The particular hunger of the forceful but adaptable heart is the key of him. Behold the mountain rillet, become a brook, become a torrent, how it inarms a handsome boulder: yet if the stone will not go with it, on it hurries, pursuing self in extension, down to where perchance a dam has been raised of a sufficient depth to enfold and keep it from inordinate restlessness. Lætitia represented this peaceful restraining space in prospect.

But she was a faded young woman. He was aware of it; and systematically looking at himself with her upturned orbs, he accepted her benevolently, as a God grateful for worship, and used the divinity she imparted to paint and renovate her. His heart required her so. The heart works the springs of imagination; imagination received its commission from the heart, and was a cunning artist.

Cunning to such a degree of seductive genius that the masterpiece it offered to his contemplation enabled him simultaneously to gaze on Clara and think of Lætitia. Clara came through the park-gates with Vernon, a brilliant girl indeed, and a shallow one: a healthy creature, and an animal; attractive, but capricious, impatient, treacherous, foul; a woman to drag men through the mud. She approached.

CHAPTER 38

IN WHICH WE TAKE A STEP TO THE CENTRE OF EGOISM

They met; Vernon soon left them.

"You have not seen Crossjay?" Willoughby inquired.

"No," said Clara. "Once more I beg you to pardon him. He spoke falsely, owing to his poor boy's idea of chivalry."

"The chivalry to the sex which commences in lies, ends by creating the woman's hero, whom we see about the world and in certain Courts of Law."

His ability to silence her was great: she could not reply to speech like that.

"You have," said he, "made a confidante of Mrs. Mount-stuart."

" Yes."

" This is your purse."

" I thank you."

" Professor Crooklyn has managed to make your father acquainted with your project. That, I suppose, is the railway ticket in the fold of the purse. He was assured at the station that you had taken a ticket to London, and would not want the fly."

" It is true. I was foolish."

" You have had a pleasant walk with Vernon — turning me in and out ? "

" We did not speak of you. You allude to what he would never consent to."

" He's an honest fellow, in his old-fashioned way. He's a secret old fellow. Does he ever talk about his wife to you ? "

Clara dropped her purse, and stooped and picked it up.

" I know nothing of Mr. Whitford's affairs," she said, and she opened the purse and tore to pieces the railway-ticket.

" The story's a proof that romantic spirits do not furnish the most romantic history. You have the word 'chivalry' frequently on your lips. He chivalrously married the daughter of the lodging-house where he resided before I took him. We obtained information of the auspicious union in a newspaper report of Mrs. Whitford's drunkenness and rioting at a London railway terminus — probably the one whither your ticket would have taken you yesterday, for I heard the lady was on her way to us for supplies, the connubial larder being empty."

" I am sorry ; I am ignorant ; I have heard nothing ; I know nothing," said Clara.

" You are disgusted. But half the students and authors you hear of marry in that way. And very few have Vernon's luck."

" She had good qualities ? "

Her under lip hung.

It looked like disgust ; he begged her not indulge the feeling.

" Literary men, it is notorious, even with the entry to society, have no taste in women. The housewife is their object. Ladies frighten and would, no doubt, be an annoyance and hindrance to them at home."

" You said he was fortunate."

" You have a kindness for him."

" I respect him."

" He is a friendly old fellow in his awkward fashion ; honourable, and so forth. But a disreputable alliance of that sort sticks to a man. The world will talk. Yes, he was fortunate so far ; he fell into the mire and got out of it. Were he to marry again . . ."

" She . . . ? "

" Died. Do not be startled ; it was a natural death. She

responded to the sole wishes left to his family. He buried the woman, and I received him. I took him on my tour. A second marriage might cover the first: there would be a buzz about the old business: the woman's relatives write to him still, try to bleed him, I dare say. However, now you understand his gloominess. I don't imagine he regrets his loss. He probably sentimentalizes, like most men when they are well rid of a burden. You must not think the worse of him."

"I do not," said Clara.

"I defend him whenever the matter's discussed."

"I hope you do."

"Without approving his folly. I can't wash him clean."

They were at the Hall-doors. She waited for any personal communications he might be pleased to make, and as there was none, she ran upstairs to her room.

He had tossed her to Vernon in his mind not only painlessly, but with a keen acid of satisfaction. The heart is the wizard.

Next he bent his deliberate steps to Lætitia.

The mind was guilty of some hesitation; the feet went forward.

She was working at an embroidery by an open window. Colonel De Craye leaned outside, and Willoughby pardoned her air of demure amusement, on hearing him say: "No, I have had one of the pleasantest half-hours of my life, and would rather idle here, if idle you will have it, than employ my faculties on horse-back."

"Time is not lost in conversing with Miss Dale," said Willoughby.

The light was tender to her complexion where she sat in partial shadow.

De Craye asked whether Crossjay had been caught. Lætitia murmured a kind word for the boy. Willoughby examined her embroidery.

The ladies Eleanor and Isabel appeared.

They invited her to take carriage-exercise with them.

Lætitia did not immediately answer, and Willoughby remarked: "Miss Dale has been reproving Horace for idleness, and I recommend you to enlist him to do duty, while I relieve him here."

The ladies had but to look at the colonel. He was at their disposal, if they would have him. He was marched to the carriage.

Lætitia plied her threads.

"Colonel De Craye spoke of Crossjay," she said. "May I hope you have forgiven the poor boy, Sir Willoughby?"

He replied: "Plead for him."

"I wish I had eloquence."

"In my opinion you have it."

"If he offends, it is never from meanness. At school, among comrades, he would shine. He is in too strong a light; his feelings and his moral nature are over-excited."

"That was not the case when he was at home with you."

"I am severe; I am stern."

"A Spartan mother!"[1]

"My system of managing a boy would be after that model: except in this: he should always feel that he could obtain forgiveness."

"Not at the expense of justice?"

"Ah! young creatures are not to be arraigned before the higher Courts. It seems to me perilous to terrify their imaginations. If we do so, are we not likely to produce the very evil we are combating? The alternations for the young should be school and home: and it should be in their hearts to have confidence that forgiveness alternates with discipline. They are of too tender an age for the rigours of the world; we are in danger of hardening them. I prove to you that I am not possessed of eloquence. You encouraged me to speak, Sir Willoughby."

"You speak wisely, Lætitia."

"I think it true. Will not you reflect on it? You have only to do so, to forgive him. I am growing bold indeed, and shall have to beg forgiveness for myself."

"You still write? you continue to work with your pen?" said Willoughby.

"A little; a very little."

"I do not like you to squander yourself, waste yourself, on the public. You are too precious to feed the beast. Giving out incessantly must end by attenuating. Reserve yourself for your friends. Why should they be robbed of so much of you? Is it not reasonable to assume that by lying fallow you would be more enriched for domestic life? Candidly, had I authority I would confiscate your pen: I would 'away with that bauble.' You will not often find me quoting Cromwell, but his words apply in this instance.[2] I would say rather, that lancet. Perhaps it is the more correct term. It bleeds you, it wastes you. For what? For a breath of fame!"

"I write for money."

"And there — I would say of another — you subject yourself to the risk of mental degradation. Who knows? — moral! Trafficking the brains for money, must bring them to the level of the purchasers in time. I confiscate your pen, Lætitia."

"It will be to confiscate your own gift, Sir Willoughby."

"Then that proves — will you tell me the date?"

"You sent me a gold pen-holder on my sixteenth birthday."

"It proves my utter thoughtlessness then, and later. And later!"

---

1. "Spartan": severe.
2. Referring to the emblems of civil government, Cromwell said, "Away with those baubles!"

He rested an elbow on his knee and covered his eyes, murmuring in that profound hollow which is haunted by the voice of a contrite past: "And later!"

The deed could be done. He had come to the conclusion that it could be done, though the effort to harmonize the figure sitting near him, with the artistic figure of his purest pigments, had cost him labour and a blinking of the eyelids. That also could be done. Her pleasant tone, sensible talk, and the light favouring her complexion, helped him in his effort. She was a sober cup; sober and wholesome. Deliriousness is for adolescence. The men who seek intoxicating cups are men who invite their fates.

Curiously, yet as positively as things can be affirmed, the husband of this woman would be able to boast of her virtues and treasures abroad, as he could not — impossible to say why not—boast of a beautiful wife or a blue-stocking wife.[3] One of her merits as a wife would be this extraordinary neutral merit of a character that demanded colour from the marital hand, and would take it.

Lætitia had not to learn that he had much to distress him. Her wonder at his exposure of his grief counteracted a fluttering of vague alarm. She was nervous; she sat in expectation of some bursts of regrets or of passion.

"I may hope that you have pardoned Crossjay?" she said.

"My friend," said he, uncovering his face, "I am governed by principles. Convince me of an error, I shall not obstinately pursue a premeditated course. But you know me. Men who have not principles to rule their conduct are — well, they are unworthy of a half-hour of companionship with you. I will speak to you to-night. I have letters to despatch. To-night : at twelve : in the room where we spoke last. Or await me in the drawing-room. I have to attend on my guests till late."

He bowed; he was in a hurry to go.

The deed could be done. It must be done; it was his destiny.

CHAPTER 39

IN THE HEART OF THE EGOIST

But already he had begun to regard the deed as his executioner. He dreaded meeting Clara. The folly of having retained her stood before him. How now to look on her and keep a sane resolution unwavering? She tempted to the insane. Had she been away, he could have walked through the performance composed by the sense of doing a duty to

3. "blue-stocking": bookish.

himself : perhaps faintly hating the poor wretch he made happy at last, kind to her in a manner, polite. Clara's presence in the house previous to the deed, and oh, heaven ! after it, threatened his wits. [Pride ? He had none ; he cast it down for her to trample it ; he caught it back ere it was trodden on. Yes ; he had pride : he had it as a dagger in his breast : his pride was his misery. But he was too proud to submit to misery. "What I do is right." He said the words, and rectitude smoothed his path, till the question clamoured for answer : Would the world countenance and endorse his pride in Lætitia ? At one time, yes. And now ? Clara's beauty ascended, laid a beam on him.[1]

We are on board the labouring vessel of humanity in a storm, when cries and countercries ring out, disorderliness mixes the crew, and the fury of self-preservation divides : this one is for the ship, that one for his life. Clara was the former to him, Lætitia the latter. But what if there might not be greater safety in holding tenaciously to Clara than in casting her off for Lætitia ? No, she had done things to set his pride throbbing in the quick. She had gone bleeding about first to one, then to another ; she had betrayed him to Vernon, and to Mrs. Mountstuart ; a look in the eyes of Horace De Craye said, to him as well : to whom not ? He might hold to her for vengeance ; but that appetite was short-lived in him if it ministered nothing to his purposes. " I discard all idea of vengeance," he said, and thrilled burn-ingly to a smart in his admiration of the man who could be so magnanimous under mortal injury : for the more admirable he, the more pitiable. He drank a drop or two of self-pity like a poison, repelling the assaults of public pity. Clara must be given up. It must be seen by the world that, as he felt, the thing he did was right. Laocoon of his own serpents, he struggled to a certain magnificence of attitude in the muscular net of constrictions he flung around himself.[2] Clara must be given up. O bright Abominable ! She must be given up : but not to one whose touch of her would be darts in the blood of the yielder, snakes in his bed : she must be given up to an extinguisher ; to be the second wife of an old-fashioned semi-recluse, disgraced in his first. And were it publicly known that she had been cast off, and had fallen on old Vernon for a refuge, and part in spite, part in shame, part in desperation, part in a fit of good sense under the cir-cumstances, espoused him, her beauty would not influence the world in its judgement. The world would know what to think. As the instinct of self-preservation whispered to Willoughby, the world, were it requisite, might be taught to think what it assuredly would not think if she should be seen tripping to the altar with Horace De Craye. Self-pres-ervation, not vengeance, breathed that whisper. He glanced

1. "beam": a shaft, as of enchantment, perhaps also as of a balance.
2. The famous statue shows Laocoon, priest of Troy, struggling with his two sons against a tangle of serpents sent by Apollo.

at her iniquity for a justification of it, without any desire to
do her a permanent hurt : he was highly civilized : but with
a strong intention to give her all the benefit of the scandal,
supposing a scandal, or ordinary tattle.

"And so he handed her to his cousin and secretary, Vernon Whitford, who opened his mouth and shut his eyes."

You hear the world ? How are we to stop it from chattering ? Enough that he had no desire to harm her. Some
gentle anticipations of her being tarnished were imperative ;
they came spontaneously to him ; otherwise the radiance of
that bright Abominable in loss would have been insufferable ;
he could not have borne it ; he could never have surrendered
her.

Moreover, a happy present effect was the result. He
conjured up the anticipated chatter and shrug of the world
so vividly that her beauty grew hectic with the stain, bereft
of its formidable magnetism. He could meet her calmly ; he
had steeled himself. Purity in women was his principal
stipulation, and a woman puffed at, was not the person to
cause him tremours.[3]

Consider him indulgently : the Egoist is the Son of Himself. He is likewise the Father. And the son loves the
father, the father the son ; they reciprocate affection through
the closest of ties ; and shall they view behaviour unkindly
wounding either of them, not for each other's dear sake
abhorring the criminal ? They would not injure you, but
they cannot consent to see one another suffer or crave in
vain. The two rub together in sympathy besides relationship to an intenser one. Are you, without much offending,
sacrificed by them, it is on the altar of their mutual love, to
filial piety or paternal tenderness : the younger has offered a
dainty morsel to the elder, or the elder to the younger.
Absorbed in their great example of devotion, they do not
think of you. They are beautiful.

Yet is it most true that the younger has the passions of
youth : whereof will come division between them ; and this
is a tragic state. They are then pathetic. This was the
state of Sir Willoughby lending ear to his elder, until he
submitted to bite at the fruit proposed to him — with how
wry a mouth the venerable senior chose not to mark. At
least, as we perceive, a half of him was ripe of wisdom in his
own interests. The cruder half had but to be obedient to
the leadership of sagacity for his interests to be secured,
and a filial disposition assisted him ; painfully indeed ; but the
same rare quality directed the good gentleman to swallow
his pain. That the son should bewail his fate were a dishonour to the sire. He reverenced, and submitted. Thus,
to say, consider him indulgently, is too much an appeal for
charity on behalf of one requiring but initial anatomy — a
slicing in halves — to exonerate, perchance exalt him. The
Egoist is our fountain-head, primeval man : the primitive is

3. "puffed at": touched by the breath of scandal.

born again, the elemental reconstituted. Born again, into new conditions, the primitive may be highly polished of men, and forfeit nothing save the roughness of his original nature. He is not only his own father, he is ours ; and he is also our son. We have produced him, he us. Such were we, to such are we returning: not other, sings the poet, than one who toilfully works his shallop against the tide, "si brachia forte remisit" : — let him haply relax the labour of his arms, however high up the stream, and back he goes, " in pejus," to the early principle of our being, with seeds and plants, that are as carelessly weighed in the hand and as indiscriminately husbanded as our humanity.[4]

Poets on the other side may be cited for an assurance that the primitive is not the degenerate : rather is he a sign of the indestructibility of the race, of the ancient energy in removing obstacles to individual growth ; a sample of what we would be, had we his concentrated power. He is the original innocent, the pure simple. It is we who have fallen ; we have melted into Society, diluted our essence, dissolved. He stands in the midst monumentally, a landmark of the tough and honest old Ages, with the symbolic alphabet of striking arms and running legs, our early language, scrawled over his person, and the glorious first flint and arrow-head for his crest: at once the spectre of the Kitchen-midden and our ripest issue.[5]

But Society is about him. The occasional spectacle of the primitive dangling on a rope has impressed his mind with the strength of his natural enemy : from which uncongenial sight he has turned shuddering hardly less to behold the blast that is blown upon a reputation where one has been disrespectful of the many. By these means, through meditation on the contrast of circumstances in life, a pulse of imagination has begun to stir, and he has entered the upper sphere, or circle of spiritual Egoism : he has become the civilized Egoist ; primitive still, as sure as man has teeth, but developed in his manner of using them.

Degenerate or not (and there is no just reason to suppose it), Sir Willoughby was a social Egoist, fiercely imaginative in whatsoever concerned him. He had discovered a greater realm than that of the sensual appetites, and he rushed across and around it in his conquering period with an Alexander's pride. On these wind-like journeys he had carried Constantia, subsequently Clara ; and however it may have been in the case of Miss Durham, in that of Miss Middleton it is almost certain she caught her glimpse of his interior from sheer fatigue in hearing him discourse of it. What he revealed was not the cause of her sickness : women can bear revelations — they are exciting : but the monotonousness. He slew imagination. There is no direr

4. "si brachia forte remiset": i.e., if by chance he relaxes his efforts . . . down the stream he goes, "in pejus," for the worse: Virgil, *Georgics* I, 202.

5. "Kitchen-midden": the garbage-heap of shards and bones and rubble that generally constitutes our record of the earliest civilizations.

disaster in love than the death of imagination. He dragged her through the labyrinths of his penetralia, in his hungry coveting to be loved more and still more, more still, until imagination gave up the ghost, and he talked to her plain hearing like a monster.[6] It must have been that; for the spell of the primitive upon women is masterful up to the time of contact.

"And so he handed her to his cousin and secretary Vernon Whitford, who opened his mouth and shut his eyes."

The urgent question was, how it was to be accomplished. Willoughby worked at the subject with all his power of concentration: a power that had often led him to feel and say, that as a barrister, a diplomatist, or a general, he would have won his grades: and granting him a personal interest in the business, he might have achieved eminence: he schemed and fenced remarkably well.

He projected a scene, following expressions of anxiety on account of old Vernon and his future settlement: and then — Clara maintaining her doggedness, to which he was now so accustomed that he could not conceive a change in it — says he: "If you determine on breaking, I give you back your word *on one condition*." Whereupon she starts: he insists on her promise: she declines: affairs resume their former footing; she frets, she begs for the disclosure: he flatters her by telling her his desire to keep her in the family: she is unilluminated, but strongly moved by curiosity: he philosophizes on marriage — "What are we? poor creatures! we must get through life as we can, doing as much good as we can to those we love; and think as you please, I love old Vernon. Am I not giving you the greatest possible proof of it?" She will not see. Then flatly out comes the one condition. That and no other. "Take Vernon and I release you." She refuses. Now ensues the debate, all the oratory being with him. "Is it because of his unfortunate first marriage? You assured me you thought no worse of him: &c." She declares the proposal revolting. He can distinguish nothing that should offend her in a proposal to make his cousin happy if she will not him. Irony and sarcasm relieve his emotions, but he convinces her he is dealing plainly and intends generosity. She is confused; she speaks in maiden fashion.

He touches again on Vernon's early escapade. She does not enjoy it. The scene closes with his bidding her reflect on it, and remember the one condition of her release. Mrs. Mountstuart Jenkinson, now reduced to believe that he burns to be free, is then called in for an interview with Clara. His aunts Eleanor and Isabel besiege her. Lætitia in passionate earnest besieges her. Her father is wrought on to besiege her. Finally Vernon is attacked by Willoughby and Mrs. Mountstuart: — and here, Willoughby

---

6. "penetralia": bowels, inmost feelings.

chose to think, was the main difficulty. But the girl has
money ; she is agreeable; Vernon likes her ; she is fond of
his " Alps," they have tastes in common, he likes her father,
and in the end he besieges her. Will she yield ? De Craye
is absent. There is no other way of shunning a marriage
she is incomprehensibly but frantically averse to. She is in
the toils. Her father will stay at Patterne Hall as long as
his host desires it. She hesitates, she is overcome; in
spite of a certain nausea due to Vernon's preceding alliance,
she yields.

Willoughby revolved the entire drama in Clara's presence. It helped him to look on her coolly. Conducting
her to the dinner-table, he spoke of Crossjay, not unkindly ;
and at table he revolved the set of scenes with a heated
animation that took fire from the wine and the face of his
friend Horace, while he encouraged Horace to be flowingly
Irish. He nipped the fellow good-humouredly once or
twice, having never felt so friendly to him since the day of
his arrival ; but the position of critic is instinctively taken
by men who do not flow : and Patterne Port kept Dr. Middleton in a benevolent reserve when Willoughby decided
that something said by De Craye was not new, and laughingly accused him of failing to consult his anecdotal note-
book for the double-cross to his last sprightly sally.
" Your sallies are excellent, Horace, but spare us your Aunt
Sallies ! " De Craye had no repartee, nor did Dr. Middleton challenge a pun. We have only to sharpen our wits to
trip your seductive rattler whenever we may choose to
think proper; and evidently, if we condescended to it, we
could do better than he. The critic who has hatched a
witticism is impelled to this opinion. Judging by the
smiles of the ladies, they thought so too.

Shortly before eleven o'clock, Dr. Middleton made a
Spartan stand against the offer of another bottle of Port.
The regulation couple of bottles had been consumed in equal
partnership, and the Rev. Doctor and his host were free to
pay a ceremonial visit to the drawing-room, where they were
not expected. A piece of work of the elder ladies, a silken
boudoir sofa-rug, was being examined, with high approval
of the two younger. Vernon and Colonel De Craye had
gone out in search of Crossjay, one to Mr. Dale's cottage,
the other to call at the head and under game-keepers. They
were said to be strolling and smoking, for the night was
fine. Willoughby left the room and came back with the
key of Crossjay's door in his pocket. He foresaw that the
delinquent might be of service to him.[7]

Lætitia and Clara sang together. Lætitia was flushed,
Clara pale. At eleven they saluted the ladies Eleanor and
Isabel. Willoughby said, " Good night" to each of them,

7. What Willoughby's schemes are for
using Crossjay, and how locking the door
of his bedroom will serve them, we are
deliberately not told; he is a man devious
even to himself.

contrasting as he did so the downcast look of Lætitia with Clara's frigid directness. He divined that they were off to talk over their one object of common interest, Crossjay. Saluting his aunts, he took up the rug, to celebrate their diligence and taste; and that he might make Dr. Middleton impatient for bed, he provoked him to admire it, held it out and laid it out, and caused the courteous old gentleman some confusion in hitting on fresh terms of commendation.

Before midnight the room was empty. Ten minutes later, Willoughby paid it a visit, and found it untenanted by the person he had engaged to be there. Vexed by his disappointment, he paced up and down, and chanced abstractedly to catch the rug in his hand; for what purpose, he might well ask himself; admiration of ladies' work, in their absence, was unlikely to occur to him. Nevertheless the touch of the warm soft silk was meltingly feminine. A glance at the mantel-piece clock told him Lætitia was twenty minutes behind the hour.

Her remissness might endanger all his plans, alter the whole course of his life. The colours in which he painted her were too lively to last; the madness in his head threatened to subside. Certain it was that he could not be ready a second night for the sacrifice he had been about to perform.

The clock was at the half hour-after twelve. He flung the silken thing on the central ottoman, extinguished the lamps, and walked out of the room, charging the absent Lætitia to bear her misfortune with a consciousness of deserving it.

CHAPTER 40

MIDNIGHT: SIR WILLOUGHBY AND LÆTITIA: WITH YOUNG CROSSJAY UNDER A COVERLET

YOUNG Crossjay was a glutton at holidays and never thought of home till it was dark. The close of the day saw him several miles away from the Hall, dubious whether he would not round his numerous adventures by sleeping at an inn; for he had lots of money, and the idea of jumping up in the morning in a strange place was thrilling. Besides, when he was shaken out of sleep by Sir Willoughby, he had been told that he was to go, and not to show his face at Patterne again. On the other hand, Miss Middleton had bidden him come back. There was little question with him which person he should obey: he followed his heart.

Supper at an inn, where he found a company to listen to his adventures, delayed him, and a short cut, intended to make up for it, lost him his road. He reached the Hall very late, ready to be in love with the horrible pleasure of a night's rest under the stars, if necessary. But a candle burned at one of the back windows. He knocked, and a kitchen-maid let him in. She had a bowl of hot soup prepared for him. Crossjay tried a mouthful to please her. His head dropped over it. She roused him to his feet, and he pitched against her shoulder. The dry air of the kitchen department had proved too much for the tired youngster. Mary, the maid, got him to step as firmly as he was able, and led him by the back-way to the hall, bidding him creep noiselessly to bed. He understood his position in the house, and though he could have gone fast to sleep on the stairs, he took a steady aim at his room and gained the door cat like. The door resisted. He was appalled and unstrung in a minute. The door was locked. Crossjay felt as if he were in the presence of Sir Willoughby. He fled on ricketty legs, and had a fall and bumps down half-a-dozen stairs. A door opened above. He rushed across the hall to the drawing-room, invitingly open, and there staggered in darkness to the ottoman and rolled himself in something sleek and warm, soft as hands of ladies, and redolent of them ; so delicious that he hugged the folds about his head and heels. While he was endeavouring to think where he was, his legs curled, his eyelids shut, and he was in the thick of the day's adventures, doing yet more wonderful things.

He heard his own name : that was quite certain. He knew that he heard it with his ears, as he pursued the fleetest dreams ever accorded to mortal. It did not mix : it was outside him, and like the danger-pole in the ice, which the skater shooting hither and yonder comes on again, it recurred ; and now it marked a point in his career, now it caused him to relax his pace ; he began to circle, and whirled closer round it, until, as at a blow, his heart knocked, he tightened himself, thought of bolting, and lay dead-still to throb and hearken.

" Oh ! Sir Willoughby," a voice had said.

The accents were sharp with alarm.

" My friend ! my dearest ! " was the answer.

" I came to speak of Crossjay."

" Will you sit here, on the ottoman ? "

" No, I cannot wait. I hoped I had heard Crossjay return. I would rather not sit down. May I entreat you to pardon him when he comes home ? "

" You, and you only, may do so. I permit none else. Of Crossjay to-morrow."

" He may be lying in the fields. We are anxious."

" The rascal can take pretty good care of himself."

" Crossjay is perpetually meeting accidents."

" He shall be indemnified if he has had excess of punishment."

" I think I will say good night, Sir Willoughby."

" When freely and unreservedly you have given me your hand."

There was hesitation.

" To say good night ? "

" I ask for your hand."

" Good night, Sir Willoughby."

" You do not give it. You are in doubt ? Still ? What language must I use to convince you ? And yet you know me. Who knows me but you ? You have always known me. You are my home and my temple. Have you forgotten your verses for the day of my majority ?

> " ' The dawn-star has arisen
>   In plenitude of light . . . ' "

" Do not repeat them, pray ! " cried Lætitia with a gasp.

" I have repeated them to myself a thousand times : in India, America, Japan : they were like our English skylark carolling to me.

> " ' My heart, now burst thy prison
>   With proud aerial flight ! ' "

" Oh ! I beg you will not force me to listen to nonsense that I wrote when I was a child. No more of those most foolish lines ! If you knew what it is to write and despise one's writing, you would not distress me. And since you will not speak of Crossjay to-night, allow me to retire."

" You know me, and therefore you know my contempt for verses, as a rule, Lætitia. But not for yours to me. Why should you call them foolish ? They expressed your feelings — I hold them sacred. They are something religious to me, not mere poetry. Perhaps the third verse is my favourite . . . "

" It will be more than I can bear ! "

" You were in earnest when you wrote them ? "

" I was very young, very enthusiastic, very silly."

" You were and are my image of constancy ! "

" It is an error, Sir Willoughby ; I am far from being the same."

" We are all older, I trust wiser. I am, I will own ; much wiser. Wise at last ! I offer you my hand."

She did not reply.

" I offer you my hand and name, Lætitia ! "

No response.

" You think me bound in honour to another ? "

She was mute.

" I am free. Thank heaven ! I am free to choose my mate — the woman I have always loved ! Freely and unreservedly, as I ask you to give your hand, I offer mine. You are the mistress of Patterne Hall ; my wife ! "

She had not a word.

" My dearest ! do you not rightly understand ? The hand I am offering you is disengaged. It is offered to the lady I respect above all others. I have made the discovery that I cannot love without respecting ; and as I will not marry without loving, it ensues that I am free — I am yours. At

last ? — your lips move : tell me the words. *Have always
loved*, I said. You carry in your bosom the magnet of constancy, and I, in spite of apparent deviations, declare to
you that I have never ceased to be sensible of the attraction. And now there is not an impediment. We two
against the world! we are one. Let me confess to an old
foible — perfectly youthful, and you will ascribe it to youth:
once I desired to absorb. I mistrusted; that was the reason:
I perceive it. You teach me the difference of an alliance
with a lady of intellect. The pride I have in you, Lætitia,
definitively cures me of that insane passion — call it an insatiable hunger. I recognize it as a folly of youth. I have,
as it were, gone the tour, to come home to you — at last? —
and live our manly life of comparative equals. At last,
then! But remember, that in the younger man you would
have had a despot — perhaps a jealous despot. Young men,
I assure you, are orientally inclined in their ideas of love.
Love gets a bad name from them. We, my Lætitia, do not
regard love as a selfishness. If it is, it is the essence of
life. At least it is our selfishness rendered beautiful. I
talk to you like a man who has found a compatriot in a
foreign land. It seems to me that I have not opened my
mouth for an age. I certainly have not unlocked my heart.
Those who sing for joy are not unintelligible to me. If I
had not something in me worth saying, I think I should
sing. In every sense you reconcile me to men and the
world, Lætitia. Why press you to speak ? I will be the
speaker. As surely as you know me, I know you;
and . . . "

Lætitia burst forth with, "No!"

" I do not know you ? " said he, searchingly mellifluous.

" Hardly."

" How not ? "

" I am changed."

" In what way ? "

" Deeply."

" Sedater ? "

" Materially."

" Colour will come back: have no fear; I promise it. If
you imagine you want renewing, *I* have the specific, I, my
love, I ! "

" Forgive me — will you tell me, Sir Willoughby, whether
you have broken with Miss Middleton ? "

" Rest satisfied, my dear Lætitia. She is as free as I am.
I can do no more than a man of honour should do. She
releases me. To-morrow or next day she departs. We,
Lætitia, you and I, my love, are home birds. It does not do
for the home bird to couple with the migratory. The little
imperceptible change you allude to, is nothing. Italy will
restore you. I am ready to stake my own health — never
yet shaken by a doctor of medicine : — I say medicine ad-
visedly, for there are Doctors of Divinity who would shake

giants: — that an Italian trip will send you back — that I shall bring you home from Italy a blooming bride.[1] You shake your head — despondently? My love, I guarantee it. Cannot I give you colour? Behold! Come to the light, look in the glass."

"I may redden," said Lætitia. "I suppose that is due to the action of the heart. I am changed. Heart, for any other purpose, I have not. I am like you, Sir Willoughby, in this: I could not marry without loving, and I do not know what love is, except that it is an empty dream."

"Marriage, my dearest . . . "

"You are mistaken."

"I will cure you, my Lætitia. Look to me, I am the tonic. It is not common confidence, but conviction. I, my love, I!"

"There is no cure for what I feel, Sir Willoughby."

"Spare me the formal prefix, I beg. You place your hand in mine, relying on me. I am pledged for the remainder. We end as we began: my request is for your hand — your hand in marriage."

"I cannot give it."

"To be my wife!"

"It is an honour: I must decline it."

"Are you quite well, Lætitia? I propose in the plainest terms I can employ, to make you Lady Patterne — mine."

"I am compelled to refuse."

"Why? Refuse? Your reason!"

"The reason has been named."

He took a stride to inspirit his wits.

"There's a madness comes over women at times, I know. Answer me, Lætitia: — by all the evidence a man can have, I could swear it: — but answer me: you loved me once?"

"I was an exceedingly foolish, romantic girl."

"You evade my question: I am serious. Oh!" he walked away from her, booming a sound of utter repudiation of her present imbecility, and hurrying to her side, said: "But it was manifest to the whole world! It was a legend. To love like Lætitia Dale, was a current phrase. You were an example, a light to women: no one was your match for devotion. You were a precious cameo, still gazing! And I was the object. You loved me. You loved me, you belonged to me, you were mine, my possession, my jewel; I was prouder of your constancy than of anything else that I had on earth. It was a part of the order of the universe to me. A doubt of it would have disturbed my creed. Why, good heaven! where are we? Is nothing solid on earth? You loved me!"

"I was childish indeed."

---

1. "Doctors of Divinity": His mind is on Dr. Middleton.

"You loved me passionately!"

"Do you insist on shaming me through and through, Sir Willoughby? I have been exposed enough."

"You cannot blot out the past: it is written, it is recorded. You loved me devotedly, silence is no escape. You loved me."

"I did."

"You never loved me, you shallow woman! 'I did!' As if there could be a cessation of a love! What are we to reckon on as ours? We prize a woman's love; we guard it jealously, we trust to it, dream of it; *there* is our wealth; there is our talisman! And when we open the casket, it has flown! — barren vacuity! — we are poorer than dogs. As well think of keeping a costly wine in potter's clay as love in the heart of a woman! There are women — women! Oh! they are all of a stamp — coin! Coin for any hand! It's a fiction, an imposture — they cannot love! They are the shadows of men. Compared with men, they have as much heart in them as the shadow beside the body! Lætitia!"

"Sir Willoughby."

"You refuse my offer?"

"I must."

"You refuse to take me for your husband?"

"I cannot be your wife."

"You have changed? . . . You have set your heart? . . . You could marry? . . . there is a man? . . . You could marry one! I will have an answer, I am sick of evasions. What was in the mind of heaven when women were created, will be the riddle to the end of the world! Every good man in turn has made the inquiry. I have a right to know who robs me — We may try as we like to solve it. — Satan is painted laughing! — I say I have a right to know who robs me. Answer me."

"I shall not marry."

"That is not an answer."

"I love no one."

"You loved me. — You are silent? — but you confessed it. Then you confess it was a love that could die! Are you unable to perceive how that redounds to my discredit? You loved me, you have ceased to love me. In other words, you charge me with incapacity to sustain a woman's love. You accuse me of inspiring a miserable passion that cannot last a lifetime! You let the world see that I am a man to be aimed at for a temporary mark! And simply because I happen to be in your neighbourhood at an age when a young woman is impressionable! You make a public example of me as a man for whom women may have a caprice, but that is all; he cannot enchain them; he fascinates passingly; they fall off. Is it just, for me to be taken up and cast down at your will? Reflect on that scandal! Shadows? Why, a man's shadow is faithful to him at least. What are women? There is not a comparison in nature that does not tower above them! not one that does not hoot at them! I, throughout my life guided by absolute deference to their weakness — paying them politeness, courtesy — whatever I touch I am happy in, except when I touch women! How is it? What is the mystery? Some monstrous explanation must exist. What can it be? I am favoured by fortune from my birth until I enter into relations with women! But will you be so good as to account for it in your defence of them? Oh! were the relations dishonourable, it would be quite another matter. *Then* they . . . I could recount . . . I disdain to chronicle such victories. Quite another matter! But they are flies, and I am something more stable. They are flies. I look beyond the day; I owe a duty to my line. They are flies. I foresee it, I shall be crossed in my fate so long as I fail to shun them — flies! Not merely born for the day, I maintain that they are spiritually ephemeral. — Well, my opinion of your sex is directly traceable to you. You may alter it, or fling another of us men out on the world with the old bitter experience. Consider this, that it is on your head if my ideal of women is wrecked. It rests with you to restore it. I love you. I discover that you are the one woman I have always loved. I come to you, I sue you, and suddenly — you have changed![2] 'I have changed: I am not the same.' What can it mean? 'I cannot marry: I love no one.' And you say you do not know what love is — avowing in the same breath that you did love me! Am I the empty dream? My hand, heart, fortune, name, are yours, at your feet: you kick them hence. I am here — you reject me. But why, for what mortal reason am I here other than my faith in your love? You drew me to you, to repel me, and have a wretched revenge."

"You know it is not that, Sir Willoughby."

"Have you any possible suspicion that I am still entangled, not, as I assure you I am, perfectly free in fact and in honour?"

"It is not that."

"Name it; for you see your power. Would you have me kneel to you, madam?"

"Oh! no; it would complete my grief."

"You feel grief? Then you believe in my affection, and you hurl it away. I have no doubt that as a poetess, you would say, love is eternal. And you have loved me. And you tell me you love me no more. You are not very logical, Lætitia Dale."

"Poetesses rarely are: if I am one, which I little pretend to be for writing silly verses. I have passed out of that delusion, with the rest."

2. "sue": woo.

"You shall not wrong those dear old days, Lætitia. I see them now; when I rode by your cottage and you were at your window, pen in hand, your hair straying over your forehead. Romantic, yes; not foolish. Why were you foolish in thinking of me? Some day I will commission an artist to paint me that portrait of you from my description. And I remember when we first whispered . . . I remember your trembling. You have forgotten — I remember. I remember our meeting in the park on the path to church. I remember the heavenly morning of my return from my travels, and the same Lætitia meeting me, stedfast and unchangeable. Could I ever forget? Those are ineradicable scenes; pictures of my youth, interwound with me. I may say, that as I recede from them, I dwell on them the more. Tell me, Lætitia, was there not a certain prophecy of your father's concerning us two? I fancy I heard of one. There was one."

"He was an invalid. Elderly people nurse illusions."

"Ask yourself, Lætitia, who is the obstacle to the fulfilment of his prediction? — truth, if ever a truth was foreseen on earth! You have not changed so far that you would feel *no* pleasure in gratifying him? I go to him to-morrow morning with the first light."

"You will compel me to follow, and undeceive him."

"Do so, and I denounce an unworthy affection you are ashamed to avow."

"That would be idle, though it would be base."

"Proof of love, then! For no one but you should it be done, and no one but you dare accuse me of a baseness."

"Sir Willoughby, you will let my father die in peace." *like DR. M*

"He and I together will contrive to persuade you."

"You tempt me to imagine that you want a wife at any cost."

"You, Lætitia, you."

"I am tired," she said. "It is late, I would rather not hear more. I am sorry if I have caused you pain. I suppose you to have spoken with candour. I defend neither my sex nor myself. I can only say, I am a woman as good as dead: happy to be made happy in my way, but so little alive that I cannot realize any other way. As for love, I am thankful to have broken a spell. You have a younger woman in your mind; I am an old one: I have no ambition and no warmth. My utmost prayer is to float on the stream — a purely physical desire of life: I have no strength to swim. Such a woman is not the wife for you, Sir Willoughby. Good night."

"One final word. Weigh it. Express no conventional regrets. Resolutely you refuse?"

"Resolutely I do."

"You refuse?"

"Yes."

"I have sacrificed my pride for nothing! You refuse?"

"Yes."

"Humbled myself! And this is the answer! You do refuse?"

"I do."

"Good night, Lætitia Dale."

He gave her passage.

"Good night, Sir Willoughby."

"I am in your power," he said in a voice between supplication and menace that laid a claw on her, and she turned and replied, —

"You will not be betrayed."

"I can trust you? . . ."

"I go home to-morrow before breakfast."

"Permit me to escort you upstairs."

"If you please: but I see no one here either to-night or to-morrow."

"It is for the privilege of seeing the last of you."

They withdrew.

Young Crossjay listened to the drumming of his head. Somewhere in or over the cavity a drummer rattled tremendously.

Sir Willoughby's laboratory-door shut with a slam.

Crossjay tumbled himself off the ottoman. He stole up to the unclosed drawing-room door, and peeped. Never was a boy more thoroughly awakened. His object was to get out of the house and go through the night avoiding everything human, for he was big with information of a character that he knew to be of the nature of gunpowder, and he feared to explode. He crossed the hall. In the passage to the scullery, he ran against Colonel De Craye.

"So there you are," said the colonel, "I've been hunting you."

Crossjay related that his bed-room door was locked and the key gone, and Sir Willoughby sitting up in the laboratory.

Colonel De Craye took the boy to his own room, where Crossjay lay on a sofa, comfortably covered over and snug in a swelling pillow; but he was restless; he wanted to speak, to bellow, to cry; and he bounced round to his left side, and bounced to his right, not knowing what to think, except that there was treason to his adored Miss Middleton.

"Why, my lad, you're not half a campaigner," the colonel called out to him; attributing his uneasiness to the material discomfort of the sofa: and Crossjay had to swallow the taunt, bitter though it was. A dim sentiment of impropriety in unburdening his overcharged mind on the subject of Miss Middleton to Colonel De Craye, restrained him from defending himself; and so he heaved and tossed about till daybreak. At an early hour, while his hospitable friend, who looked very handsome in profile half breast and head above the sheets, continued to slumber,

Crossjay was on his legs and away.

"He says I'm not half a campaigner, and a couple of hours of bed are enough for me," the boy thought proudly, and snuffed the springing air of the young sun on the fields. A glance back at Patterne Hall dismayed him, for he knew not how to act, and he was immoderately combustible, too full of knowledge for self-containment; much too zealously-excited on behalf of his dear Miss Middleton to keep silent for many hours of the day.

CHAPTER 41

THE REV. DR. MIDDLETON, CLARA, AND SIR WILLOUGHBY

WHEN Master Crossjay tumbled down the stairs, Lætitia was in Clara's room, speculating on the various mishaps which might have befallen that battered youngster; and Clara listened anxiously after Lætitia had run out, until she heard Sir Willoughby's voice; which in some way satisfied her that the boy was not in the house.

She waited, expecting Miss Dale to return; then undressed, went to bed, tried to sleep. She was tired of strife. Strange thoughts for a young head shot through her: as, that it is possible for the sense of duty to counteract distaste; and that one may live a life apart from one's admirations and dislikes: she owned[1] the singular strength of Sir Willoughby in outwearying: she asked herself how much she had gained by struggling: — every effort seemed to expend her spirit's force, and rendered her less able to get the clear vision of her prospects, as though it had sunk her deeper: the contrary of her intention to make each further step confirm her liberty. Looking back, she marvelled at the things she had done. Looking round, how ineffectual they appeared! She had still the great scene of positive rebellion to go through with her father.

The anticipation of that was the cause of her extreme discouragement. He had not spoken to her since he became aware of her attempted flight: but the scene was coming; and besides the wish not to inflict it on him, as well as to escape it herself, the girl's peculiar unhappiness lay in her knowledge that they were alienated and stood opposed, owing to one among the more perplexing masculine weaknesses, which she could not hint at, dared barely think of, and would not name in her meditations. Diverting to other subjects, she allowed herself to exclaim: "Wine! wine!" in renewed wonder of what there could be in wine to entrap venerable men and obscure their judge-

1. Confessed.

ments. She was too young to consider that her being very much in the wrong gave all the importance to the cordial glass in a venerable gentleman's appreciation of his dues. Why should he fly from a priceless wine to gratify the caprices of a fantastical child guilty of seeking to commit a breach of faith ? He harped on those words. Her fault was grave. No doubt the wine coloured it to him, as a drop or two will do in any cup: still her fault was grave.

She was too young for such considerations. She was ready to expatiate on the gravity of her fault, so long as the humiliation assisted to her disentanglement: her snared nature in the toils would not permit her to reflect on it further. She had never accurately perceived it: for the reason perhaps that Willoughby had not been moving in his appeals: but, admitting the charge of waywardness, she had come to terms with conscience, upon the understanding that she was to perceive it and regret it and do penance for it by-and-by: — by renouncing marriage altogether ? How light a penance !

In the morning, she went to Lætitia's room, knocked and had no answer.

She was informed at the breakfast-table of Miss Dale's departure. The ladies Eleanor and Isabel feared it to be a case of urgency at the cottage. No one had seen Vernon, and Clara requested Colonel De Craye to walk over to the cottage for news of Crossjay. He accepted the commission, simply to obey and be in her service: assuring her, however, that there was no need to be disturbed about the boy. He would have told her more, had not Dr. Middleton led her out.

Sir Willoughby marked a lapse of ten minutes by his watch. His excellent aunts had ventured a comment on his appearance, that frightened him lest he himself should be the person to betray his astounding discomfiture. He regarded his conduct as an act of madness, and Lætitia's as no less that of a madwoman — happily mad ! Very happily mad indeed ! Her rejection of his ridiculously generous proposal seemed to show an intervening hand in his favour, that sent her distraught at the right moment. He entirely trusted her to be discreet; but she was a miserable creature, who had lost the one last chance offered her by Providence, and furnished him with a signal instance of the mediocrity of woman's love.

Time was flying. In a little while Mrs. Mountstuart would arrive. He could not fence her without a design in his head; he was destitute of an armoury if he had no scheme: he racked the brain only to succeed in rousing phantasmal vapours. Her infernal "Twice !" would cease now to apply to Lætitia: it would be an echo of Lady Busshe. Nay, were all in the secret, *Thrice* jilted ! might become the universal roar. And this, he reflected bitterly, of a man whom nothing but duty to his line had arrested from being the most mischievous of his class with women! Such is our reward for uprightness!

At the expiration of fifteen minutes by his watch, he struck a knuckle on the library-door. Dr. Middleton held it open to him.

"You are disengaged, sir?"

"The sermon is upon the paragraph which is toned to awaken the clerk," replied the Rev. Doctor.

Clara was weeping.

Sir Willoughby drew near her solicitously.

Dr. Middleton's mane of silvery hair was in a state bearing witness to the vehemence of the sermon, and Willoughby said: "I hope, sir, you have not made too much of a trifle."

"I believe, sir, that I have produced an effect, and that was the point in contemplation."

"Clara! my dear Clara!" Willoughby touched her.

"She sincerely repents her conduct, I may inform you," said Dr. Middleton.

"My love!" Willoughby whispered. "We have had a misunderstanding. I am at a loss to discover where I have been guilty, but I take the blame, all the blame. I implore you not to weep. Do me the favour to look at me. I would not have had you subjected to any interrogation whatever."

"You are not to blame," Clara said on a sob.

"Undoubtedly Willoughby is not to blame. It was not he who was bound on a runaway errand in flagrant breach of duty and decorum, nor he who inflicted a catarrh on a brother of my craft and cloth," said her father.[2]

"The clerk, sir, has pronounced Amen," observed Willoughby.

"And no man is happier to hear an ejaculation that he has laboured for with so much sweat of his brow than the parson, I can assure you," Dr. Middleton mildly groaned. "I have notions of the trouble of Abraham. A sermon of that description is an immolation of the parent, however it may go with the child."

Willoughby soothed his Clara.

"I wish I had been here to share it. I might have saved you some tears. I may have been hasty in our little dissensions. I will acknowledge that I have been. My temper is often irascible."

"And so is mine!" exclaimed Dr. Middleton. "And yet I am not aware that I made the worse husband for it. Nor do I rightly comprehend how a probably justly excite-able temper can stand for a plea in mitigation of an attempt at an outrageous breach of faith."

"The sermon is over, sir."

"Reverberations!" the Rev. Doctor waved his arm pla-

2. Professor Crooklyn's sniffles are laid to Clara's account.

cably. "Take it for thunder heard remote."

"Your hand, my love," Willoughby murmured.

The hand was not put forth.

Dr. Middleton remarked the fact. He walked to the window, and perceiving the pair in the same position when he faced about, he delivered a cough of admonition.

"It is cruel!" said Clara.

"That the <u>owner</u> of your hand should petition you for it?" inquired her father.

She sought refuge in a fit of tears.

Willoughby bent above her, mute.

"Is a scene that is hardly conceivable as a parent's obligation once in a lustrum, to be repeated within the half hour?" shouted her father.[3]

She drew up her shoulders and shook; let them fall and dropped her head.

"My dearest! your hand!" fluted Willoughby.

The hand surrendered; it was much like the <u>icicle</u> of a sudden thaw.

Willoughby squeezed it to his ribs.

Dr. Middleton marched up and down the room with his arms locked behind him. The silence between the young people seemed to denounce his presence.

He said cordially: "Old Hiems has but to withdraw for buds to burst. ' Jam ver egelidos refert tepores.'[4] The equinoctial fury departs. I will leave you for a term."

Clara and Willoughby simultaneously raised their faces with opposing expressions.

"My girl?" her father stood by her, laying gentle hand on her.

"Yes, papa, I will come out to you," she replied to his apology for the rather heavy weight of his vocabulary, and smiled.

"No, sir, I beg you will remain," said Willoughby.

"I keep you frost-bound."

Clara did not deny it.

Willoughby emphatically did.

Then which of them was the more lover-like? Dr. Middleton would for the moment have supposed his daughter.

Clara said: "Shall you be on the lawn, papa?"

Willoughby interposed. "Stay, sir; give us your blessing."

"That you have." Dr. Middleton hastily motioned the paternal ceremony in outline.

"A few minutes, papa," said Clara.

"Will she name the day?" came eagerly from Willoughby.

"I cannot!" Clara cried in extremity.

3. "once in a lustrum": once in five years.
4. "Now spring brings back balmy warmth": Catullus XLVI; "equinoctial fury": seasonal storms.

"The day is important on its arrival," said her father,
"but I apprehend the decision to be of the chief importance
at present. First prime your piece of artillery, my
friend."

"The decision is taken, sir."

"Then I will be out of way of the firing. Hit what day
you please."

Clara checked herself on an impetuous exclamation.
It was done that her father might not be detained.

Her astute self-compression sharpened Willoughby as
much as it mortified and terrified him. He understood
how he would stand in an instant were Dr. Middleton
absent. Her father was the tribunal she dreaded, and
affairs must be settled and made irrevocable while he was
with them. To sting the blood of the girl, he called her his
darling, and half enwound her, shadowing forth a salute.[5]

She strung her body to submit, seeing her father take it
as a signal for his immediate retirement.

Willoughby was upon him before he reached the door.

"Hear us out, sir. Do not go. Stay, at my entreaty.
I fear we have not come to a perfect reconcilement."

"If that is your opinion," said Clara, "it is good reason
for not distressing my father."

"Dr. Middleton, I love your daughter. I wooed her
and won her; I had your consent to our union, and I was
the happiest of mankind. In some way, since her coming
to my house, I know not how — she will not tell me, or
cannot — I offended. One may be innocent and offend. I
have never pretended to impeccability, which is an admission that I may very naturally offend. My appeal to her
is for an explanation or for pardon. I obtain neither.
Had our positions been reversed, oh! not for any real
offence — not for the worst that can be imagined — I think
not — I hope not — could I have been tempted to propose
the dissolution of our engagement. To love is to love,
with me; an engagement a solemn bond. With all my
errors I have that merit of utter fidelity — to the world
laughable! I confess to a multitude of errors; I have that
single merit, and am not the more estimable in your
daughter's eyes on account of it, I fear. In plain words,
I am, I do not doubt, one of the fools among men; of the
description of human dog commonly known as faithful —
whose destiny is that of a tribe. A man who cries out
when he is hurt is absurd, and I am not asking for sympathy. Call me luckless. But I abhor a breach of faith.
A broken pledge is hateful to me. I should regard it in
myself as a form of suicide. There are principles which
civilized men must contend for. Our social fabric is
based on them. As my word stands for me, I hold others
to theirs. If that is not done, the world is more or less

5. Threatening a kiss.

a carnival of counterfeits. In this instance — Ah! Clara, my love! and you have principles: you have inherited, you have been indoctrinated with them: have I, then, in my ignorance offended past penitence, that you, of all women? . . . And without being able to name my sin! — Not only for what I lose by it, but in the abstract, judicially — apart from the sentiment of personal interest, grief, pain, and the possibility of my having to endure that which no temptation would induce me to commit: — judicially; — I fear, sir, I am a poor forensic orator . . ."

"The situation, sir, does not demand a Cicero: proceed," said Dr. Middleton, balked in his approving nods at the right true things delivered.

"Judicially, I am bold to say, though it may appear a presumption in one suffering acutely, I abhor a breach of faith."

Dr. Middleton brought his nod down low upon the phrase he had anticipated. "And I," said he, "personally, and presently, abhor a breach of faith. Judicially? Judicially to examine, judicially to condemn: but does the judicial mind detest? I think, sir, we are not on the Bench when we say that we abhor: we have unseated ourselves. Yet our abhorrence of bad conduct is very certain. You would signify, impersonally: which suffices for this exposition of your feelings."

He peered at the gentleman under his brows, and resumed: "She has had it, Willoughby; she has had it in plain Saxon and in uncompromising Olympian. There is, I conceive, no necessity to revert to it."

"Pardon me, sir, but I am still unforgiven."

"You must babble out the rest between you. I am about as much at home as a turkey with a pair of pigeons."

"Leave us, father," said Clara.

"First join our hands, and let me give you that title, sir."

"Reach the good man your hand, my girl; forthright, from the shoulder, like a brave boxer. Humour a lover. He asks for his own."

"It is more than I can do, father."

"How, it is more than you can do? You are engaged to him, a plighted woman."

"I do not wish to marry."

"The apology is inadequate."

"I am unworthy . . ."

"Chatter! chatter!"

"I beg him to release me."

"Lunacy!"

"I have no love to give him."

"Have you gone back to your cradle, Clara Middleton?"

"Oh! leave us, dear father."

"My offence, Clara, my offence! What is it? Will you only name it?"

"Father, will you leave us? We can better speak together . . ."

"We have spoken, Clara, how often!" Willoughby resumed, "with what result? — that you loved me, that you have ceased to love me: that your heart was mine, that you have withdrawn it, plucked it from me: that you request me to consent to a sacrifice involving my reputation, my life. And what have I done? I am the same, unchangeable. I loved and love you: my heart was yours, and is, and will be yours for ever. You are my affianced — that is, my wife. What have I done?"

"It is indeed useless," Clara sighed.

"Not useless, my girl, that you should inform this gentleman, your affianced husband, of the ground of the objection you conceived against him."

"I cannot say."

"Do you know?"

"If I could name it, I could hope to overcome it."

Dr. Middleton addressed Sir Willoughby.

"I verily believe we are directing the girl to dissect a caprice. Such things are seen large by these young people, but as they have neither organs nor arteries, nor brains, nor membranes, dissection and inspection will be alike profitlessly practised. Your inquiry is natural for a lover, whose passion to enter into relations with the sex is ordinarily in proportion to his ignorance of the stuff composing them. At a particular age they traffic in whims, which are, I presume, the spiritual of hysterics; and are indubitably preferable, so long as they are not pushed too far. Examples are not wanting to prove that a flighty initiative on the part of the male is a handsome corrective. In that case, we should probably have had the roof off the house, and the girl now at your feet. Ha!"

"Despise me, father. I am punished for ever thinking myself the superior of any woman," said Clara.

"Your hand out to him, my dear, since he is for a formal reconciliation: and I can't wonder."

"Father! I have said I do not . . . I have said I cannot . . ."

"By the most merciful! what? what? the name for it! words for it!"

"Do not frown on me, father. I wish him happiness. I cannot marry him. I do not love him."

"You will remember that you informed me aforetime that you did love him."

"I was ignorant . . . I did not know myself. I wish him to be happy."

"You deny him the happiness you wish him!"

"It would not be for his happiness were I to wed him."

"Oh!" burst from Willoughby.

"You hear him. He rejects your prediction, Clara

Middleton."

She caught her clasped hands up to her throat. "Wretched, wretched, both!"

"And you have not a word against him, miserable girl!"

"Miserable! I am."

"It is the cry of an animal!"

"Yes, father."

"You feel like one? Your behaviour is of that shape. You have not a word?"

"Against myself: not against him."

"And I, when you speak so generously, am to yield you? give you up?" cried Willoughby. "Ah! my love, my Clara, impose what you will on me; not that. It is too much for man. It is, I swear it, beyond my strength."

"Pursue, continue the strain: 't is in the right key," said Dr. Middleton, departing.

Willoughby wheeled and waylaid him with a bound.

"Plead for me, sir; you are all-powerful. Let her be mine, she shall be happy, or I will perish for it. I will call it on my head.—Impossible! I cannot lose her. Lose you, my love? It would be to strip myself of every blessing of body and soul. It would be to deny myself possession of grace, beauty, wit, all the incomparable charms of loveliness of mind and person in woman, and plant myself in a desert. You are my mate, the sum of everything I call mine. Clara, I should be less than man to submit to such a loss. Consent to it? But I love you! I worship you! How can I consent to lose you? . . ."

He saw the eyes of the desperately wily young woman slink sideways. Dr. Middleton was pacing at ever shorter lengths closer by the door.

"You hate me?" Willoughby sank his voice.

"If it should turn to hate!" she murmured.

"Hatred of your husband?"

"I could not promise," she murmured more softly in her wilyness.

"Hatred?" he cried aloud, and Dr. Middleton stopped in his walk and flung up his head; "Hatred of your husband? of the man you have vowed to love and honour? Oh! no. Once mine, it is not to be feared. I trust to my knowledge of your nature; I trust in your blood, I trust in your education. Had I nothing else to inspire confidence, I could trust in your eyes. And Clara, take the confession: I would rather be hated than lose you. For if I lose you, you are in another world, out of this one holding me in its death-like cold: but if you hate me, we are together, we are still together. Any alliance, any, in preference to separation!"

Clara listened with a critical ear. His language and tone were new; and comprehending that they were in part addressed to her father, whose phrase: "A breach of

faith:" he had so cunningly used, disdain of the actor
prompted the extreme blunder of her saying — frigidly
though she said it, —

"You have not talked to me in this way before."

"Finally," remarked her father, summing up the situation to settle it from that little speech, "he talks to you
in this way now; and you are under my injunction to
stretch your hand out to him for a symbol of union, or to
state your objection to that course. He, by your admission, is at the terminus, and there, failing the why not,
must you join him."

Her head whirled. She had been severely flagellated
and weakened previous to Willoughby's entrance. Language to express her peculiar repulsion eluded her. She
formed the words, and perceived that they would not
stand to bear a breath from her father. She perceived too
that Willoughby was as ready with his agony of supplication as she with hers. If she had tears for a resource, he
had gestures, quite as eloquent; and a cry of her loathing
of the union would fetch a countervailing torrent of the
man's love. — What could she say? he is an Egoist? The
epithet has no meaning in such a scene. *Invent!*
shrieked the hundred-voiced instinct of dislike within her,
and alone with her father, alone with Willoughby, she could
have invented some equivalent, to do her heart justice for
the injury it sustained in her being unable to name the
true and immense objection: but the pair in presence paralyzed her. She dramatized them each springing forward
by turns, with crushing rejoinders. The activity of her
mind revelled in giving them a tongue, but would not do it
for herself. Then ensued the inevitable consequence of an
incapacity to speak at the heart's urgent dictate: heart and
mind became divided. One throbbed hotly, the other hung
aloof; and mentally, while the sick inarticulate heart kept
clamouring, she answered it with all that she imagined for
those two men to say. And she dropped poison on it to
still its reproaches: bidding herself remember her fatal
postponements in order to preserve the seeming of consistency before her father; calling it hypocrite; asking
herself, what was she! who loved her! And thus beating
down her heart, she completed the mischief with a piercing
view of the foundation of her father's advocacy of Willoughby, and more lamentably asked herself what her value
was, if she stood bereft of respect for her father.

Reason, on the other hand, was animated by her better
nature to plead his case against her: she clung to her respect for him, and felt herself drowning with it: and she
echoed Willoughby consciously, doubling her horror with
the consciousness, in crying out on a world where the most
sacred feelings are subject to such lapses. It doubled her
horror, that she should echo the man; but it proved that
she was no better than he: only some years younger.

Those years would soon be outlived: after which, he and she would be of a pattern. She was unloved: she did no harm to any one by keeping her word to this man: she had pledged it, and it would be a breach of faith not to keep it. No one loved her. Behold the quality of her father's love! To give him happiness was now the principal aim for her, her own happiness being decently buried; and here he was happy: why should she be the cause of his going and losing the poor pleasure he so much enjoyed?

The idea of her devotedness flattered her feebleness. She betrayed signs of hesitation; and in hesitating, she looked away from a look at Willoughby, thinking (so much against her nature was it to resign herself to him) that it would not have been so difficult with an ill-favoured man. With one horribly ugly, it would have been a horrible exultation to cast off her youth and take the fiendish leap.

Unfortunately for Sir Willoughby, he had his reasons for pressing impatience; and seeing her deliberate, seeing her hasty look at his fine figure, his opinion of himself combined with his recollection of a particular maxim of the Great Book to assure him that her resistance was over: chiefly owing, as he supposed, to his physical perfections.

Frequently indeed, in the contest between gentlemen and ladies, have the maxims of the Book stimulated the assailant to victory. They are rosy with blood of victims. To hear them is to hear a horn that blows the mort: has blown it a thousand times.[6] It is good to remember how often they have succeeded, when, for the benefit of some future Lady Vauban, who may bestir her wits to gather maxims for the inspiriting of the Defence, the circumstance of a failure has to be recorded.[7]

Willoughby could not wait for the melting of the snows. He saw full surely the dissolving process; and sincerely admiring and coveting her as he did, rashly this ill-fated gentleman attempted to precipitate it, and so doing arrested.

Whence might we draw a note upon yonder maxim, in words akin to these: Make certain ere a breath come from thee that thou be not a frost.

"Mine! She is mine!" he cried: "mine once more! mine utterly! mine eternally!" and he followed up his devouring exclamations in person as she, less decidedly, retreated. She retreated as young ladies should ever do, two or three steps, and he would not notice that she had become an angry Dian, all arrows: her maidenliness in surrendering pleased him.[8] Grasping one fair hand, he just allowed her to edge away from his embrace, crying: "Not a syllable of what I have gone through! You shall not have

6. "horn that blows the mort": the call sounded at the death of the stag.
7. "Lady Vauban": Vauban was a seventeenth-century French expert in defensive fortifications; jocularly, a lady intent on saying no.
8. "Dian, all arrows": The goddess of the hunt is always portrayed with bow and sharp arrows.

to explain it, my Clara. I will study you more diligently, to be guided by you, my darling. If I offend again, my wife will not find it hard to speak what my bride withheld — I do not ask why : perhaps not able to weigh the effect of her reticence : not at that time, when she was younger and less experienced, estimating the sacredness of a plighted engagement. It is past, we are one, my dear sir and father. You may leave us now."

"I profoundly rejoice to hear that I may," said Dr. Middleton.

Clara writhed her captured hand.

"No, papa, stay. It is an error, an error. You must not leave me. Do not think me utterly, eternally, belonging to any one but you. No one shall say I am his but you."

"Are you quicksands, Clara Middleton, that nothing can be built on you? Whither is a flighty head and a shifty will carrying the girl ? "

"Clara and I, sir," said Willoughby.

"And so you shall," said the Doctor, turning about.

"Not yet, papa : " Clara sprang to him.

"Why, you, you, you, it was you who craved to be alone with Willoughby ! " her father shouted ; "and here we are rounded to our starting-point, with the solitary difference that now you do not want to be alone with Willoughby. First I am bidden go ; next I am pulled back ; and judging by collar and coat-tail, I suspect you to be a young woman to wear an angel's temper threadbare before you determine upon which one of the tides driving him to and fro you intend to launch on yourself. Where is your mind ? "

Clara smoothed her forehead.

"I wish to please you, papa."

"I request you to please the gentleman who is your appointed husband."

"I am anxious to perform my duty."

"That should be a satisfactory basis for you, Willoughby ; — as girls go ! "

"Let me, sir, simply entreat to have her hand in mine before you."

"Why not, Clara ? "

"Why an empty ceremony, papa ? "

"The implication is, that she is prepared for the important one, friend Willoughby."

"Her hand, sir ; the reassurance of her hand in mine under your eyes : — after all that I have suffered, I claim it, I think I claim it reasonably, to restore me to confidence."

"Quite reasonably ; which is not to say, necessarily ; but, I will add, justifiably ; and it may be, sagaciously, when dealing with the volatile."

"And here," said Willoughby, "is my hand."

Clara recoiled.

He stepped on. Her father frowned. She lifted both her

hands from the shrinking elbows, darted a look of repulsion at her pursuer, and ran to her father, crying: " Call it my mood! I am volatile, capricious, flighty, very foolish. But you see that I attach a real meaning to it, and feel it to be binding: I cannot think it an empty ceremony, if it is before you. Yes, only be a little considerate to your moody girl. She will be in a fitter state in a few hours. Spare me this moment; I must collect myself. I thought I was free; I thought he would not press me. If I give my hand hurriedly now, I shall, I know, immediately repent it. There is the picture of me! But, papa, I mean to try to be above that, and if I go and walk by myself, I shall grow calm to perceive where my duty lies . . ."

" In which direction shall you walk ? " said Willoughby.

" Wisdom is not upon a particular road," said Dr. Middleton.

" I have a dread, sir, of that one which leads to the railway-station."

" With some justice!" Dr. Middleton sighed over his daughter.

Clara coloured to deep crimson: but she was beyond anger—and was rather gratified by an offence coming from Willoughby.

" I will promise not to leave his grounds, papa."

" My child, you have threatened to be a breaker of promises."

" Oh ! " she wailed. "But I will make it a vow to you."

" Why not make it a vow to me this moment, for this gentleman's contentment, that he shall be your husband within a given period! "

" I will come to you voluntarily. I burn to be alone."

" I shall lose her ! " exclaimed Willoughby in heartfelt earnest.

" How so ? " said Dr. Middleton. " I have her, sir, if you will favour me by continuing in abeyance.— You will come within an hour voluntarily, Clara: and you will either at once yield your hand to him, or you will furnish reasons, and they must be good ones, for withholding it."

" Yes, papa."

" You will ? "

" I will."

" Mind, I say *reasons*."

" Reasons, papa. If I have none . . ."

" If you have none that are to my satisfaction, you implicitly, and instantly, and cordially obey my command."

" I will obey."

" What more would you require ? " Dr. Middleton bowed to Sir Willoughby in triumph.

" Will she . . ."

" Sir! Sir!"

" She is your daughter, sir. I am satisfied."

" She has perchance wrestled with her engagement, as the

aboriginals of a land newly discovered by a crew of adventurous colonists do battle with the garments imposed on them by our considerate civilization ; — ultimately to rejoice with excessive dignity in the wearing of a battered cocked-hat and trowsers not extending to the shanks : but she did not break her engagement, sir ; and we will anticipate, that moderating a young woman's native wildness, she may, after the manner of my comparison, take a similar pride in her fortune in good season."

Willoughby had not leisure to sound the depth of Dr. Middleton's compliment. He had seen Clara gliding out of the room during the delivery ; and his fear returned on him that, not being won, she was lost.

"She has gone ;" her father noticed her absence. "She does not waste time in the mission to procure that astonishing product of a shallow soil, her reasons; if such be the object of her search. But no : it signifies that she deems herself to have need of composure — nothing more. No one likes to be turned about; we like to turn ourselves about: and in the question of an act to be committed, we stipulate that it shall be our act — girls and others. After the lapse of an hour, it will appear to her as her act. — Happily, Willoughby, we do not dine away from Patterne to-night."

"No, sir."

"It may be attributable to a sense of deserving, but I could plead guilty to a weakness for old Port to-day."

"There shall be an extra bottle, sir."

"All going favourably with you, as I have no cause to doubt," said Dr. Middleton, with the motion of wafting his host out of the library.

CHAPTER 42

SHOWS THE DIVINING ARTS OF A PERCEPTIVE MIND

STARTING from the Hall, a few minutes before Dr. Middleton and Sir Willoughby had entered the drawing-room overnight, Vernon parted company with Colonel De Craye at the park-gates, and betook himself to the cottage of the Dales, where nothing had been heard of his wanderer ; and he received the same disappointing reply from Dr. Corney, out of the bed-room window of the genial physician, whose astonishment at his covering so long a stretch of road at night for news of a boy like Crossjay — gifted with the lives of a cat — became violent and rapped Punch-like blows on the window-sill at Vernon's refusal to take shelter and rest.[1] Vernon's excuse was that he had "no one but that fellow to

---

1. "Punch-like blows": In puppet shows,   of a cudgel.
the dwarf Punch always makes free use

care for," and he strode off, naming a farm five miles distant.
Dr. Corney howled an invitation to early breakfast to him,
in the event of his passing on his way back, and retired to
bed to think of him. The result of a variety of conjectures
caused him to set Vernon down as Miss Middleton's knight,
and he felt a strong compassion for his poor friend.
"Though," thought he, "a hopeless attachment is as pretty
an accompaniment to the tune of life as a gentleman might
wish to have, for it's one of those big doses of discord which
make all the minor ones fit in like an agreeable harmony,
and so he shuffles along as pleasantly as the fortune-favoured, when they come to compute!"

Sir Willoughby was the fortune-favoured in the little
doctor's mind; that high-stepping gentleman having wealth,
and public consideration, and the most ravishing young lady
in the world for a bride. Still, though he reckoned all these
advantages enjoyed by Sir Willoughby at their full value,
he could imagine the ultimate balance of good fortune to be
in favour of Vernon. But to do so, he had to reduce the
whole calculation to the extreme abstract, and feed his lean
friend, as it were, on dew and roots; and the happy effect
for Vernon lay in a distant future, on the borders of old age,
where he was to be blest with his lady's regretful preference,
and rejoice in the fruits of good constitutional habits. The
reviewing mind was Irish. Sir Willoughby was a character
of man profoundly opposed to Dr. Corney's nature; the
latter's instincts bristled with antagonism — not to his race,
for Vernon was of the same race, partly of the same blood,
and Corney loved him: the type of person was the annoyance. And the circumstance of its prevailing successfulness
in the country where he was placed, while it held him silent
as if under a law, heaped stores of insurgency in the Celtic
bosom. Corney contemplating Sir Willoughby, and a trotting kern governed by Strongbow, have a point of likeness
between them;[2] with the point of difference, that Corney
was enlightened to know of a friend better adapted for eminent station, and especially better adapted to please a lovely
lady — could these high-bred Englishwomen but be taught
to conceive another idea of manliness than the formal
carved-in-wood idol of their national worship!

Dr. Corney breakfasted very early, without seeing Vernon. He was off to a patient while the first lark of the
morning carolled above, and the business of the day not yet
fallen upon men in the shape of cloud, was happily inter-
mixed with nature's hues and pipings. Turning off the
highroad up a green lane, an hour later, he beheld a youngster prying into a hedge head and arms, by the peculiar
strenuous twist of whose hinder parts, indicative of a frame
plunged on the pursuit in hand, he clearly distinguished
young Crossjay. Out came eggs. The doctor pulled up.

2. "kern governed by Strongbow": an   Englishman.
Irish bog-warrior ruled by an invading

"What bird?" he bellowed.

"Yellowhammer," Crossjay yelled back.

"Now, sir, you'll drop a couple of those eggs in the nest."

"Don't order me," Crossjay was retorting: "Oh! it's you, Dr. Corney. Good morning. I said that, because I always do drop a couple back. I promised Mr. Whitford I would, and Miss Middleton too."

"Had breakfast?"

"Not yet."

"Not hungry?"

"I should be if I thought about it."

"Jump up."

"I think I'd rather not, Dr. Corney."

"And you'll just do what Dr. Corney tells you; and set your mind on rashers of curly fat bacon and sweetly-smoking coffee, toast, hot cakes, marmalade and damson-jam. Wide go the fellow's nostrils, and there's water at the dimples of his mouth! Up, my man."

Crossjay jumped up beside the doctor, who remarked, as he touched his horse: "I don't want a man this morning, though I'll enlist you in my service if I do. You're fond of Miss Middleton?"

Instead of answering, Crossjay heaved the sigh of love that bears a burden.

"And so am I," pursued the doctor: "You'll have to put up with a rival. It's worse than fond: I'm in love with her. How do you like that?"

"I don't mind how many *love* her," said Crossjay.

"You're worthy of a gratuitous breakfast in the front parlour of the best hotel of the place they call Arcadia.[3] And how about your bed last night?"

"Pretty middling."

"Hard, was it, where the bones haven't cushion?"

"I don't care for bed. A couple of hours, and that's enough for me."

"But you're fond of Miss Middleton anyhow, and that's a virtue."

To his great surprise, Dr. Corney beheld two big round tears force their way out of this tough youngster's eyes, and all the while the boy's face was proud.

Crossjay said, when he could trust himself to disjoin his lips: "I want to see Mr. Whitford."

"Have you got news for him?"

"I've something to ask him. It's about what I ought to do."

"Then, my boy, you have the right name addressed in the wrong direction: for I found you turning your shoulders on Mr. Whitford. And he has been out of his bed, hunting you all the unholy night you've made it for him. That's

3. The idyllic pastoral paradise of Greek legend is Arcadia.

melancholy. What do you say to asking my advice?"

Crossjay sighed. "I can't speak to anybody but Mr. Whitford."

"And you're hot to speak to him?"

"I want to."

"And I found you running away from him. You're a curiosity, Mr. Crossjay Patterne."

"Ah! so'd anybody be who knew as much as I do," said Crossjay, with a sober sadness that caused the doctor to treat him seriously.

"The fact is," he said, "Mr. Whitford is beating the country for you. My best plan will be to drive you to the Hall."

"I'd rather not go to the Hall," Crossjay spoke resolutely.

"You won't see Miss Middleton anywhere but at the Hall."

"I don't want to see Miss Middleton, if I can't be a bit of use to her."

"No danger threatening the lady, is there?"

Crossjay treated the question as if it had not been put.

"Now, tell me," said Dr. Corney, "would there be a chance for me, supposing Miss Middleton were disengaged?"

The answer was easy. "I'm sure she would n't."

"And why, sir, are you so cock sure?"

There was no saying; but the doctor pressed for it, and at last Crossjay gave his opinion that she would take Mr. Whitford.

The doctor asked why; and Crossjay said it was because Mr. Whitford was the best man in the world. To which, with a lusty "Amen to that," Dr. Corney remarked: "I should have fancied Colonel De Craye would have had the first chance: he's more of a lady's man."

Crossjay surprised him again by petulantly saying: "Don't."

The boy added: "I don't want to talk, except about birds and things. What a jolly morning it is! I saw the sun rise. No rain to-day. You're right about hungry, Dr. Corney!"

The kindly little man swung his whip. Crossjay informed him of his disgrace at the Hall, and of every incident connected with it, from the tramp to the baronet, save Miss Middleton's adventure, and the night-scene in the drawing-room. A strong smell of something left out struck Dr. Corney, and he said: "You'll not let Miss Middleton know of my affection. After all, it's only a little bit of love. But, as Patrick said to Kathleen, when she owned to such a little bit, 'that's the best bit of all!' and he was as right as I am about hungry."

Crossjay scorned to talk of loving, he declared. "I never tell Miss Middleton what I feel. Why, there's Miss Dale's cottage!"

"It's nearer to your empty inside than my mansion," said the doctor, "and we'll stop just to inquire whether a bed's to be had for you there to-night, and if not, I'll have you with me, and bottle you, and exhibit you, for you're a rare specimen. Breakfast you may count on, from Mr. Dale. I spy a gentleman."

"It's Colonel De Craye."

"Come after news of you."

"I wonder!"

"Miss Middleton sends him; of course she does."

Crossjay turned his full face to the doctor. "I haven't seen her for such a long time! But he saw me last night, and he might have told her that, if she's anxious.— Good morning, colonel. I've had a good walk and a capital drive, and I'm as hungry as the boat's crew of Captain Bligh."[4]

He jumped down.

The colonel and the doctor saluted smiling.

"I've rung the bell," said De Craye.

A maid came to the gate, and upon her steps appeared Miss Dale, who flung herself at Crossjay, mingling kisses and reproaches. She scarcely raised her face to the colonel more than to reply to his greeting, and excuse the hungry boy for hurrying indoors to breakfast.

"I'll wait," said De Craye. He had seen that she was paler than usual. So had Dr. Corney; and the doctor called to her concerning her father's health. She reported that he had not yet risen, and took Crossjay to herself.

"That's well," said the doctor, "if the invalid sleeps long. The lady is not looking so well, though. But ladies vary; they show the mind on the countenance, for want of the punching we meet with to conceal it; they're like military flags for a funeral or a gala; one day furled, and next day streaming. Men are ships' figure-heads, about the same for a storm or a calm, and not too handsome, thanks to the ocean. It's an age since we encountered last, colonel: on board the Dublin boat, I recollect, and a night it was."

"I recollect that you set me on my legs, doctor."

"Ah, and you'll please to notify that Corney's no quack at sea, by favour of the monks of the Chartreuse, whose elixir has power to still the waves.[5] And we hear that miracles are done with!"

"Roll a physician and a monk together, doctor!"

"True: it'll be a miracle if they combine. Though the cure of the soul is often the entire and total cure of the body: and it's maliciously said, that the body given over to our treatment is a signal to set the soul flying. By the way, colonel, that boy has a trifle on his mind."

"I suppose he has been worrying a farmer or a game-keeper."

---

4. Of "Mutiny on the Bounty" fame—a legendary hero/villain of the British navy.
5. To prevent De Craye from getting sea-sick on the Dublin boat, Corney evidently prescribed the liqueur known as Chartreuse.

"Try him. You'll find him tight. He's got Miss Middleton on the brain. There's a bit of a secret; and he's not so cheerful about it."

"We'll see," said the colonel.

Dr. Corney nodded. "I have to visit my patient here presently. I'm too early for him: so I'll make a call or two on the lame birds that are up," he remarked, and drove away.

De Craye strolled through the garden. He was a gentleman of those actively perceptive wits which, if ever they reflect, do so by hops and jumps: upon some dancing mirror within, we may fancy. He penetrated a plot in a flash; and in a flash he formed one; but in both cases, it was after long hovering and not over-eager deliberation, by the patient exercise of his quick perceptives. The fact that Crossjay was considered to have Miss Middleton on the brain, threw a series of images of everything relating to Crossjay for the last forty hours into relief before him: and as he did not in the slightest degree speculate on any one of them, but merely shifted and surveyed them, the falcon that he was in spirit as well as in his handsome face leisurely allowed his instinct to direct him where to strike. A reflective disposition has this danger in action, that it commonly precipitates conjecture for the purpose of working upon probabilities with the methods and in the tracks to which it is accustomed: and to conjecture rashly is to play into the puzzles of the maze. He who can watch circling above it awhile, quietly viewing, and collecting in his eye, gathers matter that makes the secret thing discourse to the brain by weight and balance; he will get either the right clue or none; more frequently none; but he will escape the entanglement of his own cleverness, he will always be nearer to the enigma than the guesser or the calculator, and he will retain a breadth of vision forfeited by them. He must, however, to have his chance of success, be acutely besides calmly perceptive, a reader of features, audacious at the proper moment.

De Craye wished to look at Miss Dale. She had returned home very suddenly, not, as it appeared, owing to her father's illness: and he remembered a redness of her eyelids when he passed her on the corridor one night. She sent Crossjay out to him as soon as the boy was well filled. He sent Crossjay back with a request. She did not yield to it immediately. She stepped to the front door reluctantly, and seemed disconcerted. De Craye begged for a message to Miss Middleton. There was none to give. He persisted. But there was really none at present, she said.

"You won't entrust me with the smallest word?" said he, and set her visibly thinking whether she could despatch a word. She could not; she had no heart for messages.

"I shall see her in a day or two, Colonel De Craye."

"She will miss you severely."

"We shall soon meet."

"And poor Willoughby!"

Lætitia coloured and stood silent.

A butterfly of some rarity allured Crossjay.

"I fear he has been doing mischief," she said. "I cannot get him to look at me."

"His appetite is good?"

"Very good indeed."

De Craye nodded. A boy with a noble appetite is never a hopeless lock.

The colonel and Crossjay lounged over the garden.

"And now," said the colonel, "we'll see if we can't arrange a meeting between you and Miss Middleton. You're a lucky fellow, for she's always thinking of you."

"I know I'm always thinking of her," said Crossjay.

"If ever you're in a scrape, she's the person you must go to."

"Yes, if I know where she is!"

"Why, generally she'll be at the Hall."

There was no reply: Crossjay's dreadful secret jumped to his throat. He certainly was a weaker lock for being full of breakfast.

"I want to see Mr. Whitford so much," he said.

"Something to tell him?"

"I don't know what to do: I don't understand it!" The secret wriggled to his mouth. He swallowed it down: "Yes, I want to talk to Mr. Whitford."

"He's another of Miss Middleton's friends."

"I know he is. He's true steel."

"We're all her friends, Crossjay. I flatter myself I'm a Toledo when I'm wanted.[6] How long had you been in the house last night before you ran into me?"

"I don't know, sir: I fell asleep for some time, and then I woke! . . ."

"Where did you find yourself?"

"I was in the drawing-room."

"Come, Crossjay, you're not a fellow to be scared by ghosts? You looked it when you made a dash at my midriff."

"I don't believe there are such things. Do you, colonel? You can't!"

"There's no saying. We'll hope not; for it would n't be fair fighting. A man with a ghost to back him'd beat any ten. We could n't box him, or play cards, or stand a chance with him as a rival in love. Did you, now, catch a sight of a ghost?"

"They were n't ghosts!" Crossjay said what he was sure of, and his voice pronounced his conviction.

6. "Toledo": a blade of Toledo steel, the best.

"I doubt whether Miss Middleton is particularly happy," remarked the colonel. "Why? Why, you upset her, you know, now and then."

The boy swelled. "I'd do . . . I'd go . . . I would n't have her unhappy . . . It's that! that's it! And I don't know what I ought to do. I wish I could see Mr. Whitford."

"You get into such headlong scrapes, my lad."

"I was n't in any scrape yesterday."

"So you made yourself up a comfortable bed in the drawing-room? Lucky Sir Willoughby did n't see you."

"He did n't, though!"

"A close shave, was it?"

"I was under a cover of something silk."

"He woke you?"

"I suppose he did. I heard him."

"Talking?"

"He was talking."

"What! talking to himself?"

"No."

The secret threatened Crossjay to be out or suffocate him.

De Craye gave him a respite.

"You like Sir Willoughby, don't you?"

Crossjay produced a still-born affirmative.

"He's kind to you," said the colonel; "he'll set you up and look after your interests."

"Yes, I like him," said Crossjay, with his customary rapidity in touching the subject; "I like him; he's kind, and all that, and tips and plays with you, and all that; but I never can make out why he would n't see my father when my father came here to see him ten miles, and had to walk back ten miles in the rain, to go by rail a long way, down home, as far as Devonport, because Sir Willoughby would n't see him, though he was at home, my father saw. We all thought it so odd: and my father would n't let us talk much about it. My father's a very brave man."

"Captain Patterne is as brave a man as ever lived," said De Craye.

"I'm positive you'd like him, colonel."

"I know of his deeds, and I admire him, and that's a good step to liking."

He warmed the boy's thoughts of his father.

"Because, what they say at home is, a little bread and cheese, and a glass of ale, and a rest, to a poor man — lots of great houses will give you that, and we would n't have asked for more than that. My sisters say they think Sir Willoughby must be selfish. He's awfully proud; and perhaps it was because my father was n't dressed well enough. But what can we do? We're very poor at home, and lots of us, and all hungry. My father says he is n't paid very well for his services to the Government. He's only a marine."

"He 's a hero!" said De Craye.

"He came home very tired, with a cold, and had a doctor. But Sir Willoughby did send him money, and mother wished to send it back, and my father said she was not like a woman — with our big family. He said he thought Sir Willoughby an extraordinary man."

"Not at all; very common; indigenous," said De Craye. "The art of cutting is one of the branches of a polite education in this country, and you 'll have to learn it, if you expect to be looked on as a gentleman and a Patterne, my boy. I begin to see how it is Miss Middleton takes to you so. Follow her directions. But I hope you did not listen to a private conversation. Miss Middleton would not approve of that."

"Colonel De Craye, how could I help myself? I heard a lot before I knew what it was. There was poetry!"

"Still, Crossjay, if it was important! — was it?"

The boy swelled again, and the colonel asked him: "Does Miss Dale know of your having played listener?"

"She!" said Crossjay. "Oh! I could n't tell *her*."

He breathed thick: then came a threat of tears. "She would n't do anything to hurt Miss Middleton. I 'm sure of that. It was n't her fault. She — there goes Mr. Whitford!" Crossjay bounded away.

The colonel had no inclination to wait for his return. He walked fast up the road, not perspicuously conscious that his motive was to be well in advance of Vernon Whitford: to whom, after all, the knowledge imparted by Crossjay would be of small advantage. That fellow would probably trot off to Willoughby to row him for breaking his word to Miss Middleton! There are men, thought De Craye, who see nothing, feel nothing.

He crossed a stile into the wood above the lake, where, as he was in the humour to think himself signally lucky, espying her, he took it as a matter of course that the lady who taught his heart to leap should be posted by the Fates. And he wondered little at her power, for rarely had the world seen such union of princess and sylph as in that lady's figure. She stood holding by a beech-branch, gazing down on the water.

She had not heard him. When she looked she flushed at the spectacle of one of her thousand thoughts, but she was not startled; the colour overflowed a grave face.

"And 't is not quite the first time that Willoughby has played this trick!" De Craye said to her, keenly smiling with a parted mouth.

Clara moved her lips to recall remarks introductory to so abrupt and strange a plunge.

He smiled in that peculiar manner of an illuminated comic perception : for the moment he was all falcon; and he surprised himself more than Clara, who was not in the mood to take surprises. It was the sight of her which had animated him to strike his game; he was down on it.

Another instinct at work (they spring up in twenties oftener than in twos when the heart is the hunter) prompted him to directness and quickness, to carry her on the flood of the discovery.

She regained something of her mental self-possession as soon as she was on a level with a meaning she had not yet inspected; but she had to submit to his lead, distinctly perceiving where its drift divided to the forked currents of what might be in his mind and what was in hers.

"Miss Middleton, I bear a bit of a likeness to the messenger to the glorious despot — my head is off if I speak not true! Everything I have is on the die.[7] Did I guess wrong your wish? — I read it in the dark, by the heart. But here's a certainty: Willoughby sets you free."

"You have come from him?" she could imagine nothing else, and she was unable to preserve a disguise; she trembled.

"From Miss Dale."

"Ah!" Clara drooped: "she told me that once."

"'T is the fact that tells it now."

"You have not seen him since you left the house?"

"Darkly: clear enough: not unlike the hand of destiny — through a veil. He offered himself to Miss Dale last night, about between the witching hours of twelve and one."

"Miss Dale? . . ."

"Would she other? Could she? The poor lady has languished beyond a decade. She's love in the feminine person."

"Are you speaking seriously, Colonel De Craye?"

"Would I dare to trifle with you, Miss Middleton?"

"I have reason to know it cannot be."

"If I have a head, it is a fresh and blooming truth. And more — I stake my vanity on it!"

"Let me go to her." She stepped.

"Consider," said he.

"Miss Dale and I are excellent friends. It would not seem indelicate to her. She has a kind of regard for me, through Crossjay. — Oh! can it be? There must be some delusion. You have seen — you wish to be of service to me; you may too easily be deceived. Last night? — he last night . . . ? And this morning!"

"'T is not the first time our friend has played the trick, Miss Middleton."

"But this is incredible: that last night . . . and this morning, in my father's presence, he presses! . . . You have seen Miss Dale? — Everything is possible of him: they were together, I know. Colonel De Craye, I have not the slightest chance of concealment with you. I think I

---

7. On one cast of the dice.

felt that when I first saw you.   Will you let me hear why
you are so certain ? "

"Miss Middleton, when I first had the honour of looking
on you, it was in a posture that necessitated my looking up,
and morally so it has been since.   I conceived that Willoughby had won the greatest prize on earth.   And next
I was led to the conclusion that he had won it to lose it.
Whether he much cares, is the mystery I have n't leisure to
fathom.   Himself is the principal consideration with himself, and ever was."

"You discovered it ! " said Clara.

"He uncovered it," said De Craye.   "The miracle was,
that the world would n't see.   But the world is a piggy-
wiggy world for the wealthy fellow who fills a trough for
it, and that he has always very sagaciously done.   Only
women besides myself have detected him.   I have never
exposed him ; I have been an observer pure and simple :
and because I apprehended another catastrophe — making
something like the fourth, to my knowledge, one being
public. . . ."

"You knew Miss Durham ? "

"And Harry Oxford too.   And they 're a pair as happy
as blackbirds in a cherry-tree, in a summer sunrise, with the
owner of the garden asleep.   Because of that apprehension
of mine, I refused the office of best man till Willoughby had
sent me a third letter.   He insisted on my coming.   I came,
saw, and was conquered.[8]   I trust with all my soul I did not
betray myself.   I owed that duty to my position of concealing it.   As for entirely hiding that I had used my eyes, I
can't say : they must answer for it."

The colonel was using his eyes with an increasing suavity
that threatened more than sweetness.

"I believe you have been sincerely kind," said Clara.
"We will descend to the path round the lake."

She did not refuse her hand on the descent, and he let it
escape the moment the service was done.   As he was per-
forming the admirable character of the man of honour, he
had to attend to the observance of details ; and sure of her
though he was beginning to feel, there was a touch of the
unknown in Clara Middleton which made him fear to stamp
assurance ; despite a barely resistible impulse, coming of his
emotions and approved by his maxims.   He looked at the
hand, now a free lady's hand.   Willoughby settled, his
chance was great.   Who else was in the way ?   No one.
He counselled himself to wait for her : she might have
ideas of delicacy.   Her face was troubled, speculative ; the
brows clouded, the lips compressed.

"You have not heard this from Miss Dale ? " she said.

"Last night they were together : this morning she fled.
I saw her this morning distressed.   She is unwilling to send

8. De Craye adapts Caesar's laconic "I came, I saw, I conquered."

you a message : she talks vaguely of meeting you some days
hence. And it is not the first time he has gone to her for
his consolation."

"That is not a proposal," Clara reflected. "He is too
prudent. He did not propose to her at the time you mention. Have you not been hasty, Colonel De Craye ? "

Shadows crossed her forehead. She glanced in the direction of the house, and stopped her walk.

"Last night, Miss Middleton, there was a listener."

"Who ? "

"Crossjay was under that pretty silk coverlet worked by
the Miss Patternes. He came home late, found his door
locked, and dashed downstairs into the drawing-room, where
he snuggled up and dropped asleep. The two speakers
woke him ; they frightened the poor dear lad in his love for
you, and after they had gone, he wanted to run out of the
house, and I met him, just after I had come back from my
search, bursting, and took him to my room, and laid him on
the sofa, and abused him for not lying quiet. He was restless as a fish on a bank. When I woke in the morning he
was off. Dr. Corney came across him somewhere on the
road and drove him to the cottage. I was ringing the bell.
Corney told me the boy had you on his brain, and was
miserable, so Crossjay and I had a talk."

"Crossjay did not repeat to you the conversation he had
heard ? " said Clara.

"No."

She smiled rejoicingly, proud of the boy, as she walked on.

"But you 'll pardon me, Miss Middleton — and I 'm for
him as much as you are — if I was guilty of a little
angling."

"My sympathies are with the fish."

"The poor fellow had a secret that hurt him. It rose to
the surface crying to be hooked, and I spared him twice or
thrice, because he had a sort of holy sentiment I respected,
that none but Mr. Whitford ought to be his father con-
fessor."

"Crossjay ! " she cried, hugging her love of the boy.

"The secret was one not to be communicated to Miss
Dale of all people."

"He said that ? "

"As good as the very words. She informed me too, that
she could n't induce him to face her straight."

"Oh ! that looks like it. And Crossjay was unhappy ?
Very unhappy ? "

"He was just where tears are on the brim, and would
have been over, if he were not such a manly youngster."

"It looks . . ." She reverted in thought to Willoughby,
and doubted, and blindly stretched hands to her recollection of the strange old monster she had discovered in him.
Such a man could do anything.

That conclusion fortified her to pursue her walk to the

house and give battle for freedom. Willoughby appeared
to her scarce human, unreadable, save by the key that she
could supply. She determined to put faith in Colonel De
Craye's marvellous divination of circumstances in the dark.
Marvels are solid weapons when we are attacked by real
prodigies of nature. Her countenance cleared. She conversed with De Craye of the polite and the political world,
throwing off her personal burden completely, and charming
him.

At the edge of the garden, on the bridge that crossed the
haha from the park, he had a second impulse, almost a
warning within, to seize his heavenly opportunity to ask for
thanks and move her tender lowered eyelids to hint at his
reward.[9] He repressed it, doubtful of the wisdom.

Something like "heaven forgives me!" was in Clara's
mind, though she would have declared herself innocent
before the scrutator.[10]

CHAPTER 43

IN WHICH SIR WILLOUGHBY IS LED TO THINK THAT THE ELEMENTS HAVE CONSPIRED AGAINST HIM

CLARA had not taken many steps in the garden before she
learnt how great was her debt of gratitude to Colonel De
Craye. Willoughby and her father were awaiting her. De
Craye, with his ready comprehension of circumstances,
turned aside unseen among the shrubs. She advanced
slowly.

"The vapours, we may trust, have dispersed?" her father
hailed her.

"One word, and these discussions are over, we dislike
them equally," said Willoughby.

"No scenes," Dr. Middleton added. "Speak your decision,
my girl, pro formâ, seeing that he who has the right
demands it, and pray release me." [1]

Clara looked at Willoughby.

"I have decided to go to Miss Dale for her advice."

There was no appearance in him of a man that has been
shot.

"To Miss Dale? — for advice?"

Dr. Middleton invoked the Furies. "What is the signification of this new freak?"

"Miss Dale must be consulted, papa."

"Consulted with reference to the disposal of your hand
in marriage?"

"She must be."

"Miss Dale, do you say?"

"I do, papa."

---

9. "haha": a hedged ditch, named from
the echo it created.

10. A careful scrutinizer.
1. "pro fôrma": formally.

Dr. Middleton regained his natural elevation from the bend of body habitual with men of an established sanity, pedagogues and others, who are called on at odd intervals to inspect the magnitude of the infinitesimally absurd in human nature : small, that is, under the light of reason, immense in the realms of madness.

His daughter profoundly confused him. He swelled out his chest, remarking to Willoughby : "I do not wonder at your scared expression of countenance, my friend. To discover yourself engaged to a girl as mad as Cassandra, without a boast of the distinction of her being sun-struck, can be no specially comfortable enlightenment.[2] I am opposed to delays, and I will not have a breach of faith committed by daughter of mine."

"Do not repeat those words," Clara said to Willoughby.

He started. She had evidently come armed. But how, within so short a space ? What could have instructed her ? And in his bewilderment he gazed hurriedly above, gulped air, and cried: "Scared, sir ? I am not aware that my countenance can show a scare. I am not accustomed to sue for long: I am unable to sustain the part of humble supplicant. She puts me out of harmony with creation — We are plighted, Clara. It is pure waste of time to speak of soliciting advice on the subject."

"Would it be a breach of faith for me to break my engagement ?" she said.

"You ask ?"

"It is a breach of sanity to propound the interrogation," said her father.

She looked at Willoughby ! "Now ?"

He shrugged haughtily.

"Since last night ?" said she.

"Last night ?"

"Am I not released ?"

"Not by me."

"By your act."

"My dear Clara!"

"Have you not virtually disengaged me ?"

"I who claim you as mine ?"

"Can you ?"

"I do and must."

"After last night ?"

"Tricks! shufflings! Jabber of a barbarian woman upon the evolutions of a serpent!" exclaimed Dr. Middleton. "You were to capitulate, or to furnish reasons for your refusal. You have none. Give him your hand, girl, according to the compact. I praised you to him for returning within the allotted term, and now forbear to disgrace yourself and me."

2. Apollo, the sun-god, gave to the Trojan princess Cassandra the gift of prophecy, but with this curse: that nobody would ever believe her. People naturally thought her mad: sunstroke is Dr. Middleton's learned joke.

"Is he perfectly free to offer his ? Ask him, papa."

"Perform your duty. Do let us have peace!"

"Perfectly free! as on the day when I offered it first," Willoughby frankly waved his honourable hand.

His face was blanched: enemies in the air seemed to have whispered things to her: he doubted the fidelity of the Powers above.

"Since last night ? " said she.

"Oh! if you insist, I reply, since last night."

"You know what I mean, Sir Willoughby."

"Oh! certainly."

"You speak the truth ? "

"'*Sir* Willoughby'!" her father ejaculated in wrath. "But will you explain what you mean, epitome that you are of all the contradictions and mutabilities ascribed to women from the beginning! 'Certainly,' he says, and knows no more than I. She begs grace for an hour, and returns with a fresh store of evasions, to insult the man she has injured. It is my humiliation to confess that our share in this contract is rescued from public ignominy by his generosity. Nor can I congratulate him on his fortune, should he condescend to bear with you to the utmost; for instead of the young woman I supposed myself to be bestowing on him, I see a fantastical planguncula enlivened by the wanton tempers of a nursery chit.[3] If one may conceive a meaning in her, in miserable apology for such behaviour, some spirit of jealousy informs the girl."

"I can only remark, that there is no foundation for it," said Willoughby. "I am willing to satisfy you, Clara. Name the person who discomposes you. I can scarcely imagine one to exist: but who can tell ? "

She could name no person. The detestable imputation of jealousy would be confirmed if she mentioned a name: and indeed Lætitia was not to be named.

He pursued his advantage: "Jealousy is one of the fits I am a stranger to, — I fancy, sir, that gentlemen have dismissed it. I speak for myself. — But I can make allowances. In some cases, it is considered a compliment; and often a word will soothe it. The whole affair is so senseless! However, I will enter the witness-box, or stand at the prisoner's bar! Anything to quiet a distempered mind."

"Of you, sir," said Dr. Middleton, "might a parent be justly proud."

"It is not jealousy; I could not be jealous!" Clara cried, stung by the very passion; and she ran through her brain for a suggestion to win a sign of meltingness if not esteem from her father. She was not an iron maiden, but one among the nervous natures which live largely in the moment, though she was then sacrificing it to her

---

3. "planguncula": a silly little doll—the word is from Cicero; "chit": baggage, minx.

nature's deep dislike. "You may be proud of me again, papa."

She could hardly have uttered anything more impolitic.

"Optume: but deliver yourself *ad rem*," he rejoined, alarmingly pacified. "Firmavit fidem. Do you likewise, and double on us no more like puss in the field."[4]

"I wish to see Miss Dale," she said.

Up flew the Rev. Doctor's arms in wrathful despair resembling an imprecation.

"She is at the cottage. You could have seen her," said Willoughby.

Evidently she had not.

"Is it untrue, that last night, between twelve o'clock and one, in the drawing-room, you proposed marriage to Miss Dale?"

He became convinced that she must have stolen downstairs during his colloquy with Lætitia, and listened at the door.

"On behalf of old Vernon?" he said, lightly laughing. "The idea is not novel, as you know. They are suited, if they could see it.—Lætitia Dale and my cousin Vernon Whitford, sir."

"Fairly schemed, my friend, and I will say for you, you have the patience, Willoughby—of a husband!"

Willoughby bowed to the encomium, and allowed some fatigue to be visible. He half yawned: "I claim no happier title, sir," and made light of the weariful discussion.

Clara was shaken: she feared that Crossjay had heard incorrectly, or that Colonel De Craye had guessed erroneously. It was too likely that Willoughby should have proposed Vernon to Lætitia.

There was nothing to reassure her save the vision of the panic amazement of his face at her persistency in speaking of Miss Dale. She could have declared on oath that she was right, while admitting all the suppositions to be against her. And unhappily all the Delicacies (a doughty battalion for the defence of ladies until they enter into difficulties and are shorn of them at a blow, bare as dairymaids), all the body-guard of a young gentlewoman, the drawing-room sylphides, which bear her train, which wreathe her hair, which modulate her voice and tone her complexion, which are arrows and shield to awe the creature man, forbade her utterance of what she felt, on pain of instant fulfilment of their oft-repeated threat of late to leave her to the last remnant of a protecting sprite. She could not, as in a dear melodrama, from the aim of a pointed finger denounce him, on the testimony of her instincts, false of speech, false in deed. She could not even declare that she doubted his truthfulness. The refuge of a sullen fit, the refuge of tears,

---

4. "Optume": fine, splendid; "ad rem": pertinent to the matter at hand. "Firmavit fidem": he has given his word; "puss in the field": the hare, which dodges and turns to elude the hounds.

the pretext of a mood, were denied her now by the rigour of those laws of decency which are a garment to ladies of pure breeding.

"One more respite, papa," she implored him, bitterly conscious of the closer tangle her petition involved, and, if it must be betrayed of her, perceiving in an illumination how the knot might become so woefully Gordian that haply in a cloud of wild events the intervention of a gallant gentleman out of heaven, albeit in the likeness of one of earth, would have to cut it : her cry within, as she succumbed to weakness, being fervider : "Anything but marry this one ! "[5] She was faint with strife and dejected, a condition in the young when their imaginative energies hold revel uncontrolled and are projectively desperate.

"No respite !" said Willoughby genially.

"And I say, no respite !" observed her father. "You have assumed a position that has not been granted you, Clara Middleton."

"I cannot bear to offend you, father."

"Him ! Your duty is not to offend him. Address your excuses to him. I refuse to be dragged over the same ground, to reiterate the same command perpetually."

"If authority is deputed to me, I claim you," said Willoughby.

"You have not broken faith with me ? "

"Assuredly not, or would it be possible for me to press my claim ? "

"And join the right hand to the right," said Dr. Middleton : "no, it would not be possible. What insane root she has been nibbling, I know not, but she must consign herself to the guidance of those whom the gods have not abandoned, until her intellect is liberated. She was once . . . there : I look not back : — if she it was, and no simulacrum of a reasonable daughter. I welcome the appearance of my friend Mr. Whitford. He is my sea-bath and supper on the beach of Troy, after the day's battle and dust."

Vernon walked straight up to them : an act unusual with him, for he was shy of committing an intrusion.

Clara guessed by that, and more by the dancing frown of speculative humour he turned on Willoughby, that he had come charged in support of her. His forehead was curiously lively, as of one who has got a surprise well under, to feed on its amusing contents.

"Have you seen Crossjay, Mr. Whitford ? " she said.

"I 've pounced on Crossjay ; his bones are sound."

"Where did he sleep ? "

"On a sofa, it seems."

She smiled, with good hope — Vernon had the story.

Willoughby thought it just to himself that he should defend his measure of severity.

<hr />

5. "knot . . . Gordian": The great knot in Gordium, Asia Minor, was so intricate that nobody could untie it. Alexander on his way to the East cut it with his sword.

" The boy lied ; he played a double game."

" For which he should have been reasoned with at the Grecian portico of a boy," said the Rev. Doctor.[6]

" My system is different, sir. I could not inflict what I would not endure myself."

" So is Greek excluded from the later generations ; and you leave a field, the most fertile in the moralities in youth, unploughed and unsown. Ah ! well. This growing too fine is our way of relapsing upon barbarism. Beware of over-sensitiveness, where nature has plainly indicated her alternative gateway of knowledge. And now, I presume, I am at liberty."

" Vernon will excuse us for a minute or two."

" I hold by Mr. Whitford now I have him."

" I 'll join you in the laboratory, Vernon," Willoughby nodded bluntly.

" We will leave them, Mr. Whitford. They are at the time-honoured dissension upon a particular day, that for the sake of dignity, blushes to be named."

" What day ? " said Vernon, like a rustic.

" *The* day, these people call it."

Vernon sent one of his vivid eyeshots from one to the other. His eyes fixed on Willoughby's with a quivering glow, beyond amazement, as if his humour stood at furnace heat, and absorbed all that came.

Willoughby motioned him to go.

" Have you seen Miss Dale, Mr. Whitford ? " said Clara.
He answered : " No.   Something has shocked her."

" Is it her feeling for Crossjay ? "

" Ah," Vernon said to Willoughby, " your pocketing of the key of Crossjay's bed-room door was a masterstroke ! "

The celestial irony suffused her, and she bathed and swam in it, on hearing its dupe reply : " My methods of discipline are short.   I was not aware that she had been to his door."

" But I may hope that Miss Dale will see me," said Clara.
" We are in sympathy about the boy."

" Mr. Dale might be seen. He seems to be of a divided mind with his daughter," Vernon rejoined.   " She has locked herself up in her room."

" He is not the only father in that unwholesome predicament," said Dr. Middleton.

" He talks of coming to you, Willoughby."

" Why to me ? "   Willoughby chastened his irritation :
" He will be welcome, of course.   It would be better that the boy should come."

" If there is a chance of your forgiving him," said Clara.

" Let the Dales know I am prepared to listen to the boy, Vernon.   There can be no necessity for Mr. Dale to drag himself here."

6. "Grecian portico of a boy": his bottom, by which, through schoolmasterly
beatings, he might be induced to learn
Greek.

" How are Mr. Dale and his daughter of a divided mind, Mr. Whitford ? " said Clara.

Vernon simulated an uneasiness. With a vacant gaze that enlarged around Willoughby and was more discomforting than intentness, he replied : " Perhaps she is unwilling to give him her entire confidence, Miss Middleton."

"In which respect, then, our situations present their solitary point of unlikeness in resemblance, for I have it in excess," observed Dr. Middleton.

Clara dropped her eyelids for the wave to pass over. " It struck me that Miss Dale was a person of the extremest candour."

" Why should we be prying into the domestic affairs of the Dales ! " Willoughby interjected, and drew out his watch, merely for a diversion ; he was on tiptoe to learn whether Vernon was as well instructed as Clara, and hung to the view that he could not be, while drenching in the sensation that he was : — and if so, what were the Powers above but a body of conspirators ? He paid Lætitia that compliment. He could not conceive the human betrayal of the secret. Clara's discovery of it had set his common sense adrift.

" The domestic affairs of the Dales do not concern me," said Vernon.

" And yet, my friend," Dr. Middleton balanced himself, and with an air of benevolent slyness, the import of which did not awaken Willoughby until too late, remarked : " They might concern you. I will even add, that there is a probability of your being not less than the fount and origin of this division of father and daughter, though Willoughby in the drawing-room last night stands accuseably the agent."

" Favour me, sir, with an explanation," said Vernon, seeking to gather it from Clara.

Dr. Middleton threw the explanation upon Willoughby.

Clara communicated as much as she was able in one of those looks of still depth which say, Think ! and without causing a thought to stir, take us into the pellucid mind.

Vernon was enlightened before Willoughby had spoken. His mouth shut rigidly, and there was a springing increase of the luminous wavering of his eyes. Some star that Clara had watched at night was like them in the vivid wink and overflow of its light. Yet, as he was perfectly sedate, none could have suspected his blood to be chasing wild with laughter, and his frame strung to the utmost to keep it from volleying. So happy was she in his aspect, that her chief anxiety was to recover the name of the star whose shining beckons and speaks, and is in the quick of spirit-fire. It is the sole star which on a night of frost and strong moonlight preserves an indomitable fervency : that she remembered, and the picture of a hoar earth and a lean Orion in flooded heavens, and the star beneath, Eastward of him : but the name ! the name ! — She heard Willoughby indistinctly.[7]

"Oh, the old story ; another effort ; you know my wish ; a failure, of course, and no thanks on either side, I suppose I must ask your excuse. — They neither of them see what's good for them, sir."

"Manifestly, however," said Dr. Middleton, "if one may opine from the division we have heard of, the father is disposed to back your nominee."

"I can't say ; as far as I am concerned, I made a mess of it."

Vernon withstood the incitement to acquiesce, but he sparkled with his recognition of the fact.

"You meant well, Willoughby."

"I hope so, Vernon."

"Only you have driven her away."

"We must resign ourselves."

"It won't affect me, for I'm off to-morrow."

"You see, sir, the thanks I get."

"Mr. Whitford," said Dr. Middleton, "you have a tower of strength in the lady's father."

"Would you have me bring it to bear upon the lady, sir ? "

"Wherefore not ? "

"To make her marriage a matter of obedience to her father ? "

"Ay, my friend, a lusty lover would have her gladly on those terms, well knowing it to be for the lady's good. What do you say, Willoughby ? "

"Sir ! Say ? What can I say ? Miss Dale has not plighted her faith. Had she done so, she is a lady who would never dishonour it."

"She is an ideal of constancy, who would keep to it though it had been broken on the other side," said Vernon, and Clara thrilled.

"I take that, sir, to be a statue of constancy, modelled upon which, a lady of our flesh may be proclaimed as graduating for the condition of idiocy," said Dr. Middleton.

"But faith is faith, sir."

"But the broken is the broken, sir, whether in porcelain or in human engagements : and all that the one of the two continuing faithful, I should rather say, regretful, can do, is to devote the remainder of life to the picking up of the fragments ; an occupation properly to be pursued, for the comfort of mankind, within the enclosure of an appointed asylum."

"You destroy the poetry of sentiment, Dr. Middleton."

"To invigorate the poetry of nature, Mr. Whitford."

"Then you maintain, sir, that when faith is broken by one, the engagement ceases, and the other is absolutely free ? "

7. "Orion": Orion the hunter is a constellation suggesting Vernon Whitford the lean pedestrian; but it is not the star Clara is trying to think of, just near to it.

"I do; I am the champion of that platitude, and sound that knell to the sentimental world; and since you have chosen to defend it, I will appeal to Willoughby, and ask him if he would not side with the world of good sense in applauding the nuptials of man or maid married within a month of a jilting?"

Clara slipped her arm under her father's.

"Poetry, sir," said Willoughby, "I never have been hypocrite enough to pretend to understand or care for."

Dr. Middleton laughed. Vernon too seemed to admire his cousin for a reply that rang in Clara's ears as the dullest ever spoken. Her arm grew cold on her father's. She began to fear Willoughby again.

He depended entirely on his agility to elude the thrusts that assailed him. Had he been able to believe in the treachery of the Powers above, he would at once have seen design in these deadly strokes, for his feelings had rarely been more acute than at the present crisis; and he would then have led away Clara, to wrangle it out with her, relying on Vernon's friendliness not to betray her to her father: but a wrangle with Clara promised no immediate fruits, nothing agreeable; and the lifelong trust he had reposed in his protecting genii, obscured his intelligence to evidence he would otherwise have accepted on the spot, on the faith of his delicate susceptibility to the mildest impressions which wounded him. Clara might have stooped to listen at the door: she might have heard sufficient to create a suspicion. But Vernon was not in the house last night; she could not have communicated it to him, and he had not seen Lætitia, who was besides trustworthy, an admirable if a foolish and ill-fated woman.

Preferring to consider Vernon a pragmatical moralist played upon by a sententious drone, he thought it politic to detach them, and vanquish Clara while she was in the beaten mood, as she had appeared before Vernon's vexatious arrival.

"I'm afraid, my dear fellow, you are rather too dainty and fussy for a very successful wooer," he said. "It's beautiful on paper, and absurd in life. We have a bit of private business to discuss. We will go inside, sir, I think. I will soon release you."

Clara pressed her father's arm.

"More?" said he.

"Five minutes. There's a slight delusion to clear, sir. My dear Clara, you will see with different eyes."

"Papa wishes to work with Mr. Whitford."

Her heart sank to hear her father say: "No, 't is a lost morning. I must consent to pay tax of it for giving another young woman to the world. I have a daughter! You will, I hope, compensate me, Mr. Whitford, in the afternoon. Be not downcast. I have observed you meditative of late. You will have no clear brain so long as that stuff is on the mind.

I could venture to propose to do some pleading for you, should it be needed for the prompter expedition of the affair."

Vernon briefly thanked him, and said:

"Willoughby has exerted all his eloquence, and you see the result: you have lost Miss Dale and I have not won her. He did everything that one man can do for another in so delicate a case: even to the repeating of her famous birthday verses to him, to flatter the poetess. His best efforts were foiled by the lady's indisposition for me."

"Behold," said Dr. Middleton, as Willoughby, electrified by the mention of the verses, took a sharp stride or two, "you have in him an advocate who will not be rebuffed by one refusal, and I can affirm that he is tenacious, pertinacious as are few. Justly so. Not to believe in a lady's No, is the approved method of carrying that fortress built to yield. Although unquestionably to have a young man pleading in our interests with a lady, counts its objections. Yet Willoughby being notoriously engaged, may be held to enjoy the privileges of his elders."

"As an engaged man, sir, he was on a level with his elders in pleading on my behalf with Miss Dale," said Vernon.

Willoughby strode and muttered. Providence had grown mythical in his thoughts, if not malicious: and it is the peril of this worship, that the object will wear such an alternative aspect when it appears no longer subservient.

"Are we coming, sir?" he said, and was unheeded. The Rev. Doctor would not be defrauded of rolling his billow.

"As an honourable gentleman faithful to his own engagement and desirous of establishing his relatives, he deserves, in my judgement, the lady's esteem as well as your cordial thanks; nor should a temporary failure dishearten either of you, notwithstanding the precipitate retreat of the lady from Patterne, and her seclusion in her sanctum on the occasion of your recent visit."

"Supposing he had succeeded," said Vernon, driving Willoughby to frenzy, "should I have been bound to marry?"

Matter for cogitation was offered to Dr. Middleton.

"The proposal was without your sanction?"

"Entirely."

"You admire the lady?"

"Respectfully."

"You do not incline to the state?"

"An inch of an angle would exaggerate my inclination."

"How long are we to stand and hear this insufferable nonsense you talk?" cried Willoughby.

"But if Mr. Whitford was not consulted . . ." Dr. Middleton said, and was overborne by Willoughby's hurried: "Oblige me, sir. — Oblige me, my good fellow!" he swept his arm to Vernon, and gestured a conducting hand to Clara.

"Here is Mrs. Mountstuart!" she exclaimed.

Willoughby stared. Was it an irruption of a friend or a foe? He doubted, and stood petrified between the double question.

Clara had seen Mrs. Mountstuart and Colonel De Craye separating: and now the great lady sailed along the sward like a royal barge in festival trim.

She looked friendly, but friendly to everybody, which was always a frost on Willoughby, and terribly friendly to Clara.

Coming up to her she whispered: "News indeed! Wonderful! I could not credit his hint of it yesterday. Are you satisfied?"

"Pray, Mrs. Mountstuart, take an opportunity to speak to papa," Clara whispered in return.

Mrs. Mountstuart bowed to Dr. Middleton, nodded to Vernon, and swam upon Willoughby, with: "Is it? But *is* it? Am I really to believe? You have? My dear Sir Willoughby? Really?"

The confounded gentleman heaved on a bare plank of wreck in mid sea.

He could oppose only a paralyzed smile to the assault.

His intuitive discretion taught him to fall back a step, while she said: "So!" the plummet word of our mysterious deep fathoms; and he fell back further, saying: "Madam?" in a tone advising her to speak low.

She recovered her volubility, followed his partial retreat and dropped her voice, —

"Impossible to have imagined it as an actual fact! You were always full of surprises, but this! this! Nothing manlier, nothing more gentlemanly has ever been done: nothing: nothing that so completely changes an untenable situation into a comfortable and proper footing for everybody. It is what I like: it is what I love: — sound sense! Men are so selfish: one cannot persuade them to be reasonable in such positions. But you, Sir Willoughby, have shown wisdom and sentiment: the rarest of all combinations in men."

"Where have you? . . . " Willoughby contrived to say.

"Heard? The hedges, the housetops, everywhere. All the neighbourhood will have it before nightfall. Lady Busshe and Lady Culmer will soon be rushing here, and declaring they never expected anything else, I do not doubt. I am not so pretentious. I beg your excuse for that 'twice' of mine yesterday. Even if it hurt my vanity, I should be happy to confess my error: I was utterly out. But then I did not reckon on a fatal attachment, I thought men were incapable of it. I thought we women were the only poor creatures persecuted by a fatality. It *is* a fatality! You tried hard to escape, indeed you did. And she will do honour to your final surrender, my dear friend. She is gentle, and very clever, very: she is devoted to you: she will entertain excellently. I see her like a flower in sunshine. She will expand to a perfect hostess. Patterne will shine under her reign; you have my warrant for that. And so will you. Yes, you flourish best when adored. It must be adoration. You have been under a cloud of late. Years ago I said it was a match, when no one supposed you could stoop. Lady Busshe would have it was a screen, and she was deemed high wisdom. The world will be with you. All the women will be: excepting, of course, Lady Busshe, whose pride is in prophesy; and she will soon be too glad to swell the host. There, my friend, your sincerest and oldest admirer congratulates you. I could not contain myself; I was compelled to pour forth. And now I must go and be talked to by Dr. Middleton. How does he take it? They leave?"

"He is perfectly well," said Willoughby, aloud, quite distraught.

She acknowledged his just correction of her for running on to an extreme in low-toned converse, though they stood sufficiently isolated from the others. These had by this time been joined by Colonel De Craye, and were all chatting in a group — of himself, Willoughby horribly suspected.

Clara was gone from him! Gone! but he remembered his oath and vowed it again: not to Horace De Craye! She was gone, lost, sunk into the world of waters of rival men, and he determined that his whole force should be used to keep her from that man. the false friend who had supplanted him in her shallow heart, and might, if he succeeded, boast of having done it by simply appearing on the scene.

Willoughby intercepted Mrs. Mountstuart as she was passing over to Dr. Middleton: "My dear lady! spare me a minute."

De Craye sauntered up, with a face of the friendliest humour: "Never was man like you, Willoughby, for shaking new patterns in a kaleidoscope."

"Have you turned punster, Horace?" Willoughby replied, smarting to find yet another in the demon secret, and he drew Dr. Middleton two or three steps aside, and hurriedly begged him to abstain from prosecuting the subject with Clara. "We must try to make her happy as we best can, sir. She may have her reasons — a young lady's reasons!" He laughed, and left the Rev. Doctor considering within himself under the arch of his lofty frown of stupefaction.

De Craye smiled slyly and winningly as he shadowed a deep droop on the bend of his head before Clara, signifying his absolute devotion to her service, and this present good fruit for witness of his merits.

She smiled sweetly though vaguely. There was no concealment of their intimacy.

"The battle is over," Vernon said quietly, when Willoughby had walked some paces beside Mrs. Mountstuart, adding: " You may expect to see Mr. Dale here. He knows."

Vernon and Clara exchanged one look, hard on his part, in contrast with her softness, and he proceeded to the house.

De Craye waited for a word or a promising look. He was patient, being self-assured, and passed on.

Clara linked her arm with her father's once more, and said, on a sudden brightness: " Sirius, papa! "

He repeated it in the profoundest manner: " Sirius! And is there," he asked, " a feminine scintilla of sense in that ? "

" It is the name of the star I was thinking of, dear papa."

" It was the star observed by King Agamemnon before the sacrifice in Aulis.[8] You were thinking of that ? But, my love, my Iphigeneia, you have not a father who will insist on sacrificing you."

" Did I hear him tell you to humour me, papa ? "

Dr. Middleton humphed.

" Verily the dog-star rages in many heads," he responded.

CHAPTER 44

DR. MIDDLETON: THE LADIES ELEANOR AND ISABEL: AND MR. DALE.

CLARA looked up at the flying clouds. She travelled with them now, and tasted freedom, but she prudently forebore to vex her father; she held herself in reserve.

They were summoned by the mid-day bell.

Few were speakers at the meal, few were eaters. Clara was impelled to join it by her desire to study Mrs. Mountstuart's face. Willoughby was obliged to preside. It was a meal of an assembly of mutes and plates, that struck the ear like the well-known sound of a collection of offerings in church after an impressive exhortation from the pulpit. A sally of Colonel De Craye's met the reception given to a charity-boy's muffled burst of animal spirits in the silence of the sacred edifice. Willoughby tried politics with Dr. Middleton, whose regular appetite preserved him from uncongenial speculations when the hour for appeasing it had come; and he alone did honour to the dishes, replying to his host, —

" Times are bad, you say, and we have a Ministry doing with us what they will. Well, sir, and that being so, and opposition a manner of kicking them into greater stability, it is the time for wise men to retire within themselves, with

---

8. Sirius, the dog-star, is emphatically mentioned in the first lines of Euripides' play *Iphigenia in Aulis*, which is about a daughter, Iphigenia, threatened with sacrifice on the altar by her father, Agamemnon.

the steady determination of the seed in the earth to grow. Repose upon nature, sleep in firm faith, and abide the seasons. That is my counsel to the weaker party."

The counsel was excellent, but it killed the topic.

Dr. Middleton's appetite was watched for the signal to rise and breathe freely ; and such is the grace accorded to a good man of an untroubled conscience engaged in doing his duty to himself, that he perceived nothing of the general restlessness ; he went through the dishes calmly, and as calmly he quoted Milton to the ladies Eleanor and Isabel, when the company sprang up all at once upon his closing his repast. Vernon was taken away from him by Willoughby. Mrs. Mountstuart beckoned covertly to Clara. Willoughby should have had something to say to him, Dr. Middleton thought : the position was not clear. But the situation was not disagreeable ; and he was in no serious hurry, though he wished to be enlightened.

" This," Dr. Middleton said to the spinster aunts, as he accompanied them to the drawing-room, " shall be no lost day for me if I may devote the remainder of it to you."

" The thunder, we fear, is not remote," murmured one.

" We fear it is imminent," sighed the other.

They took to chanting in alternation.

" — We are accustomed to peruse our Willoughby, and we know him by a shadow."

" — From his infancy to his glorious youth and his established manhood."

" — He was ever the soul of chivalry."

" — Duty : duty first. The happiness of his family : the well-being of his dependents."

" — If proud of his name, it was not an over-weening pride ; it was founded in the conscious possession of exalted qualities."

" — He could be humble when occasion called for it."

Dr. Middleton bowed to the litany, feeling that occasion called for humbleness from him.

" Let us hope ! . . ." he said, with unassumed penitence on behalf of his inscrutable daughter.

The ladies resumed : —

" — Vernon Whitford, not of his blood, is his brother ! "

" — A thousand instances ! Lætitia Dale remembers them better than we."

" — That any blow should strike him ! "

" — That another should be in store for him ! "

" — It seems impossible he can be quite misunderstood ! "

"Let us hope ! . . ." said Dr. Middleton.

" — One would not deem it too much for the dispenser of goodness to expect to be a little looked up to ! "

" — When he was a child he one day mounted a chair, and there he stood in danger, would not let us touch him, because he was taller than we, and we were to gaze. Do you remember him, Eleanor ? ' I am the sun of the house ! ' It was inimitable ! "

" — Your feelings; he would have your feelings! He was fourteen when his cousin Grace Whitford married, and we lost him. They had been the greatest friends; and it was long before he appeared among us. He has never cared to see her since."

" — But he has befriended her husband. Never has he failed in generosity. His only fault is — "

" — His sensitiveness. And that is — "

" — His secret. And that — "

" — You are not to discover! It is the same with him in manhood. No one will accuse Willoughby Patterne of a deficiency of manliness: but what is it? — he suffers, as none suffer, if he is not loved. He himself is inalterably constant in affection."

" — What it is no one can say. We have lived with him all his life, and we know him ready to make any sacrifice: only, he does demand the whole heart in return. And if he doubts, he looks as we have seen him to-day."

" — Shattered: as we have never seen him look before."

"We will hope," said Dr. Middleton, this time hastily. He tingled to say "what it was": he had it in him to solve perplexity in their inquiry. He did say, adopting familiar speech to suit the theme: "You know, ladies, we English come of a rough stock. A dose of rough dealing in our youth does us no harm, braces us. Otherwise we are likely to feel chilly: we grow too fine where tenuity of stature is necessarily buffetted by gales, namely, in our self-esteem. We are barbarians, on a forcing soil of wealth, in a conservatory of comfortable security; but still barbarians. So, you see, we shine at our best when we are plucked out of that, to where hard blows are given, in a state of war. In a state of war we are at home, our men are high-minded fellows, Scipios and good legionaries.[1] In the state of peace we do not live in peace: our native roughness breaks out in unexpected places, under extraordinary aspects — tyrannies, extravagances, domestic exactions: and if we have not had sharp early training . . . within and without . . . the old-fashioned island-instrument to drill into us the civilization of our masters, the ancients, we show it by running here and there to some excess.[2] Ahem. Yet," added the Rev. Doctor, abandoning his effort to deliver a weighty truth obscurely for the comprehension of dainty spinster ladies, the superabundance of whom in England was in his opinion largely the cause of our decay as a people, " Yet I have not observed this ultra-sensitiveness in Willoughby. He has borne to hear more than I, certainly no example of the frailty, could have endured."

"He concealed it," said the ladies. " It is intense."

" Then is it a disease? "

" It bears no explanation; it is mystic."

---

1. Scipio and his legions represent Roman soldiers of the rough and ready republican era

2. "old-fashioned-island instrument": the birch rod.

"It is a cultus, then, a form of self-worship."

"Self!" they ejaculated. "But is not Self indifferent to others? Is it Self that craves for sympathy, love and devotion?"

"He is an admirable host, ladies."

"He is admirable in all respects."

"Admirable must he be who can impress discerning women, his life-long housemates, so favourably. He is, I repeat, a perfect host."

"He will be a perfect husband."

"In all probability."

"It is a certainty. Let him be loved and obeyed, he will be guided. That is the secret for her whom he so fatally loves. That, if we had dared, we would have hinted to her. She will rule him through her love of him, and through him all about her. And it will not be a rule he submits to, but a love he accepts. If she could see it!"

"If she were a metaphysician!" sighed Dr. Middleton.

"— But a sensitiveness so keen as his might —"

"— Fretted by an unsympathizing mate —"

"— In the end become, for the best of us is mortal —"

"— Callous!"

"— He would feel perhaps as much —"

"— Or more! —"

"— He would still be tender —"

"— But he might grow outwardly hard!"

Both ladies looked up at Dr. Middleton, as they revealed the dreadful prospect.

"It is the story told of corns!" he said, sad as they.

The three stood drooping: the ladies with an attempt to digest his remark; the Rev. Doctor in dejection lest his gallantry should no longer continue to wrestle with his good sense.

He was rescued.

The door opened and the footman announced,—

"Mr. Dale."

Miss Eleanor and Miss Isabel made a sign to one another of raising their hands.

They advanced to him, and welcomed him.

"Pray be seated, Mr. Dale. You have not brought us bad news of our Lætitia?"

"So rare is the pleasure of welcoming you here, Mr. Dale, that we are in some alarm, when, as we trust, it should be matter for unmixed congratulation."

"Has Dr. Corney been doing wonders?"

"I am indebted to him for the drive to your house, ladies," said Mr. Dale, a spare, close-buttoned gentleman, with an Indian complexion deadened in the sick-chamber.[3] "It is unusual for me to stir from my precincts."

"The Rev. Dr. Middleton."

---

3. Sunburnt by service in India, also withered by Oriental fevers.

Mr. Dale bowed. He seemed surprised.

"You live in a splendid air, sir," observed the Rev. Doctor.

"I can profit little by it, sir," replied Mr. Dale. He asked the ladies: "Will Sir Willoughby be disengaged?"

They consulted: "He is with Vernon. We will send to him."

The bell was rung.

"I have had the gratification of making the acquaintance of your daughter, Mr. Dale, a most estimable lady," said Dr. Middleton.

Mr. Dale bowed. "She is honoured by your praises, sir. To the best of my belief — I speak as a father — she merits them. Hitherto I have had no doubts."

"Of Lætitia?" exclaimed the ladies; and spoke of her as gentleness and goodness incarnate.

"Hitherto I have devoutly thought so," said Mr. Dale.

"Surely she is the very sweetest nurse, the most devoted of daughters!"

"As far as concerns her duty to her father, I can say she is that, ladies."

"In all her relations, Mr. Dale!"

"It is my prayer," he said.

The footman appeared. He announced that Sir Willoughby was in the laboratory with Mr. Whitford, and the door locked.

"Domestic business," the ladies remarked. "You know Willoughby's diligent attention to affairs, Mr. Dale."

"He is well?" Mr. Dale inquired.

"In excellent health."

"Body and mind?"

"But, dear Mr. Dale, he is never ill."

"Ah! For one to hear that who is never well! And Mr. Whitford is quite sound?"

"Sound? The question alarms me for myself," said Dr. Middleton. "Sound as our Constitution, the Credit of the country, the reputation of our Prince of poets. I pray you to have no fears for him."

Mr. Dale gave the mild little sniff of a man thrown deeper into perplexity.

He said: "Mr. Whitford works his head; he is a hard student; he may not be always, if I may so put it, at home on worldly affairs."

"Dismiss that defamatory legend of the student, Mr. Dale; and take my word for it, that he who persistently works his head has the strongest for all affairs."

"Ah! Your daughter, sir, is here?"

"My daughter is here, sir, and will be most happy to present her respects to the father of her friend Miss Dale."

"They are friends?"

"Very cordial friends."

Mr. Dale administered another feebly pacifying sniff to himself.

"Lætitia!" he sighed in apostrophe, and swept his forehead with a hand seen to shake.

The ladies asked him anxiously whether he felt the heat of the room; and one offered him a smelling-bottle.

He thanked them. "I can hold out until Sir Willoughby comes."

"We fear to disturb him when his door is locked, Mr. Dale; but, if you wish it, we will venture on a message. You have really no bad news of our Lætitia? She left us hurriedly this morning, without any leave-taking, except a word to one of the maids, that your condition required her immediate presence."

"My condition! And now her door is locked to me! We have spoken through the door, and that is all. I stand sick and stupefied between two locked doors, neither of which will open, it appears, to give me the enlightenment I need more than medicine."

"Dear me!" cried Dr. Middleton, "I am struck by your description of your position, Mr. Dale. It would aptly apply to our humanity of the present generation; and were these the days when I sermonized, I could propose that it should afford me an illustration for the pulpit. For my part, when doors are closed I try not their locks; and I attribute my perfect equanimity, health even, to an uninquiring acceptation of the fact that they are closed to me. I read my page by the light I have. On the contrary, the world of this day, if I may presume to quote you for my purpose, is heard knocking at those two locked doors of the secret of things on each side of us, and is beheld standing sick and stupefied because it has got no response to its knocking. Why, sir, let the world compare the diverse fortunes of the beggar and the postman: knock to give, and it is opened unto you: knock to crave, and it continues shut. I say, carry a letter to your locked door, and you shall have a good reception: but there is none that is handed out. For which reason . . ."

Mr. Dale swept a perspiring forehead, and extended his hand in supplication. "I am an invalid, Dr. Middleton," he said. "I am unable to cope with analogies. I have but strength for the slow digestion of facts."

"For facts, we are bradypeptics to a man, sir.[4] We know not yet if nature be a fact or an effort to master one. The world has not yet assimilated the first fact it stepped on. We are still in the endeavour to make good blood of the fact of our being."

Pressing his hands at his temples, Mr. Dale moaned: "My head twirls; I did unwisely to come out. I came on an impulse; I trust, honourable. I am unfit — I cannot follow you, Dr. Middleton. Pardon me."

4. "bradypeptics": slow of digestion.

"Nay, sir, let me say, from my experience of my countrymen, that, if you do not follow me, and can abstain from abusing me in consequence, you are magnanimous," the Rev. Doctor replied, hardly consenting to let go the man he had found to indemnify him for his gallant service of acquiescing as a mute to the ladies, though he knew his breathing robustfulness to be as an East wind to weak nerves, and himself an engine of punishment when he had been torn for a day from his books.

Miss Eleanor said: "The enlightenment you need, Mr. Dale? Can we enlighten you?"

"I think not," he answered faintly. "I think I will wait for Sir Willoughby . . . or Mr. Whitford. If I can keep my strength. Or could I exchange — I fear to break down — two words with the young lady who is, was . . . ?"

"Miss Middleton, my daughter, sir? She shall be at your disposition; I will bring her to you." Dr. Middleton stopped at the window. "She, it is true, may better know the mind of Miss Dale than I. But I flatter myself I know the gentleman better. I think, Mr. Dale, addressing you as the lady's father, you will find me a persuasive, I could be an impassioned, advocate in his interests."

Mr. Dale was confounded; the weakly sapling caught in a gust falls back as he did.

"Advocate?" he said. He had little breath.

"His impassioned advocate, I repeat: for I have the highest opinion of him. You see, sir, I am acquainted with the circumstances. I believe," Dr. Middleton half turned to the ladies, "we must, until your potent inducements, Mr. Dale, have been joined to my instances, and we overcome what feminine scruples there may be, treat the circumstances as not generally public. Our Strephon may be chargeable with shyness.[5] But if for the present it is incumbent on us, in proper consideration for the parties, not to be nominally precise, it is hardly requisite in this household that we should be. He is now for protesting indifference to the state. I fancy we understand that phase of amatory frigidity. Frankly, Mr. Dale, I was once in my life myself refused by a lady, and I was not indignant, merely indifferent to the marriage-tie."

"My daughter *has* refused him, sir?"

"Temporarily it would appear that she has declined the proposal."

"He was at liberty? . . . he could honourably? . . ."

"His best friend and nearest relative is your guarantee."

"I know it; I hear so: I am informed of that; I have heard of the proposal, and that he could honourably make it. Still, I am helpless, I cannot move, until I am assured that my daughter's reasons are such as a father need not underline."

5. "Strephon" is a pastoral name, generally signifying a lover; his usual beloved is Chloe.

"Does the lady, perchance, equivocate?"

"I have not seen her this morning; I rise late. I hear an astounding account of the cause for her departure from Patterne, and I find her door locked to me — no answer."

"It is that she has no reasons to give, and she feared the demand for them."

"Ladies!" dolorously exclaimed Mr. Dale.

"We guess the secret, we guess it!" they exclaimed in reply; and they looked smilingly, as Dr. Middleton looked.

"She had no reasons to give?" Mr. Dale spelt these words to his understanding. "Then, sir, she knew you not adverse?"

"Undoubtedly, by my high esteem for the gentleman, she must have known me not adverse. But she would not consider me a principal. She could hardly have conceived me an obstacle. I am simply the gentleman's friend. A zealous friend, let me add."

Mr. Dale put out an imploring hand; it was too much for him.

"Pardon me; I have a poor head. And your daughter the same, sir?"

"We will not measure it too closely, but I may say, my daughter the same, sir. And likewise — may I not add? — these ladies."

Mr. Dale made sign that he was overfilled. "Where am I! And Lætitia refused him?"

"Temporarily, let us assume. Will it not partly depend on you, Mr. Dale?"

"But what strange things have been happening during my daughter's absence from the cottage!" cried Mr. Dale, betraying an elixir in his veins. "I feel that I could laugh if I did not dread to be thought insane. She refused his hand, and he was at liberty to offer it? My girl! We are all on our heads. The fairy-tales were right and the lesson-books were wrong. But it is really, it is really very demoralizing. An invalid — and I am one, and no momentary exhilaration will be taken for the contrary — clings to the idea of stability, order. The slightest disturbance of the wonted course of things unsettles him. Why, for years I have been prophesying it! and for years I have had everything against me, and now when it is confirmed, I am wondering that I must not call myself a fool!"

"And for years, dear Mr. Dale, this union, in spite of counter-currents and human arrangements, has been our Willoughby's constant preoccupation," said Miss Eleanor.

"His most cherished aim," said Miss Isabel.

"The name was not spoken by me," said Dr. Middleton. "But it is out, and perhaps better out, if we would avoid the chance of mystifications. I do not suppose we are seriously committing a breach of confidence, though he might have wished to mention it to you first himself. I have it from Willoughby that last night he appealed to your daughter, Mr. Dale — not for the first time, if I apprehend him correctly; and unsuccessfully. He despairs. I do not: supposing, that is, your assistance vouchsafed to us. And I do not despair, because the gentleman is a gentleman of worth, of acknowledged worth. You know him well enough to grant me that. I will bring you my daughter to help me in sounding his praises."

Dr. Middleton stepped through the window to the lawn on an elastic foot, beaming with the happiness he felt charged to confer on his friend Mr. Whitford.

"Ladies! it passes all wonders," Mr. Dale gasped.

"Willoughby's generosity does pass all wonders," they said in chorus.

The door opened: Lady Busshe and Lady Culmer were announced.

CHAPTER 45

THE PATTERNE LADIES: MR. DALE: LADY BUSSHE AND LADY CULMER: WITH MRS. MOUNTSTUART JENKINSON

LADY BUSSHE and Lady Culmer entered spying to right and left. At the sight of Mr. Dale in the room, Lady Busshe murmured to her friend: "Confirmation!"

Lady Culmer murmured: "Corney is quite reliable."

"The man is his own best tonic."

"He is invaluable for the country."

Miss Eleanor and Miss Isabel greeted them.

The amiability of the Patterne ladies, combined with their total eclipse behind their illustrious nephew, invited enterprising women of the world to take liberties, and they were not backward.

Lady Busshe said: "Well? the news! we have the outlines. Don't be astonished: we know the points: we have heard the gun. I could have told you as much yesterday. I *saw* it. And I guessed it the day before. Oh! I do believe in fatalities now. Lady Culmer and I agree to take that view: it is the simplest. Well, and are you satisfied, my dears?"

The ladies grimaced interrogatively. "With what?"

"With it! with all! with her! with him!"

"Our Willoughby?"

"Can it be possible that they require a dose of Corney?" Lady Busshe remarked to Lady Culmer.

"They play discretion to perfection," said Lady Culmer. "But, my dears, we are in the secret."

"How did she behave?" whispered Lady Busshe. "No high flights and flutters, I do hope. She was well-connected, they say; though I don't comprehend what they mean by a line of scholars — one thinks of a row of pinafores: and she was pretty. That is well enough at the start. It never will

stand against brains. He had the two in the house to contrast them, and . . . the result! A young woman with
brains — in a house — beats all your Beauties. Lady Culmer
and I have determined on that view. He thought her a
delightful partner for a dance, and found her rather tiresome
at the end of the gallopade.[1] I saw it yesterday, clear as
daylight. She did not understand him, and he did understand her. That will be our report."

" She is young : she will learn," said the ladies, uneasily,
but in total ignorance of her meaning.

" And you are charitable, and always were. I remember
you had a good word for that girl Durham."

Lady Busshe crossed the room to Mr. Dale, who was
turning over leaves of a grand book of the heraldic devices
of our great Families.[2]

" Study it," she said, " study it, my dear Mr. Dale; you
are in it, by right of possessing a clever and accomplished
daughter. At page 300 you will find the Patterne crest.
And mark me, she will drag you into the Peerage before she
has done — relatively, you know. Sir Willoughby and wife
will not be contented to sit down and manage the estates.
Has not Lætitia immense ambition? And very creditable,
I say."

Mr. Dale tried to protest something. He shut the book,
examined the binding, flapped the cover with a finger,
hoped her ladyship was in good health, alluded to his own
and the strangeness of the bird out of the cage.

" You will probably take up your residence here, in a
larger and handsomer cage, Mr. Dale."

He shook his head. " Do I apprehend . . . ? " he said.

" I *know*," said she.

" Dear me, can it be ? "

Mr. Dale gazed upward, with the feelings of one awakened
late to see a world alive in broad daylight.

Lady Busshe dropped her voice. She took the liberty
permitted to her with an inferior in station, while treating
him to a tone of familiarity in acknowledgement of his ex
pected rise : which is high breeding, or the exact measurement of social dues.

" Lætitia will be happy, you may be sure. I love to see a
long and faithful attachment rewarded — love it ! Her tale
is the triumph of patience. Far above Grizzel![3] No woman
will be ashamed of pointing to Lady Patterne. You are
uncertain ? You are in doubt ? Let me hear — as low as
you like. But there is no doubt of the new shifting of the
scene ? — no doubt of the proposal ? Dear Mr. Dale! a very
little louder. You are here because — ? of course you wish
to see Sir Willoughby. She ? I did not catch you quite.
She ? . . . it seems, you say ? . . ."

1. A lively dance.
2. Burke's *Complete Peerage*, sometimes
known in county sporting circles as the
stud-book.
3. Far beyond patient Griselda.

Lady Culmer said to the Patterne ladies, —

"You must have had a distressing time. These affairs always mount up to a climax, unless people are very well bred. We saw it coming. Naturally we did not expect such a transformation of brides: who could? If I had laid myself down on my back to think, I should have had it. I am unerring when I set to speculating on my back. One is cooler: ideas come; they have not to be forced. That is why I am brighter on a dull winter afternoon, on the sofa, beside my tea-service, than at any other season. However, your trouble is over. When did the Middletons leave?"

"The Middletons leave?" said the ladies.

"Dr. Middleton and his daughter."

"They have not left us."

"The Middletons are here?"

"They are here, yes. Why should they have left Patterne?"

"Why?"

"Yes. They are likely to stay some days longer."

"Goodness!"

"There is no ground for any report to the contrary, Lady Culmer."

"No ground!"

Lady Culmer called out to Lady Busshe.

A cry came back from that startled dame.

"She has refused him!"

"Who?"

"*She* has!"

"She? — Sir Willoughby?"

"Refused! — declines the honour."

"Oh! never! No, that carries the incredible beyond romance! But is he perfectly at . . . ?"

"Quite, it seems. And she was asked in due form and refused."

"No, and no again!"

"My dear, I have it from Mr. Dale."

"Mr. Dale, what can be the signification of her conduct!"

"Indeed, Lady Culmer," said Mr. Dale, not unpleasantly agitated by the interest he excited, in spite of his astonishment at a public discussion of the matter in this house, "I am in the dark. Her father should know, but I do not. Her door is locked to me; I have not seen her. I am absolutely in the dark. I am a recluse. I have forgotten the ways of the world. I should have supposed her father would first have been addressed."

"Tut-tut. Modern gentlemen are not so formal; they are creatures of impulse and take a pride in it. He spoke. We settle that. But where did you get this tale of a refusal?"

"I have it from Dr. Middleton."

"From Dr. Middleton!" shouted Lady Busshe.

"The Middletons are here," said Lady Culmer.

"What whirl are we in?" Lady Busshe got up, ran two or three steps and seated herself in another chair. "Oh! do let us proceed upon system. If not, we shall presently be rageing; we shall be dangerous. The Middletons are here, and Dr. Middleton himself communicates to Mr. Dale that Lætitia Dale has refused the hand of Sir Willoughby, who is ostensibly engaged to his own daughter! And pray, Mr. Dale, how did Dr. Middleton speak of it? Compose yourself; there is no violent hurry, though our sympathy with you and our interest in all the parties does perhaps agitate us a little. Quite at your leisure — speak!"

"Madam . . . Lady Busshe." Mr. Dale gulped a ball in his throat. "I see no reason why I should not speak. I do not see how I can have been deluded. The Miss Patternes heard him. Dr. Middleton began upon it, not I. I was unaware, when I came, that it was a refusal. I had been informed that there was a proposal. My authority for the tale was positive. The object of my visit was to assure myself of the integrity of my daughter's conduct. She had always the highest sense of honour. But passion is known to mislead, and there was this most strange report. I feared that our humblest apologies were due to Dr. Middleton and his daughter. I know the charm Lætitia can exercise. Madam, in the plainest language, without a possibility of my misapprehending him, Dr. Middleton spoke of himself as the advocate of the suitor for my daughter's hand. I have a poor head. I supposed at once an amicable rupture between Sir Willoughby and Miss Middleton, or that the version which had reached me of their engagement was not strictly accurate. My head is weak. Dr. Middleton's language is trying to a head like mine; but I can speak positively on the essential points : he spoke of himself as ready to be the impassioned advocate of the suitor for my daughter's hand. Those were his words. I understood him to entreat me to intercede with her. Nay, the name was mentioned. There was no concealment. I am certain there could not be a misapprehension. And my feelings were touched by his anxiety for Sir Willoughby's happiness. I attributed it to a sentiment upon which I need not dwell. Impassioned advocate, he said."

"We are in a perfect maelstrom!" cried Lady Busshe turning to everybody.

"It is a complete hurricane!" cried Lady Culmer.

A light broke over the faces of the Patterne ladies. They exchanged it with one another.

They had been so shocked as to be almost offended by Lady Busshe, but their natural gentleness and habitual submission rendered them unequal to the task of checking her.

"Is it not," said Miss Eleanor, "a misunderstanding that a change of names will rectify?"

"This is by no means the first occasion," said Miss Isabel, "that Willoughby has pleaded for his cousin Vernon."

"We deplore extremely the painful error into which Mr. Dale has fallen."

"It springs, we now perceive, from an entire misapprehension of Dr. Middleton's."

"Vernon was in his mind. It was clear to us."

"Impossible that it could have been Willoughby!"

"You see the impossibility, the error!"

"And the Middletons here!" said Lady Busshe. "Oh! if we leave unilluminated, we shall be the laughing-stock of the county. Mr. Dale, please, wake up. Do you see? You may have been mistaken."

"Lady Busshe," he woke up, "I may have mistaken Dr. Middleton; he has a language that I can compare only to a review-day of the field forces. But I have the story on authority that I cannot question: it is confirmed by my daughter's unexampled behaviour. And if I live through this day I shall look about me as a ghost to-morrow."

"Dear Mr. Dale!" said the Patterne ladies compassionately.

Lady Busshe murmured to them: "You know the two did not agree; they did not get on: I saw it; I predicted it."

"She will understand him in time," said they.

"Never. And my belief is, they have parted by consent, and Letty Dale wins the day at last. Yes, now I do believe it."

The ladies maintained a decided negative, but they knew too much not to feel perplexed, and they betrayed it, though they said: "Dear Lady Busshe! is it credible, in decency?"

"Dear Mrs. Mountstuart!" Lady Busshe invoked her great rival appearing among them: "You come most opportunely; we are in a state of inextricable confusion: we are bordering on frenzy. You, and none but you, can help us. You know, you always know; we hang on you. Is there any truth in it? a particle?"

Mrs. Mountstuart seated herself regally. "Ah! Mr. Dale!" she said, inclining to him. "Yes, dear Lady Busshe, there is a particle."

"Now, do not roast us! You can; you have the art. I have the whole story. That is, I have a part. I mean, I have the outlines. I cannot be deceived, but you can fill them in, I know you can. I saw it yesterday. Now, tell us, tell us. It must be quite true or utterly false. Which is it?"

"Be precise."

"His fatality! you called her. Yes, I was sceptical. But here we have it all come round again, and if the tale is true, I shall own you infallible. Has he? — and she?"

"Both."

"And the Middletons here? They have not gone; they keep the field. And more astounding, she refuses him! And to add to it, Dr. Middleton intercedes with Mr. Dale for Sir Willoughby!"

"Dr. Middleton intercedes!" This was rather astonishing to Mrs. Mountstuart.

"For Vernon," Miss Eleanor emphasized.

"For Vernon Whitford, his cousin," said Miss Isabel, still more emphatically.

"Who," said Mrs. Mountstuart, with a sovereign lift and turn of her head, "speaks of a refusal?"

"I have it from Mr. Dale," said Lady Busshe.

"I had it, I thought, distinctly from Dr. Middleton," said Mr. Dale.

"That Willoughby proposed to Lætitia for his cousin Vernon, Dr. Middleton meant," said Miss Eleanor.

Her sister followed: "Hence this really ridiculous misconception!— sad indeed," she added, for balm to Mr. Dale. "Willoughby was Vernon's proxy. His cousin, if not his first, is ever the second thought with him."

"But can we continue? . . ."

"Such a discussion!"

Mrs. Mountstuart gave them a judicial hearing. They were regarded in the county as the most indulgent of non-entities, and she as little as Lady Busshe was restrained from the burning topic in their presence. She pronounced:

"Each party is right and each is wrong."

A cry: "I shall shriek!" came from Lady Busshe.

"Cruel!" groaned Lady Culmer.

"Mixed, you are all wrong. Disentangled, you are each of you right. Sir Willoughby does think of his cousin Vernon; he is anxious to establish him; he is the author of a proposal to that effect."

"We know it!" the Patterne ladies exclaimed. "And Lætitia rejected poor Vernon once more!"

"Who spoke of Miss Dale's rejection of Mr. Whitford?"

"Is he not rejected?" Lady Culmer inquired.

"It is in debate, and at this moment being decided."

"Oh! do be seated, Mr. Dale," Lady Busshe implored him, rising to thrust him back to his chair if necessary. "Any dislocation, and we are thrown out again! We must hold together if this riddle is ever to be read. Then, dear Mrs. Mountstuart, we are to say that there is no truth in the other story?"

"You are to say nothing of the sort, dear Lady Busshe."

"Be merciful! And what of the fatality?"

"As positive as the Pole to the needle."

"She has not refused him?"

"Ask your own sagacity."

"Accepted?"

"Wait."

"And all the world's ahead of me! Now, Mrs. Mountstuart, you are oracle. Riddles, if you like — only speak!
If we can't have corn, give us husks."

"Is any one of us able to anticipate events. Lady Busshe?"

"Yes. I believe that you are. I bow to you. I do sin
cerely. So it's another person for Mr. Whitford? You nod.
And it is our Lætitia for Sir Willoughby? You smile. You
would not deceive me? A very little, and I run about crazed
and howl at your doors. And Dr. Middleton is made to play
blind man in the midst? And the other person is — now I
see day! An amicable rupture, and a smooth new arrangement! She has money; she was never the match for our
hero; never; I saw it yesterday, and before, often: and so
he hands her over — tuthe-rum-tum-tum, tuthe-rum-tum-
tum." Lady Busshe struck a quick march on her knee:
"Now isn't that clever guessing? The shadow of a clue
for me! And because I know human nature. One peep,
and I see the combination in a minute. So he keeps the
money in the family, becomes a benefactor to his cousin by
getting rid of the girl, and succumbs to his fatality. Rather
a pity he let it ebb and flow so long. Time counts the tides,
you know. But it improves the story. I defy any other
county in the kingdom to produce one fresh and living to
equal it. Let me tell you I suspected Mr. Whitford, and I
hinted it yesterday."

"Did you indeed!" said Mrs. Mountstuart, humouring
her excessive acuteness.

"I really did. There is that dear good man on his feet
again. And looks agitated again."

Mr. Dale had been compelled both by the lady's voice and
his interest in the subject, to listen. He had listened more
than enough: he was exceedingly nervous. He held on by
his chair, afraid to quit his moorings, and "Manners!" he
said to himself unconsciously aloud, as he cogitated on the
libertine way with which these chartered great ladies of
the district discussed his daughter.[4] He was heard and unnoticed. The supposition, if any, would have been that he
was admonishing himself.

At this juncture Sir Willoughby entered the drawing-
room by the garden-window, and simultaneously Dr. Middleton by the door.

4. "chartered": privileged.

CHAPTER 46

THE SCENE OF SIR WILLOUGHBY'S GENERALSHIP

HISTORY, we may fear, will never know the qualities of leadership inherent in Sir Willoughby Patterne to fit him for the post of Commander of an army, seeing that he avoided the fatigues of the service and preferred the honours bestowed in his country upon the quiet administrators of their own estates : but his possession of particular gifts, which are military, and especially of the proleptic mind, which is the stamp and sign-warrant of the heaven-sent General, was displayed on every urgent occasion when, in the midst of difficulties likely to have extinguished one less alert than he to the threatening aspect of disaster, he had to manœuvre himself.[1]

He had received no intimation of Mr. Dale's presence in his house, nor of the arrival of the dreaded women Lady Busshe and Lady Culmer: his locked door was too great a terror to his domestics. Having finished with Vernon, after a tedious endeavour to bring the fellow to a sense of the policy of the step urged on him, he walked out on the lawn with the desire to behold the opening of an interview not promising to lead to much, and possibly to profit by its failure. Clara had been prepared, according to his directions, by Mrs. Mountstuart Jenkinson, as Vernon had been prepared by him. His wishes, candidly and kindly expressed both to Vernon and Mrs. Mountstuart, were, that since the girl appeared disinclined to make him a happy man, she would make one of his cousin. Intimating to Mrs. Mountstuart that he would be happier without her, he alluded to the benefit of the girl's money to poor old Vernon, the general escape from a scandal if old Vernon could manage to catch her as she dropped, the harmonious arrangement it would be for all parties. And only on the condition of her taking Vernon, would he consent to give her up. This he said imperatively : adding, that such was the meaning of the news she had received relating to Lætitia Dale. From what quarter had she received it? he asked. She shuffled in her reply, made a gesture to signify that it was in the air, universal, and fell upon the proposed arrangement. He would listen to none of Mrs. Mountstuart's woman-of-the-world instances of the folly of pressing it upon a girl who had shown herself a girl of spirit. She foretold the failure. He would not be advised; he said : "It is my scheme ;" and perhaps the look of mad benevolence about it induced the lady to try whether there was a chance that it would hit the madness in our nature, and somehow succeed or lead to

---

1. "proleptic": prophetic, far-seeing.

a pacification. Sir Willoughby condescended to arrange
things thus for Clara's good ; he would then proceed to
realize his own. Such was the face he put upon it. We can
wear what appearance we please before the world until we are
found out, nor is the world's praise knocking upon hollowness always hollow music ; but Mrs. Mountstuart's laudation
of his kindness and simplicity disturbed him ; for though he
had recovered from his rebuff enough to imagine that Lætitia
could not refuse him under reiterated pressure, he had let it
be supposed that she was a submissive handmaiden throbbing for her elevation ; and Mrs. Mountstuart's belief in it
afflicted his recent bitter experience; his footing was not
perfectly secure. Besides, assuming it to be so, he considered the sort of prize he had won ; and a spasm of downright hatred of a world for which we make mighty sacrifices
to be repaid in a worn, thin, comparatively valueless coin,
troubled his counting of his gains. Lætitia, it was true, had
not passed through other hands in coming to him, as Vernon
would know it to be Clara's case : time only had worn her :
but the comfort of the reflection was annoyed by the physical
contrast of the two. Hence an unusual melancholy in his
tone that Mrs. Mountstuart thought touching. It had the
scenic effect on her which greatly contributes to delude the
wits. She talked of him to Clara as being a man who had
revealed an unsuspected depth.

Vernon took the communication curiously. He seemed
readier to be in love with his benevolent relative than with
the lady. He was confused, undisguisedly moved, said the
plan was impossible, out of the question, but thanked Willoughby for the best of intentions, thanked him warmly.
After saying that the plan was impossible, the comical fellow allowed himself to be pushed forth on the lawn to see
how Miss Middleton might have come out of her interview
with Mrs. Mountstuart. Willoughby observed Mrs. Mountstuart meet him, usher him to the place she had quitted
among the shrubs, and return to the open turf-spaces. He
sprang to her.

"She will listen," Mrs. Mountstuart said : "she likes
him, respects him, thinks he is a very sincere friend, clever,
a scholar, and a good mountaineer ; and thinks you mean
very kindly. So much I have impressed on her, but I have
not done much for Mr. Whitford."

"She consents to listen," said Willoughby, snatching at
that as the death-blow to his friend Horace.

"She consents to listen, because you have arranged it so
that if she declined she would be rather a savage."

"You think it will have no result ? "

"None at all."

"Her listening will do."

"And you must be satisfied with it."

"We shall see."

"'Anything for peace,' she says : and I don't say that a

gentleman with a tongue would not have a chance. She wishes to please you."

"Old Vernon has no tongue for women, poor fellow! You will have us be spider or fly, and if a man can't spin a web, all he can hope is not to be caught in one. She knows his history too, and that won't be in his favour. How did she look when you left them?"

"Not so bright: like a bit of china that wants dusting. She looked a trifle *gauche*, it struck me; more like a country girl with the hoyden taming in her than the well-bred creature she is.[2] I did not suspect her to have feeling. You must remember, Sir Willoughby, that she has obeyed your wishes, done her utmost: I do think we may say she has made some amends: and if she is to blame she repents, and you will not insist too far."

"I do insist," said he.

"Beneficent, but a tyrant!"

"Well, well." He did not dislike the character.

They perceived Dr. Middleton wandering over the lawn, and Willoughby went to him to put him on the wrong track: Mrs. Mountstuart swept into the drawing-room. Willoughby quitted the Rev. Doctor, and hung about the bower where he supposed his pair of dupes had by this time ceased to stutter mutually:—or what if they had found the word of harmony? He could bear that, just bear it. He rounded the shrubs, and behold, both had vanished. The trellis decorated emptiness. His idea was, that they had soon discovered their inability to be turtles: and desiring not to lose a moment while Clara was fretted by the scene, he rushed to the drawing-room with the hope of lighting on her there, getting her to himself, and finally, urgently, passionately offering her the sole alternative of what she had immediately rejected.[3] Why had he not used passion before, instead of limping crippled between temper and policy? He was capable of it: as soon as imagination in him conceived his personal feelings unwounded and un-imperilled, the might of it inspired him with heroical confidence, and Clara grateful, Clara softly moved, led him to think of Clara melted. Thus anticipating her he burst into the room.

One step there warned him that he was in the jaws of the world. We have the phrase, that a man is himself, under certain trying circumstances. There is no need to say it of Sir Willoughby: he was thrice himself when danger menaced, himself inspired him. He could read at a single glance the Polyphemus eye in the general head of a company.[4] Lady Busshe, Lady Culmer, Mrs. Mountstuart, Mr. Dale, had a similarity in the variety of their expressions that made up one giant eye for him, perfectly, if awfully,

2. "*gauche*": awkward, unsophisticated.
3. "turtles": turtle-doves, lovebirds.
4. "Polyphemus eye": the glaring single eye of the giant Cyclops in Homer's *Odyssey*.

legible.   He discerned the fact that his demon secret was abroad, universal.   He ascribed it to fate.   He was in the jaws of the world, on the world's teeth.   This time he thought Lætitia must have betrayed him, and bowing to Lady Busshe and Lady Culmer, gallantly pressing their fingers and responding to their becks and archnesses, he ruminated on his defences before he should accost her father.   He did not want to be alone with the man, and he considered how his presence might be made useful.

" I am glad to see you, Mr. Dale.   Pray, be seated.   Is it nature asserting her strength ? or the efficacy of medicine ? I fancy it can't be both.   You have brought us back your daughter ? "

Mr. Dale sank into a chair, unable to resist the hand forcing him.

" No, Sir Willoughby, no.   I have not; I have not seen her since she came home this morning from Patterne."

" Indeed ?   She is unwell ? "

" I cannot say.   She secludes herself."

" Has locked herself in," said Lady Busshe.

Willoughby threw her a smile.   It made them intimate.

This was an advantage against the world, but an exposure of himself to the abominable woman.

Dr. Middleton came up to Mr. Dale to apologize for not presenting his daughter Clara, whom he could find neither in nor out of the house.

" We have in Mr. Dale, as I suspected," he said to Willoughby, "a stout ally."

" If I may beg two minutes with you, Sir Willoughby," said Mr. Dale.

" Your visits are too rare for me to allow of your numbering the minutes," Willoughby replied.   " We cannot let Mr. Dale escape us now that we have him, I think, Dr. Middleton."

" Not without ransom," said the Rev. Doctor.

Mr. Dale shook his head.   " My strength, Sir Willoughby, will not sustain me long."

" You are at home, Mr. Dale."

" Not far from home, in truth, but too far for an invalid beginning to grow sensible of weakness."

" You will regard Patterne as your home, Mr. Dale," Willoughby repeated for the world to hear.

" Unconditionally ? "   Dr. Middleton inquired with a humourous air of dissenting.

Willoughby gave him a look that was coldly courteous, and then he looked at Lady Busshe.   She nodded imperceptibly.   Her eyebrows rose, and Willoughby returned a similar nod.

Translated, the signs ran thus : —

" — Pestered by the Rev. gentleman : — I see you are.   Is the story I have heard correct ? — Possibly it may err in a few details."

This was fettering himself in loose manacles.

But Lady Busshe would not be satisfied with the compliment of the intimate looks and nods. She thought she might still be behind Mrs. Mountstuart; and she was a bold woman, and anxious about him, half-crazed by the riddle of the pot she was boiling in, and having very few minutes to spare.

Not extremely reticent by nature, privileged by station, and made intimate with him by his covert looks, she stood up to him. " One word to an old friend. Which is the father of the fortunate creature ? I don't know how to behave to them."

No time was afforded him to be disgusted with her vulgarity and audacity.

He replied, feeling her rivet his gyves: "The house will be empty to-morrow."[5]

" I see. A decent withdrawal, and very well cloaked. We had a tale here of her running off to decline the honour, afraid, or on her dignity or something."

How was it that the woman was ready to accept the altered posture of affairs in his house — if she had received a hint of them ? He forgot that he had prepared her in self-defence.

" From whom did you have that ? " he asked.

" Her father. And the lady aunts declare it was the cousin she refused ! "

Willoughby's brain turned over. He righted it for action, and crossed the room to the ladies Eleanor and Isabel. His ears tingled. He and his whole story discussed in public! Himself unroofed ! And the marvel that he of all men should be in such a tangle, naked and blown on, condemned to use his cunningest arts to unwind and cover himself, struck him as though the lord of his kind were running the gauntlet of a legion of imps. He felt their lashes.

The ladies were talking to Mrs. Mountstuart and Lady Culmer of Vernon and the suitableness of Lætitia to a scholar. He made sign to them, and both rose.

" It is the hour for your drive. To the cottage ! Mr. Dale is ill. She must come. Her sick father ! No delay, going or returning. Bring her here at once."

" Poor man ! " they sighed : and " Willoughby," said one, and the other said : " There is a strange misconception you will do well to correct "

They were about to murmur what it was. He swept his hand round, and excusing themselves to their guests, obediently they retired.

Lady Busshe at his entreaty remained, and took a seat beside Lady Culmer and Mrs. Mountstuart.

She said to the latter : " You have tried scholars. What do you think ? "

" Excellent, but hard to mix," was the reply.

5. "rivet his gyves": hammer tight the chains on his ankles.

"I never make experiments," said Lady Culmer.

"Some one must!" Mrs. Mountstuart groaned over her dull dinner-party.

Lady Busshe consoled her. "At any rate, the loss of a scholar is no loss to the county."

"They are well enough in towns," Lady Culmer said.

"And then I am sure you must have them by themselves."

"We have nothing to regret."

"My opinion."

The voice of Dr. Middleton in colloquy with Mr. Dale swelled on a melodious thunder: "For whom else should I plead as the passionate advocate I proclaimed myself to you, sir? There is but one man known to me who would move me to back him upon such an adventure. Willoughby, join me. I am informing Mr. Dale . . ."

Willoughby stretched his hands out to Mr. Dale to support him on his legs, though he had shown no sign of a wish to rise.

"You are feeling unwell, Mr. Dale."

"Do I look very ill, Sir Willoughby?"

"It will pass. Lætitia will be with us in twenty minutes."

Mr. Dale struck his hands in a clasp. He looked alarmingly ill, and satisfactorily revealed to his host how he could be made to look so.

"I was informing Mr. Dale that the petitioner enjoys our concurrent good wishes: and mine in no degree less than yours, Willoughby," observed Dr. Middleton, whose billows grew the bigger for a check. He supposed himself speaking confidentially. "Ladies have the trick; they have, I may say, the natural disposition for playing enigma now and again. Pressure is often a sovereign specific. Let it be tried upon her all round, from every radiating line of the circle. You she refuses. Then I venture to propose myself to appeal to her. My daughter has assuredly an esteem for the applicant that will animate a woman's tongue in such a case. The ladies of the house will not be backward. Lastly, if necessary, we trust the lady's father to add his instances. My prescription is, to fatigue her negatives; and where no rooted objection exists, I maintain it to be the unfailing receipt for the conduct of a siege. No woman can say No for ever. The defence has not such resources against even a single assailant, and we shall have solved the problem of continuous motion before she will have learnt to deny in perpetuity. That I stand on."

Willoughby glanced at Mrs. Mountstuart.

"What is that?" she said. "Treason to our sex, Dr. Middleton?"

"I think I heard, that no woman can say No for ever!" remarked Lady Busshe.

"To a loyal gentleman, ma'am: assuming the field of the

recurring request to be not unholy ground; consecrated to affirmatives rather."

Dr. Middleton was attacked by three angry bees. They made him say Yes and No alternately so many times that he had to admit in men a shiftier yieldingness than women were charged with.

Willoughby gesticulated as mute chorus on the side of the ladies; and a little show of party spirit like that, coming upon their excitement under the topic, inclined them to him genially.

He drew Mr. Dale away while the conflict subsided in sharp snaps of rifles and an interval rejoinder of a cannon.

Mr. Dale had shown by signs that he was growing fretfully restive under his burden of doubt.

"Sir Willoughby, I have a question. I beg you to lead me where I may ask it. I know my head is weak."

"Mr. Dale, it is answered when I say that my house is your home, and that Lætitia will soon be with us."

"Then this report is true!"

"I know nothing of reports. You are answered."

"Can my daughter be accused of any shadow of falseness, dishonourable dealing?"

"As little as I."

Mr. Dale scanned his face. He saw no shadow.

"For I should go to my grave bankrupt if that could be said of her; and I have never yet felt poor, though you know the extent of a pensioner's income. Then this tale of a refusal . . .?"

"Is nonsense."

"She has accepted?"

"There are situations, Mr. Dale, too delicate to be clothed in positive definitions."

"Ah, Sir Willoughby, but it becomes a father to see that his daughter is not forced into delicate situations. I hope all is well. I am confused. It may be my head. She puzzles me. You are not . . . Can I ask it here? You are quite? . . . Will you moderate my anxiety? My infirmities must excuse me."

Sir Willoughby conveyed by a shake of the head and a pressure of Mr. Dale's hand, that he was not, and that he was quite.

"Dr. Middleton?" said Mr. Dale.

"He leaves us to-morrow."

"Really!" The invalid wore a look as if wine had been poured into him. He routed his host's calculations by calling to the Rev. Doctor. "We are to lose you, sir?"

Willoughby attempted an interposition, but Dr. Middleton crashed through it like the lordly organ swallowing a flute.

"Not before I score my victory, Mr. Dale, and establish my friend upon his rightful throne."

"You do not leave to-morrow, sir?"

"Have you heard, sir, that I leave to-morrow?"

Mr. Dale turned to Sir Willoughby.

The latter said: "Clara named to-day. To-morrow, I thought preferable."

"Ah?" Dr. Middleton towered on the swelling exclamation, but with no dark light. He radiated splendidly. "Yes, then, to-morrow. That is, if we subdue the lady."

He advanced to Willoughby, seized his hand, squeezed it, thanked him, praised him. He spoke under his breath, for a wonder; but: "We are in your debt lastingly, my friend," was heard, and he was impressive, he seemed subdued, and saying aloud: "Though I should wish to aid in the reduction of that fortress," he let it be seen that his mind was rid of a load.

Dr. Middleton partly stupefied Willoughby by his way of taking it, but his conduct was too serviceable to allow of speculation on his readiness to break the match. It was the turning-point of the engagement.

Lady Busshe made a stir.

"I cannot keep my horses waiting any longer," she said, and beckoned. Sir Willoughby was beside her immediately. "You are admirable! perfect! Don't ask me to hold my tongue. I retract, I recant. It *is* a fatality. I have resolved upon that view. You could stand the shot of beauty, not of brains. That is our report. There! And it's delicious to feel that the county wins you. No tea. I cannot possibly wait. And, oh! here she is. I must have a look at her. My dear Lætitia Dale!"

Willoughby hurried to Mr. Dale.

"You are not to be excited, sir: compose yourself. You will recover and be strong to-morrow: you are at home; you are in your own house; you are in Lætitia's drawing-room. All will be clear to-morrow. Till to-morrow we talk riddles by consent. Sit, I beg. You stay with us."

He met Lætitia and rescued her from Lady Busshe, murmuring, with the air of a lover who says, "my love! my sweet!" that she had done rightly to come and come at once.

Her father had been thrown into the proper condition of clammy nervousness to create the impression. Lætitia's anxiety sat prettily on her long eyelashes as she bent over him in his chair.

Hereupon Dr. Corney appeared; and his name had a bracing effect on Mr. Dale. "Corney has come to drive me to the cottage," he said. "I am ashamed of this public exhibition of myself, my dear. Let us go. My head is a poor one."

Dr. Corney had been intercepted. He broke from Sir Willoughby with a dozen little nods of accurate understanding of him, even to beyond the mark of the communications. He touched his patient's pulse lightly, briefly sighed with professional composure, and pronounced: "Rest.

Must not be moved. No, no, nothing serious," he quieted
Lætitia's fears, "but rest, rest. A change of residence for
a night will tone him. I will bring him a draught in the
course of the evening. Yes, yes, I'll fetch everything
wanted from the cottage for you and for him. Repose on
Corney's forethought."

"You are sure, Dr. Corney?" said Lætitia, frightened on
her father's account and on her own.

"Which aspect will be the best for Mr. Dale's bed-room?"
the hospitable ladies Eleanor and Isabel inquired.

"Southeast, decidedly : let him have the morning sun,
a warm air, a vigorous air, and a bright air, and the patient
wakes and sings in his bed."

Still doubtful whether she was in a trap, Lætitia
whispered to her father of the privacy and comforts of his
home.

He replied to her that he thought he would rather be in
his own home.

Dr. Corney positively pronounced No to it.

Lætitia breathed again of home, but with the sigh of one
overborne.

The ladies Eleanor and Isabel took the word from
Willoughby, and said : "But you are at home, my dear.
This is your home. Your father will be at least as well
attended here as at the cottage."

She raised her eyelids on them mournfully, and by chance
diverted her look to Dr. Middleton, quite by chance.

It spoke eloquently to the assembly of all that Willoughby
desired to be imagined.

"But there is Crossjay," she cried. "My cousin has gone,
and the boy is left alone. I cannot have him left alone. If
we, if, Dr. Corney, you are sure it is unsafe for papa to be
moved to-day, Crossjay must . . . he cannot be left."

"Bring him with you, Corney," said Sir Willoughby : and
the little doctor heartily promised that he would, in the
event of his finding Crossjay at the cottage, which he
thought a distant probability.

"He gave me his word he would not go out till my
return," said Lætitia.

"And if Crossjay gave you his word," the accents of a
new voice vibrated close by, "be certain that he will not
come back with Dr. Corney unless he has authority in your
handwriting."

Clara Middleton stepped gently to Lætitia, and with a
manner that was an embrace, as much as kissed her for
what she was doing on behalf of Crossjay. She put her
lips in a pouting form to simulate saying : "Press it."

"He is to come," said Lætitia.

"Then, write him his permit."

There was a chatter about Crossjay and the sentinel true
to his post that he could be, during which Lætitia dis-
tressfully scribbled a line for Dr. Corney to deliver to him.
Clara stood near. She had rebuked herself for a want of

reserve in the presence of Lady Busshe and Lady Culmer, and she was guilty of a slightly excessive containment when she next addressed Lætitia. It was, like Lætitia's look at Dr. Middleton, opportune: enough to make a man who watched as Willoughby did, a fatalist for life: the shadow of a difference in her bearing toward Lætitia sufficed to impute acting, either to her present coolness or her previous warmth. Better still, when Dr. Middleton said: "So we leave to-morrow, my dear, and I hope you have written to the Darletons," Clara flushed and beamed, and repressed her animation on a sudden, with one grave look, that might be thought regretful, to where Willoughby stood.

Chance works for us when we are good captains.

Willoughby's pride was high, though he knew himself to be keeping it up like a fearfully dexterous juggler, and for an empty reward: but he was in the toils of the world.

"Have you written? The post-bag leaves in half an hour," he addressed her.

"We are expected, but I will write," she replied: and her not having yet written counted in his favour.

She went to write the letter. Dr. Corney had departed on his mission to fetch Crossjay and medicine. Lady Busshe was impatient to be gone. "Corney," she said to Lady Culmer, "is a deadly gossip."

"Inveterate," was the answer.

"My poor horses!"

"Not the young pair of bays?"

"Luckily, my dear. And don't let me hear of dining to-night!"

Sir Willoughby was leading out Mr. Dale to a quiet room, contiguous to the invalid gentleman's bed-chamber. He resigned him to Lætitia in the hall, that he might have the pleasure of conducting the ladies to their carriage.

"As little agitation as possible. Corney will soon be back," he said, bitterly admiring the graceful subservience of Lætitia's figure to her father's weight on her arm.

He had won a desperate battle, but what had he won? What had the world given him in return for his efforts to gain it? Just a shirt, it might be said: simple scanty clothing, no warmth. Lady Busshe was unbearable; she gabbled; she was ill-bred, permitted herself to speak of Dr. Middleton as ineligible, no loss to the county. And Mrs. Mountstuart was hardly much above her, with her inevitable stroke of caricature:—"You see Dr. Middleton's pulpit scampering after him with legs!" Perhaps the Rev. Doctor did punish the world for his having forsaken his pulpit, and might be conceived as haunted by it at his heels, but Willoughby was in the mood to abhor comic images: he hated the perpetrators of them and the grinners. Contempt of this laughing empty world, for which he had performed a monstrous immolation, led him to associate Dr. Middleton in his mind, and Clara too, with the desireable things he had sacrificed — a shape of youth and health; a sparkling companion; a face of innumerable charms; and his own veracity; his inner sense of his dignity; and his temper, and the limpid frankness of his air of scorn, that was to him a visage of candid happiness in the dim retrospect. Haply also he had sacrificed more; he looked scientifically into the future: he might have sacrificed a nameless more. And for what? he asked again. For the favourable looks and tongues of these women whose looks and tongues he detested!

"Dr. Middleton says he is indebted to me: I am deeply in *his* debt," he remarked.

"It is we who are in *your* debt for a lovely romance, my dear Sir Willoughby," said Lady Busshe, incapable of taking a correction, so thoroughly had he imbued her with his fiction, or with the belief that she had a good story to circulate.

Away she drove, rattling her tongue to Lady Culmer.

"A hat and horn, and she would be in the old figure of a post-boy on a hue-and-cry sheet," said Mrs. Mountstuart.[6]

Willoughby thanked the great lady for her services, and she complimented the polished gentleman on his noble self-possession. But she complained at the same time of being defrauded of her "charmer" Colonel De Craye since luncheon. An absence of warmth in her compliment caused Willoughby to shrink and think the wretched shirt he had got from the world no covering after all: a breath flapped it.

"He comes to me, to-morrow, I believe," she said, reflecting on her superior knowledge of facts in comparison with Lady Busshe, who would presently be hearing of something novel, and exclaiming: "So, *that* is why you patronized the colonel!" And it was nothing of the sort, for Mrs. Mountstuart could honestly say she was not the woman to make a business of her pleasure.

"Horace is an enviable fellow," said Willoughby, wise in The Book, which bids us ever, for an assuagement, to fancy our friend's condition worse than our own, and recommends the deglutition of irony as the most balsamic for wounds in the whole moral pharmacopœia.[7]

"I don't know," she replied with a marked accent of deliberation.

"The colonel is to have you to himself to-morrow!"

"I can't be sure of what I shall have in the colonel!"

"Your perpetual sparkler?"

Mrs. Mountstuart set her head in motion. She left the matter silent.

"I'll come for him in the morning," she said, and her carriage whirled her off.

Either she had guessed it, or Clara had confided to her the treacherous passion of Horace De Craye!

However, the world was shut away from Patterne for the night.

---

6. "Hue-and-cry sheets" used to be circulated to advertise for criminals; "post-boys" would sometimes be shown on them, crying aloud a description of the fugitive.

7. "deglutition": swallowing; balsamic: generally efficacious.

CHAPTER 47

SIR WILLOUGHBY AND HIS FRIEND HORACE DE CRAYE

WILLOUGHBY shut himself up in his laboratory to brood awhile after the conflict. Sounding through himself, as it was habitual with him to do, for the plan most agreeable to his taste, he came on a strange discovery among the lower circles of that microcosm. He was no longer guided in his choice by liking and appetite : he had to put it on the edge of a sharp discrimination and try it by his acutest judgment before it was acceptable to his heart : and knowing well the direction of his desire, he was nevertheless unable to run two strides on a wish. He had learnt to read the world : his partial capacity for reading persons had fled. The mysteries of his own bosom were bare to him ; but he could comprehend them only in their immediate relation to the world outside. This hateful world had caught him and transformed him to a machine. The discovery he made was, that in the gratification of the egoistic instinct we may so beset ourselves as to deal a slaughtering wound upon Self to whatsoever quarter we turn.

Surely there is nothing stranger in mortal experience. The man was confounded. At the game of Chess it is the dishonour of our adversary when we are stale-mated : but in life, combatting the world, such a winning of the game questions our sentiments.

Willoughby's interpretation of his discovery was directed by pity : he had no other strong emotion left in him. He pitied himself, and he reached the conclusion that he suffered because he was active ; he could not be quiescent. Had it not been for his devotion to his house and name, never would he have stood twice the victim of womankind. Had he been selfish, he would have been the happiest of men ! He said it aloud. He schemed benevolently for his unborn young, and for the persons about him : hence he was in a position forbidding a step under pain of injury to his feelings. He was generous : otherwise would he not in scorn of soul, at the outset, straight off, have pitched Clara Middleton to the wanton winds ? He was faithful in affection : Lætitia Dale was beneath his roof to prove it. Both these women were examples of his power of forgiveness, and now a tender word to Clara might fasten shame on him — such was her gratitude ! And if he did not marry Lætitia, laughter would be devilish all around him — such was the world's ! Probably Vernon would not long be thankful for the chance which varied the monotony of his days. What of Horace ? Willoughby stripped to enter the ring with Horace : he cast away disguise. That man had been the first to divide him in the all but equal slices of his egoistic from his amatory self : murder of his individuality was the crime of Horace

De Craye. And further, suspicion fixed on Horace (he knew not how, except that The Book bids us be suspicious of those we hate) as the man who had betrayed his recent dealings with Lætitia.

Willoughby walked the thoroughfares of the house to meet Clara and make certain of her either for himself or, if it must be, for Vernon, before he took another step with Lætitia Dale. Clara could reunite him, turn him once more into a whole and an animated man; and she might be willing. Her willingness to listen to Vernon promised it. "A gentleman with a tongue would have a chance," Mrs. Mountstuart had said. How much greater the chance of a lover! For he had not yet supplicated her: he had shown pride and temper. He could woo, he was a torrential wooer. And it would be glorious to swing round on Lady Busshe and the world, with Clara nestling under an arm, and protest astonishment at the erroneous and utterly unfounded anticipations of any other development. And it would righteously punish Lætitia.

Clara came downstairs, bearing her letter to Miss Darleton.

"*Must* it be posted?" Willoughby said, meeting her in the hall.

"They expect us any day, but it will be more comfortable for papa," was her answer. She looked kindly in her new shyness.

She did not seem to think he had treated her contemptuously in flinging her to his cousin, which was odd.

"You have seen Vernon?"

"It was your wish."

"You had a talk?"

"We conversed."

"A long one?"

"We walked some distance."

"Clara, I tried to make the best arrangement I could."

"Your intention was generous."

"He took no advantage of it?"

"It could not be treated seriously."

"It was meant seriously."

"There I see the generosity."

Willoughby thought this encomium, and her consent to speak on the subject, and her scarcely embarrassed air and richness of tone in speaking, very strange: and strange was her taking him quite in earnest. Apparently she had no feminine sensation of the unwontedness and the absurdity of the matter.

"But, Clara! am I to understand that he did not speak out?"

"We are excellent friends."

"To miss it, though his chance were the smallest!"

"You forget that it may not wear that appearance to him."

"He spoke not one word of himself?"

" No."

" Ah! the poor old fellow was taught to see it was hopeless — chilled. May I plead? Will you step into the laboratory for a minute? We are two sensible persons . . ."

" Pardon me, I must go to papa."

" Vernon's personal history perhaps . . . ? "

" I think it honourable to him."

" Honourable! — 'hem! "

" By comparison."

" Comparison with what? "

" With others."

He drew up to relieve himself of a critical and condemnatory expiration of a certain length. This young lady knew too much. But how physically exquisite she was!

" Could you, Clara, could you promise me — I hold to it. I must have it, I know his shy tricks — promise me to give him ultimately another chance? Is the idea repulsive to you? "

" It is one not to be thought of."

" It is not repulsive? "

" Nothing could be repulsive in Mr. Whitford."

" I have no wish to annoy you, Clara."

" I feel bound to listen to you, Willoughby. Whatever I can do to please you, I will. It is my life-long duty."

" Could you, Clara, could you conceive it, could you simply conceive it; — give him your hand? "

" As a friend, Oh! yes."

" In marriage."

She paused. She, so penetrative of him when he opposed her, was hoodwinked when he softened her feelings: for the heart, — though the clearest, is not the most constant instructor of the head; the heart, unlike the often obtuser head, works for itself and not for the commonwealth.

" You are so kind . . . I would do much . . . " she said.

" Would you accept him — marry him? He is poor."

" I am not ambitious of wealth."

" *Would* you marry him? "

" Marriage is not in my thoughts."

" But could you marry him? "

Willoughby expected no. In his expectation of it he hung inflated.

She said these words: "I could engage to marry no one else."

His amazement breathed without a syllable.

He flapped his arms, resembling for the moment those birds of enormous body which attempt a rise upon their wings and achieve a hop.

" Would you engage it? " he said, content to see himself stepped on as an insect if he could but feel the agony of his false friend Horace — their common pretensions to win her were now of that comparative size.

"Oh! there can be no necessity. And an oath — no!" said Clara, inwardly shivering at a recollection.

"But you could?"

"My wish is to please you."

"You could?"

"I said so."

It has been known of the patriotic mountaineer of a hoary pile of winters, with little life remaining in him, but that little on fire for his country, that by the brink of the precipice he has flung himself on a young and lusty invader, dedicating himself exultingly to death if only he may score a point for his country by extinguishing in his country's enemy the stronger man. So likewise did Willoughby, in the blow that deprived him of hope, exult in the toppling over of Horace De Craye. They perished together, but which one sublimely relished the headlong descent? And Vernon taken by Clara would be Vernon simply tolerated. And Clara taken by Vernon would be Clara previously touched, smirched. Altogether he could enjoy his fall.

It was at least upon a comfortable bed, where his pride would be dressed daily and would never be disagreeably treated.

He was henceforth Lætitia's own. The bell telling of Dr. Corney's return was a welcome sound to Willoughby, and he said good-humouredly : "Wait, Clara, you will see your hero Crossjay."

Crossjay and Dr. Corney tumbled into the hall. Willoughby caught Crossjay under the arms to give him a lift in the old fashion pleasing to Clara to see. The boy was heavy as lead.

"I had work to hook him and worse to net him," said Dr. Corney. "I had to make him believe he was to nurse every soul in the house, you among them, Miss Middleton."

Willoughby pulled the boy aside.

Crossjay came back to Clara heavier in looks than his limbs had been. She dropped her letter in the hall-box, and took his hand to have a private hug of him. When they were alone, she said : "Crossjay, my dear, my dear! You look unhappy."

"Yes, and who wouldn't be, and you're not to marry Sir Willoughby!" his voice threatened a cry. "I know you're not, for Dr. Corney says you are going to leave."

"Did you so very much wish it, Crossjay?"

"I should have seen a lot of you, and I sha'n't see you at all, and I'm sure if I'd known I wouldn't have — and he has been and tipped me this."

Crossjay opened his fist in which lay three gold pieces.

"That was very kind of him," said Clara.

"Yes, but how can I keep it?"

"By handing it to Mr. Whitford to keep for you."

"Yes, but, Miss Middleton, ought n't I to tell him? I mean Sir Willoughby."

"What?"

"Why, that I," Crossjay got close to her, "why, that I, that I — you know what you used to say. I would n't tell a lie, but ought n't I, without his asking . . . and this money! I don't mind being turned out again."

"Consult Mr. Whitford," said Clara.

"I know what you think, though."

"Perhaps you had better not say anything at present, dear boy."

"But what am I to do with this money?"

Crossjay held the gold pieces out as things that had not yet mingled with his ideas of possession.

"I listened, and I told of him," he said. "I could n't help listening, but I went and told; and I don't like being here, and his money, and he not knowing what I did. Have n't you heard? I 'm certain I know what you think, and so do I, and I must take my luck, I 'm always in mischief, getting into a mess or getting out of it. I don't mind, I really don't, Miss Middleton, I can sleep in a tree quite comfortably. If you 're not going to be here, I 'd just as soon be anywhere. I must try to earn my living some day. And why not a cabin-boy? Sir Cloudesley Shovel was no better.[1] And I don't mind his being wrecked at last, if you 're drowned an admiral. So I shall go and ask him to take his money back, and if he asks me I shall tell him, and there. You know what it is: I guessed that from what Dr. Corney said. I 'm sure I know you 're thinking what 's manly. Fancy me keeping his money, and you not marrying him! I would n't mind driving a plough. I should n't make a bad gamekeeper. Of course I love boats best, but you can't have everything."

"Speak to Mr. Whitford first," said Clara, too proud of the boy for growing as she had trained him, to advise a course of conduct opposed to his notions of manliness, though now that her battle was over she would gladly have acquiesced in little casuistic compromises for the sake of the general peace.

Some time later Vernon and Dr. Corney were arguing upon the question. Corney was dead against the sentimental view of the morality of the case propounded by Vernon as coming from Miss Middleton and partly shared by him. "If it 's on the boy's mind," Vernon said, "I can't prohibit his going to Willoughby and making a clean breast of it, especially as it involves me, and sooner or later I should have to tell him myself."

Dr. Corney said no at all points. "Now hear me," he said finally. "This is between ourselves, and no breach of confidence, which I 'd not be guilty of for forty friends, though

1. Sir Cloudesley Shovell was a picturesquely named British admiral of the eighteenth century.

I 'd give my hand from the wrist-joint for one — my left, that 's to say. Sir Willoughby puts me one or two searching interrogations on a point of interest to him, his house and name. Very well, and good night to that, and I wish Miss Dale had been ten years younger, or had passed the ten with no heartrisings and sinkings wearing to the tissues of the frame and the moral fibre to boot. She 'll have a fairish health, with a little occasional doctoring; taking her rank and wealth in right earnest, and shying her pen back to Mother Goose.[2] She 'll do. And, by the way, I think it 's to the credit of my sagacity that I fetched Mr. Dale here fully primed, and roused the neighbourhood, which I did, and so fixed our gentleman, neat as a prodded eel on a pair of prongs — namely, the positive fact and the general knowledge of it. But mark me, my friend. We understand one another at a nod. This boy, young Squire Crossjay, is a good stiff hearty kind of a Saxon boy, out of whom you may cut as gallant a fellow as ever wore epaulettes. I like him, you like him, Miss Dale and Miss Middleton like him; and Sir Willoughby Patterne of Patterne Hall and other places won't be indisposed to like him mightily in the event of the sun being seen to shine upon him with a particular determination to make him appear a prominent object, because a solitary, and a Patterne." Dr. Corney lifted his chest and his finger: "Now, mark me, and verbum sap: Crossjay must not offend Sir Willoughby.[3] I say no more. Look ahead. Miracles happen, but it 's best to reckon that they won't. Well, now, and Miss Dale. She 'll not be cruel."

"It appears as if she would," said Vernon, meditating on the cloudy sketch Dr. Corney had drawn.

"She can't, my friend. Her position 's precarious; her father has little besides a pension. And her writing damages her health. She can't. And she likes the baronet. Oh, it 's only a little fit of proud blood. She 's the woman for him. She 'll manage him — give him an idea that he has got a lot of ideas. It 'd kill her father if she was obstinate. He talked to me, when I told him of the business, about his dream fulfilled, and if the dream turns to vapour, he 'll be another example that we hang more upon dreams than realities for nourishment, and medicine too. Last week I could n't have got him out of his house with all my art and science. Oh, she 'll come round. Her father prophesied this, and I 'll prophesy that. She 's fond of him."

"She was."

"She sees through him ?"

"Without quite doing justice to him now," said Vernon. "He can be generous — in his way."

"How ?" Corney inquired, and was informed that he should hear in time to come.

<hr/>

2. Laetitia will not wear herself out trying to write literature anymore, but will confine her efforts to the nursery.

3. "verbum sap": a word to the wise.

Meanwhile Colonel De Craye, after hovering over the park and about the cottage for the opportunity of pouncing on Miss Middleton alone, had returned, crest-fallen, for once, and plumped into Willoughby's hands.

"My dear Horace," Willoughby said, "I've been looking for you all the afternoon. The fact is — I fancy you'll think yourself lured down here on false pretences : but the truth is, I am not so much to blame as the world will suppose. In point of fact, to be brief, Miss Dale and I . . . I never consult other men how they would have acted. The fact of the matter is, Miss Middleton . . . I fancy you have partly guessed it."

"Partly," said De Craye.

"Well, she has a liking that way, and if it should turn out strong enough, it's the best arrangement I can think of."

The lively play of the colonel's features fixed in a blank inquiry.

"One can back a good friend for making a good husband," said Willoughby. "I could not break with her in the present stage of affairs without seeing to that. And I can speak of her highly, though she and I have seen in time that we do not suit one another. My wife must have brains."

"I have always thought it," said Colonel De Craye, glistening and looking hungry as a wolf through his wonderment.

"There will not be a word against her, you understand. You know my dislike of tattle and gossip. However, let it fall on me; my shoulders are broad. I have done my utmost to persuade her, and there seems a likelihood of her consenting. She tells me her wish is to please me, and this will please me."

"Certainly. Who's the gentleman ? "

"My best friend, I tell you. I could hardly have proposed another. Allow this business to go on smoothly just now."

There was an uproar within the colonel to blind his wits, and Willoughby looked so friendly that it was possible to suppose the man of projects had mentioned his best friend to Miss Middleton.

And who was the best friend ?

Not having accused himself of treachery, the quick-eyed colonel was duped.

"Have you his name handy, Willoughby ? "

"That would be unfair to him at present, Horace — ask yourself — and to her. Things are in a ticklish posture at present. Don't be hasty."

"Certainly. I don't ask. Initials 'll do."

"You have a remarkable aptitude for guessing, Horace, and this case offers you no tough problem — if ever you acknowledge toughness. I have a regard for her and for him — for both pretty equally ; you know I have, and I should be thoroughly thankful to bring the matter about."

"Lordly!" said De Craye.

"I don't see it. I call it sensible."

"Oh! undoubtedly. The style, I mean. Tolerably antique?"

"Novel, I should say and not the worse for that. We want plain practical dealings between men and women. Usually we go the wrong way to work. And I loath sentimental rubbish."

De Craye hummed an air. "But the lady?" said he.

"I told you, there seems a likelihood of her consenting."

Willoughby's fish gave a perceptible little leap now that he had been taught to exercise his aptitude for guessing.

"Without any of the customary preliminaries on the side of the gentleman?" he said.

"We must put him through his paces, friend Horace. He's a notorious blunderer with women; has n't a word for them, never marked a conquest."

De Craye crested his plumes under the agreeable banter. He presented a face humourously sceptical.

"The lady is positively not indisposed to give the poor fellow a hearing?"

"I have cause to think she is not," said Willoughby, glad of acting the indifference to her which could talk of her inclinations.

"Cause?"

"Good cause."

"Bless us!"

"As good as one can have with a woman."

"Ah?"

"I assure you."

"Ah! Does it seem like her, though?"

"Well, she would n't engage herself to accept him."

"Well, that seems more like her."

"But she said she could engage to marry no one else."

The colonel sprang up, crying: "Clara Middleton said it?" He curbed himself. "That's a bit of wonderful compliancy."

"She wishes to please me. We separate on those terms. And I wish her happiness. I've developed a heart lately and taken to think of others."

"Nothing better. You appear to make cock sure of the other party — our friend?"

"You know him too well, Horace, to doubt his readiness."

"Do *you*, Willoughby?"

"She has money and good looks. Yes, I can say I do."

"It would n't be much of a man who 'd want hard pulling to that lighted altar!"

"And if he requires persuasion, you and I, Horace, might bring him to his senses."

"Kicking, 't would be!"

"I like to see everybody happy about me," said Willoughby, naming the hour as time to dress for dinner.

The sentiment he had delivered was De Craye's excuse for grasping his hand and complimenting him; but the colonel betrayed himself by doing it with an extreme fervour almost tremulous.

"When shall we hear more?" he said.

"Oh, probably to-morrow," said Willoughby. "Don't be in such a hurry."

"I'm an <u>infant asleep</u>!" the colonel replied, departing.

He resembled one, to Willoughby's mind: or a <u>traitor drugged</u>.

"There is a fellow I thought had some brains!"

Who are not fools to be set spinning if we choose to whip them with their vanity! It is the consolation of the great to watch them spin. But the pleasure is loftier, and may comfort our unmerited misfortune for a while, in making a false friend drunk.

Willoughby, among his many preoccupations, had the satisfaction of seeing the effect of drunkenness on Horace De Craye when the latter was in Clara's presence. He could have laughed. Cut in keen epigram were the marginal notes added by him to that chapter of The Book which treats of friends and a woman: and had he not been profoundly preoccupied, troubled by recent intelligence communicated by the ladies, his aunts, he would have played the two together for the royal amusement afforded him by his friend Horace.

CHAPTER 48

THE LOVERS

THE hour was close upon eleven at night. Lætitia sat in the room adjoining her father's bed-chamber. Her elbow was on the table beside her chair, and two fingers pressed her temples. The state between thinking and feeling, when both are molten and flow by us, is one of our nature's intermissions, coming after thought has quieted the fiery nerves, and can do no more. She seemed to be meditating. She was conscious only of a struggle past.

She answered a tap at the door, and raised her eyes on Clara.

Clara stepped softly. "Mr. Dale is asleep?"

"I hope so."

"Ah! dear friend."

Lætitia let her hand be pressed.

"Have you had a pleasant evening?"

"Mr. Whitford and papa have gone to the library."

"Colonel De Craye has been singing?"

"Yes — with a voice! I thought of you upstairs, but

could not ask him to sing piano."[1]

"He is probably exhilarated."

"One would suppose it: he sang well."

"You are not aware of any reason?"

"It cannot concern me."

Clara was in rosy colour, but could meet a steady gaze.

"And Crossjay has gone to bed?"

"Long since. He was at dessert. He would not touch anything."

"He is a strange boy."

"Not very strange, Lætitia."

"He did not come to me to wish me good night."

"That is not strange."

"It is his habit at the cottage and here; and he professes to like me."

"Oh! he does. I may have wakened his enthusiasm, but you he loves."

"Why do you say it is not strange, Clara?"

"He fears you a little."

"And why should Crossjay fear me?"

"Dear, I will tell you. Last night — You will forgive him, for it was by accident: his own bed-room door was locked and he ran down to the drawing-room and curled himself up on the ottoman, and fell asleep, under that padded silken coverlet of the ladies — boots and all, I am afraid!"

Lætitia profited by this absurd allusion, thanking Clara in her heart for the refuge.

"He should have taken off his boots," she said.

"He slept there, and woke up. Dear, he meant no harm. Next day he repeated what he had heard. You will blame him. He meant well in his poor boy's head. And now it is over the county. Ah! do not frown."

"That explains Lady Busshe!" exclaimed Lætitia.

"Dear, dear friend," said Clara. "Why — I presume on your tenderness for me; but let me: to-morrow I go — why will you reject your happiness? Those kind good ladies are deeply troubled. They say your resolution is inflexible; you resist their entreaties and your father's. Can it be that you have any doubt of the strength of this attachment? I have none. I have never had a doubt that it was the strongest of his feelings. If before I go I could see you . . . both happy, I should be relieved, I should rejoice."

Lætitia said quietly: "Do you remember a walk we had one day together to the cottage?"

Clara put up her hands with the motion of intending to stop her ears.

"Before I go!" said she. "If I might know this was to be, which all desire, before I leave, I should not feel as I do now. I long to see you happy . . . him, yes, him too. Is

it like asking you to pay my debt? Then, please! But,
no; I am not more than partly selfish on this occasion. He
has won my gratitude. He can be really generous."

"An Egoist?"

"Who is?"

"You have forgotten our conversation on the day of our
walk to the cottage?"

"Help me to forget it — that day, and those days, and all
those days! I should be glad to think I passed a time
beneath the earth, and have risen again. I was the Egoist.
I am sure, if I had been buried, I should not have stood up
seeing myself more vilely stained, soiled, disfigured — oh!
Help me to forget my conduct, Lætitia. He and I were
unsuited — and I remember I blamed myself then. You
and he are not: and now I can perceive the pride that can be
felt in him. The worst that can be said is, that he schemes
too much."

"Is there any fresh scheme?" said Lætitia.

The rose came over Clara's face.

"You have not heard? It was impossible, but it was
kindly intended. Judging by my own feeling at this moment, I can understand his. We love to see our friends
established."

Lætitia bowed. "My curiosity is piqued, of course."

"Dear friend, to-morrow we shall be parted. I trust to
be thought of by you as a little better in grain than I have
appeared, and my reason for trusting it is, that I know I
have been always honest — a boorish young woman in my
stupid mad impatience; but not insincere.[2] It is no lofty
ambition to desire to be remembered in that character, but
such is your Clara, she discovers. I will tell you. It is
his wish . . . his wish that I should promise to give my
hand to Mr. Whitford. You see the kindness."

Lætitia's eyes widened and fixed, —

"You think it kindness?"

"The intention. He sent Mr. Whitford to me, and I
was taught to expect him."

"Was that quite kind to Mr. Whitford?"

"What an impression I must have made on you during
that walk to the cottage, Lætitia! I do not wonder; I was
in a fever."

"You consented to listen?"

"I really did. It astonishes me now, but I thought I
could not refuse."

"My poor friend Vernon Whitford tried a love speech."

"He? no: Oh! no."

"You discouraged him?"

"I? no."

"Gently, I mean."

"No."

2. "grain": real nature.

"Surely you did not dream of trifling? He has a deep heart."

"Has he?"

"You ask that: and you know something of him."

"He did not expose it to me, dear; not even the surface of the mighty deep."

Lætitia knitted her brows.

"No," said Clara, "not a coquette: she is not a coquette, I assure you."

With a laugh, Lætitia replied: "You have still the 'dreadful power' you made me feel that day."

"I wish I could use it to good purpose!"

"He did not speak?"

"Of Switzerland, Tyrol, the Iliad, Antigone."

"That was all?"

"No, Political Economy.[3] Our situation, you will own, was unexampled: or mine was. Are you interested in me?"

"I should be, if I knew your sentiments."

"I was grateful to Sir Willoughby: grieved for Mr. Whitford."

"Real grief?"

"Because the task imposed on him of showing me politely that he did not enter into his cousin's ideas, was evidently very great, extremely burdensome."

"You, so quick-eyed in some things, Clara!"

"He felt for me. I saw that, in his avoidance of . . . And he was, as he always is, pleasant. We rambled over the park for I know not how long, though it did not seem long."

"Never touching that subject?"

"Not ever neighbouring it, dear. A gentleman should esteem the girl he would ask . . . certain questions. I fancy he has a liking for me as a volatile friend."

"If he had offered himself?"

"Despising me?"

"You can be childish, Clara. Probably you delight to tease. He had his time of it, and it is now my turn."

"But he must despise me a little."

"Are you blind?"

"Perhaps, dear, we both are, a little."

The ladies looked deeper into one another.

"Will you answer me?" said Lætitia.

"Your if? If he had, it would have been an act of con-descension."

"You are too slippery."

"Stay, dear Lætitia. He was considerate in forbearing to pain me."

"That is an answer. You allowed him to perceive that it would have pained you."

---

3. The dismal science of economics. Vernon has been scrupulous in not imposing his attentions on a lady who, he is afraid, does not want them.

" Dearest, if I may convey to you what I was, in a simile
for comparison : I think I was like a fisherman's float on
the water, perfectly still, and ready to go down at any instant, or up.   So much for my behaviour."

" Similes have the merit of satisfying the finder of them,
and cheating the hearer," said Lætitia.   " You admit that
your feelings would have been painful."

" I was a fisherman's float : please, admire my simile
any way you like, this way or that, or so quiet as to tempt
the eyes to go to sleep.   And suddenly I might have disappeared in the depths, or flown in the air.   But no fish
bit."

" Well, then, to follow you, supposing the fish or the
fisherman, for I don't know which is which . . .   Oh ! no,
no : this is too serious for imagery.   I am to understand
that you thanked him at least for his reserve."

" Yes."

" Without the slightest encouragement to him to break
it ? "

" A fisherman's float, Lætitia ! "

Baffled and sighing, Lætitia kept silence for a space.

The simile chafed her wits with a suspicion of a meaning
hidden in it.

" If he had spoken ? " she said.

" He is too truthful a man."

" And the railings of men at pussy women who wind
about and will not be brought to a mark, become intelligible
to me."

" Then, Lætitia, if he had spoken, if, and one could have
imagined him sincere . . . "

" So truthful a man ? "

" I am looking at myself.   If ! — why, then, I should
have burnt to death with shame.   Where have I read ? —
some story — of an inextinguishable spark.   That would
have been shot into my heart."

" Shame, Clara?   You are free."

" As much as remains of me."

" I could imagine a certain shame, in such a position,
where there was no feeling but pride."

" I could not imagine it where there was no feeling but
pride."

Lætitia mused : " And you dwell on the kindness of a
proposition so extraordinary ! "   Gaining some light, impatiently she cried : " Vernon loves you."

" Do not say it ! "

" I have seen it."

" I have never had a sign of it."

" There is the proof."

" When it might have been shown again and again ! "

" The greater proof ! "

" Why did he not speak when he was privileged ? —
strangely, but privileged."

"He feared."

"Me?"

"Feared to wound you—and himself as well, possibly. Men may be pardoned for thinking of themselves in these cases."

"But why should he fear?"

"That another was dearer to you?"

"What cause had I given . . . Ah! see! He could fear that; suspect it! See his opinion of me! Can he care for such a girl? Abuse me, Lætitia. I should like a good round of abuse. I need purification by fire. What have I been in this house? I have a sense of whirling through it like a madwoman. And to be loved, after it all!—No! we must be hearing a tale of an antiquary prizing a battered relic of the battle-field that no one else would look at. To be loved, I see, is to feel our littleness, hollowness— feel shame. We come out in all our spots. Never to have given me one sign, when a lover would have been so tempted! Let me be incredulous, my own dear Lætitia. Because he is a man of honour, you would say! But are you unconscious of the torture you inflict? For if I am — you say it—loved by this gentleman, what an object it is he loves—that has gone clamouring about more immodestly than women will bear to hear of, and she herself to think of! Oh! I have seen my own heart. It is a frightful spectre. I have seen a weakness in me that would have carried me anywhere. And truly I shall be charitable to women — I have gained that. But, loved! by Vernon Whitford! The miserable little me to be taken up and loved after tearing myself to pieces! Have you been simply speculating? You have no positive knowledge of it! Why do you kiss me?"

"Why do you tremble and blush so?"

Clara looked at her as clearly as she could. She bowed her head. "It makes my conduct worse!"

She received a tenderer kiss for that. It was her avowal, and it was understood to know that she had loved, or had been ready to love him, shadowed her in the retrospect.

"Ah! you read me through and through," said Clara, sliding to her for a whole embrace.

"Then there never was cause for him to fear?" Lætitia whispered.

Clara slid her head more out of sight. "Not that my heart . . . But I said I have seen it; and it is unworthy of him. And if, as I think now, I could have been so rash, so weak, wicked, unpardonable—such thoughts were in me! —then to hear him speak, would make it necessary for me to uncover myself and tell him—incredible to you, yes!—that while . . . yes, Lætitia, all this is true: and thinking of him as the noblest of men, I could have welcomed any help to cut my knot. So there," said Clara, issuing from her nest with winking eyelids, "you see the pain I mentioned."

" Why did you not explain it to me at once ? "

" Dearest, I wanted a century to pass."

" And you feel that it has passed ? "

" Yes ; in Purgatory — with an angel by me. My report of the place will be favourable. Good angel, I have yet to say something."

" Say it, and expiate."

" I think I did fancy once or twice, very dimly, and espe cially to-day . . . properly I ought not to have had any idea : but his coming to me, and his not doing as another would have done, seemed . . . A gentleman of real noble ness does not carry the common light for us to read him by. I wanted his voice ; but silence, I think, did tell me more : if a nature like mine could only have had faith without hearing the rattle of a tongue."

A knock at the door caused the ladies to exchange looks.

Lætitia rose as Vernon entered.

" I am just going to my father for a few minutes,'' she said.

" And I have just come from yours," Vernon said to Clara.

She observed a very threatening expression in him.

The sprite of contrariety mounted to her brain to indem nify her for her recent self-abasement. Seeing the bed-room door shut on Lætitia, she said : " And of course papa has gone to bed," implying " otherwise . . . "

" Yes, he has gone. He wished me well."

" His formula of good night would embrace that wish."

" And failing, it will be good night for good to me ! "

Clara's breathing gave a little leap. " We leave early to-morrow."

" I know. I have an appointment at Bregenz for June."[4]

" So soon ? With papa ? "

" And from there we break into Tyrol, and round away to the right, Southward."

" To the Italian Alps ! And was it assumed that I should be of this expedition ? "

" Your father speaks dubiously."

" You have spoken of me, then ? "

" I ventured to speak of you. I am not over-bold, as you know."

Her lovely eyes troubled the lids to hide their softness.

" Papa should not think of my presence with him dubiously."

" He leaves it to you to decide."

" Yes, then : many times : all that can be uttered."

" Do you consider what you are saying ? "

" Mr. Whitford, I shut my eyes and say Yes."

" Beware. I give you one warning. If you shut your eyes . . . "

4. Bregenz is a mountain-climbing center in the Austrian Alps.

"Of course," she flew from him, "big mountains must be satisfied with my admiration at their feet."

"That will do for a beginning."

"They speak encouragingly."

"One of them." Vernon's breast heaved high.

"To be at your feet makes a mountain of you?" said she.

"With the heart of a mouse if that satisfies me!"

"You tower too high; you are inaccessible."

"I give you a second warning. You may be seized and lifted."

"Some one would stoop, then."

"To plant you like the flag on the conquered peak!"

"You have indeed been talking to papa, Mr. Whitford." Vernon changed his tone.

"Shall I tell you what he said?"

"I know his language so well."

"He said—"

"But you have acted on it."

"Only partly. He said—"

"You will teach me nothing."

"He said . . ."

"Vernon, no! oh! not in this house!"

That supplication coupled with his name confessed the end to which her quick vision perceived she was being led, where she would succumb.

She revived the same shrinking in him from a breath of their great word yet: not here; somewhere in the shadow of the mountains.

But he was sure of her. And their hands might join. The two hands thought so, or did not think, behaved like innocents.

The spirit of Dr. Middleton, as Clara felt, had been blown into Vernon, rewarding him for forthright outspeaking. Over their books, Vernon had abruptly shut up a volume and related the tale of the house. "Has this man a spice of religion in him?" the Rev. Doctor asked midway. Vernon made out a fair general case for his cousin in that respect. "The complemental dot on his i of a commonly civilized human creature!" said Dr. Middleton, looking at his watch and finding it too late to leave the house before morning. The risky communication was to come. Vernon was proceeding with the narrative of Willoughby's generous plan when Dr. Middleton electrified him by calling out: "He whom of all men living I should desire my daughter to espouse!" and Willoughby rose in the Rev. Doctor's esteem: he praised that sensibly minded gentleman, who could acquiesce in the turn of mood of a little maid, albeit Fortune had withheld from him a taste of the switch at school. The father of the little maid's appreciation of her volatility was exhibited in his exhortation to Vernon to be off to her at once with his authority to finish her moods and assure him of peace in the morning. Vernon hesitated. Dr. Mid-

dleton remarked upon being not so sure that it was not he
who had done the mischief. Thereupon Vernon, to prove
his honesty, made his own story bare. " Go to her," said
Dr. Middleton. Vernon proposed a meeting in Switzerland,
to which Dr. Middleton assented, adding: " Go to her : " and
as he appeared a total stranger to the decorum of the situation, Vernon put his delicacy aside, and taking his heart up,
obeyed. He too had pondered on Clara's consent to meet
him after she knew of Willoughby's terms, and her grave
sweet manner during the ramble over the park. Her
father's breath had been blown into him ; so now, with
nothing but the faith lying in sensation to convince him of
his happy fortune (and how unconvincing that may be until
the mind has grasped and stamped it, we experience even
then when we acknowledge that we are most blest), he held
her hand. And if it was hard for him, for both, but harder
for the man, to restrain their particular word from a flight
to heaven when the cage stood open and nature beckoned,
he was practised in self-mastery, and she loved him the
more.

Lætitia was a witness of their union of hands on her
coming back to the room.

They promised to visit her very early in the morning,
neither of them conceiving that they left her to a night of
storm and tears.

She sat meditating on Clara's present appreciation of Sir
Willoughby's generosity.

CHAPTER 49

LÆTITIA AND SIR WILLOUGHBY

WE cannot be abettors of the tribes of imps whose revelry
is in the frailties of our poor human constitution. They
have their place and their service, and so long as we continue to be what we are now, they will hang on to us, rest-
lessly plucking at the garments which cover our nakedness,
nor ever ceasing to twitch them and strain at them until
they have fairly stripped us for one of their horrible Walpurgis nights : when the laughter heard is of a character to
render laughter frightful to the ears of men throughout the
remainder of their days.[1] But if in these festival hours
under the beams of Hecate they are uncontrollable by the
Comic Muse, she will not flatter them with her presence
during the course of their insane and impious hilarities,
whereof a description would out-Brocken Brockens and make
Graymalkin and Paddock too intimately our familiars.[2]

1. "Walpurgis nights": witches' sabbaths.
2. "beams of Hecate": the moon in her
aspect as patroness of hags and witches.
"Brocken": a German mountain on

which witches are said to hold their rev-
els, as in Goethe's *Faust*. "Greymalkin
and Paddock": beasts infested by diabolic
spirits.

It shall suffice to say that from hour to hour of the midnight to the grey-eyed morn, assisted at intervals by the
ladies Eleanor and Isabel, and by Mr. Dale awakened and
reawakened — hearing the vehemence of his petitioning outcry to soften her obduracy — Sir Willoughby pursued Lætitia
with solicitations to espouse him, until the inveteracy of his
wooing wore the aspect of the life-long love he raved of
aroused to a state of mania. He appeared, he departed, he
returned; and all the while his imps were about him and
upon him, riding him, prompting, driving, inspiring him
with outrageous pathos, an eloquence to move any one but
the dead, which its object seemed to be in her torpid attention. He heard them, he talked to them, caressed them ;
he flung them off and ran from them, and stood vanquished
for them to mount him again and swarm on him. There
are men thus imp-haunted. Men who, setting their minds
upon an object, must have it, breed imps. They are noted
for their singularities, as their converse with the invisible
and amazing distractions are called. Willoughby became
aware of them that night. He said to himself, upon one of
his dashes into solitude : I believe I am possessed ! And if
he did not actually believe it, but only suspected it, or
framed speech to account for the transformation he had
undergone into a desperately beseeching creature, having
lost acquaintance with his habitual personality, the opera-
tions of an impish host had undoubtedly smitten his
consciousness.

He had them in his brain : for while burning with an
ardour for Lætitia, that incited him to frantic excesses of
language and comportment, he was aware of shouts of the
names of Lady Busshe and Mrs. Mountstuart Jenkinson, the
which, freezing him as they did, were directly the cause of
his hurrying to a wilder extravagance and more headlong
determination to subdue before break of day the woman he
almost dreaded to behold by daylight, though he had now
passionately persuaded himself of his love of her. He could
not, he felt, stand in the daylight without her. She was his
morning. She was, he raved, his predestinated wife. He
cried : "Darling !" both to her and to solitude. Every
prescription of his ideal of demeanour as an example to his
class and country, was abandoned by the enamoured gentleman. He had lost command of his countenance. He
stooped so far as to kneel, and not gracefully. Nay, it is in
the chronicles of the invisible host around him, that in a fit
of supplication, upon a cry of " Lætitia !" twice repeated,
he whimpered.

Let so much suffice. And indeed not without reason do
the multitudes of the servants of the Muse in this land of
social policy avoid scenes of an inordinate wantonness,
which detract from the dignity of our leaders and menace
human nature with confusion. Sagacious are they who conduct the individual on broad lines, over familiar tracks,

under well-known characteristics. What men will do, and amorously minded men will do, is less the question than what it is politic that they should be shown to do.

The night wore through. Lætitia was bent, but had not yielded. She had been obliged to say — and how many times, she could not bear to recollect: "I do not love you; I have no love to give;" and issuing from such a night to look again upon the face of day, she scarcely felt that she was alive.

The contest was renewed by her father with the singing of the birds. Mr. Dale then produced the first serious impression she had received. He spoke of their circumstances, of his being taken from her and leaving her to poverty, in weak health; of the injury done to her health by writing for bread; and of the oppressive weight he would be relieved of by her consenting. He no longer implored her; he put the case on common ground.

And he wound up: "Pray do not be ruthless, my girl."

The practical statement, and this adjuration incongruously to conclude it, harmonized with her disordered understanding, her loss of all sentiment and her desire to be kind. She sighed to herself: "Happily, it is over!"

Her father was too weak to rise. He fell asleep. She was bound down to the house for hours; and she walked through her suite, here at the doors, there at the windows, thinking of Clara's remark "of a century passing." She had not wished it, but a light had come on her to show her what she would have supposed a century could not have effected: she saw the impossible of overnight a possible thing: not desireable, yet possible, wearing the features of the possible. Happily, she had resisted too firmly to be again besought.

Those features of the possible once beheld allured the mind to reconsider them. Wealth gives us the power to do good on earth. Wealth enables us to see the world, the beautiful scenes of the earth. Lætitia had long thirsted both for a dowering money-bag at her girdle, and the wings to fly abroad over lands which had begun to seem fabulous in her starved imagination.[3] Then, moreover, if her sentiment for this gentleman was gone, it was only a delusion gone; accurate sight and knowledge of him would not make a woman the less helpful mate. That was the mate he required: and he could be led. A sentimental attachment would have been serviceless to him. Not so the woman allied by a purely rational bond: and he wanted guiding. Happily, she had told him too much of her feeble health and her lovelessness to be reduced to submit to another attack.

She busied herself in her room, arranging for her departure, so that no minutes might be lost after her father had breakfasted and dressed.

3. Laetitia has always wanted money, in order to give it to others.

Clara was her earliest visitor, and each asked the other whether she had slept, and took the answer from the face presented to her. The rings of Lætitia's eyes were very dark. Clara was her mirror, and she said : " A singular object to be persecuted through a night for her hand ! I know these two damp dead leaves I wear on my cheeks to remind me of midnight vigils. But you have slept well, Clara."

" I have slept well, and yet I could say I have not slept at all, Lætitia. I was with you, dear, part in dream and part in thought : hoping to find you sensible before I go."

"Sensible. That is the word for me."

Lætitia briefly sketched the history of the night; and Clara said, with a manifest sincerity that testified of her gratitude to Sir Willoughby : " Could you resist him, so earnest as he is ? "

Lætitia saw the human nature without sourness : and replied : " I hope, Clara, you will not begin with a large stock of sentiment, for there is nothing like it for making you hard, matter-of-fact, worldly, calculating."

The next visitor was Vernon, exceedingly anxious for news of Mr. Dale. Lætitia went into her father's room to obtain it for him. Returning she found them both with sad visages, and she ventured, in alarm for them, to ask the cause.

"It's this," Vernon said : " Willoughby will everlastingly tease that boy to be loved by him. Perhaps, poor fellow, he had an excuse last night. Anyhow he went into Crossjay's room this morning, woke him up and talked to him, and set the lad crying, and what with one thing and another Crossjay got a berry in his throat, as he calls it, and poured out everything he knew and all he had done. I need n't tell you the consequence. He has ruined himself here for good, so I must take him."

Vernon glanced at Clara. " You must indeed," said she. " He is my boy as well as yours. No chance of pardon ? "

" It 's not likely."

" Lætitia ! "

" What can I do ? "

" Oh ! what can you not do ? "

" I do *not* know."

" Teach him to forgive ! "

Lætitia's brows were heavy and Clara forebore to torment her.

She would not descend to the family breakfast-table. Clara would fain have stayed to drink tea with her in her own room, but a last act of conformity was demanded of the liberated young lady. She promised to run up the moment breakfast was over. Not unnaturally, therefore, Lætitia supposed it to be she to whom she gave admission, half an hour later, with a glad cry of, " Come in, dear."

The knock had sounded like Clara's.

Sir Willoughby entered.

He stepped forward. He seized her hands. "Dear!" he said. "You cannot withdraw that. You called me dear. I am, I must be dear to you. The word is out, by accident or not, but, by heaven, I have it and I give it up to no one. And love me or not — marry me, and my love will bring it back to you. You have taught me I am not so strong. I must have you by my side. You have powers I did not credit you with."

" You are mistaken in me, Sir Willoughby," Lætitia said feebly, outworn as she was.

" A woman who can resist me by declining to be my wife, through a whole night of entreaty, has the quality I need for my house, and I batter at her ears for months, with as little rest as I had last night, before I surrender my chance of her. But I told you last night I want you within the twelve hours. I have staked my pride on it. By noon you are mine : you are introduced to Mrs. Mountstuart as mine, as the lady of my life and house. And to the world! I shall not let you go."

" You will not detain me here, Sir Willoughby ? "

" I will detain you. I will use force and guile. I will spare nothing."

He raved for a term, as he had done overnight.

On his growing rather breathless, Lætitia said : " You do not ask me for love ? "

" I do not. I pay you the higher compliment of asking for *you*, love or no love. My love shall be enough. Reward me or not. I am not used to be denied."

" But do you know what you ask for ? Do you remember what I told you of myself ? I am hard, materialistic ; I have lost faith in romance, the skeleton is present with me all over life. And my health is not good. I crave for money. I should marry to be rich. I should not worship you. I should be a burden, barely a living one, irresponsive and cold. Conceive such a wife, Sir Willoughby ! "

" It will be you ! "

She tried to recall how this would have sung in her ears long back. Her bosom rose and fell in absolute dejection. Her ammunition of arguments against him had been expended overnight.

" You are so unforgiving," she said.

" Is it I who am ? "

" You do not know me."

" But you are the woman of all the world who knows *me*, Lætitia."

" Can you think it better for you to be known ? "

He was about to say other words : he checked them. " I believe I do not know myself. Anything you will, only give me your hand ; give it ; trust to me ; you shall direct me. If I have faults, help me to obliterate them."

" Will you not expect me to regard them as the virtues of

meaner men?"

"You will be my wife!"

Lætitia broke from him, crying: "Your wife, your critic! Oh! I cannot think it possible. Send for the ladies. Let them hear me."

"They are at hand," said Willoughby, opening the door. They were in one of the upper rooms anxiously on the watch.

"Dear ladies," Lætitia said to them, as they entered. "I am going to wound you, and I grieve to do it: but rather now than later, if I am to be your housemate. He asks me for a hand that cannot carry a heart, because mine is dead. I repeat it. I used to think the heart a woman's marriage portion for her husband. I see now that she may consent, and he accept her, without one. But it is right that you should know what I am when I consent. I was once a foolish romantic girl; now I am a sickly woman, all illusions vanished. Privation has made me what an abounding fortune usually makes of others — I am an Egoist. I am not deceiving you. That is my real character. My girl's view of him has entirely changed; and I am almost indifferent to the change. I can endeavour to respect him, I cannot venerate."

"Dear child!" the ladies gently remonstrated.

Willoughby motioned to them.

"If we are to live together, and I could very happily live with you," Lætitia continued to address them, "you must not be ignorant of me. And if you, as I imagine, worship him blindly, I do not know how we are to live together And never shall you quit this house to make way for me. I have a hard detective eye. I see many faults."

"Have we not all of us faults, dear child?"

"Not such as he has; though the excuses of a gentleman nurtured in idolatry may be pleaded. But he should know that they are seen, and seen by her he asks to be his wife, that no misunderstanding may exist, and while it is yet time he may consult his feelings. He worships himself."

"Willoughby?"

"He is vindictive."

"Our Willoughby?"

"That is not your opinion, ladies. It is firmly mine. Time has taught it me. So, if you and I are at such variance, how can we live together? It is an impossibility."

They looked at Willoughby. He nodded imperiously.

"We have never affirmed that our dear nephew is devoid of faults. If he is offended . . . And supposing he claims to be foremost, is it not his rightful claim, made good by much generosity? Reflect, dear Lætitia. We are your friends too."

She could not chastise the kind ladies any further.

"You have always been my good friends."

"And you have no other charge against him?"

Lætitia was milder in saying, "He is unpardoning."

"Name one instance, Lætitia."

"He has turned Crossjay out of his house, interdicting the poor boy ever to enter it again."

"Crossjay," said Willoughby, "was guilty of a piece of infamous treachery."

"Which is the cause of your persecuting me to become your wife!"

There was a cry of "Persecuting!"

"No young fellow behaving so basely can come to good," said Willoughby, stained about the face with flecks of redness at the lashings he received.

"Honestly," she retorted. "He told of himself: and he must have anticipated the punishment he would meet. He should have been studying with a master for his profession. He has been kept here in comparative idleness to be alternately petted and discarded: no one but Vernon Whitford, a poor gentleman doomed to struggle for a livelihood by literature — I know something of that struggle — too much for me! — no one but Mr. Whitford for his friend."

"Crossjay is forgiven," said Willoughby.

"You promise me that?"

"He shall be packed off to a crammer at once."

"But my home must be Crossjay's home."

"You are mistress of my house, Lætitia."

She hesitated. Her eyelashes grew moist. "You can be generous."

"He is, dear child!" the ladies cried. "He is. Forget his errors in his generosity, as we do."

"There is that wretched man Flitch."

"That sot has gone about the county for years to get me a bad character," said Willoughby.

"It would have been generous in you to have offered him another chance. He has children."

"Nine. And I am responsible for them?"

"I speak of being generous."

"Dictate." Willoughby spread out his arms.

"Surely now you should be satisfied, Lætitia," said the ladies.

"Is *he?*"

Willoughby perceived Mrs. Mountstuart's carriage coming down the avenue.

"To the full." He presented his hand.

She raised hers with the fingers catching back before she ceased to speak, and dropped it: —

"Ladies, you are witnesses that there is no concealment, there has been no reserve, on my part. May heaven grant me kinder eyes than I have now. I would not have you change your opinion of him; only that you should see how I read him. For the rest, I vow to do my duty by him. Whatever is of worth in me is at his service. I am very tired. I feel I must yield or break. This is his wish, and I submit."

"And I salute my wife," said Willoughby, making her hand his own, and warming to his possession as he performed the act.

Mrs. Mountstuart's indecent hurry to be at the Hall before the departure of Dr. Middleton and his daughter, afflicted him with visions of the physical contrast which would be sharply perceptible to her this morning of his Lætitia beside Clara.

But he had the lady with brains ! He had : and he was to learn the nature of that possession in the woman who is our wife.

CHAPTER 50

UPON WHICH THE CURTAIN FALLS

"PLAIN sense upon the marriage question is my demand upon man and woman, for the stopping of many a tragedy."

These were Dr. Middleton's words in reply to Willoughby's brief explanation.

He did not say that he had shown it parentally while the tragedy was threatening, or at least there was danger of a precipitate descent from the levels of comedy. The parents of hymenæal men and women he was indisposed to consider as dramatis personæ.[1] Nor did he mention certain sympathetic regrets he entertained in contemplation of the health of Mr. Dale, for whom, poor gentleman, the proffer of a bottle of the Patterne Port would be an egregious mockery. He paced about, anxious for his departure, and seeming better pleased with the society of Colonel De Craye than with that of any of the others. Colonel de Craye assiduously courted him, was anecdotal, deferential, charmingly vivacious, the very man the Rev. Doctor liked for company when plunged in the bustle of the preliminaries to a journey.

"You would be a cheerful travelling comrade, sir," he remarked, and spoke of his doom to lead his daughter over the Alps and Alpine lakes for the Summer months.

Strange to tell, the Alps for the Summer months, was a settled project of the colonel's.

And thence Dr. Middleton was to be hauled along to the habitable quarters of North Italy in high Summer-tide.

That also had been traced for a route on the map of Colonel De Craye.

"We are started in June, I am informed," said Dr. Middleton.

1. "hymenaeal men and women": men and women about to marry; "dramatis personae": the characters in a play.

June, by miracle, was the month the colonel had fixed upon.

"I trust we shall meet, sir," said he.

"I would gladly reckon it in my catalogue of pleasures," the Rev. Doctor responded: "for in good sooth it is conjectureable that I shall be left very much alone."

"Paris, Strasburg, Basle?" the colonel inquired.

"The Lake of Constance, I am told," said Dr. Middleton.

Colonel De Craye spied eagerly for an opportunity of exchanging a pair of syllables with the third and fairest party of this glorious expedition to come.

Willoughby met him, and rewarded the colonel's frankness in stating that he was on the look-out for Miss Middleton to take his leave of her, by furnishing him the occasion. He conducted his friend Horace to the Blue Room, where Clara and Lætitia were seated circling a half embrace with a brook of chatter, and contrived an excuse for leading Lætitia forth. Some minutes later Mrs. Mountstuart called aloud for the colonel, to drive him away. Willoughby, whose good offices were unabated by the services he performed to each in rotation, ushered her into the Blue Room, hearing her say, as she stood at the entrance: "Is the man coming to spend a day with me with a face like that?"

She was met and detained by Clara.

De Craye came out.

"What are you thinking of?" said Willoughby.

"I was thinking," said the colonel, "of developing a heart, like you, and taking to think of others."

"At last!"

"Ah, you're a true friend, Willoughby, a true friend. And a cousin to boot!"

"What! has Clara been communicative?"

"The itinerary of a voyage Miss Middleton is going to make."

"Do you join them?"

"Why, it would be delightful, Willoughby, but it happens I've got a lot of powder I want to let off, and so I've an idea of shouldering my gun along the sea-coast and shooting gulls: which'll be a harmless form of committing parricide and matricide and fratricide — for there's my family, and I come of it! — the gull![2] And I've to talk lively to Mrs. Mountstuart for something like a matter of twelve hours, calculating that she goes to bed at midnight: and I would n't bet on it; such is the energy of ladies of that age!"

Willoughby scorned the man who could not conceal a blow, even though he joked over his discomfiture.

"Gull!" he muttered.

"A bird that's easy to be had, and better for stuffing than for eating," said De Craye. "You'll miss your cousin."

2. "gull": bamboozled victim, sucker.

"I have," replied Willoughby, "one fully equal to supplying his place."

There was confusion in the hall for a time, and an assembly of the household to witness the departure of Dr. Middleton and his daughter. Vernon had been driven off by Dr. Corney, who further recommended rest for Mr. Dale, and promised to keep an eye for Crossjay along the road.

"I think you will find him at the station, and if you do, command him to come straight back here," Lætitia said to Clara.

The answer was an affectionate squeeze, and Clara's hand was extended to Willoughby, who bowed over it with perfect courtesy, bidding her adieu.

So the knot was cut. And the next carriage to Dr. Middleton's was Mrs. Mountstuart's, conveying the great lady and Colonel De Craye.

"I beg you not to wear that face with me," she said to him. "I have had to dissemble, which I hate, and I have quite enough to endure, and I must be amused, or I shall run away from you and enlist that little countryman of yours, and him I can count on to be professionally restorative. Who can fathom the heart of a girl! Here is Lady Busshe right once more! And I was wrong. She must be a gambler by nature. I never should have risked such a guess as that. Colonel De Craye, you lengthen your face preternaturally, you distort it purposely."

"Ma'am," returned De Craye, "the boast of our army is never to know when we are beaten, and that tells of a great-hearted soldiery. But there's a field where the Briton must own his defeat, whether smiling or crying, and I'm not so sure that a short howl does n't do him honour."

"She was, I am certain, in love with Vernon Whitford all along, Colonel De Craye!"

"Ah!" the colonel drank it in. "I have learnt that it was not the gentleman in whom I am chiefly interested. So it was not so hard for the lady to vow to friend Willoughby she would marry no one else!"

"Girls are unfathomable! And Lady Busshe — I know she did not go by character — shot one of her random guesses, and she triumphs. We shall never hear the last of it. And I had all the opportunities. I'm bound to confess I had."

"Did you by chance, ma'am," De Craye said with a twinkle, "drop a hint to Willoughby of her turn for Vernon Whitford?"

"No," said Mrs. Mountstuart, "I'm not a mischief-maker; and the policy of the county is to keep him in love with himself, or Patterne will be likely to be as dull as it was without a lady enthroned. When his pride is at ease he is a prince. I can read men. Now, Colonel De Craye, pray, be lively."

"I should have been livelier, I'm afraid, if you had dropped a bit of a hint to Willoughby. But you're the magnanimous person, ma'am, and revenge for a stroke in the game of love shows us unworthy to win."

Mrs. Mountstuart menaced him with her parasol. "I forbid sentiments, Colonel De Craye. They are always followed by sighs."

"Grant me five minutes of inward retirement, and I'll come out formed for your commands, ma'am," said he.

Before the termination of that space De Craye was enchanting Mrs. Mountstuart, and she in consequence was restored to her natural wit.

So, and much so universally, the world of his dread and his unconscious worship wagged over Sir Willoughby Patterne and his change of brides, until the preparations for the festivities of the marriage flushed him in his county's eyes to something of the splendid glow he had worn on the great day of his majority. That was upon the season when two lovers met between the Swiss and Tyrol Alps over the Lake of Constance. Sitting beside them the Comic Muse is grave and sisterly. But taking a glance at the others of her late company of actors, she compresses her lips.

THE END

Textual Notes

The authorized edition of 1897 and following, which is the text used
by this Norton Critical Edition, is compared in the table below with
the first edition of 1879. (The reading set in bold type is that of
1897.)

4.1 **We may with effort get even him** *altered from* We may get him
4.11 *After* matter *added* **(extending well-nigh to the very Pole)**
50.12–13 **sharpened to think that after all it was not so severe a trial** *altered from*
thankful to her ordeal for being over. And, after all, it was not so severe a trial.
81.14 *After* And *added* **they are the**
97.37 **"The mountains tame luxurious dreams, you mean."** *altered from* "Luxurious
dreams, you mean; the stupid portion.
104.37 *After* **strike.** *deleted* ¶; he was anything but obtuse.
106.43 *After* **revolt** *deleted* from the Egoist.
107.26 **Her busy brain** *altered from* Her giddy brain
191.20 *After* **Lesbia Quadrantaria.** *deleted* ¶ She must be sculptured Griselda with
him not in her soul to suffer the change; she must have the power of halting between celestially good and brutishly. [But let women tell us]
204.26–27 **conscience will be made to walk the plank for being of no service to
either party.** *altered from* he will be made to walk the plank: why not? he is of no
service to either party.
213.18 **intercept** *altered from* interrupt
232.39 **"An anticipatory story** *altered from* "A ready-made story
241.22 *Beginning of paragraph deleted* He was anything but obtuse;
242.9 *After* up to *added* **the verge of**
243.31 *After* **the maid.** *deleted* Anything but obtuse, as it has been observed,
244.49 *After* **gracefully** *deleted* to escape the touch.
253.19 *After* **in season.** *deleted* The *à propos* puffs us to the heroic size.
254.36 *After* his dish *added* **behind the head.' "**
255.25 *After* **your time.** *deleted* This, which does not happen in cases of petty larceny
or felony or murder, is so positive that one need not hesitate to say it is equal to
an offence done to our animal health in the unerringness and swiftness of the
chastisement. There could be no stronger proof of the divinity of that bright and
black young person than his alacrity in hitting back, or countering.
257.21 *Before* **He spelt** *deleted* He was anything but obtuse, and
257.29 **binding** *altered from* escaping
259.18 **When the centre of him** *altered from* Anything but obtuse, when the centre
of him
260.46 *After* **earnest,** *deleted* almost inflaming,
265.6–7. *After* surrendered *added* **unto benignant sleep**
267.4 **He is a true friend."** *altered from* He is the one man who can be a friend."
293.32 **the outer conflagration.** *altered from* the conflagration.
305.3 *After* and he, *deleted* anything but obtuse,
313.6 *After* **ominous;** *deleted* he was anything but obtuse;
317.44 *After* accompanied *added* **and reported of**
326.11 *Before* **Willoughby** *deleted* Anything but obtuse,
353.47 *After* **flying.** *deleted* Well, perhaps we do manage somehow to work in common, without sticking. We did, that night.
390.45 *Before* **He could read** *deleted* Anything but obtuse,
417.25 **through her suite, here at the doors, there at the windows,** *altered from*
round her room, here at the door, there at the window,
424.32 *After* "She was *added* **, I am certain,**
424.37 *After* **she would marry no one else?"** *deleted* ¶"Now would you, could you

have judged from her physiognomy that she was a girl to fall in love with a man like Mr. Whitford?"

"Going by the mythology, ma'am, I should have suspected the god Mars."

In addition, the text of the 1897 edition has been corrected as follows, without authority from the editions but on the score of obvious need:

11.27   Louis IV *changed to* Louis XIV
193.40–41   business should be sift *changed to* business should be to sift
204.32   realized the out of prison *changed to* realized the way out of prison
256.4   the project she had so frequently *changed to* the project he had so frequently
342.27–28   she has had it plain Saxon *changed to* she has had it in plain Saxon

Backgrounds

Just two years before *The Egoist* appeared in print, George Meredith delivered at the London Institution a lecture "On the Idea of Comedy and the Uses of the Comic Spirit." Meredith was not commonly given to delivering lectures, but this topic was much on his mind, and he showed the importance he attached to it by publishing the original lecture, with some modifications, in the *New Quarterly Magazine* for April 1877. Many of the ideas glanced at in the lecture can be observed at work in the novel; most interestingly of all, the frame of values within which Meredith created his comedy can be seen to derive not so much from English authors as from the example of the seventeenth-century French drama, above all from the supreme figure of Molière. Our text is from the edition of Lane Cooper, Cornell University Press, Ithaca, New York, 1956. All footnotes are the editor's.

GEORGE MEREDITH

An Essay on Comedy and the Uses of the Comic Spirit

* * *

Politically, it is accounted a misfortune for France that her nobles thronged to the Court of Louis Quatorze.[1] It was a boon to the comic poet. He had that lively quicksilver world of the animalcule passions, the huge pretensions, the placid absurdities, under his eyes in full activity; vociferous quacks and snapping dupes, hypocrites, posturers, extravagants, pedants, rose-pink ladies and mad grammarians, sonnetteering marquises, high-flying mistresses, plain-minded maids, interthreading as in a loom, noisy as at a fair. A simply bourgeois circle will not furnish it, for the middle class must have the brilliant, flippant, independent upper for a spur and a pattern; otherwise it is likely to be inwardly dull, as well as outwardly correct. Yet, though the King was benevolent toward Molière, it is not to the French Court that we are indebted for his unrivaled studies of mankind in society. For the amusement of the Court the ballets and farces were written, which are dearer to the rabble upper, as to the rabble lower, class than intellectual comedy. The French bourgeoisie of Paris were sufficiently quick-witted and enlightened by education to welcome great works like *le Tartuffe, Les Femmes savantes*, and

1. Louis XIV, who ruled France from 1643 to 1715, creating during that period one of the great ages of French civilization.

le Misanthrope, works that were perilous ventures on the popular intelligence, big vessels to launch on streams running to shallows.[2] The *Tartuffe* hove into view as an enemy's vessel; it offended, not *'Dieu, mais . . . les dévots,'* as the Prince de Condé explained the cabal raised against it to the King.[3]

The *Femmes savantes* is a capital instance of the uses of comedy in teaching the world to understand what ails it. The farce of the *Précieuses* ridiculed, and put a stop to, the monstrous romantic jargon made popular by certain famous novels.[4] The comedy of the *Femmes savantes* exposed the later and less apparent, but more finely comic, absurdity of an excessive purism in grammar and diction, and the tendency to be idiotic in precision. The French had felt the burden of this new nonsense; but they had to see the comedy several times before they were consoled in their suffering by seeing the cause of it exposed.

The *Misanthrope* was yet more frigidly received. Molière thought it dead. 'I can not improve on it, and assuredly never shall,' he said. It is one of the French titles of honor that this quintessential comedy of the opposition of Alceste and Célimène was ultimately understood and applauded. In all countries the middle class presents the public which, fighting the world, and with a good footing in the fight, knows the world best. It may be the most selfish, but that is a question leading us into sophistries. Cultivated men and women who do not skim the cream of life, and are attached to the duties, yet escape the harsher blows, make acute and balanced observers. Molière is their poet.

Of this class in England, a large body, neither Puritan nor Bacchanalian, have a sentimental objection to face the study of the actual world. They take up disdain of it, when its truths appear humiliating; when the facts are not immediately forced on them, they take up the pride of incredulity. They live in a hazy atmosphere that they suppose an ideal one. Humorous writing they will endure, perhaps approve, if it mingles with pathos to shake and elevate the feelings. They approve of satire, because, like the beak of the vulture, it smells of carrion, which they are not. But of comedy they have a shivering dread, for comedy enfolds them with the wretched host of the world, huddles them with us all in an ignoble assimilation, and cannot be used by any exalted variety as a scourge and a

---

2. *Tartuffe, The Learned Ladies,* and *The Misanthrope,* serious intellectual comedies by Molière.
3. "Not God, but the bigots."
4. Molière's two plays ridiculing feminine literary affectation appeared at a distance from one another, *Les Précieuses ridicules (Those Affected Females)* in 1659, *Les Femmes savantes (The Learned Ladies)* in 1672.

broom. Nay, to be an exalted variety is to come under the calm, curious eye of the Comic Spirit, and be probed for what you are. Men are seen among them, and very many cultivated women. You may distinguish them by a favorite phrase: 'Surely we are not so bad!' and the remark: 'If that is human nature, save us from it!'—as if it could be done; but in the peculiar paradise of the wilful people who will not see, the exclamation assumes the saving grace.

Yet, should you ask them whether they dislike sound sense, they vow they do not. And question cultivated women whether it pleases them to be shown moving on an intellectual level with men, they will answer that it does; numbers of them claim the situation. Now comedy is the fountain of sound sense; not the less perfectly sound on account of the sparkle; and comedy lifts women to a station offering them free play for their wit, as they usually show it, when they have it, on the side of sound sense. The higher the comedy, the more prominent the part they enjoy in it. Dorine in the *Tartuffe* is common sense incarnate, though palpably a waiting-maid. Célimène is undisputed mistress of the same attribute in the *Misanthrope*; wiser as a woman than Alceste as man. In Congreve's *Way of the World*, Millamant overshadows Mirabell, the sprightliest male figure of English comedy.

But those two ravishing women, so copious and so choice of speech, who fence with men and pass their guard, are heartless! Is it not preferable to be the pretty idiot, the passive beauty, the adorable bundle of caprices, very feminine, very sympathetic, of romantic and sentimental fiction? Our women are taught to think so. The Agnès of the *École des femmes* should be a lesson for men.[5] The heroines of comedy are like women of the world, not necessarily heartless from being clear-sighted; they seem so to the sentimentally reared, only for the reason that they use their wits, and are not wandering vessels crying for a captain or a pilot. Comedy is an exhibition of their battle with men, and that of men with them; and as the two, however divergent, both look on one object, namely, life, the gradual similarity of their impressions must bring them to some resemblance. The comic poet dares to show us men and women coming to this mutual likeness; he is for saying that when they draw together in social life their minds grow liker; just as the philosopher discerns the similarity of boy and girl, until the girl is marched away to the nursery. Philosopher and

5. In *The School for Wives*, Arnolphe, who is training Agnès from childhood to be his wife, on the principle of keeping her strictly ignorant, finds that she is still clever enough to subvert his tyranny.

comic poet are of a cousinship in the eye they cast on life; and they are equally unpopular with our wilful English of the hazy region and the ideal that is not to be disturbed.

Thus, for want of instruction in the comic idea, we lose a large audience among our cultivated middle class that we should expect to support comedy. The sentimentalist is as averse as the Puritan and as the Bacchanalian.

Our traditions are unfortunate. The public taste is with the idle laughers, and still inclines to follow them. It may be shown by an analysis of Wycherley's *Plain Dealer*, a coarse prose adaption of the *Misanthrope*, stuffed with lumps of realism in a vulgarized theme to hit the mark of English appetite, that we have in it the key-note of the comedy of our stage. It is Molière travestied, with the hoof to his foot, and hair on the pointed tip of his ear.[6] And how difficult it is for writers to disentangle themselves from bad traditions is noticeable when we find Goldsmith, who had grave command of the comic in narrative, producing an elegant farce for a comedy;[7] and Fielding, who was a master of the comic both in narrative and in dialogue, not even approaching to the presentable in farce.

These bad traditions of comedy affect us, not only on the stage, but in our literature, and may be tracked into our social life. They are the ground of the heavy moralizings by which we are outwearied, about life as a comedy, and comedy as a jade,[8] when popular writers, conscious of fatigue in creativeness, desire to be cogent in a modish cynicism; perversions of the idea of life, and of the proper esteem for the society we have wrested from brutishness, and would carry higher. Stock images of this description are accepted by the timid and the sensitive, as well as by the saturnine, quite seriously; for not many look abroad with their own eyes—fewer still have the habit of thinking for themselves. Life, we know too well, is not a comedy, but something strangely mixed; nor is comedy a vile mask. The corrupted importation from France was noxious, a noble entertainment spoilt to suit the wretched taste of a villainous age;[9] and the later imitations of it, partly drained of its poison and made decorous, became tiresome, notwithstanding their fun, in the perpetual recurring of the same situations, owing to the absence of original study and vigor of conception. Scene 5, Act 2, of the *Misanthrope*, owing, no

6. The goat-foot and pointed ear are marks of the uncivilized satyr; real comedy is urbane.

7. The "serious" comedy of *The Vicar of Wakefield* is contrasted with the farcical comedy of *She Stoops to Conquer*. Fielding's farces are very rough, but not as

unworthy as Meredith says.

8. Slut.

9. Meredith refers to the Restoration comedy of sexual intrigue, softened but repeated in the sentimental comedies of the next age.

doubt, to the fact of our not producing matter for original study, is repeated in succession by Wycherley, Congreve, and Sheridan, and, as it is at second hand, we have it done cynically—or such is the tone—in the manner of 'below stairs.'[1] Comedy thus treated may be accepted as a version of the ordinary worldly understanding of our social life; at least, in accord with the current dicta concerning it. The epigrams can be made; but it is uninstructive, rather tending to do disservice. Comedy justly treated, as you find it in Molière, whom we so clownishly mishandled—the comedy of Molière throws no infamous reflection upon life. It is deeply conceived, in the first place, and therefore it cannot be impure. Meditate on that statement. Never did man wield so shrieking a scourge upon vice; but his consummate self-mastery ·is not shaken while administering it. Tartuffe and Harpagon, in fact, are made each to whip himself and his class—the false pietists, and the insanely covetous. Molière has only set them in motion. He strips Folly to the skin, displays the imposture of the creature, and is content to offer her better clothing, with the lesson Chrysale reads to Philaminte and Bélise.[2] He conceives purely, and he writes purely, in the simplest language, the simplest of French verse. The source of his wit is clear reason; it is a fountain of that soil, and it springs to vindicate reason, common sense, rightness, and justice—for no vain purpose ever. The wit is of such pervading spirit that it inspires a pun with meaning and interest. His moral does not hang like a tail, or preach from one character incessantly cocking an eye at the audience, as in recent realistic French plays, but is in the heart of his work, throbbing with every pulsation of an organic structure. If life is likened to the comedy of Molière, there is no scandal in the comparison.

Congreve's *Way of the World* is an exception to our other comedies, his own among them, by virtue of the remarkable brilliancy of the writing, and the figure of Millamant. The comedy has no idea in it, beyond the stale one that so the world goes; and it concludes with the jaded discovery of a document at a convenient season for the descent of the curtain. A plot was an afterthought with Congreve. By the help of a wooden villain (Maskwell), marked gallows to the flattest eye,[3] he gets a sort of plot in *The Double-Dealer*. His *Way of*

1. Act II, scene 4, of *The Misanthrope* is, as scenes are commonly numbered, a confrontation of Célimène's wit with Alceste's rough honesty. It's not clear from what he says if Meredith had this scene in mind or some other.

2. In *The Learned Ladies.* Harpagon above is the central figure of *l'Avare* (*The Miser*).

3. A man marked "gallows" was born to be hanged—as is evident to the dullest observer (the flattest eye).

the World might be called 'The Conquest of a Town Coquette'; and Millamant is a perfect portrait of a coquette,
both in her resistance to Mirabell and the manner of her surrender, and also in her tongue. The wit here is not so salient as
in certain passages of *Love for Love*, where Valentine feigns
madness, or retorts on his father, or Mrs. Frail rejoices in the
harmlessness of wounds to a woman's virtue, if she keeps them
'from air.' In *The Way of the World*, it appears less prepared
in the smartness, and is more diffused in the more characteristic style of the speakers. Here, however, as elsewhere, his
famous wit is like a bully-fencer, not ashamed to lay traps for
its exhibition, transparently petulant[4] for the train between
certain ordinary words and the powder-magazine of the im-
proprieties to be fired. Contrast the wit of Congreve with
Molière's. That of the first is a Toledo blade, sharp, and wonderfully supple for steel; cast for dueling, restless in the
scabbard, being so pretty when out of it. To shine, it must
have an adversary. Molière's wit is like a running brook, with
innumerable fresh lights on it at every turn of the wood
through which its business is to find a way. It does not run in
search of obstructions, to be noisy over them; but when dead
leaves and viler substances are heaped along the course, its
natural song is heightened. Without effort, and with no dazzling flashes of achievement, it is full of healing, the wit of
good breeding, the wit of wisdom.

'Genuine humor and true wit,' says Landor, 'require a
sound and capacious mind, which is always a grave one. . . .
Rabelais and La Fontaine are recorded by their countrymen
to have been *rêveurs*.[5] Few men have been graver than Pascal;
few have been wittier.' To apply the citation of so great a brain
as Pascal's to our countryman would be unfair. Congreve had a
certain soundness of mind; of capacity, in the sense intended
by Landor, he had little. Judging him by his wit, he performed
some happy thrusts; and, taking it for genuine, it is a surface
wit, neither rising from a depth nor flowing from a spring:

On voit qu'il se travaille à dire de bons mots.[6]

He drives the poor hack-word, 'fool,' as cruelly to the market
for wit as any of his competitors. Here is an example, that has
been held up for eulogy:

4. Meredith uses the word for its Latin
root, giving it the sense of "in search of."
5. François Rabelais of the sixteenth century, Jean de la Fontaine of the seventeenth century were French humorists;
rêveurs are dreamers.
6. "You see that he works at saying
bright things."

WITWOUD. He has brought me a letter from the fool my
brother. . . .

MIRABEL. A fool, and your brother, Witwoud!

WITWOUD. Ay, ay, my half-brother. My half-brother he is; no
nearer, upon honor.

MIRABEL. Then 'tis possible he may be but half a fool.

—By evident preparation. This is a sort of wit one remembers
to have heard at school, of a brilliant outsider; perhaps to have
been guilty of oneself a trifle later. It was, no doubt, a blaze of
intellectual fireworks to the bumpkin squire who came to
London to go to the theatre and learn manners.

Where Congreve excels all his English rivals is in his literary
force, and a succinctness of style peculiar to him. He had
correct judgment, a correct ear, readiness of illustration within
a narrow range—in snap-shots of the obvious at the obvious—
and copious language. He hits the mean of a fine style and a
natural in dialogue. He is at once precise and voluble. If you
have ever thought upon style, you will acknowledge it to be a
signal accomplishment. In this he is a classic, and is worthy of
treading a measure with Molière. *The Way of the World* may
be read out currently[7] at a first glance, so sure are the accents
of the emphatic meaning to strike the eye, perforce of the
crispness and cunning polish of the sentences. You have not to
look over them before you confide yourself to him; he will
carry you safe. Sheridan imitated, but was far from surpassing,
him. The flow of boudoir billingsgate in Lady Wishfort is
unmatched for the vigor and pointedness of the tongue. It
spins along with a final ring, like the voice of Nature in a fury,
and is, indeed, racy eloquence of the elevated fishwife.[8]

Millamant is an admirable, almost a lovable, heroine. It is a
piece of genius in a writer to make a woman's manner of
speech portray her. You feel sensible of her presence in every
line of her speaking. The stipulations with her lover in view of
marriage, her fine lady's delicacy, and fine lady's easy evasions
of indelicacy, coquettish airs, and playing with irresolution,
which in a common maid would be bashfulness, until she
submits to 'dwindle into a wife,' as she says, form a picture
that lives in the frame, and is in harmony with Mirabell's
description of her:

Here she comes, i' faith, full sail, with her fan spread and
her streamers out, and a shoal of fools for tenders.

7. Fluently.

8. See *The Way of the World*, act V,

scene 1, where Lady Wishfort reviles
Foible, her maid.

And, after an interview:

> Think of you? To think of a whirlwind, though 't were in a whirlwind, were a case of more steady contemplation; a very tranquillity of mind and mansion.

There is a picturesqueness, as of Millamant and no other, in her voice, when she is encouraged to take Mirabell by Mrs. Fainall, who is 'sure' she has 'a mind to him':

> MILLAMANT. Are you? I think I have—and the horrid man looks as if he thought so too.—

One hears the tones, and sees the sketch and color of the whole scene, in reading it.

Célimène[9] is behind Millamant in vividness. An air of bewitching whimsicality hovers over the graces of this comic heroine, like the lively conversational play of a beautiful mouth. But in wit she is no rival of Célimène. What she utters adds to her personal witchery, and is not further memorable. She is a flashing portrait, and a type of the superior ladies who do not think, not of those who do. In representing a class, therefore, it is a lower class, in the proportion that one of Gainsborough's full-length aristocratic women is below the permanent impressiveness of a fair Venetian head.

Millamant, side by side with Célimène, is an example of how far the realistic painting of a character can be carried to win our favor, and of where it falls short. Célimène is a woman's mind in movement, armed with an ungovernable wit; with perspicacious, clear eyes for the world, and a very distinct knowledge that she belongs to the world, and is most at home in it. She is attracted to Alceste by her esteem for his honesty; she cannot avoid seeing where the good sense of the man is diseased.

Rousseau, in his letter to D'Alembert on the subject of the *Misanthrope*,[1] discusses the character of Alceste as though Molière had put him forth for an absolute example of misanthropy; whereas Alceste is only a misanthrope of the circle he finds himself placed in—he has a touching faith in the virtue residing in the country, and a critical love of sweet simpleness. Nor is he the principal person of the comedy to which he gives a name. He is only passively comic. Célimène

9. Célimène is the chief female character —not exactly the heroine, but the leading lady—of *The Misanthrope*. In comparing her to one of the fine ladies painted by the eighteenth-century portrait painter Gainsborough, Meredith seems to deny her spiritual qualities that might be found in "a fair Venetian head," as painted for example by Titian.

1. Jean-Jacques Rousseau's letter to Jean D'Alembert (1758) is on the subject of establishing a comic theater in Geneva— a subject of great concern to the two philosophers.

is the active spirit. While he is denouncing and railing, the trial is imposed upon her to make the best of him, and control herself, as much as a witty woman, eagerly courted, can do. By appreciating him she practically confesses her faultiness, and she is better disposed to meet him half-way than he is to bend an inch; only she is *'une âme de vingt ans,'*[2] the world is pleasant, and, if the gilded flies of the Court are silly, uncompromising fanatics have their ridiculous features as well. Can she abandon the life they make agreeable to her, for a man who will not be guided by the common sense of his class, and who insists on plunging into one extreme—equal to suicide in her eyes—to avoid another? That is the comic question of the *Misanthrope*. Why will he not continue to mix with the world smoothly, appeased by the flattery of her secret and really sincere preference of him, and taking his revenge in satire of it, as she does from her own not very lofty standard, and will by and by do from his more exalted one?

Célimène is worldliness; Alceste is unworldliness. It does not quite imply unselfishness; and that is perceived by her shrewd head. Still, he is a very uncommon figure in her circle, and she esteems him, *'l'homme aux rubans verts,'*[3] who 'sometimes diverts,' but more often horribly vexes her—as she can say of him when her satirical tongue is on the run. Unhappily the soul of truth in him, which wins her esteem, refuses to be tamed, or silent, or unsuspicious, and is the perpetual obstacle to their good accord. He is that melancholy person, the critic of everybody save himself; intensely sensitive to the faults of others, wounded by them; in love with his own indubitable honesty, and with his ideal of the simpler form of life befitting it—qualities which constitute the satirist. He is a Jean-Jacques of the Court.[4] His proposal to Célimène, when he pardons her, that she should follow him in flying humankind, and his frenzy of detestation of her at her refusal, are thoroughly in the mood of Jean-Jacques. He is an impracticable creature of a priceless virtue; but Célimène may feel that to fly with him to the desert (that is, from the Court to the country),

Oú d'être homme d'honneur on ait la liberté,[5]

she is likely to find herself the companion of a starving satirist, like that poor princess who ran away with the waiting-man,

2. "A lady of twenty."
3. "The man with the green ribbons": it is Célimène's phrase for Alceste, the Misanthrope himself.
4. Jean-Jacques Rousseau, who posed as, and to some extent was, a blunt teller of plain truths.
5. "Where one is free to be a man of honor."

and, when both were hungry in the forest, was ordered to give him flesh. She is a *fieffée*[6] coquette, rejoicing in her wit and her attractions, and distinguished by her inclination for Alceste in the midst of her many other lovers; only she finds it hard to cut them off—what woman with a train does not?—and when the exposure of her naughty wit has laid her under their rebuke, she will do the utmost she can: she will give her hand to honesty, but she cannot quite abandon worldliness. She would be unwise if she did.

The fable is thin. Our pungent contrivers of plots would see no indication of life in the outlines. The life of the comedy is in the idea. As with the singing of the skylark out of sight, you must love the bird to be attentive to the song, so in this highest flight of the comic Muse, you must love pure comedy warmly to understand the *Misanthrope*; you must be receptive of the idea of comedy. And to love comedy you must know the real world, and know men and women well enough not to expect too much of them, though you may still hope for good.

* * *

Eastward you have total silence of comedy among a people intensely susceptible to laughter, as the *Arabian Nights* will testify. Where the veil is over women's faces, you cannot have society, without which the senses are barbarous and the Comic Spirit is driven to the gutters of grossness to slake its thirst. Arabs in this respect are worse than Italians—much worse than Germans,—just in the degree that their system of treating women is worse.

M. Saint-Marc Girardin,[7] the excellent French essayist and master of critical style, tells of a conversation he had once with an Arab gentleman on the topic of the different management of these difficult creatures in Orient and in Occident; and the Arab spoke in praise of many good results of the greater freedom enjoyed by Western ladies, and the charm of conversing with them. He was questioned why his countrymen took no measures to grant them something of that kind of liberty. He jumped out of his individuality in a twinkling, and entered into the sentiments of his race, replying, from the pinnacle of a splendid conceit, with affected humility of manner: '*You* can look on them without perturbation—but *we*! . . .' And, after this profoundly comic interjection, he added, in deep tones: 'The very face of a woman!' Our representative of temperate notions demurely consented that the Arab's pride of

---

6. Downright, absolute.
7. A French journalist who wrote a number of books about the Middle East.

inflammability should insist on the prudery of the veil as the civilizing medium of his race.

There has been fun in Bagdad. But there never will be civilization where comedy is not possible; and that comes of some degree of social equality of the sexes. I am not quoting the Arab to exhort and disturb the somnolent East; rather for cultivated women to recognize that the comic Muse is one of their best friends. They are blind to their interests in swelling the ranks of the sentimentalists. Let them look with their clearest vision abroad and at home. They will see that, where they have no social freedom, comedy is absent; where they are household drudges, the form of comedy is primitive; where they are tolerably independent, but uncultivated, exciting melodrama takes its place, and a sentimental version of them. Yet the comic will out, as they would know if they listened to some of the private conversations of men whose minds are undirected by the comic Muse; as the sentimental man, to his astonishment, would know likewise, if he in similar fashion could receive a lesson. But where women are on the road to an equal footing with men, in attainments and in liberty—in what they have won for themselves, and what has been granted them by a fair civilization—there, and only waiting to be transplanted from life to the stage, or the novel, or the poem, pure comedy flourishes, and is, as it would help them to be, the sweetest of diversions, the wisest of delightful companions.

Now, to look about us in the present time, I think it will be acknowledged that, in neglecting the cultivation of the comic idea, we are losing the aid of a powerful auxiliar. You see Folly perpetually sliding into new shapes in a society possessed of wealth and leisure, with many whims, many strange ailments and strange doctors. Plenty of common sense is in the world to thrust her back when she pretends to empire. But the first-born of common sense, the vigilant Comic, which is the genius of thoughtful laughter, which would readily extinguish her at the outset, is not serving as a public advocate.

You will have noticed the disposition of common sense, under pressure of some pertinacious piece of light-headedness, to grow impatient and angry. That is a sign of the absence, or at least of the dormancy, of the comic idea. For Folly is the natural prey of the Comic, known to it in all her transformations, in every disguise; and it is with the springing delight of hawk over heron, hound after fox, that it gives her chase, never fretting, never tiring, sure of having her, allowing her no rest.

Contempt is a sentiment that cannot be entertained by comic intelligence. What is it but an excuse to be idly-minded, or personally lofty, or comfortably narrow, not perfectly humane? If we do not feign when we say that we despise Folly, we shut the brain. There is a disdainful attitude in the presence of Folly, partaking of the foolishness to comic perception; and anger is not much less foolish than disdain. The struggle we have to conduct is essence against essence. Let no one doubt of the sequel when this emanation of what is firmest in us is launched to strike down the daughter of Unreason and Sentimentalism—such being Folly's parentage, when it is respectable.

Our modern system of combating her[8] is too long defensive, and carried on too ploddingly with concrete engines of war in the attack. She has time to get behind entrenchments. She is ready to stand a siege, before the heavily-armed man of science and the writer of the leading article or elaborate essay have primed their big guns. It should be rememberd that she has charms for the multitude; and an English multitude, seeing her make a gallant fight of it, will be half in love with her, certainly willing to lend her a cheer. Benevolent subscriptions assist her to hire her own man of science, her own organ in the press. If ultimately she is cast out and overthrown, she can stretch a finger at gaps in our ranks. She can say that she commanded an army, and seduced men, whom we thought sober men and safe, to act as her lieutenants. We learn rather gloomily, after she has flashed her lantern, that we have in our midst able men, and men with minds, for whom there is no pole-star in intellectual navigation. Comedy, or the comic element, is the specific for the poison of delusion while Folly is passing from the state of vapor to substantial form.

O for a breath of Aristophanes, Rabelais, Voltaire, Cervantes, Fielding, Molière! These are spirits that, if you know them well, will come when you do call.[9] You will find the very invocation of them act on you like a renovating air—the southwest coming off the sea, or a cry in the Alps.

* * *

* * * A centenarian does not necessarily provoke the comic idea, nor does the corpse of a duke. It is not provoked in the

---

8. I.e., Folly.
9. Meredith is half-quoting Shakespeare, *Henry IV, Part 1*, act III, scene 1, lines 52–54:
   GLENDOWER. I can call spirits from the vasty deep.
   HOTSPUR. Why, so can I, or so can any man;
   But will they come when you do call for them?

order of nature, until we draw its penetrating attentiveness to some circumstance with which we have been mixing our private interests, or our speculative obfuscation. Dulness, insensible to the comic, has the privilege of arousing it; and the laying of a dull finger on matters of human life is the surest method of establishing electrical communications with a battery of laughter—where the comic idea is prevalent.

But if the comic idea prevailed with us, and we had an Aristophanes to barb and wing it, we should be breathing air of Athens. Prosers now pouring forth on us like public fountains would be cut short in the street and left blinking, dumb as pillar-posts with letters thrust into their mouths. We should throw off incubus, our dreadful familiar—by some called boredom—whom it is our present humiliation to be just alive enough to loathe, never quick enough to foil. There would be a bright and positive, clear Hellenic perception of facts. The vapors of unreason and sentimentalism would be blown away before they were productive. Where would pessimist and optimist be? They would in any case have a diminished audience. Yet possibly the change of despots, from good-natured old obtuseness to keen-edged intelligence, which is by nature merciless, would be more than we could bear. The rupture of the link between dull people, consisting in the fraternal agreement that something is too clever for them, and a shot beyond them, is not to be thought of lightly; for, slender though the link may seem, it is equivalent to a cement forming a concrete of dense cohesion, very desirable in the estimation of the statesman.

* * *

In our prose literature we have had delightful comic writers. Besides Fielding and Goldsmith, there is Miss Austen, whose *Emma* and Mr. Elton might walk straight into a comedy, were the plot arranged for them. Galt's[1] neglected novels have some characters and strokes of shrewd comedy. In our poetic literature the comic is delicate and graceful above the touch of Italian and French. Generally, however, the English elect excel in satire, and they are noble humorists. The national disposition is for hard-hitting, with a moral purpose to sanction it; or for a rosy, sometimes a larmoyant,[2] geniality, not unmanly in its verging upon tenderness, and with a singular attraction for thickheadedness, to decorate it with asses' ears and the most beautiful sylvan haloes. But the comic is a different spirit.

1. John Galt (1779–1839), minor novel-ist of Scottish rural life.   2. Tearful.

You may estimate your capacity for comic perception by being able to detect the ridicule of them you love without loving them less; and more by being able to see yourself somewhat ridiculous in dear eyes, and accepting the correction their image of you proposes.

Each one of an affectionate couple may be willing, as we say, to die for the other, yet unwilling to utter the agreeable word at the right moment; but if the wits were sufficiently quick for them to perceive that they are in a comic situation, as affectionate couples must be when they quarrel, they would not wait for the moon or the almanac, or a Dorine,[3] to bring back the flood-tide of tender feelings, that they should join hands and lips.

If you detect the ridicule, and your kindliness is chilled by it, you are slipping into the grasp of Satire.

If, instead of falling foul of the ridiculous person with a satiric rod, to make him writhe and shriek aloud, you prefer to sting him under a semi-caress, by which he shall in his anguish be rendered dubious whether indeed anything has hurt him, you are an engine[4] of Irony.

If you laugh all round him, tumble him, roll him about, deal him a smack, and drop a tear on him, own his likeness to you, and yours to your neighbor, spare him as little as you shun, pity him as much as you expose, it is a spirit of Humor that is moving you.

The comic, which is the perceptive, is the governing spirit, awakening and giving aim to these powers of laughter, but it is not to be confounded with them; it enfolds a thinner form of them, differing from satire in not sharply driving into the quivering sensibilities, and from humor in not comforting them and tucking them up, or indicating a broader than the range of this bustling world to them.

Fielding's Jonathan Wild presents a case of this peculiar distinction, when that man of eminent greatness remarks upon the unfairness of a trial in which the condemnation has been brought about by twelve men of the opposite party; for it is not satiric, it is not humorous; yet it is immensely comic to hear a guilty villain protesting that his own 'party' should have a voice in the law. It opens an avenue into villains' ratiocination. And the comic is not canceled though we should suppose Jonathan to be giving play to his humor. (I may have dreamed this, or had it suggested to me, for, on referring to

---

3. Dorine is the saucy maid in Molière's *Tartuffe*, who reconciles the quarreling lovers.

4. Tool, agent.

Jonathan Wild, I do not find it.)[5] Apply the case to the man of deep wit, who is ever certain of his condemnation by the opposite party, and then it ceases to be comic, and will be satiric.

The look of Fielding upon Richardson is essentially comic.[6] His method of correcting the sentimental writer is a mixture of the comic and the humorous. Parson Adams is a creation of humor. But both the conception and the presentation of Alceste and of Tartuffe, of Célimène and Philaminte, are purely comic, addressed to the intellect; there is no humor in them, and they refresh the intellect they quicken to detect their comedy, by force of the contrast they offer between themselves and the wiser world about them—that is to say, society, or that assemblage of minds whereof the comic spirit has its origin.

Byron had splendid powers of humor, and the most poetic satire that we have example of, fusing at times to hard irony. He had no strong comic sense, or he would not have taken an anti-social position, which is directly opposed to the comic; and in his philosophy, judged by philosophers, he is a comic figure by reason of this deficiency. *'Sobald er reflectirt ist er ein Kind,'* Goethe says of him.[7] Carlyle sees him in this comic light, treats him in the humorous manner.

The satirist is a moral agent, often a social scavenger, working on a storage of bile.

The ironist is one thing or another, according to his caprice. Irony is the humor of satire; it may be savage, as in Swift, with a moral object, or sedate, as in Gibbon, with a malicious.[8] The foppish irony fretting to be seen, and the irony which leers, that you shall not mistake its intention, are failures in satiric effort pretending to the treasures of ambiguity.

The humorist of mean order is a refreshing laugher, giving tone to the feelings, and sometimes allowing the feelings to be too much for him; but the humorist of high has an embrace of contrasts beyond the scope of the comic poet.

Heart and mind laugh out at Don Quixote, and still you brood on him. The juxtaposition of the knight and squire is a

5. Meredith was evidently quoting from memory, for what he has in mind is Fielding's account of James Wild, Jonathan's father, who took up arms against society but was captured and "put basely and cowardly to death by a combination between twelve men of the enemy's party, who, after some consultation, unanimously agreed on the said murder."
6. Fielding satirized Samuel Richardson's *Pamela* in *Shamela*, and continued the parody in *Joseph Andrews*. Parson Adams is a character in the latter novel.
7. "As soon as he starts to think, he is a child": Goethe, the famous German poet-philosopher, in conversation with his disciple Eckermann.
8. Edward Gibbon, the historian of the Roman Empire's decline and fall.

comic conception, the opposition of their natures most humorous. They are as different as the two hemispheres in the time of Columbus, yet they touch, and are bound in one, by laughter. The knight's great aims and constant mishaps, his chivalrous valiancy exercised on absurd objects, his good sense along the high road of the craziest of expeditions, the compassion he plucks out of derision, and the admirable figure he preserves while stalking through the frantically grotesque and burlesque assailing him, are in the loftiest moods of humor, fusing the tragic sentiment with the comic narrative. The stroke of the great humorist is world-wide, with lights of tragedy in his laughter.

* * *

If you believe that our civilization is founded in common sense (and it is the first condition of sanity to believe it), you will, when contemplating men, discern a Spirit overhead; not more heavenly than the light flashed upward from glassy surfaces, but luminous and watchful; never shooting beyond them, nor lagging in the rear; so closely attached to them that it may be taken for a slavish reflex, until its features are studied. It has the sage's brows, and the sunny malice of a faun lurks at the corners of the half-closed lips drawn in an idle wariness of half-tension. That slim feasting smile, shaped like the long-bow, was once a big round satyr's laugh, that flung up the brows like a fortress lifted by gunpowder. The laugh will come again, but it will be of the order of the smile, finely-tempered; showing sunlight of the mind, mental richness rather than noisy enormity. Its common aspect is one of unsolicitous observation, as if surveying a full field and having leisure to dart on its chosen morsels, without any fluttering eagerness. Men's future upon earth does not attract it; their honesty and shapeliness in the present does; and whenever they wax out of proportion, overblown, affected, pretentious, bombastical, hypocritical, pedantic, fantastically delicate; whenever it sees them self-deceived or hoodwinked, given to run riot in idolatries, drifting into vanities, congregating in absurdities, planning short-sightedly, plotting dementedly; whenever they are at variance with their professions, and violate the unwritten but perceptible laws binding them in consideration one to another; whenever they offend sound reason, fair justice; are false in humility or mined with conceit, individually, or in the bulk; the Spirit overhead will look humanely malign, and cast an oblique light on them, followed by volleys of silvery laughter. That is the Comic Spirit.

Not to distinguish it is to be bull-blind to the spiritual, and to deny the existence of a mind of man where minds of men are in working conjunction.

You must, as I have said, believe that our state of society is founded in common sense, otherwise you will not be struck by the contrasts the Comic Spirit perceives, or have it to look to for your consolation. You will, in fact, be standing in that peculiar oblique beam of light, yourself illuminated to the general eye as the very object of chase and doomed quarry of the thing obscure to you. But to feel its presence, and to see it, is your assurance that many sane and solid minds are with you in what you are experiencing; and this of itself spares you the pain of satirical heat, and the bitter craving to strike heavy blows. You share the sublime of wrath, that would not have hurt the foolish, but merely demonstrate their foolishness. Molière was contented to revenge himself on the critics of the *École des femmes* by writing the *Critique de l'École des femmes*, one of the wisest as well as the playfullest of studies in criticism.[9] A perception of the Comic Spirit gives high fellowship. You become a citizen of the selecter world, the highest we know of in connection with our old world, which is not supermundane. Look there for your unchallengeable upper class! You feel that you are one of this our civilized community, that you cannot escape from it, and would not if you could. Good hope sustains you; weariness does not overwhelm you; in isolation you see no charms for vanity; personal pride is greatly moderated. Nor shall your title of citizenship exclude you from worlds of imagination or of devotion. The Comic Spirit is not hostile to the sweetest songfully poetic. Chaucer bubbles with it; Shakespeare overflows; there is a mild moon's ray of it (pale with super-refinement through distance from our flesh and blood planet) in *Comus*. Pope has it, and it is the daylight side of the night half-obscuring Cowper.[1] It is only hostile to the priestly element when that, by baleful swelling, transcends and overlaps the bounds of its office; and then, in extreme cases, it is too true to itself to speak, and veils the lamp—as, for example, the spectacle of Bossuet over the dead body of Molière, at which the dark angels may, but men do not, laugh.[2]

* * *

9. Molière ridiculed the critics of his play *The School for Wives* in a little playlet, *Criticism of the School for Wives*.

1. William Cowper, the late-eighteenth-century poet, when not under the grip of obsession, was one of the most genial and jovial of authors, as in "John Gilpin's Ride."

2. The very learned bishop Bossuet did not literally stand over Molière's dead body, but twenty years after his death reviled the playwright as an immoral author.

The laughter heard in circles not pervaded by the comic idea will sound harsh and soulless, like versified prose, if you step into them with a sense of the distinction. You will fancy you have changed your habitation to a planet remoter from the sun. You may be among powerful brains, too. You will not find poets—or but a stray one, over-worshiped. You will find learned men undoubtedly, professors, reputed philosophers, and illustrious dilettanti. They have in them, perhaps, every element composing light, except the comic. They read verse, they discourse of art; but their eminent faculties are not under that vigilant sense of a collective supervision, spiritual and present, which we have taken note of. They build a temple of arrogance; they speak much in the voice of oracles; their hilarity, if it does not dip in grossness, is usually a form of pugnacity.

Insufficiency of sight in the eye looking outward has deprived them of the eye that should look inward. They have never weighed themselves in the delicate balance of the comic idea, so as to obtain a suspicion of the rights and dues of the world; and they have, in consequence, an irritable personality. A very learned English professor crushed an argument in a political discussion by asking his adversary angrily: 'Are you aware, Sir, that I am a philologer?'

The practice of polite society will help in training them, and the professor on a sofa, with beautiful ladies on each side of him, may become their pupil and a scholar in manners without knowing it; he is at least a fair and pleasing spectacle to the comic Muse. But the society named polite is volatile in its adorations, and to-morrow will be petting a bronzed soldier, or a black African, or a prince, or a spiritualist; ideas cannot take root in its ever-shifting soil. It is besides addicted in self-defence to gabble exclusively of the affairs of its rapidly revolving world, as children on a whirli-go-round bestow their attention on the wooden horse or cradle ahead of them, to escape from giddiness and preserve a notion of identity. The professor is better out of a circle that often confounds by lionizing, sometimes annoys by abandoning, and always confuses. The school that teaches gently what peril there is lest a cultivated head should still be coxcomb's, and the collisions which may befall high-soaring minds, empty or full, is more to be recommended than the sphere of incessant motion supplying it with material.

Lands where the Comic Spirit is obscure overhead are rank with raw crops of matter. The traveler accustomed to smooth highways and people not covered with burrs and prickles is amazed, amid so much that is fair and cherishable, to come upon such curious barbarism. An Englishman paid a visit of admiration to a professor in the land of culture,[3] and was introduced by him to another distinguished professor, to whom he took so cordially as to walk out with him alone one afternoon. The first professor, an erudite entirely worthy of the sentiment of scholarly esteem prompting the visit, behaved (if we exclude the dagger) with the vindictive jealousy of an injured Spanish beauty. After a short prelude of gloom and obscure explosions, he discharged upon his faithless admirer the bolts of passionate logic familiar to the ears of flighty caballeros:[4] 'Either I am a fit object of your admiration, or I am not. Of these things, one: either you are competent to judge, in which case I stand condemned by you; or you are incompetent, and therefore impertinent, and you may betake yourself to your country again, hypocrite!' The admirer was for persuading the wounded scholar that it is given to us to be able to admire two professors at a time. He was driven forth.

Perhaps this might have occurred in any country, and a comedy of The Pedant, discovering the greedy humanity within the dusty scholar, would not bring it home to one in particular. I am mindful that it was in Germany, when I observe that the Gemans have gone through no comic training to warn them of the sly, wise emanation eyeing them from aloft, nor much of satirical. Heinrich Heine[5] has not been enough to cause them to smart and meditate.

* * *

I do not know that the fly in amber is of any particular use, but the comic idea enclosed in a comedy makes it more generally perceptible and portable, and that is an advantage. There is a benefit to men in taking the lessons of comedy in congregations,[6] for it enlivens the wits; and to writers it is beneficial, for they must have a clear scheme, and even if they have no idea to present, they must prove that they have made the public sit to them before the sitting, to see the picture. And writing for the stage would be a corrective of a too-incrusted scholarly style, into which some great ones fall at times. It keeps minor writers to a definite plan, and to English. Many of them now swelling a plethoric market in the composition of novels, in pun-manufactories, and in journalism—attached to

3. The land of culture (*Kultur*) is Germany.
4. Literally, "horsemen"; in context, "admirers."
5. Heinrich Heine (1797–1856) was famous for his light, scoffing humor, more in the French than the German vein, though he wrote primarily in German. Not enough Germans followed in his cosmopolitan footsteps.
6. The audiences of stage plays.

the machinery forcing perishable matter on a public that swallows voraciously and groans—might, with encouragement, be attending to the study of art in literature. Our critics appear to be fascinated by the quaintness of our public, as the world is when our beast-garden has a new importation of magnitude, and the creature's appetite is reverently consulted.[7] They stipulate for a writer's popularity before they will do much more than take the position of umpires to record his failure or success. Now the pig supplies the most popular of dishes, but it is not accounted the most honored of animals, unless it be by the cottager. Our public might surely be led to try other, perhaps finer, meat. It has good taste in song. It might be taught as justly, on the whole (and the sooner when the cottager's view of the feast shall cease to be the humble one of our literary critics), to extend this capacity for delicate choosing in the direction of the matter arousing laughter.

Readers of *The Egoist* who are intrigued by the prominence of the star Sirius in the thoughts of Clara Middleton, at a time when she has many other matters to occupy her mind, may find it useful to meditate on a poem that Meredith wrote specifically for this heavenly body. Sirius, it's helpful to know, is one of the brightest stars in the sky, and a major component of Canis Major, one of two constellations supposed to represent dogs which follow Orion the keen hunter across the heavens.

GEORGE MEREDITH
The Star Sirius

Bright Sirius! that when Orion pales
To dotlings under moonlight still art keen
With cheerful fervour of a warrior's mien
Who holds in his great heart the battle-scales:
Unquenched of flame though swift the flood assails,
Reducing many lustrous to the lean:
Be thou my star, and thou in me be seen
To show what source divine is, and prevails.
Long watches through, at one with godly night,
I mark thee planting joy in constant fire;
And thy quick beams, whose jets of life inspire
Life to the spirit, passion for the light,
Dark Earth since first she lost her lord from sight
Has viewed and felt them sweep her as a lyre.

7. In fact, the enormous growth of population in the nineteenth century and the spread of limited literacy had created new audiences for sub-literature or semi-literature, or new guises of literature itself, with which the Victorian sages were busily trying to cope.

Criticism

It is not to be pretended that either George Meredith or his novel *The Egoist* pose such central problems for our time that grand critical issues have to be fought over them. Modern appreciation of Meredith as a novelist has had to be much muted by doubt over his pretensions as a Victorian sage; and even his technical innovations have been clouded by the company he keeps. Falling inescapably among the Victorians, he has been read through eyes prepared by Dickens and George Eliot, rather than by the Continental authors with whom he claimed kinship. The Continental tradition might very well render his silent negatives more speaking and positive: and this, I think, is the real problem with Meredith, after which criticism is still groping. We've got used to not reading him for his lectures and sermons, but how to see into his reticences and discretions we're still learning. They may be the most important, as they are certainly the most difficult, parts of his novels; it is hoped that the commentaries that follow will help make some of them more evident.

Wherever called for, page references to *The Egoist* in the following materials have been corrected to conform with the pagination of this edition.

ROBERT D. MAYO

The Egoist and the Willow Pattern†

No one has yet pointed out the full significance of Sir Willoughby Patterne's name in *The Egoist*. It has, in the first place, an obvious association with *pattern*, and tends to recall Sir Willoughby's exemplary traits as a wealthy young land-owner—"a picture of an English gentleman," and a model of excellence and eligibility. This is the effect intended in such passages as that in which he is contrasted with his cousin, Vernon Whitford:

> But one was a Patterne; the other a Whitford. One had genius; the other pottered after him with the title of student. One was the English gentleman wherever he went; the other was a new kind of thing, nondescript . . .[1]

Here Meredith is matching Sir Willoughby's name with one of his dominant characteristics, and is following the old tradition of satirical comedy. But from a number of other passages in the novel it is clear that the name is meant to arouse other associations, less obvious, but none the less intentional. To the alert reader Sir Willoughby Patterne is supposed also to sug-

† From *English Literary History* (*ELH*)
IX (1942), pp. 71–78.   1. *The Egoist*, p. 23.

gest *Willow Pattern*, as a close inspection of the novel will bear witness. It is this view of *The Egoist* which seems to have escaped previous commentators, although to overlook it is to obtain an incomplete picture of the book's design.

The blue Willow Pattern, named for the willow tree which figures in its center, is undoubtedly the most popular single design ever to be employed on English earthenware. The pattern originated about 1780 at the Caughley porcelain factory in Shropshire, where it was adapted from conventional forms on Chinese porcelain. It was widely copied by other manufacturers of English china, and soon attained an extraordinary popularity. According to a writer in 1849, "the sale of the common blue plate, known as the 'willow-pattern' exceeds that of all the others put together."[2] References to "Blue Willow" are fairly common in nineteenth century writings, but a surer mark than these of its popular favor is the number of nursery verses referring to it which were current during the middle and late years of the century.[3] In Meredith's day, as in our own, Willow-ware was undoubtedly the best known variety of English china.

Early in its history a romantic legend became associated with the Willow Pattern, and owing to the great popularity of the latter, acquired a considerable currency in England. The legend itself is probably not oriental in origin, but merely represents an attempt to explain the scenes on the universally familiar blue willow-plate. The story was told in some detail in the first volume of *The Family Friend* (1849), but it is likely that this is but an elaboration of what had already circulated for some years before.[4] In December, 1851, the Willow story formed the subject of an extravaganza presented at the Strand Theatre in London, entitled *The Mandarin's Daughter; or, The Willow Pattern Plate*. From April 19 to July 3, 1875—four years before the publication of *The Egoist*—another version of the same story, by F. C. Burnand, was offered as a German Reed entertainment at St. George's Hall, London,[5] and some years later the tale was made the subject of a Savoy opera.[6] In

2. *The Family Friend*, London, 1 (1849), 124.

3. Cf. *Notes and Queries* 6. 6. 345; 6. 7. 32; 6. 10. 329; 8. 12. 326, 413, 514; 9. 1. 212; 10. 9. 437; 12. 7. 236.

4. "The Story of the Common Williow-Pattern Plate," *The Family Friend* 1 (1849). 124–27, 151–54. The writer believes in the Chinese origin of the story, and presumably, therefore, is reworking earlier material. See also "A True History of the Celebrated Wedgewood Hieroglyph, commonly called the Willow Pattern," *Bentley's Miscellany* 3 (1838). 61–65. This sketch by Mark Lemon, although largely nonsensical, involves a very similar story.

5. *A Tale of Old China*, written by F. C. Burnand, with music by J. L. Molloy. Cf. *Notes and Queries* 10. 10. 98; 12. 9. 175. F. C. Burnand was a friend of Meredith.

6. *The Willow Pattern*, a comic operetta in two episodes, by Basil Hood, music by Cecil Cook, produced at the Savoy Theatre, November 14, 1901.

naming his hero Sir Willoughby Patterne, therefore, and in duplicating certain features of the Willow legend, Meredith was not presuming acquaintance with totally unfamiliar material.

The Willow story is variously told, but practically all versions agree in outline. According to most of these the rich and influential mandarin who inhabited the stately mansion depicted on the right in the design was a widower possessed of a lovely daughter named Koong-see. He intended to marry his daughter to a wealthy suitor of high degree, but the maiden opposed her parent's wish. She had chosen for her lover a poor and honorable man serving as her father's secretary and had exchanged vows with him in clandestine meetings under the blossoming trees of the Willow Pattern. Suspecting his daughter's defection, the mandarin imprisoned her in a pavilion in his garden, and commanded her to marry the husband of his choice when the peach tree should be in blossom. Here Koong-see pined for her freedom, and prayed that she might find release. Her chosen lover found means to communicate with her, invaded her prison, and carried her off, while her father feted the promised bridgeroom in the banquet hall. The lovers were hotly pursued by the mandarin (in some versions by Ta-jin, the rejected suitor), but they escaped over the Willow bridge. After further adventures the gods turned them into birds in token of their fidelity.

It is this romantic tale, curiously, which seems to have provided Meredith with the groundplan of *The Egoist*. The resemblance between the two is obvious, but the triumph of true love over parental veto is a theme so common to fiction that the likeness might escape notice had the novelist not drawn particular attention to it by the name he gave his hero. In his relation to Clara Middleton, Sir Willoughby Patterne, the representative of a great country family, and in spirit (we are told) "a despotic prince," assumes the double role of tyrannical father and frustrated lover (although in Dr. Middleton's support of his suit, and in their *rapprochement* over the wine cups there may be an echo of the original relationship). Like Koong-see Clara resolves to escape from a seemingly brilliant match because it promises to fetter her to a man she does not love. Her captivity is hardly physical, no more than Sir Willoughby's "despotism," but her struggle is no less real and leads to one abortive attempt at flight. Like the maiden of the Willow story, also, she takes for her lover a dowerless scholar and secretary. In *The Egoist*, it is true, the sequence is reversed, and Clara makes her bid for freedom before she and Whitford are acknowledged lovers. The reasons for Clara's revolt occupy Meredith's interest more than her new love— here there has been a shift of accent—but Vernon is no less her liberator from "dolorous bondage,"[7] and she assures Sir Willoughby before he releases her that she could marry no one else. In "Vernon's Holy Tree," in fact, the soaring "double-blossom wild cherry," under which Clara first awakens to a serious interest in Whitford, we may find a reflection of the lush floral background of the Willow love story.

In view of these parallels, which, from his later references to the Willow Pattern, Meredith evidently intended us to recognize, we are able to attach new significance to Mrs. Mountstuart Jenkinson's enigmatical reference to Clara as "a dainty rogue in porcelain." This phrase, which figures recurrently in the narrative, both puzzles and displeases Sir Willoughby, who objects that "rogue and mistress of Patterne do not go together." But to his repeated query of "why rogue?" his friend cryptically answers that "porcelain explains it," and declines to clarify her meaning further. "Like all rapid phrasers," says Meredith, "Mrs. Mountstuart detested the analysis of her sentence. It had an outline in vagueness, and was flung out to be apprehended, not dissected."[8] May not the elusive meaning be its reference to the independent action of Clara's prototype in the Willow story? Sir Willoughby, we are told, "detested but was haunted by the phrase," and with his progressive dissatisfaction with Clara's attitude towards himself, he came to feel that he could glimpse something of her "roguishness" —that is, her self-willed determination to maintain her integrity of spirit against his "Egoist ideal of a waxwork sex."

She certainly had at times the look of a nymph that has gazed too long on the faun, and has unwittingly copied his lurking lip and long sliding eye. Her play with young Crossjay resembled a return of the lady to the cat; she flung herself into it as if her real vitality had been in suspense till she saw the boy. Sir Willoughby by no means disapproved of a physical liveliness that promised him health in his mate; but he began to feel in their conversations that she did not sufficiently think of making herself a nest for him. Steely points were opposed to him when he, figuratively, bared his bosom to be taken to the softest and fairest.[9]

7. *The Egoist*, p. 197. Clara thinks of herself as being held prisoner.

8. *Ibid.*, pp. 37–39.
9. *Ibid.*, p. 75.

Once introduced by Mrs. Mountstuart, the "rogue-in-porcelain" motif is caught up like a musical theme, and repeated, alluded to, and periodically re-scrutinized by the principal characters through the greater part of the book.[1] The figure, furthermore, is pursued beyond mere recapitulation. Now Clara is "prettily moulded in a delicate substance"; later she is one of those "delicate vessels" that "ring sweetly to a finger nail"; and, after her struggle for freedom, she looks "like a bit of china that wants dusting"[2]—until as we approach the end of the story we feel, like Clara, that we have been "overdone with porcelain" and are constrained to exclaim with Mrs. Mountstuart "Porcelain again!" and *"Toujours la porcelaine!"*[3]

In addition to the frequent recurrence of what might be termed Clara's *leitmotif*, it is important to recall that Meredith has twice carried over the "porcelain-idea" into the plot itself. Both incidents are skillfully linked with the "rogue-in-porcelain" theme and must represent a conscious attempt on his part to extend his original conceit to another plane of the narrative. The arrival of Colonel De Craye at Patterne Hall marks a decisive stage of Sir Willoughby's relations with his bride-to-be, in providing him with a definite focus for his discontent. In Chapter 17, entitled "The Porcelain Vase"—which begins, significantly, with a reversion by Mrs. Mountstuart and Sir Willoughby to the subject of the "rogue in porcelain" —the Colonel's appearance is signalized by the arrival of a carriage bearing, not the guest, but the fragments of a porcelain vase. This was to have been De Craye's wedding gift to his friend, but it has been broken through an accident on the road which has abruptly brought Clara and the handsome Colonel together. Here Meredith is employing the "thematic material" symbolically, suggesting the shattering of his hero's earlier illusion of a perfect match.

"Well, now the gift can be shared, if you're either of you for a division," Mrs. Mountstuart declares, returning to the subject of their earlier conversation. "At any rate, there was a rogue in *that* porcelain"—"What was meant by Clara being seen walking on the highroad alone?" queries the novelist. "What snare, traceable ad inferas,[4] had ever induced Willoughby Patterne to make her the repository and fortress of his honour!" And the next moment he brings Clara into the scene, "chatting and laughing with Colonel de Craye . . . a dazzling

---

1. Cf. *The Egoist*, pp. 36, 37 ff., 45, 75, 92, 134–35, 137, 139, 196, 225, 240, 279, 284, 285–86, 290, 316.
2. *Ibid.*, pp. 32, 289, 390.

3. "Always this porcelain!" [*Editor.*] *Ibid.*, pp. 240, 285, 293.
4. "To the lower regions." [*Editor.*]

offender as if she wished to compel the spectator to recognize the dainty rogue in porcelain."[5]

> ". . . the broken is the broken, sir, [exclaims Dr. Middleton to Vernon Whitford later] whether in porcelain or in human engagements: and all that the one of the two continuing faithful, I should rather say, regretful, can do, is to devote the remainder of life to the picking up of the fragments . . ."[6]

After Clara's mutiny the remainder of *The Egoist* is devoted to Sir Willoughby's regretful gathering of the fragments.

In the second half of the novel, again, it is Lady Busshe's wedding present—likewise porcelain—which becomes the center of converging lines of interest. The gift, a porcelain service which Clara archly terms "another dedicatory offering to the *rogue* in me!"—becomes the occasion for a battle of wits in Patterne Hall. For Lady Busshe, with her "passion to foretell disasters," it provides a means of testing her suspicion of a rift between Sir Willoughby and his bride; for Clara, "incapable of decent hypocrisy," it presents an obstacle to her resolve to add no further tie to those which already bind her; to Sir Willoughby it offers a threat to his desire to present to the world a serenely unbroken facade. In the dinner scene which follows, one of the most brilliantly comic in the book, Sir Willoughby scarcely succeeds in concealing his predicament from Lady Busshe. Her victorious trumpeting is thus communicated by Mrs. Mountstuart:

> " 'I shall have that porcelain back,' says Lady Busshe to me, when we were shaking hands last night: 'I think,' says she, 'it should have been the Willow Pattern.' And she really said: 'he's in for being jilted a second time!' "
> Sir Willoughby restrained a bound of his body that would have sent him up some feet into the air. He felt his skull thundered at within.[7]

Lady Busshe's parting thrust, typically Meredithian in its obliquity, acquires meaning only with reference to Koongsee's jilting of Ta-jin in the Willow legend. The extravagance of Sir Willoughby's horror is not otherwise explainable. Mrs. Mountstuart may translate for emphasis Lady Busshe's gibe into more direct terms, but she does not need to explain the pun. Like other Meredithian characters, Sir Willoughby has a hypersensitive ear for overtones, hints, and side-hits, and is acutely aware of her meaning in raising at this juncture the

5. *Ibid.*, p. 139.
6. *Ibid.*, p. 368.

7. *Ibid.*, p. 286.

name of Willow Patttern. "In her bitter vulgarity, that beaten rival of Mrs. Mountstuart Jenkinson for the leadership of the county had taken his nose for a melancholy prognostic of his fortunes; she had recently played on his name: she had spoken the hideous English of his fate."[8] It is this portentous linking of his plight with that of the jilted suitor of the sentimental Willow story which goads Sir Willoughby into a course of action that eventually gains Clara her freedom. Alarmed by the possibility of losing face a second time in the county's eyes he admits the alternative of marrying Laetitia Dale and relinquishing his promised bride to Vernon Whitford.

> He was bound to marry: he was bound to take to himself one of them: and whichever one he selected would cast a lustre on his reputation. At least she would rescue him from the claws of Lady Busshe, and her owl's hoot of "Willow Pattern," and her hag's shriek of "twice jilted."[9]

The Willow legend thus becomes a factor in the *dénouement* of *The Egoist* and an integral part of the book's design. If we may judge from the evidence collected, moreover, it provided Meredith with a rough outline for his novel, which he consciously held in mind from the outset. Though he never explicitly identifies his "source," it is implied by a wealth of allusion from the moment Sir Willoughby makes his first appearance to the time when Lady Busshe utters her "owl's hoot of 'Willow Pattern.' " But beyond providing Mrs. Mountstuart with a topic for conversational skirmishing and Lady Busshe with an armour-piercing taunt, it is difficult to assign to the Willow "theme" any very important function in the novel. The resemblance between the two stories is too much obscured by indirectness to heighten appreciably our feeling of *pattern or form* in the narrative, or to serve effectively as an ironic augury of Sir Willoughby's fate. Meredith's unsuccess in these respects is shown by the failure of readers to respond to his hints. The link between the name "Willoughby Patterne" and "rogue in porcelain" is lost on most of his audience, who pass over Lady Busshe's pun as mere freakishness. Even when rescued from obscurity the Willow "theme" seems a superfluous piece of ingenuity. It cannot be said to illuminate in any essential way the relationship of Clara to her father or her two lovers, or—apart from revealing the intensity of Sir Willoughby's humiliation—throw light on the springs of action. Not-

8. *Ibid.*, pp. 310–11. On the day of his majority Lady Busshe had declared that Sir Willoughby had "the nose of a monarch destined to lose a throne."

9. *Ibid.*, p. 288.

withstanding Meredith's pronouncement in the "Prelude" to
The Egoist, that "the Comic Spirit conceives a definite situation for a number of characters, and rejects all accessories in
the exclusive pursuit of them and their speech,"[1] this device
would seem to be more an *accessory* than anything else. He was
rarely content to occupy himself with the "exclusive pursuit"
of any story. In his abiding anxiety to avoid the hackneyed
and the obvious, he was impelled to dazzle his readers with
feats of virtuosity. This the use of the Willow story certainly
is—an exercise in adroitness, an elaborate conceit which adds
to the effect of quaintness and artificiality in the novel, but
advances nowhere. It is in some degree the artifice for artifice's
sake of a writer who, as Paul Elmer More says, like Mrs.
Mountstuart, was "mad for cleverness."

RICHARD B. HUDSON

The Meaning of Egoism
in George Meredith's *The Egoist*†

I

George Meredith's *The Egoist*, published in 1879, is a novel
of life among the landed gentry in which a wealthy member
of that class is forced to undergo humiliation because of his
preposterous absorption in himself, his concern for his own
comfort and convenience, and his appearance to the world at
large. His nemesis is not an aroused and militant proletariat,
nor an indignant society, but the Comic Spirit and her attendant imps, who catch him off guard and apply the corrective
of laughter. The casual reader might infer that there is no
more to the novel. On the surface no tremendous issues seem
to be at stake in the drawing room at Patterne Hall; the action
centers on Sir Willoughby Patterne and his presumptions and
apparently has no meaning in the vast world outside, except
perhaps in its implications for the conduct of all young men in
love. Indeed, according to Meredith, the Comic Spirit has no
concern with such matters as philosophic import: she is concerned with the actions of men in the here and now. "Men's
future on earth does not attract [the Comic Spirit], their hon-

1. *Ibid.*, p. 1.
† From *The Trollopian* (*Nineteenth Century Fiction*), III (1948–49), 163–76.

esty and shapeliness in the present does . . ."[1] Reason triumphs over the sentimental egoism of Sir Willoughby, and the comic imps are satisfied.

When one looks at Meredith's poetry, however, he finds that egoism is mentioned again and again and taken far more seriously than it seems to be in the novel. Meredith the writer of social comedy seems to be amused by the absurdity of Sir Willoughby's egoism; Meredith the philosophical poet is not. The purpose of this study is to show that the full meaning of the novel depends in part upon an understanding of what egoism stood for in Meredith's philosophy and that, despite the spirit of comedy in which the novel is conceived, its underlying aim is serious indeed. How seriously Meredith took egoism appears clearly whenever he writes in his poetry of the intellectual evolution of society or of the goals toward which society as a whole is moving.[2] In the light of what Meredith says here, the egoism of Sir Willoughby Patterne is more than mere conceit or self-worship; it is a reversal of the evolutionary process, a bar to progress.

II

Meredith's conception of the intellectual evolution which produced society and which now controls it grew out of his belief in biological evolution. This belief has been examined at length, and I need recapitulate only a few of the most important points.[3] Evolution provided Meredith with an acceptable answer to the question of what man's relation to nature is. Given the starting point that man evolved from lower to higher form on earth, Meredith deduces the relationship between man and society as a further evolutionary process. According to Meredith, there are three stages in man's evolutionary development: blood, brain, and spirit. These are, of course, mere animation, which man shares with all animals;

1. "On the Idea of Comedy and the Uses of the Comic Spirit," *The Works of George Meredith*, Memorial Edition (27 vols., Constable, 1909–1911), XXIII, 46 f. See also p. 446, above. References to Meredith's works in the notes that follow are all to the Memorial Edition. [But references to *The Egoist* have been corrected to reflect the pagination of the present edition.—*Editor*.]
2. The poems which have bearing on this study were published in or after 1883, the year in which *Poems and Lyrics of the Joy of Earth* appeared. Except for a few pieces in magazines, Meredith published no poetry between 1862 and 1883. There is evidence in his letters for these years, however, that he was writing poetry, and

there can be little doubt that most of the poems published in 1883 were written in the 'seventies. Some of the poems I have used were published long after *The Egoist* (1879), and were probably written much later, but I do not feel that this fact injures my argument since Meredith's thought is consistent throughout, and it is immaterial whether he conceived the comic aspects of egoism first or, as I feel certain, the serious philosophical aspects.
3. See Lionel Stevenson, *Darwin among the Poets* (Chicago: University of Chicago Press, 1932), pp. 183–236; and Joseph Warren Beach, *The Concept of Nature in Nineteenth Century English Poetry* (New York: Macmillan, 1936), pp. 470–499.

intellect, in which he differs from animals; and spirit, that toward which he is always striving. Man does not pass through each stage and leave it behind; he absorbs each stage and contains it. As he says in "The Woods of Westermain,"

> Each of each in sequent birth,
> Blood and brain and spirit, three
> (Say the deepest gnomes of Earth),
> Join for true felicity.
> Are they parted, then expect
> Someone sailing will be wrecked:
> Separate hunting are they sped,
> Scan the morsel coveted.
> Earth that Triad is: she hides
> Joy from him who that divides;
> Showers is when the three are one
> Glassing her in union.[4]

Man, then, is an animal that has evolved directly out of nature through compliance with nature's laws, however unconscious that compliance has been at times. To those that do not understand her, nature appears cruel and ruthless, apparently random in her law of survival of the fittest, but actually this law has developed intellect in man and prompts him to progress. In "Hard Weather" Meredith says:

> Behold the life at ease; it drifts.
> The sharpened life commands its course.
> She winnows, winnows roughly; sifts,
> To dip her chosen in her source:
> Contention is the vital force,
> Whence pluck they brain, her prize of gifts,
> Sky of the senses! on which height,
> Not disconnected, yet released,
> They see how spirit comes to light,
> Through conquest of the inner beast,
> Which Measure tames to movement sane,
> In Harmony with what is fair.[5]

Man's absorption in the second and third stages of evolution shows him that life has a meaning and a purpose when regulated according to nature and leads him to form a society as the most intelligent method of regulating his life in relation to others. In deriving the intellectual and spiritual aspects of life from nature and evolution, Meredith goes far beyond the dis-

4. XXV, 43. ["Glassing" perhaps implies putting a window or shield between man and nature—something to close off her crudities yet allow light, if not air, to penetrate.—*Editor*.]

5. XXV, 213.

coveries of science, as Mr. Stevenson points out.[6] The scientist will not proclaim as true what he cannot demonstrate experimentally. Meredith, however, felt that the implications of science were clear and that the bearing of these implications on the future was the most important contribution of science, especially the theory of biological evolution. Science alone—science without philosophy—will not explain man's intellectual progress. As he says in *The Egoist*:

> We drove in a body to Science the other day for an antidote . . . and Science introduced us to our o'er-hoary ancestry—them in the Oriental posture: whereupon we set up a primaeval chattering to rival the Amazon forest nigh nightfall, cured, we fancied. And before daybreak our disease was hanging on to us again, with the extension of a tail. We had it fore and aft. We were the same, and animals into the bargain. That is all we got from Science.[7]

Thus man in society finds himself in the position of being an animal with all the instincts of an animal and at the same time a thinking being whose continued existence depends upon his ability to adjust himself to living in a society with other men. Often, of course, conflict arises: the demands of the animal run counter to the demands of the member of the social organization.

III

The place of egoism in this philosophical structure and its relation to *The Egoist* has not, however, been pointed out. Egoism, as Meredith depicts it in his poems, is a demand of the animal, a holdover from man's brutish past. It is the primitive desire of the animal for self-preservation, refined somewhat now that man is in society. Thus egoism is opposed to the social organization because egoism seeks to preserve the individual at the expense of society as a whole. To primitive man, egoism, as instinctive self-preservation, was necessary if the individual were to survive the rigors of his existence; but since brain has led man to form a society, the individual no longer has the right to seek survival at the expense of his fellows. Survival of society as a whole—society in the largest and most cosmopolitan sense of the word—is far more important than the survival of the single individual. Yet egoism as the instinct for self-preservation was given to man by nature; he cannot simply wipe out an instinct as he might remove a law from the statute books. All creatures of earth have this instinct for self-preservation, and the only answer to the

6. Stevenson, *op. cit.*, p. 223.   7. *Egoist*, p. 4.

dilemma, according to Meredith, is that intellectual evolution must put egoism to the uses of society. In "The Woods of Westermain" he says:

> Muffled by his cavern-cowl
> Squats the scaly Dragon-fowl,
> Who was lord ere light you drank,
> And lest blood of knightly rank
> Stream, let not your fair princess
> Stray: he holds the leagues in stress,
>   Watches keenly there.
> Oft has he been riven; slain
> Is no force in Westermain.
> Wait, and we shall forge him curbs,
> Put his fangs to uses, tame,
> Teach him, quick as cunning herbs,
> How to cure him sick and lame.
> Much restricted, much enringed,
> Much he frets, the hooked and winged,
>   Never known to spare.
>
> . . . .
>
>   Self, his name declare.
> Him shall Change, transforming late,
> Wonderously renovate.
> Hug himself the creature may:
> What he hugs is loathed decay.
> Crying, slip thy scales, and slough!
> Change will strip his armour off;
> Make of him who was all maw,
> Inly only thrilling-shrewd,
> Such a servant as none saw
> Through his days of dragonhood:
> Days when growling o'er his bone,
> Sharpened he for mine and thine;
> Sensitive within alone;
> Scaly as in clefts of pine.
> Change, the strongest son of Life,
> Has the Spirit here to wife.[8]

Throughout Meredith's poetry, egoism is always identified with primitive brutishness; Meredith personifies the selfish individualism of man, the tendency of man to batten on his kind, as a predatory beast or monster that has not moved forward with "Change," that is, evolution. He means, of course, that the egoist has not passed beyond the first stage of evolution and remains in many ways a mere animal, appearances to the contrary. The egoist will fail to understand na-

8. XXV, 39 f.

ture, for he will see in her only foul shapes, disorder and death. He will see nature as the destroyer of the self, not as the preserver of the race. In "Earth and Man" Meredith says:

> He will not read her good,
> Or wise, but with the passion Self obscures;
> Through that old devil of the thousand lures,
> Through that dense hood:
>
> Through terror, through distrust,
> The greed to touch, to view, to have, to live:
> Through all that makes of him a sensitive
> Abhorring dust.[9]

As Meredith depicts him in the poems, then, the egoist is out of tune with nature in failing to understand her evolutionary purpose and out of tune with society in opposing the aim of society, which we may take to be the general good rather than the individual good. But how serious is this failure of the egoist to catch up with evolution? Is it anything more than a deviation from the norm that can be laughed off the stage? From the novel one might think not, although Meredith does give some hints of how seriously he regards Sir Willoughby's offense. In the poetry, however, he takes it seriously indeed. It represents a halt in the course of evolution; the egoist remains at the first stage of evolution—the animal—in opposition to progress. In "Foresight and Patience" Meredith says:

> Now must the brother soul alive in each
> His traitorous individual devildom
> Hold subject lest the grand destruction come.
> Dimly men see it menacing apace
> To overthrow, perhance uproot, the race.[1]

A force that can stop evolution and return man to the primitive is important indeed. The reason lies in the distinction that Meredith makes between physical evolution, the first stage, and the evolution of the intellect; the former is an automatic process directed by the laws of nature over which man has no control. The latter is not inevitable, but dependent upon man himself and his ability to construct a society in harmony with nature. Nature reigns, but nature has only started man on his road: his destiny ultimately is in his own hands. He says in "The Test of Manhood":

> Inconscient, insensitive, she reigns
> In iron laws, though rapturous fair her face.

9. XXV, 94 f.   1. XXVI, 93 f.

> Back to the primal brute shall he retrace
> His path, doth he permit to force her chains
> A soft Persuader coursing through his veins,
> An icy Huntress stringing to the chase . . .[2]

It is in the life of the senses that egoism has its roots, and Meredith believed that man's frantic desire to retain his individual senses is one of his most harmful instincts if not properly controlled in society. He does not mean simply that man is sensual: Meredith always believed in the right use of the senses, condemning both the "Huntress" and the "Persuader." He means that man's primitive instincts are continually keeping him from seeing how the evolution of the intellect leads him into society and how this society is his insurance for survival as a race. Man, in his egocentric fear of change and of death, places too much importance upon the individual and ignores the vast, cosmic plan of nature that clearly operates only by generalities. The enduring reality is the abstraction.

Life is a war on sensation, or blood, the first stage of evolution, because sensation is a product of man's animal past and is the opposite of the direction in which evolution is traveling. The war is not to wipe out sensation, however; the war is to teach man the right use of it in the present order, to teach him that sensation on the level of blood is one thing, on the level of brain another. The faculty that wages this war is reason, evolved, as we have seen, painfully out of nature's law of survival of the fittest. Man's instincts and fears—all heritages from his brutish past—must submit to the control of reason. In "A Faith on Trial" Meredith says:

> But this in my self did I know,
> Not needing a studious brow,
> Or trust in a governing star,
> While my ears held the jangled shout
> The children were lifting afar:
> That natures at interflow
> With all of their past and the now,
> Are chords to the Nature without,
> Orbs to the greater whole:
> First then, nor utterly then
> Till our lord of sensations at war,

2. XXVI, 204. This passage is interesting in that it shows not only man's relation to nature, but also elements in his make-up other than egoism that may cause a retrogression to the primitive. The "Persuader" and the "Huntress" symbolize sensuality on the one hand and asceticism on the other, both of which Meredith looked upon as contrary to nature and both of which represent retrogression rather than progress. Four poems discuss these tendencies in man: "The Vital Choice," "With the Huntress," "With the Persuader," and "The Test of Manhood."

> The rebel, the heart, yields place
> To brain, each prompting the soul.
> Thus our dear earth we embrace
> For the milk, her strength to men.[3]

The triumph of reason over all forms of self-indulgence causes the individual to sink his desire for personal happiness and satisfaction in a social idea, and thus he finds a larger self and substitutes an abstract, intellectual ideal for a selfish concern with immediate satisfactions. In "Earth and Man" he says:

> But that the senses still
> Usurp the station of their issue mind,
> He would have burst the chrysalis of the blind:
> As yet he will;
>
> As yet he will, she prays,
> Yet will when his distempered devil of Self;—
> The glutton of her fruits, the wily elf
> In shifting rays;—
>
> That captain of the scorned;
> The coveter of life in soul and shell,
> The fratricide, the thief, the infidel,
> The hoofed and horned;—
>
> He singularly doomed
> To what he execrates and writhes to shun;—
> When fire has passed him vapour to the sun,
> And sun relumed,
>
> Then shall the horrid pall
> Be lifted, and a spirit nigh divine,
> "Live in thy offspring as I live in mine,"
> Will hear her call.[4]

Submission to nature's laws and to the governing of reason cause one to suppress the primitive self and to understand the meaning of life in terms of service and subordination of the self to the good of the group.

> Drink the sense the notes infuse,
> You a larger self will find:
> Sweetest fellowship ensues
> With the creatures of your kind.[5]

The individual will not then fear death and express that fear in his selfish desire for a personal immortality. He will be

3. XXV, 250.
4. XXV, 97.

5. XXV, 36.

content with the immortality he achieves through service to humanity. The task he performs will live after him. Meredith does not specifically deny the immortality of the spirit, but he considers the desire of man for a personal immortality, like his prayers for gifts, another instance of his egoism, his inordinate desire to preserve the identity of the self. "Live in thy off-spring, as I live in mine," nature tells him. Man must do his duty on earth and place his trust in nature. Meredith sees that earth, or nature, has no interest in the personal; she is interested in the race. She "winnows out" the best. In "The Test of Manhood" he says:

> As only for the numbers Nature's care
> Is shown, and she the personal nothing heeds,
> So to Divinity the spring of prayer
> From brotherhood the one way upward leads.[6]

And again in "Foresight and Patience":

> Advantage to the Many: that we name
> God's voice; have there the surety in our aim.[7]

Therefore man, following nature's lead, must labor for the advancement of humanity as a whole, not merely for his own personal gain. This use of life, all of which he found implicit in biological evolution, he thought to be the chief lesson that man must learn if the evolution of the intellect is to continue to progress. In a letter to G. P. Baker he says:

> My dear Sir,—When at the conclusion of your article on my works, you say that a certain change in public taste, should it come about, will be to some extent due to me, you hand me the flowering wreath I covet. For I think that all right use of life, and the one secret of life, is to pave ways for the firmer foot-ing of those who succeed us; as to my works, I know them faulty, think them of worth only when they point and aid to that end.[8]

Meredith believed, to summarize, in an intellectual and spir-itual progress that would advance much as physical evolution has advanced. The advance will be slow, never in a straight line, but by devious paths. He compares progress in "The World's Advance" to the homeward journey of the inebriate, who "plays diversions on the homeward line."[9] The inebriate does not take the shortest, most direct path to his goal; he

6. XXVI, 202.
7. XXVI, 98.
8. *The Letters of George Meredith*, col-lected and edited by his son (2 vols.; New York: Scribner's, 1912), II, 398.
9. XXV, 17.

staggers, he is often delayed, but he instinctively moves in the right direction. Nothing can divert him more than momentarily. The part played by the individual in this intellectual evolution is, of course, important. He must strive to understand nature and nature's evolutionary plan, to master and put to use his primitive instincts, and to leave behind him some work that furthers the progress of man.

IV

The comic tone of *The Egoist* may tend to obscure the seriousness of its aim, but there can be no doubt that Sir Willoughby Patterne, the egoist of the novel, is the flesh-and-blood representation of the primitive beasts of the poems. The difference lies in the fact that, in the poems, Meredith discusses egoism in relation to society; but in the novel, he follows the egoist in love, where his qualities are closer to the surface and more easily demonstrated. "The love-season is the carnival of egoism, and it brings the touchstone to our natures."[1] Meredith's thinking throughout the novel, however, is consistent with that in his poetry. Egoism is an instinct given man by nature. Egoism put to the uses of society is good. Egoism that is no more than blind instinct for self-preservation is retrogression to the primitive.

When the primitive instinct that has made man survive is controlled and aimed toward the advancement of society, Meredith has no quarrel with it. He says: "[The comic imps] dare not be chuckling while Egoism is valiant, while sober, while socially valuable, nationally serviceable. They wait."[2] The House of Patterne owes its rise to such an egoism, an egoism that has been put to the uses of society; and with it the comic imps have no game. "Aforetime a grand old Egoism built the House [of Patterne]. It would appear that even finer essences of it are demanded to sustain the structure; but especially would it appear that a reversion to the gross original, beneath a mask and in a vein of fineness, is an earthquake at the foundations of the House."[3]

Sir Willoughby is the "gross original," the reversion to the primitive, though carefully cloaked. In society, the preservation of the individual is less important than the preservation of the race. Sir Willoughby's egoism is calculated to preserve himself and his appearance to the world at large. It retains the power of primitive egoism to inflict deadly injury, but substitutes for the present-day directive intelligence a sentimental concern for the self above all else.

1. *Egoist*, p. 92.
2. *Egoist*, p. 6.
3. *Egoist*, pp. 6–7.

One of the most revealing passages in the novel, one which explains the egoist in prose much as egoism had been developed in the poetry, comes in the chapter entitled appropriately "In the Heart of the Egoist." Meredith says:

The Egoist is our fountain-head, primeval man: the primitive is born again, the elemental reconstituted. Born again, into new conditions, the primitive may be highly polished of men, and forfeit nothing save the roughness of his original nature. He is not only his own father, he is ours; and he is also our son. We have produced him, he us. Such were we, to such are we returning: not other, sings the poet, than one who toilfully works his shallop against the tide, "si brachia forte remisit":—let him haply relax the labour of his arms, however high up the stream! and back he goes, "in pejus," to the early principle of our being, with seeds and plants, that are as carelessly weighed in the hand and as indiscriminately husbanded as our humanity.

Poets on the other side may be cited for an assurance that the primitive is not the degenerate: rather is he a sign of the indestructability of the race, of the ancient energy in removing obstacles to individual growth; a sample of what we would be, had we his concentrated power. He is the original innocent, the pure simple. It is we who have fallen; we have melted into Society, diluted our essence, dissolved. He stands in the midst monumentally, a landmark of the tough and honest old Ages, with the symbolic alphabet of striking arms and running legs, our early language, scrawled over his person, and the glorious first flint and arrow-head for his crest: at once the spectre of the Kitchen-midden and our ripest tissue.

But Society is about him. The occasional spectacle of the primitive dangling on a rope, has impressed his mind with the strength of his natural enemy: from which uncongenial sight he has turned shuddering hardly less to behold the blast that is blown upon a reputation where one has been disrespectful of the many. By these means, through meditation on the contrast of circumstances in life, a pulse of imagination has begun to stir, and he has entered the upper sphere, or circle of spiritual Egoism: he has become the civilized Egoist; primitive still, as sure as man has teeth, but developed in his manner of using them.

Degenerate or not (and there is no just reason to suppose it), Sir Willoughby was a social Egoist, fiercely imaginative in whatsoever concerned him. He had discovered a greater realm than that of the sensual appetites, and he rushed across and around it in his conquering period with an Alexander's pride.[4]

By making Sir Willoughby wealthy and not without brains and ability, Meredith shows how wasteful of the best in mankind is an overindulgence in the ego. The comic purpose of the novel often makes Sir Willoughby's superficial interest in intellectual pursuits appear fatuous, but the point is that Sir Willoughby puts whatever brains, ability, and material wealth he has to the enhancement of his own ego, rather than to the service of mankind.

There is an obvious contrast between Sir Willoughby and Nevil Beauchamp, the central character in *Beauchamp's Career* (1874). Beauchamp, although a member of the upper classes by birth, tries to throw off class distinctions and to work for the advancement of mankind as a whole. His honest efforts are misunderstood by his own social group and regarded with suspicion by those whose lot he would advance. In a letter to Moncure D. Conway, June 18, 1874, Meredith describes the novel thus: "It is philosophical-political, with no powerful stream of adventure: an attempt to show the forces around a young man of the present day, in England, who would move them, and finds them unutterably solid, though it is seen in the end that he does not altogether fail, has not lived quite in vain."[5]

Beauchamp fails mainly because he does not understand the evolutionary process by which man develops; he is a revolutionist who wants to change the world overnight. But Beauchamp follows reason in an unselfish devotion to an abstract principle. Sir Willoughby, on the other hand, eschews reason and follows brute sensation to an exaltation of the self.

Sir Willoughby should have been a leader, as Beauchamp was, accepting responsibility not only in the immediate world of Patterne Hall but also in the larger world outside. Instead, he demanded of others a devotion to his person that was against the laws of nature and that denied the intellectual progress of mankind. For all his position, his wealth, his refinement, and his native endowments he stood for the primitive past rather than for the present and future. His guide was the heart, the seat of sensation, not the brain, the seat of the intellect. The Sir Willoughbys of the world can turn back the course of intellectual evolution—for it is not inevitable—and cause a retrogression of society to the primitive.

4. *Egoist*, pp. 324–25.   5. *Letters*, I, 242.

The comedy of the novel, in which the author has obviously taken so much delight, may cause it to be taken as little more than polite comedy castigating a social vice of the weight of miserliness or hypocrisy, but when one sees the meaning of egoism to Meredith and its importance in his serious philosophy as expressed in his poetry one cannot doubt that the Comic Spirit is doing battle in earnest.

JENNI CALDER

The Insurrection of Women†

When in 1870 women were enabled to own money and property in their own names it became more difficult to regard women themselves as property, though in most respects they continued to have little independent existence. As long as they could be persuaded to believe that marriage was their major occupation in life, and as long as there were men who could afford to buy wives, either with money or with social status, ideally with both, it would be possible for men such as Sir Willoughby Patterne in Meredith's *The Egoist* to consider their destined brides as precious items of furniture, tributes to their own good taste. This is one of the reasons why Meredith writes about an upper class in which he himself is an alien. He is concerned with exposing features of upper-class life which traditionally have been lauded, and which are woven into the fabric of upper-class aspirations. Among the wealthier classes a woman is almost inevitably a symbol. A desirable residence needs a desirable woman. Meredith's men tend to woo images embodying their attitudes to land, property, and their place in society. Meredith concentrates on a clearly defined sphere. Like Jane Austen, although for different reasons, he can examine a world in some completeness. He has all the advantages of writing as an outsider, both envious and critical, who is attracted and also repelled by what he has the opportunity to observe. He often uses as an important, sometimes a central, character an intruder into this world: *Evan Harrington* (1861) is about such an intrusion, to a certain extent so is *Beauchamp's Career* (1876). Aminta in *Lord Ormont and his Aminta* (1894) and Carinthia in *The Amazing Marriage* (1895) are intruders. And intruders feature significantly in

† From *Women and Marriage in Victorian Fiction* (New York, Oxford University Press, 1976), pp. 181–88.

The Egoist (1879). These intrusions are a vital part of Meredith's method of exposure. He cannot rely wholly on either comedy or irony to do this work for him. He must have positive, incisive, disruptive characters who can stir things up, prevent alternatives, refuse to be entirely swayed by the dominant ethos. Vernon Whitford in *The Egoist* is a good example.

But perhaps the most important aspect of Meredith's preoccupation with the upper classes is the question of property. Raynham Abbey[1] and Patterne Hall are commanding centres of their respective novels. As houses and land they have their own profound influence on the plot. It is these things that make Sir Austin and Sir Willoughby much of what they are, and lurk as insistent motives behind their actions. Men of property need wives and they need heirs. It is important that, in *The Amazing Marriage*, Carinthia refuses to take up residence on her husband's property: she does not consider either herself in terms of her husband's possession or her son as heir to his property.

In *The Egoist* the diagnosis of a class situation is central. Mrs. Mountstuart, intimate of the family, says: 'Sir Willoughby is a splendid creature; only wanting a wife to complete him' (Chapter 2). Sir Willoughby's splendour consists partly of his ownership, to which he needs to add a wife, and partly of his consciousness of status, which the right wife will heighten. For him personally a wife will enhance his situation in a peculiarly satisfactory way, for he seeks in women a reflection of his own image of himself, and that sums up what he wants to find permanently established in a wife.

Patterne Hall is full of ladies only too ready to admire and obey Sir Willoughby and to enhance his self-image. 'He ruled arrogantly in the world of women.' The world of women is perhaps his proper sphere, and they are mostly ladies without individuality, vague aunts, middle-aged and elderly ladies, whose major interest in life derives from him. The fact that Sir Willoughby has no particular occupation is a part of his class characterization; he is able to devote himself to nourishing the admiration of lifeless women.

Clara, his intended bride, is not lifeless. Her sheer physical vigour commands our respect of her as a heroine. She is too strong, too swift, to be imprisoned even in the copious nest of Patterne Hall. *The Egoist* is about a woman's discovery that she cannot be a prize awarded to a man, whatever the man

---

1. Raynham Abbey is the residence of Sir Austin Feverel, father of Richard Feverel, hero of Meredith's first major novel, *The Ordeal of Richard Feverel* (1859). [*Editor.*]

has to offer, although her youth and beauty conventionally characterize her as this. The egoist we understand to be Sir Willoughby, yet Clara describes herself as an egoist, and it is her 'egoism' that prompts her rebellion, her awareness of herself as an independent, individual woman. This idea of egoism, which runs through practically everything that Meredith wrote, is double-edged. Egoism is on the one hand the core of selfish, limited, self-aggrandizing behaviour; on the other it is the spur to what Meredith calls insurrection. A sense of oneself is vital. An ignorance of self in others is disastrous. Sir Willoughby and Clara demonstrate the two facets of the same idea.

Clara's problem is that in many ways she is the perfect wife for Sir Willoughby. 'With the wit to understand him, and the heart to worship, she had a dignity rarely seen in young ladies' (Chapter 5). Sir Willoughby dwells on her qualities:

> Clara was young, healthy, handsome; she was therefore fitted to be his wife, the mother of his children, his companion picture. Certainly they looked well side by side. In walking with her, in drooping to her, the whole man was made conscious of the female image of himself by her exquisite unlikeness. She completed him, added the softer lines wanting to his portrait before the world. He had wooed her rageingly; he courted her becomingly; with the manly self-possession enlivened by watchful tact which is pleasing to girls. He never seemed to undervalue himself in valuing her: a secret priceless in the courtship of young women that have heads; the lover doubles their sense of personal worth through not forfeiting his own. (Chapter 5)

This picture of Sir Willoughby bending to Clara, patronizing, self-congratulatory, calculating, stays throughout the novel. We see them together perambulating the gardens of Patterne Hall, restrained and sedate. We see Clara alone roaming the countryside, running, gathering flowers. We see Sir Willoughby sustained by admiring company, often by the best of food, claret and port as well. Sir Willoughby's dignity renders him ultimately ridiculous because he clings to it so rigidly, but the damage which his dignity receives makes him also ultimately sympathetic. Clara's dignity is voluntarily shed when she insists that, after all, she cannot marry him, and risks the anger, scorn and bewilderment of all who surround her.

The tension is indicated early on. Meredith makes it quite explicit that the superbly polite and well-bred Sir Willoughby's view of Clara is as an oriental slave. The suggestions of the harem are obvious. But Clara has 'a natural love of liberty'.

'She preferred to be herself' (Chapter 6). Yet, 'She has no character yet. You are forming it,' says Mrs Mountstuart, whose function as a misleading interpreter is similar to that of Adrian in *Richard Feverel* (Chapter 5). And, 'You are mine, my Clara, utterly mine,' insists Sir Willoughby.

Meredith maintains the tension by showing us Clara's progress towards freedom. She has nothing to sustain her but her own conscience and instinct: instinct, again—it is crucial in *Richard Feverel*—is important. From these she painfully attempts to rationalize and articulate her compulsion to tear herself away from her betrothal. Her association with Crossjay, the active, free-roaming, truant-playing fourteen-year-old boy, and her literal escape in the rain from Patterne Hall are instinctive. Her gradual understanding that she must have it all out in words with both her father and her intended husband, a battle in which she is at an immense disadvantage as neither believes she has a mind of her own, is an act of conscience.

The novel proceeds by means of groups of images illuminated by almost formally dramatic dialogue. Here Mrs Mountstuart and Sir Willoughby discuss the former's characterization of Clara as 'a rogue in porcelain':

> 'Why rogue?' he insisted with Mrs Mountstuart.
> 'I said—in porcelain,' she replied.
> 'Rogue perplexes me.'
> 'Porcelain explains it.'
> 'She has the keenest sense of honour.'
> 'I am sure she is a paragon of rectitude.'
> 'She has beautiful bearing.'
> 'The carriage of a young princess!'
> 'I find her perfect.'
> 'And still she may be a dainty rogue in porcelain.'
> 'Are you judging by the mind or the person, ma'am?'
> 'Both.'
> 'And which is which?'
> 'There's no distinction.'
> 'Rogue and mistress of Patterne do not go together.'
> 'Why not? She will be a novelty to our neighbourhood and an animation of the Hall.' (Chapter 5)

This kind of antithetical, dramatically pointed dialogue emphasizes the particular quality of contained controversy that is maintained throughout. No other novel of Meredith's is so carefully worked out and fulfilled as regards this sort of momentum. This, and the clarity and tension of the images, are reasons for the high regard in which it has been held. The impression in this passage is of the energetic Clara rigidified into an ornament. Her wild running becomes 'beautiful bearing', her creative conscience becomes 'a sense of honour', her whole personality is seen in terms of her future as 'mistress of Patterne'.

Clara as an *objet d'art* is one of the central images. She will ornament Sir Willoughby's house and his life. She will be static, at home; Sir Willoughby pictures her awaiting his return from masculine pursuits; it is the classic Victorian male image of the wife. Closely linked with this is the image of possession, of enslavement, which recurs varied and insistent throughout. Words such as 'authority' and 'subjugates' surround Sir Willoughby, for although he is negative in personality he is powerful in status. 'Was it possible he did not possess her entirely?' Sir Willoughby wonders as Clara is beginning to indicate her disquiet. There is a passage in which Meredith explicitly draws together the two images of ornament and ownership:

. . . the possession of land is not without obligation both to the soil and the tax-collector; the possession of fine clothing is oppressed by obligation; gold, jewelry, works of art, enviable household furniture, are positive fetters: the possession of a wife we find surcharged with obligation. In all these cases, possession is a gentle term for enslavement, bestowing the sort of felicity attained to by the helot drunk. You can have the joy, the pride, the intoxication of possession: you can have no free soul.

But there is one instance of possession, and that the most perfect, which leaves us free, under not a shadow of obligation, receiving ever, never giving, or if giving, giving only of our waste; as it were (sauf votre respect), by form of perspiration, radiation, if you like: unconscious poral bountifulness; and it is a beneficial process for the system. Our possession of an adoring female's worship, is this instance.
(Chapter 13)

The ownership of things constitutes enslavement to them. But the possession of a woman's adoration makes her less than a thing. The irony is that she has less life even than a porcelain vase—there is an actual vase in the book which is broken as the result of an accident, thus suggesting the shattering of Willoughby's image of Clara. For a woman to worship a man is a denial of being, or so Meredith persuades us in this particular class context, and Clara understands this. To be the recipient of Willoughby's 'poral bountifulness'—a memorable and genially ironic phrase, and delightfully apt—is just what she rejects.

A second group of images sharpens the focus. These are images of hunting, prey and sacrifice. Meredith describes Clara running like a hare pursued by hounds. She is also 'a victim decked for the sacrifice'. This particular phrase returns us to the ornament image for she goes on to describe herself as 'the garlanded heifer you see on Greek vases' (Chapter 16). Sir Willoughby is trying to insist that she wear the family jewels.

The tension surrounding Clara is heightened by the fact that she is the only character in the book who sees herself in this light. Although she turns to Crossjay and Vernon for support, and to a lesser extent to the engaging Colonel de Craye, who misjudges her motives, they do not understand the way she sees herself. Clara does think that Vernon perceives her dilemma—'A scrutiny so penetrating under its air of abstract thoughtfulness, though his eyes did but rest on her a second or two, signified that he read her line by line'—but he refrains from commitment. It is significant that finally, when it becomes clear that he and Clara will marry, an event which is not fully convincing or pleasing, it is Clara who chooses him.

Education, an important substitute for experience, is something Meredith is much concerned with. Clara has been brought up by an erudite father and is versed in the classics, but Dr Middleton is totally traditional, and although her education has helped her to understand him and other men, his own learning has not enabled him to understand her. The problem of education, Meredith suggests, is a problem of communication between generations. Crossjay can learn from Clara because there is something they share, a pleasure in open-air life. Vernon, Crossjay's tutor, shares this too. It is a theme that crops up again in *The Amazing Marriage* and *Lord Ormont*, and to a certain extent in *Diana of the Crossways*: shared experience of open-air activities aids communication.

The picture of Dr Middleton and Sir Willoughby discussing Clara over their third bottle of port is suggestive. This is the sphere of *their* communication. It is a totally male world in which the idea that women might appreciate the quality of the wine from the Patterne cellars is outrageous. Good wine is linked with a male dominated world, with an established generation and status, with the ownership of property built over 'cool vaulted cellars' (Chapter 20), containing wine laid down generations before. They discuss the mutability of women— 'The choicest of them will furnish us examples of a strange perversity,' says Dr Middleton. 'Choicest' sounds like wine, but wine is more reliable. When Sir Willoughby brings forth another bottle Dr Middleton says, 'I have but a girl to give' (Chapter 20). He fears Sir Willoughby might think it an unequal exchange, yet tries to enhance his daughter's worth. 'She goes to you from me, from me alone, from her father to her husband.'

We cannot for long escape the idea of possession. As Sir Willoughby's wine is his to use as he likes, so is Dr Middleton's daughter. Clara reacts against the idea that women must be 'cloistral'. This means more than the indication of a virgin bride, which is what Dr Middleton is talking about. Clara resents the fact that 'young women are trained to cowardice' when they are faced with problems they have no courage with which to handle them:

> For them to front an evil with plain speech is to be guilty of effrontery and forfeit the waxen polish of purity, and therewith their commanding places in the market. They are trained to please man's taste, for which purpose they soon learn to live out of themselves, and look on themselves as he looks, almost as little disturbed as he by the undiscovered. (Chapter 25)

'The undiscovered': this perhaps is the crux. Meredith's fiction is about women making discoveries hitherto beyond their reach. No writer in the nineteenth century anatomized the problem in such psychological depth. Clara gains stature as she sees her own particular problem as symptomatic of a much wider dilemma.

After Clara's attempted escape Sir Willoughby is mortified, and ruthlessly, yet sympathetically, exposed.

We now witness a kind of moral disintegration. He turns to Laetitia Dale, who was once devoted to him and whom he has always used to illuminate his own idea of himself. His egoism makes it very hard for him to believe in Clara's treason; at the same time he feels damaged. He needs to bask in what he assumes is Laetitia's continued worship, and proposes to her: she is colourless, he will be able to make his own imprint on her. She refuses him, and he cannot tolerate the thought that he has been totally defeated by women. He reveals the depth of his contempt:

> What are women? There is not a comparison in nature that does not tower above them! not one that does not hoot at them! I throughout my life guided by absolute deference to

their weakness—paying them politeness, courtesy. . . . Not merely born for the day, I maintain that they are spiritually ephemeral. (Chapter 40)

So we now see the courtesy and deference of the upper-class male to the upper-class female as, what perhaps we suspected all the time, unequivocally empty. Politeness to women means, simply, a calculated emphasis of their uselessness.

It is Laetitia in fact who puts most succinctly what Clara has for so long felt. She knows that Sir Willoughby will drink her dry. 'She scarcely felt that she was alive' (Chapter 48). Laetitia is the ultimate victim, the last ounce of her resistance used up by Sir Willoughby's prideful demands, and he makes no secret of the fact that he wants her because he cannot bear to face the world without a bride. But if Laetitia is the ultimate victim, Sir Willoughby himself is the most instructive one. 'This hateful world had caught him and transformed him to a machine. The discovery he made was, that in the gratification of the egoistic instinct we may so beset ourselves as to deal a slaughtering wound upon Self to whatsoever quarter we turn' (Chapter 47).

Clara escapes the final sacrifice; Laetitia does not. The book is structured as comedy, and reminds us, in its particular emphases, that Meredith used the word 'comedy' in a very specific way to suggest a strictly limited sphere of action, 'no dust of the struggling outer world' (Prelude)—in other words Meredith rejects naturalism—and the operation of an anarchic spirit within it. In his 'Essay on Comedy' he makes it quite clear that one of the most significant ways in which he saw the anarchic spirit in operation was in reversing the role of women. He writes:

The heroines of Comedy are like women of the world, not necessarily heartless from being clear-sighted: they seem so to the sentimentally-reared only for the reason that they use their wits, and are not wandering vessels crying for a captain or a pilot. Comedy is an exhibition of their battle with men, and that of men with them: and as the two, however divergent, both look on one object, namely, Life, the gradual similarity of their impressions must bring them to some resemblance. The comic poet dares to show us men and women coming to this mutual likeness; he is for saying that when they draw together in social life their minds grow liker; just as the philosopher discerns the similarity of boy and girl, until the girl is marched away to the nursery. Philosopher and comic poet are of a cousinship in the eye they cast on

life: and they are equally unpopular with our wilful English
of the hazy region and the ideal which is not to be disturbed.

This passage provides many clues to Meredith's work. It
emphasizes the crucial significance of Meredith's heroines, and
emphasizes similarly Meredith's uniqueness as a Victorian
novelist. Was there any other novelist in the century whose
most important theme concerned the 'mutual likeness' of men
and women? He saw himself, this passage suggests, as a fusion
of comic poet and philosopher. Critics have often been concerned with the process of this operation of Meredith's, but
not so much with its motives or results. Both seem to me
rather important. We can also see how certain subsidiary
themes that occur frequently in his novels are of great importance. His belief that boys and girls should be educated together is one.

Inevitably, within the confines of the society Meredith
chooses to write about, if women are to achieve male freedom
of action and decision, an insurrection will be required (it is
no coincidence that it involves that child-parent theme that we
see in *Richard Feverel*). Clara rebels against her father and
her intended husband and the assumptions of all around her.
Later, in *Diana of the Crossways*, his most popular novel in his
own lifetime, Meredith deals with a heroine who is free of a
restrictive context of family and society. *Diana of the Crossways* begins where *The Egoist* leaves off, yet Meredith demonstrates that the problems of both heroines are closely akin and
traceable to the same source.

Meredith's later novels from *The Egoist* onwards are about
non-marriages, that is, about marriages that do not take place,
or marriages that are formal contracts but not complete relationships. There is a sexual theme here, and although Meredith conforms outwardly to Victorian convention in this
respect he is much more suggestive and psychologically explicit than most Victorian writers. Sexual relations are closely
allied with property and possession. Clara cannot bear Sir
Willoughby to touch her; he deems a kiss a right of ownership.
When Carinthia gets over her longing for her neglectful husband she sees him in terms of his possession of thousands of
acres of land and numerous properties. She rejects the land,
the houses and sexual ownership. When in *Lord Ormont*
Aminta marries the elderly general she has admired from
childhood, it is clear that the marriage is a sexual failure. She
becomes not even a sexual object, merely a decorative thing.

* * *

GILLIAN BEER

The Two Masks and the Idea of Comedy†

On 1 February 1877 Meredith delivered a lecture which later became known as *An Essay on Comedy and the Uses of the Comic Spirit*. The essay was printed in the *New Quarterly Magazine* in April 1877, but first separately published in 1897, when it was reviewed by Bernard Shaw.[1] Although its general critical influence was delayed, its composition was artistically crucial for Meredith himself. Meredith's own avowed favourite among his novels, *Beauchamp's Career*, was written during the preceding years, and *The Egoist*, which immediately succeeds the *Essay*, is often taken to be his masterpiece.

Many of the effects in *The Egoist* can be traced directly to Meredith's theories on comedy, and its introductory chapter presents an epitome of the main ideas of the *Essay*. Meredith creates a rather laboured comic detachment by presenting the ideas in a burlesque of Carlyle's style and then explaining them to us in his own somewhat similar and equally idiosyncratic manner. In the *Essay* Meredith elaborated at length, and with examples drawn from many strands of European literature, the idea that true comedy was 'the fountain of sound sense' and that the comic spirit was directed against 'Unreason and Sentimentalism'. In *The Egoist* he warned those who would be free from the scrutiny of the comic spirit: 'Do not offend reason' (Prelude, p. 5). The imps of comedy malignly 'love to uncover ridiculousness in imposing figures' (Prelude, p. 6). Comedy is concerned to correct pretensions and exaggerations, not to laugh at genuine emotion, though 'A lover pretending too much by one foot's length of pretence, will have that foot caught in her trap' (Prelude, p. 5). Comedy must be distinguished from humour and from satire: it is more intellectual than humour, less derisive than satire. 'Incidents of a kind casting ridicule on our unfortunate nature instead of our conventional life, provoke derisive laughter, which thwarts the Comic idea. But derision is foiled by the play of the intellect' (*Essay*). It is 'the play of the intellect' which Meredith uses as his primary weapon of comedy in *The Egoist*.

Two minor works which he wrote while thinking out the *Essay* shed light on its implications for him as an artist. Mere-

† Chapter 4 in *Meredith: A Change of Masks* (London, 1970), pp. 114–139.   1. *Saturday Review*, 27 March, 1897.

dith had already begun to test his critical formulations
through the stresses of writing an original work. The unpub-
lished play 'The Satirist', is particularly relevant because it
was written during the time that Meredith was at work on the
Essay.[2] One of the *Essay*'s themes is Meredith's attempt to
differentiate comedy from both humour and satire:

> The Comic, which is the perceptive, is the governing spirit,
> awakening and giving aim to these powers of laughter, but
> it is not to be confounded with them: it enfolds a thinner
> form of them, differing from satire, in not sharply driving
> into the quivering sensibilities, and from humour, in not
> comforting them and tucking them up, or indicating a
> broader than the range of this bustling world to them.
> (*Essay*)

Whereas comedy appeals to reason and exhibits folly only in
order to cure it, satire appeals to more murderous instincts:
'The laughter of satire is a blow in the back or the face.'
Instead of the 'sunny malice' of the comic spirit, satire 'smells
of carrion'. Meredith describes Alceste in Molière's *Le Misanthrope* in this way:

> He is that melancholy person, the critic of everybody save
> himself; intensely sensitive to the faults of others, wounded
> by them; in love with his own indubitable honesty, and with
> his ideal of the simpler form of life befitting it: qualities
> which constitute the satirist. (*Essay*)

Raphael, the hero of 'The Satirist', strikingly resembles this
character sketch. The play explores in dramatic human terms
the central discussion of the *Essay*: What is the function of the
comic poet in society? The play is incomplete but coherent: it
consists of a hundred consecutive holograph pages forming
fourteen scenes of Act I of the drama: its theme seems fully
worked out. Perhaps Meredith abandoned it because he had
expressed the idea of the work in the extremely long first act.
The play's theme is the way in which the hero discovers his
responsibility for the consequences of his destructive attitude
towards society. Raphael, the Satirist, thinks himself superior
to the corrupt society in which he lives: in the course of the
play he is forced to see that he is himself a part of its corruption. Raphael is accused of killing a young nobleman, Octavius, in a duel—the evidence is that the assailant had
taunted Octavius with satirical verses written by Raphael.

2. Altschul Collection, Yale University
Library. See G. Beer, "George Meredith
and 'The Satirist,'" *Review of English
Studies*, n.s., XV (1964), 283–295.

Raphael denies all responsibility and refuses to flee: he is confronted by Amatista, Octavius's betrothed, with whom he has himself had an equivocal relationship (she in fact, during a period of estrangement, had persuaded him to write the verses against Octavius). At last, he discovers that the killer of Octavius was Manuel, his own disciple, and that Octavius believed that he was fighting Raphael. Abandoned by his employer, Don Beltran, Raphael cryptically obeys a summons to appear before the king. The manuscript ends with the exchange:

RAPHAEL: Ten minutes with the King!
MANUEL: You're lost.
RAPHAEL: Made! Made!
        There do I quit the ladder and plant foot
        Upon the highest stage, and there begins
                                        (End of manuscript)

We are left uncertain what 'begins'—is it material advantage, or the status of tragic hero? The second would be a more emotionally satisfying solution, but the unfulfilled dénouement makes it impossible fully to judge the play's meaning. Meredith's attitude to his villain-hero remains ambiguous. Pehaps it was this basic ambiguity of feeling which made it impossible for him to finish the play as a '5 Act comedy in verse': the comic spirit which could see Raphael's predicament as material for comedy would be savage indeed, and yet, in terms of Meredith's philosophy, Raphael's Timonesque bitterness cannot be shown as a heroic force. As it stands, the play shows how irresponsible any attempt to condemn the world must be if we remain disengaged from society. The theme is taken up in a different way in Willoughby's desire to banish the world.

Meredith is again exploring, in dramatic form, two of his most insistent themes: the need for a harmonious balance between instinct and reason; and, second, the ease with which we see through others while remaining blind about ourselves. The function of comedy, as he sees it, is to show us the true nature of our actions—particularly those acts of impulse and self-seeking which appear to us disguised as reason and 'good citizenship'. The issue of 'good citizenship' is fraught with artistic difficulties, and Meredith did not solve them all. The fruitful relationship of the comic poet to society is everywhere asserted in the *Essay*. He says there that it is necessary to believe that

> our state of society is founded in common-sense, otherwise you will not be struck by the contrasts the Comic Spirit perceives, or have it to look to for your consolation. You will, in

fact, be standing in that peculiar oblique beam of light, yourself illuminated to the general eye as the very object of chase and doomed quarry of the thing obscure to you. But to feel its presence and to see it is your assurance that many sane and solid minds are with you in what you are experiencing: and this of itself spares you the pain of satirical heat, and the bitter craving to strike heavy blows.

By setting 'The Satirist' in Spain, Meredith immediately complicated the issue: Raphael is plainly living in a society *not* founded on common sense and so is unable to find any 'sweet pleasant juice of contrast'. He feels himself isolated and develops 'the bitter craving to strike heavy blows'. He becomes a destructive anti-rational force and the result is lurid melodrama instead of the 'clear reason' of comedy. Apart from the first scene (which is in prose), the play is almost entirely un-comic. It shows the tragic result of misusing the weapons of comedy.

A major criticism which has been made of Meredith's theory of comedy is that he placed too much faith in the *status quo*; society is seen as the norm and any sharp deviation opens the culprit to chastisement by the comic spirit. This attitude is not always carried through in the novels, but it is certainly part of his thought in the *Essay*. The construction of 'The Satirist' places it closer to the *Essay* than to a novel like *The Tragic Comedians* where the hero is ruined by attempting to come to terms with bourgeois society. In 'The Satirist' Meredith sets the play in an environment where there are implied grounds for the wrath of the satirist, but he does not follow up this hint. He says in the *Essay*: 'The Satirist is moral agent, often a social scavenger, working on a storage of bile'—but Raphael is denied any adequate focus for his anger until he experiences injustice personally. Moreover, he is himself involved in the corruption of the time (for example, in his relations with Amatista). We never know what Raphael wrote in his satires or what are the particular abuses of the people against whom Raphael directs his spleen. The implication is that Raphael is actuated by petty motives—but this is never proved. By thus undermining the moral position of his satirist hero, Meredith avoids the question of the satirist's duty in a corrupt society.

While preparing the *Essay on Comedy* Meredith studied the works of Aristophanes and several pages of his working manuscript notes, apparently written about that time, are preserved in the Altschul collection.[3] In Aristophanes he was

---

3. Aristophanes Portfolio. All the quotations are from the first page of notes on Aristophanes.

confronted with 'a lusty and strong-smelling wit', but he says of him: 'He was not only a satirist: he was a critic of politicians, poets, philosophers.' The rather curious antithesis in this sentence is to some extent explained by his marginal comparison with 'Our English Foote' who 'was a meaner kind of Aristophanes, and with some garlic in him, but none of the sacred fire, and no sense of public interests'. The sacred fire and the sense of public interests are also lacking in Raphael. I think it more likely that Meredith's hostility to satire in the *Essay* derives to some extent from his feelings towards his own creation, Raphael, than that Raphael is purely a dramatic projection of Meredith's views on satire. With a writer like Meredith, whose characters existed to him as living beings, the passage of ideas is two-way; the comedy may 'be in the idea' but the characters who figure forth the idea become human beings to whom the author then reacts emotionally—as he reacts to Sir Willoughby. Raphael is satisfactory only as an individual representing one kind of satirical impulse. He is not an adequate criticism of the function of satire itself.

As so often in Meredith's work, one feels the urgency of a personal argument in the way he explores the implications of satire both in the *Essay* and the play. His own position had some affinities with that of Raphael: like him he had felt the pain of isolation which brings with it the 'craving to strike heavy blows'; he had himself been accused of cynicism, and there is a considerable element of cruelty in his comedies, particularly those of the late eighteen-seventies such as 'General Ople and Lady Camper' and *The Egoist.* Yet he admired Molière's wit most because 'it is full of healing'. In a letter later in his life to an American admirer (15 November 1886) he defended himself against the charge of cynicism: 'There has been a confounding of the tone of irony (or satire in despair) with cynicism. I must have overcharged the dose to produce such an impression' (*Letters*, ii, 387). 'Satire in despair' well describes Raphael's speech of self-discovery. In Raphael Meredith embodied his own temptations towards the contempt of society which he rebukes in the *Essay* and for which he reproves himself some ten years later in a letter to George Stevenson (15 January 1888): 'Without placing myself high—or anywhere—I am, I moan to think, disdainful of an English public, and am beset with devils of satire when I look on it. That is not a good state for composition' (*Letters*, II, 406). This determination to reject Raphael's intellectual position while feeling an unwilling emotional sympathy with him enriches the ambiguity of characterisation in the play; but it may also account for its unfinished state.

The short story 'The Case of General Ople and Lady Camper' is the most doctrinaire 'comedy' among his works, and it is correspondingly less successful as fiction. The story describes the persecution of General Ople by his eccentric neighbour, Lady Camper. General Ople is a retired officer well pleased with life, 'in good humour with himself', and given to genteel phrases. Blinded by his own wishes, he believes that Lady Camper, socially his superior, is favourably inclined to receiving a marriage proposal from him. In fact she is concerned only to prevent the intimacy between his daughter and her nephew which General Ople has failed to notice. Lady Camper goes abroad and sends a fleet of cartoons to the General, each showing him in a ridiculous situation and emphasising his self-importance. The twist which makes the story more than a malicious retailing of a practical joke is that General Ople is obscurely flattered as well as hurt by her attentions and cannot resist showing the cartoons around the neighbourhood, rousing ridicule and pity among his acquaintances. Lady Camper's function is corrective. When she has finally reduced his self-esteem and persuaded him to think of his daughter Elizabeth before himself, she marries him. Such is her acuteness that: 'The senses of General Ople were struck by the aspect of a lurid Goddess, who penetrated him, read him through, and had both power and will to expose and make him ridiculous for ever'.[4] Lady Camper clearly has the functions of the Comic Spirit, and she claims that she exaggerates only in order to bring home the truth: 'Could any caricature of mine exceed in grotesqueness your sketch of yourself? You are a brave and a generous man all the same: and I suspect it is more hoodwinking than egotism—or extreme egotism—that blinds you'.[5] This speech gives us the clue to what is wrong with the story. Throughout we see things from the general's point of view. Lady Camper remains remote, her motives obscure, whereas we are made to feel that he is indeed a 'brave and generous man' driven to the verge of insanity by an apparently pointless persecution. The punishment he undergoes is ludicrously out of proportion to the crime, and though this may be true to tragedy, to life, and to the comedy of buffoonery, it runs counter to the 'comic spirit' because it arouses an atmosphere of hysteria, not of reason-

4. Memorial Edition, Vol. XXI, Chap.   5. *Ibid.*, Chap. viii, p. 183.
vi, p. 163.

ableness. It is true that in the *Essay* Meredith wrote that 'keen-edged intelligence is by nature merciless' and that some of the highest comedy 'refines even to pain'. Nevertheless by giving one of his characters the impregnable position and power of the comic spirit, he alienates our sympathies from her. There is too much unacknowledged and unsatirised self-esteem in Lady Camper for us to enjoy her triumph.

In this story Meredith faces the problem, even more acute in *The Egoist*, inherent in his metaphor for the Idea of comedy.

> For Folly is the natural prey of the Comic, known to it in all her transformations, in every disguise; and it is with the springing delight of hawk over heron, hound after fox, that it gives her chase, never fretting, never tiring, sure of having her, allowing her no rest.

The reader is predisposed to feel sympathy for the hunted rather than the hunter, and although this can serve a satiric purpose by making the reader undergo the character's punishment, he must be convinced that the punishment is just.

These two works test certain of the *Essay*'s assertions in action, but they are limited in scope and achievement—curiously less humane than the *Essay* itself. Though this is presented as an attempt to *define* comedy, the method used is poetic: it works through metaphor and paradox, illuminating the comic spirit by its closeness to it, rather than by building a close-structured argument. It is a *representation* of the spirit of comedy.

Meredith's description of the comic spirit sheds light on his attitude as narrator in *The Egoist*, his 'comedy in narrative' as he sub-titled it. *The Egoist* was his first full-length novel after writing the *Essay*. He had begun it by June 1877, and finished it by the middle of February 1879, at a heavy cost to his health. 'The Satirist' was written from about August 1876 to some time after April 1877. 'The House on the Beach' which he had begun fifteen years earlier was recast and appeared in the *New Quarterly* in January 1877. 'The Case of General Ople and Lady Camper', printed in the *New Quarterly*, July 1877, was probably written during the April in which the *Essay* was published. During the two months after finishing *The Egoist* Meredith wrote a draft of the first quarter of *The Amazing Marriage* which he was not to finish until 1894. All these works represent in some degree his changing attitude to comedy.

In *The Egoist* he examines many of the epitomised observa-

tions of the *Essay* against the shifting world of human personalities and relationships. The book is his only attempt to
write a sustained 'comedy' invoking the conventions of the
stage, and particularly of Molière's comedies, the source of
whose wit, Meredith says, is pure reason. 'He strips Folly to
the skin, displays the imposture of the creature, and is content
to offer her better clothing'; that is, as he says in *The Egoist*,
'In Comedy is the singular scene of charity issuing of disdain
under the stroke of honourable laughter'.

The comedy he most often cites in the *Essay* is *Le Misanthrope*, and this has some obvious plot connections with
The Egoist: it is about an unfulfilled engagement, and one in
which the hero, although a good man, makes demands upon
the heroine which it is impossible for her to fulfil without
running counter to her nature. Just as the first cause of the
dissension between Sir Willoughby and Clara is his wish to
banish the world, so that between Alceste and Célimène is his
wish to retire into a deserted countryside far from the corrup-
tions of the court. Just as Sir Willoughby offers his hand to
Laetitia, so Alceste attempts at one point to revenge himself
on Célimène by proposing marriage to her cousin, who is
devoted to him. Here however the resemblance ends. Alceste
is shown as truly (and unreasonably) in love with Célimène,
whereas we see nothing of the relationship of the lovers in *The
Egoist* until Clara's withdrawal has begun. The suggestion is
that there has never been any relationship. The attitude of the
two writers to their characters has less in common than might
at first appear: Molière is the more truly reasonable because
more truly charitable. Alceste is endearing as well as infuriating, whereas there is a coldness in Sir Willoughby and in
Meredith's treatment of him which creates an effect of cruelty.
Meredith gives himself the position of comic spirit—detached,
disengaged; but he uses it in a way that sometimes seems self-
flagellatory and reminds us that Sir Willoughby represents
much that Meredith wants to drive out of himself as well as
others.

The effect of near-hysteria in parts of *The Egoist* does not,
of course, derive always from autobiographical pressures; it is
also a dramatisation of Clara's state of mind. Meredith's apparent detachment from the characters in *The Egoist* (he is
even at a distance from the comic imps) helps him to keep the
control which he admired in Molière, but the violent image he
uses to describe Molière's achievement suggests the enormous
self-discipline needed to retain his impartiality: 'Never did
man wield so shrieking a scourge upon vice, but his consum-

mate self-mastery is not shaken while administering it'. Molière's comedies support Meredith in his attempt to reach ideal comic detachment: 'the laughter of reason refreshed' (*Egoist*, Prelude).

Robert Louis Stevenson reports that when a young friend complained that Meredith had based Sir Willoughby on him, Meredith replied, 'No, my dear fellow, he is all of us'.[6] But Meredith's other comments on the book suggest that he felt that Sir Willoughby did not represent the whole of us. He wrote to Stevenson on 16 April 1879: 'It is a comedy with only half of me in it' (*Letters*, I, 297), and to Foote he wrote: 'It comes mainly from the head and has nothing to kindle imagination' (*Letters*, I, 300). Allowing for Meredith's usual dissatisfaction with recently finished work, these comments show how oppressed he was by the narrow intensity of the book's form. Its power derives from a sense of barely, exquisitely, contained emotion.

The Egoist becomes an exploration of the boundaries beyond which comedy cannot venture. 'Life, we know too well, is not a Comedy, but something strangely mixed', he wrote in the *Essay*; *The Egoist* ranges beyond what Meredith had earlier declared to be the province of comedy: social follies rather than man's inescapable nature. 'Do not offend reason', enjoin Essay and Prelude—but as soon as Meredith is dealing with human figures he shows a heightened consciousness of how narrow is reason's power in human conduct: and he sees further that since the flouting of reason is the root of comedy, comedy may have a tragic issue in the lives of human beings. When the control of reason is removed, the result may be the ludicrous spectacle of Tinman in 'The House on the Beach' adorning himself in his court suit for his private admiration, or it may equally be the hideous frenzy of Alvan in *The Tragic Comedians* struggling against ever-increasing odds to regain his loved Clotilde. The entirely reasonable man is quite as likely to be a cold self-seeker, like Cecil Baskelett in *Beauchamp's Career* who can only see *through* men, as he is to be a self-abnegating rational lover, like Vernon Whitford in *The Egoist*. Although tragedy is not in question, the special emotional edge of *The Egoist* comes from a sense of poignancy held at bay.

The narrative language represents the characters' active inner life and sets it off against their elaborately controlled dialogue exchanges.

6. "Books Which Have Influenced Me," in *Essays in the Art of Writing* (London, 1905).

An example to which *The Westminster Review* took exception in its notice of *The Egoist* is the passage in which Laetitia Dale has her first unwilling doubts about Sir Willoughby's perfection. Having engaged her affections without declaring his, he has abruptly left for a three year trip abroad. On his return he greets her enthusiastically but withdraws again and some time later Laetitia is told by young Crossjay that he has seen Willoughby riding with a young lady fifteen miles away.

> Still . . . the tale seemed fictitious to Laetitia until Crossjay related how that he had stood to salute on the road to the railway, and taken off his cap to Sir Willoughby, and Sir Willoughby had passed him, not noticing him, though the young lady did, and looked back and nodded. The hue of truth was in that picture.
>
> Strange eclipse, when the hue of truth comes shadowing over our bright ideal planet. It will not seem the planet's fault, but truth's. Reality is the offender; delusion our treasure that we are robbed of. Then begins with us the term of wilful delusion, and its necessary accompaniment of the disgust of reality; exhausting the heart much more than patient endurance of starvation.[7]

The Westminster Review says that the last paragraph quoted is 'wrapping up such a simple, we might almost say commonplace, proposition in such mysterious terms' and dismisses Meredith as 'over-fastidious, or what the world would vulgarly call too clever'.[8] The general truth conveyed *may* be commonplace (that we prefer to be deluded rather than face unpleasant truth) : but through the image of the eclipse 'shadowing over our bright ideal planet' Meredith also renders the intensity of this ordinary truth when it is actually experienced.[9] The darkening of the sky, the chilling greyness of familiar objects, the forebodings associated with eclipse: these are suggested in order to convey Laetitia's feelings at that moment. Sir Willoughby is her planet, and the silent overcasting is also the emotional process within Laetitia which goes unrecognised in speech and finds an issue into consciousness only much later in the novel. The half-submerged violence of the image of appetite and starvation is the end of a sequence suggesting the voracious emotion which Laetitia always suppresses in her active life. When Sir Willoughby seems to be returning to her,

7. *Egoist*, chapter 4.
8. *Westminster Review*, n.s., VIII (1880), 287.

9. Willoughby imagines himself as the Sun King: cf. chapters 14, 37.

The starveling of patience awoke to the idea of a feast. The sense of hunger came with it, and hope came, and patience fled.

He leaves her again:

Patience travelled back to her sullenly. As we must have some kind of food, and she had nothing else, she took to that and found it dryer than of yore. It is a composing but a lean dietary. The dead are patient, and we get a certain likeness to them in feeding on it unintermittingly overlong.[1]

The grandiloquence of the comparison with the dead allows Laetitia's despair its full stature. Through metaphor we are made inward with her. Instead of hearing a well worn story about a stock figure—the blue-stocking, slightly faded, devoted spinster—we enter into the quality of her experience. This has other effects in the book: we are made to see the crassness of Sir Willoughby's conventional view of her and are further alienated from him. By devoting a chapter to Laetitia's inner life so early in the book, Meredith awakens our sympathetic understanding of her so that he is able to assume her life for much of the rest of the time. The structural tour-de-force praised by E. M. Forster in *Aspects of the Novel* draws heavily on this early vein of imagery.[2] When Laetitia at last declares her changed feelings for Willoughby we can greet the stroke not with incredulity but with delighted recognition.

Meredith says in the *Essay* that comedy does not deal with 'periods of fervour' but in the novel both Clara and Willoughby are in a state of ferment, swelling beneath the glossy surface of polite interchange in which a raised eyebrow is the only possible representation of rage. The basis of the novel is the struggle between the instinctual demands of a man or woman's nature and the social forms they adopt by demand or as disguise. The struggle is not judged easily: Meredith believes in civilisation and evolution. What he shows is that a man like Willoughby may use the forms of civilisation to disguise from himself an uncontained and animal voraciousness, and that the same civilised forms may prevent a woman like Clara from responding in her own full identity because they present her with a model of what a lady should feel and be—a model which is static and anti-evolutionary.

The clash takes its crucial form in the disparity between the pre-ordained conventional patterns of fiction and actual existential feeling. Sir Willoughby Patterne is a 'model' gentleman

1. *Egoist*, chapter 4.
2. *Aspects of the Novel* (London, 1927), pp. 87–88.

('He has a leg', as Mrs Mountstuart cryptically observes). He is the ideal hero of popular Victorian fiction—handsome, intelligent, wealthy, generous, and admired by all about him. Clara, the girl to whom he is engaged, seems to have all the qualities of a typical novel heroine: she is pretty, absolutely 'pure' and inexperienced sexually, with means of her own and the only daughter of an elderly scholar-gentleman. Everyone is preparing for a conventional courtship and wedding. But this is an anti-conventional novel which takes the easy expectations of society and the plot judgments of fiction and turns them askew. Thus, Clara who has been swept off her feet by Willoughby's romantic whirlwind courtship begins to realise that whirlwind courtships may be a form of aggression and a prelude to annihilation. She comes to understand (all unwillingly) that Sir Willoughby's ideal of marriage is not partnership but absorption. The narrator interprets Willoughby's view of it thus:

> She would not burn the world for him; she would not, though a purer poetry is little imaginable, reduce herself to ashes, or incense, or essence, in honour of him, and so, by love's transmutation, literally be the man she was to marry. She preferred to be herself, with the egoism of women! She said it: she said: 'I must be myself to be of any value to you, Willoughby.'[3]

He uses everyone to act as a flattering mirror for himself and is incapable of dialogue:

> 'So entirely one, that there never can be question of external influences. I am, we will say, riding home from the hunt: I see you awaiting me: I read your heart as though you were beside me. And I know that I am coming to the one who reads mine! You have me, you have me like an open book, you, and only you!'
> 'I am to be always at home?' Clara said, unheeded, and relieved by his not hearing.[4]

Meeting his faithful first love, Laetitia, after a journey abroad of three years, this is how he greets her:

> 'Laetitia Dale!' he said. He panted. 'Your name is sweet English music! And you are well?' The anxious question permitted him to read deeply in her eyes. He found the man he sought there, squeezed him passionately, and let her go . . .[5]

Clara's growing dislike of Willoughby's possessiveness de-

3. *Egoist*, chapter 6.
4. *Egoist*, chapter 7.
5. *Egoist*, chapter 4.

velops into a sullen physical antagonism. She cannot bear him to kiss her.

> The gulf of a caress hove in view like an enormous billow hollowing under the curled ridge.
> She stooped to a buttercup; the monster swept by.[6]

These passages show the range of strategies by which the reader is led to judge Sir Willoughby; the representation of his consciousness in which his thoughts and the narrator's overlap; direct speech; motives imputed to him by an epitomising commentator; mock-heroic aggrandising metaphor. Willoughby is indeed pursued.

Meredith does not entirely avoid rousing our sympathy for Sir Willoughby by the end of the book. As he says in the Prelude: 'The Egoist surely inspires pity. He who would desire to clothe himself at everybody's expense, and is of that desire condemned to strip himself stark naked, he, if pathos ever had a form, might be taken for the actual person.' What makes us stand apart from Sir Willoughby, even while feeling the ironic truth of this passage, is that the last thing he himself wants is to rouse pity. Most of his activity in the second half of the book is part of the effort to save face, to allow the world no opportunity to pity him. Meredith denies him tragic stature by allowing him to be successul in his efforts. The book ends with him handing Clara over to the cousin whom he still sees as inferior to himself, discomfiting his friend De Craye who has tried to get Clara, and presenting Laetitia to a not entirely sceptical world as his inescapable destiny. He remains much the same man at the end as he was at the beginning. The Comedy has corrected but not reclaimed him. Although the function of comedy is 'to teach the world what ails it', it never really teaches Sir Willoughby.

If the reader's role is to be primarily that of judge, it is necessary that our detachment should be sustained. Meredith's usual method of rousing and flouting our expectations has to be modified. Elsewhere he emphasises the devious flow of life, the often undynamic nature of significant emotion, the pressure of free will on circumstances and of circumstances on individuality, and in his later works he begins to abandon belief in congruity of character. In some of his novels where he claims to be writing internal history, such as *Sandra Belloni*, recognisable plot patterns are more or less obliterated, while in others he uses patterns the reader will recognise but

6. *Egoist*, chapter 13.

which give only a deliberately limited insight into the conduct of the action. Only in *The Egoist* does he use reassuring analogues within the work whose promise is fulfilled: our concern for Clara is tempered because we have been told at the outset that the book is 'a comedy in narrative': because Sir Willoughby's previous, ironically-named fiancée, Constantia, escaped, and because we know that he is selfish before Clara does.

The book begins with the episode of the valiant but unromantically plebeian and middle-aged sailor Patterne to whom Willoughby is 'not at home'—because he does not fit the dashing version of him that Willoughby has been purveying to the county. This man is the father of young Crossjay who acts in the novel as the touchstone of character other than the test of love. Love is not the only, though the most fiery, test men meet: social relationships test too. By using a prepubertal child to test the behaviour of his characters, Meredith can subject them to different demands.

Besides the analogues within the novel, Meredith suggests several other parallels to give the reader a sense of control and detachment and to avoid an avid emotional involvement in the characters' experience. The areas of disturbance are clearly defined: the shocks the reader undergoes, such as Laetitia's change of mind, are in part foreseen. There is the satisfying congruity of promise and performance, a stability larger than the individual surprises, which is common to classical comic novels. Fielding's comic masterpieces *Joseph Andrews* and *Tom Jones* have this kind of dependable harmony.

One foresight into the plot is on the whole lost to modern readers: the clue given us in Sir Willoughby Patterne's name. R. D. Mayo pointed out in his article '*The Egoist* and the Willow Pattern' that not only is there the element of Pattern (a model of manhood); there is also a reference to the Willow Pattern story.[7] This story, constructed from the figures on the popular blue willow pattern plate, runs thus: a widower mandarin intends to marry his daughter to a wealthy suitor but the maiden chooses a poor but honourable man serving as her father's secretary. She and the secretary escape, hotly pursued by father and betrothed and are turned into birds for their fidelity. The story had been used as the basis of a successful pantomime in 1875 by Francis Burnand, editor of *Punch* and a close friend of Meredith. In the novel Clara's father, the mandarin-scholar, Dr Middleton, is determined that she shall marry Willoughby, while during the course of the book we see

7. See above, pp. 453–60. [*Editor.*]

her gradually awakening feeling for Vernon Whitford, Willoughby's scholar-secretary.

The parallels are clear though not insistent. The willow-pattern analogue gives a meaningful edge to the persistent references to porcelain throughout the story. Mrs. Mountstuart perturbs Willoughby by harping on her definition of Clara as 'a dainty rogue in porcelain' and (gnomic as ever) refusing to explain herself. Austin Dobson's 'Proverbs in Porcelain', French-style amorous dialogues, appeared in 1877, two years before *The Egoist*, and these, I think, may be another pointer to Willoughby's unease. Colonel De Craye, Sir Willoughby's friend who hopes to win Clara from him, brings a wedding present of a porcelain vase which is immediately smashed in an accident on the way from the station—and here Meredith may be invoking echoes from Restoration and Augustan comedy: the famous double-entendre scene of 'viewing the china' in Wycherley's *The Country Wife*, Pope's image in *The Rape of the Lock*:

> Whether the nymph shall break Diana's law,
> Or some frail china-jar receive a flaw.[8]

Toward the end of the book Clara's unwillingness to accept a china dinner-service reveals to the county gossips her unwillingness to go through with the marriage. The willow-pattern story and the images from porcelain work together with exacerbating significance: they are an additional emotional restraint on us as readers because they give us controlling knowledge, but the nagging repetition of the porcelain imagery grates after a time in a way which makes us share something of Sir Willoughby's exasperation.

For although our sympathy is in the main invited for Clara, Meredith is too subtle an observer to refuse a measure of fellow-feeling to Willoughby or to suggest that he has a monopoly of egoism. 'The love-season is the carnival of egoism, and brings the touchstone to our natures'.[9] Meredith is showing the workings of egoism in *all* his characters and particularly in Clara, and in this way he suggests that egoism is common to us all. Nor does he suggest that egotism is *necessarily* destructive. In the youthful Crossjaye, egotism is part of a sturdy, growing identity and the other characters are judged by their response to his demands. Vernon wants to send him

---

8. Breaking china is associated metaphorically with breaking chastity in William Wycherley's bawdy Restoration farce when Horner acts out Lady Fidget's seduction in terms of this metaphor (Act IV). Diana's law: the law of chastity. [*Editor.*]
9. *Egoist*, chapter 11.

to train in London at his own expense because it is best for the boy; Laetitia behaves like an anxious, upright mother towards him; Willoughby spoils him but is ready to abandon him if he goes against his wishes (as he has done the wretched Flitch and will do Vernon if he leaves); Clara delights him and uses him in her escape. She forgets him (having bound him to wait for her by a childish obsessional promise) and she plays on his awakening sexuality.

Laetitia's declaration at the end of the book, 'I am an Egoist', is a declaration of growth as well as of hardening. Her timid self-abnegation has given way to independence. Clara's egotism is inextricable from her discovery of her self, which includes her sexual self—and *The Egoist* is exceptional among Victorian novels in the closeness and intensity with which it suggests sexual revulsion (just as *The Tragic Comedians* is exceptional in the ferocity with which it depicts sexual obsession). Clara realises 'the tragedy of the embrace' which will come to her if she dutifully fulfills her engagement and 'the clash of a sharp physical thought: "The difference! the difference!" told her she was woman and never could submit'.[1] In this struggle 'physical pride' and 'incandescent reason' unite to affirm her distinctness—while at the same time they lead her to understand how essential love is to her.

> With her body straining in her dragon's grasp, with the savour of loathing, unable to contend, unable to speak aloud, she began to speak to herself, and all the health of her nature made her outcry womanly:—'If I were loved!'—not for the sake of love, but for free breathing; and her utterance of it was to ensure life and enduringness to the wish, as the yearning of a mother on a drowning ship is to get her infant to shore.[2]

To Willoughby the essentially feminine is 'a parasite—a chalice': Clara's twistings, false starts, half lies have, in contrast, the hectic serpentine movement of the hunted. She is saved from Willoughby's portentous self-absorption not only by her capacity to love but by her humour. Meredith's language to describe her is similar to his description of the comic spirit: 'her equable shut mouth threw its long curve to guard the small round chin from that effect; her eyes wavered only in humour'.[3] But her close resemblance to the spirit of the work ('that slim feasting smile, shaped like the long-bow') does not protect her from the consequences of her human complexity.

1. *Egoist*, chapter 21.
2. *Egoist*, chapter 10.
3. *Egoist*, chapter 5.

The book is an intricate account of the duel between Willoughby and Clara: neither of them is a particularly scrupulous fighter. Both are fighting defensively to preserve the same thing: their identity. Willoughby *cannot* release Clara from her engagement because his love for her is intimately entangled with his assurance of his own worth—if she goes he will no longer be Sir Willoughby Patterne, cynosure of the county, but a twice-jilted man. Clara *cannot* marry Willoughby to be absorbed by his voracious love. Although the original cause of his dispute with Clara is his vaunted wish to 'banish the world' and live in total absorbed intimacy with her, he is really entirely dependent on the world's estimate of him. He exists to himself only through the mirror image it reflects of him, and his relationship with Clara was to have been a rosy and enlarging mirror—extending his image beyond death.

Clara 'was the first who taught him what it was to have sensations of his mortality'.[4] The concerns of the book are lofty and the suffering of the characters is allowed its full stature and inwardness. We *realise* the experience of Willoughby's self-pity through the imagery:

> This was the ground of his hatred of the world: it was an appalling fear on behalf of his naked eidolon, the tender infant Self swaddled in his name before the world, for which he felt as the most highly civilised of men alone can feel, and which it was impossible for him to stretch out hands to protect. There the poor little loveable creature ran for any mouth to blow on; and frost-nipped and bruised, it cried to him, and he was of no avail![5]

(This is strikingly close to the imagery used by Clara, in the passage quoted above.) The mingling of parental tenderness and infantilism measures both the intensity and the inadequacy of Willoughby's capacity to love. The ultimate thinness and repetitiveness of his characterisation is seen to represent the actual thinness and repetitiveness of egotism.[6]

The book is long (about 600 pages): it may seem an excessive length for the breaking of an engagement—even so solemn a betrothal as Willoughby has enforced. Until two-thirds of the way through there is little physical action. This is partly because Willoughby owns everything within sight except the railway; Clara's flight to the railway station is in itself an assertion of freedom. Her vision of the Alps is the only

4. *Egoist*, chapter 23.
5. *Egoist*, chapter 29.
6. Dorothy Van Ghent in *The English*

Novel: Form and Function (New York, 1961) complains of this effect.

glimpse of a free world beyond the confines of the book. In contrast to the lush, privately-owned landscape of the home-counties is set the crystalline freedom of the mountains. The length of the book corresponds to the density of the emotional life described: it is swift, not leisurely, but 'The slave of a passion thinks in a ring, as hares run: he will cease where he began'.[7] The claustrophobia of the relationship between Willoughby and Clara, which is the cause of its dissolution, also makes it almost impossible to dissolve.

In order to underline the claustrophobic effect Meredith follows a form of three unities: the action is continuous, in one place, and never moves out of its narrow range of emotions, chief among which is frustration (Laetitia, Vernon, Clara and Willoughby are all frustrated). He adds the further, fictive, unity that the book is seen largely from a single point of view, that of Clara. He does, however, allow us to know Sir Willoughby's thoughts: he transcribes them apparently quite straightforwardly and often without commentary. But the mind of the reader scrutinises them. In this way he allows us to make the same discoveries about Sir Willoughby as Clara does, by a means additional to, and to some extent independent of, hers. At times it seems scarcely believable that Sir Willoughby should fail to recognise his motives for what they are, so clearly does he state grossly selfish ideas to himself; but it is precisely the failure to take that final step to self-consciousness which involves self-criticism which makes Sir Willoughby what he is. By making us share Sir Willoughby's stream-of-consciousness, Meredith further suggests that we all think, quite lucidly, many more thoughts than we dare scrutinise.

His observation of the two principal characters is scrupulously exact. For example the deliberately uncharming account of the way Clara desperately annexes confidants: first Laetitia, then Vernon, then Mrs Mountstuart (it is important for our estimate of her that she only *seems* to have confided in Horace de Craye). This series of incidents is both a comic exaggeration of the conventional role of the confidante (a role found in French neo-classical *tragedy*) and a representation of the hysterical urge to be understood and justified which is common to most of us in emotional crises. This realism and inwardness (which reaffirms the emotional meaning of literary conventions) is seen also in the picture of Laetitia. It combines uneasily with the extremely formal dramatic structure of

7. *Egoist*, chapter 23.

the last part of the book, in which all the devices of high comedy are deployed: the hidden listener, Crossjay, who unintentionally hears Sir Willoughby's midnight proposal to Laetitia; the chapter headings from stage directions; the comic chorus of county ladies; the crowding of all the characters onto the stage for the scintillating untying of knots.

The delight of the book's conclusion (as well as its drop in intensity) comes because the solutions imposed derive from a more familiar literary world. Willoughby has been made to look ridiculous (to the reader, but not entirely to the other characters). His victories may be hollow, but they clothe his nakedness—and for him this preserves his identity, which is vested in appearances. (His favourite image of himself is as *le roi soleil*.) [8] Clara has won her battle—but at the end of the book is a little withdrawn, so that she seems again just an ordinary young woman.

The sense of comic release at the end of the novel is in part a sense of release from the stringency of Meredith's comic vision. He said himself that the book contained 'only half myself'; the tart rationality of the scrutinising Comic Spirit cannot fully contain the emotional force of the characters. The comic imps are not our representatives. They come from a different world. They inhibit our involvement with the characters, but we are not like them. It is a situation akin to the fourth book of *Gulliver's Travels*: we cannot comfortably identify ourselves with either group. Comic imps and Houhyhynyms, however admirable, are ineffacably different from us. At times the primness of the narrative insistence on folly seems limited in the face of the characters' suffering, whether or not the suffering is self-imposed. We are not kept at the 'point fixe'[9] of comedy: we move into the characters, then very far away, to where they seem like comic china ornaments caught in grotesque attitudes. The emotional energy of the book is such that at times the rigid comic form is almost shattered.

In his next novel, *The Tragic Comedians*, Meredith treats a similar story: an engagement broken by the woman and the man's frantic attempts to restore the relationship. This time his sources were in life not art and he was attempting to draw forth some meaningful pattern from an apparently arbitrary waste. Instead of suppressing the relationships as in *The Egoist*, in *The Tragic Comedians* he shows us the genuine and growing richness of love between a man and a woman (in

8. The Sun King, Louis XIV. [*Editor.*]
9. Literally, fixed point; in a comedy, the point on which the action turns. [*Editor.*]

history Ferdinand Lassalle and Helene von Dönniges) and the destruction of this love relationship through the pressures of society and through the weaknesses of the lovers themselves.

Meredith's sources were Helene von Racowitza's *Meine Beziehungen zu Ferdinand Lassalle*[1] and J. M. Ludlow's article 'Ferdinand Lassalle, the German Social Democrat' in the *Fortnightly Review*.[2] His relation to his story is more complicated in *The Tragic Comedians* than in *The Egoist*. The facts are historical, and he is determined to present them as he knows them, without any fictional manipulation. But his interpretation of the facts differs from that of Frau von Racowitza so radically that his view of the events becomes a judgment on hers. He is involved in a dispute with the heroine. Equally, however, his view of Alvan (Lassalle), the hero, differs from that of J. M. Ludlow. Ludlow adopted a superficially Meredithian attitude of sound common sense towards Lassalle's pretensions, but Meredith sees that this is an inadequate response to Alvan's genuine if flawed nobility. Life and non-fictional literary sources become involved in a complicated interplay. Meredith undergoes a process of disillusionment with Clotilde, who was a real living woman, not merely a character of his imagination. The tragic strain is far more potent because the events really happened. Instead of creating an artefact designed specifically to figure forth the artist's ideas, Meredith is attempting to draw some instructive pattern out of a seemingly meaningless waste of talent and life. It must be remembered that Ferdinand Lassalle, the original of Alvan, was a politician of real importance, as influential in the Labour movement of his time as Marx himself. Meredith therefore has a situation artistically akin to Greek tragedy, in which the story is already known to the audience, who are assumed to have preconceptions about it. He wants to undermine the obvious meanings which others have assigned to the story.

He will accept it neither as a romantic Romeo-and-Juliet tragedy nor as a picture of vice leading to its own undoing. He

1. *My Recollections of Ferdinand Lassalle* (Breslau, 1879). [*Editor*.]
2. *Fortnightly Review*, n.s. V (1869) 419–453. For a more detailed discussion of Meredith's handling of his sources, see G. Beer, "Meredith's Revisions of *The Tragic Comedians*," *Review of English Studies*, n. s. XIV (1963), 33–53. [Basic background information is that Lassalle (1825–1864) was a fiery German-Jewish socialist who died in a duel as a result of his infatuation with Helene von Dönniges. Meredith was naturally intrigued by this anachronistic, anomalous romantic.—*Editor*.]

shows with considerable irony how both Alvan and Clotilde refuse to recognise the weaknesses of their own natures: her craving to be dominated, which leads her to worship power instead of an individual, and his yearning for respectability and denial of his own capacity for violence. Alvan, Meredith insists, is not a self-inflated figure like Sir Willoughby. He is 'hugely man', and if he had also accepted his own animality he would not have been a prey for the comic spirit. Clotilde bears the brunt of Meredith's pursuit of Folly, but there is no simple division between hero and heroine. The heroine behaves in a conventionally laudable fashion in submitting to the wishes of her family, but she forms an unfavourable contrast with Clara in *The Egoist*, who pursues her will to escape with more energy than Clotilde can muster for her will to love.

True reason, it seems, cannot necessarily be equated with the conventional attitudes of society, although Meredith had written in the *Essay* that it was the first condition of sanity to believe that our civilisation is founded on common sense. In the *Essay* Meredith says of women that: 'Comedy is an exhibition of their battle with men, and that of men with them'. This battle is the root of both the novels, but in the comic *Egoist* Clara is victorious and keeps her integrity, whereas in *The Tragic Comedians* Clotilde's vacillation results in her self-destruction. By the end of the book she is incapable of feeling. In *The Tragic Comedians* the man is the centre of sympathy and by allowing us to sympathise primarily with the character who is striving for a fulfillment of love instead of with a character who is fleeing an intolerable love as in *The Egoist*, Meredith swings the balance of *The Tragic Comedians* decisively away from the appraising light of comedy towards a more generous sense of the tragic potential of life—a sense which persisted and grew through the works of his last years.

The Egoist is high comedy of the kind which 'refines even to pain'. Despite his belief in the power of reason, Meredith's own creative sympathy is usually given to passionate feeling. Clara is justified by her passionate revulsion against Sir Willoughby in which both mind and instincts play a part. The characters speak with grace and wit; they are allusive, urbane, epigrammatic, apparently articulate—but what they say nearly always serves as a foil to their urgent, often ugly feelings. Meredith sets up a fruitful tension between the poise of high comedy and the primitive emotions with which the characters are grappling. It is the abrasion between comedy and passion which makes the book both witty and poignant.

JOHN GOODE

The Egoist: Anatomy or Striptease?†

Yes! Mr. Meredith is the Harvey[1] of the Ego.
  —Le Gallienne

Four species of idols beset the human mind, to which (for distinction's sake) we have assigned names, calling the first Idols of the Tribe, the second Idols of the Den, the third Idols of the Market, the fourth Idols of the Theatre.
  —Bacon

I

Criticism is a game played to throw reflections on the literary work in order to exhibit the way in which it deals with human nature. But *The Egoist* seems to be an inward mirror: it throws its own reflections, so that, for example, to discover that the willow pattern or the symbolic status of hands are important is to do no more than restate what the author, and, indeed, his protagonists, tell us. How do we muscle in on a game of patience?[2] The novel states its own terms, works itself out in perfect accord with those terms, and the critic either paraphrases (Beach), makes doubtful analogies with life (Priestley) or becomes something else, a metacritic questioning the terms themselves.[3]

Thus Gillian Beer. She measures the achievement of *The Egoist* against works not so committed to a specific aesthetic, notably *The Tragic Comedians*, and she sees it finally as a *parenthetical* work in which Meredith works out schematically the role of authorial distance before he moves on to the later novels, 'in which Meredith shows an enhanced tenderness toward his characters and a willingness to move through the emotions and not only through the head'.[4] I don't really know what *The Egoist* 'moves' through if it is not the generation of an emotional commitment (think only of the way in which Meredith links Clara, Crossjay and the wild weather). But, more importantly, Gillian Beer's placing seems to me to demolish the novel altogether. She sees it as an experiment in a deliberately enclosed form: 'in contrast with *The Egoist, The*

† From *Meredith Now*, ed. Ian Fletcher (London, 1971), pp. 205–221.
1. The allusion is to William Harvey, the seventeenth-century discoverer of the circulation of the blood. Richard LeGallienne wrote in 1890 an early and enthusiastic appreciation of Meredith. [*Editor.*]
2. Solitaire. [*Editor.*]
3. Joseph Warren Beach and J. B. Priest-

ley are critics of Meredith, their major contributions listed in the bibliography at the back of the present volume. A "metacritic" is, perhaps, a critic of criticism. [*Editor.*]
4. G. Beer, "Meredith's Idea of Comedy, 1876–1880," *Nineteenth Century Fiction*, XX (September 1965), 176.

Tragic Comedians derives from real life, not from literature.'[5] It explicitly is such an experiment, of course, but the enclosure has no point unless it enables the novel to relate more vividly to life. It invokes 'the embracing and condensing spirit', and thus to argue that it derives, more than most other literary artefacts, from 'literature', is to condemn it outright. Meredith is claiming a definite social role for art in the Prelude ('Art is the specific'), so that the only way we can evaluate the novel is to evaluate its terms and the claims those terms make to offer a meaningful impression of the actual.

II

The very title seems to reduce the 'original psychological notation' which is the most recognizable development in later-nineteenth-century fiction, to a simple moral typology. George Steiner's history of the words 'egoism' and 'egotism' concludes that, on the whole, they 'betray the survival of a neo-classical façade long after Rousseau and Romanticism had subdued the feelings which had originally animated these words'.[6] If he is right, and if *The Egoist*, therefore, is merely the elaboration of a pre-Romantic psychology, its theme is anachronistic, and its extensive exploration within the formal terms of the novel is gratuitous. For the most successful realizations of pre-Romantic characterization depend precisely on their allusive brevity. We are alerted to the complexity of Atossa, for example, because we recognize that the moral framework of *The Moral Essays* demands a rhetorical process of typification through epigram and pictorial fixity.[7] *The Egoist* seems to be trying to create a profound world out of that highly achieved surface.

But Steiner is inaccurate, at least about the latter half of the nineteenth century. He fails to make any real distinction between 'egotist' and 'egoist', and yet the N.E.D. would have told him that *The Saturday Review* saw Meredith's use of the French orthography as an adoption of 'the current slang'. Although the word was used in the eighteenth century as a philosophical term, the most extensive use of it in the 1870s in that way was by Henry Sidgwick, who was concerned to take it seriously as a possible moral attitude, so that he hardly conceals a neo-classical anti-individualism.[8] Its most important use, however, is as a biological/psychological term, with,

5. *Ibid.*, 174.
6. F. G. Steiner, "Contributions to a Dictionary of Critical Terms: 'Egoism' and 'Egotism,' " *Essays in Criticism* II (October 1952), 452.
7. "Atossa" is a blind reference; it may be a way of referring to someone better known under another name, but no author named "Atossa" is listed by the major library catalogues and reference books of the world. [*Editor.*]
8. Henry Sidgwick (1838–1900), English philosopher; the allusion is probably to his *Method of Ethics*, published in 1874. [*Editor.*]

to be sure, moral implications, by Spencer and Comte. 'Egoism' belongs to a technical context, and we can gauge how technical if we note that whereas Comte himself uses the word in a fairly general way (it does, of course, have a consistent history in French) when he says, for example, *'Le Positivisme conçoit directement l'art moral comme consistant à faire, autant que possible, prévaloir les instincts sympathiques sur impulsions égoistes'*,[9] the English translation renders this last phrase as 'selfish instincts'[1] and uses 'egoistic' in the specific context of the section on biology. What I am emphasizing is that 'egoist' re-enters the English language between the mid-fifties and mid-seventies with a renewed connotative force—linking it with the attempt to find a basis for human conduct in empirical scientific discourse. And with this renewed force, it is connected not with attempts to resurrect pre-Romantic attitudes, but with attempts to find post-Romantic ideas, ideas which would cope with that aspect of human experience which is not coherently explained in terms of individual consciousness. Such an attempt dominates the speculative thought of the mid-Victorians. It pervades, for example, Leslie Stephen's *Thought in the Eighteenth Century,* in which he speaks for the generation reflected in Meredith's novel when, commenting on Hartley, he writes: 'The purely selfish solution . . . has a terrible plausibility, especially when all philosophy is obliged to start from the individual mind, instead of contemplating the social organism.'[2] 'Egoism', through its links with Comte and Spencer, becomes involved with the movement to create sociology—that is, to confront fully the romantic self and to transcend it in social terms. Positivism is the most influential system to cater for this desire, but Bradley, in his own terms, was also engaged in affirming extra-personal forces which motivate individuals as social beings.[3] We shall see that *The Egoist* needs to be referred to all these contexts, and that, consequently, it is at the pulse of its own epoch.

9. A. Comte, *Système de politique positive* (Paris, 1851), I, 91. [Comte's sentence says: "Positivism specifically conceives the art of morality as consisting, so far as possible, of making the sympathetic instincts prevail over the egoistic impulses."—Auguste Comte (1798–1857) was the founder of "positivism," a kind of philosophy which aimed to marry science and religion. Herbert Spencer (1820–1903) was a philosopher, psychologist, and exponent of progress, sympathetic to Comte.—*Editor.*]
1. John Henry Bridges, tr., A. Comte, *System of Positive Polity* (1875), I, 559–560.
2. L. Stephen, *A History of English Political Thought in the Eighteenth Century* (1962), II, 58. [Leslie Stephen (1832–1904), in addition to his work on the *Dictionary of National Biography* and his fame as the father of Virginia Woolf, was the model for Vernon Whitford in *The Egoist.* Hartley is David Hartley (1705–57), the associationist psychologist. —*Editor.*]
3. Bradley is probably F. H. Bradley, the author of *Appearance and Reality* (1893). [*Editor.*]

The Prelude rejects the scientific description of human nature, but to reject it is not to dismiss it. *The Egoist* echoes in its title and in the connotations of its theme Comte's biological account of human emotion, the theory of cerebral functions. Comte analyses the cerebral functions in terms of a progressive scale moving from egoism to altruism, a scale which exists statically in the mind of every individual and dynamically in individual growth and social evolution. The fundamental law of the scale is that 'cerebral functions are higher in quality and inferior in force as we proceed from behind forwards'.[4] He categorizes the egoistic functions in three stages, moving progressively towards the individual's awareness of and involvement in society. At the base are the defensive instincts—self-preservation and procreation; above them are the instincts which make for self-improvement, military (destructive) and industrial (constructive). Intermediary between these purely egoistic instincts and the social affections are pride (which is defined as love of power) and vanity (love of approbation). Both of these 'are essentially personal, whether in their origin or in their object. But the means through which these instincts are to be gratified give them a social character, and render their tendencies far more modifiable'.[5] One final relevant point is made by Comte, and that is that the organism which provides the bridge between egoistic instincts and social affections is the family:

> If, on the one hand, domestic life is that which prepares us best to feel the charm of living for others, on the other hand it places us in the situation that best enables each of us to abuse this power over others ... For Society continually acts in purifying the leading characteristics of Family.[6]

The Egoist is not, of course, a Positivist manifesto; on the contrary, as we shall see, much of its didactic impetus is directed against Comte's seductive and dangerous complacency. Nor does it reflect Comte schematically: it is rather that it is saturated with the Comtist ambience. The implicit way it tends to find itself in the novel is best exemplified in the episode of the rumour about the widow 'who had very nearly snared him'.[7] It requires an aggressive act on the widow's integrity in order to quash it:

> Sir Willoughby unbent. His military letter I took a careless glance at itself lounging idly and proudly at ease in the glass

4. A. Comte, *System of Positive Polity*, I, 559, 560.
5. *Ibid.*, I, 564.
6. *Ibid.*, tr. Frederic Harrison, II, 178.
7. *Egoist*, chapter 3.

of his mind, decked with a wanton wreath, as he dropped a hint, generously vague, just to show the origin of the rumour, and the excellent basis it had for not being credited.[8]

Marriage at this point is an act of self improvement: 'His duty to his House was a foremost thought with him'[9] and he has moved in 'his admirable passion to excel'[1] from hunting to the pursuit of Constantia Durham. The constructive act of building the new generation has to be preceded by the military training of the hunt (which Meredith explicitly links to a stage in society in which the State demands no personal service, just as Comte makes the modification of egoism dependent on the ability of society to exert its influence), and it is thus natural that, in this description of Willoughby's exertion to the destruction of the threatened snare, he should use Comte's adjective 'military'. Comte is important for *The Egoist*, not because of a deliberate commitment to or confrontation with that philosopher in particular, but because the general tenor of his thinking pervades so much English thought in the 1870s (the decade of the official translation and the heyday of figures like Beesly and Harrison).[2]

In a general way, therefore, the structure of egoism in the novel has to be related to this biological scheme. The most important point (and this is true as well of Herbert Spencer) is that Comte maintains an air of moral neutrality about the word—egoism is the starting-point of what transcends it. Up to a point, which we shall have to define precisely, *The Egoist* shares this neutrality. The Book of Egoism is the Book of the Earth. 'The Egoist is our fountain-head, primeval man' (Chapter 39) and thus, without irony, Meredith can go on to say he is 'a sign of the indestructibility of the race'. This is why it is a grand old Egoism that built the house: it is not endorsed in absolute terms, but it is granted its role: man's instinct for self-preservation, which Comte defines as nutrition and which is both affirmatively and ironically imaged in the novel as Crossjay's appetite and Dr Middleton's gastronomic vulnerability, is what has created the society whose finest manifestation is the Comic Spirit. The primitive force which determines Willoughby is a potential for good, and Clara's own rebellion begins with a necessary self-assertion: 'She preferred to be herself, with the egoism of women' (Chapter 6). It is those who deny themselves for Willoughby's sake who are the per-

8. *Ibid.*
9. *Ibid.*
1. *Egoist*, chapter 2.
2. Frederic Harrison and E. S. Beesly were among those active in the movement to establish the philosophical religion of Comte in England. [*Editor.*]

petrators of the social ill-health which enables him to remain unexposed—the Patterne ladies, Lætitia and, to a very large extent, Vernon. For Willoughby is a *degenerate* egoist essentially. What he seeks in love is not self-preservation, but something more, 'the pacification of a voracious aesthetic *gluttony*' (Chapter 11). This implies that in one sense he is retarded, so that, for example, the procreative instinct is perverted to a narrower appetite: 'Miss Middleton was different: she was the true ideal, fresh gathered morning fruit in a basket, warranted by her bloom' (Chapter 5). But equally he is, in the Comtist perspective, highly advanced, a *social egoist* whose main motives are pride and vanity, which, as Comte says himself, are the most difficult to modify for two reasons: first, they are in 'perpetual antagonism' with each other, and, second, the most developed society has a tendency to stimulate both.

Egoism ceases to be a morally neutral word in Meredith's novel as soon as it becomes involved with a social structure, particularly that of the family. In the first place, it becomes linked to competitiveness—Willoughby uses a Darwinian vocabulary of natural selection about Flitch or Vernon (they are 'extinct' if they thwart him). Secondly, its involvement with property—property that is not built, but inherited and used as an instrument of power and a claim to applause (this emerges in Willoughby's patronage of Vernon)—provides not a modification of the beast, but a protective cover. Willoughby's jealousy is defined as 'the primitive egoism seeking to refine in a blood gone to savagery under apprehension of an invasion of rights' (Chapter 23). George Woodcock, in his excellent Introduction to the Penguin edition of *The Egoist*, says that Meredith may have been aware of Stirner (and that Stirner was known in England at this time is confirmed by F. H. Bradley's use of him to admonish Henry Sidgwick).[3] And if that is the case, he would have read (I'm quoting here from Woodcock's book, *Anarchism*, 94):

> He who, to hold his own, must count on the absence of will in others is a thing made by those others, as the master is a thing made by the servant.

Certainly Willoughby, because of his competitive and property-based sensitivity, is finally exposed as a thing, a leg, we may say, whose life consists of dancing to the tunes and leaping the obstacles provided by those over whom he has power.

3. "Max Stirner" was the pseudonym of a philosophical anarchist, Kaspar Schmidt, whose mid-century reflections on individuality and identity were widely influential in England. [*Editor.*]

But this makes the novel a very radical challenge to Comte's version of social evolution. For in so far as Willoughby grows away from primitive egoism, he clearly grows not towards society, but towards a more inexorably alienated relationship to it. Comte's assertion that pride and vanity require social *means* is endorsed by the novel, but that this makes them more accessible to modification is exposed as absurd. In fact, the very title implicitly attacks the Comtist (and equally Spencerian) biological/ethical relation through the concepts of egoism and altruism. Strictly speaking, for Comte, though there is egoism, there can be no Egoist, for egoism is merely a part of the pattern which is in all of us at various phases of growth: it is an element in an evolutionary process, and hence cannot be a fixed attribute. That Meredith should use the phrase 'social egoist' and make his consummate example embody not so much the basic features of egoism, but the intermediary features, pride and vanity, is a direct challenge to Comte's social faith. For what the 'scientific' explanation of ethics fails to account for is the divorce between self and self-communication. The Carlylean clothes image[4] is invoked only briefly in the Prelude, but it is enough to alert us to the special claims of insight which art makes in the face of sociology (and this is one reason why we have little to learn of apes). Self-consciousness, which is what differentiates pride and vanity from the other egoistic instincts, is not the same as self-awareness. Art offers an 'inward mirror'. It is the psychology of the social egoist that matters, not just his position in the evolution of society.

We should recall here that one of the earliest uses of the word 'egoist' in England was by Thomas Reid, and that Reid used it in an epistemological framework to describe those (unspecified) philosophers who were trapped in a post-Cartesian solipsism.[5] In the 1870s it is Henry Sidgwick who devotes most coherent attention to the egoist world-view, this time within a discourse on ethics. Both Reid and Sidgwick assume that 'egoist' defines a tenable and permanent *attitude*. Meredith could hardly have been unconscious of Sidgwick at least (and if he was, Stephen would have sufficiently evoked self-interest as a possible consciously held attitude). He commits himself neither to the simply biological nor to the overtly ideological uses of the word, but the coexistence of the two

4. See *Sartor Resartus*. [*Editor*.]
5. Thomas Reid, Scottish philosopher (1710–96). The point is that Reid uses the word "egoist" in connection with the problem of being. Anyone who accepts the formula of Descartes, "I think therefore I am," is bound to be preoccupied with the processes of his own mind. [*Editor*.]

demands psychological dramatization of the interaction of biologically enforced will and ethically based idea. It is the rationalization of the first by the second which becomes the most obvious theme of the novel, and it is this that commits him to take account of egoism at precisely the point where it accounts for itself in terms of 'the world', in pride and vanity.

Willoughby himself uses the word 'egoist' in a traditional pejorative sense. Nevertheless, his most explicit *idea* is hatred of the world: 'up in London you are nobody,' he says, '. . . a week of London literally drives me home to discover the individual where I left him' (Chapter 11). His enemy is the world, but this means only, of course, that the world has to be continually squared. This is the simplest paradox of the novel, and Clara rapidly recognizes it. In Comtist terms it should make Willoughby ripe for modification, but the novel sees the psychology of self-consciousness primarily in terms of reflection and therefore of enclosure. Given the epistemological and ethical connotations of the word, it becomes possible for pride and vanity to become motives which not only use society as a means of personal gratification, but which attempt to transform the means themselves into functions of the egoistic mind. This is why to be a social egoist is to be 'arcadian by the aesthetic route'. The golden world of grand old egoism (Meredith is, of course, using 'arcadian' with ironic undertones) is recovered through the assimilation of the outer world into personal images. The dominant motif of the novel has to do with mirrors (which are servants both of vanity and art) : 'In his more reflective hour the attractiveness of that lady which held the mirror to his features was paramount' (Chapter 3). The image undergoes many repetitions and variations until it enters explicitly into his calculations about Lætitia, with an almost insanely obsessive intonation: 'It would be marriage with a mirror, with an echo; marriage with a shining mirror, a choric echo (Chapter 37). The point is that pride and vanity, so far from being intermediate in the evolution from egoism, are its terminus ad quem; they formulate, as long as they are not completely antagonistic to each other, an enclosed world from which there is no escape. Thus Meredith uses the motif to encapsulate an immediate reflex action springing from an apparently selfless concern:

> He sprang to the ground and seized her hand. 'Lætitia Dale!' he said. He panted. 'Your name is sweet English music! And you are well?' The anxious question permitted him to read deeply in her eyes. He found the man he sought there, squeezed him passionately, and let her go. . . . (Chapter 4).

It is a reflex, but it is the reflex of the reflective man. Most of his reflections, it is true, are mediated by sentimental stereotypes: he accuses Clara of seeing the world through popular romances, but his hilarious projections of the ruined and penitent Clara are, of course, all highly literary, and Meredith makes it quite explicit 'as his popular romances would say' (Chapter 23). The mirror works both ways: in order that society should reflect Willoughby, Willoughby has to shape himself to society. Comte is ironically half right. But the primary concern is with the process of reflection itself, so that the mirror motif enters into his carefully chosen language: 'You hit me to the life' (Chapter 4) he says to Lætitia, and, later: 'Where I do not find myself—that *I* am *essentially* I—no applause can move me' (Chapter 31). It is because he seeks a mirror that he is so anxious to reveal himself first to Clara and later to Lætitia: 'But try to enter into my mind; think with me, feel with me' (Chapter 6).

The image is linked, as a phrase such as this suggests, to another motif which equally embodies the enclosed psychology of social egoism, and which manifests itself in terms of the imprisonment of the reflected image. At the end of Chapter 9, Willoughby reflects with a systematic aesthetic gluttony which looks forward to that of Will Brangwen,[6] on the physical beauties of Clara. In the following chapter he makes a decisive bid to appropriate her mind by 'revealing' his fault in a way which makes him into a Darwinian natural force and a 'fallen archangel'. Clara realizes that she is now in 'the inner temple of him.' He rejects the bid Vernon is making for independence because it threatens the walls of 'our magic ring'. 'One small fissure,' he says, 'and we have the world with its muddy deluge' (Chapter 10). Later in the chapter Willoughby supplies his own title, and by the end of the episode Clara feels herself trapped:

> The idea of the scene ensuing upon her petition for release, and the being dragged round the walls of his egoism, and having her head knocked against the corners, alarmed her with sensations of sickness (Chapter 10).

The temple, externalized as the house itself, becomes an image of the reflective mind, again making for an extreme scepticism about Comte's theory. For this image finds a parallel on a narrative plane, when Willoughby, to secure Dr Middleton, Clara's social guardian, takes him to the inner cellar of Patterne Hall. On this level, the procedure works. Pride is able to

6. The allusion is to D. H. Lawrence's novel *The Rainbow*. [*Editor.*]

exploit social means to its own end. What prevents it ultimately from asserting domination is not society, but the opposing *self* of Clara's egoism—courage to be dishonourable.
Mirror and cave are total defences against the social world
they respond to. What happens, of course, is that the enclosed,
reflective mind destroys itself. The key image modulates from
mirror to web: 'And this female, shaped by that informing
hand, would naturally be in harmony with him, from the centre of his profound identity to the raying circle of his variations' (Chapter 11). This image has overtones both of mirror
('raying') and web. Once Clara has broken out of the house,
Vernon has placed him with the zoological image:

> His insane dread of a detective world makes him artificially
> blind. As soon as he fancies himself seen, he sets to work
> spinning a web, and he discerns nothing else. It's generally a
> clever kind of web; but if it's a tangle to others it's the
> same to him and a veil as well (Chapter 30).

Willoughby is no longer in an inclusive world of self: there are
other spiders, and Clara's flight makes him feel 'as we may
suppose a spider to feel when plucked from his own web and
set in the centre of another's' (Chapter 29). Pride and vanity
are henceforth at war.

These images are not substitutes for the dramatic realization
of the process. The gyrations Willoughby gets caught in the
attempt to preserve the mirror-cave are manifest in the outstanding moments of the novel—the interviews with Lætitia,
the pursuit of Clara and the struggle with Clara for Dr Middleton's mind. What the images do is to transpose the biological source of egoism into a psychological drama growing out
of an ethical and epistemological commitment. It is not biological growth that transforms egoism; it is a fundamental intellectual error that exposes it—through very love of self himself
he slew. Sidgwick argued that empirical hedonism (which is
the 'method' of egoism) was likely to be self-defeating, and
went on to say 'that a rational method of attaining the end at
which it aims requires that we should to some extent put it out
of sight and not directly aim at it . . . (is) . . . the "fundamental Paradox of Egoistic Hedonism" '.[7] Stephen made a similar,
slightly positivized point in his commentary on Bishop Butler.[8] The comedy of *The Egoist* grows out of the 'twists of the

7. H. Sidgwick, *The Method of Ethics*, 1874, p. 136. [Hedonism is defined as the pursuit of pleasure.—*Editor*.]

8. L. Stephen, *History of English Political Thought*, II, 45–46.

heart', the ironic contradictions which are inherent in the relationship between the idols of the tribe and the idols of the den, and it is given moral depth by the careful placing of moral discriminations at the point at which the human mind, in its self-realization, is confronted with a choice between being directed outwards towards love or turning in on itself to form a cave of possession in which there is no fissure.

III

I don't think I need to insist on its value in these terms. George Woodcock argues that Meredith gives us not just two-dimensional characters defined simply by inward feeling and pretension, as do Fielding, Congreve and Wilde, but manifests 'a probing complexity' which presents the comic victim in process.[9] But though this may be enough to make us read the novel, it clearly isn't enough to make it a great or even good one. Woodcock's comparatives are significant: two minor dramatists and an eighteenth-century novelist do not offer much of a challenge. The critical question is whether *The Egoist* doesn't fade into insignificance beside *Middlemarch* and *The Portrait of a Lady*. Fade because Willoughby may seem to be only a stylized, and therefore harmless, version of Casaubon and Osmond. Dorothy Van Ghent compares the novel at some length with *Portrait of a Lady*, and the comparison becomes the most damaging attack on *The Egoist* which has been written. She points out that although Willoughby ought, on the face of it, to be a characterization which offers meaningful insights into human psychology (he demonstrates, as she points out, 'the fetal and infantile proclivities of the adult'),[1] he remains so distant that our response is at best admiration for Meredith's cleverness, and in the end an inevitable indifference. The distance is not merely the result of the comic form (though I think that, implicitly, she is querying the validity of the conventions), but comes from the fact that Willoughby has no dramatized causal connection with the world he inhabits—he is without 'internal relations' with the society he dominates, like the giant in 'Jack and the Beanstalk'.

I don't think we can escape the fact that there is, on the face of it, a good deal of confusion between what Meredith claims the form of the novel to be and the themes that he proposes to handle within that form. Both the 'Essay on Comedy' and the

9. G. Meredith, *The Egoist*, ed. with an introduction by George Woodcock, 1968.
1. D. Van Ghent, *The English Novel: Form and Function* (New York, 1961), p. 188. [Edward Casaubon of *Middle-march* and Gilbert Osmond of *Portrait of a Lady* are figures comparable to Willoughby because they too are dry, demanding, and unsympathetic.—*Editor.*]

'Ode to the Comic Spirit' show that Meredith was very conscious of the particular social context of comedy. The comic spirit is the sword of common sense; it is the dramatization of 'our united social intelligence'. In the past, therefore, the best comedy, like that of Molière, appears when society is one wherein 'ideas are current and the perceptions quick'. It depends on the assumption that 'our civilization is based on common sense' because, for example, 'Molière's comedy . . . appeals to the individual mind to perceive and participate in the social'. Meredith is surely right about Molière. The social criticism voiced within the plays can be devastating, but it never queries the structure of society because it sees social evils as deviationist. Thus Philinte[2] is, if anything, more bitter about the world in which he finds himself than Alceste : but he knows that to criticize society is as deviationist and ridiculous as any of its vices *'Le monde par vos soins ne se changera pas'*[3] : Alceste is absurd because he judges society by social criteria (those of the *honnête homme*[4]), and then tries to become free of it. The social status of Molière's comedy can be defined by the end of *Tartuffe*, in which, after a devastating portrayal of hypocrisy, the exposure is brought about by the King himself, and the constable he sends identifies the King with the comic spirit : *'Nous vivons sous un prince ennemi de la fraude.'*[5] Comedy reflects the social artifice of good government. Both simplify human relationships sufficiently to affirm a normative code which guarantees the triumph of reason.

'Comedy' is the first word of *The Egoist,* and its predicate acknowledges its artificiality : it will exclude the dust and mire of the outside world. It will be played in the drawing-room, not because Meredith is concerned with a particular social class, but because he wishes to create a social paradigm, which will hunt 'the *spirit* in men' and therefore the spirit in society. That spirit is 'the Book of our Common Wisdom'. The rhetoric doesn't make it clear whether this Book is different from the Book of Earth, but clearly Egoism and Common Wisdom are the concepts which do battle with one another.

There are two points to be made here. The first is that it is difficult to know what in *The Egoist* is meant to stand for 'Common Wisdom'. Is it merely the author himself? In which case it seems very abstract and tenuous. Or is it the society at

---

2. Philinte is the friend of Alceste in *The Misanthrope*. [*Editor.*]
3. "The world won't be changed by your efforts." [*Editor.*]

4. "Honest, straightforward man." [*Editor.*]
5. "We live under a prince who hates fraud." [*Editor.*]

large? It cannot be the latter, because most of the characters who surround Willoughby are either social cast-offs, such as Vernon, Crossjay and finally Clara; or they are fools—the Patterne ladies, Lady Busshe and Lady Culmer, and, though at a somewhat different level, Mrs Mountstuart Jenkinson and De Craye (who turns out in the end to be 'a Willoughby butterfly'). We may say perhaps that it is the grouping of these characters at the end which exposes Willoughby, but it isn't true, since it is the combined assertiveness of Clara and Lætitia, aided by the elements which *create* the situation. And in any case when Willoughby finds himself in the jaws of the world, he seems much less ridiculous than the outrageous crowd who are waiting to consume him. We have already seen that *The Egoist* offers a radical challenge to the most accepted ideology of social man in the late nineteenth century. It is difficult to see how Meredith proposes a different order or a different ideal.

The trouble is that Willoughby is the consummate product of the social structure, not merely a moral type it yields. Mirror, temple and web are motifs which imply social relationships, but they are of a very general kind: they define only the attitude of man to woman, man to family and man to 'the world'. In this way Willoughby's social status is merely paradigmatic: Meredith chooses a country gentleman because this enables him to present these relationships, uncluttered by economic pressure or class antagonism. Indeed, for a moment, in Ch. XXIII, when Willoughby assesses his position after Clara's flight and return, there is a perfect coalescence between the particularity of Willoughby's position and the generalizations it is meant to bear: although it defines 'the feelings of a man hereditarily sensitive to property', we are conscious that the egoism is conditioned only by biological and cultural determinations: 'The capricious creature probably wanted a whipping to bring her to the understanding of the principle called mastery, which is in man' (Chapter 23). The difficulty is that Willoughby's feelings are not seen to be completely subjective, and hence they cannot be characterized as an abnormal development of normal traits. Another of the major motifs in the novel *is* very specifically social, and as such is deterministic:

The little prince's education teaches him that he is other than you, and by virtue of the instruction he receives, and also something, we know not what, within, he is enabled to maintain his posture where you would be tottering (Chapter 2).

It is true that 'something, we know not what, within' alerts us to the portrayal of Willoughby as a moral type, but the whole image emphasizes the differentiation (the use of 'you' here is crucial) in social terms. A social determinism heightens and grants cover to the moral individuality. Metaphors suggesting a German prince or the sun-king pervade the novel, and are linked inextricably with the voracious aesthetic appetite for applause and devotion: 'At least I have you for my tenant,' he tells Lætitia, 'and wherever I am, I see your light at the end of my park' (Chapter 4). And later, speaking of Vernon, he says: 'Feudalism is not an objectionable thing if you can be sure of the lord. You know, Clara, and you should know me in my weakness too. I do not claim servitude. I stipulate for affection' (Chapter 9). The social structure, the great house giving power to the central figure, becomes thus the agent of Willoughby's sentimentality. At the end of the novel the Patterne ladies, themselves hard-drilled soldiery of the proper emotions, ask Dr Middleton:

'Is it Self that craves for sympathy, love and devotion?'
'He is an admirable host, ladies' (Chapter 44).

Middleton's reply is not merely bathetic: it is importantly true. Craving for sympathy is what the self of the little prince, the host of the great house, is educated to. Lætitia is not wrong when she says, 'the excuses of a gentleman nurtured in idolatry may be pleaded' (Chapter 49).

This cannot be explained away by saying that the social contains inherent dangers which have to be moderated by the sword of common sense. For it depends for its very existence on the egoism it creates. In dramatic terms, Willoughby is the centre and linchpin of the social world. Vernon recognizes this when he says to Lætitia:

'We none of us know what will be done. We hang on Willoughby, who hangs on whatever it is that supports him: and there we are in a swarm' (Chapter 18).

The hold Willoughby has over Dr Middleton is not merely the hold of sensual pleasure over an epicure: 'A house having a great wine stored below, lives in our imagination as a joyful house fast and splendidly rooted in the soil' (Chapter 20). It is the house which holds also Vernon, Lætitia and all of the characters who do not specifically break out. The power the house has over others is its rootedness, and its rootedness is epitomized in the inner cellar which is itself related to Willoughby's egoism. It is thus not enough to say that the social order permits egoism—egoism is the social order.

This is made explicit in the opening passage of the novel proper:

> There was an ominously anxious watch of eyes visible and invisible over the infancy of Willoughby, fifth in descent from Simon Patterne, of Patterne Hall, premier of this family, a lawyer, a man of solid acquirements and stout ambition, who well understood the foundation-work of a House, and was endowed with the power of saying No to those first agents of destruction, besieging relatives. He said it with the resonant emphasis of death to younger sons. For if the oak is become a stately tree, we must provide against the crowding of timber. Also the tree beset with parasites prospers not. A great House in its beginning, lives, we may truly say, by the knife (Chapter 1).

It is a passage which leads us to expect a much greater social specificity than the terms in which we have seen the novel so far (moral drama based on biological and cultural universals) allow for. For it points very precisely to the *bourgeois* foundation (the lawyer) of a paternalistic social structure (the gentry). And, more importantly, it draws attention to the Hobbesian reality behind the Burkeian affirmation of an organic society (the tree prospers by pruning).[6] As the novel progresses, such precision comes to seem irrelevant. But we are reminded of it again when Willoughby rejects marriage to the aristocracy, when, with unconscious irony, he describes the Americans as the sons of Roundheads, and when he has to forgo the *ancien régime* role of 'the Gallican courtier' for that of the more *bourgeois* 'model gentleman'.[7] The specific bases and limitations of egoism are not on the surface, but they are stubbornly recurrent.

To note this is to offer some kind of answer to Van Ghent's criticism. Willoughby is not only related to the social context; he is, in his major characteristic, the very essence of the social structure. But this only moves the question on to a different plane. In the last chapter Meredith is drawing attention very emphatically to the theatrical basis of the novel—'the curtain falls', 'so the knot was cut'. But immediately after this latter

6. Edmund Burke, the conservative eighteenth-century statesman, saw society as a tree, its elements organically related; Thomas Hobbes, the seventeenth-century philosopher, saw it as growing out of a contract. [*Editor.*]

7. The *ancien régime* (the old order) of pre-revolutionary France is contrasted with the more middle-class (*bourgeois*) ideals of Willoughby and county gentry of his stripe. [*Editor.*]

phrase, Mrs Mountstuart Jenkinson, with her habitual helpless shrewdness, says, 'and the policy of the county is to keep him in love with himself, or Patterne will be likely to be as dull as it was without a lady enthroned' (Chapter 1). Willoughby's egoism has to be preserved because that is what an ordered society (the swarm) is based on. It is the transfixed spectators of Willoughby's exposure who compel him to preserve his egoism intact. And his most loyal tenant, seeing through him, nevertheless sacrifices herself to this preservation. Patterne Hall closes its gates. The swarm loses two or three bees, but reforms itself. If the knot has been loosened, it has not been cut.

What, then, we ask, is the comedy trying to achieve? In this perspective, it seems that it wishes only to define egoism, so that it challenges not the principle itself, but merely the folly of its trying to transcend itself. Willoughby has to learn to be a model gentleman, obedient to the limited social contract, rather than a *grand monarque*. He must acknowledge liberty of mind. He must choose his own tenant to preserve the house, and not make conquests beyond his property. In this odd way, the comedy seems to bid self-love and social be the same. This is how Meredith saw Molière, but it hardly fits with the 'probing complexity' with which Willoughby is presented as a moral type, for that doesn't allow for the *reform* of egoism towards social accommodation. The comedy seems thus to retreat from a full confrontation with the social implications of egoism. On the one hand we see egoism as an extension of biological self-assertion into the realm of social relationships in which it plays what is fundamentally an anti-social role. On the other we see it as the essence of the social order. The paradox is not an impossible one, but it is difficult to see in what way comedy can expose it and resolve its tensions. For comedy asserts the social order, but here the social order seems to depend on what it is asserted against. It is as though Tartuffe should turn out to be Louis XIV in disguise: the comic scapegoat, so far from rushing off the stage with exasperation like Alceste, or being carried off to gaol like Tartuffe, turns out to be the instrument of order.

Le Gallienne praised Meredith as the Harvey of the ego, but in the end we have to ask the question whether the unmasking of Willoughby is anatomy or striptease. For anatomy uncovers something about the structure of all of us, and offers the possibilities of cure. Whereas striptease is a process we go through to reassure us of our own clothing—the stripping happens to someone else. And we are not concerned with the nakedness so much as with the clothing: clothing is what matters because it relates us to everyone else. And equally striptease stops short at the g-string, for what is important is that finally the real animal truth shouldn't be revealed, should remain intact. The plot finally resolves itself to recover Willoughby before the final exposure. The exposure he has been submitted to comes to seem a reassurance: the curtain falls, we may feel in the end, not because the comedy is complete, but because finally it is ashamed of the nakedness it has hinted at. We seem bound to come away feeling either that Willoughby has never stood a chance, and so that his stripping is almost authorial sadism (the view that Meredith was relentlessly, almost hysterically, punishing himself is enticing), or that he is so harmless, the stooge that society creates the ultimately cherishes with a sceptical smile, that the analysis is superfluous. Both views depend on seeing the novel as comedy, artifically limited to establish a paradigm and affirming our united social intelligence against abnormality. But I think this simplifies the novel too much. Comedy is only one of the perspectives it uses. We have seen how Meredith builds a psychological drama out of the relationship between the idols of the tribe and the idols of the den. It is a drama which seems to be distanced for the sake of the idols of the market-place. In so far as he is a representative type, Willoughby is stripped, but he is also a proprietor, and he must be recovered. He is indeed, made to perform 'a monstrous immolation for this laughing empty world' (Chapter 46). But this is Meredith's phrase and Willoughby's consciousness. Such a self-evaluation compels us to look more precisely at the comic structure.

CHARLES J. HILL
Theme and Image in *The Egoist*†

It is generally acknowledged that *The Egoist*, published in 1879, represents the quintessential Meredith. Nowhere else is his analysis of motives more penetrating, or his idea of comedy more steadily exemplified. Moreover, in dealing with the predicament of Clara Middleton, Meredith comes to grips with the position of women in Victorian society, a theme which was to figure, in one way or another, in all of his later books. In fact, the subjection of women in a world governed

† From *The University of Kansas City Review*, vol. 20, no. 4 (Summer 1954), pp. 281–85.

in the interests of men becomes, inevitably, a salient theme in the author's remorseless exposure of the masculine ego. Inseparable from the central theme of egoism, it has in the final analysis an almost equal importance. For the significant action of the story is all related to Sir Willoughby's efforts to bind the woman of his choice, and Clara's struggle to break her engagement. It is illuminating to discover how the repetition of appropriate imagery assists the development of these themes in the carefully ordered structure of the novel.[1]

In the presentation of Sir Willoughby Patterne, Meredith gives us not only the character of an individual but the portrait of a type. The dignity of the Egoist is sacred. Not only must he think well of himself, but he must have the approval of others. Sir Willoughby holds the most exalted opinion of himself, because all his life he has been nourished upon adulation. He has a sensitiveness extremely tender, is "fiercely imaginative" in whatever concerns himself. It is characteristic of the Egoist that he is perpetually looking at himself, perpetually listening to himself, and that he must have his environment minister to his ideal conception of himself. Sir Willoughby expects his relatives and his friends to serve as satellites, who will give him back his own image and make him shine the brighter by their subservient admiration. And what Sir Willoughby demands in a wife, it is made unmistakably clear, is one who will be an obedient slave, a fixed star, one who will read and reverence him, one who will be as faithful to him as a mirror or an echo.

It is precisely because Clara Middleton comes to see that marriage with him would in fact be "marriage with a shining mirror, a choric echo,"[2] that she resolves to make her fight for

1. It has frequently been observed that the plot of *The Egoist* is exceptionally simple, approximating in design a drama based upon the Unities. [The Unities of time, space, and action are traditional restrictions on the representational field of a drama.—*Editor.*] No subordinate issues distract the reader's attention from the central problem, and the main action, which is confined to Patterne Hall and its environs, covers only a few weeks; most of it is compressed into less than one. The significance of the Willow Pattern and the procelain imagery related to it, which has been admirably treated by Robert D. Mayo in *"The Egoist and the Willow Pattern,"* ELH, IX (1942), 71–78, will not be discussed here. [See above, pp. 453–60.—*Editor.*]
2. *The Egoist*, p. 317. Images of reflecting and of reflection occur with some frequency in the pattern of the novel, point-

ing up the narcissism of Sir Willoughby so that it cannot be missed. Thus it is early said of him that 'His military letter I took a careless glance at itself lounging idly and proudly at ease in the glass of his mind" (p. 16). The presence of Laetitia Dale "illuminated him as the burning taper lights up consecrated plate" (p. 68). Clara's features "were treated as the mirror of himself" (p. 39). "We do," says Sir Willoughby of himself and Laetitia, "bring one another out, reflecting, counter-reflecting" (p. 108). But the supremely revealing context describes Sir Willoughby's greeting of Laetitia after a protracted absence. " 'Laetitia Dale!' he said. He panted. 'Your name is sweet English music! And you are well?' The anxious question permitted him to read deeply in her eyes. He found the man he sought there, squeezed him passionately, and let her go" (p. 24).

freedom. Clara cannot bring herself to sink her identity in his. She is determined not to "reduce herself to ashes, or incense, or essence, in honour of him, and so . . . literally be the man she was to marry."[3] But to Sir Willoughby betrothal means possession, complete, exclusive, and eternal; and the extreme of his vanity is displayed when he begs her, in the event of his death, to promise him a worshipful widowhood! Clara listens to him gravely, "conceiving the infinity as a narrow dwelling where a voice droned and ceased not."[4] Though she has much to endure before she is liberated, this is the beginning of the end.

The egoism represented by Sir Willoughby is related to Meredith's serious thinking about man in society. His view of man, as everybody is now aware, had its basis in the evolutionary theory which was the outstanding contribution to the scientific thought of his time and which he adapted after his own fashion.[5] In a word, Meredith looked upon egoism as a reversion to primitive brutishness. The primitive in modern man may be subtly disguised, for the civilized egoist is a sophisticated animal, skilled in concealing his predatory motives, but he is animal nonetheless.

The conception of egoism as a survival of primitive brutishness becomes, indeed, the informing idea in Meredith's novel. It inspires not only a number of important statements but an impressive body of interpretive imagery. We encounter, for example, the direct pronouncement:

> The Egoist is our fountain-head, primeval man; the primitive is born again, the elemental reconstituted. Born again, into new conditions, the primitive may be highly polished of men, and forfeit nothing save the roughness of his original nature . . . he has become the civilized Egoist; primitive still, as sure as man has teeth, but developed in his manner of using them.[6]

The Egoist's sentimental idea of women, demanding of them ("to be named innocent") cloistral purity and ignorance of the world they live in, is seen by Meredith as a "voracious æsthetic gluttony," a refinement of the gross original instinct of the predatory male to possess. Whether women "distinguish the ultra-refined but lineally great-grandson of the Hoof in

3. *Egoist*, p. 41.
4. *Egoist*, p. 39.
5. For Meredith's "evolutionary philosophy," see J. B. Priestley, *George Meredith* (London: Macmillan & Co., 1926), pp. 59–85, and Richard B. Hudson, "The Meaning of Egoism in George Meredith's The Egoist," *The Trollopian*, III (December, 1948), 163–176. [For the latter essay, see above, pp. 460–72.—*Editor*.]
6. *Egoist*, pp. 324–25.

this vast and dainty exacting appetite, is uncertain. They probably do not; the more the damage."[7] "The devouring male Egoist," Meredith goes on to say, wants women fashioned as "precious vessels . . . for him to walk away with hugging, call his own, drink of, and fill and drink of, and forget that he stole them."[8] Here the idea of the Egoist as rapaciously possessive is related to the position of women in Victorian society, and the image of the "devouring male Egoist" is supported throughout the narrative by many related images drawn from eating and drinking.

Clara Middleton once speaks in terms which echo the words of her author just now quoted. "Men who are egoists," she says in an important conversation with Laetitia Dale, "have *good* women for their victims; women on whose devoted constancy they feed; they drink it like blood."[9] Thus, to Sir Willoughby, Laetitia is a "feast," which he snatches at "hungrily if contemptuously."[1] Her eyes give him the "food" that he enjoys.[2] It is notable that the Egoist wishes to keep the woman he would consume as a morsel reserved for himself. Therefore Sir Willoughby had resented the fact that Constantia Durham had had many suitors: "She had been nibbled at, all but eaten up," while he waited. "He wished for her to have come to him out of an eggshell, somewhat more astonished at things than a chicken, but as completely inclosed before he tapped the shell."[3] By contrast, he somehow rationalized that he had caught Clara from the crowd before she had been contaminated. She was not like other girls who "run about the world nibbling and nibbled at, until they know one sex as well as the other."[4]

Sir Willoughby covets her as "fresh-gathered morning fruit . . . warranted by her bloom,"[5] and tastes in imagination the felicity that she promises. But when he becomes vexed and frightened by her his emotions are quite different. Then he would like to "burn and devour her."[6] In his annoyance he makes "devouring exclamations";[7] he suffers from a "gnawing jealousy," and Meredith speaks of the "jaw-chasm of his greed."[8] Clara thinks of herself as being caught and consumed, but the images which come most frequently to *her* mind are those of the hunted quarry and the captive.

Women are in the position of inferiors, she once observes to

7. *Egoist*, p. 92.
8. *Egoist*, p. 93.
9. *Egoist*, p. 133.
1. *Egoist*, p. 264.
2. *Egoist*, p. 116.
3. *Egoist*, pp. 17–18.

4. *Egoist*, p. 35.
5. *Ibid.*
6. *Egoist*, p. 190.
7. *Egoist*, p. 346.
8. *Egoist*, p. 190.

Laetitia Dale. "They are hardly out of their nursery when a lasso is round their necks."[9] Clara admires Vernon Whitford because he does not flatter her or "practice the fowler's arts."[1] But Sir Willoughby is "a falcon,"[2] and Clara's case is likened to that of "a captured wild creature" crying for help.[3] She feels her position as the betrothed of Sir Willoughby palpably, "as a shot in the breast of a bird."[4] She sees herself trapped, caught in "the jaws of her aversion."[5] Willoughby's house is a "cage," a "dungeon" in which she appears fated to spend a "life-long imprisonment."[6] The imagery of devouring is joined with the figure of the prison when Clara conceives of herself as "fixed at the mouth of a mine," condemned to descend into it daily, "to be chilled in subterranean sunlessness . . . in those caverns of the complacent-talking man."[7]

Now it was with *The Egoist* that Meredith began to make the marriage problem a major issue. The predicament of Clara Middleton, plighted to a despot from whom she must be liberated, is as much his concern as is the anatomy of Sir Willoughby's egoism; and Meredith is frequently moved to generalize from Clara's particular case. "What of wives miserably wedded?" he exclaims in a crucial passage. "What aim in view have these woeful captives?"[8] "Clara," he writes, "had shame of her sex. They cannot take a step without becoming bondswomen: into what a slavery!"[9] But Meredith was no facile generalizer.[1] He knew that not every man is an egoist and that many women of his day enjoyed a rational and companionable partnership with their husbands. He was acutely aware, nev-

9. *Egoist*, p. 132.
1. *Egoist*, p. 63.
2. *Egoist*, p. 357. [But this is De Craye who is a falcon.—*Editor*.]
3. *Egoist*, p. 85. Earlier it is said that Clara "was implored to enter the state of captivity by the pronunciation of vows" (p. 34).
4. *Egoist*, p. 50.
5. *Egoist*, p. 79.
6. *Ibid*. "Oh, to be caught up out of this prison of thorns and brambles!" Clara exclaims to herself (p. 85).
7. Opposed to the idea of the dungeon is Clara's yearning for the mountains, which become a quite explicit symbol of her desire for freedom. Clara thinks of the mountains, yearning for an Alpine holiday, whenever she is most oppressed by her sense of bondage, and her delight in mountains (see pp. 46, 97–98, 168–69) is appropriately shared by Vernon Whitford, who is destined to win her in the end. Readers of Meredith will recall in this connection the passage in *Harry Richmond* ("Carry your fever to the Alps, you of minds diseased") and will remember that for Diana of the Crossways the exhilaration of the Salvatore became an emblem of happiness and of a liberty craved.
8. *Egoist*, p. 97.
9. *Egoist*, p. 50. And Clara meditates, "We women are nailed to our sex" (p. 172).
1. He made it clear elsewhere that if women were denied the rights and privileges which were due to them, the fault lay not only with male egoists, but also with themselves; for thousands of them have been too ready to accept the domination of the male, contributing to their own enslavement by their relish for the pedestal. In *Sandra Belloni* (1864), where he made a penetrating study of sentimentalism, he admonished women on this very point. "If," he said, "you will smile on men, because they adore you as vegetable products, take what ensues. . . ." George Meredith, *Works*, The Memorial Edition (New York: Scribners, 1910), III, 181.

ertheless, of the limitations and the taboos imposed upon the sex in regard to education and opportunity, and of all the consequences for women arising out of their dependence in the married state. The position of women, in fact, seemed to him to be not only a test of men but a measure of the society in which they live.

> Women have us back to the condition of primitive man, or they shoot us higher than the top-most star . . . They are to us what we hold of best or worst within. By their state is our civilization judged; and if it is hugely animal still, that is because primitive men abound and will have their pasture.[2]

It is significant that in this highly characteristic utterance the imagery associated with "the devouring male egoist" should reappear.

If Meredith's conception of egoism as a reversion to primitive brutishness is related to his "evolutionary philosophy," his thinking about the dependence of women and the marriage problem owes much to the essay of John Stuart Mill on "The Subjection of Women." Meredith had read this essay when it appeared, in 1869, and his whole-hearted acceptance of Mill's arguments[3] is reflected not only in the substance of *The Egoist* (and elsewhere) but in the very language of that novel. Indeed, the correspondences are so striking that it is strange they have not been noticed, since Meredith's appreciation of Mill has long been common knowledge. What Meredith has done in *The Egoist* is to dramatize the ideas of Mill, and since the thematic material of the novel has already been examined, the parallels with the essay can be quickly pointed out.

It is notable in the first place that Mill describes the legal dependence of women as "the primitive state of slavery" which has not lost "the taint of its brutal origin."[4] Women are in the situation of bond-servants, educated to accept their captive state.[5] "Men do not want solely the obedience of women, they want their sentiments," Mill writes, expressing the thesis of *The Egoist* precisely.[6] "How many are the forms and gradations of animalism and selfishness, often under an outward varnish of civilization and even cultivation!" he exclaims in a voice that could as well be Meredith's.[7] "There is nothing

---

2. *Egoist*, pp. 190–91.
3. John Morley describes Meredith's excitement about the essay. "One morning in 1869, I put into his hands Mill's new little volume . . . on the *Subjection of Women*. Meredith eagerly seized the book, fell to devouring it in settled silence, and could not be torn from it all day." *Recollections* (New York: The Macmillan Co., 1917), I, 47.
4. John Stuart Mill, *On Liberty. The Subjection of Women* (New York: Henry Holt and Co., 1898), pp. 215–16.
5. *Ibid.*, p. 233.
6. *Ibid.*, p. 232.
7. *Ibid.*, p. 271.

which men so easily learn as this self-worship," he is observing a little later,[8] and to all that Mill has to say about the effect upon men and women alike, and upon the harmony of their relations in the state of marriage, which the inferiority imposed upon women is bound to produce, Meredith is in fullest accord. Mill's contention that women cannot expect emancipation, or be expected to devote themselves to gaining it, "until men in considerable number are prepared to join with them in the undertaking,"[9] must also have made a deep impression upon him. *The Egoist*, which reads almost as if it were a document in the campaign, shows the extent to which Meredith was already committed to the cause and the debt which he owed to Mill.

From this time to the day of his death, Meredith was to be counted a champion of women. The novels that followed *The Egoist* all treat some aspect or other of the marriage problem, and Meredith was frequently solicited for support of the feminist cause. "Women who read my books," he wrote to a female correspondent, "have much to surmount in the style, and when they have mastered it and come to the taste, I am well assured of their having discovered in me one who is much at heart with them."[1] But it was to a male friend, curiously enough, that Meredith communicated what may be taken as his testament of faith. He said:

> Since I began to reflect, I have been oppressed by the injustice done to women, the constraint put upon their natural aptitudes and their faculties, generally much to the degradation of the race. I have not studied them more closely than I have men, but with more affection . . . being assured that women of independent mind are needed for any sensible degree of progress . . . I have no special choice among the women of my books. Perhaps I gave more colour to 'Diana of the Crossways' and 'Clara Middleton' of the 'Egoist,' and this on account of their position.[2]

MICHAEL C. SUNDELL

The Functions of Flitch in *The Egoist*†

As Clara Middleton begins to phrase her first, tentative request for freedom from Sir Willoughby Patterne, the supreme

8. *Ibid.*, p. 283.
9 *Ibid.*, p. 351.
1. *Letters of George Meredith*, Collected and edited by his son (New York: Scribners, 1912), II, 418–19.

2. *Ibid.*, II, 562.
† Reprinted from *Nineteenth-Century Fiction*, vol. 24, no. 2 (September 1969), pp. 227–235.

egoist interrupts by ejaculating the word "Flitch!" (Chapter 11, p. 106). This sudden explosion bewilders the reader almost as much as it does Clara, for only in the next few lines does Sir Willoughby identify "Flitch" as a person, not merely an expletive. While half-listening to Clara's plea, Willoughby has sighted hovering in the background a former servant of that name. Having risen from stableboy to groom to coachman at Patterne, as his father had before him, Flitch forsook Sir Willoughby's service for the independence of running his own shop, a venture which soon failed. Now Flitch defies the Master's orders by presenting himself periodically at Patterne to beg for reinstatement. Willoughby consistently refuses this boon, despite the ties of old associations and the needs of Flitch's wife and nine hungry children.

The character Meredith introduces in this surprising manner seems peripheral to the central concerns of the novel. Flitch appears in person only four times and provides a subject of conversation not many times more, most notably at the end, when Laetitia Dale makes his return one of the conditions of her acceptance of Sir Willoughby's hand. Yet so skillfully does Meredith choreograph *The Egoist*, so intricately does he weave its various strands, that even Flitch serves innumerable functions in the book, heightening major themes, parodying characters of greater importance, and establishing necessary links in the plot. Intruding his pleas for restoration at crucial moments during the process of Clara's perception and then assertion of her need for freedom, Flitch accentuates her desire by its contrast to his own. At the same time, he helps demonstrate to her and others the extent to which Willoughby is ruled by a brutal egoism which makes him indifferent to the needs of anyone else and intransigent in insisting on the validity of his own whims. Furthermore, as a man bound to the consequences of a single decision, Flitch parodies in his fate the destinies of the major characters. For, ruled by the Goddess of Poetic Justice as they are observed by the Comic Muse, each must accept the future he essentially chooses, live with the results of his primary desire.

Each time he enters the scene, Flitch also serves more limited functions, sometimes advancing the plot, sometimes acting as a foil, sometimes reinforcing a motif. By and large, in his first and fourth appearances he acts mainly as a parodic figure; in his second and third, as an unwitting agent of providence, as Clara's unconscious guardian spirit. When Willoughby incomprehensibly shouts out his name, the world embodied in the novel seems momentarily to fall into chaos.

Language becomes nonsense, reduced to an indecipherable expletive. Though order and meaning soon reassert themselves, as we learn the significance of the word "Flitch," the experience Meredith provides of a possible failure of language prepares us for occasions when language truly either ceases to convey meaning or eludes the conscious control of the person using it. When Dr. Middleton, for example, is confronted by his paternal responsibilities, he escapes behind a smokescreen of pointless classical or philological allusions. Well before she is conscious of her love for Vernon Whitford, Clara makes it clear by her verbal slips, as she substitutes for his name that of Captain Oxford, the man who eloped with Willoughby's earlier *fiancée*. Most striking is Willoughby's lapse into incoherence when Clara finally petitions for release. His brains thoroughly scattered, the baronet evades her demand with a burst of jargon consisting of disconnected references to the uncleared breakfast dishes, the peculiarities of American diction, and the relative advantages of travel in different countries:

> He squeezed both her hands, threw the door wide open, and said, with countless blinkings: "In the laboratory we are uninterrupted. I was at a loss to guess where the most unpleasant effect on the senses came from. They are always 'guessing' through the nose. I mean, the remainder of breakfast here. Perhaps I satirized them too smartly—if you know the letters. When they are not 'calculating.' More offensive than debris of a midnight banquet. An American tour is instructive, though not so romantic. Not so romantic as Italy, I mean. Let us escape" (Chapter 15).

Here Willoughby too is throwing up a smoke screen, more to blind himself than to blind Clara. By this passage, as by numerous others, Meredith insists on the supple and volatile nature of language. Like every other medium of relationship between people, it can be used to obscure as well as to convey meaning. Like every mode of behavior, it easily escapes voluntary control.[1]

In a scene shortly before Willoughby shouts out "Flitch," he and Vernon have been arguing about what the baronet considers Vernon's irrational desire to quit Patterne for a literary life in London. Flitch's appearance provides Willoughby with an apt illustration as he continues to discuss the subject with

---

1. For further comment on Meredith's use of idiosyncracies of speech and thought for characterization, see Lionel Stevenson, *The Ordeal of George Mere-* *dith* (New York, 1953), pp. 226–29, and Deborah S. Austin, "Meredith on the Nature of Metaphor," *UTQ*, XXVII (1957), 96–102.

Clara. Drawing an explicit parallel between his cousin and his former coachman, Willoughby asserts that if Vernon leaves his protection, the divorce between them must be absolute. As Flitch has ceased to exist for Willoughby, so too will Vernon. Willoughby's insistent comparison of the two men convinces us that Vernon indeed is in peril, but we of course read that peril in a way wholly opposite to Willoughby's. By postponing his departure, Vernon risks becoming what Flitch now wishes to be, a bondsman. At Patterne he relinquishes his independent manhood, deprives himself of the chance to gain the individuality which Willoughby mistakenly assures him he can keep only by remaining. Meredith implies at the end of the chapter in which this conversation occurs that Vernon's present state even entails an essential barrenness. Clara comes upon him asleep under the tree he worships, the beautiful but unproductive double-blossom wild cherry, symbolic of nature tamed by artifice to a lovely sterility. In having Clara awaken him, Meredith suggests that she must awaken his manhood so that he may escape the graceful sterility of life at Patterne. Otherwise he faces the danger of becoming little more than an intellectual Flitch.

Flitch comes onto the scene for the second time driving the railway fly which bears the luggage of Willoughby's prospective best man, Horace De Craye. With De Craye's boxes are the fragments of his intended wedding-gift, a porcelain vase, smashed when Flitch was forced to swerve on the highway to avoid hitting Clara. This incident carries numerous symbolic implications, some of them obvious.[2] The destruction of the best man's present prefigures the destruction of the engagement, in large part through the agency of the best man himself. Furthermore, the circumstances of the accident represent Clara's present situation and her alternative courses of future action. Against the rules of Patterne, she has escaped for relief from Willoughby's smothering presence to the highway—to the "world" which Willoughby claims to abhor and from which he intends to isolate her. As her temporary escape endangers her physically, her larger movement for freedom does so socially and morally. In seeking to break her engagement, she risks the loss of her position as impeccable, well-bred young lady. To gain her escape, she will in effect have to submit to the destruction of another porcelain object, the artificial quality implicit in Mrs. Mountstuart Jenkinson's descrip-

2. R. D. Mayo discusses extensively the images of porcelain and especially the importance of the Willow Pattern. See *"The Egoist* and the Willow Pattern," *ELH*, IX (1942), 71–78. [Reprinted above, pp. 453–60.—*Editor.*]

tion of her as "a dainty rogue in porcelain." But the chinaware prison must be smashed if Clara is to be more than an object of fixed daintiness, indeed if she is to grow from a "rogue" into a woman. The alternative is that her essential nature be violated. Flitch is the agent who makes these alternatives clear when he causes the fly to overturn, saving Clara from personal harm but occasioning the destruction of the porcelain vase.

The accident which tumbles Horace De Craye's gift to the side of the highway tumbles Horace himself to Miss Middleton's feet, in a posture of clumsy adoration. This method of introduction benefits Clara invaluably. By encouraging a superficial intimacy between her and De Craye, it provides her with a willing ally. By suggesting an easy topic of conversation for them, it gives her an indirect means of expressing to him her situation and desire. With Vernon figuratively asleep, unable to offer substantial help, Clara needs the assistance of just such a facile man of the world as Horace De Craye: quick to understand social relations, sharp at reading hints, and adept at intrigue. She can maintain her honor while avoiding submission to Willoughby only if appearances are manipulated in such a way that Willoughby is forced to relinquish her voluntarily. For if she simply leaves him, she will be labeling herself a "jilt," and more importantly she will be breaking her word. De Craye, alerted to Clara's desire by her banter about Willoughby's inflexible harshness to Flitch, aids her by his social agility and by his very presence as the object of Willoughby's jealousy. In a larger sense, Horace creates the opportunity for Clara to gain the command of artificial behavior which every young girl must have to achieve—but not suppress—her natural desires.

Because of his very usefulness, however, De Craye presents a threat to Clara. Eager to take personal advantage of her situation, he suavely but ostentatiously presses himself upon her. Should Clara weaken sufficiently to run away, all the world will attribute her behavior to love for De Craye. Most significantly, Vernon Whitford will concur, and Clara will thus be prevented from gaining the husband she should have. By aiding her selfishly instead of disinterestedly, De Craye earns the fate he suffers at the end of the novel, when he sits figuratively where Flitch had deposited him literally—at Clara's feet, in an awkward position of worship.

Flitch continues to serve Clara's interests in his third appearance, which occurs at the turning point of the action: the moment when Clara, intolerably wearied by Willoughby's cleverness in maintaining her captive, is about to board a train for sanctuary with her friend Lucy Darleton. Vernon has just left her, unable to persuade her to return to Patterne. As Clara prepares to embark, Flitch drives up in the railway fly, carrying Horace De Craye. This situation engenders multiple misunderstandings which lead to the unraveling of the plot. More significantly, it presents Clara with crucial knowledge of her own desires, and it forces her to behave in the only way worthy of her. Fearing that Vernon may have seen De Craye, she goes back to Patterne lest he assume that she and Horace were acting in concert. Though not yet fully aware of her love for Whitford, she now knows that what she most values is his good opinion. Only the opportune arrival of Flitch saves her from breaking her promise and thus meriting the inevitable disapproval of society and of Vernon himself.

In arriving with De Craye and in transporting Clara back to the Patterne, Flitch acts as her unconscious good angel, as he did earlier when he presented Horace to her at the edge of the highway. Meredith emphasizes this role when he later shows the coachman returning a purse Clara had left in the fly. As Flitch says, the purse is "intact" (Chapter 34), and in effect Flitch has also returned Clara "intact," unflawed by dishonesty or by the compromising protection which Horace threatens to force upon her. Though Meredith never says so, Flitch's unknowing services seem the direct—if inexplicable—result of Clara's championing of him. Later in the novel, the boy Crossjay is also given the accidental chance to aid her, apparently because of the love and care with which she has watched over him. In the world of *The Egoist*, the gods work deviously and often invisibly to assure that one reaps what one sows.

On Flitch's final entrance, Meredith permits him briefly to command the stage with his own voice. Licensed by his return of the purse and fortified in the classical manner, the coachman addresses an eloquent plea for reinstatement to Willoughby and Mrs. Mountstuart, who are gathered with most of the other characters in the gardens at Patterne. Flitch bases his petition not on the needs of his family, but on his nostalgic recollection of the good old days, when he used to toast the young heir at Christmas in the old port wine. Indulging himself in what Meredith calls a "feast of pathos," he likens himself to Adam cast out of Paradise and to the Hebrew people in the bondage of Egypt (Chapter 34).

In this scene, Flitch serves as a sharp parody of two of the prime egoists of the book, Dr. Middleton and especially Willoughby himself. Flitch's drunkenness, reminiscences about the old wine, and failure to mention his family bring to mind

Dr. Middleton's recent disregard of paternal duty under the Circean spell of Willoughby's ninety-year-old port. As Clara thinks, the wine "expelled reasonableness, fatherliness" from Dr. Middleton (Chapter 24). Despite his usual temperance and hard good sense, Dr. Middleton becomes changed by the superb port into a slothful glutton, concerned only with his own comfort, a man no better than the ludicrous Flitch.

In his "feast of pathos," Flitch also resembles the master of Patterne. A great egoist, Willoughby is no less a great sentimentalist, forever casting his thoughts and speeches in the language of fifth-rate romantic fiction. Upon Clara's arrival at Patterne early in the novel, for example, he greets her with a characteristic burst of lover's rhetoric:

> "You are mine, my Clara—utterly mine; every thought, every feeling. We are one: the world may do its worst. I have been longing for you, looking forward. You save me from a thousand vexations. One is perpetually crossed. That is all outside us. We two! With you I am secure! Soon! I could not tell you whether the world's alive or dead. My dearest!" (Chapter 7).

Later, furiously jealous, he soothes himself by imagining the future in terms of a pulp novel: Clara—cast-off, humiliated, and penitent—begs forgiveness for having left Willoughby, wishing only to be allowed to think of him as her friend. He, gently condescending, comforts her with just sufficient intimacy to compromise her reputation further.

In moments of tension, Willoughby almost always fortifies himself with a strong dose of self-pity. But in pity, as in all else, he cannot be self-sufficient. He needs the concurrence of at least part of the world he pretends to despise. Eternally protective of his pride, however, he must evoke the comforting pity he requires while obscuring the true reasons he requires it. These complex desires result in two scenes with Laetitia Dale which are riots of pathos. The first, which comes not long before Flitch indulges in his own pathetic feast, appears in a chapter aptly entitled "Sir Willoughby Attempts and Achieves Pathos" (Chapter 31). In it, Willoughby dazzles Laetitia with a series of sentimental non sequiturs meant simultaneously to brand Clara a traitor, conceal the extent of her betrayal, and demonstrate the largeness of spirit with which the baronet views that betrayal as a sad example of human frailty. Even more, Willoughby wishes to solace himself by provoking in Laetitia some sign that she still worships him. The satisfaction with which he sees her break into tears is ironic, for she weeps in fact for the loss of her illusion of his perfection. This loss causes her torture in Willoughby's next great venture into pathos, his midnight proposal of marriage. In this scene, Willoughby becomes another Flitch, waxing nostalgic about the past as he insists to Laetitia on her legendary adoration of him and even goes so far as to quote the idolatrous verses she wrote on his coming of age.

Though Laetitia resists this appeal, she of course later accepts Willoughby, but only after forcing him to perceive—however briefly—her lack of love and his own faults.[3] We may feel sorry for Laetita, but she gets only what she deserves and what she has most strongly desired. So it is with all the characters, save Dr. Middleton perhaps, in the cluster of marriages, literal and figurative, with which the novel concludes. Willoughby is able to maintain appearances, though at the cost of taking an unloving and faded wife, a heavy price for a man who wished all women to worship him and who could not bear that the bloom of any young girl go untouched by his hand. Horace De Craye and Mrs. Mountstuart ride off together into an eternity of witty banter. Crossjay, who had been threatened with being made an idle dependent of Sir Willoughby, will study with a tutor in preparation for the Navy. Clara and Vernon, perfected by their responses to each other, will soon become united in the Alps, the geographical symbol opposed to Patterne throughout the book. And Adam Flitch, the perennial servitor, released from the bondage of freedom to the freedom of bondage, will return to the Eden which could be a Paradise for him alone.

VIRGINIA WOOLF

The Novels of George Meredith†

Twenty years ago[1] the reputation of George Meredith was at its height. His novels had won their way to celebrity through all sorts of difficulties, and their fame was all the

---

3. John Espey has pointed out to me that Laetitia's insistence on Flitch's restoration intensifies Meredith's irony, for Flitch's name would have recalled to Victorian readers the "Dunmow flitch," a side of bacon traditionally awarded at Dunmow in Essex to any married couple who could prove that they had lived in conjugal harmony for a year and a day. Such plays on names are, of course, common in *The Egoist*. De Craye's remark to Willoughby (Chapter 18, p. 142) makes this reference clear when he says: " '. . . 'Tis Flitch, my dear Willoughby, has been and stirred the native in me, and we'll present him to you for the like good office when we hear after a number of years that you've not wrinkled your forehead once at your liege lady.' "
† From *The Second Common Reader* (New York, 1932; reprinted 1960).
1. Written in January, 1928.

brighter and the more singular for what it had subdued. Then, too, it was generally discovered that the maker of these splendid books was himself a splendid old man. Visitors who went down to Box Hill reported that they were thrilled as they walked up the drive of the little suburban house by the sound of a voice booming and reverberating within. The novelist, seated among the usual knick-knacks of the drawing-room, was like the bust of Euripides to look at. Age had worn and sharpened the fine features, but the nose was still acute, the blue eyes still keen and ironical. Though he had sunk immobile into an arm-chair, his aspect was still vigorous and alert. It was true that he was almost stone-deaf, but this was the least of afflictions to one who was scarcely able to keep pace with the rapidity of his own ideas. Since he could not hear what was said to him, he could give himself whole-heartedly to the delights of soliloquy. It did not much matter, perhaps, whether his audience was cultivated or simple. Compliments that would have flattered a duchess were presented with equal ceremony to a child. To neither could he speak the simple language of daily life. But all the time this highly wrought, artificial conversation, with its crystallised phrases and its highpiled metaphors, moved and tossed on a current of laughter. His laugh curled round his sentences as if he himself enjoyed their humorous exaggeration. The master of language was splashing and diving in his element of words. So the legend grew; and the fame of George Meredith, who sat with the head of a Greek poet on his shoulders in a suburban villa beneath Box Hill, pouring out poetry and sarcasm and wisdom in a voice that could be heard almost on the high road, made his fascinating and brilliant books seem more fascinating and brilliant still.

But that is twenty years ago. His fame as a talker is necessarily dimmed, and his fame as a writer seems also under a cloud. On none of his successors is his influence now marked. When one of them whose own work has given him the right to be heard with respect chances to speak his mind on the subject, it is not flattering.

> Meredith [writes Mr. Forster in his *Aspects of Fiction*] is not the great name he was twenty years ago. . . . His philosophy has not worn well. His heavy attacks on sentimentality—they bore the present generation. . . . When he gets serious and noble-minded there is a strident overtone, a bullying that becomes distressing. . . . What with the faking, what with the preaching, which was never agreeable and is now

said to be hollow, and what with the home counties posing as
the universe, it is no wonder Meredith now lies in the trough.

The criticism is not, of course, intended to be a finished estimate; but in its conversational sincerity it condenses accurately enough what is in the air when Meredith is mentioned. No, the general conclusion would seem to be,
Meredith has not worn well. But the value of centenaries lies
in the occasion they offer us for solidifying such airy impressions. Talk, mixed with half-rubbed-out memories, forms a
mist by degrees through which we scarely see plain. To open
the books again, to try to read them as if for the first time, to
try to free them from the rubbish of reputation and accident
—that, perhaps, is the most acceptable present we can offer to
a writer on his hundredth birthday.

And since the first novel is always apt to be an unguarded
one, where the author displays his gifts without knowing how
to dispose of them to the best advantage, we may do well to
open *Richard Feverel* first. It needs no great sagacity to see
that the writer is a novice at his task. The style is extremely
uneven. Now he twists himself into iron knots; now he lies flat
as a pancake. He seems to be of two minds as to his intention.
Ironic comment alternates with long-winded narrative. He
vacillates from one attitude to another. Indeed, the whole
fabric seems to rock a little insecurely. The baronet wrapped
in a cloak; the county family; the ancestral home; the uncles
mouthing epigrams in the dining-room; the great ladies flaunt-
ing and swimming; the jolly farmers slapping their thighs: all
liberally if spasmodically sprinkled with dried aphorisms from
a pepper-pot called the Pilgrim's Scrip—what an odd con-
glomeration it is! But the oddity is not on the surface; it is not
merely that whiskers and bonnets have gone out of fashion: it
lies deeper, in Meredith's intention, in what he wishes to bring
to pass. He has been, it is plain, at great pains to destroy the
conventional form of the novel. He makes no attempt to preserve the sober reality of Trollope and Jane Austen; he has
destroyed all the usual staircases by which we have learnt to
climb. And what is done so deliberately is done with a purpose. This defiance of the ordinary, these airs and graces, the
formality of the dialogue with its Sirs and Madams are all
there to create an atmosphere that is unlike that of daily life,
to prepare the way for a new and an original sense of the
human scene. Peacock, from whom Meredith learnt so much,
is equally arbitrary, but the virtue of the assumptions he asks

us to make is proved by the fact that we accept Mr. Skionar
and the rest with natural delight.[2] Meredith's characters in
Richard Feverel, on the other hand, are at odds with their
surroundings. We at once exclaim how unreal they are, how
artificial, how impossible. The baronet and the butler, the hero
and the heroine, the good woman and the bad woman are
mere types of baronets and butler, good women and bad. For
what reason, then, has he sacrificed the substantial advantages
of realistic common sense—the staircase and the stucco? Because, it becomes clear as we read, he possessed a keen sense
not of the complexity of character, but of the splendour of a
scene. One after another in this first book he creates a scene to
which we can attach abstract names—Youth, The Birth of
Love, The Power of Nature. We are galloped to them over
every obstacle on the pounding hoofs of rhapsodical prose.

Away with Systems! Away with a corrupt World! Let us
breathe the air of the Enchanted Island! Golden lie the meadows; golden run the streams; red gold is on the pine stems.

We forget that Richard is Richard and that Lucy is Lucy;
they are youth; the world runs molten gold. The writer is a
rhapsodist, a poet then; but we have not yet exhausted all the
elements in this first novel. We have to reckon with the author
himself. He has a mind stuffed with ideas, hungry for argument. His boys and girls may spend their time picking daisies
in the meadows, but they breathe, however unconsciously, an
air bristling with intellectual question and comment. On a
dozen occasions these incongruous elements strain and
threaten to break apart. The book is cracked through and
through with those fissures which come when the author
seems to be of twenty minds at the same time. Yet it succeeds
in holding miraculously together, not certainly by the depths
and originality of its character drawing but by the vigour of its
intellectual power and by its lyrical intensity.

We are left, then, with our curiosity aroused. Let him write
another book or two; get into his stride; control his crudities:
and we will open *Harry Richmond*[3] and see what has happened now. Of all the things that might have happened this
surely is the strangest. All trace of immaturity is gone; but
with it every trace of the uneasy adventurous mind has gone
too. The story bowls smoothly along the road which Dickens
has already trodden of autobiographical narrative. It is a boy

2. Thomas Love Peacock was the father
of Meredith's first wife; Mr. Skionar is a
character in his novel *Crotchet Castle*.

[*Editor.*]
3. The novel in question is *The Adventures of Harry Richmond*. [*Editor.*]

speaking, a boy thinking, a boy adventuring. For that reason, no doubt, the author has curbed his redundance and pruned his speech. The style is the most rapid possible. It runs smooth, without a kink in it. Stevenson, one feels, must have learnt much from this supple narrative, with its precise adroit phrases, its exact quick glance at visible things.

> Plunged among dark green leaves, smelling wood-smoke, at night; at morning waking up, and the world alight, and you standing high, and marking the hills where you will see the next morning and the next, morning after morning, and one morning the dearest person in the world surprising you just before you wake: I thought this a heavenly pleasure.

It goes gallantly, but a little self-consciously. He hears himself talking. Doubts begin to rise and hover and settle at last (as in *Richard Feverel*) upon the human figures. These boys are no more real boys than the sample apple which is laid on top of the basket is a real apple. They are too simple, too gallant, too adventurous to be of the same unequal breed as David Copperfield, for example. They are sample boys, novelist's specimens; and again we encounter the extreme conventionality of Meredith's mind where we found it, to our surprise, before. With all his boldness (and there is no risk that he will not run with probability) there are a dozen occasions on which a reach-me-down character will satisfy him well enough. But just as we are thinking that the young gentlemen are altogether too pat, and the adventures which befall them altogether too slick, the shallow bath of illusion closes over our heads and we sink with Richmond Roy and the Princess Ottilia into the world of fantasy and romance, where all holds together and we are able to put our imagination at the writer's service without reserve. That such surrender is above all things delightful: that it adds spring-heels to our boots: that it fires the cold scepticism out of us and makes the world glow in lucid transparency before our eyes, needs no showing, as it certainly submits to no analysis. That Meredith can induce such moments proves him possessed of an extraordinary power. Yet it is a capricious power and highly intermittent. For pages all is effort and agony; phrase after phrase is struck and no light comes. Then, just as we are about to drop the book, the rocket roars into the air; the whole scene flashes into light; and the book, years after, is recalled by that sudden splendour.

If, then, this intermittent brilliancy is Meredith's characteristic excellence, it is worth while to look into it more closely.

And perhaps the first thing that we shall discover is that the scenes which catch the eye and remain in memory are static; they are illuminations, not discoveries; they do not improve our knowledge of the characters. It is significant that Richard and Lucy, Harry and Ottilia, Clara and Vernon, Beauchamp and Renée[4] are presented in carefully appropriate surroundings—on board a yacht, under a flowering cherry tree, upon some river-bank, so that the landscape always makes part of the emotion. The sea or the sky or the wood is brought forward to symbolise what the human beings are feeling or looking.

> The sky was bronze, a vast furnace dome. The folds of light and shadow everywhere were satin rich. That afternoon the bee hummed of thunder and refreshed the ear.

That is a description of a state of mind.

> These winter mornings are divine. They move on noiselessly. The earth is still as if waiting. A wren warbles, and flits through the lank, drenched branches; hillside opens green; everywhere is mist, everywhere expectancy.

That is a description of a woman's face. But only some states of mind and some expressions of face can be described in imagery—only those which are so highly wrought as to be simple and, for that reason, will not submit to analysis. This is a limitation; for though we may be able to see these people, very brilliantly, in a moment of illumination, they do not change or grow; the light sinks and leaves us in darkness. We have no such intuitive knowledge of Meredith's characters as we have of Stendhal's, Tchehov's, Jane Austen's. Indeed, our knowledge of such characters is so intimate that we can almost dispense with "great scenes" altogether. Some of the most emotional scenes in fiction are the quietest. We have been wrought upon by nine hundred and ninety-nine little touches; the thousandth, when it comes, is as slight as the others, but the effect is prodigious. But with Meredith there are no touches; there are hammer-strokes only, so that our knowledge of his characters is partial, spasmodic, and intermittent.

Meredith, then, is not among the great psychologists who feel their way, anonymously and patiently, in and out of the fibres of the mind and make one character differ minutely and completely from another. He is among the poets who identify the character with the passion or with the idea; who symbolise

---

4. Richard and Lucy, Harry and Ottilia, Clara and Vernon, Beauchamp and Renée are the romantic leads of *The Ordeal of Richard Feverel*, *The Adventures of Harry Richmond*, *The Egoist*, and *Beauchamp's Career*. [*Editor.*]

and make abstract. And yet—here lay his difficulty perhaps—
he was not a poet-novelist wholly and completely as Emily
Brontë was a poet-novelist. He did not steep the world in one
mood. His mind was too self-conscious, and too sophisticated
to remain lyrical for long. He does not sing only; he dissects.
Even in his most lyrical scenes a sneer curls its lash round the
phrases and laughs at their extravagance. And as we read on,
we shall find that the comic spirit, when it is allowed to dominate the scene, licked the world to a very different shape. *The
Egoist* at once modifies our theory that Meredith is pre-
eminently the master of great scenes. Here there is none of
that precipitate hurry that has rushed us over obstacles to the
summit of one emotional peak after another. The case is one
that needs argument; argument needs logic; Sir Willoughby,
"our original male in giant form", is turned slowly round before a steady fire of scrutiny and criticism which allows no
twitch on the victim's part to escape it. That the victim is a
wax model and not entirely living flesh and blood is perhaps
true. At the same time Meredith pays us a supreme compliment to which as novel-readers we are little accustomed. We
are civilised people, he seems to say, watching the comedy of
human relations together. Human relations are of profound
interest. Men and women are not cats and monkeys, but beings of a larger growth and of a greater range. He imagines us
capable of disinterested curiosity in the behaviour of our kind.
This is so rare a compliment from a novelist to his reader that
we are at first bewildered and then delighted. Indeed his
comic spirit is a far more penetrating goddess than his lyrical.
It is she who cuts a clear path through the brambles of his
manner; she who surprises us again and again by the depth of
her observations; she who creates the dignity, the seriousness,
and the vitality of Meredith's world. Had Meredith, one is
tempted to reflect, lived in an age or in a country where
comedy was the rule, he might never have contracted those
airs of intellectual superiority, that manner of oracular solem-
nity which it is, as he points out, the use of the comic spirit to
correct.

But in many ways the age—if we can judge so amorphous a
shape—was hostile to Meredith, or, to speak more accurately,
was hostile to his success with the age we now live in—the
year 1928. His teaching seems now too strident and too optimistic and too shallow. It obtrudes; and when philosophy is
not consumed in a novel, when we can underline this phrase
with a pencil, and cut out that exhortation with a pair of
scissors and paste the whole into a system, it is safe to say that

there is something wrong with the philosophy or with the novel or with both. Above all, his teaching is too insistent. He cannot, even to hear the profoundest secret, suppress his own opinion. And there is nothing that characters in fiction resent more. If, they seem to argue, we have been called into existence merely to express Mr. Meredith's views upon the universe, we would rather not exist at all. Thereupon they die; and a novel that is full of dead characters, even though it is also full of profound wisdom and exalted teaching, is not achieving its aim as a novel. But here we reach another point upon which the present age may be inclined to have more sympathy with Meredith. When he wrote, in the seventies and eighties of the last century, the novel had reached a stage where it could only exist by moving onward. It is a possible contention that after those two perfect novels, *Pride and Prejudice* and *The Small House at Allington*, English fiction had to escape from the dominion of that perfection, as English poetry had to escape from the perfection of Tennyson. George Eliot, Meredith, and Hardy were all imperfect novelists largely because they insisted upon introducing qualities, of thought and of poetry, that are perhaps incompatible with fiction at its most perfect. On the other hand, if fiction had remained what it was to Jane Austen and Trollope, fiction would by this time be dead. Thus Meredith deserves our gratitude and excites our interest as a great innovator. Many of our doubts about him and much of our inability to frame any definite opinion of his work comes from the fact that it is experimental and thus contains elements that do not fuse harmoniously—the qualities are at odds: the one quality which binds and concentrates has been omitted. To read Meredith, then, to our greatest advantage we must make certain allowances and relax certain standards. We must not expect the perfect quietude of a traditional style nor the triumphs of a patient and pedestrian psychology. On the other hand, his claim, "My method has been to prepare my readers for a crucial exhibition of the personae, and then to give the scene in the fullest of their blood and brain under stress of a fierce situation", is frequently justified. Scene after scene rises on the mind's eye with a flare of fiery intensity. If we are irritated by the dancing-master dandyism which made him write "gave his lungs full play" instead of laughed, or "tasted the swift intricacies of the needle" instead of sewed, we must remember that such phrases prepare the way for the "fierce situations". Meredith is creating the atmosphere from which we shall pass naturally into a highly pitched state of emotion.

Where the realistic novelist, like Trollope, lapses into flatness
and dullness, the lyrical novelist, like Meredith, becomes
meretricious and false; and such falsity is, of course, not only
much more glaring than flatness, but it is a greater crime
against the phlegmatic nature of prose fiction. Perhaps Meredith had been well advised if he had abjured the novel altogether and kept himself wholly to poetry. Yet we have to
remind ourselves that the fault may be ours. Our prolonged
diet upon Russian fiction, rendered neutral and negative in
translation, our absorption in the convolutions of psychological Frenchmen, may have led us to forget that the English
language is naturally exuberant, and the English character full
of humours and eccentricities. Meredith's flamboyancy has a
great ancestry behind it; we cannot avoid all memory of
Shakespeare.

When such questions and qualifications crowd upon us as
we read, the fact may be taken to prove that we are neither
near enough to be under his spell nor far enough to see him in
proportion. Thus the attempt to pronounce a finished estimate
is even more illusive than usual. But we can testify even now
that to read Meredith is to be conscious of a packed and
muscular mind; of a voice booming and reverberating with its
own unmistakable accent even though the partition between
us is too thick for us to hear what he says distinctly. Still, as
we read we feel that we are in the presence of a Greek god
though he is surrounded by the innumerable ornaments of a
suburban drawing-room; who talks brilliantly, even if he is
deaf to the lower tones of the human voice; who, if he is rigid
and immobile, is yet marvellously alive and on the alert. This
brilliant and uneasy figure has his place with the great eccen-
trics rather than with the great masters. He will be read, one
may guess, by fits and starts; he will be forgotten and discovered and again discovered and forgotten like Donne, and
Peacock, and Gerard Hopkins. But if English fiction continues
to be read, the novels of Meredith must inevitably rise from
time to time into view; his work must inevitably be disputed
and discussed.

JOHN LUCAS
Meredith's Reputation†

Anyone who so much as glances over the history of Meredith's reputation is bound to notice how very odd it is. It may

† From *Meredith Now*, ed. Ian Fletcher (London, 1971).

even be unique, at least as far as English literature is concerned. Certainly it is not easy to think of a parallel. Meredith is not the object of a cult-worship, for example. There is no evidence that successive generations of admirers have for him the sort of smouldering affection that occasionally breaks out into flame, a flame that is always kept well-stoked and banked. He is not, let us say, like Kipling. But then neither is he like Philip James Bailey. His reputation came to him late, grew steadily until his death, and a few years later was gone. He never had the following of a Dickens or even a George Eliot. Yet amongst his admirers he was unswervingly regarded as a great artist. When they spoke of him, it tended to be in reverential whispers. 'Of course,' Richard Le Gallienne wrote, recalling a visit to Box Hill during the 1890s, 'the wonderful thing was that the novelist who wrote of Lucy and Richard by the river and the poet of "Love in the Valley" should actually be reading to me at all. It was almost like listening to Shakespeare read *Hamlet*."[1] But a few years after his death the whispers turned into rude noises. In 1918 Ezra Pound wrote to tell John Quinn that Meredith is 'chiefly a stink'.[2] It seems a remark of terrible finality.

Not even Pound, however, can so easily dispose of a writer. And Meredith, after all, has had later critics. Since the Second World War there have been full-length studies by such critics as Sassoon, Jack Lindsay, Lionel Stevenson and Norman Kelvin; and there will no doubt be others.

Yet if the growing library of Meredith studies proves anything it is that Meredith is more or less a dead issue. He may help establish an academic reputation or boost a publications list, but he is not essentially a living force. Every so often a well-intentioned person spots him, dusty and neglected, takes him down from the shelf of forgotten writers and sticks the label 're-discovered' on him. But it comes off. Nobody notices. And back on the shelf he goes. To be sure, there is the *Egoist*, there is 'Modern Love'; there is even the *Comic Spirit*. But for the rest? Little is reprinted. Very little is read. Hardly anything is known. Meredith seems one with Revett, with Lever, with Dallas. Sixty years ago the books on him poured out, all intended to help establish or simply salute the deathless reputation. And such titles! *George Meredith, His Life, Genius and Teaching; George Meredith, a Primer to the Novels; George Meredith, His Life and Art in Anecdote and Criticism; George Meredith, Novelist, Poet, Reformer; The Philosophy and Po-*

1. Richard Le Gallienne, *The Romantic 90s*, 1926, 40.

2. *The Letters of Ezra Pound, 1907–1941*, 1950, 137.

etry of George Meredith; George Meredith, a Study (a sober
enough title, but the authoress makes up for it by a breathless
insistence that 'Shakespearian is the word to describe Meredith').[3] 'His words wing on as live words will', Hardy wrote at
the time of Meredith's death.[4] In fact, they have plummeted
out of sight—or almost. How did it happen?

The nature of the reputation itself must take most of the
blame. It is a fact of literary history that Meredith became
accepted as a great master in the 1890s. In 1898, for example,
T.H.S. Escott wrote that Meredith is 'the foremost of English
novelists now living', and he remarked that although, like
Browning, Meredith had suffered from years of neglect and
indifference the situation was now being corrected. In both
cases the invincible indifference of the inappreciative has

> been coerced into a meek acquiescence in the beauties of a
> genius which it would require the same courage to deny to
> the one as to the other.[5]

Escott's praise is a form of canonization. This does not mean
that Meredith was suddenly discovered in the 1890s, or that his
election to the Presidency of the Society of Authors following
Tennyson's death in 1892 was unpredictable. But the plain
fact is that in the 1890s the audience which Meredith himself
had called the 'acute but honourable minority' became both
larger and more assertive. It is in the 1890s that comparisons
between Meredith and Shakespeare become commonplace.
Hannah Lynch and Richard Le Gallienne are not alone in
coupling the names; most commentators on Meredith did.
Perhaps the first was W. E. Henley. In an essay of 1879 he
called Meredith Shakespearian, four years later Mark Pattison
repeated the claim,[6] and R. L. Stevenson told an American
reporter that *Rhoda Fleming* 'is the strongest thing in English
letters since Shakespeare died, and if Shakespeare could have
read it he would have jumped and cried, "Here's a fellow!"'[7]
By the time Meredith died it seemed unthinkable not to make
the comparison. Sturge Henderson noted that Meredith's novels 'include a horizon, they allow for the uncluttered part of
our speech; and this is probably the truth that has been aimed
at in the comparison of his works with Shakespeare's'.[8] J. A.
Hammerton quotes Elton's essay in which Elton says that

3. Hannah Lynch, *George Meredith. A
Study*, 1891, 39.
4. T. Hardy, 'George Meredith', *Collected
Poems*, 1960, 280.
5. T. H. S. Escott, *Personal Forces of the
Period*, 1898, 254, 256.

6. See *George Meredith, Some Early Appreciations*, ed. Forman, 1909, 193, 227.
7. L. Stevenson, *The Ordeal of George
Meredith*, 1954, 277.
8. M. Sturge Henderson, *George Meredith, Novelist, Poet, Reformer*, 1907, 42.

'Meredith is sound like Shakespeare',[9] Photiadès simply asserts that 'Meredith bears a greater resemblance to Shakespeare than any other novelist', and Trevelyan claims that 'Modern Love' has the 'same kind of spiritual and intellectual beauty as saves *Othello* from being morbid, and *Hamlet* from being decadent'.[1]

The comparison with Shakespeare is not really a studied or suggestive one. It is merely a way of asserting Meredith's stature. And the very interesting feature of Meredith criticism in the 1890s is that most of his admirers insist that his greatness is more or less proved by the fact that he had been for so long ignored or treated with contempt. This brings us to the famous argument about Meredith's obscurity. The sceptical insisted that Meredith was difficult and rapidly getting worse. But for the admirers obscurity, so called, required commendation. Meredith, they argued, was obscure or difficult only for those who had neither the patience, intelligence nor sensitivity to understand him. He did not pander to his audience, he challenged his readers to follow him. '[Meredith] reaches his thought by means of ladders which he kicks away', James Barrie wrote. 'Too sluggish to climb, the public sit in the rear, flinging his jargon at his head, yet aware, if they have heads themselves, that one of the great intellects of the age is on in front.'[2] Amy Cruse, who lived through the period of Meredith's greatest fame, reaches to the heart of the matter:

> For the true Meredithians . . . it was this intellectual brilliance that gave his works their greatest attraction. It attracted also a large number of painstaking readers who, admiring intellect above all things, and longing to be—and to be recognized as—its possessors, often succeeded in persuading themselves—and others—that they read with pleasure. Earnest young men and women belonging to Literary Societies wrote papers full of psychology and sociology, ethics and dialectics on the works of Meredith, but usually failed to convince the unregenerate majority among their fellow members.[3]

As the tone of that passage very clearly shows, Amy Cruse was herself one of the unregenerate; and altogether Meredith and the Meredithians had to put up with a good deal of mockery throughout the 1890s. Quite apart from Oscar Wilde's famous

9. J. A. Hammerton, *George Meredith, Life and Art in Anecdote and Criticism*, rev. ed., 1911, 310.

1. G. M. Trevelyan, *The Philosophy and Poetry of George Meredith*, 1906, 21.

2. Quoted in Amy Cruse, *After the Victorians*, 1935, 174.

3. *Ibid.*, 175.

gibe about Meredith and Browning (a commonplace comparison that had been given an early airing in the *Tobacco Plant* for May 1879, where it was suggested that Meredith was the 'Robert Browning of our novelists' and that 'his day is bound to come, as Browning's at length has come')[4] there is Mrs Windsor of the *Green Carnation*, who remarks that

> Mr. Amarinth says that he is going to bring out a new edition of [Meredith's works], 'done into English' by himself. It is such a good idea and would help the readers so much. I believe he could make a lot of money by it, but it would be very difficult to do, I suppose. However, Mr. Amarinth is so clever that he might manage it.[5]

Still, gibes, jeers and jokes clearly mean that Meredith had become a force to be reckoned with. The interesting point is that not all could make up their minds as to what sort of a force he was. George Saintsbury, for example. In 1896 Saintsbury published a *History of Nineteenth Century Literature*, and in the chapters 'The Second Poetical Period' and 'The Novel since 1860' Meredith is conspicuous by his absence. Browning, Arnold, the Rossettis, Thomson, George Eliot, Kingsley, the Trollopes, Stevenson—yes, they and many more are there. But not Meredith. And yet he is listed as part of the achievement of English fiction in the nineteenth century. Not even France, Saintsbury says, can 'show such a "gallaxy-gallery" as the British novelists'.[6] And he mentions Dickens, Thackeray and Meredith. It is something of a facing-all-ways position.

But if Saintsbury and a few others hedged their bets, most commentators backed Meredith wholeheartedly. 'Meredith is one of the greatest artists of our time', James Oliphant declared in 1899, 'indeed [he is] the only living writer of English novels who can be ranked unhesitatingly among the giants.'[7] As for his obscurity—well, 'No one has ever tried to make words convey so much meaning as Meredith, and very few have had so much meaning to express.'[8] And most of Meredith's champions saw in his alleged obscurity an opportunity to attack the hostile, indifferent or plain ignorant public. The champions are not merely the young and earnest whom Amy Cruse indicates. There are also practising writers, Le Gallienne, Stevenson, Henley, and above all Gissing.

---

4. *George Meredith: Some Early Appreciations*, 194.
5. Robert Hichens, *The Green Carnation*, 1894, 44.
6. G. Saintsbury, *A History of Nineteenth Century Literature*, 1896, 444.
7. J. Oliphant, *Victorian Novelists*, 1899, 143.
8. *Ibid.*, 146.

Gissing may not have been of substantial help in building Meredith's reputation, but he does provide substantial reasons for its immense authority. For what Gissing says about Meredith is clear proof of how Meredith's reputation belongs to the history of taste and was *bound* to rise at the end of the nineteenth century. 'He is great, there is no doubt of it', Gissing wrote to his brother in 1885, 'but too difficult for the British public. What good thing is not?'[9] A little later he is telling the same person that

> George Eliot never did such work, and Thackeray is shallow in comparison. . . . For the last thirty years he has been producing work unspeakably above the best of any living writer and yet no one reads him outside a small circle of highly cultured people. Perhaps that is better than being popular, a hateful word.[1]

There is no doubt that Gissing takes Meredith's cause very much to heart, since his own comparative failure to attract attention embittered him against popularity and the public. Meredith indeed could easily become the hero for all those writers who in the last years of the nineteenth century saw a wedge being driven between art and popularity and for whom the rise of the best-seller spelled the doom of the novel as a serious literary form. From now on to be good was to be unpopular. In an important essay on the art of fiction in the 1880s, John Goode has pointed out that it is during the penultimate decade of the nineteenth century that a really radical and apparently unbridgeable gap between good and popular novels begins to open up. Gissing's attitude to Meredith may well have been sharpened by the debate between Sir Walter Besant and Henry James on the art of fiction, which had taken place in 1884.[2] Certainly, he himself was deeply concerned with what he took to be the impossibility of his ever achieving much fame or due notice; and what he says of Edwin Reardon in the semi-autobiographical *New Grub Street* of 1891 comes very close to what he had said of Meredith in 1885: 'Strong characterization was within his scope, and an intellectual fervour, appetising to a small section of refined readers, marked all his best pages.'[3] Reardon is not Meredith, but Jasper Milvain's remark that Reardon is 'the old type of unpractical artist' who 'won't make concessions, or rather . . . can't make

9. *Letters of George Gissing to Members of his Family*, 1927, 155.
1. *Ibid.*, 170–72.
2. See 'The Art of Fiction: Walter Besant and Henry James', in *Tradition and Tolerance in Nineteenth Century Fiction*, Howard, Lucas and Goode, 1966.
3. *New Grub Street*, Penguin Books, 1968, 93.

them; he can't supply the market'[4]—that might easily have
been said of Meredith. The fact that he did not write the sort
of novels which would assure him of a sizeable audience came
to be seen as an essential part of his integrity. And, in all
fairness, it has to be said that Meredith was a novelist of
integrity. As far as his reputation is concerned, the result of
this refusal to supply the market could be seen as proof of his
unswerving dedication to his art, so that it was customary to
admire—indeed venerate—him less for what he had accomplished than for what he stood for. Meredith, quite simply,
became a cause to rally round. His obscurity was a useful
pointer to his integrity, and where in the 1860s Justin Mc-
Carthy might regret that 'Meredith is too much the thinking
man';[5] by the latter half of the 1880s he could not be too much
of a thinking man for his admirers. 'Get hold of *Diana of the
Crossways*', Gissing told his brother. 'It needs to be read twice
or even three times, but that is because there is more "brain
stuff" in the book, than many I have read for long.'[6] No use
for Conan Doyle to grumble that Meredith was 'clever, but
neither interesting nor intelligible'.[7] Lafcadio Hearn put the
case for the admirers when, in an essay of 1900, he declared
Meredith to be

> the poet of scholars; the poet of men of culture. Only a man
> of culture can really like him—just as only a man long ac-
> customed to good living can appreciate the best kinds of
> wine. Give wine to a poor man accustomed only to drink
> coarse spirits, and he will not care about it. So the common
> reader cannot care about Meredith. He is what we call a
> 'test-poet'—your culture, your capacity to think and feel, is
> tested by your ability to like such a poet. The question, 'Do
> you like Meredith?' is now in English and even in French
> literary circles, a test.[8]

Reading that now, you feel that with friends like Hearn
Meredith hardly needs enemies. And there is no doubt that it
was Hearn's sort of snobbish adulation that helped create such
a sharp reaction against the reputation. Still, Hearn's remarks
are justified to the extent that in poetry and prose alike Meredith's 'obscurity' sprang from his wanting to be taken seriously
as a great thinker. Indeed, he wanted to be a philosophical
writer. Perhaps his admirers found it easier to convert ambi-

4. *Ibid.*, 38.
5. Quoted in L. Stevenson, *The Ordeal
of George Meredith*, 135.
6. *Letters of George Gissing*, 156.

7. *After the Victorians*, 174.
8. Lafcadio Hearn, *Pre-Raphaelite and
Other Poets*, ed. J. Erskine, 1923, 373.

tion into achievement just because of the neglect from which he suffered. There is a real sense in which the history of Meredith's career opens him up to a variety of clichés: a prophet without honour in his own country, the 'difficult' artist who is called obscure only by the philistines, the artist of integrity who can expect to win only scorn, etc.

This brings us to an important point. Much of Meredith's reputation is founded on his being a man of ideas. A glance at the books people wrote about him will establish that much. It is not necessary here to detail what the ideas were: enough to note that they were taken to stand for a radical reappraisal of lines of thought associated with Victorian England. Feminism, little England, paganism, advanced liberalism, scepticism, the Comic Spirit even: whatever marked a rejection of high-Victorianism could be attributed to Meredith. He became the figure who embodied modernity, a man for the times. One can go further, of course, and claim that Meredith at the end of the nineteenth century was seen as a truth-teller, a sage. And as soon as we put the matter that way, we see that he is very recognizably in the line that finds one dominant point in Arnold's claim that

> Without poetry, our science will appear incomplete; and most of what passes with us for religion and philosophy will be replaced by poetry.[9]

For while the matter of Meredith's ideas may be said to represent a denial of high-Victorianism, in manner he is entirely a product of Victorian ideas and assumptions about literature and the artist. Meredith took himself to be, and was accepted as, a spokesman, consoler and sage. 'He is essentially a psychological poet,' Hearn remarked, 'but he is also an evolutionary philosopher . . . he alone of all living Englishmen really expresses the whole philosophy of the modern scientific age.'[1]

For Hannah Lynch

> Mr. Meredith is above and beyond all a thinker, less simple and direct, less wholly preoccupied with the mission of improving humanity and beautfying life, than either George Eliot or Tolstoi. Perhaps he has a healthier conviction that the world is very well as it is, and that in the main it is all the better that we are neither so muddy nor so pink as realists and sentimentalists would have us believe, but are just com-

9. M. Arnold, *Essays in Criticism*, 2nd Series, 1908, 2–3.

1. *Pre-Raphaelite and Other Poets*, 312.

fortably spotted and well-meaning to escape excess of censure
or admiration.[2]

Yet, she laments, the British public has been too stupid to
recognize the presence of a 'prophet in its midst'.[3] It is not
very easy to understand from Hannah Lynch just what Meredith is supposed to be a prophet of, but there is no doubting
the fervency of her campaign for establishing him as a great
modern thinker. Sturge Henderson's campaign has an even
more exalted note:

> Intermittently, Mr. Meredith is a great artist; primarily and
> consistently, he is a moralist—a teacher. He has pondered on
> man and his destiny till his insight has perceived whole re-
> gions and vistas of human possibility that as yet are unten-
> anted, and he has made it the object of his existence to nerve
> his fellows to seize and enter on the fullness of their inheri-
> tance. It may appear paradoxical that pages which would not
> have been published by lesser writers, should have found fa-
> vour with an artist towering head and shoulders above any
> but the masters, but the explanation is simple enough. It is to
> be found in Meredith's conviction that he has a message to
> deliver and in his willingness to sacrifice all other considera-
> tions to its delivery.[4]

We go in dread of what praise such as Henderson's implies,
but Meredith himself would have welcomed it. As Kenneth
Graham points out, Meredith saw his art as aiding a 'vague
ethical idealism' (very Victorian, that):

> As an enemy of the conventional prudery implied in the word
> 'morality', he uses instead such words as 'philosophy',
> 'thought', 'problems of life', 'the Spirit', and 'Idea' to describe
> his aims. The novel, he holds, must be an instrument of Civil-
> ization and the Comic Spirit, opposed to scientific material-
> ism, and uncovering 'the laws of existence' and the 'destinies
> of the world.'[5]

Graham is almost certainly wrong to think Meredith opposed
scientific materialism, though in his defence it can be suggested that he was probably misled by Meredith's rather
murky desire to be on both sides of just about every fence. But
he is quite right to see that Meredith makes the novel a ve-
hicle for his messages (the fact that Meredith also said that

2. H. Lynch, *George Meredith, A Study*,
7–8.
3. *Ibid.*, 8.

4. M. Sturge Henderson, *George Meredith*, 2–3.
5. Kenneth Graham, *English Criticism of
the Novel 1865–1900*, 1965, 74.

the novel should be dramatic and free from the omniscient author does not alter the truth of what Graham and Henderson say; it merely provides another example of Meredith's wanting to have it both ways). Even contemporary admirers sometimes regretted his willingness to sacrifice the drama or organic unity of the novel to abstract theorizing or musing. 'In Meredith,' Katherine Bradley remarked, 'the living heat rarely kindles the overplus of intellect.'[6] And Graham quotes J. A. Noble on Meredith's lack of ' "organic integrity" ("The one thing needful in the novel is that it should be a whole")'.[7] On the other hand, if you wanted your artist to be a thinker you had to be prepared to accept an occasional blemish in the art. And all the evidence points to the fact that Meredith's champions saw him as exonerated just because he was a great thinker. Photiadès puts the case in its most strident form:

> As Meredith grew older he gained in wisdom what he lost in imagination, so that the didactic tendencies of his art and teaching became still more intensified. His reason waged a pitiless war against his fancy . . . the master's decision was irrevocable and high-minded; he knew that his works would give pleasure only to an *élite*.[8]

Oh, that's all right, then.

Meredith, of course, came to look the part of the great thinker and teacher. It is one more clïché. Crusty, deaf, increasingly lame, he is the image of what might seem to epitomize the remorselessly honest seeker after truth, willing to endure the world's slings and arrows in his pursuit of . . . of what exactly? At this point the admirers are apt to grow a little coy. After all, if you know, you don't need telling. If you don't know—well, that is what the 'test-case' is all about. Not that the admirers resist any analysis or explanation of Meredith's ideas. But the ideas are apt to look more than a little obvious when brutally exposed to plain statement. And one notices that even the most devoted give the impression of looking uneasily over their shoulders in case there should be any ignorant non-*élite* and test-case failure ready to announce that the Emperor isn't wearing any clothes.

I do not wish to be cynical about Meredith. If he became his admirers, it was not entirely his fault. He did suffer for his art, he was unjustly and even outrageously neglected for many years, he was treated with brutish stupidity by critics and

6. *After the Victorians*, 175.
7. Kenneth Graham, op. cit., 115.
8. C. Photiadès, *George Meredith, His*
Life, His Genius, His Teaching, 1913, 250–52.

readers, many of whom should have known better; and even after he had become the sage of Box Hill it is clear that he derived little enjoyment from his late fame. He cannot be blamed because in old age he becomes eminently one to be painted, photographed and peered-at, his head beautiful, gnarled, leonine—everyman's ideal philosopher. Nor can he be blamed because young people saw in him an image of the writer who embodied a rejection of what they took Victorianism to be (Meredith is the unofficial Laureate of the 1890s, inevitably opposed to Alfred Austin). But the unavoidable truth is that the sort of reputation which Meredith acquired has done him lasting damage. To praise him because he was an intellectual novelist whose style was properly opaque and to insist that he was a great intellectual and a fearless spokesman for modern ideas was to invite disaster. Sooner or later someone in full retreat from Victorianism or in pursuit of new gods would be bound to shout that the Emperor really wasn't wearing any clothes. And that, of course, is what happened.

There is no need to trace in detail the catastrophic collapse of Meredith's reputation. But one or two of the more important contributions may be noted. There is Pound's attack on the famous style, for example. Writing of *Tarr*, Pound remarked that on occasions Lewis's expression is 'as bad as that of Meredith's floppy sickliness'. But at least 'In place of Meredith's mincing we have something active'.[9] The phrases are disconcertingly memorable. They also typify much twentieth-century response to Meredith as a writer of prose and, for that matter, of poetry. To his admirers Meredith was the Glad Day of modernity and the dedicated artist. To later generations he was merely the false dawn.

After Pound, the deluge. In particular, Forster's demolition of Meredith the great thinker:

> His philosophy has not worn well. His attacks on sentimentality—they bore the present generation, which pursues the same quarry but with neater instruments. . . . And his visions of Nature—they do not endure like Hardy's, there is too much Surrey about them, they are fluffy and lush. . . . What is really tragic and enduring in the scenery of nature was hidden from him, and so is what is really tragic in life. Where he gets serious and noble-minded there is a strident overtone, a bullying that becomes distressing. . . . And his novels: most of the social values are faked. The tailors are

9. *Literary Essays of Ezra Pound*, ed. T. S. Eliot, 1954, 425.

not tailors, the cricket matches are not cricket, the railway
trains do not even seem to be trains, the county families give
the air of having been only just that moment unpacked. . . .[1]

And, of course, Dr Leavis. Forster knocks Meredith down;
Leavis counts him out. The poetry is 'the flashy product of
unusual but vulgar cleverness working upon cheap emotion'.[2]
And the novels?

As for Meredith, I needn't add anything to what is said about
him by Mr. E. M. Forster, who, having belonged to the original *milieu* in which Meredith was erected into a great
master, enjoys peculiar advantages for the demolition-work.[3]

There is no doubt that the destruction of Meredith's reputation had to come. For it was absurd. Meredith is not a great
stylist, he is not a great intellectual, not for the reasons his
admirers gave, anyway. Yet destroying the reputation should
not have meant destroying Meredith. And at least some of the
demolition workers clearly felt that by knocking down the
Meredith created by erring admirers, Meredith himself would
emerge plain. After the passage in which Forster breaks down
the image of Meredith the thinker, he adds: 'And yet he is in
one way a great novelist. He is the finest contriver that English fiction has ever produced.'[4] Clearly it was not *that* remark which Leavis had in mind when he suggested that
Forster had said all that was needed about Meredith. Leavis
also quotes James's famous letter to Gosse about *Lord Ormont
and his Aminta*: 'It fills me with a critical rage, an artistic fury,
utterly blighting in me the indispensable principle of *respect*.'[5]
He does not, however, quote James's remark in an essay of
1905, in which Meredith is called 'that bright particular genius
of our day'.[6] Virginia Woolf, echoing Forster in saying that
Meredith's teaching 'seems now too strident and too optimistic
and too shallow', adds, 'to read Meredith is to be conscious of
a packed and muscular mind'.[7] And even in the 1890s it is
possible to find critics like Lionel Johnson and Arthur Symons
writing about Meredith with tactful good sense. Both see
much to regret and also much to acclaim.

But it was not measured praise that won Meredith his reputation, and it does seem to be the case that in demolishing the
nonsense later writers have, no matter what their intention,

1. E. M. Forster, *Aspects of the Novel*,
1953, 85–86.
2. F. R. Leavis, *New Bearings in English
Poetry*, Penguin Edn., 1963, 25 (he is
talking specifically of 'Modern Love').
3. *Ibid.*, *The Great Tradition*, 1948, 23.

4. *Aspects of the Novel*, 86.
5. *The Great Tradition*, 23.
6. 'The Lesson of Balzac', in *The House
of Fiction*, ed. Edel, 1957, 67.
7. 'The Novels of George Meredith', *The
Common Reader*, 1932, 235–36.

more or less buried Meredith in the rubble. He ought to survive the worst his reputation did for him and the worst that has been done to his reputation. But it is not certain that he has. If we are to try to recover Meredith, therefore, we have to begin by clearing the rubble away. He can never again be taken seriously as a great philosopher, and as for the style—we are properly less ready to turn its defects into virtues, even if improperly reluctant to recognize its virtues for what they are. The reluctance is understandable. Meredith is badly flawed, often infuriating, sometimes downright silly and vulgar. But he is also—or he ought·to be—of permanent interest, and at his best he is probably a master.

ROBERT M. ADAMS

A Counter Kind of Book

By 1877, when he sat down to write *The Egoist*, George Meredith had accumulated a good deal of past. He was nearly fifty years old. He had outlived the humiliation of a father who was a bankrupt tailor, and adjusted to the social and intellectual consequences of not attending a university. He had failed as a student of the law, tried a career as a poet, and undergone the disaster of a bitterly unsuccessful first marriage. He had long since cut his teeth as a storyteller and novelist, suffering a good many bitter failures and some modest success; he had been an editor and a writer of editorials, and for years he had earned his living by the steady grind of serving as publisher's reader for Chapman & Hall. Apart from all this personal history, he was able to look back upon the entire literary careers of Dickens, Thackeray, George Eliot, and most of the work of Trollope, not to mention Bulwer-Lytton, Disraeli, and a mass of lesser Victorian novelists, bottoming out among the lady fictioneers who supplied, once every year, a three-decker for the shelves of Mudie's Lending Library. The point is simply that *The Egoist* appeared late in the history of the Victorian novel, when many of the green fields of fiction had been pretty heavily trampled over. It represents a set of variations on standard themes and arrangements which give it the appearance of a very *different* novel indeed. What it *isn't* (in terms of traditional fictions) takes us a long way toward seeing what it *is*. A crashing set of negatives is where we have to begin.

In the first place, a novel in which the central figure is violently antipathetic—hateful, in fact—from beginning to end, runs directly against the current of Victorian fiction, which even more than most fiction operates through manipulating currents of sympathy around a central figure or couple. Most Victorian novels build toward a marriage; Meredith's works overwhelmingly toward a breakup, a separation. Unlike the extended, episodic Victorian novel, *The Egoist* takes place on a single country estate, with a sharply limited cast of characters (not even a proper covey of maids, butlers, gamekeepers, and picturesque confidants to set off the protagonists), and over a period of little more than a week. Its prose style, though toned down from earlier extravagances, is mannered beyond the norm of any Victorian writer but Carlyle; it is elliptical, metaphoric, and epigrammatic to the point where the author seems sometimes out to distract attention from its characters. It declines almost all sympathetic and reverberant effects—big scenes are not made, medium scenes are sometimes avoided entirely. The properties of life are scanted— Victorian activities like a long, rich breakfast, like card games, like prayers with the servants, like a run with the hounds, simply evaporate. There is little description—for example, of Colonel De Craye, of Mrs. Mountstuart Jenkinson. The novel is short on *body*, where most Victorian novels are long.

In general, the persons of the novel are wealthy, if not beyond the need for work, at least to the point of regarding work as a disagreeable imposition. They have no social reforms to propose, no political issues to urge. A few of them have a bare minimum of the most perfunctory religious sentiment: the rest, quietly and without the slightest consequence, have none at all. The most attractive male of the lot is out of the marriage game entirely, being at least a decade and a half too young; the second most attractive male is still a bachelor at the end of the book, and likely to remain so. Number one girl marries number three man, apparently because he is least likely to compromise the freedom she has fought so hard to establish in the course of the action. Number two girl marries the last man on the totem pole, last from the aspect of sympathy, though he is number one on the social scale. Poetic justice simply doesn't happen in the book; virtue doesn't get much rewarded, vice is hardly punished. Apart from divine providence, it doesn't look as if the author believes in that other special dispensation of the Victorian novelist, bilateral symmetry.

Finally, the novel—unlike all other Victorian novels except

those of Thomas Love Peacock—is not particularly interested
in morality. Within the action, people are moral and immoral,
of course; but the problems are hardly defined in these heavy
terms, and when simpleminded bystanders like Dr. Middleton
occasionally do so, the moment is so brief that one can hardly
be sure where the weight of the comment is falling. (Can a
man who will sell his daughter for a bottle of wine be trusted
to pass moral judgment on anyone or anything?) In a properly
moralistic novel, the moralist ought to have the last or at least
a special, authoritative word, so that we can be sure he is
right, i.e., seriously meant. Here he is just another voice,
maybe even a ridiculous one. From the traditional perspective,
it's all very distressing. But it is part of a curious quality in
Meredith, for which one could perhaps find a metaphor in his
special fictional *touch*. When points are scored in his games, it
is in such brief, ironic glints of perception that a hasty reader
may well remain in doubt whether they have been scored at
all. "Saints and sinners" isn't the name of the game. Yet serious
issues are at stake: the pressures on Clara are so heavy, her
resources against them are so reduced, that at times the lady
really seems reduced to grappling with the dragon bare-
handed, while her knights stand around and make phrases.
This is upsetting. For a French farce (which it partly is), the
novel is too grave, almost Gothic, in its menaces; for a novel
based on cruel sexual threat, it's too urbane and verbal. The
whole plot rests, precariously, via some doubtful puns, on a
Chinese legend; and when one adds a few aggressive but
inconsequential outcries about women's liberation, it seems as
if there were very little more one could add to define the book
as peculiar.

Its "strangeness" causes *The Egoist* to stand out among
books of its class, but also to make clear what a curious class
that was to begin with. Novels in general, and Victorian novels in particular, are commonly assumed to be like what we
nowadays call "problems"—that is, they present a set of disarranged events which are capable, not only of an optimal but
of a perfect arrangement. The "solution" of the problem is the
dénouement of the novel. Only, as the social scientists are
slowly finding out now, the solution to problem A may interfere with problem B or even, seen in a new context, constitute
problem C. The central erotic knot of *The Egoist* is intrinsically and irredeemably incapable of resolution, if only because
there are five participants in a game of sexual fascination and
evasion which is to be settled by pairing off. Clara, Willoughby, Laetitia, Vernon, and Horace De Craye are the

comedians; and, until the last minute, none of them is conclusively eliminated from the possibility of any match. Obviously the game isn't going to work out like *Pride and Prejudice*, with number one girl lining up with number one boy, number two with number two, and so on down the line. An extra element of instability lies in the character of Willoughby, who has radically different standings on two different scales—he's both a prize and a booby prize and has to be radically ground down before even Laetitia is asked to endure him.

On this level, however, both his advantages and disadvantages are traditional: he is Fitzwilliam Darcy, the snob of *Pride and Prejudice*, but petrified in one direction, anxious in the other. The first fault is really fatal; it is the rigidity of temper made manifest in the affair of Flitch which renders Willoughby intolerable. By that one inflexible decision alone he is entered in the company of Victorian insensitives and inhumans, with Dickensian fiends like Murdstone, Bounderby, and their ilk. Yet at the same time, he has the old high-strung irritability of temper traditional to the House of Stuart (Charles I and II) and their cavalier attendants. Actually, his social advantages are more painful to the reader than impressive. His wealth is never made tangible, his library is for the use of others, his laboratory is a pretense, and his stable merely an occasion to show off before others—no wonder his position as master of Patterne and social luminary of the county wears thin, as his primitive ferocities are felt to be hardening within him.

Actually, it is only the prospect that Laetitia can, by an equivalent severity, dominate this self-righteousness of Willoughby's that renders their union conceivable—and so paves the way for that still more factitious union, between Vernon and Clara, with which the package is, after a fashion, tied up. Meredith, it may be felt, had to use the symbol of marriage, if not much of the actuality, to top off his fable; but the institution as such did not answer very well to the ends he asked it to serve. In similar fashion, Spenser (with whom Meredith has a lot in common) sometimes in the course of the *Faerie Queene* has a couple of ironclad knights meet in a grove for a set of fencing and foining—when in fact the kind of spiritual endeavor in which they're engaged might better be represented as a course of therapy in a hospital or the reassembly of a shattered image.

By long-standing tradition, comedies (and novels as a comic class) are supposed to end with a marriage; Meredith's

comedians manage at least the phantom of a couple of ceremonies, but not from the heart—not at all. Each of them
seems to be writing and enacting a private comedy, the last
scene of which is an enthronement, not a marriage. Nowhere
is this more striking than in the case of Laetitia Dale, who
winds up holding absolutely all the unbeatable moral cards in
her trim little hands. She has been a dutiful daughter to her
ailing father and a loyal friend to Clara, has protected Crossjay's interests, and has got everybody in the county out of
immense social trouble by agreeing to be Willoughby's lady.
In the marriage itself she has stipulated, with brutal honesty,
to be just as much of a wife as she chooses, and not an iota
more. And she has forgiven but not forgotten (as she makes
icily clear) such an intolerable deal of Willoughby's worst
conduct that he can never again possibly stand on an even
footing with her. This comedy of sexual shuffling and matching clearly ends in an act of hard sexual conquest, as if to
make evident that the traditional matrimonial knot could not
suffice to tie up the comic problems and insights present in the
story. Another way to say this would be that *The Egoist* takes
the comic socializing process too seriously to represent contemporary society, or its institutions, as a triumphant solution
to the needs of contemporary people.

The fact is that Meredith baffles a practiced reader of Victorian fiction because he doesn't find society thick and resis-
tant or people deep and resourceful. Lady Busshe, Lady
Culmer, and Mrs. Mountstuart Jenkinson can do no more than
caricature the rest of the county—the squires, yeomen, bank-
ers, burghers, clergymen, MPs, lawyers, and their ladies,
whom Trollope and Dickens would have given us in such
profusion.[1] And by the same token, the only person who is
seen in depth in *The Egoist* is Willoughby, and the only thing
inside him is a cold and cavernous primitive void. (Mining is a
frequent metaphor for descent into Willoughby.) Society is
evidently an interminable bore, and the resources of people
against that boredom are appallingly scant. Vernon and Dr.
Middleton plunge like ostriches into the dry sand of Classical
scholarship; the Colonel peloothers and blarneys; and for the
rest, people walk, walk, walk, and talk, talk, talk. What they
will talk about when there are no more matches to be made is

---

1. "His themes in public," Meredith tells
us in chapter 15, "were those of an English gentleman: horses, dogs, game,
sport, intrigue, scandal, politics, wines,
the manly themes; with a condescension
to ladies' tattle and approbation of a racy
anecdote." How could he have lived in
the county, with these tastes, for twenty-
seven years and know so few persons,
have so limited a history?

far from clear. One reason why young Crossjay is such an appealing fellow, in the story, is that (unlike the grownups) he always seems to have enough to do.

It isn't a matter of the idle rich being better off for some honest labor, but of what one could call exoskeletal personalities, people looking for a role without being particularly sure whether they have yet found an identity. Even vigorous Vernon doesn't have anything to propose for himself, when he takes his pen to London, except drudgery—in effect, literary pedestrianism. Apart from getting Clara free of Willoughby, the plot doesn't have any powerful or sustaining objective: it doesn't bother with an interlaced subplot, and doesn't seem to exercise more than a fraction of the total human energies engaged in it. Rather than a striving- or a growth-plot, one could describe it, even without the pun, as a pattern-plot. This brings up the question of the willow plate.

The idea of taking a French comedy set in an English country-house and constructing it on a narrative taken from an old Chinese legend is already enough to suggest cross-cultural indigestion; and Mr. Robert Mayo, who in 1942 first called attention to the parallel with the story told in the deep-blue plate pattern, confessed, with a directness which did him all sorts of credit, that he didn't see much function for it, except as incidental and distracting decoration. And indeed, so long as one thinks of a plot as unfolding steadily down a temporal sequence from the known toward the as-yet-unknown, there is no point in calling attention to analogies which reveal the whole plot, seen as a totality.

In the old days, it was customary to defend Meredith against the charge of playing clever, irrelevant games with aphorisms, analogies, and puzzles by suggesting that he offered us psychology in depth—or, alternatively, that he forced his reader, in some unspecified way, to think, as if this were a useful exercise whether relevant or not. But neither of these statements, though both may be true after a fashion, offers much of a rationale for the willow-ware pattern in a social comedy of the home counties. Actually, the lurking congruence, made sensible only from time to time in an Oriental image or an isolated outcry from Lady Busshe, serves to reinforce a sense of fatality and deep pre-arrangement—as if the characters were not working out their destinies but re-enacting a schema which existed before them, alongside them, independent of times. A good part of their comedy (as perhaps of most comedy) lies in their thinking themselves people when in fact they are figures.

Comedy, I think, does not want to and cannot afford to look very carefully into the causes of things. It does not wish to see people as layered, motivated, committed; it does not wish to tease out the tangled roots of the past. Its game is with the momentary present incongruity, the glint and flash of discordant surfaces. The willow plate serves much the same function in *The Egoist* that Homer's *Odyssey* serves in Joyce's *Ulysses*. The point is not that it controls or orders modern experience, nor that it offers ironic contrast. What it does is arrest and condense the action into a moment of time, miniaturizing it into three little figures fleeing across a bridge; and at the same time it renders the social surface transparent to the analogue behind it. The story doesn't have to be *told*, with all the infantile and passive overtones of that process: it's already present behind the foreground comedy, backlighting it, so to speak. The clatter and collision of two-dimensional characters on a brightly lit stage is one description of comedy: it applies pretty well to Meredith's, at least. And the willow-plate background, precisely because it's an anti-story device, is one of the most important technical innovations that Meredith made in *The Egoist*.

I don't suppose, though, that it's more than a small part of the reason for the novel's success and continuing popularity, which are primarily due to its stylistic and dramatic content. The characteristic action of Meredith's style is a sting—a small, unobtrusive puncture is made, a bit of acid is silently injected—and only after a while does a large, itchy red patch appear to remind us of something actively at work which our complacencies don't gladly tolerate. Meredith actually represents this delayed, subcutaneous reaction several times in the novel—Willoughby in particular is apt to pass off a comment airily, then respond to it with a thud in the middle of other discourse some moments later. But Meredith's own prose works on the reader in the same way. The best of his comedy is made with phrases, usually dropped by the wayside, in the midst of syntactical or psychological distractions. In a famous passage, Sir Willoughby greets Laetitia on his return to England by looking deep into her eyes: "He found the man he sought there, squeezed him passionately, and let her go" (Chapter 4). It is the agile play of pronouns that makes the comedy. Or again, we are told that Willoughby thought Clara "essentially feminine, in other words, a parasite and a chalice" (Chapter 5). The coalescence of the contemptuous and the sacred in a single swift phrase couldn't be caught more concisely.

Less epigrammatic, but equally rich in its working out, is the splendid scene of Chapter 43, in which Vernon turns Sir Willoughby slowly, slowly over the fire. Though he knows all about the previous night's proposal to Laetitia, down to such details as a recital of the famous birthday poem, Vernon pretends to accept the story that Willoughby's proposal was made in his name. He toys with the wretched egoist as cruelly as a cat with a mouse—and only at the last minute does he raise with Dr. Middleton, in the most indirect of all possible ways, the most awkward of all possible questions. Supposing Willoughby successful in his "proxy" suit, would Vernon then be bound by a proposal he had never authorized? With that still-hypothetical question, the fat is in the fire. In fact, Willoughby· is allowed to bluster his way out of the scene. But his total defeat is apparent, and Vernon has won the whole game simply by indicating his hand to Willoughby and Clara. Now the curious thing is the remoteness of Clara's mind from this entire scene. She is trying to think of the name of a star near Orion; and the fact that four hundred pages of the novel are coming to a climax doesn't impress her at all. Why is she trying to bring to mind this particular astronomical detail? A bright star is suggested by the look in Vernon's eye; but any glittering, frosty light in the sky would serve to suggest this effect, and hanging her up on a particular name still lacks point. At the very end of the chapter we learn that she has been trying to think of Sirius. Well, Sirius is the Dog Star; and perhaps this implies that the light in Vernon's eye is cynical or satirical. Perhaps Clara reaches for the word because Vernon is now for the first time her cynosure, a celestial sign by which to navigate. But the Dog Star is also said to threaten sanity, it presages madness. Vernon is by no means out of his mind; but is he perhaps out of control, especially from Willoughby's point of view? Dr. Middleton recalls at the very end of the chapter that Sirius is mentioned in a play by Euripides, describing how Agamemnon, to appease an oracle, tried to sacrifice his daughter Iphigenia. Here is perhaps another cross-cultural parallel, akin to the willow-plate paradigm. But Sirius had nothing to do with the moment of Iphigenia's rescue; she was preserved by Artemis, goddess of chastity, whom we do not particularly want to see in Vernon Whitford's eye at this point. Only recently (1862) Sirius had been discovered to be not one star, but two; does Clara take this as a prognosis of matrimony? In addition to nursing a premature addiction to Freudian slips, Clara is her father's pun-loving daughter, and may, in her search for the star's name, be intimating to herself that for the first time Vernon is "serious" about her. Our speculations might continue, with the help of Meredith's curious sonnet to this particular star (see above, p. 450). The fact is that Meredith simply gestures the vacancy of Clara's astral thoughts to stretch as we will across her horizon—and this at the crucial instant of her liberation. He doesn't render, he doesn't control his own meaning or his character's, simply flings up a very specific symbol in her mind, and lets light pulse out of it. It is a non-technique with a large future in twentieth-century literature.

On the whole, though, there's no use in pointing up Meredith, any more than Gerard Manley Hopkins, as the writer, far less the thinker, of the future. When he died at the age of eighty-one, in 1909, Meredith was acclaimed and lamented as the last of the Victorians—and for once the public phrase was exactly right. He was Victorian not just in the components of his literary personality but in the way they were put together. For example, a cult of personal energy combined somewhere inside him with a deep-rooted streak of puritanism—he preached an ethic of work and strenuous physical exercise as if that were the only aspect of nature worth worshiping. His atheism was more scrupulous than a devotee's creed. He spoke for women's rights, but rather in the manner of Ibsen, because he wanted them to be fearless Vikings—vigorous, rigorous, ethical athletes, very much like the sort of man he liked best. For all his various liberal views, he was a deep-rooted imperalist, jingoist, militarist, and racist; he was as anti-Semitic (in a gentlemanly way, of course) as Henry James himself and contemptuous beyond words of most other inferior breeds. Perhaps the aspect of him that we can least endure today is his blowhard assurance and opinionative volubility on topics of which he knew no more than any other crackerbox philosopher. Recollections of Meredith, from the days of his youth and energy, are unanimous on the point—again and again, we hear of ten- or twenty-mile walks across the fields during which Meredith indulged in "splendid" talk. His conversation is often described in terms borrowed from the taproom, as foamy, bubbling, zesty, yeasty, exuberant, heady, intoxicating, and so forth and so on—generally leading to the lame admission that there was rather more of it than anyone, except Meredith himself, could stand.

For Meredith talked as he walked, to lay an uncertain and doubtfully legitimate ghost within himself; his impulse to shine, to be accepted by worshipers, to triumph over "the world" was at least as avid as Willoughby's and under only a little better control. He was an appalling Egoist. Of course one can't say there is a great deal of Meredith in Willoughby without immediately adding that there is a great deal of Willoughby in every man, and men since the dawn of time have been struggling to come to terms with it. Call it hubris, or love of glory, or pride, or self-assertion, it is the sphinx within us, which we all encounter sooner or later, asking us various riddles to which the answer is always a deeper enigma—man and what it means to be a man. The pride of the warrior, which is an arrogance only to be placated by fawning and submission, is in us all: we testify to it most eloquently in our modern impulses to seek out a moral equivalent for war. It is the root of the social order and the civilization which that makes possible; it is the root of that social order's destruction. How to live with it? Meredith asks and does not answer. Vernon Whitford is the symbol, or, as some might say, the caricature of an answer. But even Vernon, selfless, upright, honorable Vernon Whitford, has been eaten out by an irony of history. His figure was modeled, we know, on Leslie Stephen in his youth; and we have another portrait of Leslie Stephen, painted many years later by his daughter, Virginia Woolf. Mr. Ramsay, of *To the Lighthouse*, is the later Leslie Stephen; and this safest refuge from egoism (in Meredith's book) has become, alas, the very symbol of avid, brazen egoism in his daughter's.

There's no beating this. It implies that any success we have in overcoming our primal egotism is simply evidence of its renewed vitality. One might as well be crowned, to the applause of thousands, victor in a humility-contest. But the fact that Meredith has posed an insoluble problem is simply the best evidence that he has really transcended the mode of Victorian fiction, where problems as a rule are all too soluble. Some dissolve in the water of a few easily jerked tears. *The Egoist*, for all its dated manners and odd rhetoric, presents a view of life too serious, too deep (as well as too shallow) for moral formulas, or moral solutions. The counterpoint of primeval patterns with meticulous observation of modern manners—while the whole middle ground of moral problem solving is left out—represents at least one major mode of contemporary fiction. Not many men are better qualified to serve as godfather to this view of fiction's field than Mr. George Meredith; and *The Egoist* is his book.

Bibliography

BIOGRAPHICAL MATERIAL

Stevenson, Lionel. *The Ordeal of George Meredith*. New York, 1953.
Cline, C. L., ed. *The Letters of George Meredith*. 3 vols. Oxford, 1970.
Johnson, Diane. *The True History of the First Mrs. Meredith*. New York, 1972.

CRITICAL AND SCHOLARLY WORKS

Critical and scholarly discussion of Meredith to 1964 is summarized in C. L. Cline's chapter on the novelist in *Victorian Fiction: A Guide to Research*, ed. Lionel Stevenson (Cambridge, Mass., 1964), pp. 324–348. Two subsequent collections provide handy compendia of critical opinion: *Meredith Now*, ed. Ian Fletcher (London, 1971) contains novel-by-novel contemporary revaluations; *Meredith, the Critical Heritage*, ed. Ian M. Williams (London, 1971) reprints nineteenth-century reviews and articles. Other articles and studies of special interest include the following:

Bartlett, Phyllis. "The Novels of George Meredith," *Review of English Literature*, III (1962), 31–46.
Beach, Joseph W. *The Comic Spirit in George Meredith*. New York, 1911; reprinted 1963.
Buchen, Irving H. "Science, Society, and Individuality: *The Egoist*," *University of Kansas City Review*, XXX (1964), 185–192.
Campbell, O. J. "Some Influences of Meredith's Philosophy on His Fiction," *Wisconsin Studies in Language and Literature*, II (1918), 323–339.
Fanger, D. S. "Joyce and Meredith," *Modern Fiction Studies*, VI (Summer 1960), 125–130.
Lindsay, Jack. *George Meredith: His Life and Work*. London, 1956.
Priestley, J. B. *George Meredith*. New York, 1926.
Pritchett, V. S. *George Meredith and English Comedy*. New York, 1970.
Woods, Alice. *George Meredith as Champion of Women and of Progressive Education*. Oxford, 1937.
Wright, W. F. *Art and Substance in George Meredith*. Lincoln, Neb., 1953.

BACKGROUND STUDIES

Background studies, not immediately related to Meredith but very useful in estimating his achievement, include:

Buckley, Jerome H. *The Victorian Temper*. Cambridge, Mass., 1951.
Houghton, Walter E. *The Victorian Frame of Mind*. New Haven, 1957.
Young, G. M. *Victorian England: Portrait of an Age*. London, 1936.

Studies with special emphasis on Victorian attitudes toward sex include:

Crow, Duncan. *The Victorian Woman*. New York, 1971.
Hewitt, Margaret. *Wives and Mothers in Victorian Industry*. London, 1958.
Marcus, Steven. *The Other Victorians*. New York, 1966.
Vicinus, Martha. *Suffer and Be Still: Women in the Victorian Age*. Bloomington, Ind., 1972.

NORTON CRITICAL EDITIONS

Missing mother — JE

Vic — Becky's
Becky

LD — Aunt Arthur

Gost — Clara